The Handbook of

Equipment
Leasing
Volume One

The Handbook of

Equipment Leasing
Volume One

Shawn D. Halladay

Sudhir P. Amembal

Amembal, Deane & Associates
International Lease Educators and Consultants

Managing Editor: Shawn D. Halladay
Project Manager: Trudy McEwan
Project Editor: Christine Pickett
Cover Design: Bailey-Montague & Associates
Layout: Trudy McEwan
Printing: Publishers Press, Salt Lake City, Utah

Library of Congress Catalog Card Number: 95-79541

ISBN (The Handbook of Equipment Leasing): 0-945988-10-9
ISBN (Volume One): 0-945988-08-7

Printed in the United States of America

Address orders to:

Amembal, Deane & Associates
International Lease Educators and Consultants
4 Triad Center, Suite 850
Salt Lake City, UT 84180-1408 U.S.A.
Telephone: (801) 533-8555
Fax: (801) 533-8778

Dedicated to the equipment leasing industry
of today and tomorrow. May we continue to grow together.

About Amembal, Deane & Associates

Amembal, Deane & Associates is recognized as the worldwide authority in the field of equipment lease education and consulting. Our goal continues to be the provision of superior services across a broad range of products and services. In this respect, Amembal, Deane & Associates has played a critical role in the growth and advancement of the leasing industry, contributing knowledge, ideas and techniques currently used within the industry.

Over 45,000 professionals have benefited from the knowledge and insight obtained through attendance at a broad range of leasing seminars and conferences throughout North and South America, Africa, Asia, Australia and Europe. In 1991, Euromoney Publications, Plc., a publicly-held company based in London, acquired a working interest in Amembal, Deane & Associates. This relationship has created additional advantages for the international leasing community. Amembal, Deane & Associates also manages, on behalf of Euromoney, the most prestigious international leasing event, the annual World Leasing Convention.

Amembal, Deane & Associates prides itself on being the premier provider of education, consulting and M&A services to the leasing industry and continually strives to initiate change and advancement within the leasing industry. In keeping with this tradition, we provide the following full complement of products and services:

- Public leasing seminars, conferences and leasing schools covering a broad spectrum of topics, including leasing fundamentals, accounting, taxes, credit, documentation, law and pricing

- Video training including an orientation to leasing, off balance sheet leases and lease versus purchase

- Leasing publications addressing many aspects of leasing including accounting, securitizations and the current bestseller, *The Handbook of Equipment Leasing (second edition.)*

- Inhouse seminars tailored to individual corporate environments, available at any location

- Consulting covering a wide range of leasing issues

- Mergers, acquisitions and financial services

We have built our company on a commitment to provide high quality seminars, services and products that are accurate, relevant and recognized as the most effective in the industry. We intend to continue this commitment. In this regard, Amembal, Deane & Associates plans to offer several new products in addition to the constant updating of our seminar offerings. These actions are based upon the firm belief that continued growth in the industry is a direct function of the increased recognition of opportunities that knowledge provides.

Preface

The worldwide equipment leasing industry has experienced substantial growth over the last several years. This growth has caused many changes within the industry, such as those attributable to tax, accounting and regulatory rules. Keeping pace with these changes, from an educational and consulting standpoint, has been a challenge. The *Handbook of Equipment Leasing* has successfully met this challenge.

This third edition represents a fresh view of the world of equipment leasing. The information contained in its two volumes is relevant and informative, and incorporates both current theories and practical applications. In addition to the requisite basics of tax, accounting, finance, etc., it also includes new topics such as securitizations, asset management and venture leasing.

The *Handbook of Equipment Leasing* is the culmination of thousands of hours of research, years of experience in the leasing industry and significant effort on the part of all those involved. It also represents the culmination of Shawn Halladay's career with the firm. With his departure, the name of the firm is changing to Amembal, Deane & Associates, which is reflective of the much broader range of services the firm now provides to the leasing industry.

The equipment leasing industry is diverse, with various ticket sizes, differing practices and many levels of experience. Even so, we intend for the *Handbook of Equipment Leasing* to be used by all segments of the industry; lessors, lessees, funding sources and the various groups of professionals serving the industry. Although the contents have a U. S. emphasis, international readers will find the information to be extremely relevant and valuable in their countries, as well. The book is organized by general topics for ease of use. You also will find a complete index and table of contents in each volume.

The *Handbook of Equipment Leasing* is a complete reference guide for the leasing industry. It is current in content and easy to read. I hope you enjoy the *Handbook of Equipment Leasing* and use it as a valuable resource.

Sudhir P. Amembal
President and Chief Executive Officer
July 31, 1995

Acknowledgments

The authors wish to gratefully acknowledge the many parties who aided in making this book possible. Special thanks are due to:

Shawn Halladay, who, in addition to bringing this project to completion, authored the majority of the *Handbook of Equipment Leasing*.

Trudy McEwan, whose skills, commitment and determination helped make the *Handbook of Equipment Leasing* the valuable and complete resource that it is.

Joseph N. Cannon, who authored the chapter on credit. Mr. Cannon is a Senior Lease Consultant with Amembal, Deane & Associates.

Steve Gilyeart, Attorney, who wrote the chapters on lease documentation and legal issues. Mr. Gilyeart teaches courses and provides consulting services on behalf of Amembal, Deane & Associates. Questions concerning the subject matter or his chapters may be addressed to him at 220 23rd Avenue East #202, Seattle WA 98112, or at (206) 325-5031.

Greg Harper, who contributed to the chapter on lease versus buy. Mr. Harper is Vice President at Chancellor Fleet Corporation, Boston Massachusetts.

Gregory Keever, Partner, assisted by Gary Vyneman, Associate, who contributed the state and local tax chapter. Questions concerning this chapter may be addressed to them at Buchalter, Nemer, Fields & Younger, 601 So. Figueroa Street, Suite 2400, Los Angeles, California 90017, or at (213) 891-0700, fax (213) 896-0400.

Bruce E. Kropschot, who authored the chapter on mergers and acquisitions. Mr. Kropschot is President of Kropschot Financial Services, a subsidiary of Amembal, Deane & Associates. Questions concerning the subject matter of this chapter may be addressed to him at 3341 Monet Drive, Palm Beach Gardens, Florida 33410, (561) 694-7700, fax (561) 694-7706.

James Marchant, who helped write the chapter on structuring principles. Mr. Marchant is a former instructor for Amembal, Deane & Associates.

Jeffrey D. Negri, who contributed to several of the accounting and tax chapters. Mr. Negri is a former instructor for Amembal, Deane & Associates.

Mark F. Rea, who contributed the chapter on asset management. Mr. Rea has provided services to Amembal, Deane & Associates in the past.

Jonathan M. Ruga, who provided the sample documentation in the book. Mr. Ruga is the CEO of Sentry Financial Corporation of Salt Lake City, Utah.

Jeffrey Taylor, who authored the chapter on management information systems. Mr. Taylor is a Senior Lease Consultant with Amembal, Deane & Associates.

GE Capital Corporation, which so graciously gave of its vast knowledge and skills by contributing 'Methods of Servicing Vendor Lessors by Third-party Lessors' to the chapter on captives and vendor leasing.

The Financial Accounting Standards Board for allowing us to quote portions of their literature. This literature is copyrighted by the Financial Accounting Standards Board, 401 Merritt 7, P.O. Box 5116, Norwalk, Connecticut 06856-5116, U.S.A., and is reprinted with permission. Copies of the complete documents are available from the Financial Accounting Standards Board.

In addition we would like to extend our appreciation to Christine Pickett for her editing skills and insights. Our greatest thanks go to those at Amembal, Deane & Associates, who, as always, put forth their best efforts.

Table of Contents

VOLUME ONE

About Amembal, Deane & Associates   vii

Preface   ix

Acknowledgments   xi

Section One: General Issues   1

CHAPTER ONE: OVERVIEW OF THE INDUSTRY   3
  Evolution of Leasing   3
    Early History   4
    Leasing in the U.K.   5
    Development of the U.S. Leasing Industry   6
  Equipment Leasing Today   11
    Market Segments   11
    Today's Lessors   12
    Industry Associations   15
    Why Leasing   16
  Elements of a Lease   16
    Parties to a Lease   16
    Lease Payments and Residual Value   18
    End-of-term Options   19
    Bundled Services   20
    Funding Aspects   21
    Tax and Accounting Attributes   23

CHAPTER TWO: DYNAMICS OF THE INDUSTRY   25
  Lessee Reasons to Lease   25
    Technological   26
    Financial Reporting   28
    Cash Management   30
    Income Tax   33
    Ownership   36
    Flexibility and Convenience   38
    Economic   43
    Less Restrictive Form of Financing   44
    Economies of Scale in Lessor Purchasing and Servicing . . .   45
    Lower Cost   45
  Lessor Motivations to Provide Leasing Services   46
    Lessor Earnings and Profitability   46
    Income Tax Benefits   47
    Financial Leverage Considerations   48
    Residual Speculation Motivations   48
    Vendor Leasing Issues   49
    Integration Opportunities   50
    International Leasing   51

CHAPTER THREE: TRENDS IN LEASING   53
  Trends in the Leasing Industry   53
    Changing Lessor Base   54
    Evolving Lessee Perspective   55
    Changes in Lease Products   55
    Factors Affecting Profitability   57
    Tax and Accounting Changes   58
    Factors Necessary for Volume to Increase   59
    Emergence of International Markets   60
    Key Economic Factors   61
    Increased Interest in Consumer Leasing   61
  Key Factors for Success   62
    Competitive Advantages   62
    Specialization   63
    Customer Service and Flexibility   63
    Funding Ability   63
    Control of Back-office Costs   64
    Highly-trained Workforce   64
    Appropriate Strategies   64
    Adaptability to Market Shifts   65
    Maintaining Objectives   65

CHAPTER FOUR: INTERNATIONAL LEASING   67
  Global Leasing   67
    The Leasing Cycle   68
    Leasing Differences   70
    Substance Versus Form   71
    Role of Leasing   72
    Funding   74
    Regional Overview   82
    Lease Clubs   87
  Cross-border Transactions   88
    Double-dips   88
  Outbound U.S. Leasing   89
    Conditional Sale Versus True Tax Lease   91
    Foreign Tax Credit   92
    Pickle Leases   95
    Outbound Double-dip Leasing   97
  Foreign Sales Corporations (FSC)   99
    Types of FSCs   99

Section Two: Taxation   107

CHAPTER FIVE: IRS QUALIFICATIONS OF A LEASE . .   109
  Definitions of a Lease   109
    Lease   110
    Sale   110
    Service Contract   111
  Lease or Sale: Issues of Concern   111
    Federal Income Tax Consequences   112
    Financial Reporting Requirements   113
    Uniform Commercial Code Ramifications   114
  True Lease or Sale: Factors, Guidelines and Tests   114
    Statutory Basis   114
    Judicial Tests and Criteria   115
    IRS Tests and Criteria   120
    Application of the Judicial and Administrative Factors   132
    The TRAC Lease   137

CHAPTER SIX: INCOME TAX BENEFITS   139
  Corporate Tax Rates   139
    Timing of Taxes Paid   140

Modified Accelerated Cost Recovery System 144
    Recovery Classes 144
    Cost Recovery Methodology 145
    Effective Dates 145
    Value of Depreciation 146
    Elective Alternatives to MACRS 151
    Short Taxable Years 156
Deferred Intercompany Transactions 159
    Requirements 159
    Application to Leasing 160
Investment Tax Credit 163

CHAPTER SEVEN: INCOME TAX LIMITATIONS 165
Midquarter Convention 165
Antichurning Rules 170
    Examples 170
Alternative Minimum Tax 172
    General Provisions 172
    Tax Preference Items 174
    Credits and Losses 181
    AMT Small Corporation Exemption 182
    Minimum Tax Credit 183
Uneven Rents 185
    Applicable Leases 185
    Application of the Rules 186
At-risk Provisions 188
    Affected Taxpayers 189
    Limitations 190
    Applicable Activities 191
Passive Losses 192
    Affected Taxpayers 192
    Application of the Rules 192

CHAPTER EIGHT: STATE AND LOCAL TAXES 197
Franchise and Income Taxes 197
    Tax Structure 198
    Nexus 202
    Miscellaneous Issues 208
Sales Tax 215
    Continuing Sale 216
    Nexus 217

Sales for Resale 218
Exempt Property 218
Other Issues 220
Personal Property Taxes 224
Owner of Record 225
Situs of Personal Property 226
Effect of Contractual Obligations Borne by the Lessee 226
Valuation Issues 227
Exempt Tangible Personal Property 228
Exempt Lessee 228

Section Three: Financial Reporting 231

**CHAPTER NINE: INTRODUCTORY LEASE
ACCOUNTING** 233
Accounting and Leasing 233
Accounting Perspective 233
Role of Accounting in the Leasing Industry 238
An Introduction to FASB 13 239
Definitions of a Lease 239
FASB 13 242
Capital Versus Operating Leases 246
Four Criteria 246
FASB 13 Terminology 250
The 90% Test 258
Disclosure Requirements 261

CHAPTER TEN: LESSOR ACCOUNTING 267
Direct Financing Leases 267
FASB 13 Requirements 268
Direct Financing Lease Example 270
Disclosure Requirements 287
Sales-type Leases 293
Characteristics 293
FASB 13 Requirements 294
Sales-type Lease Example 296
Operating Leases 311
Characteristics 311
FASB 13 Requirements 313
Operating Lease Example 314

CHAPTER ELEVEN: LESSEE ACCOUNTING 329
  Capital Lease Accounting 329
    FASB 13 Requirements 330
    Illustration 332
  Operating Lease Accounting 336
    FASB 13 Requirements 336
    Illustration 338
  Comparative Differences 342
    Assumptions 345
    Comparative Financial Statements 349
  Sale-leasebacks 357
    Reasons for Entering Into Sale-leasebacks 357
    Accounting Requirements 359
    Sale-leaseback Illustrations 363

CHAPTER TWELVE: STRUCTURING
FASB 13 OPERATING LEASES 371
  FASB 13 and Operating Lease Structuring 371
  FASB 13 Operating Lease Test 372
    Step One 373
    Step Two 373
    Step Three 374
    Examples of the FASB 13 Test 374
  Operating Lease Structuring Methodology 378
    Increase the Lessee's Discount Rate 379
    High Fair Market Value 380
    Reduce the Minimum Lease Payments 381
    Contingent Rentals 383
    Executory Costs 383
    Higher Residual 384
    Shorter Lease Term 384
    Step Payments 385
    Short-term Loan Followed by a Sale-leaseback 387
    Splitting the Transaction 387
    Early Out 388
  Structuring Operating Leases 388
    Computing the Maximum Payment 388
    Computing the Maximum Guaranteed Residual 393

Section Four: Finance 397

CHAPTER THIRTEEN: LEASE VERSUS BUY 399
  The Investment Decision 399
    Changing the Investment Profile 400
    The Mini-investment Decision 404
  Financing Alternatives 404
    Debt 405
    Deferred Taxes 405
    Retained Earnings and Equity 405
    Optimizing Capital Investment Through Leasing 406
  Decision Methodology 407
    Decision Inputs 408
    Appropriate Discount Rates 416
    Methods of Analysis 421
  Examples 426
    Case One 428
    Case Two 433
  Advanced Issues 434
    Dual Rate Method 434
    Alternative Minimum Tax Impact 440
    Foreign Tax Credit Impact 449

CHAPTER FOURTEEN: LEASE ANALYSIS 455
  Approaches to Yield 455
    Yield-oriented Methods 456
    Present and Future Value Methods 456
    Managerial-oriented Indices 457
    Marketing-related Techniques 457
    Integrated Approaches 458
  Types of Yields 459
    Gross Versus Net Yields 459
    Pretax Versus After-tax Yields 460
    ROA, ROE and ROI Yields 460
    IRR Versus ERR Yields 462
  Yield Analysis 462
    Gross, Pretax Yields 463
    Net, After-tax Yields 467
    Conversion to a Pretax IRR 482
    External Rate of Return Analysis (ERR) 483
  Comparing Proposals 487
    Implicit Cost 488
    NPV 489

CHAPTER FIFTEEN: STRUCTURING PRINCIPLES 491
 Purpose of Structuring 491
  Structuring Theory 492
 Structuring Factors To Be Considered 494
  Inputs 496
  Structuring Variables 500
 Pretax Targeted Yield Structuring 502
  Example One 504
  Example Two 505
  The Three-step Method 507
  Effect of Deposits, Fees and IDC 510
 Structuring Unusual Payment Streams 518
  Structuring Step-up or Step-down Leases 519
  Structuring Leases With Known Initial Payments 523
  Structuring a Skipped Payment Lease 525
  Uneven or Step Payments (IRS Tests) 527

CHAPTER SIXTEEN: ADVANCED STRUCTURING 533
 Pricing Theory 533
  Quality of Earnings 534
  Quantity of Earnings 541
 Quantification of Tax Variables 545
  Structuring Variables 547
 After-tax Structuring Techniques 554
  Structuring Steps 554
  After-tax Structuring Example 557
  Structuring Unusual Payment Streams 563
  ROE Structuring (Match Funded) 566
  GPTD Structuring 574
  Alternative Minimum Tax Considerations 575

APPENDIX ONE 583

GLOSSARY 589

INDEX I-1

ADVERTISEMENTS A-1
 Equipment Leasing Association of America A-2
 Kropschot Financial Services A-3
 LeaseTeam, Inc. A-4
 McCue Systems Incorporated A-5

VOLUME TWO

About A&H   v

Acknowledgments   vii

Section Five: Operations   631

CHAPTER SEVENTEEN: CREDIT ANALYSIS   633
 Role of Credit   633
  Impact on Lessor Profitability   634
  Credit Risk and Residual Risk   636
  Evaluating Credit Risk   640
  Summary   642
 Credit Information Requirements   642
  Initial Credit Investigation   644
  Accept/Reject Decision   644
 Credit Evaluation Tools   646
  Credit Scoring   647
  Financial Statements   659
  Financial Ratios   662
  Cash Flow Analysis   681
  Projecting Future Results   688
 Risk Adjustment   690
  Increase the Lease Yield   692
  Require a Security Deposit   692
  Use Advance Payments   692
  Write a Step-down Lease   692
  Shorten the Lease Term   692
  Require a Personal Guarantee   693
  Require Additional Collateral   693
  Increase Late Fees   693
  Require Credit Life Insurance   693
  Obtain Vendor Guarantees   693
  Require a Letter of Credit or Certificate of Deposit   694
  Utilize Other Credit Enhancements   694

CHAPTER EIGHTEEN: LEASE DOCUMENTATION   695
 Documentation and the Marketplace   695
  Small Ticket Documentation   696
  Middle Market Documentation   696
  Big Ticket Documentation   696

The Three-party Structure 696
Lessor-lessee Documents 697
   Lease Proposal 697
   Lease Application 697
   Credit Application 698
   Commitment Letter 699
   Lease Agreement 701
   Remedies 711
   Lease Agreement Addenda 717
Lessor-vendor Documents 729
   Supply Contract (or Purchase Agreement) 729
Intercreditor Documents 730
   Landlord's Waiver 731
   Mortgagee's Waiver 732
   Other Credit Waivers 733

CHAPTER NINETEEN: LEGAL ISSUES 735
The Historical Perspective 735
   The Traditional Law of Bailments and Rentals 736
   Leasing and the Uniform Commercial Code 736
The Definition of a Lease 737
   Enhancing the Distinction Between Secured
   Transactions and Leases 737
   Case Law Perspective 739
   Essence of a True Lease 749
Article 2A-Leases 750
   The Finance Lease 751
   Warranties and Article 2A 758
   Risk of Loss and Article 2A 760
   Fixtures 760
   Transfers and Assignments of Lessor and Lessee Interests .. 761
   Rights and Remedies 763
Article 9-Secured Transactions 770
   The Nature of a Security Interest 770
   The Creation of a Security Interest 771
   The Perfection of a Security Interest 771
   Goods Subject to Certificates of Title 775
   Secured Transaction Remedies 775
Bankruptcy 777
   The Different Chapters 778
   Payment Priorities 782
   Performance of Lease Obligations after 60 Days 783

CHAPTER: TWENTY: TERMINATIONS 793
  Termination Types 793
  Termination Factors 794
    Documentation Rights 794
    Accounting and Tax Treatment 796
    Residual Acceleration 797
    Lost Tax Benefits 797
    Lost Rents 798
    Lost Opportunity Cost 798
    Administrative Charges 799
    Income Recognition 799
    Fee Income 799
  Termination Formulae 799
    Implicit Rate Method 800
    Rule of 78 Method 802
    After-tax Method 804
    Summary of Methods 808
  Termination Example 809
    Pretax Payoff Amount 809
    Rule of 78 Payoff 810
    After-tax Payoff 811

CHAPTER TWENTY-ONE: ASSET MANAGEMENT 819
  Overview of Asset Management 819
    The Four Phases of Asset Management 821
  New Business Processing 822
    Residual Value Analysis Procedures 822
    Use of Forms in the Residual Evaluation Process 832
    Residual Risk Documentation 833
  Disposition of Equipment 845
    End-of-lease Strategy 846
    Strategy Development 849
    Equipment Remarketing Procedures 852

CHAPTER TWENTY-TWO: THE MIS FUNCTION 859
  Leasing Systems 859
    Accounting Systems 860
    Pricing Systems 861
    Credit Scoring Systems 862
    Income Tax Systems 863
    Sales/Property Tax Systems 863

Document Storage Systems 864
Residual Valuation Systems 864
Management Information Systems 865
Hardware and Software Platforms 865
Hardware Platforms 865
Software Platforms 867
The Evaluation Process 868
The Off-the-shelf Solution 869
The Inhouse Solution 870
The Development Process 870
Implementation Issues 871
Leasing Systems Trends 871

Section Six: Advanced Topics 873

**CHAPTER TWENTY-THREE: GOVERNMENTAL
LEASING** 875
Reasons for Public Sector Leasing 875
Obsolescence Avoidance 876
Budgetary Reasons 876
Lower-level Decision Making 877
Cash Management Considerations 877
Ownership Aspects 878
Flexibility and Convenience 879
Economic Reasons 880
Potential Lessees 881
Federal Government 881
Prime Contractors 886
State and Local Governments 887
Tax Consequences 891
Tax Benefits 892
Tax Limitations 896
The Decision to Lease 904
Federal Government 904
Prime Contractors 907
State and Local Government 908
Financial Reporting Ramifications 908
Lease Accounting Rules 909
Nonappropriation Clauses 910

CHAPTER TWENTY-FOUR: CAPTIVES
AND VENDOR PROGRAMS 913
  Vendor Leasing Programs 913
    Market Control 914
    Market Enhancement 918
    Ancillary Income 921
  Program Forms 925
    Types of Programs 926
    Captive or Third Party? 930
  Risks and Pitfalls 932
    Consolidation 932
    Business Collapse 933
    Management 933
    Scarce Resources 934
    The Parent 934
    Tax 934
  Tax and Accounting Issues 935
    Taxation 935
    Accounting 947
  The Role of Third-party Lessors 948
    Services Provided 949
    Funding Methods 952

CHAPTER TWENTY-FIVE: OTHER PRODUCTS 955
  Residual Participations 955
    Methodology 956
    Example One 958
    Example Two 960
  Venture Leasing 961
    Motivations 961
    Stages of Development 962
    Transaction Profile 964
  Sale-leasebacks 966
    Sale-leaseback Transactions 966
    Lessee Motivations for Sale-leasebacks 971
    Marketing Opportunities 977
  Income Funds 979
    Description 979
    Objectives 983
    Partnership Risks 983
    Illustration 986
    Phases of the Program 989

CHAPTER TWENTY-SIX: LEVERAGED LEASING 991
Definitions 991
  Industry Viewpoint 992
  FASB Viewpoint 993
  IRS Viewpoint 993
Types of Transactions 993
  Basic Leveraged Lease 995
  Sold Leveraged Lease 997
  Use of Trusts 999
Economics of Leveraged Leasing 999
  Methods of Analysis 999
  Disinvestment Balances 1002
  IRR Versus ERR 1004
  Debt Optimization 1017
Accounting Considerations 1022
  Balance Sheet Presentation 1023
  Income Statement Presentation 1027
  Financial Statement Format 1035

CHAPTER TWENTY-SEVEN: SECURITIZATION 1041
Asset-backed Financings 1041
Lease Securitization 1042
  Structure 1043
  History 1044
Product Characteristics 1046
  Structures 1046
  Parties Involved 1049
  Motivations and Benefits 1054
  Pitfalls 1058
  Investor Criteria 1062
The Securitization Process 1064
  Making the Decision 1064
Tax, Accounting and Legal Aspects 1078
  Tax 1078
  Accounting 1082
  Legal 1089
Economic Analysis 1093
  Components 1093
  Establishing the Cost 1096
  Impact on Returns 1099

**CHAPTER TWENTY-EIGHT: MERGERS AND
ACQUISITIONS** 1101
　Merger and Acquisition Trends 1101
　　Seller Motivations 1102
　　Tax Legislation 1104
　　Buyers 1105
　　Growth and Profitability Prospects 1107
　Planning for the Sale of a Leasing Company 1108
　　Methods of Sale 1109
　　Timing of the Sale 1110
　　Preparation for the Sale 1111
　Acquisition Pricing 1112
　　Factors Affecting the Price 1113
　　Methods of Valuing the Business 1114
　　Structuring the Transaction 1116

Section Seven: Management 1119

**CHAPTER TWENTY-NINE: HURDLE
RATE DEVELOPMENT** 1121
　Return Expectations 1121
　　The Cost of Capital 1122
　　Other Costs 1126
　Base Pricing Model 1126
　　Components 1127
　　Utility 1130
　Approaches to Hurdle Rates 1131
　　Layered Approach 1133
　　Additive Approach 1137
　　Alternative Approaches 1142

CHAPTER THIRTY: DEBT MANAGEMENT 1147
　Funding the Company 1147
　　Capital Structure 1149
　　The Effects of Leverage 1153
　Funding Risks 1153
　　Capital Structure Risk 1153
　　Interest Rate Risk 1154
　Leverage and Yield 1163
　　Debt Repayment Example 1164
　Funding Techniques 1169
　　Pooling 1170

Match Funding 1173
Combinations 1175
Tax and Accounting Issues 1176
Assignments 1176
Accounting 1177
Taxation 1181

**CHAPTER THIRTY-ONE: MONITORING
PERFORMANCE** 1185
Risk and Control Issues 1185
Risks 1186
Historical Problems 1190
Checks and Balances 1191
Financial Statement Issues 1192
Balance Sheet 1193
Income Statement 1195
Statement of Cash Flows 1197
Understanding Income Patterns 1197
Summary 1203
Measures and Benchmarks 1204
Establishing Performance Standards 1205
Production Standards 1206
Cost Standards 1207
Measuring Performance 1208
Management Focus 1221

APPENDIX TWO 1223

INDEX I-1

ADVERTISEMENTS A-1
Equipment Leasing Association of America A-2
Kropschot Financial Services A-3
LeaseTeam, Inc. A-4
McCue Systems Incorporated A-5

Section One

General Issues

Chapter One

Overview of the Industry

Equipment leasing is, without doubt, the creative financing alternative of today. It is an imposing industry in terms of scope, size and potential, as more and more of the world's equipment needs are met through this unique form of financing. What is the genesis of this complex yet exciting industry? Why has it caught the imagination and attention of the press, business world and consuming public?

Leasing offers many benefits to all parties in the transaction, including low payments and off balance sheet financing to the lessee and financing income to the lessor. The range of equipment being leased is vast, from basic copier leases to extremely complex leveraged leases involving nuclear facilities. Leasing truly has something to offer everyone.

In order to provide perspective on this fascinating industry, and as a basis for the remaining portions of this book, this chapter addresses the following topics:

- Evolution of Leasing
- Equipment Leasing Today
- Elements of a Lease.

EVOLUTION OF LEASING

Equipment leasing has a rich and lengthy history. Although the complex leases of today may be a far cry from the simple leases of old, they share many similarities based upon the utility and demand for the leasing mechanism. In gaining an understanding of the lease process it is important to have perspective into where leasing came from and why it has become what it is today.

Early History

Although the exact date of the first leasing transaction is unknown, the earliest records of leasing are those of transactions occurring sometime before 2000 B.C., in the ancient Sumerian city of Ur. Sumerian lease documents, which were produced in damp clay, recorded transactions ranging from leases for agricultural tools and land and water rights to oxen and other animals. The clay tablets, some of which were found as recently as 1984, indicate the priests of the temples (lessors) leased to the local farmers (lessees). These early documents do not preclude the possibility that leasing may have existed elsewhere in the world at an earlier date but no documentation of such leases has been preserved.

Many early legal systems make mention of the financial tool called leasing. The most noteworthy record of leasing laws relates to roughly 1700 B.C., when the famous Babylonian king, Hammurabi, incorporated ancient Sumerian and Achaian mores concerning leasing into his extensive collection of laws.

Just southeast of Babylon, in the ancient city of Nippur, the Murashu family established what was to become a well-known bank and leasing house in approximately 400 to 450 B.C. The Murashus provided financial services that reflected the current economic and social conditions of the Persian Empire. They specialized in land leasing, but also leased oxen and agricultural equipment, as well as seed.

Other ancient civilizations, including the Greeks, Romans and Egyptians, found leasing to be attractive and affordable and, at times, the only viable method of financing equipment, land and livestock. The ancient Phoenicians, long known for their expertise in shipping and trade, chartered their ships. The charters resembled a very pure form of an equipment lease. Many short-term charters provided for use of the crew as well as the ship. Longer-term charters also were written for periods covering the estimated economic life of the ships and required the lessee to assume most of the benefits and obligations of ownership. Many of the same kinds of negotiating issues that today's lessors and lessees face were addressed in these ancient ship charters.

Leasing in earlier times was not limited to the leasing of only one or two types of property. In fact, historical evidence provides illustrations of the leasing of various types of agricultural and industrial equipment, as well as equipment used in militaristic endeavors. As an example, in 1066 A.D., two large invasion fleets (one Norwegian and one Norman) sailed towards England within a two-week period. Both voyages were great undertakings for their time. Neither the Norwegian king nor Norman duke possessed the economic resources to finance such large projects; therefore, they utilized forms of lease financing to secure the necessary ships, crews and equipment.

In medieval times, lease-related activities were limited primarily to farming implements and horses, although unique opportunities to utilize leasing occasionally occurred. Many knights of old were known to have leased their armor. For instance, in 1248, Bonfils Manganella of Gaeta leased a suit of armor for the Seventh Crusade, paying a lease rental of close to 25% of its original value.

Leasing in the U.K.

For centuries, the leasing of personal property was not recognized under British common law. The long-term leasing of real property was allowed, however, and was, in many cases, the only means available to acquire the use of land, because of a very rigid system of land laws. Eventually, with the writing of the Statute of Wales in 1284, the leasing of personal property became permissible. Some people, however, used leasing as a means to secretly transfer property, with the intention of defrauding creditors who had based credit decisions on the strength of the apparent ownership of the property. An act was passed in 1571 that prohibited such fraudulent practices, but that still allowed legitimate leases entered into for reasonable consideration.

The early 1800s saw a great increase in the amount and types of equipment being leased in the United Kingdom. The development of the agricultural, manufacturing and transportation industries required new types of equipment, many of which were suitable for lease financing. The concomitant expansion of the railroads also brought about major advances in the development and use of leasing. Most early railroad companies were able to supply only the track and charged tolls for the use of their lines. This left open the opportunity for many entrepreneurs to separately provide the railroad companies and independent shippers with locomotives and railcars.

Development of the U.S. Leasing Industry

As the demand for lease financing of all kinds and types of equipment continued to grow in the United Kingdom, so too did the need for a similarly creative form of finance in the U.S. In the U.S. the first recorded leases of personal property in the 1700s provided for the leasing of horses, buggies and wagons by liverymen. Leasing developed further as the types of, and need for, equipment increased. The real growth in U.S. leasing, however, was caused by the railroad industry.

HISTORIC FACTORS

Railroad companies in the U.S. faced many of the same problems as their counterparts in the United Kingdom. Because expansion was called for, yet conventional financing was hard to come by, the railroad companies searched for ways either to obtain use of the railcars or to have the cars provided directly to the private shippers.

This need created opportunities for investors to earn a profitable return by providing financing for locomotives and railcars through equipment trusts. Banks or trust companies set up and administered these trusts and equipment trust certificates, representing the right to receive a return of principal and interest on invested funds, were sold to the investors. The trust's administrator paid the manufacturer for the equipment and collected rentals from the end-user during the term of the trust. The rentals covered the obligation of the equipment trust certificates issued to the investors.

Many variations of the equipment trust came into being. The most widely recognized type of railroad financing was the Philadelphia Plan, which allowed for the transfer of ownership to the end-user upon completion of an initial term. The Philadelphia Plan became the forerunner of today's conditional sales contracts and money-over-money leases.

In the early 1900s, many railroad leasing companies recognized that a growing number of shippers did not want the long-term control or ownership of railcars inherent in the equipment trust, but, instead, wanted only their short-term use. These leasing companies began offering shorter-term contracts, at the expiration of which the railcar was to be returned to the leasing company, which continued to retain title. These types of leases marked the beginning of the true, or operating, leases that are offered so commonly today.

In other areas of leasing growth, a developing economy as well as the desire of manufacturers to provide financing for their products caused a surge of installment credit in the U.S. during the early 1900s. Manufacturers or vendors believed they would be able to sell more products if they were able to offer an affordable payment plan along with the desired equipment; hence, the beginning of lease financing provided by vendors. Apparently those early manufacturers were right, as vendor leasing is continuing as a significant force in the equipment leasing industry today.

Certain manufacturers, however, were looking for something more. Although definitely interested in the profits that could be made by offering financial services, manufacturers were equally interested in protecting the proprietary technology they had developed and built into their new machinery. Many viewed the leasing (versus selling) of equipment as a way to protect the ownership of such technology, thereby creating a monopoly of sorts.

As early as 1877, the Bell Telephone Company made it a policy to provide equipment in a customer's home or office on a rental basis. Similarly, the Hughes Tool Company kept strict control over the amount paid for its specialized 166-edged drill bit by providing it to wellhead operators on a lease basis. Other examples followed, most notably U.S. Shoe Machinery, which manufactured boot and shoe making equipment and also employed clauses tying customers to its products exclusively. Eventually, however, the enforcement of federal antitrust legislation required manufacturers to offer their equipment for sale.

The U.S. government's use of cost-plus contracts in World War II was another important impetus to the development of the leasing industry. In most contracts, government contractors were allowed to earn only a certain amount above and beyond their costs. These contractors realized that many of their goods or services were needed by the government only during wartime, and that the government would not, in all likelihood, renew those contracts once the war was over. A company that purchased machinery for a specific governmental project could be exposed to a high degree of risk if the contract was not renewed because the contractor may have not yet recovered its equipment purchase costs. Furthermore, if the equipment was specialized, it may have had little market value. Government contractors recognized that leasing, as opposed to buying, of production equipment during a specific contract period minimized their exposure to contract non-renewals. In some cases in which large specialized machinery and tools were required, the government had to act as the lessor to the contractors.

During this same time period, the vehicle leasing industry was beginning to develop on a large scale. Although the first car rental business dates back to 1918, Zollie Frank, a Chicago car dealer who offered long-term fleet leasing of automobiles in the early 1940s, is credited as being the originator of the vehicle leasing industry.

As was previously mentioned, many manufacturers recognized the value of providing financing for their products throughout the development of the U.S. leasing industry. Some manufacturers even set up their own finance organizations. The manufacturers who chose not to, or who were unable to provide financing, were left with two options: to let the customer independently seek financing, as before, or to work with an independent financial concern to set up some type of vendor financing arrangement or program. Independent, or third-party, leasing companies were formed to provide this specific product financing for manufacturers and dealers. Eventually independent leasing companies also began providing leasing services directly to the lessee for other, unrelated equipment.

MODERN-DAY LEASING

The tax attributes of equipment ownership, which have become a major force in the leasing industry, did not become so until the advent of accelerated depreciation and the Investment Tax Credit (ITC) during the 1950s and 1960s. These tax benefits, inuring to the owners of equipment, had little value to companies that could not fully utilize them. Lessors and lessees soon realized that the lessor in a tax-oriented lease could claim the tax benefits of ownership and pass them back to the lessee in the form of reduced rentals, which were often much lower than the payment on a corresponding equipment loan. This type of lease created a twofold benefit: (1) lower lease payments and (2) a pass-through of tax benefits to lessees that otherwise could not use them.

In order to realize the expected tax benefits of ownership in a tax-oriented lease, however, lessors had to be very careful to make certain their agreement with the lessee was, in fact, a lease in the eyes of the Internal Revenue Service (IRS). In 1955, the IRS issued Revenue Ruling 55-540, which outlined what characteristics should (or should not) be included in a tax lease.

The technology revolution of the 1960s had a major impact upon the growth of modern-day equipment lease financing, as firms recognized the competitive advantages of using equipment, such as computers and communication systems, that incorporated the most advanced technology.

Although these firms needed this new equipment, they were often wary of its future economic value. They found leasing to be a flexible way to hedge against potential technological obsolescence. Additionally, the cost of acquiring this new technology was, at times, prohibitive. Many firms that could not afford the down payment required by the bank, let alone the full purchase price, found leasing to be an affordable means of acquiring the necessary equipment. The significant amount of computers and other office equipment leased during the 1960s was very critical to the growth of the leasing industry, as those leases represented the introduction of many companies to equipment leasing.

Independent and manufacturer-related leasing companies have continued to grow in size and number over the years, as can be seen from the previous discussions. This growth, however, has not been to the exclusion of financial institution lessors such as banks, savings and loans and insurance companies. Banks were given the go-ahead to lease equipment in 1963, when the U.S. Comptroller of the Currency issued a ruling that permitted national banks to own and lease personal property. The involvement of banks in equipment leasing was further legitimized in 1970 through an amendment to the Bank Holding Company Act, allowing banks to form holding companies, under which they could engage in a number of nontraditional financing activities, such as equipment leasing.

Although officially in the leasing business, banks at first were allowed (because of regulatory constraints) to offer only leases that, in form, resembled long-term financing. Many of the legislative barriers for bank-related leasing companies are coming down, however. The Competitive Equality Banking Act of 1987, for instance, removed the maximum residual value limit for a portion of bank lessors' business, thus allowing them to competitively enter the operating lease marketplace.

TAX AND ACCOUNTING FACTORS

The modern leveraged lease structure came of age during the 1970s. An investor, or equity participant, in a leveraged lease was entitled to 100% of the available tax benefits of ownership, while paying out only a portion of the leased equipment's cost. The rest was borrowed from a nonrecourse funding source. Investors in this type of lease were concerned over the availability of tax benefits in a specific transaction, as these benefits represented a major portion of the investor's return in the lease.

Because of this concern, the entities putting these complex transactions together would often apply for an advance ruling from the IRS as to the actual tax status of a proposed lease transaction. By 1975, the IRS was so completely inundated with such requests that it issued a set of guidelines that must be adhered to for an advanced ruling (Revenue Procedure (Rev. Proc.) 75-21). Although initially intended as a mechanism for the handling of advance rulings, the impact of Rev. Proc. 75-21 has been felt across the board for all tax leases, as it further clarifies what a lease should be from an IRS viewpoint.

The tides of tax law changes have had a significant impact on the growth and direction of the equipment leasing industry. ITC, which fueled many tax-oriented leases, has changed in amount over the years, and has been made available and taken away three times since its introduction in 1962. As can be expected, a major force in the tax-oriented lease market is absent whenever ITC is unavailable.

The value of accelerated depreciation in lease structures also has been impacted by tax law change. The Economic Recovery Tax Act of 1981 (ERTA 81) did away with the use of the Asset Depreciation Range for depreciation purposes and replaced it with the Accelerated Cost Recovery System (ACRS). ACRS has since been modified by both the Tax Equity and Fiscal Responsibility Act of 1982 (TEFRA 82) and the Tax Reform Act of 1986 (TRA 86).

The constantly changing tax laws have altered not only the tax benefits of equipment ownership, and, hence, the economics of tax-oriented leasing, but also the specific definitions of what constitutes a lease in the eyes of the IRS. Safe harbor leases, including tax benefit transfer leases, were introduced by ERTA 81, but were repealed shortly thereafter by TEFRA 82. TEFRA 82 also introduced the finance lease, which later was modified by the Tax Reform Act of 1984.

The financial reporting attributes of a lease have faced no less a dynamic history. The rapid growth of tax-oriented leases in the 1960s and early 1970s brought about many questions as to the appropriate financial reporting treatment for such transactions. Attempts were made to formulate accounting guidelines; however, it was not until 1976, prompted by pressure on the accounting profession from the Securities and Exchange Commission, that the newly formed Financial Accounting Standards Board (FASB) issued FASB Statement No. 13 (FASB 13). FASB 13 sets forth comprehensive guidelines for both lessor and lessee lease accounting. FASB 13 has given much greater uniformity to the financial reporting of equipment leases, although, since 1976, many other statements, interpretations and technical bulletins have been issued by the FASB in an attempt to further clarify FASB 13.

SUMMARY

The leasing industry has evolved from and been impacted by various significant events. Many of these important events, such as the technology boom, the proliferation of sales-aid financing and tax and accounting guidelines, have occurred in the past 20 to 30 years. In spite of all the changes, however, the core leasing concepts of over 4,000 years ago are still a part of today's industry. Because of this, it should be evident to both outsider and insider alike that the leasing industry is very dynamic. The strength of the industry as a whole is characterized by its resiliency and its ability to make the most of a changing environment.

EQUIPMENT LEASING TODAY

Today, the equipment leasing industry remains a significant force in equipment finance. Whether due to the benefits of obsolescence avoidance, off balance sheet financing, income tax factors, 100% financing or flexibility, leasing remains the single most widely-used method of external finance in the U.S. today. The leasing industry generates around $140 billion in new lease volume each year and provides one-third of the external financing for investment in capital equipment in the U.S. Worldwide, this number approaches $500 billion.

Market Segments

Now, more than ever before, all types of equipment are leased. Automobiles, aircraft, personal computers, mainframes, laboratory equipment, nuclear magnetic imagers, adding machines, satellites, trucks and ships are all commonly leased. The differing types of equipment and respective price ranges help to divide the overall leasing industry into three core segments: the small, middle and large ticket market. (Some lessors further subdivide these categories; for example, the small ticket can be broken down into mini-ticket and micro-ticket leasing.) Each market is characterized by the range of its transaction sizes, the key decision factors influencing lessees and the most common types of lease products available.

The small ticket market is that portion of the overall marketplace that concentrates on leasing lower-priced equipment, such as copiers, fax machines, personal computers and word processors. The cut-off point between the small ticket and middle markets ranges from $25,000 to $100,000, depending upon individual firms' interpretations. The lessee in this market is more concerned with the convenience of acquisition, maintenance and disposal than it is with cost. Although tax-oriented leases can be written in the small ticket market, money-over-money leases and conditional sales contracts are more common.

The large ticket market, on the other hand, is very price sensitive, as it focuses on higher-priced equipment such as aircraft, mainframe computers, ships and telecommunications equipment. The large ticket market typically is defined as equipment having a cost of $1,000,000 or more. This market is quite competitive because of the number of interested parties vying for these transactions. This market, for the most part, consists of large, tax-oriented leveraged leases. Documentation tends to be more involved than in the small ticket market because of the size and complexity of each individual transaction.

The middle market, by definition, fills the very wide gap between the small and large ticket markets, both in size and complexity. This market is influenced by a number of different and, at times, conflicting factors. Price and convenience are common issues surfacing in the negotiation process. Lessors focusing on the middle market often offer both tax and money-over-money leases, depending upon the specific needs of an individual lessee.

Today's Lessors

Industry estimates approximate the number of active equipment lessors at roughly 2,000 to 3,000 companies. Few accurate statistics exist concerning the proportion of the leasing industry that any individual lessor group represents. Nevertheless, all leasing companies can be classified into one of three groups: independent leasing companies, captive finance organizations and lease brokers, or packagers.

Independent leasing companies represent a large part of the leasing industry. These companies are independent of any one manufacturer. They purchase equipment from various manufacturers and then lease the equipment to the end-user or lessee. Independent leasing companies often are referred to as third-party lessors. The three parties are the lessor, the unrelated manufacturer and, of course, the lessee (see Exhibit 1-1). Financial institutions involved in leasing, such as banks, thrift institutions and insurance companies, also are considered independent lessors. Many of these financial institution lessors provide lease financing to lessees as well as funding to other leasing companies. Independent lessors also may provide lease financing plans (called vendor programs) to equipment manufacturers.

The second type of lessor is a captive lessor. Such a lessor is created when a manufacturer (or equipment dealer) decides to establish a leasing company to finance its products. The manufacturer realizes that, by providing lease financing, it can increase the sales of its products over the level of

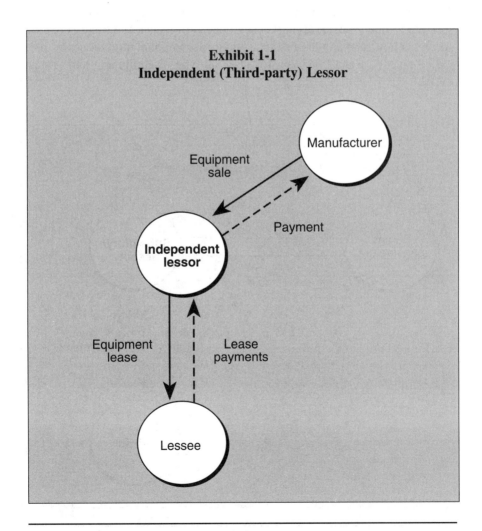

Exhibit 1-1
Independent (Third-party) Lessor

sales utilizing traditional financing alone. The captive lessor also is referred to as a two-party lessor. One party consists of the consolidated parent and captive leasing subsidiary, and the other party is the lessee (or actual user) of the equipment (see Exhibit 1-2).

The final type of leasing company is the lease broker, or packager. The lease broker may find the interested lessee, arrange for the equipment with the manufacturer, secure debt financing for the lessor to use in purchasing the leased equipment and locate the ultimate lessor in the lease transaction (see Exhibit 1-3). The lease broker typically does not own the equipment or retain the lease transaction for its own account. The broker provides one or more various services, depending upon what is needed in a given lease transaction.

The leasing companies just described offer a wide range of products and services to many different market segments. However, the trend is toward specialization, as many lessors are finding substantial market niches by providing tailored lease financing for just one type of equipment and/or customer.

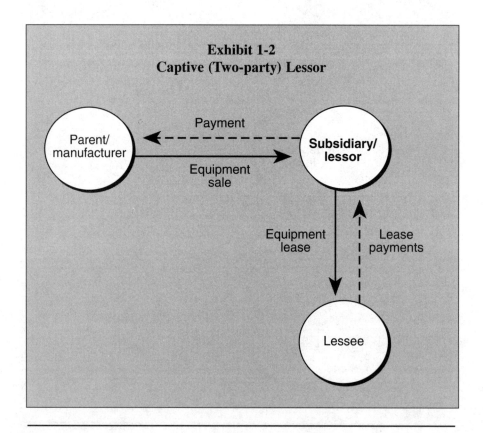

Exhibit 1-2
Captive (Two-party) Lessor

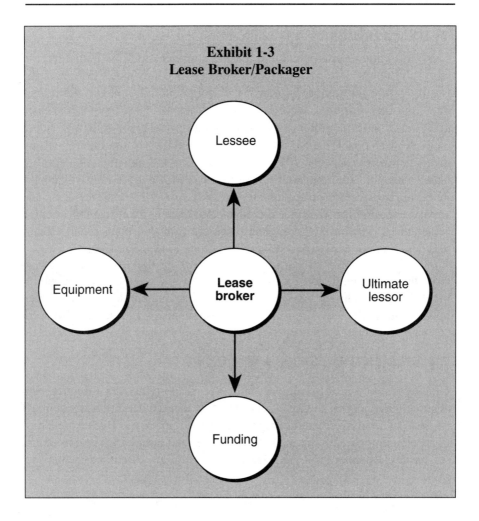

Exhibit 1-3
Lease Broker/Packager

Industry Associations

Over the years, a number of leasing associations have emerged to assist their member firms in identifying and maximizing the opportunities available in this burgeoning industry. Some associations are geographically-specific, such as national or regional, whereas many others focus on a specific type of leased equipment, such as computers, aircraft or vehicles. Each association, regardless of its specific focus, provides its member firms with a wide variety of valuable services.

Why Leasing

The bottomline reason equipment leasing continues to grow is that leasing meets the needs of so many types and sizes of companies. For example, mature, profitable companies may lease equipment to keep bank credit lines open for other purposes. Young, start-up companies lease to conserve cash, and firms requiring state-of-the-art technology lease equipment to avoid technological obsolescence and preserve the ability to upgrade. Leasing meets the different needs of each company: large companies that want to leave managers free to acquire small, noncapital budget items of equipment; midsized companies that cannot tap the stock or bond markets; and small companies that like the convenience of leasing all utilize this creative financing alternative. A complete discussion on the many other reasons why lessors and lessees find leasing beneficial is found in Chapter Two.

Now that an appreciation for the development and evolution of the equipment leasing industry in the financial products marketplace has been gained, the fundamental concepts and components of a lease are discussed.

ELEMENTS OF A LEASE

Leasing is a multidisciplinary industry, embodying tax, finance and accounting concepts, among others. The fact that the lease transaction itself consists of many elements compounds this complexity. Because each of these elements directly impacts the character and nature of the transaction, the basic elements of a typical lease transaction are discussed in this section.

Parties to a Lease

An equipment lease is a usage agreement between an equipment owner (a lessor) and a user of the property (a lessee). The lessee remits to the lessor a periodic rental fee as compensation for the usage of the property. An example of a basic lease is illustrated in Exhibit 1-4.

Lease agreements take the form of written contracts and specifically set forth the various terms and conditions of the lease transaction. Such terms and conditions include the number of periods the equipment is to be used, the amount and timing of the lease payments, the specifications of the equipment leased and any end-of-term conditions.

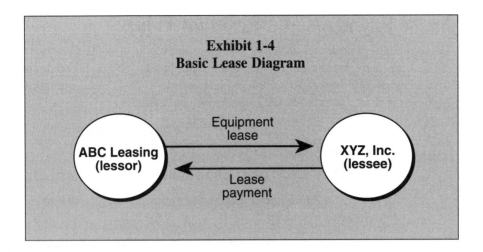

How the lease is viewed and utilized varies throughout the world, although there are two basic forms: the finance lease and the operating lease. The finance lease is the same as a loan, in many respects, because the lessor does not assume any residual risk. The lessor does assume residual risk in an operating lease, however. The finance lease is the most common lease throughout the world. Only in the U.S., and other mature markets, do lessors offer many operating leases to their customers.

Lessors provide the equipment to be leased and may supply services and add value as well. They purchase, manage and remarket equipment as part of the lease process, and also tailor the financing to fit the individual, sometimes highly complex, needs of each equipment user. Typically, the lessor is viewed as the owner of the equipment. However, such a view does not imply ownership from an IRS perspective. If the lease agreement does not meet various tax lease criteria, the lessor is unable to claim the normal tax benefits of equipment ownership. Instead, the lessee is considered the owner for tax purposes and is, therefore, entitled to the tax benefits.

The lessee is the user of the equipment. The lessee, at this point, has gone through the preliminary steps necessary to acquire the equipment and has made the decision to use lease financing. The lessee's equipment, servicing and financing needs, of course, are critical in the development of an appropriate lease product and overall transaction.

Lease Payments and Residual Value

Lessees pay a periodic rental fee or charge to the lessor over the prescribed term of the lease for the use of the leased equipment. The rental payment compensates the lessor for numerous investment costs and operating expenses incurred to provide the leased services, including:

1. Depreciation of the equipment (physical wear and tear as well as technological obsolescence)

2. Interest expense on the debt used to fund the lease

3. General and administrative expenses supporting the operations of the lease company

4. Initial direct costs, such as sales commissions, attorney's fees, credit check fees, etc., incurred at the inception of the lease

5. Costs of bundled services, such as maintenance, warranties, supplies, reagents, etc.

6. Reasonable profit on the outstanding investment over its economic life.

PAYMENTS

Lease payments generally are structured on a monthly basis, although quarterly, semiannual and annual repayment schedules also are used. (Leasing is a very flexible financing tool because of the wide range of possible lease payment schedules.) Payments are commonly structured in advance, with the payment due at the beginning of each period. Payments also can be structured in arrears, with the payment due at the end of each period. Most leases call for equal or even payments over the term of the lease; however, to meet the cash flow of the lessee, payments can be varied in amount and/or timing, as in step leases or skip leases.

A step-up lease consists of increasingly larger lease payments during the lease term. Frequently, a start-up company may be interested in step-up payments, which enable it to conserve cash while securing the equipment necessary to get the business moving. A step-down lease consists of decreasing or declining lease payments over the term of the lease. A company that is currently cash rich might request a step-down lease. Occasionally, a lessee has a seasonal or cyclical cash flow constraint. This type of lessee may opt for a skipped payment lease, in which payments are required only during those business periods when the lessee's expected cash flow is sufficient to make the lease payments.

Lease payment amounts, whether even, stepped or skipped, normally are determined up front and specified in the lease documentation. In some cases, however, a lease may call for a fixed base rental plus an additional contingency rental based upon future usage. A lease also may contain a variable (as opposed to fixed) rate that has been tied to an external index, such as the prime rate or consumer price index. As the external rate increases or decreases, so too does the lease payment. Such indexed contingent rentals usually serve to reimburse the lessor for increases in its underlying costs of providing the lease services (debt costs, maintenance expenses, etc.).

RESIDUAL

Regardless of the method used to arrive at the rental payment, the future expected residual value of the equipment is taken into consideration in pricing most types of leases. Residual value and lease payments both represent potential cash inflow to the lessor. The higher the assumed residual value, the less the lessor needs to charge in the form of lease payments. As an example, if the lessor expects to sell the equipment at the end of the lease for 10% of its original cost, it needs to recover only 90% of the equipment cost through the lease payments (see Exhibit 1-5). The higher the expected residual value, the lower the lease payment is to the lessee.

If a lessor recovers, through the lease payments, all costs incurred in the lease plus an acceptable rate of return, without any reliance on a future residual value, the lease is referred to as a full-payout lease. In an operating lease (not to be confused with an operating lease for financial reporting purposes), however, the lessor does rely on the residual for payment (takes a residual position). In the operating lease, the lessor must receive a certain value for the equipment at the end of the term in order to earn its rate of return.

End-of-term Options

At the termination of a lease, lessors allow lessees to select one of three alternatives:

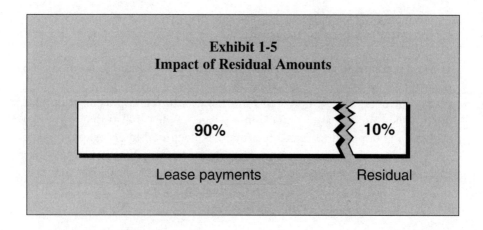

Exhibit 1-5
Impact of Residual Amounts

90%   10%

Lease payments   Residual

1. Return the equipment without further obligation except for, perhaps, deinstallation and shipping costs

2. Purchase the equipment at an exercise price determined by appraisal at the lease termination (fair market value purchase option), or by agreement at the lease inception (fixed purchase option)

3. Renew the lease at a renewal rate determined by appraisal or by earlier agreement.

Some lessors do not provide purchase or renewal rights to the lessee. Such leases are referred to as closed-end leases because renewal or purchase rights are closed off to the lessee.

Certain leases require that the lessor receive a predetermined value (termed a guaranteed residual value) upon return of the equipment to the lessor. If the equipment is appraised or salvaged for an amount less than this value, the deficiency is paid by the lessee guarantor. Lessees, equipment vendors and/or manufacturers, insurance companies, etc., can all guarantee lessor residual values. It should be noted, however, that the inclusion of certain end-of-term options or obligations in a lease contract, such as bargain purchase options or lessee guaranteed residual values, can affect the specific tax and financial reporting attributes of the lease.

Bundled Services

An equipment lease can include other services, such as maintenance, product warranties, supplies, software, consulting time, swaps (replacement equipment to be used while waiting for a major repair on the leased property), etc. The equipment portion of a service package may be minimal depending upon how many other products and services have been bundled. Such bundled service packages are referred to as full-service leases. Net leases, on the other hand, have few, if any, services included in the lease, which implies the lessee must arrange for the services apart from the lease agreement. Service bundling is very natural in leasing, especially when a lease is viewed as a service (temporary equipment usage for a rental fee) as opposed to an equipment purchase.

Funding Aspects

Lessors fund their leased equipment in different ways. In a single-investor lease, the cash paid for the equipment represents the lessor's own equity as well as pooled funds that have been borrowed from a variety of sources, normally on a recourse basis. In a recourse borrowing, the lessor is fully at-risk for any borrowed funds (see Exhibit 1-6).

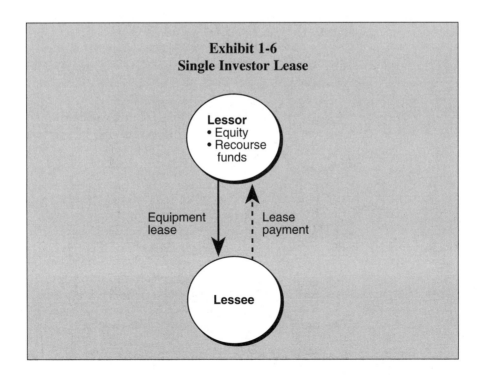

Exhibit 1-6
Single Investor Lease

In a leveraged lease, the lessor borrows a significant amount of nonrecourse money by assigning, or discounting, the lease payment stream to the lender, in return for up-front cash. This cash amount represents the amount of the loan and is equal to the present value of the future lease payments discounted at the lessor's borrowing rate (see Exhibit 1-7). The assignment or discounting of lease payments represents a funding technique used by a large segment of the leasing industry for both single investor and leveraged leases.

In a nonrecourse borrowing, the lender looks to the creditworthiness of the lessee and the value of the equipment for payment, not to the lessor. In fact, the lessee generally makes lease payments directly to the lender in a leveraged lease. The lessor puts equity (cash and/or recourse borrowings) into the transaction in the amount of the difference between the cost of the equipment and the debt. In an assignment, the debt is equal to the present value of the assigned lease payments.

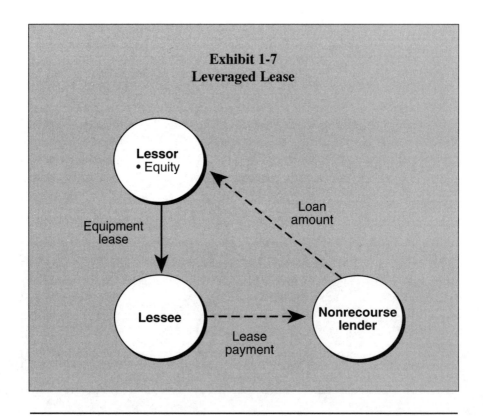

Exhibit 1-7
Leveraged Lease

Tax and Accounting Attributes

From an industry standpoint, a lease is a contract that has been labeled a lease and that contains many of the elements mentioned earlier. Aside from this somewhat generic definition of a lease, each contract also has certain tax and accounting attributes. These various attributes help delineate the tax status and financial reporting treatment of the lease.

TAX ATTRIBUTES

As mentioned earlier, federal tax law, as interpreted by the IRS, dictates the classification of a lease from a tax perspective. The determination as to whether the IRS views a transaction as a lease is outlined in several IRS pronouncements, offering both general and specific insights. The issue of who is at-risk is the major criterion for determining whether a lease is a tax lease or a nontax lease. If the lease is to be a tax lease, the lessor must be considered at-risk. In a tax lease, the lessor receives the tax benefits of ownership and the lessee is entitled to deduct the lease payments as a business expense.

In those cases in which the lease conditions fail to meet the IRS tax lease criteria, the transaction is referred to as a nontax, or money-over-money, lease. This transaction is nothing more than an installment sale contract in the guise of a lease. A money-over-money lease is the opposite of a tax lease. The lessee is bearing the risks of ownership and is entitled to the tax benefits, such as depreciation. It is not, however, entitled to deduct the entire lease payments as it does in a tax lease.

If the lessor is to claim the tax benefits of ownership, risk of ownership must be evident. For instance, a tax lease should not contain a bargain purchase option or specify a lessee guaranteed residual value. Either of these two events removes the residual risk from the lessor. If the lessor bears the risks of ownership, the lease is deemed a tax lease. If the lessee bears those risks, the lease is deemed a money-over-money lease.

ACCOUNTING ATTRIBUTES

The financial reporting treatment of a lease is separate from its tax treatment. Rather than being concerned with the tax characteristics of a lease, the various financial reporting criteria, as determined by the FASB (not the IRS), determine how a lease should be reported in a firm's financial statements.

Because in-depth treatments of lessor and lessee lease accounting are accomplished in subsequent chapters, suffice it to say here that the focus of the financial reporting criteria is to determine whether a lease transaction resembles a purchase or a usage agreement. If a lease contains the characteristics of a purchase agreement it is classified as a capital lease. Characteristics of a purchase agreement include (1) an automatic transfer of ownership from the lessor to the lessee, (2) a purchase option that is considerably less than expected fair market value or (3) terms and conditions that allow the lessee control of the equipment for the major portion of its economic life, or require the lessee to pay for a major portion of the equipment cost.

If, on the other hand, the lease has more of the characteristics of a usage agreement, as in the concept of a true, fixed-period rental arrangement, the agreement is classified as an operating lease. The term operating lease has become synonymous with off balance sheet financing for the lessee because the lease obligation is not reflected on the lessee's balance sheet. The operating lease, because of financial reporting treatment, appears as a lease in the financial statements, whereas the capital lease appears as an installment sale/purchase.

The mere representation or appearance of a lease does not necessarily mean a lease is truly a lease from either a tax or a financial reporting standpoint. Independent guidelines must be considered for both areas of classification. The major determinants for both tax and financial reporting purposes, however, are risk and intent.

CONCLUSION

Simplicity of concept has given leasing a timeless value. It has been a useful equipment financing tool for 4,000 years. Today the need for equipment leasing has only increased, with the many benefits it has to offer contributing to its huge popularity. The affordability and desirability of leasing, particularly as portrayed in the press, have heightened businesses' awareness of the value of the equipment lease as a means for acquiring equipment. Leasing is a dynamic and creative (albeit complex) industry that is still undergoing significant changes – changes that will result in an industry of tomorrow that is even more flexible in solving the financial needs of lessees.

Chapter Two

Dynamics of the Industry

The demand for leasing is high, as evidenced by the amount of equipment being leased each year. Leasing currently accounts for approximately one-third of all capital expenditures in the U.S. and is increasing in popularity throughout the world. Corporations and individuals alike are more and more aware of the many advantages offered by this creative form of financing. Aircraft, computers, railcars and machinery are just a few of the many types of equipment that are leased. To meet this increasingly diverse set of financial needs, leasing companies of varying size, type and market focus are emerging all around the globe.

This chapter reviews the many benefits of leasing and the underlying forces shaping today's leasing industry. This review is presented in the context of how these benefits apply to the two principal parties to the lease transaction:

- Lessee Reasons to Lease
- Lessor Motivations to Provide Services.

LESSEE REASONS TO LEASE

There are 35 to 40 reasons why lessees consider the lease alternative. Some lessees lease for only one reason, others for a variety of reasons. These reasons can be broken down into the following major categories:

1. Technological
2. Financial reporting

3. Cash management

4. Income tax

5. Ownership

6. Flexibility and convenience

7. Economic.

Technological

Keeping up with changing technology is a constant battle for some equipment users. Leasing is an effective means of coping with this problem. Several of the technological reasons for leasing are presented in this subsection.

A NATURAL OBSOLESCENCE HEDGE

One of the major reasons for acquiring equipment through leasing, as opposed to purchasing, is that leasing helps lessees avoid many risks of ownership. Much of today's equipment is based upon rapidly changing technology, making it subject to technological obsolescence. For example, a computer that is expected to be worth 20% of its original value at the end of five years can easily be worthless in three years, given the advances in technology that are constantly occurring. The risk of owning technologically-sensitive equipment is that it may become economically useless much earlier than expected. In fact, in many situations, the equipment becomes useless before the obligations incurred to acquire the equipment have been satisfied.

Leasing helps lessees avoid the risk of technological obsolescence by initially transferring that risk to a lessor. In other words, let the leasing company, as owner of the equipment, worry about the obsolescence. When entering into a short-term lease, a leasing company assumes the technological risk to the extent that it has built an assumed residual value into the lease pricing. If a piece of leased equipment, in which a residual position has been taken, is completely worthless at the end of a lease term, the lessor will not recover all its costs or earn its targeted return. The lessee, on the other hand, has benefited by paying less than 100% of the cost of equipment that is now technologically useless.

Since residual realization is a component of the lessor's return in the lease, lessors cannot take unjustifiable residual positions and remain viable for very long. Lessors, however, long ago recognized two very important market realities that enable them to take the risk of technological obsolescence. First, what is obsolete to one user is not necessarily obsolete to another. Therefore, leasing companies realize the importance of remarketing their equipment that comes off lease. Many leasing companies move used equipment all over the world trying to find the right user.

Second, a lessor's equipment knowledge, combined with its greater access to secondary equipment markets, may cause the equipment to be of greater value in the hands of the lessor than in those of the lessee. Leasing companies are equipment specialists. Their understanding of the equipment markets allows lessors to often sell the equipment for a higher price than if the lessee had purchased the equipment outright and then salvaged it on its own. These two market realities create a business environment that allows lessors to take residual positions in the equipment. The lessor's residual assumption transfers the risk of obsolescence from the lessee to the lessor.

TAKEOUTS, ROLLOVERS AND UPGRADES

Short-term leases in which the lessor assumes a residual position help the lessee avoid the risk of obsolescence at the end of the lease term. Two common lease options, takeouts and rollovers, also give the lessee flexibility during the lease term should the leased equipment become obsolete prior to the termination of the lease.

A takeout occurs when a lessor replaces obsolete equipment with updated equipment. The lessee is "taken out" of the outmoded equipment and then leased equipment incorporating the newer technology. Sometimes a lessee may need only an upgrade of its current equipment as opposed to complete replacement. Many contracts contain upgrade provisions that allow additional equipment to be added to the existing system (through leasing) to increase either its efficiency or capacity. In both a takeout and an upgrade, the lessee may incur costs such as termination fees and payoffs. A rollover occurs when the lessor finances these costs as part of the new lease. This "rolling over" of costs is a benefit to the lessee.

Leasing, therefore, transfers the technological obsolescence risk from the lessee to the lessor throughout the lease term. This is made quite easy because of the many flexible options that can be built into a lease agreement. Purchasing equipment, on the other hand, forces the equipment owner to assume all the risks of ownership, including that of obsolescence.

Financial Reporting

Financial reporting reasons, or accounting presentation, play an important role in many equipment acquisition decisions. Leasing versus purchasing a piece of equipment results in a very different accounting presentation. Loans from banks and capital raised from stockholders are often dependent upon the financial statements of a company. Therefore, this reason for leasing is of great importance to many lessees. Several other reasons are presented in this subsection.

OFF BALANCE SHEET FINANCING

When a company purchases equipment, it must capitalize the equipment on its balance sheet as an asset and recognize a corresponding liability for any loans used to finance the purchase. Because the cost of the capitalized equipment is amortized over its economic life, depreciation expense appears on the company's income statement. Depreciation expense and interest expense on the loan represent the financial statement cost of purchasing and financing the equipment. Capital leases, per Financial Accounting Standards Board Statement No. 13 (FASB 13), although not actual purchases of equipment, are treated much the same way.

If a lease is classified as an operating lease for financial reporting purposes, however, it is not required to be capitalized in the financial statements. (Neither an asset nor a liability appear on the lessee's balance sheet, although certain information is required to be included in a footnote; hence, the term off balance sheet financing.) Furthermore, the only expense appearing on the lessee's income statement that is attributable to the lease is the lease rental expense.

Off balance sheet financing is sought for many different reasons. The use of operating leases helps a firm to "window dress" its financial statements. Many, if not all, the firm's financial ratios and measurements are improved, at least initially. Therefore, the firm appears to be stronger, more liquid and more profitable. Also, there is no debt or liability on the balance sheet, creating the illusion that the firm is less leveraged.

Many companies use operating leases as a way to maintain certain loan covenants. If lenders are not fully on top of the situation, they may be more willing to lend additional funds to such a seemingly less indebted company. Keep in mind, however, that the actual cash flow of the lease is not affected by whether it is treated as a capital or operating lease. Only the allocation of the rental payment in the lessee's financial statements is altered.

IMPROVED REPORTED EARNINGS

The operating lease has a more favorable impact than the capital lease on a lessee's income statement in the early years of the lease. Initially, the operating lease expense is less than the depreciation and interest expense for the capital lease, thus boosting the lessee's overall reported earnings. This concept is illustrated in Exhibit 2-1.

INCREASED RETURN ON ASSETS

Because it lowers the asset base and increases reported earnings, an operating lease helps a lessee report a higher return on assets (ROA). Many managers are sensitive to the ROA, as oftentimes bonus arrangements and profitability goals are tied to the ROA attained by the division or company.

Companies constantly strive to make their financial statements look as strong and healthy as possible to shareholders and lenders. Operating lease treatment, which is discussed in further detail in Chapter Eleven, helps lessees accomplish this goal.

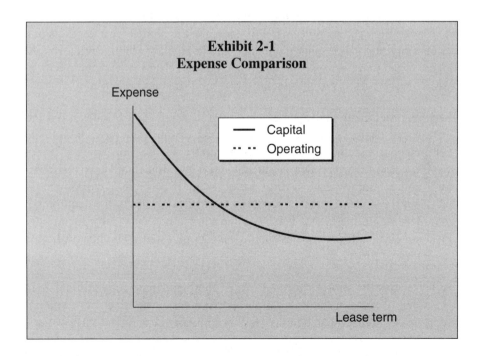

Exhibit 2-1
Expense Comparison

Expense

—— Capital
·· ·· Operating

Lease term

LOWER-LEVEL DECISION MAKER

Managers who wish to acquire equipment, but who do not have the authority to expend the funds, find leasing to be a convenient method of acquiring equipment. Through a lease they are able to pay monthly lease rentals out of the operating budget of the department or division. The amount of the monthly lease payment oftentimes falls within their spending authority guidelines.

Cash Management

Leasing is an effective cash management tool. In fact, cash management is the most often cited reason for companies to utilize leasing. Several cash management considerations are discussed in this subsection.

AFFORDABILITY TO LESSEES

Acquiring assets through leasing, as opposed to purchasing, becomes even more desirable as the cost of equipment rises. As new and more sophisticated (and expensive) equipment is available in the marketplace, many companies choose to acquire equipment through leasing, as opposed to purchasing, for affordability reasons.

First, as a general rule, leasing companies require lower down payments than other financial institutions. For example, the typical lease requires one or possibly two lease rental payments paid in advance (representing roughly 2 to 4% down), whereas many banks require a 10 to 20% down payment (see Exhibit 2-2). This is especially true for used equipment.

Second, other incidental costs of acquiring the asset, such as sales taxes and installation charges, can be included as part of the lease payment. If the equipment is purchased, these costs generally are paid up front. By not tying up cash in large down payments and other incidental costs, a company is able to employ cash savings for other, more profitable, working capital needs. Frequently, the opportunity cost of tying up cash in equipment may necessitate the use of leasing as an alternative, especially for rapidly growing companies whose available cash is invested in highly profitable inventory and receivables.

A lease may be more affordable to a company than conventional loan financing because of the lower monthly payment of the lease. The amount of the lease payment can be impacted by a number of variables. These vari-

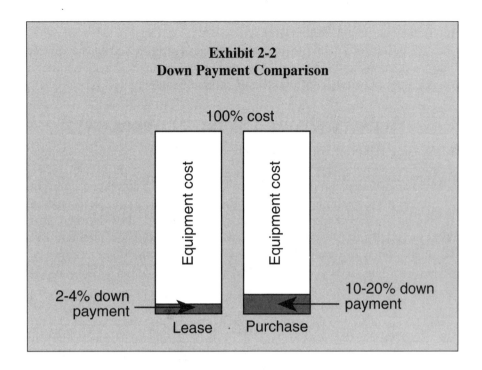

Exhibit 2-2
Down Payment Comparison

ables include the value of the tax benefits received by the lessor in a tax lease, the residual position taken and the longer lease terms available in the marketplace. Leasing helps a firm conserve working capital for its intended purpose.

In today's marketplace, both large and small companies seek financing alternatives with affordable repayment options. Leasing provides these alternative methods of acquiring equipment because of its low, if any, up-front costs, the resulting conservation of working capital, the general ability to finance soft costs (delivery, installation, etc.) and lower periodic lease payments.

IMPROVED CASH FORECASTING

In a lease, the lessee uses the equipment for a specific period of time and, in return, pays a periodic usage or rental charge. The fixed contractual nature of the lease obligation eliminates any uncertainties regarding the future cost of the equipment, thus enabling companies to prepare more accurate cash forecasts and plans. In addition, a company knows a decision must be made at the end of the base lease term to purchase the equipment, return the equipment or renew the lease. Once the decision has been made, the cost of the chosen end-of-term option can be determined and integrated into the planning and forecasting process. In this manner, leasing facilitates the accurate preparation of the overall company budget.

CIRCUMVENTING CAPITAL BUDGET CONSTRAINTS

Many large and profitable firms choose to lease for one very real reason: to circumvent various capital budget constraints. A division or department may have sufficient funds to purchase a new piece of equipment outright. However, if the group has already utilized its capital expenditures budget, it may be precluded from purchasing the equipment. The department or division could request additional capital expenditure funds, but that process is all too often unsuccessful. Even if successful, the steps required to acquire equipment beyond the capital budget are onerous and time-consuming and, therefore, unpopular.

On the other hand, the department or division can lease the necessary equipment and pay for the lease rentals out of its operating budget instead of the capital budget. (As previously mentioned, a lease structured as an operating lease for financial reporting purposes appears as a periodic expense on the lessee's income statement, is not reflected on the lessee's balance sheet and is paid for out of its operating budget.) By utilizing leasing, the department obtains the equipment it needs and avoids the capital budget scrutiny that may not have worked in its favor.

Along the same lines, many state and local governments are required to have special capital appropriations made by the legislature or decision-making bodies to acquire equipment through purchasing. Others require voter approval to issue a debt. These capital appropriations may prohibit acquisition of equipment required for unanticipated needs or emergencies. In these cases leasing can solve the problem, as lease payments can be paid out of operating budgets rather than the already depleted capital acquisition appropriation. Operating expenses generally require only days or weeks for approval as compared to the annual capital appropriations approval. Lastly, leases traditionally have been held to not constitute debt, which requires voter approval.

REIMBURSEMENT POLICIES

Companies operating in certain regulated industries, as well as prime contractors for the federal government, are reimbursed in various ways for the expenses they have incurred, depending upon the nature of the expense. Oftentimes, lease expense can be recovered more quickly than depreciation and interest expense incurred in purchasing an asset. In many cases lease expense is viewed as an expense tied to a certain project or time period. The total interest expense or depreciation for a long-lived asset may not be accepted as a project expense and, therefore, may not be immediately reimbursable.

Income Tax

The tax laws impact all aspects of leasing. The acquisition of equipment by the lessee creates tax consequences. These consequences occur whether the asset is acquired through leasing or purchasing. Their magnitude and characteristics, however, differ significantly depending on whether or not leasing is used. Income tax motivations are presented in this subsection.

RECIPROCITY OF TAX BENEFITS

When leases are structured such that they qualify as tax leases per Internal Revenue Service (IRS) criteria, the lessor is considered the tax owner of the equipment. As the owner, the lessor receives tax benefits that may be considered when determining the lessee's monthly payment. The lessor may fully or partially pass these benefits on to the lessee, allowing the lessee to share indirectly in the tax benefits. This reciprocity, or exchange of tax benefits for a lower lease rate, is particularly important for a lessee that is currently in a nontaxpaying position, and, therefore, cannot utilize the tax benefits of ownership directly. If the same company purchases the equipment, its payments are higher than the tax lease payments and it is unable to benefit from current tax benefits such as accelerated depreciation.

Equipment leasing increasingly is used by nonprofit organizations (the federal government, churches, organizations such as the Boy Scouts of America, nonprofit hospitals, etc.) who cannot take advantage of the tax benefits resulting from equipment ownership. Although tax advantages are not available to these nonprofit organizations, they still can receive indirect benefit if any tax benefits retained by the lessor in a tax lease are partially or fully passed on to them in the form of lower lease rental payments.

In certain leases (municipal leases) to state, local or county governments there are no tax benefits, such as accelerated depreciation, available to the lessor. The municipal lease resembles a conditional sales contract in form, usually having a nominal purchase option (one dollar), stated interest rate, etc. However, the interest income to the lessor in this conditional sales contract is exempt from federal income taxes. The lessor can pass part of these tax savings on to the municipal lessee by charging a lower payment than it would normally need to charge a taxable organization.

LOWER LEVERAGED LEASE RATES

Other benefits can be obtained from the use of financial leverage in addition to the tax savings derived by the lessor in a tax lease. In a leveraged lease the lessor of the equipment provides roughly 10 to 20% of the capital necessary to acquire the equipment. The remainder of the capital is borrowed from a funding source on a nonrecourse basis. The nonrecourse loan is secured by an assignment of the lease payments and a collateral lien on the equipment itself. The advantage to the lessor in the leveraged lease is that all tax benefits incidental to ownership of the equipment pass through to the lessor. This occurs even though its equity interest in the lease is only 10 to 20%. This financial leverage creates greater than proportionate tax savings to the lessor. For example, first year depreciation benefits alone can come close to offsetting a lessor's 10% equity investment. This leveraging of tax benefits results in a lower lease payment being charged to the lessee.

Leveraged lease rates also are impacted by the size of the specific transaction. Generally, leveraged leases are written for very large dollar amounts; therefore, lessors attempt to fine-tune their bids to be competitive, thereby lowering lease rates even more.

DEDUCTIBILITY OF RENTALS

Lease payments in a tax lease are fully deductible by the lessee for federal income tax purposes. Although the lessee, as user, not owner, does not receive any accelerated depreciation benefits, the deductibility of the payments provides a clear tax benefit. In regard to deductibility of lease payments, short-term leases provide an even greater tax incentive to lease.

When leases are written for noncancellable terms shorter than the equipment's Modified Accelerated Cost Recovery (MACRS) classlife, an incremental tax advantage is created to the degree that the deductible lease payments exceed the expenses plus MACRS deductions that would have been available to the user had the equipment been purchased. For example, if an equipment user were to purchase office equipment, it would have to depreciate the 7-year MACRS equipment over eight years, because of the half-year convention, as shown in Exhibit 2-3. However, if the equipment user were to lease the equipment through a four-year, full-payout lease, it would be able to write off 100% of the equipment cost in four years, as shown in Exhibit 2-4. Had the lessee purchased the equipment instead, the equipment-user would have received only cost recovery (depreciation) benefits equal to roughly 69% of the equipment cost over the same four-year period.

NEGATIVE IMPACT OF ADDITIONAL PURCHASES

Current tax law places many companies in the position of being penalized from a tax standpoint when purchasing additional equipment. The impact of federal income tax law on leasing is discussed in Chapters Six and Seven, but it is important to mention here that companies either facing or approaching the alternative minimum tax (AMT) or the midquarter depreciation convention are penalized when purchasing new equipment because such companies have to pay more taxes with the loss or reduction in the value of certain tax benefits.

For a company in or approaching an AMT position it makes more sense to lease. Purchases of equipment may cause the company to pay additional taxes under AMT because of excess accelerated depreciation.

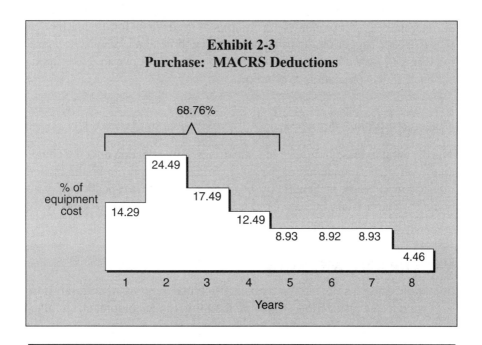

Exhibit 2-3
Purchase: MACRS Deductions

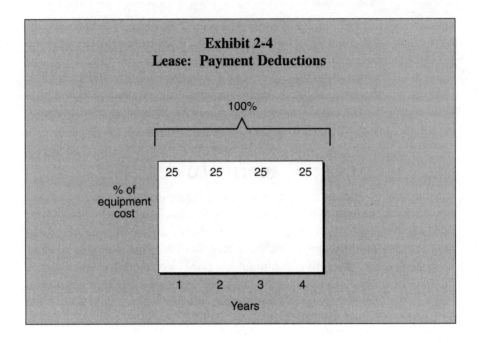

Exhibit 2-4
Lease: Payment Deductions

In addition, a company in need of new equipment in the fourth quarter of its fiscal year may fall subject to the midquarter depreciation convention through purchasing the equipment. This aspect of tax law lessens the over-all first year depreciation benefits for all personal property placed in service during that year. A company with equipment needs in its fourth quarter that also is facing triggering the midquarter convention should choose to lease. Leasing and leased assets have no effect on the rules governing the application of this depreciation convention.

Ownership

The decision to lease or buy is, in many cases, dependent on how the equipment user views ownership of the asset. Some users want to be the owner, others simply want to benefit by utilizing the asset, irrespective of who owns it. The reasons for lessees to lease relating to ownership aspects are covered in this subsection.

USE VERSUS OWNERSHIP

For years, business people have realized the use of equipment is far more important to the production of income than title to the equipment. In other words, it is the use of equipment that produces profit, not the ownership. In fact, if equipment can be used for most of its economic life without the user having the full legal responsibilities, risk and burdens of ownership, then little value exists in owning the equipment.

Although many people are unwilling or unable to separate the concept of asset use from asset ownership, a growing number of individuals and firms are finding that ownership of equipment is not nearly as important as other aspects of equipment acquisition. For example, ownership of equipment may not be as important to a firm as acquiring use of the equipment at the lowest possible cost. This is especially true in today's cash and debt conscious business community. Obtaining the use of equipment through leasing may result in lower acquisition costs, which in turn leads to greater profitability for a firm.

OWNERSHIP NOT AVAILABLE OR FEASIBLE

In certain cases, the only realistic means of acquiring an asset's use is through leasing, as ownership may be unavailable or impractical. For instance, a company may need a satellite to transmit data from its headquarters to regional offices in various parts of the world. The cost of the entire satellite may be prohibitive, especially if the company needs only a fraction of the satellite's power and capabilities. Through leasing, however, the company can obtain the use of a portion of the satellite's capacity in exchange for affordable, periodic rental payments.

AVOIDING STRANDED ASSETS

For financial reporting purposes, equipment that has been capitalized on a firm's balance sheet is depreciated over its estimated economic life. Occasionally estimates are missed, or changes in technology make original estimates of economic life inaccurate. If equipment becomes obsolete before the end of its depreciable life, the company owns a worthless piece of equipment that is not fully depreciated on its books. If the company is able to sell the equipment, it will be sold at a loss, creating a negative impact on reported earnings.

When the firm decides to hold such equipment until it is fully depreciated, simply to avoid a current loss on the sale for reported earnings, the equipment is deemed a stranded asset. To avoid the risk of a stranded asset on its financial statements, a firm should lease the equipment because an operating lease is not reported as an asset on the lessee's balance sheet.

Therefore, by selecting a short-term lease that specifies reasonable renewal terms for additional periods of use, the lessee avoids stranded assets.

LESSEE'S POTENTIAL FOR OWNERSHIP

Another important aspect of leasing is the lessee's general ability to purchase the equipment at the end of the lease term and, thus, eventually become the owner of the equipment. Some purchase options are set at prestated amounts but many leases state the purchase option amount to be equal to the equipment's established fair market value at the end of the lease term. Given economic volatility, fixed purchase option amounts can vary from the equipment's actual value at the end of the term. This practice, therefore, may appear risky for the lessee intending to purchase the leased equipment upon lease termination. Determining purchase options at fair market value, however, is certainly acceptable to those lessees that expect to use the equipment for many more years beyond the initial lease term.

Flexibility and Convenience

Leasing is a very flexible and convenient method of acquiring equipment with few of the restrictions traditionally imposed by lenders. The leasing industry is relatively young and unregulated and, thus, tends to be more aggressive. Leasing companies, therefore, are often in a position to adapt to the specific needs of lessees. This adaptability translates directly into convenience and flexibility for the lessee.

CONVENIENCE TO THE LESSEE

Leasing offers many convenience advantages over conventional forms of financing. Acquiring an asset through a lease can involve less red tape and time than conventional financing. Furthermore, many, if not all, of the headaches of ownership are transferred to the lessor in a lease. As an example, the lessee can simply return the equipment to the lessor upon termination of the lease without further obligation. The lessor bears the burden and risk of disposing of the equipment for an adequate price.

Leasing also provides for very convenient "one-stop shopping." When acquiring a piece of equipment, a company has many product and model options, plus several financing options (including leasing) available from several sources. A lessor takes some of the legwork out of this process by providing product variety and knowledge, the product itself, financing, maintenance, insurance and many flexible options, all under one roof. Documentation can be standardized such that the necessary paperwork is ready for the lessor and lessee to immediately consummate a transaction.

Additional convenience and cost savings are obtained with operating leases. These leases require much less bookkeeping than outright purchases. Purchased assets are capitalized and depreciated in the financial statements, and loan payments are separated into principal and interest. All of this requires additional time and effort.

Cash flow projections, as mentioned earlier, are made easy through leasing because most leases have fixed, equal payments. Commercial loan financing of equipment, on the other hand, may require payments that fluctuate with the prime rate or other index. Furthermore, financing with internal funds is subject to the vagaries of changing costs of capital. Likewise, most firms require a rigorous capital budgeting analysis prior to purchasing equipment. Oftentimes, these companies do not require the same lengthy analysis for leasing equipment, possibly because of the perceived shorter-term nature of a lease. Government agencies frequently can acquire assets through leasing rather than waiting for time-consuming appropriations for purchases.

A few of the many reasons to lease have been reviewed from a convenience standpoint. Each of the remaining reasons builds upon the overall concept of the flexibility and convenience inherent in leasing as opposed to purchasing equipment.

FLEXIBILITY IN LEASE STRUCTURING

Leases are a flexible tool in meeting the various needs of lessees. A brief description of several unique types of leases best illustrates the flexibility of leasing.

1. **Step leases:** A lease agreement that allows the lessee's payments to either increase (step-up lease) or decrease (step-down lease) over the term of the lease to better meet the lessee's cash flow constraints (see Exhibit 2-5)

2. **Skipped payment leases:** A lease agreement that requires the lessee to make payment only during certain months or periods each year. Skipped payment leases are structured to meet the seasonal or other cash flow constraints of a specific lessee (see Exhibit 2-5). For example, a farmer may prefer a lease with

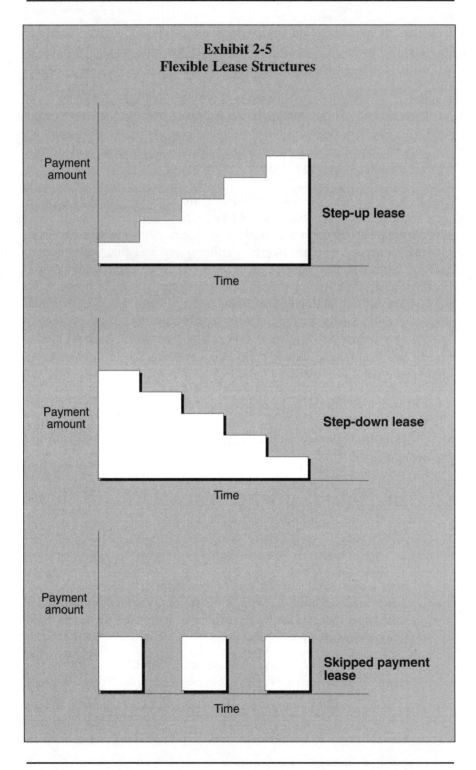

**Exhibit 2-5
Flexible Lease Structures**

payments required only in late summer and fall, when the cash flow from the sale of harvested crops is available to service the lease obligation

3. **Swap lease:** A lease that allows the lessee to temporarily exchange equipment in need of major repair with properly working replacement equipment to avoid costly maintenance and repair delays. Of course, lessors that carry inventory of equipment would be the most able to provide such services

4. **Upgrade lease:** An option that allows additions to existing leased equipment to improve its capacity or efficiency; or an exchange during the lease of outmoded equipment with newer model upgraded equipment

5. **Master lease:** An agreement that contains the boilerplate provisions of the lease. It allows a lessee to add equipment to a lease (by schedule) under the same basic terms and conditions, without having to renegotiate a new lease contract. The lease rate generally is set for each equipment schedule as it is placed in service and put on lease

6. **Short-term or experimental lease:** A lease that provides for short periods of use or for trial use periods. During this time the lessee decides whether the equipment will accomplish the required task and, more importantly, generate revenue. This removes a good deal of the speculative risk from the lessee's acquisition of an asset.

BUNDLED SERVICES

Usually, the subject of a lease is tangible personal property. However, other products or services can be bundled with the lease to offer a full-service package. This bundled package may be more convenient for the lessee, or in many cases, may be less expensive than if the lessee were to separately purchase the same services. Products or services that are commonly bundled into a full-service or bundled lease include maintenance, insurance and property taxes. As manufacturing companies utilize leasing as a marketing tool, they offer full-service leases because they typically can offer bundled services more readily and profitably than independent leasing companies because of their in-depth knowledge of the product and customer needs.

PLANNED REPLACEMENT OF EQUIPMENT

Many managers prefer to lease equipment because leasing facilitates the planned replacement of existing equipment with new technology. A lease contract is written for a specific period, after which the lessee must purchase the equipment, return it or renew the lease. High technology equipment often is returned to the lessor at the end of the lease term, because newer and better technology is available; therefore, new equipment is acquired upon lease termination. If the equipment is purchased, however, no outside forces (i.e., a lease agreement) exist to compel the company to replace its existing equipment. Also, a manager's intent to replace equipment at a certain point easily could be side-tracked by a temporary corporate freeze on capital expenditures.

EXCESSIVE USE OF LEASED EQUIPMENT

Many lessees prefer to lease when they expect to overuse the equipment, which generally results in little, if any, residual value at the end of the lease term. They would rather lease, not own, a rapidly depreciating asset. This perceived benefit of leasing may be a misconception, however. The leasing company also realizes that the lessee will use the equipment excessively. The lessor, therefore, prices the excess wear and tear on the equipment into the lease structure.

PRIORITY DELIVERY

When a company has an immediate need for new equipment, delivery delays might cost it a great deal in terms of lost sales, customer goodwill and incremental profits. From time to time, certain equipment may be in such high demand that a long lead time is required between order and delivery of the equipment. Companies with a dire need will consider every conceivable means of shortening this market-established lead time. If the company has little clout with the manufacturer, it is wise to contact a large leasing company, or one that specializes in that type of equipment and purchases regularly from the manufacturer. The leasing company may be able to obtain a priority delivery of equipment because of its relationship with the manufacturer. Leasing, therefore, may result in speedier delivery of equipment, thereby preserving potentially lost sales, profits and goodwill.

CONTROL OVER THE VENDOR

Some lessees lease from the manufacturer's leasing company so that if, for any reason, the equipment does not perform as it should, the lessee can withhold lease payments to the lessor until the equipment is in working order. In other words, the lessee believes that a vendor leasing company provides implicit warranties for the equipment being leased. This notion, from a legal perspective, is false. Even though the leasing company is related to the manufacturing parent, the parent normally provides, and is at-risk for, all warranty claims. Therefore, regardless of outstanding warranty claims, the lessee still must make regular lease payments to the leasing company according to the lease agreement.

If a lessee ignores its legal responsibility to continue paying lease rentals during a warranty dispute with the manufacturer, the lessor generally approaches the manufacturing parent and tries to resolve the dispute before aggressively seeking payment from the lessee. In this case, the lessee has de facto but not necessarily de jure control over the lessor. This de facto control causes the lessor to act as an arbitrator in settling warranty claims once lease payments have been withheld.

Economic

Lessees constantly review the options for financing their equipment acquisitions. Some lessees use leasing for qualitative reasons; others focus on the economic benefits of leasing. Many of the economic reasons for lessees to lease are discussed in this subsection.

DIVERSIFICATION OF FINANCING SOURCES

National economies always experience swings in the availability of conventional bank financing. Many businesses are acutely aware of the dangers of depending solely upon conventional sources of equipment financing. Diversification of financing sources makes good business sense whether credit is in short supply or not. It is important to note that banks have, by regulatory law, built-in limits on the availability of loanable funds to any single customer.

ADDITIONAL SOURCE OF DEBT FINANCING

Adding to the rapid growth in the volume of leasing since the 1960s have been the continued capital needs for business expansion and modernization.

This growth has occurred in an environment of limited availability of capital funds from the usual channels of equity issues and bond financing. Many economic factors have led to the drying up of conventional capital financing sources, notably the use of loanable funds for government spending and consumer credit.

This dearth of conventional capital forced many companies to seek installment loans from banks for equipment financing. Yet banks and other similar financial institutions had been suffering from their own capital shortages during the same period and could not solve the problem effectively. In order to sell their products, many manufacturing companies turned to leasing to make financing for their equipment available to those customers who otherwise could not obtain the use of the equipment. Thus, during periods of capital shortages stemming from numerous underlying economic factors, leasing's popularity is enhanced by its capacity to provide an additional source of funds not otherwise available.

Often, even when bank financing is generally available, credit may not be obtainable for many businesses. Start-up companies or companies with less than investment grade credit may not be able to borrow additional funds. Fortunately, leasing provides an additional source of financing that is available when conventional financing is not obtainable. Because of their knowledge of asset values and access to secondary equipment markets, lessors are generally more willing than conventional lenders to take the value of the leased equipment into consideration when granting credit approval for a transaction.

Less Restrictive Form of Financing

When lending to a company, a banker typically builds restrictive loan covenants into the loan agreement. The covenants are used by the bank to help minimize, or at least bring to its attention, any potential default on the loan by the borrower. Restrictive covenants typically include current ratio and debt-to-equity ratio limits, a minimum times-interest-earned ratio level and certain other minimum measures of profitability. The violation of any of the covenants flags potential default risk for the lender, who then has the option to demand repayment of the loan obligation.

Loan covenants attempt to minimize the lender's risk but oftentimes can be very restrictive. If the lessee is subject to numerous restrictive covenants then its decision-making autonomy or independence is greatly reduced. Some covenants state the company cannot incur any additional debt without the bank's prior approval.

Lease agreements rarely contain restrictive covenants. The lessor builds its perceived risk into the pricing of the lease by adjusting yield requirements, the amount of refundable security deposits, up-front fees or the number of advance rentals. Of course, the leasing company also considers the value of its collateral in the lease (the leased equipment), along with the viability of repossession if the need should arise. Leasing can offer greater freedom or flexibility than a loan, as it does not tie up a company's future financing options through restrictive covenants.

Economies of Scale in Lessor Purchasing and Servicing

Certain leasing companies, because of their large size, can generate savings in the form of quantity discounts received through volume purchasing. Such savings might be partially passed on to the lessee. Additional savings from economies of scale can be obtained through the full-service lease, for which the cost of maintaining the leased equipment is included as part of each rental payment. If the leasing company is able to procure low-cost maintenance because of its large size, savings can be passed on to the lessee. However, it does not always follow that large size and reduced cost go hand-in-hand. Therefore, savings must be ascertained by comparison with lease rates charged by competing companies.

In addition, large leasing companies have greater access to secondary markets in which returned equipment may be resold. A lessor's ability to quickly sell returned equipment for a high resale amount allows it to take a higher residual position for lease pricing purposes. This greater reliance on residual value permits the lessor to charge a lower lease payment to the lessee. Though large scale operations do not guarantee savings to lessees, at least they present the possibility of savings. With proper negotiation the lessee can receive some of the savings of economies of scale in cases in which the lessor is receiving such efficiency benefits.

Lower Cost

Leasing not only provides the many advantages discussed so far, but also, at times, can be the less expensive method of acquiring equipment. Typically, financial alternatives, such as a lease versus a loan, are compared on a present value, after-tax basis. The alternative with the lower cost, adjusted for the impact of taxes and the time value of money, is selected. Leasing can be the less expensive form of financing for a variety of reasons. In order to properly make a determination as to whether a lease will cost less than an outright purchase of equipment, however, a formal analysis should be performed. The techniques used in the lease versus buy decision are the subject of Chapter Thirteen.

Conclusion

The reasons for leasing's popularity – why 8 out of 10 companies lease today – have been presented in the preceding pages. From this, it can be seen that lessees lease for a variety of reasons. A lessee leases to avoid the risks of technological obsolescence, to benefit from off balance sheet operating leases or to take advantage of the many flexible structuring options available in a lease.

The benefits of leasing to the lessee are numerous. Some of the benefits mentioned may be the only motivation for a company to lease. Other benefits, when combined with technological, financial reporting, cash management, income tax, ownership, flexibility, convenience and economic reasons, overwhelmingly support the case for leasing versus purchasing equipment.

LESSOR MOTIVATIONS TO PROVIDE LEASING SERVICES

At least two parties are involved in any lease – the lessor and the lessee. Lessors, like lessees, have many reasons to be in the leasing business. Understanding these reasons can be beneficial for both parties to the lease transaction.

Lessor Earnings and Profitability

Lessors provide leasing products and services to meet the various market-driven needs of the lessee. In so doing, the lessor's main objective is to assure reasonable profitability in each lease transaction entered into.

A lessor realizes that each lease transaction is not without its associated risks. The lessor requires little, if any, up-front payments and typically charges lower lease payments throughout the lease term; therefore, a lessor's earnings and profitability are at risk in most leases. To minimize the risk, a lessor structures leases that are based upon a number of complex components. These many components and related opportunities, including income tax benefits, residual value and so forth, are discussed in the remainder of this chapter.

Income Tax Benefits

When leases have been structured in conformity with the various IRS criteria defining tax lease status, the lessor is considered the tax owner of the leased equipment. As such, it is entitled to the numerous tax benefits of ownership. The primary benefits are accelerated depreciation, gross profit tax deferral, the Investment Tax Credit (ITC) and tax-exempt interest income on municipal leases to qualifying state, county and city governments. The complexities of the tax benefits of leasing preclude an indepth discussion at this time. They are, however, discussed in detail in Chapter Six.

Accelerated depreciation provides the lessor with a write-off of its equipment acquisition costs according to the MACRS guidelines. For example, the first- and second-year deductions for 5-year classlife equipment (computers, buses, certain manufacturing equipment) are 20% and 32%, respectively, of the equipment cost. Therefore, the lessor can write off over 50% of its equipment acquisition costs over a short two-year period.

Gross profit tax deferral provides manufacturer-lessors or dealer-lessors with a valuable tax benefit. Any gross profit to the manufacturer in the overall transaction is deferred and recognized over time. Since the taxes on the deferred gross profit in a tax lease are paid over the MACRS classlife of the leased asset, the parent manufacturer pays fewer taxes on a present value basis.

ITC, when available, has significant value to lessors who have sufficient tax appetite to utilize it. Tax credits, unlike tax deductions, represent dollar for dollar reductions in a lessor's tax liability. As an example, for a 35% tax bracketed lessor, a 10% ITC is worth the same as a 15.38% deduction (as a percent of the leased equipment's cost). However, the Tax Reform Act of 1986 eliminated ITC.

Tax-exempt interest earnings are available to lessors leasing to qualifying state, local and county governments. The lease agreement resembles a conditional sales contract in that it states an interest rate and provides for a nominal purchase option at lease termination. The lessor does not qualify for any tax benefits of ownership, such as depreciation, but receives interest earnings that are exempt from federal income taxes.

Financial Leverage Considerations

One of the more significant economic aspects of leasing is financial leverage. Contractually fixed lease rentals permit lessors to finance the acquisition cost of their leased equipment with large proportions of debt relative to equity. To the degree the debt costs less than the interest rate charged in the lease, the lessor can earn substantial returns on its equity. Use of significant amounts of financial leverage is commonplace in leasing because of the contractual nature of lease revenue and the availability of tax benefits, as well as the additional expectation of residual value.

Debt acquired by the lessor for use in purchasing the equipment to be leased is obtained on either a recourse or a nonrecourse basis. If a lessor borrows funds on a recourse basis, it must honor this obligation to the bank or lending institution whether or not the lessee defaults on the underlying lease. If the lessor borrows funds on a nonrecourse basis, however, and the lessee subsequently defaults on the lease, the lending institution cannot demand repayment from the lessor. Instead, the lending institution must seek recovery of any losses from the lessee or from the salvage of the leased equipment (collateral).

Lessors in large leveraged lease transactions generally are able to offer very favorable lease pricing to lessees. A lessor typically borrows from 80 to 90% of the equipment cost, thus paying for only a fraction of the cost from its own funds, or equity. The lessor can afford to offer lower tax lease rates because it is receiving 100% of the tax benefits available in the lease in exchange for payment up front of a fraction (10 to 20%) of the equipment's cost.

Residual Speculation Motivations

The residual value of leased equipment may represent an important cash inflow to the lessor. It also may be a significant part of the lessor's overall return in the lease. At the end of the lease term, assuming no purchase or renewal option has been exercised, the lessee returns the leased equipment to the lessor. The lessor then re-leases or sells it for the highest possible amount. In order to offer competitive lease pricing, the lessor must factor some of this expected future value into the lease rates.

For instance, if the lessor is confident the equipment will be worth at least 10% of its original value at lease termination, it may price the lease payments so that it recovers 90% of the equipment cost. The lessor hopes the remaining 10% will be realized once the equipment is returned and subsequently salvaged or re-leased. Keep in mind that the amount of the residual used in the lessor's pricing is not the exact amount the lessor expects to receive at the end of the term, but, rather, the amount the lessor is willing to be at-risk for in the lease. The lessor must receive the at-risk residual amount in order to recover all of its costs and earn a pretargeted return.

Leasing companies also are motivated by the opportunity to earn higher than expected returns from the realization of residual values that exceed the values used in pricing their leases. Of course, the downside risk to leasing companies is that the residual value in a lease will be less than the amount assumed on the lease pricing. Lessors, however, generally are conservative in the residual value used in pricing. This conservative approach increases their confidence of earning at least the required residual value, if not more.

In a leveraged lease, the lessor's return comes from two primary sources: the tax benefits (as previously discussed) and the residual value of the equipment. Since the lease transaction is highly leveraged with nonrecourse borrowings, the lease payments will most likely go to the lending institution to cover the lessor's loan obligations. Therefore, the lessor's other sources of income – the residual value at lease termination and the tax benefits throughout the lease term – become even more crucial to its overall return in the leveraged lease transaction.

Vendor Leasing Issues

Since the inception of the leasing industry, manufacturers of equipment have recognized that providing lease financing for their customers helps them realize many of their objectives. Vendor leasing, whether provided by the manufacturer's captive finance company or by an independent lessor, is increasing in importance and value today.

Providing lease financing is a successful way for manufacturers to distinguish their products. Providing the equipment as well as the financing may entice a potential customer to choose a certain manufacturer's product because of the convenience offered. Convenience, however, is not the only benefit of one-stop shopping. By locking in the sale with financing so it will not be lost to a competitor as the customer searches for financing, the vendor lessor exerts a considerable amount of market control.

Market control also is experienced because the vendor lessor is providing leasing services for the manufacturer. The manufacturer, therefore, knows when its customer, the lessee, will be in need of a new piece of equipment (i.e., at the termination of the existing lease term). This knowledge allows the manufacturer to market a new piece of equipment to its current leasing customer long before a competitor is aware a potential transaction exists.

Increased revenue and profitability also can accompany a vendor leasing program. Incremental sales of equipment may be made, as leasing makes equipment acquisition affordable for customers who could not purchase the equipment outright. Along the same lines, customers may be able and willing to lease more expensive models or additional accessories now that leasing has put these extras within their reach.

Manufacturers also can benefit greatly from the marketing synergy, as well as profitability, that exists in providing bundled services as a part of a full-service lease contract. The vendor lessor can augment the concept of one-stop shopping by providing maintenance, insurance and payment of property taxes for the lessee. The vendor lessor is at a real, or at least highly perceived, advantage in providing these services because it is in some way related to the equipment manufacturer. The vendor lessor may be able to provide these services at a cost below what the lessee could separately procure them for, and as a result, profit from the additional revenues.

Some products are necessary to the operation of the equipment. For example, a vendor lessor that manufactures and leases copy machines also can provide toner and paper for the copier. These ancillary products add to the one-stop shopping feature of a lease and to the overall profitability of the lease.

Integration Opportunities

Integration refers to ways in which a company can expand operations. Vertical integration refers to acquisition of the means of producing a product from the raw material sources, through production and transportation, to the final wholesale and retail outlets. Horizontal integration refers to expansion into the sales and production of related products (like wax production for an oil company). With conglomerate integration, a company enters into a wholly unrelated business venture.

Manufacturing firms, as discussed, use leasing as an additional way to sell goods. Establishing a vendor leasing program to further promote sales is an important step in vertically integrating a company. An additional advantage of such integration is that the leasing company can better serve the client because of its extensive knowledge of the product. For example, knowledge of the product permits the lessor to predict with greater accuracy residual values, which removes some risk from leasing. This enhanced knowledge of residual values may enable the vendor leasing company to fine tune the lease payment amount charged the lessee. Control over residuals also allows the vendor lessor to sell new equipment at the termination of the lease to a somewhat captive clientele.

Some vendor lease companies find leasing so profitable that they begin leasing equipment other than that manufactured by the parent company. This expansion into new, unrelated product leasing is a form of horizontal integration that is becoming popular among manufacturer-lessors.

Some other companies enter into the leasing business as a totally unrelated business opportunity in relation to their normal operations. New business ventures involved with leasing represent a form of conglomerate integration. A utility acquiring a lease company is an example of conglomerate integration. However, a bank acquiring a leasing company is a form of horizontal integration because the leasing service is closely related to the bank's loan service.

The natural expansion from a vertically integrated manufacturing company beginning to lease others' products (horizontal integration) to other companies acquiring lease companies as new investment opportunities (conglomeration) has led to an increase in leasing's popularity.

International Leasing

Overseas leasing is expected to expand significantly in order to serve large multinational companies abroad as well as foreign companies that are seeking new forms of asset financing. Although equipment leasing abroad by U.S. companies started only 20 years ago, the amount of equipment on lease in other parts of the world has grown significantly. One of the reasons for the growing popularity of leasing as a form of financing new equipment abroad is that many foreign banks generally offer loans for about three years and equipment buyers are, therefore, required to negotiate two or three loans during the life of a particular piece of equipment.

As in the U.S., all types of equipment are being leased abroad: tankers, railroad cars, computers, machine tools, printing presses, aircraft, restaurant equipment, mining equipment and drilling rigs. Many international leases do not offer the same benefits of depreciation or the possibility of residual value gains, because foreign tax laws differ from U.S. tax laws.

Despite restrictive foreign government regulations concerning percent local ownership requirements, varying tax laws, foreign exchange fluctuations and export laws, many equipment leasing companies are still interested in the expanding leasing markets abroad. Many U.S.-based multinationals use leasing to promote foreign sales. In addition, numerous tax, import and investment tax credit benefits are available to the experienced international lessor. In essence, the same reasons that led to an expansion of leasing in this country have stimulated leasing abroad. Thus, international markets have created another factor leading to the popularity of leasing.

CONCLUSION

The dynamics of the leasing industry is not a topic to quickly dismiss as too elementary or straightforward. Many important reasons or motivations to lease exist for the two primary parties to the lease transaction. A full understanding of the dynamic forces that drive this multibillion dollar industry, therefore, is absolutely necessary for success today. Lessors that understand lessee needs are better positioned to offer lease products that will be acceptable to the lessee marketplace. Indeed, those lessors that more clearly understand lessee needs sell more leases.

Successful lessors continue to satisfy their main goal, that of greater earnings and profitability, through careful consideration of the many components of a lessor's return in a lease. By the same token, all parties involved in the industry (lessors, lessees, other professionals, etc.) are more effective in their roles in this exciting industry if they have a solid feel for its dynamics.

Chapter Three

Trends in Leasing

Any discussion of leasing is incomplete without looking to what the future may bring and the role of lessors in that future. A&H has been fortunate over the last 15 years to have had the opportunity to meet many people, see diverse practices, encounter unique situations and enjoy a broad range of experiences. These experiences and our daily contact with all segments of the leasing industry allow us to register the pulse of the industry. By combining this feel for the industry with our knowledge and experience, A&H has been able to identify trends developing within the leasing industry and key factors for success. Therefore, this chapter is broken into the following two sections:

- Trends in the Leasing Industry

- Key Factors for Success.

TRENDS IN THE LEASING INDUSTRY

The key trends expected to significantly influence the leasing industry over the next several years can be separated into the following categories:

1. Changing lessor base

2. Evolving lessee perspective

3. Changes in lease products

4. Factors affecting profitability

5. Tax and accounting changes

6. Factors necessary for volume to increase

7. Emergence of international markets

8. Key economic factors

9. Increased interest in consumer leasing.

Changing Lessor Base

As the leasing industry in the U.S. continues to mature, it is still experiencing change and consolidation, although not at the same rate as a few years ago. For example, firms attempting to hedge against or plan for future changes in the leasing industry are diversifying their businesses from equipment, marketplace or geographic standpoints. Although this diversification can be accomplished internally, many firms will move to a quicker resolution through external means, such as mergers and acquisitions.

Oftentimes the quickest way for a lessor to enter into a specific niche market such as medical equipment may be to acquire a leasing company that specializes in that area. Other reasons for strategic acquisitions include achieving operational economies of scale, enhancing growth without the associated sales costs and increasing market share.

The lessor base will change because of sales of leasing subsidiaries by their parents, usually for one of two reasons. The first is a desire by the parent to return to its core business. This decision can be based on any number of factors, such as reduced bond ratings from the additional debt placed on the balance sheet by the captive or a lack of understanding of the finance business on the part of the parent. The second reason is that many companies have experienced lower earnings because of external economic factors. Several of these companies have sold their subsidiaries to generate bottom-line income and clean up their balance sheets.

Another factor contributing to a changing lessor base is the impact of the lessor's tax capacity and the alternative minimum tax (AMT). The AMT consequences of owning equipment have impacted the way lessors, both large and small, do business. For some lessors, AMT has forced the creation of different products or altered pricing strategies. For others, the impact has been severe enough to cause them to leave the marketplace. The level of industry participation of some entities, such as banks, is tied directly to their tax capacity.

Some leasing companies have left the industry because of the economy, unfavorable borrowing rates and ill-advised business decisions. The economic environment will continue to be an important factor in determining who succeeds and who fails.

All the factors discussed above have contributed, to one degree or another, to the ever-changing lessor base. The next few years will bring more of the same, albeit at a much slower pace. The lessor landscape will continue to change. However, few new players will enter the market, especially from the manufacturing arena, where third-party lessors are filling the financing needs of most manufacturers.

Evolving Lessee Perspective

In spite of tax law changes, adverse economic conditions and constantly changing government fiscal policies, leasing has continued to grow over the years. Much of this growth is caused by an increase in lessee awareness and sophistication. More lessees than ever are taking the time to understand the many benefits leasing has to offer. Often this education process is provided by the lessors themselves through sales calls and information campaigns.

This increase in awareness is a double-edged sword for lessors. Lessees increasingly will take tougher stands when negotiating with lessors as their knowledge level of leasing increases. They will seek more assurances regarding end-of-term consequences, such as demanding fixed or capped purchase and renewal options. These demands result in new products such as window leases that provide early-out opportunities for the lessee. In addition, lessees are exercising more care in their selection of a lessor. Lessees are creating their own master lease agreements rather than signing those of the lessors. The combination of more knowledgeable and aggressive lessees with inexpensive analytical tools will force lessors to be more competitive and customer driven.

Changes in Lease Products

The leasing industry is not regulated in the U.S. This has allowed leasing companies to quickly adapt to changes in tax laws, accounting rules or the economic climate. This adaptability leads directly to an evolving mix of lease products. For example, as funding from the federal government to states and municipalities continues to decline, lessors are offering more tax-exempt user leases to meet the needs of this marketplace.

One product trend is that operating leases will continue to expand in terms of market share. This in part relates to the increase in lessee awareness. As lessees more clearly understand the financial reporting, cash flow and technological benefits of operating leases, they will request off-balance sheet lease structures. To the extent possible, lessors still try to structure the lease as operating for the lessee and as capital for themselves. However, this is becoming more and more difficult in today's marketplace, resulting in new and innovative structures.

A variety of tax, economic and financial reporting considerations will add to the number of operating leases in the marketplace. Flexibility in keeping pace with technological change is one of the factors. One of the more popular structures used to achieve flexibility through operating leases is the window lease. The many variations of this lease allow lessees to get out of the lease at various points, or windows. Within the sometimes vague provisions of Financial Accounting Standards Board Statement No. 13 (FASB 13), the lease can be classified as an operating lease for the lessee if structured properly. Unfortunately, this structure most often makes the lease operating for the lessor.

The industry also is seeing more fixed or capped purchase options in the structures requested by lessees because lessees are seeking more end-of-term assurances. As lessors provide these assurances, different lease products will evolve. Lessors will have to continue to be creative in designing products that meet lessee needs and comply with tax and accounting rules. Synthetic leases are products that fall in this category.

Lessors also are being forced to take higher residual positions because of an increase in competition. With more dependence on residual realization to meet their yield requirements, lessors often are caught in a vise when offering fixed purchase or renewal options. On one side is the desire to generate new business in a very competitive marketplace. On the other side is the need to maintain yields and profitability. It is expected that lessors will continue to face this dilemma, perhaps on an increasing level.

We also expect to see an increase in full-service leasing. Offering other services such as maintenance, insurance or ancillary products is one way in which lessors can distinguish their products from those of the competition. In addition, there will be more facility management contracts, in which a lessor not only leases the equipment but also manages and staffs the facility. The facility management contract is becoming a popular product offered by manufacturer-lessors.

As the rapid increases in technological advancement seen in the 1980s slow, and differences between high-technology products such as computers continue to diminish, more and more lessees are deciding not to upgrade to the latest technology. The result is that more used equipment will be leased than ever before. This trend also is caused in part by continued uncertainty about the economy and any related downturns. Lessors, therefore, will be forced to take creative approaches in structuring leases containing more used equipment. The near future should see an increase in the amount of used equipment being leased, utilizing a variety of different structures.

Factors Affecting Profitability

It is difficult to look at lessor profitability in general terms. Profitability will vary significantly, depending on the characteristics of the leasing company. Favorable borrowing rates, economies of scale and a variety of products are just some of the reasons the very large companies operate on a different level of expected profitability. A small leasing company, on the other hand, can charge a premium for a higher level of individualized service. Regardless of size, though, all leasing companies are faced with the challenge of maintaining or increasing profitability.

Competition in the leasing industry will remain intense, particularly as lease financing is increasingly viewed as a commodity. As the number and sophistication of lessees continue to increase, all leasing companies will continue to look at strategies leading to an increase in market share. As a natural consequence of this competition, the industry is experiencing an increasing emphasis on residual and term as lessors attempt to lower their lease rates relative to the competition. This has resulted in lower profit margins – profit margins that are not expected to improve in the near future.

Lessors are being forced to look at additional sources of profit because of the intense competition in the marketplace, and the resultant lower profit margins. One strategy has been to examine other financial service products. For example, some traditional equipment lessors have become involved in commercial real estate leasing and others have entered the insurance business. In addition, most leasing companies are focusing on the inner sources of additional profit. More than ever, they are monitoring their selling, general and administrative expenses to improve the bottom line. Leasing companies also are relying more on better software and systems to help lower back-office costs. Many, for instance, utilize computerized credit scoring systems that are both time and cost efficient.

The rise in residual risk that is being experienced by lessors has increased the need for asset management. In many leasing companies asset management will be the fastest growing department as lessors search for new and innovative ways to realize the residual. Also, given the increase in used equipment being leased, equipment refurbishment and remarketing will be key to residual realization and, hence, profitability.

Another important source of profitability is the employees of the leasing company. Just as other industries are reengineering their workforces and operating strategies, so too is the leasing industry. This has led to a reduced workforce that requires more from the employees. As this trend continues, the need for an educated workforce increases as many employees now wear more than one hat. Training helps keep employees motivated, leading to increases in productivity.

Tax and Accounting Changes

Congress is endlessly tinkering with the tax code to meet myriad social and economic goals. This trend will continue, but likely will not have a significant impact on the way lessors do business in the near future. However, the AMT will influence not only how lessors do business, but also whether or not they stay in business. For many lessors, AMT is causing effective tax rates significantly in excess of the top corporate rate of 35%. Leasing companies are endlessly seeking new ways to avoid the AMT, maintain profitability and remain competitive. This is a challenge that must be met by leasing companies large and small.

For now, though, and in the near future, AMT and the other subtle changes that are filtering into the tax code will continue to increase the overall tax burden, forcing lessors to adjust their products and structures accordingly. Major structural changes to the tax code, such as changes to the Modified Accelerated Cost Recovery System or the reinstatement of the investment tax credit, are not expected in the foreseeable future.

From an accounting perspective, lease accounting continues to evolve, although not from specific changes to FASB 13. For example, new FASB statements regarding special purpose corporations will affect the accounting and structuring of securitizations as well as new and innovative domestic and cross-border transactions. All indications are, however, that specific changes to lease accounting are not part of the foreseeable future.

The continued stretching of the spirit of FASB 13, especially with regard to structuring operating leases, may force the FASB to rethink FASB 13. For now, however, the status quo will remain, from both an accounting and a tax perspective.

Factors Necessary for Volume to Increase

An increase in overall capital spending is the first factor necessary for leasing volume to increase. The adverse economic climate throughout the world in the last few years has made most companies wary of acquiring new equipment – whether by leasing or purchasing. The current trend has been that of an improving world economy and an increase in capital spending. Given that a certain percentage of all equipment is acquired with the lease alternative, an increase in capital spending means more equipment will be leased.

Another key factor necessary for lease volume to increase is an increase in interest rates. As bank borrowing rates increase so too do lease rates – although typically not as quickly. Therefore, the gap between the two rates shrinks, making leasing more attractive to lessees that previously had been seeking the lower bank rates. Economic forecasts indicate that interest rates will, in the near future, continue to rise, thereby leading to more volume.

Historically, one of the most popular reasons to lease has been to avoid technological obsolescence. Because technology is still an important reason to lease, changes in technology in areas such as telecommunications will lead to an improvement in leasing volume.

Many lessees often lease because they have been educated about the benefits of leasing. Therefore, another key factor in achieving greater lease volume is further education of lessees about the complexities of leasing. Such education can be accomplished either by the lessor or through more formal, external training programs. As discussed earlier, a better educated lessee community increases leasing volume.

Manufacturers and dealers will continue to provide leasing services in order to boost sales of their products, either through their own financing organization or through vendor leasing agreements.

Whether through a captive subsidiary or through a third-party leasing company, manufacturers have enjoyed an improvement in sales and gross profit by offering lease products to their customers. This trend is expected to continue as most leasing companies have vendor programs available to their customers and vendors continue to recognize the benefits of a vendor program.

Finally lessors must continue to instill confidence in leasing through quality products and service. Leasing companies have for years combated the perception that leasing is a form of second rate financing or a last resort. Too often, these perceptions are based on a few transactions. The effect of these transactions has been lasting and will require diligence on the part of leasing companies to overcome.

Emergence of International Markets

Leasing continues to grow at different rates around the world. Emerging countries, attempting to meet their growing capital requirements, typically have few lessors willing to take the associated credit, equipment, currency and interest rate risks. These countries often do not have favorable accounting or tax regulations and, more importantly, lessors do not have the ability to evaluate the creditworthiness of the lessee. Therefore, leasing, although it has high potential, is usually done on a limited basis.

On the other hand, the leasing industry is very developed in many countries. These are the established, industrialized countries in North America and Europe and a few countries such as Australia, India, Japan and Korea in the Pacific Rim. These countries typically have a large number of lessors chasing a limited number of high quality transactions. As competition increases, they increasingly look to international markets for growth.

Aiding the recent growth in international lease markets is the formation of economic trade unions such as the European Economic Community and the North American Free Trade Agreement. These unions are designed to eliminate many of the trade barriers that currently exist between countries. The affected leasing industries will benefit from these unions, although to what extent is not yet known. Other free trade zones, specifically in Central and South America and the Pacific Rim, are being discussed.

Several U.S. lessors have tried, with varying degrees of success, to establish operations in foreign countries. Failure has often been a result of not understanding the local market conditions, rules and regulations, procedures and, most importantly, the local customs and ways of doing business.

Some lessors have overcome these barriers by establishing a joint venture with a local partner that understands the nuances of doing business in that particular country. Many of these ventures are not currently profitable because of the large investment required to get the venture off the ground. The groundwork for future profitability has been laid, however, and U.S. investors will continue to expand their international markets.

Key Economic Factors

A strong economy, which is necessary for equipment acquisition to increase, also leads to an increase in leasing volume. It is impractical to discuss the economic forecast for all countries but the general economic outlook is favorable.

Past economic problems have caused restructurings, renewals and sale/leasebacks in the industry. Lessors in the past have seen a slight increase in their provisions for losses and have experienced slightly higher charge-offs compared to other years. However, this trend will moderate because of an improving economic climate. The status of the economy also has led to more used equipment being leased. This trend will continue.

Another consequence of economic conditions has been an increase in lessee requests for tailored structuring to more adequately match their cash flow needs. More step and skipped payment leases are required than ever before. Lessees, having been exposed to these structures, will continue to request them. Lessees also will seek more full-service leases that bundle facility management contracts into the lease, allowing the lessee to decrease its overhead costs.

Finally, economic conditions have forced those lending to leasing companies to more closely evaluate the financial condition of the lessor. More time is being spent by funding sources to understand the complex financial reporting requirements of leasing companies. As a result, lessors will be required to spend more time seeking and managing funding relationships.

Increased Interest in Consumer Leasing

An increase in the volume and types of consumer leasing is expected. Over the past 20 to 30 years many consumers have been introduced to the leasing industry through vehicle leasing. Vehicle leasing recently has gained considerable momentum, as many consumers have opted for the lower up-front costs and monthly payments of a lease.

Vehicle leasing experts predict that approximately 50% of all new automobiles will be leased in the next 5 to 10 years. The acceptance of leasing as a financing tool in the vehicle market is spreading to other consumer marketplaces as well. Personal computers and other types of office equipment for home use are now being leased more often than before. This trend is expected to increase dramatically as the number of consumers exposed to consumer equipment leasing increases.

CONCLUSION

The fundamental benefits of leasing that have existed for over 4,000 years continue to provide impetus for the growth of equipment leasing. These benefits, combined with the creativity of the leasing industry, will continue to increase the acceptability of leasing as a means to finance equipment.

KEY FACTORS FOR SUCCESS

The commercial equipment leasing marketplace has become much more competitive. Even as margins remain narrow, lessees are demanding more and better service. Success in such a market is not an accident, but, instead, is the result of a well-conceived strategy. This section presents several key factors that are directly related to the level of success a lessor will enjoy.

1. Competitive advantages

2. Specialization

3. Customer service and flexibility

4. Funding ability

5. Controlled back-office costs

6. Highly-trained workforce

7. Appropriate strategies

8. Adaptability to market shifts

9. Maintenance of objectives.

Competitive Advantages

One of the key strategies for success is to establish a competitive advantage. Such an advantage can take many different forms. For example, some leasing companies use their size as an advantage. They can offer every possible structure, finance every type of equipment and market their products to the entire world, giving them a very distinct advantage in the marketplace.

Other leasing companies create an advantage by finding funding sources that are diverse or that allow them to borrow favorably. Over the years, lessors have diversified away from traditional bank and public borrowing by utilizing insurance companies, pension funds, venture capitalists, income funds and securitizations as alternative funding sources.

There are other competitive advantages, one of which is the tax status of the leasing company. Certain provisions of the tax code, such as the midquarter convention and the AMT, create an unlevel playing field when pricing transactions. For example, a lessor not in AMT may price more favorably than a competitor who is in AMT. A strong parent, a relationship with a manufacturer or superior and individualized service are other competitive advantages.

Specialization

Specializing in a specific niche market, another competitive advantage, is important enough to warrant its own section. Many lessors, large and small, have been successful by focusing on one particular product or market segment. Sometimes the focus is on equipment type, such as mainframe computers or rail cars. The focus also may be by transaction size, a geographic area or technical expertise. Regardless of the niche, specialization can lead to success in a market through superior knowledge, uncompromising service and value-added products.

Customer Service and Flexibility

It is easy, in a world of interest rates, lease rates and residual values, to forget that leasing is, to a large degree, a business of relationships. People do business with those they like and trust. Good relationships begin with quality customer service. Regardless of the size of a leasing company, customers will look elsewhere if the service is not what they expect. In addition, flexibility, with regard to products offered and lessor responsiveness, is an important consideration for customers when selecting a lessor.

Funding Ability

One key strategy for success is to establish and maintain a premier funding ability. Although this ability translates into a competitive advantage, it also is a cornerstone of long-term viability.

A premier funding ability consists of many facets. One of the most important of these is reliable sources of funds. Without continued funding, the company cannot grow. Another facet of a premier funding ability is a low cost of funds. The lessor also should diversify its funding and make certain the funding methods are consistent with its business plans. By establishing a strong funding program, and constantly monitoring it, the lessor can ensure its long-term success.

Control of Back-office Costs

The cash flow generated by a leasing company is applied to three different areas. First and foremost is the payment of debt. Because leasing companies are highly leveraged, debt costs constitute their largest expense. The cash flow generated also must cover the company's overhead costs. What is left over is profit that is either retained for future operations or distributed to the shareholders.

In order to generate more profit, either the debt costs or the back-office costs must be lowered. Most leasing companies are somewhat limited in terms of controlling debt costs, although as mentioned earlier, lessor ingenuity has opened new and innovative sources of funds in the last few years. As a result, many successful lessors have devoted time and effort to enhancing profits through reengineering their companies to achieve economies of scale, lower costs and eliminate waste to enhance profits. Reevaluation and upgrading of systems and a more streamlined workforce are two of the strategies that have helped lessors achieve higher margins in this very competitive marketplace.

Highly-trained Workforce

As a company pursues the strategy of a streamlined workforce, the education of that workforce becomes more important. With fewer employees, oftentimes performing more than one function, leasing companies need to dedicate the necessary resources to properly educate and train the employees or profitability will suffer. Many of the most successful leasing companies, both in the U.S. and abroad, adopted this strategy many years ago, and now reap the benefits from a highly trained workforce.

Appropriate Strategies

Some leasing companies have failed because they adopted strategies that were based on assumptions over which they had little or no control. For example, some companies based their business on true tax leases, assuming the tax laws would never change. Unfortunately, tax benefits, such as the investment tax credit, which for many lessors was a primary source of profit, come and go in the tax code. Often Congress enacts tax limitations, such as the midquarter convention or the AMT, that severely limit the availability of tax benefits.

Another example of an inappropriate strategy is to plan future business based on an endless supply of available capital. Many leasing companies in the past relied on one or two good sources of funds, rather than diversifying. When economic or other conditions eliminated these sources such lessors were left with transactions for which they could not find funding.

Adaptability to Market Shifts

Leasing companies must, within reason, be able to effectively shift in and out of different markets as profitability changes or those markets experience shifts themselves. For example, a lessor may find it necessary to shift its emphasis from mainframe computers to PCs, or from computers to medical equipment if its traditional market undergoes significant change. This ability to adapt has helped some lessors weather the storm as particular markets or equipment types experience cyclical downturns. It is unrealistic, however, to expect a company that has been in the computer leasing business to enter the aircraft leasing market overnight.

Maintaining Objectives

Keeping focused on the lessor's core business sounds like a simple strategy to adopt and follow. Many leasing companies, however, have either failed altogether or suffered a significant loss of business by losing sight of the original objectives that made them successful. These leasing companies achieved an enviable level of success, only to make decisions outside the spirit and philosophy of their original business plan, causing their share of the market to evaporate. This is not to say that leasing companies should not be constantly evaluating the marketplace and adopting new strategies to remain competitive. Such an approach is critical to success. It is important, however, that the overall philosophies that generated success in the first place be maintained and fine tuned, not replaced or forgotten.

CONCLUSION

The growth experienced by the leasing industry in the late 1980s and early 1990s has slowed. This slowdown means lessors must be more creative and work harder at satisfying their customers. It also means lessors must focus on all aspects of the business, both external and internal. Many opportunities for success still exist and steady growth worldwide in the coming years is predicted. Given this scenario, companies that adopt the simple yet critical strategies discussed in this chapter will position themselves to maximize opportunities and enjoy continued success.

Chapter Four

International Leasing

The need for lease financing continues to increase as the world becomes smaller and more economically intertwined. At the same time, the U.S. leasing industry has become a mature marketplace. The growth rates of the past have slowed, margins have thinned and lessors have consolidated. In this environment, many U.S. lessors are looking outside the country to maintain their targeted growth and earnings requirements. These lessors are finding many opportunities in all parts of the world, although U.S. companies traditionally have focused their efforts in Western Europe.

This chapter addresses various leasing markets throughout the world and some of the issues lessors will encounter as they expand beyond their domestic markets. Topics include:

- Global Leasing

- Cross-border Transactions

- Outbound U.S. Leasing

- Foreign Sales Corporations.

GLOBAL LEASING

On a worldwide basis, lease financing currently provides approximately one-eighth of the world's equipment financing. The percentage of leasing (the penetration rate) as a form of financing equipment, however, varies significantly among countries. In the U.S., for instance, leasing accounts for one-third of total equipment financing. In some countries of the world, in which the leasing industry is in a nascent stage, the penetration rate of lease financing is very low.

The Leasing Cycle

Although the leasing industry within each country develops at its own pace, all industries tend to follow a certain evolutionary cycle. This leasing cycle is illustrated in Exhibit 4-1. Familiarity with the various phases of the cycle helps lessors better understand the competitive environment they face when entering foreign markets.

FINANCE LEASES

The leasing cycle in most countries begins with finance leases. In this phase, lessors offer a leasing product that is very similar in structure to a loan. The leases are full payout and noncancellable. The rents are level and the lessee is responsible for maintaining and insuring the equipment. Furthermore, the lessee invariably buys the asset at the end of the term.

These finance leases are generally tax leases. The lessor keeps the benefits of tax depreciation and the lessee writes off the lease payments. The other source of profit for the lessor is the spread in the transaction. At this point in the cycle there are no tax or accounting guidelines and most of the business is vendor-driven.

FLEXIBLE/CREATIVE FINANCE LEASES

Lessors begin to offer additional features with the lease product in this phase of the cycle. These features include residual options, such as renewals and fixed purchase options, and structures that better meet the cash flow needs of the lessee. Simple leveraged leases are developed and captive leasing companies are formed in this phase.

OPERATING LEASES

As competition increases, lessors continue to look for new ways to sell leases. Development of the operating lease product, with its residual feature, is the next step in the leasing cycle. This phase usually is preceded by a developing or developed secondary equipment market. Such a market is

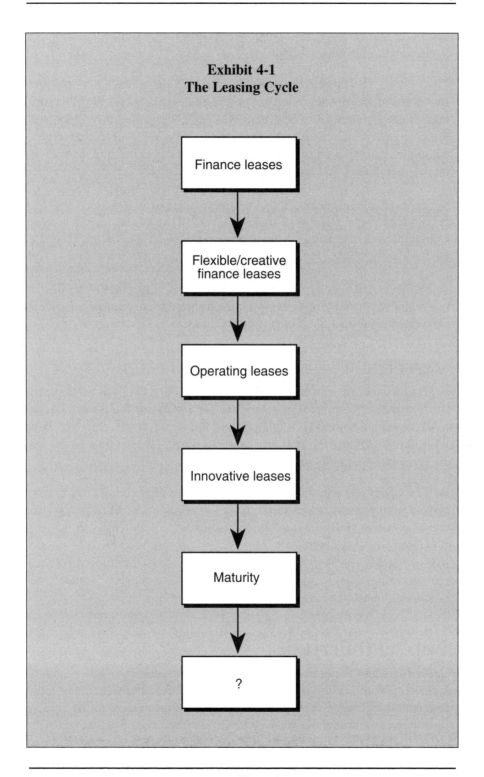

Exhibit 4-1
The Leasing Cycle

Finance leases

Flexible/creative finance leases

Operating leases

Innovative leases

Maturity

?

necessary for development of the operating lease product because lessors begin to take true residual risk.

This residual risk creates the need for a strong asset management function. In this phase, lessors begin to incorporate after-tax concepts into their pricing. Since operating leases generally do not run to maturity, lessors are forced to develop remarketing expertise. Vehicles are the first type of equipment to be put on operating leases. Other types of equipment leased include computers, telecommunication gear and aircraft.

INNOVATIVE LEASES AND PRODUCTS

Competition is very keen by the time a leasing industry reaches this phase of the leasing cycle. Just as with operating leases, lessors need to create unique products. Unexploited niches also are sought to increase volume and profits. The types of products introduced in this phase of the leasing cycle include income funds, wrap leases, venture leasing, project financing and securitizations.

MATURITY

No country has yet moved beyond the maturity phase of the leasing cycle so, for all practical purposes, this is the final phase of the cycle. Leasing has become a commodity at this point in the cycle. It is readily available, with all products sharing common characteristics. Competition is pervasive and very intense in this phase.

New products are very difficult to find, or even nonexistent. As a result, lessors attempt to add value through additional services and responsiveness and as a means of differentiating their products. The intensity of competition also forces lessors to shift from an external (product) focus to an internal (operations) focus to increase profitability. This shift in focus results in reengineering of company processes, more research and development and a continuing quest to be a low-cost provider of services.

Leasing Differences

Lease financing is not defined the same in all countries of the world. In some countries, leasing provides only the use of property for a portion of the property's life. The lessor retains a significant interest in the value of the equipment throughout its useful life, and the lessee has a range of termination options available to it at the conclusion of the lease term. In other countries, however, leasing is nothing more than disguised lending. The lessor does not take residual risk and the lessee always acquires the equipment at the end of the lease term. In this instance, the form of the transaction is a lease, but the substance of the transaction is a loan.

The level of government support also varies significantly among countries. The governments in some countries provide incentives to lessors, whereas others have restrictions that limit the availability and growth of lease financing. It is because of these differences that U.S. lessors doing business on an international basis encounter both opportunities and obstacles.

For example, in economies that require a high down payment or additional collateral to obtain installment financing, lease financing is very popular because neither is required. In countries with a high rate of inflation, however, operating leases (those in which the lessor accepts residual risk) are not popular. The lessee wishes to have ownership at lease termination because inflation has kept the residual value of the equipment very high in current terms. In fact, in economies with high inflation, the equipment is often sold at termination for nominal values greater than its original cost.

Substance Versus Form

The concept of substance versus form is critical in determining ownership of leased assets, not only from a legal perspective but also for tax and accounting purposes. In many countries, the lessor remains the owner of the equipment throughout the lease term, irrespective of the economic substance of the transaction. As long as the contract is referred to as a lease the lessor is considered the owner (i.e., the form of the transaction governs). Elsewhere in the world, the economic substance of the transaction governs.

In the U.S., for instance, a lessor may or may not be the legal owner of the equipment under lease. The terms and conditions of the contract may be such that the lessee bears all the risks and responsibilities of ownership. In this case, the lessee is the beneficial owner of the equipment, or owner in substance. The issue of form versus substance is a very important consideration when a U.S. lessor is considering expansion into foreign countries.

Various criteria are used for determining when, in substance, the lessee is the owner of equipment. One such criterion is the existence of a bargain purchase option. For example, an agreement that allows the lessee to acquire the equipment for one dollar at lease conclusion may be titled a lease. The substance of the transaction, however, is such that the lessee will be the owner of the equipment at lease end. Thus, the form of the transaction is a lease but the substance is that of a loan. Some countries may not allow the lessee a purchase option if the transaction is to qualify as a lease. In others, it is a requirement that a purchase right be extended to the lessee at lease termination.

The leasing industries of the world are divided over whether it is more appropriate to follow substance over form or form over substance. For example, Leaseurope rejects an approach to accounting that requires the economic owner to capitalize the leased asset. It does not believe that such an approach based on substance would bring about greater comparability of annual accounts or provide more financial information to investors. Leaseurope is of the opinion that the concept of economic ownership does not fully reflect the nature of lease transactions, and, therefore, fails to convey a true and fair view of the affairs of a company to users of accounts.

This divergence of views among countries of the world has created benefits and problems when dealing cross-border. The U.S. lessor, accustomed to dealing with the concept of substance over form, may find it difficult to adjust to doing business in a country governed by form over substance. It is very important, therefore, for lessors doing business outside their domestic market to fully understand the legal, accounting and tax requirements of each particular country.

Role of Leasing

The U.S. leasing market comprises approximately 37% of the total lease financing volume in the world. Most recent statistics indicate the annual volume of leasing in the U.S. is equal to the volume of the next four countries combined. In fact, the U.S. leasing industry is double the size of the world's second largest industry, Japan, and four times the size of the third largest, Germany. Obviously there is room for growth in leasing outside the U.S.

Economic conditions in a country play a major role in the level of leasing activity. Leasing has grown during both good and bad times, and in expanding and contracting economies. In some cases leasing activity actually increases more rapidly in bad economic times. Such an increase usually is caused by a credit crunch that forces equipment users to seek alternative sources of capital. As a general rule, however, leasing is at its strongest when the economy is healthy.

The past years have brought into focus the correlation between the economy and the level of leasing activity, as leasing's record of continued worldwide growth was broken for the first time. During this period, the major developed countries in the world experienced economic problems, ranging from simple stagnation to near depression. The leasing industries of these countries have suffered declines in volume. Countries that are experiencing robust economic activity, such as those in Latin America, have seen leasing rapidly expand, especially if supported by the government and a strong domestic leasing association.

Nations in the process of industrialization require significant amounts of capital. Leasing industries the world over help meet this need for capital, furthering economic development wherever they exist. Many developing countries use leasing as a means of attracting foreign capital. Governments and world agencies such as the Asian Development Bank (ADB) are encouraging this process. The means of developing the domestic leasing industry are diverse but a sizable amount of assistance from the public and private sector is required.

Given the many benefits of leasing, it is somewhat puzzling why emerging nations have taken so long to adopt leasing as a means of solving capital shortages. It now appears that recognition of lease financing on a worldwide basis is accelerating. The greatest challenge to further expansion of leasing lies in the legal complexities involving repossession and other problems connected with collection. The establishment of a secondary market for equipment also is critical to this expansion.

Since leasing is predominantly a domestic product, constrained by the individual legal, tax and accounting guidelines of each jurisdiction, it is not easy to compare leasing with other international capital market products. This does not mean that cross-border leasing is an insignificant business. Extremely sophisticated international lease transactions have been designed to provide equipment at a low cost and protect the rights and yields of the funding sources and equity participants.

U.S. lessors also must be aware of increasing foreign competition in their domestic markets and react accordingly. This competition is coming from leasing subsidiaries of foreign manufacturers, foreign banks and foreign independent leasing companies. The entrance of foreign banks into leasing is natural because the same factors prompting U.S. banks to favor leasing are now impacting foreign financial institutions. Furthermore, foreign banks constantly are looking for ways to expand their presence and gain a toehold in the largest leasing market in the world. The enormous size of certain of these entities could lead to a significant penetration of the U.S. leasing market as they offer leasing to existing as well as new customers.

Funding

The lessor's ability to access adequate financing and to understand the economic, legal, tax and accounting environments of each country is critical for success in leasing within multiple countries. Finding financing, however, remains one of the most important keys for success.

Lessors must realize that the methods for raising money in one country may not function well in another because of the individual characteristics of each locale. For example, match funding is a problem in some countries because funds have become scarce and unacceptably priced. In others, lessors must provide fixed rate lease payments to the lessee, even though the lessor is borrowing on a floating rate basis.

When it comes to funding, involvement in the international marketplace requires a great deal of sophistication and knowledge. Foreign exchange risk, interest rate hedges and political risk arrangements are part of everyday life for an international lessor. Country-specific problems may inhibit the growth of leasing and the types of leases offered. In some countries, for instance, all debt funding must be fully recourse to the lessor if it expects to receive tax benefits. Tax depreciation is not available with non-recourse borrowing because of the limited risk to the lessor.

Most often, lessor funding is accomplished by sourcing traditional funds such as banks and the public market. Other techniques may be required, however. In some countries, large lessors have accessed commodity funds or directly tapped the institutional and public markets. Companies also are using sophisticated arbitrage techniques for increasing available funds and lowering their cost. Regional development agencies are becoming more willing to finance leasing companies, and more lessors are turning to securitization.

In some countries the sale of receivables to fund operations is common. Other countries almost mandate the sale of receivables because they assess taxes on debt amounts or asset values. Some do not allow the securitization of leases in any form, instead requiring lessors to source funds from the interbank market or to raise issues in the public market. Other lessor financing arrangements may take the form of joint ventures, syndications or correspondent relationships.

UNIQUE FINANCING SOURCES

Many quasi-governmental agencies as well as multigovernment agencies support and finance leasing companies throughout the world. In addition, unique financing arrangements are required under certain religious laws.

Eximbank

The Export-Import Bank of the U.S. (Eximbank), an independent U.S. government agency, facilitates export financing of U.S. goods and services by matching the effect of export credit subsidies from other governments. It also absorbs reasonable credit risks beyond the current reach of the private sector. The major benefits Eximbank provides are listed in Exhibit 4-2.

Exhibit 4-2
Benefits of Eximbank

1. Helps U. S. exporters obtain preexport financing by guaranteeing their repayment of export-related working capital loans from commercial lenders

2. Helps exporters extend credit to their foreign customers by covering the political and commercial risks of nonpayment

3. Encourages commercial financing of U.S. exports by guaranteeing repayment of loans and leases made to foreign buyers of U. S. exports

4. Encourages foreign buyers to purchase U.S. exports by offering competitive, fixed-rate loans and leases.

Eximbank can support the sale of U.S. goods or services to a creditworthy foreign buyer when competitive private financing is unavailable. To qualify for Eximbank support, the product or service must have at least 50% U.S. content and cannot be military-related. There must be a reasonable assurance of repayment and the transaction must not adversely impact the U.S. economy.

Companies leasing products of U.S. origin outside the U.S. can reduce their risks by insuring the stream of lease payments and the fair market value of the leased products through Eximbank's lease policies. The coverage protects against credit risks, both political and commercial. Coverage is available for a cross-border lease or an international lease (a lease in which both the lessor and lessee are in the same country, other than the U.S.).

Eximbank offers two credit insurance policies for the leasing industry – an operating lease policy and a financing lease policy. Each provides a unique system of coverage. The choice of the operating or financing lease policy is solely the lessor's and is based upon an evaluation of which coverage structure fits the specific transaction.

An eligible lessor is any leasing company, manufacturer, bank, trust, partnership or other entity, foreign or domestic, that leases or participates in the financing of leases of U.S.-manufactured equipment and services outside the U.S. Lease coverage can apply to new or used equipment and related services.

Generally, no more than 15% of the value of the leased products, exclusive of price mark-up, may consist of labor, raw materials, component parts or any combination thereof, originating or manufactured outside the U.S. Any foreign content in the leased products must be approved by Eximbank. The transaction must be subject to a lease agreement that is valid and enforceable in the U.S. and the lessee's country at the time the policy becomes effective.

The operating lease policy divides coverage into two parts: (1) coverage for the stream of payments and (2) coverage against governmental prevention of repossession. The two parts may be purchased together or separately. Eximbank's coverage for operating leases applies to lease transactions in which:

1. The sum of the payments is less than the full value of the leased products

2. A residual value is associated with the leased products

3. The lessor intends to repossess the leased products and re-lease, sell or otherwise dispose of them

4. The lessor bears the risk that the leased products will decline in market value at a rate greater than expected.

Eximbank's financing lease policy was designed around a lease concept in which little residual value generally remains in the leased products and ownership is transferred to the lessee at the end of the lease. Eximbank views the structure as similar to a medium-term sale transaction. Accordingly, it requires a 15% advance payment from the lessee to the lessor on or before delivery of the leased products. (Eximbank will insure only 85% of the lease transaction.) Generally, the advance payment may not be financed by the insured, by a financial institution with recourse back to the insured or by any financial institution that requires any share of the leased products as security against the loan.

Should the lessee default, coverage is provided for the insured percentage of each lease payment as it falls due until the end of the lease term. Coverage usually is provided at a maximum of 100% for sovereign lessees and 90% for all others. Both the operating and financing lease policies cover single transactions. Under both policies, the insured is obligated to transfer the lease obligations to Eximbank at time of claim payment. It also is obligated to transfer title to the leased products to Eximbank for claims paid.

IFC

The International Finance Corporation (IFC), an affiliate of the World Bank, promotes private sector investments in developing countries. IFC shares the same board of directors and many common members with the World Bank. IFC was founded in 1956. Member countries include both developed and developing nations. IFC's mandate is to assist in the development of the private sector of developing countries by complementing the role played by the World Bank in the public sector.

IFC makes both equity investments and loans, never funding over 25% of the project cost. IFC finances viable private sector projects on a commercial basis, mobilizes investment capital and provides advisory services. Although its role is developmental, IFC does not accept government guarantees nor does it provide subsidized financing. Its aim is to be profitable, although it is not necessarily a profit-maximizing institution.

IFC has been active in leasing activities since its first leasing company investment in 1977. It has been able to promote the development of domestic financial markets by introducing leasing as an alternative source of equipment finance for industrial, agricultural and commercial enterprises. In addition, IFC has encouraged competition and efficiency in the financial sector by participating in leasing companies whose performance serves to demonstrate the financial and economic viability of leasing activity.

The fundamental role of IFC in its leasing investments is that of project catalyst. IFC brings together domestic sponsors, foreign technical and financial partners and government authorities to ensure the project is commercially viable; organized on sound management, operating, and financial principles; and operated in a reasonable regulatory environment.

IFC has played an important role as a provider of finance for new leasing companies. It structures major fund-raising programs to offer new companies a strong base of term funds, and introduces them to the international markets by facilitating their first foreign loan syndications. In general, IFC requires leverage of no more than about 12 times net worth, but, in fact, most of its leasing companies maintain lower leverage ratios, usually between eight and nine times net worth.

ADB

The ADB has supported the leasing industry's development in Asia over the past 10 years. It views lease financing as an important financing technique in the region's fledgling capital markets. ADB's program was developed as a result of studies that indicated leasing was a flexible and convenient form of financing that could be used in relatively unsophisticated capital markets. There was, however, little governmental supervision or monitoring of the activities of individual companies. The bank decided to concentrate on nurturing and strengthening the existing industry, rather than contributing to the proliferation of unnecessary leasing companies in the region.

The most important role of the ADB is as an adviser to governments of developing member countries. The main attribute of the ADB is its impartiality in negotiating industry regulation. The involvement of the bank is most important in areas in which leasing is a relatively new form of financing, as new leasing companies face tough competition from commercial banks.

ADB is active in advising governments against unfair competition between privately-owned leasing companies and development banks with access to inexpensive government funding. It also is involved in direct funding via both debt and equity injections in the targeted areas. Sourcing long-term debt presents a serious problem to leasing companies in Asia, as lessors are unable to match their borrowings to future lease receivables. As a result, the ADB concentrates on providing such financing to companies for which it would otherwise be unobtainable.

EIB

The European Investment Bank (EIB) was established in 1958 and receives its operational mandate from the Treaty of Rome. Under the treaty, the objective of the EIB is to facilitate the balanced development of the European Community (EC). EIB's aims are to invest in regional development in the economically less favored areas, to increase environmental protection and to help in the development of transport, telecommunications, industrial and energy projects.

The EIB finances only fixed assets. In principle, the bank contributes only 50% of the total costs of a project. Of its total financing, approximately 95% is made for projects within the EC. The capital for lending and lease funding is raised by issuing public and private bonds. The EIB issues bonds in the European and international capital markets in 13 currencies. The European currency unit has become the primary currency in most recent years.

The EIB was not established with a profit making motive; however it has shown positive results to date. It lends at a rate of 15 basis points above that which it has to pay on the capital markets; the margin is absorbed in administrative costs. Because the EIB is restricted to lending for no more than 50% of total project costs, it works side by side with commercial banks and national investment banks. The EIB also works closely with the European Bank for Reconstruction and Development, of which it is a shareholder.

ISLAMIC LEASING AND TAX CONSIDERATIONS

Islamic banks and financial institutions are playing an expanding role in worldwide economic activity, although they are required to operate within certain precepts. One of the more specific constraints is the prohibition of riba, or interest. This prohibition against interest raises concerns about the appropriateness of lease transactions under Islamic law.

The peculiarities of Islamic finance do not prevent lease financing from occurring, however. In fact, Islamic leases of all sizes have come to the forefront of financing offered by Islamic banks and financial institutions. Although speculation is not allowed under Islamic economic thought, risk-sharing is both legitimate and permissible. Consequently, any profit from a sharing of risk is regarded as a proper reward. As a result, Islamic banks and financial institutions generally base their operations on the concept of profit-sharing. This concept also applies to leasing.

Financing Products

Exhibit 4-3 describes the different modes of financing employed in Islamic cultures. There are two basic forms of leasing recognized in Islam:

Exhibit 4-3
Islamic Financing Devices

1. **Mudaraha:** A contractual arrangement whereby the entire capital of a business enterprise is provided by the Islamic bank or financial institution. Management, however, remains in the hands of the party operating the business. Profit is shared in predetermined proportions. Any loss is borne solely by the provider of the capital

2. **Musharaka:** An agreement in which the Islamic bank or financial institution provides funds that are intermingled with the funds of others participating in the business enterprise. All such participants are entitled to participate in management. Profit is distributed among the partners in preagreed upon ratios. Losses are borne by each partner in proportion to his or her capital contribution

3. **Murabaha:** A contract whereby an Islamic bank or financial institution purchases goods or equipment required by a customer and resells them to the customer at a predetermined profit

4. **Bai-Muajjal:** A transaction whereby the seller allows the buyer to pay the price of a commodity at a future date in a lump sum or installments

5. **Qard:** A regular loan transaction in which the client undertakes to repay the principal at a future time. Generally, no interest is charged. However, a service fee is permissible in some jurisdictions as long as such a fee is based on the actual cost of administering the loan.

---

1. An Ijara is the equivalent of a true lease. In practice, an Islamic bank or financial institution purchases goods, such as construction equipment or computers, on behalf of its client. Thereafter, it agrees to lease the equipment to the client for a specified sum and for a fixed period

2. An Ijara-wa-Iqtina is the equivalent of a financial lease or hire-purchase arrangement. Payment for the leased goods is made monthly or quarterly by the client. The bank's fixed rates cover most of the original purchase price of the item over the period of the contract. At the end of the contract period the lessee has the option to purchase the leased equipment. If the eventual sale to the lessee is agreed to at the time the original contract is signed, the contract could be considered to incorporate both Ijara and Murabaha elements. In this case the rental premiums are usually smaller. This mixed type of contract is increasing in popularity.

For a particular transaction to qualify as a lease under Islamic legal principles, several criteria have to be satisfied (Exhibit 4-4). To qualify as a true lease, Shari'a principles require that title to the leased item remain vested in the lessor throughout the term of the lease (form over substance). It is

---

Exhibit 4-4
Islamic Lease Criteria

1. The leased item must have a real, physical use. An asset that lies dormant and has no real use cannot be leased in accordance with Shari'a principles

2. A real and measurable economic benefit must be derived from the leased item

3. The rental payments must be preagreed upon and properly defined

4. A clear relationship must exist between the term of the lease and the actual economic life of the leased item

5. There must be no element of riba in the lease transaction or the rental cost

6. The leased item must be used for a purpose that is lawful in Islam.

---

possible to structure a transaction wherein the lessee makes payment of the purchase price in tranches in addition to rent spread over the lease period. In this case, transfer of title is gradual and the lessor's title to the property decreases proportionately.

In a true lease arrangement (no option to buy at the end of the lease term) any appreciation or depreciation of the leased asset remains with the lessor. In a lease with a binding promise to sell at a fixed time in the future, the title to the leased asset and all related risks remain with the lessor until the option is exercised.

Lease contracts often contain a hell or high water clause that covers the loss or destruction of the leased asset. Such clauses normally provide that if the leased item is lost or destroyed during the term of the lease, the lessee is still liable to make all remaining lease payments.

Taxation

Islam has a unique system of taxation. The primary tax payable by all individuals and businesses is known as zakat. Zakat is a wealth tax levied on businesses and individuals at a rate of 2.5% of their total net worth, which includes industrial assets and real estate. The proceeds of zakat are used for socially worthwhile projects and are supervised by the religious authorities in the concerned jurisdictions. Zakat serves as an incentive for businesses to employ their assets in a constructive manner, as they are liable for taxation even if the assets remain idle and unproductive.

The effect of leasing on the payment of zakat is that the leased asset is not included as part of the total net worth of the lessee in calculating the zakat payable. However, because zakat is an income-based tax, profit generated by use of the leased item will be included in any future calculation of zakat.

Regional Overview

Equipment leasing is growing around the world, albeit at different rates and in different ways. The condition of a country's leasing industry is a function, to a large extent, of the economy. The country's phase in the leasing cycle also impacts how the leasing industry performs. Because each country or geographic region has its own unique problems and circumstances, the leasing industries within these regions are developing differently. Exhibit 4-5 compares volumes by individual regions.

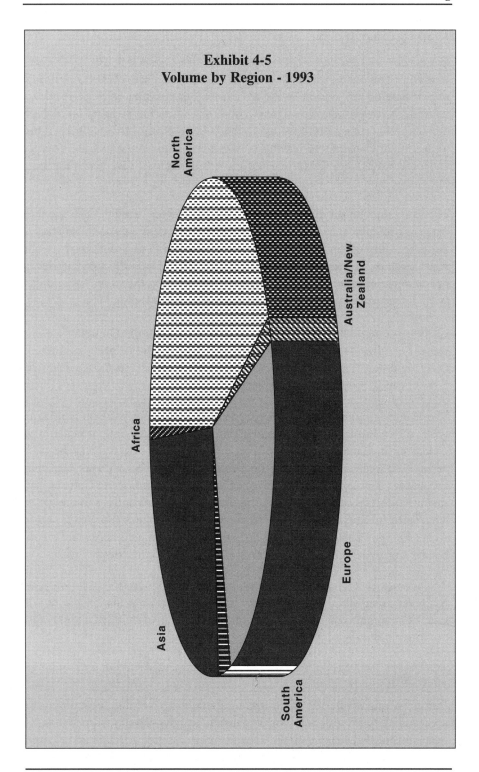

Exhibit 4-5
Volume by Region - 1993

NORTH AMERICA

For purposes of measuring leasing activity, this region consists of all countries from Panama northwards. North America has the highest level of leasing volume of any region of the world, with approximately 43% of global leasing volume conducted in these countries. Leasing penetration of capital equipment expenditure is high in the U.S. because of the maturity of this industry. In Canada, the leasing market penetration remains low. Mexico has experienced significant leasing growth in the past few years, but leasing penetration of the capital equipment finance market remains low.

The implementation of the North American Free Trade Agreement is expected to increase and expedite cross-border activity for these trading partners, although in both the U.S. and Canada a consolidation of leasing companies is creating fewer but larger lessors. This is the trend in developed countries as maturity approaches. Mexico, on the other hand, offers some of the greatest opportunities for growth in the region.

Currently, computers are the single largest type of equipment under lease in the U.S., followed by aircraft, trucks and trailers and office machines, in order by dollar volume. These four types of equipment comprise just over 50% of the U.S. leasing marketplace.

The leading market segments for Canada are computer hardware and software, office furniture and equipment, and vehicles. The rate of penetration of leasing in Canada continues to be low. This low rate reflects the competitive strategies pursued by the banking industry as well as Canadian income tax laws. In general, the existing income tax laws in Canada, particularly the 1989 changes, have eliminated any tax incentives to the lessor. This elimination has had a corresponding impact on lease rates. Accordingly, Canadian lessors who write tax-advantaged leases are significantly disadvantaged compared to lessors in other countries.

The average annual growth rate for leasing in Mexico for the past five years has been over 30%. Mexico ranks in the top 20 countries leasing in volume. The major types of equipment leased are transportation (mainly automobiles) and industrial and commercial equipment.

EUROPE

Europe is one of the top three leasing markets by volume, accounting for approximately 25% of the world's leasing activity. The most recent statistics indicate that leasing is the second largest source for financing equipment in Europe, although it has been flat to slightly down over the past few years. (The largest source is direct loans.) An analysis of leasing activity by Leaseurope members indicates automobiles represent the largest share of business, followed by industrial equipment, computers, business machines and commercial vehicles. Almost 60% of Leaseurope activity consists of automobiles and industrial equipment.

Most European countries embrace the concept of form over substance for accounting, tax and legal purposes. Great Britain is an exception to this general rule. Other countries have a mixed approach. For example, some countries have accepted International Accounting Standard 17 (the international lease accounting standard) which is based on substance over form. However, they continue to follow a form over substance format for tax purposes.

The recent economic climate has been poor in the more developed countries of Europe, however. The economic situation has created a concomitant slowdown in lease activity. Even so, Germany, Great Britain, France and Italy are ranked among the top 10 leasing industries in the world. Notwithstanding the slowing of the economies, the prospect of moderate growth for the developed countries, especially when coupled with very high growth in some of the newer leasing industries of Eastern Europe, is high.

Leasing is a relatively new activity for many Eastern European countries, for a variety of reasons. For instance, the concept of legal ownership is new to many of these countries and generally accepted accounting principles are only now being established. The need for equipment to build infrastructure and modernize facilities is enormous, however, and will require significant amounts of capital. Leasing is viewed as a form of finance that is beneficial to sustained economic activity. In spite of the need for capital and an improving regulatory climate, there are extremes in the development of the various industries.

Bulgaria, for example, finds it difficult to attract foreign investors because of unfavorable laws. The Bulgarian leasing market is very underdeveloped and little understood and there currently are not any tax breaks. Additionally, no specific law governs lease contracts in Bulgaria. A lease contract is viewed as being somewhere between a rent and a hire-purchase agreement, with the lessor as the owner of the equipment.

Hungary, on the other hand, is considered one of the more well-developed Eastern European countries. In terms of legal protection, investments in Hungary are not hindered. Furthermore, leasing is approaching the standard of Western Europe, making it likely that leasing will become an important factor in business. The government also has passed laws favorable to cross-border financing activities although the details of such structures are often complex.

ASIA

This region of the world continues to experience growth, with leasing activity in Asia comprising approximately 25% of the world's volume. The economies of newly industrialized countries such as South Korea, Hong Kong, Taiwan and Singapore have seen exceptional growth in the early nineties. These and other Asian countries will offer tremendous economic opportunities for the remainder of the decade.

Currently, 18 Asian countries have established leasing industries. Of these industries, 14 rank in the top 50 of the world. Japan is the largest lessor in this region, followed by South Korea. The single largest type of equipment leased in Japan is computers, followed by industrial machinery. In Korea, industrial equipment comprises in excess of 60% of the leased equipment market.

Hong Kong currently is ranked in the top 20 in the world for leasing activity. Leasing activity has been stable, but the future is uncertain because of the reversion of Hong Kong to China in 1997. Approximately 15% of Hong Kong's current activity is for equipment used across the border in China.

The People's Republic of China also has a growing leasing industry, although little information is available on either domestic or cross-border transactions. The Chinese economy appears to be growing and leasing is expected to play an important role in financing China's plant and equipment requirements.

SOUTH AMERICA

The overall growth of this region's leasing industry has been very strong during the early nineties. Growth is expected to continue, particularly as economic and political conditions stabilize.

Specifically, Brazil has moved into the top 10 countries of the world in annual lease volume. A strong economy in Chile has attracted foreign investment and stimulated growth. In Colombia a spectacular growth rate has increased leasing market penetration. Argentina is reestablishing a leasing industry that was virtually destroyed as a result of the economic conditions in the late eighties and early nineties.

AFRICA

South Africa is the largest producer in Africa, with a current ranking in the top 20 in leasing volume. Morocco and Malawi are the only other countries to rank in the top 50. One reason for the lack of leasing in Africa is the political and, hence, economic instability. Another is the rules and regulations promulgated in some African countries that put leasing at a disadvantage to hire-purchase arrangements and loans. Funding by international organizations has been utilized extensively, allowing leasing to grow as a means of increasing the productive capability of many African nations.

AUSTRALIA AND NEW ZEALAND

These two countries comprise approximately 2% of the world leasing market. The economies of these areas are starting to recover after suffering significantly during the early nineties, with Australia ranking in the top 10 in leasing volume. The majority of leasing in New Zealand is for vehicles.

Lease Clubs

To facilitate cross-border lease transactions, major leasing companies from various countries have formed several different associations, commonly referred to as leaseclubs, to solve difficult cross-border tax, accounting and legal differences. The members of these associations cooperate in offering to their export customers a complete international leasing service, providing significant marketing and operating cost savings to all parties involved in a lease transaction. By utilizing their membership as a marketing instrument, the members of these associations can offer both their exporting and multinational customers a worldwide leasing service.

The major benefits of membership in a leaseclub are (1) local advice and decision support for exporters' foreign equipment sales, which might include the provision of lease quotations and the conclusion of leasing contracts with customers abroad; (2) establishment of personal and commercial contacts between the various members; and (3) access to credit information on companies abroad. Members have access to this information through credit reference facilities.

CROSS-BORDER TRANSACTIONS

The international leasing market consists not only of leasing conducted within various countries but also of leases between countries. The latter transactions are referred to as cross-border leases. The very name of a cross-border lease implies that the lessor and the lessee are domiciled in different countries.

The most simple cross-border lease is one in which a lessor located in country A leases equipment to a lessee located in country B. These transactions also can be very complex and might involve more than two countries. For example, the equipment may be manufactured in country A, debt financing procured in country B, equity raised in country C, the nominal lessor located in country D and the equipment actually placed in service in country E.

Lessors and lessees must consider many factors when entering into cross-border leases, including:

1. The currency to be used for making payment and who will be assuming exchange rate risk

2. Problems to be overcome in repatriating earnings from one country to another

3. The best way to mitigate the effects of differing inflation rates

4. Potential changes in the socio-political climate over the term of the lease

5. The risks and benefits of gaining a foreign presence and reputation.

These and other considerations must be understood and incorporated into the decision process when entering into cross-border transactions. Cross-border leases can be very complex and expensive to complete. The advantages to be gained, however, oftentimes justify the cost.

Double-dips

Certain cross-border leases offer lessors the opportunity to take advantage of the different tax, accounting, legal and economic conditions of various countries. By doing so, the lessor is able to provide the lessee with low cost and creative financing for the equipment. A lease in which the lessor takes advantage of the tax differences between two countries is called a double-dip lease.

The double-dip lease involves a series of lease transactions between parties in two countries. The tax rules for leases, however, must be different between the two countries. In one type of double-dip, the lessor is located in a country that follows form over substance (a form country). The lessee is located in a country that follows substance over form (a substance country).

By properly structuring the lease, both the lessor and the lessee are able to take the tax depreciation on the equipment. This double-dip of tax benefits lowers the overall cost to the ultimate lessee. A variation of this lease involves a lease from a form country to a substance country, followed by a subsequent sublease to an actual user. (See Exhibit 4-6.)

For example, a lessor in France, which is a form country, enters into a lease (credit-bail) with a lessee (a leasing company) in the U.S. The lease is structured with a bargain purchase option. In France, the form of the transaction is respected and it qualifies as a true tax lease, so the French lessor is entitled to receive the tax benefits of depreciation. Consequently, it passes these benefits on to the U.S. leasing company, which is the original lessee in the transaction.

The U.S. is a substance country, however, so, based on the existence of the bargain purchase option, the lease is characterized as a conditional sale contract by the lessee. The U.S. leasing company, therefore, receives tax benefits in its country. At this point, the double-dip has occurred. The U.S. leasing company has received the benefit of the French lessor's depreciation plus the U.S. depreciation benefit. The U.S. lessor then enters into a sublease agreement with a U.S. lessee. This lease is characterized as a tax lease because the U.S. lessee/sublessor must remain the tax owner. The sublease is priced very attractively because both the French and U.S. depreciation are utilized.

Double-dip transactions provide significant pricing benefits to the sublessee. These transactions, however, work only between form and substance countries. Furthermore, the incidence of double-dip leases has decreased as the taxing authorities from different countries have cracked down on such structures.

OUTBOUND U.S. LEASING

An outbound cross-border lease arises when (1) a U.S. lessor enters into an agreement to lease property to a non-U.S. person or entity and (2) the lease is subject to classification and reporting requirements in at least two taxing

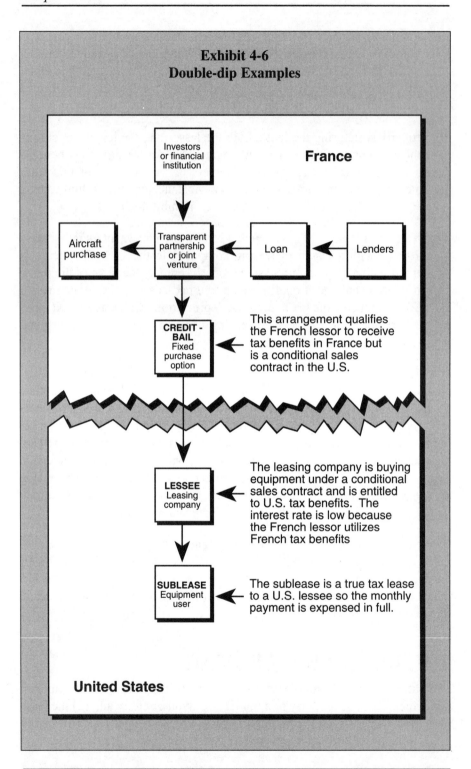

Exhibit 4-6
Double-dip Examples

France

| Investors or financial institution |

| Aircraft purchase | ← | Transparent partnership or joint venture | ← | Loan | ← | Lenders |

CREDIT - BAIL
Fixed purchase option

This arrangement qualifies the French lessor to receive tax benefits in France but is a conditional sales contract in the U.S.

LESSEE
Leasing company

The leasing company is buying equipment under a conditional sales contract and is entitled to U.S. tax benefits. The interest rate is low because the French lessor utilizes French tax benefits

SUBLEASE
Equipment user

The sublease is a true tax lease to a U.S. lessee so the monthly payment is expensed in full.

United States

jurisdictions. Numerous factors must be considered when leasing outside the U.S. Some of these factors are product-related, whereas others are a function of the tax laws. Sometimes the tax laws drive the product being offered.

Conditional Sale Versus True Tax Lease

As in domestic leases, the first step in determining the U.S. income tax consequences of a lease is to decide whether the arrangement is actually a lease, or is substantively something else. (This topic also is discussed in Chapter Five) Under U.S. tax law, a lease transaction can be recharacterized as a conditional sale. In this event, the lessee is treated as the purchaser of the property at the outset of the arrangement, and the lease itself as a debt instrument issued in payment for the property.

The substance of the arrangement, versus its form, determines whether the agreement is classified as a lease or a conditional sale contract. Typically, an agreement is subject to being classified by the Internal Revenue Service (IRS) as a conditional sale contract, and not a lease, if it meets any of the following conditions:

1. Part of each rent payment is applied toward an equity investment that the taxpayer will receive

2. Title to the property is passed upon the payment of a certain amount of the payments required by the contract

3. The amount paid for the use of the property during a short time is almost the same as the amount one would pay to receive title of the property

4. The rent being paid is substantially more than the current fair rental value for that property

5. The person renting the equipment has an option to buy the equipment at a price less than the fair market value of the property at the time the option is exercised

6. There is an option to buy the property at a price less than the total amount to be paid under the lease

7. Part of the lease payments are designated as interest by the lease contract, or it is easy to recognize that part of the lease payments is interest.

The foregoing criteria are applied by the IRS to single investor leases. The IRS also has established certain criteria to determine if a leveraged lease qualifies as a tax lease when the parties are seeking an advance ruling on the transaction. These criteria are set forth by the IRS in a series of Revenue Procedures issued between 1975 and 1979.

These revenue procedures, collectively referred to as the "Guidelines," do not purport to be the standard of law for lease classification for U.S. tax purposes. However, the IRS has ruled privately that (1) if a transaction otherwise meets the Guidelines, an examining agent should not disturb its classification, even though the taxpayer did not actually seek a ruling, and (2) the Guidelines may be helpful in testing nonleveraged lease for tax status. The Guidelines are discussed more fully in Chapter Five.

Resolving the tax lease versus conditional sale issue of a lease is critical in determining the proper method of accounting for the transaction. However the outbound transaction is classified, the typical accounting methods for income and expense recognition generally apply. When accounting for outbound cross-border lease transactions, certain exceptions to the general rule do exist, however. Some of these exceptions will be addressed below.

Foreign Tax Credit

A U.S. lessor leasing equipment into a foreign country will be subject to foreign taxes, which can include those taxes imposed via actual in-country tax return filing, foreign tax withholding on U.S.-bound lease payments, as well as value-added taxes (VAT) and others. The provisions of applicable income tax treaties can have an impact on the amount of withholding required on lease payments and other definitional matters.

A U.S. lessor paying foreign taxes must consider the following two questions: (1) is the foreign tax paid creditable against the U.S. income tax liability? (2) what are the limitations on the use of the credit?

Under § 901 of the IRS Code (the Code), a foreign tax credit (FTC) is allowed for taxes paid or accrued to a foreign country or U.S. possession during the taxable year. The taxes must be characterized as "income, war profits and excess profits" taxes. Generally, the foreign tax must arise from an event that results in the realization of income as determined under principles that mirror those in the Code.

In an effort to prevent the use of an FTC to shelter U.S. income that is not subject to a foreign tax, § 904 imposes a limitation on the amount of foreign taxes allowed as a credit against U.S. income tax. Generally, the limit is calculated as follows:

$$\frac{\text{Foreign source taxable income}}{\text{Worldwide taxable income}} \times \frac{\text{U.S. income tax liability on}}{\text{worldwide income before credits}}$$

Separate FTC limitations must be calculated for each category (basket) of income as prescribed under § 904(d)(1)(A) through 904(d)(1)(I). The categories of income include:

1. Passive income

2. High withholding tax interest

3. Financial services income

4. Shipping income

5. In the case of a corporation, dividends received from each non-controlled § 902 corporation

6. Dividends from a Domestic International Sales Corporation (DISC) or former DISC to the extent that the dividends are foreign source dividends

7. Taxable income attributable to foreign trade income as defined by § 923(b)

8. Distributions from a Foreign Sales Corporation (FSC) or former FSC out of earnings and profits attributable to foreign trade income or qualified interest and carrying charges

9. All other income that is not described in any of the preceding subparagraphs.

The primary objective of the separate limitation provisions is to discourage the mixing of low-taxed, investment income from tax havens with highly-taxed, active income from operations.

Leasing income generally is included in the passive income basket; however, certain active rental activity exceptions exist. With regard to leasing to a controlled foreign corporation (CFC), one must look to the nature of the business conducted by the CFC to determine the proper basket for such leasing income.

In order to calculate the limiting fraction previously outlined, gross income must be sourced as U.S. or foreign income. Leasing income is most commonly sourced to the location of the leased equipment. The fraction calls for taxable income; thus deductions must be allocated and/or apportioned to derive taxable income. Expenses such as fungible interest, depreciation and other related expenses must be allocated/apportioned against the leasing income, which reduces the amount of foreign taxes allowed as a credit (i.e., the FTC limitation). The regulations under § 861 set forth rules for allocating and apportioning deductions. These rules are specific and mandatory for some deductions such as interest but are more general for other deductions such as depreciation.

To the extent an entity is unable to utilize all its allowable FTC, the excess may be carried back two years and forward five years. If the U.S. lessor presently has unused FTCs, the foreign withholding tax may result in an added cost of participating in a lease, thus negatively impacting the yield from the transaction. Consequently, considerable thought should be given to the overall tax effect of the foreign taxes paid in connection with leasing arrangements.

COMPREHENSIVE EXAMPLE

In 19X1, U.S. Corporation has 2,000 of taxable service income from U.S. sources and has mining assets (asset class 10.0, per Revenue Procedure 87-56) under lease to an unrelated party in Canada with the following activity:

Cost - 19X1 purchase	10,000
Rents - current year	2,000
Interest expense (allocable to Canada)	200
Lease term	10 years
Canadian tax paid	600

The calculation of the foreign source taxable income, worldwide taxable income and the U.S. taxes that U.S. Corporation owes are shown in Exhibit 4-7. The foreign tax credit is 385, which is the lesser of:

1. The § 904 FTC limit

   $$\frac{1,400}{3,400} \times 1,190 = 490$$

2. The Canadian taxes paid of 600.

Exhibit 4-7
Worldwide Tax

Foreign source income	2,000
Less: Interest	(200)
Depreciation (10 years x 125%) = 12.5 year recovery period	(400)
Foreign source taxable income	1,400
U.S. source taxable income	2,000
Worldwide taxable income	3,400
U.S. tax at 35%	1,190

Based on a U.S. income tax liability of 1,190, the net U.S. tax paid is 700 (1,190 - 490). U.S. Corporation has an excess foreign tax credit of 110 (600 - 490) and an effective current tax rate (ignoring FTC carryover) of 38% as shown below:

$$\frac{700 \text{ (U.S.)} + 600 \text{ (Canadian)}}{3,400 \text{ (worldwide taxable income)}} = 38\%$$

Pickle Leases

One tax-based product that has gained popularity with foreign lessees is the Pickle lease. These foreign lessees are considered tax-exempt entities for U.S. tax purposes. The 1984 Tax Reform Act limited the tax benefits that can be claimed by taxpayers leasing property to tax-exempt entities. This particular piece of legislation was sponsored by Texas Representative J.J. Pickle. Leases subject to this aspect of the tax law are referred to as Pickle leases.

Essentially, the Pickle legislation requires that property leased to tax-exempt entities be depreciated using the straight-line method and a longer

---

recovery period. These tax-exempt entity leasing provisions generally apply to property placed in service after May 23, 1983, in taxable years ending after May 23, 1983. They also apply to property placed in service on or before May 23, 1983 if the lease was entered into after that date.

For purposes of applying the Pickle legislation, the term tax-exempt entity includes tax-exempt organizations, foreign persons and entities and governmental entities. The rules defining a tax-exempt entity become more complex when dealing with foreign persons and entities. As mentioned, the general rule under § 168(h)(2)(A)(iii) is that a foreign person or entity is a tax-exempt entity. § 168(h)(2)(C) further expands the definition to include foreign governments, international organizations, agencies of those governments and "any person who is not a U.S. person."

Excluded from the definition are foreign partnerships and any other form of foreign pass-through entities. Additionally, under § 168(h)(2)(B), if 50% or more of the gross income derived from the use of the property is subject to U.S. income tax, the property is not subject to the tax-exempt entity provisions.

§ 168(h) also contains a five-year lookback rule, applicable to former tax-exempt entities. If an entity was tax-exempt at any time during the five-year period ending on the date property was first used by the entity, it is treated as tax-exempt with regard to the leased property.

Leased property subject to the tax-exempt leasing rules must be depreciated using the alternative depreciation system described in § 168(g) of the Code. The depreciation deduction is determined by using the straight-line method (without regard to salvage value) and the applicable convention under § 168(d) (i.e., the half-year or midquarter convention). The recovery period will be subject to the Pickle rule. Under this rule, the depreciable life is equal to the longer of (i) the property's class life or (ii) 125% of the lease term. § 168(i)(3) generally includes options to renew in determining the length of the lease term for purposes of the 125% calculation.

The Code provides an exception that excludes short-term leases and leases of qualified technological equipment from the tax-exempt entity leasing rules. A short-term lease means any lease in which the lease period is less than three years and less than the greater of one year or 30% of the property's present class life.

In the case of qualified technological equipment, the statute excludes any equipment that qualifies under § 168(i)(2) and is subject to lease periods that do not exceed five years. High-technology equipment is excluded from the tax-exempt entity leasing rules. Because of the rapid evolution in such fields, this type of equipment could become obsolete before it actually reaches the end of its physical useful life. Chapter Six contains a more complete discussion of the alternative depreciation system.

Outbound Double-dip Leasing

A transaction respected as a lease for U.S. tax purposes may be a conditional sale for foreign tax purposes (or vice versa) because of differences in U.S. and foreign tax law with respect to asset ownership. Such differences give rise to the opportunity of claiming deductions on an asset in two separate jurisdictions simultaneously (i.e., once by the U.S. lessor for U.S. tax purposes and once again by the foreign lessee for foreign tax purposes). These leases are known as double-dip leases. Additionally, in jurisdictions where interest paid by a resident corporation gets a more favorable treatment than rent paid by such corporation, the outbound double-dip structure can sometimes help eliminate withholding taxes.

MECHANICS

The most basic double-dip structure is one in which a U.S. lessor leases property to a lessee, and the lessee takes advantage of any tax savings offered by the local tax law of that country. This structure is known as the single-tier, outbound, double-dip lease. The transaction will be easier to accomplish if the asset is leased to a company located in a jurisdiction that characterizes a true lease under U.S. tax law as a conditional sale for foreign tax purposes, conveying tax ownership to the lessee.

A second type of outbound, double-dip structure adds a new party or entity to the basic transaction. In this case, the U.S. lessor leases an asset to a lessor in a foreign jurisdiction. The foreign lessor subleases the asset to an ultimate user in a transaction that qualifies as a true lease under that jurisdiction's local law. This structure is known as a two-tier, outbound, double-dip lease.

An outbound, double-dip lease creates an opportunity for the U.S. lessor to take depreciation and interest expense deductions on the leased asset. Since the transaction qualifies as a true lease for U.S. tax purposes, the lessor will recognize the lease payments as income when they are received. In some jurisdictions, the withholding issue becomes a concern because those jurisdictions consider the lessee's payment as a payment of interest and principal. However, this situation differs from jurisdiction to jurisdiction.

Structuring a double-dip lease in a jurisdiction that requires a fixed purchase option of any type to be classified as a conditional sale for foreign jurisdiction purposes is more challenging. The objective of this transaction is to meet the requirements of the foreign jurisdiction and still qualify as a lease for U.S. tax purposes.

Another outbound, double-dip lease structure is essentially a triple-dip. A U.S. lessor leases equipment to a foreign lessee that qualifies as the tax owner in its particular jurisdiction. The lessee, respecting the law that governs its U.S. lease, leases the equipment to another person or entity, in a different tax jurisdiction, who can take advantage of the tax opportunities offered by that jurisdiction's local law. In this transaction, all three entities are taking advantage of the tax benefits of the law simultaneously in the three different jurisdictions.

The classification of lease payments as rent or interest is important in double-dip transactions because such classification will have an effect on the payment of withholding taxes. One method to avoid withholding taxes is to prepay all the rental payments because the payment will be classified as rent, not interest. However, this solution is unfavorable to the U.S. lessor because it is forced to recognize the prepayments as taxable income in the year they are received.

In some foreign jurisdictions, the local law requires that, in order to meet the tax ownership test, the lessee must hold title to the asset for U.S. tax purposes. This requirement can be met through a conditional or installment sale arrangement. The requirements of the foreign country must be satisfied so the lessee can receive a favorable tax treatment, without affecting the tax treatment of the U.S. lessor.

LEASE-SUBLEASE/SALE

In the lease-sublease structure, the lease transaction includes a third party that becomes the ultimate user of the equipment. The U.S. lessor leases the equipment to a foreign person or entity that later becomes a sublessor by leasing that same equipment to the third party from a different jurisdiction.

In this transaction, the U.S. lessor still is considered the tax owner of the asset, and the sublessor can take advantage of any tax benefits offered by the local tax jurisdiction. In addition, the rental payments made by the ultimate user benefit the sublessor because the sublease does not give tax ownership to the ultimate user. The most important benefit for the U.S. lessor in this transaction is the ability to manage the withholding requirement of the foreign country.

FOREIGN SALES CORPORATIONS

The predominantly used outside the U.S. rules and the tax-exempt entity rules also apply to complex lease structures involving the use of FSCs. The purpose of a FSC is to create an incentive for the export of goods produced in the U.S. If a FSC meets the qualifications for FSC status, a portion of its income is exempt from current U.S. taxation. The income also can be distributed to a corporate U.S. shareholder without additional U.S. tax. Because of requirements set forth in the General Agreement on Tariffs and Trade, a FSC must be a foreign corporation and must meet certain structural, annual, transactional and export property requirements to assure it has a sufficient foreign presence. The structural requirements are outlined in Exhibit 4-8.

Types of FSCs

There are two basic types of FSCs: the Commission FSC (CFSC) and the Ownership FSC (OFSC). The requirements discussed in Exhibit 4-8 apply to both types. In general, the CFSC is used when the lessee is a U.S. domestic corporation and the OFSC is used when the equipment is leased to a foreign lessee.

COMMISSION FSC STRUCTURE

In a CFSC structure, the FSC acts as a commission agent for the lessor in a leveraged lease to a domestic lessee. A CFSC structure typically is organized as follows:

1. A U.S. equity investor (the lessor) organizes the CFSC in a FSC-certified jurisdiction prior to soliciting the deal

2. The lessor enters into a commission agreement and an agency agreement with the CFSC as soon as it is organized, pursuant to which the CFSC agrees to act as the lessor's commission agent and the lessor agrees to act as the CFSC's agent in the performance of required FSC activities, respectively

Exhibit 4-8
FSC Requirements

Structural requirements

The FSC must:

1. Be incorporated in a U.S. possession or a foreign country certified for FSC purposes

2. Have no more than 25 shareholders at any time during the taxable year

3. Have no preferred stock outstanding at any time during the taxable year

4. Maintain an office and set of permanent books of account in a FSC-certified country or a U.S. possession and maintain certain required records in the U.S.

5. Have at least one non-U.S. resident on its board of directors at all times during the taxable year

6. Not be a member of a controlled group of corporations of which a DISC is a member

7. Elect to be treated as a FSC during the first 90 days of the 90-day period immediately preceding the beginning of any other taxable year in which it desires the FSC election to be effective

8. Have the same taxable year as that of the shareholder (or shareholders) who own(s) the highest percentage of voting power.

Annual requirements

Generally, the management of the FSC must take place outside the U.S. This requirement will be satisfied if all shareholders' meetings and all board of directors' meetings occur outside the U.S.; the FSC is established within 30 days after incorporation and maintains its principal bank account in a U.S. possession or a foreign country that is certified for FSC purposes; and all dividends, legal and accounting fees, and salaries of officers and directors are disbursed from bank accounts outside the U.S.

Transactional requirements

1. Foreign sales activities test. The FSC or its agent must participate outside the U.S. in the solicitation (other than advertising), negotiation or making of the contract

2. Foreign costs test. The FSC must incur either 50% of the total direct costs in each of five enumerated categories of economic activity or 85% of the total direct costs in any two of the following five categories:

   a. advertising and sales promotion

   b. processing of orders and arranging delivery

   c. transportation

   d. determination and transmittal of invoice and receipt of payment

   e. assumption of credit risk.

Export property requirements

The property must qualify as export property. Export property is property that is manufactured, produced, grown or extracted in the U.S. by a person other than a FSC and held primarily for sale, lease or rental in the ordinary course of a trade or business by, or to, a FSC for direct use, consumption or disposition outside the U.S. Additionally, no more than 50% of the property's fair market value can be attributable to articles imported into the U.S.

3. The lessor borrows up to 80% of the amount of the acquisition cost of the property leased by issuing nonrecourse notes to a U.S. lender

4. The lessor purchases the property from a U.S. manufacturer and leases the property to a U.S. lessee under a long-term, triple net lease

5. The lessee uses the property predominantly outside the U.S. for purposes contained in the FSC export property requirements

6. The property, however, will not be subject to the less favorable alternative depreciation system set forth in § 168 (g) of the Code, because the property does not constitute tax-exempt use property and will not be used predominantly outside the U.S. for purposes of the MACRS provisions.

Special rules govern the taxation of CFSCs. Approximately 65% (15/23) of the FSC's commission income is treated as foreign source income that is not effectively connected to a U.S. trade or business and, therefore, is exempt from tax in the U.S. Approximately 35% (8/23) is treated as U.S. source income that is effectively connected with a U.S. trade or business. This U.S. source income, accordingly, is subject to U.S. tax currently at regular corporate rates.

The benefit available from the CFSC structure is the ability, in years in which the lease generates positive taxable income, to allocate 23% of the lessor's net rental income from the lease to the commission FSC. The income of the CFSC is largely exempt from tax in the U.S. This exemption reduces the effective tax rate on the commission income from 35% to 29.75%. Exhibit 4-9 illustrates the CFSC structure.

Turbo FSC

The benefit of the commission FSC structure is that up to 23% of the combined taxable income of the lessor can be allocated to the FSC as a commission. However, the interest allocation rules of §861 of the Code present a problem. §861 requires that interest expense related to qualified nonrecourse indebtedness be allocated to any gross income produced by property acquired with the proceeds of the nonrecourse loan. Consequently, the combined taxable income from the lease transaction will be reduced, along with a corresponding reduction in the commission allocated to the FSC.

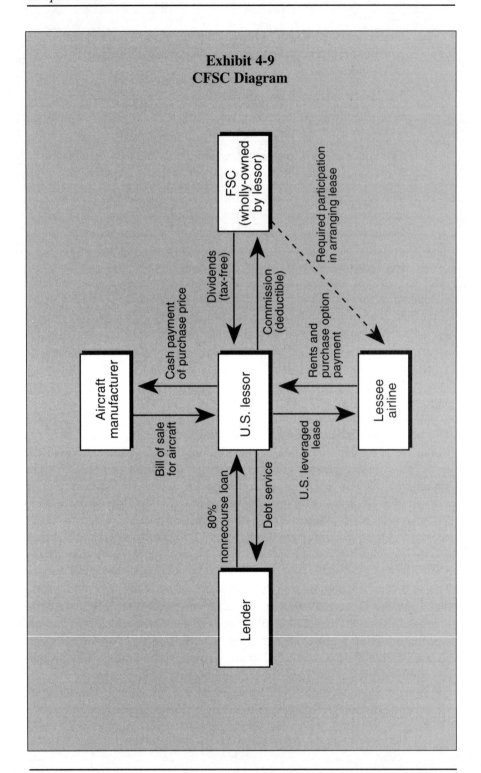

Exhibit 4-9
CFSC Diagram

The turbo FSC structure, however, provides a more favorable result. A turbo FSC transaction is designed in such a way that the acquisition indebtedness will fail one of the tests necessary to satisfy the definition of qualified nonrecourse indebtedness. Failing the test avoids the negative result previously mentioned. Through the use of the turbo FSC structure, the interest expense on the acquisition indebtedness is not directly offset against the income from the lease. Thus, the method of allocating the interest results in increased FSC benefits.

Under Treasury Regulation §1.861-10T(b)(2), qualified nonrecourse indebtedness is defined to mean any borrowing if:

(1) *it is specifically incurred for the purpose of purchasing either amortizable intangible personal property with a useful life of more than one year or depreciable tangible property with a useful life of more than one year,*

(2) *the proceeds are actually applied to purchase or improve the identified property,*

(3) *the creditor can look only to the identified property as security for payment of the principal and interest on the loan, except as permitted in a leveraged lease transaction,*

(4) *the cash flow from the property is reasonably expected to be sufficient in the first year of ownership as well as in each subsequent year of ownership to fulfill the terms and conditions of the loan agreement with respect to the amount and timing of interest and principal payments,*

(5) *there are restrictions in the loan agreement on the disposal or use of the property consistent with these conditions.*

Pursuant to the regulations, if qualified nonrecourse debt is refinanced it may no longer be considered as qualified nonrecourse debt. The refinancing of qualified nonrecourse debt will qualify as such only when the five definitional requirements are satisfied. Additionally, the principal amount of the new debt may not be more than 5% greater than the principal amount of the refinanced debt and the time until the refinanced debt matures cannot exceed that of the old debt by more than six months. Consequently, a turbo FSC transaction frequently involves the refinancing of the original debt that does not satisfy these refinancing requirements.

OWNERSHIP FSC

In an OFSC, the FSC, as a lessor, leases, under a leveraged lease, equipment to an unrelated lessee. As with CFSCs, an OFSC must satisfy the structural, annual, transactional and export property requirements.

An OFSC is generally structured as follows:

1. A U.S. equity investor (the investor) organizes an OFSC (the lessor) in an FSC-certified jurisdiction

2. The lessor enters into an agency agreement with the investor to allow the regular employees of the investor, on behalf of the lessor, to perform the requisite economic process functions

3. The investor contributes equity to the lessor in an amount equal to the acquisition cost of the property to be leased

4. The investor borrows up to 80% of the amount of its equity investment in the lessor by issuing nonrecourse notes secured solely by the lessor's stock. The exact nature of the security package for the debt generally is heavily negotiated.

The taxation of an OFSC also is complex, but results in significant tax savings. When the FSC does not purchase or lease property or receive a commission from a related person, 30% of its Foreign Trading Income (FTI) is exempt from U.S. federal income tax. The remaining 70% is nonexempt FTI. Unlike the nonexempt FTI of a typical CFSC, nonexempt FTI of an OFSC is treated as U.S. source income only to the extent income is so treated under the generally applicable rules. If the leased property is aircraft or ships, rental income is exempt from federal income taxation provided that the foreign country in which the FSC is organized grants an equivalent exemption to U.S. citizens and corporations.

At the shareholder level, 70% of the lessor's net rental income must be included currently in the shareholder's gross income. As with the CFSC, the U.S. corporate shareholder of an OFSC will not be subject to any tax on actual earnings and profits distributions from the FSC's FTI. The shareholder should be entitled to a full deduction for interest paid on notes issued to finance the capital contribution to the lessor. Exhibit 4-10 is a diagram of the OFSC structure.

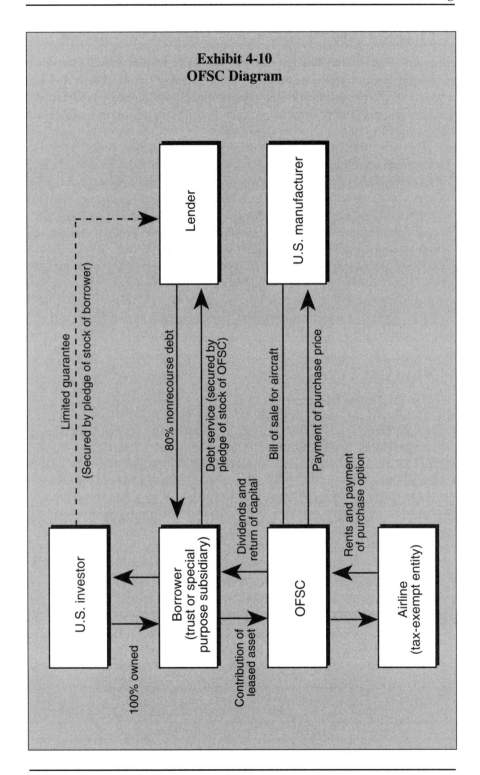

**Exhibit 4-10
OFSC Diagram**

CONCLUSION

The U.S. leasing industry has become a mature marketplace. In order to expand and maintain/increase profits, U.S. leasing companies have found they need to go overseas for new opportunities. Often, they have been able to take advantage of international tax benefits by designing financial products tailored to this fast growing marketplace.

International funding mechanisms have improved and the Eximbank, IFC, ADB and EIB have provided low cost capital to achieve these goals. Even lessees in Islamic countries have benefited from leasing structures. Furthermore, the use of special lease structures, such as FSCs, OFSCs and Pickle leases, indicates U.S. leasing companies have entered the international leasing arena and plan to stay for a long time.

Section Two

Taxation

Chapter Five

IRS Qualifications of a Lease

To someone not generally familiar with the ins and outs of tax theory and application, it is unclear why such a simple question as "Is the transaction a lease or a sale?" creates such controversy. When classifying a lease for tax purposes, the true substance of the transaction, not the form, must be examined. Since leasing made its dramatic appearance after World War II, the Internal Revenue Service (IRS), the courts and Congress have attempted to develop guidelines to determine the tax substance of transactions (i.e., whether the transactions is a true tax lease or conditional sales contract). These guidelines are used by lessors and lessees to structure transactions to avoid this continuing controversy. Unfortunately, the guidelines have, in many cases, served to complicate the situation even more.

This chapter addresses the lease versus sale question through a threefold focus:

- Definitions of a Lease

- Lease or Sale: Issues of Concern

- True Lease or Sale: Factors, Guidelines and Tests.

DEFINITIONS OF A LEASE

One of the most confusing tax issues in leasing is the tax classification of a transaction as a lease or as a sale disguised as a lease. The classification of the lease is very important because the federal income tax consequences to the parties in a lease transaction vary greatly depending on how the lease is classified. In the simplest of legal terms, a lease consists of four parts. First, there is an agreement between the owner of an asset (the lessor) and the prospective or current user of that asset (the lessee). Second, pursuant to the agreement, the lessor transfers the use (but not the ownership) of the asset to the lessee. Third, the lessee compensates the lessor for the use of the asset, usually in the form of rent. Finally, after the predetermined period of use (the lease term), which is less than the asset's economic life, the lessee returns the asset to the lessor.

From a different vantage point, a lease may be viewed as a tax advantaged installment loan with either a guaranteed or unguaranteed residual. Both this definition and the one from the paragraph above are correct and both contain a common element essential to the existence of a lease: residual value.

To determine what a lease is, it is helpful to compare it to transactions that are not leases. In today's legal environment, an owner of an asset can transfer some or all of the benefits of that asset to another party in only three different ways – a lease, a sale or a service arrangement.

Lease

A lease is commonly referred to as a true lease or a tax lease for tax purposes. A lease for federal income tax purposes treats the lessor as the owner of the asset. The federal income tax criteria of a lease are the primary focus of this chapter and are discussed later in great detail. A true, or tax, lease is a lease meeting those criteria. True leases encompass several other types of leases, including tax-exempt and terminal rental adjustment clause (TRAC) leases. These are discussed later in the chapter.

Sale

A sale, in its truest form, involves the transfer, for consideration, by the owner of an asset (the seller) to another party (the buyer) of all rights to the asset, including ownership and use. A seller generally has no continuing interest in or right to the asset. Three types of sales are common. In a conditional sales contract (CSC), the seller sells the asset and transfers possession to the purchaser, but retains title to the asset until the purchaser has fully paid for it. A secured sale occurs when the seller transfers title to the asset to the purchaser at the point of sale, but the purchaser grants the seller a security interest in the asset to secure payment of the purchase price. Upon full payment by the purchaser, the seller releases the security interest.

Finally, in an absolute sale, the seller transfers title to the asset to the purchaser and does not take back a security interest in the asset, irrespective of whether the purchase price is paid in full. In an absolute sale, if the entire purchase price is not paid at the time title is transferred, the seller relies solely on the purchaser's general financial ability to pay the purchase price.

Service Contract

The third legal method to transfer some or all of an asset's benefits to another party involves a service contract. A service contract is one in which the providing of a service (e.g., copies or computer time) requires the use of a type of asset, but not any particular asset. This arrangement differs from a lease because, among other things, it is not dependent on the use of any particular asset. Similarly, a service arrangement differs from a sale for many reasons, one of them being that title to the asset necessary to provide the service is retained by the service provider. The only benefit transferred to the service recipient is the service, e.g., copies or computer time.

The preceding discussion illustrates that the substance of the relationship between two parties has a direct bearing on how that transaction is characterized. The agreement may be a sale, or it could be a service contract. Unfortunately, no simple test can be employed in every case to determine the substance of the agreement. In many instances the distinctions become blurred and uncertain. It is important, therefore, to carefully analyze the characteristics of each transaction.

LEASE OR SALE: ISSUES OF CONCERN

The classification of the lease determines how it is treated by the lessor and the lessee. Transactions are classified as either leases or sales from four different perspectives, each with numerous subsets:

1. Federal income tax consequences

2. Financial reporting requirements

3. Uniform Commercial Code (UCC) ramifications

4. Bankruptcy effects.

This chapter deals primarily with the first perspective, that of federal income taxes. The financial reporting perspective is covered in depth in Chapters Nine through Eleven. The effects of the UCC and the Bankruptcy Reform Act are considered in much greater detail in Chapter Nineteen.

Federal Income Tax Consequences

The legal and tax infrastructure within which business must be conducted has a pervasive influence on transactions. Business people, however, are very adaptable and have learned to operate within any reasonable set of requirements and constraints. U.S. federal income tax laws have a deep and far-reaching effect on every facet of the economy, as the laws traditionally have been used to accomplish social and fiscal objectives.

If, for federal income tax purposes, a transaction is in substance a true tax lease, the lessor is entitled to all tax benefits associated with the purchase and ownership of the property. Depreciation deductions and any credits available, e.g., the Investment Tax Credit (ITC), are recognized by the lessor along with the income associated with the lease payments. Conversely, if the transaction is in substance a sale, the lessor recognizes income (generally ordinary) to the extent the sales price exceeds the lessor's investment in the property. The lease payments received from the lessee are classified as return of principal, interest income and gain. Because the property has, in substance, been sold to the lessee, the lessor is not entitled to any tax benefits attendant to ownership.

From a lessee perspective, if the transaction is a true lease the full amount of the lease payments is deductible as an ordinary and necessary business expense. If, on the other hand, the transaction is a sale of the asset to the lessee, the lessee becomes the owner of the asset and, therefore, is entitled to any tax benefits attendant to ownership. In the event of sale status, the lease payments paid by the lessee are treated as payments on the purchase price and are classified as principal and interest expense.

The classification of the agreement is, therefore, very important because of the significance of the tax treatment. The tax treatment affects the cash flows of the parties involved and has a direct effect on the yields associated with the transaction. Over the years, the lease market has become efficient in transferring the tax benefits of ownership to the parties most able to use them. Lessors are able to transfer some portion of the tax benefits to the lessees in the form of lower lease payments. This, of course, results in a lower effective cost of the equipment to lessees, which leads to greater profits and the ability to expand.

On a larger scale, the end result is a fueling of economic growth. If a lessor cannot be reasonably certain of its entitlement to the tax benefits of ownership (whatever they are at the time), however, the cost of equipment to lessees is certain to rise. The importance of tax benefits to an equipment leasing transaction does not mean they are essential to the viability of the leasing industry. Leasing also is important to lessors and lessees for a number of additional reasons.

Financial Reporting Requirements

Whether a lease is classified as a lease or as a sale also affects the way the transaction is reflected on the financial statements of the parties. The criteria used to make this decision for financial reporting purposes, however, are different (although conceptually similar) from those used for tax purposes.

A lease that is a true usage agreement is called an operating lease for accounting purposes. If the lease is an operating lease, the lessor's financial statements reflect its ownership of the asset, showing a corresponding expense for depreciation and interest, if any. That treatment is similar to true lease treatment by the lessor under the tax law. In the case of an operating lease, the only direct effect on the lessee's financial statements is a periodic expense on the income statement for lease payments, which also is similar to true lease treatment for tax purposes.

On the other hand, a lease that is really a sale is referred to as a capital lease. A capital lease is capitalized by the lessee, i.e., it is shown as an asset on the balance sheet of the lessee. In the case of a capital lease to the lessee, the lessee is treated for accounting purposes as the owner of the asset. If the lease is a capital lease to the lessor, the lessor's books indicate that it has sold the asset. Therefore, the asset is not shown on the lessor's balance sheet but is reflected as a receivable. The lessor reports any gain or loss on the sale and classifies the lease payments as return of capital, interest and gain.

A very interesting yet confusing element of the accounting rules is that a lease does not have to be classified the same for the lessor and lessee. It is possible (and in fact likely) that a lessor will classify a lease as a capital lease and the lessee, in the same transaction, will properly treat the lease as an operating lease.

Uniform Commercial Code Ramifications

Forty-nine states (all except Louisiana) have adopted a set of laws governing a variety of business transactions including, among others, the sale of goods (personal, not real, property) and secured transactions. Many states also have adopted laws dealing with lease transactions. This set of laws is referred to as the Uniform Commercial Code (UCC). The rules developed under the UCC for determining whether a lease is a lease or a sale are different (even though conceptually similar) from those existing under either the tax law or accounting standards.

BANKRUPTCY

An unpleasant reality in the equipment leasing environment is the potential of lessee bankruptcy. If it does happen, what are the lessor's rights? The answer to that question depends, to a large extent, on whether the lease is really a lease or whether it is a sale. The standards used to decide the lease versus sale controversy in the context of bankruptcy are essentially the same as those developed under the UCC. The complexities of leasing and bankruptcy are discussed in Chapter Nineteen in more detail.

TRUE LEASE OR SALE: FACTORS, GUIDELINES AND TESTS

The following discussion provides insight into the many factors considered in determining whether a transaction is a lease or a sale.

Statutory Basis

The starting point for resolution of most questions arising under federal income tax law is the Internal Revenue Code (IRC). The true lease versus sale controversy is no different. The IRC, enacted and frequently changed by Congress, contains two sections that together form the basis for the definition of a lease from a federal income tax viewpoint. These IRC sections do not answer directly the question of lease or sale, but the first of the two, IRC §167, provides that:

> *There shall be allowed as a depreciation deduction a reasonable allowance for the exhaustion, wear and tear (including a reasonable allowance for obsolescence) of property used in the trade or business, or of property held for the production of income. [IRC §1 67(a)]*

Although IRC §167 does not explicitly define who is entitled to the depreciation deduction, court decisions over many years make it clear that only the "owner in substance" is so entitled. The "owner in substance" is the person who has made a capital investment in the property and who is in a position to suffer an economic loss by reason of the wear and tear, decay, exhaustion or obsolescence of the property.

The second section of the IRC §162 that helps form the basis of the definition of a tax lease states:

> *There shall be allowed as a deduction all the ordinary and necessary expenses paid or incurred during the taxable year in carrying on any trade or business including . . . (3) rentals or other payments required to be made as a condition to the continued use or possession, for purposes of the trade or business, of property to which the taxpayer has not taken or is not taking title or in which he has no equity. [IRC §162(a)]*

IRC §162 and §167 establish the statutory foundation for the true lease versus sale determination. Both the courts and the IRS have struggled over the years to expand this foundation in an effort to provide some meaningful guidance to taxpayers. Consequently, a series of general rules have been established in the form of IRS rulings and court decisions. Unfortunately, the rules have many exceptions and are vague in their definitions and, therefore, do not adequately address all of the intricacies of equipment leasing.

Judicial Tests and Criteria

Many cases have addressed the issue of whether a transaction is a lease or a sale. The case law that has been developed, however, is by no means very clear. Nonetheless, broad concepts have been established within which most factual settings fall. Therefore, although some inconsistency exists when analyzing specific criteria, the general principles provide a sufficient basis for resolving most cases. The purpose of this subsection is to establish a general knowledge base that can be utilized by leasing professionals to avoid encountering a true lease versus conditional sale problem. This problem can be avoided only if the transaction is in the planning or structuring phase. The focus of this chapter is on how to structure equipment leasing transactions to avoid, or at least mitigate, the true lease versus sale controversy. Understanding what the courts have done in the past aids in this endeavor.

BASIC JUDICIAL TESTS

Using the IRC as the basis for answering the true lease versus sale question, the courts have developed two broad tests to be applied to a specific factual setting. The first test, applied in the context of a lessor's entitlement to depreciation of an asset, is whether the substance of the transaction is such that the lessor no longer has a sufficient connection with the property to constitute a depreciable interest therein. In other words, has the lessor retained sufficient indicia of ownership? Is the lessor still in a position to suffer an economic loss by reason of the wear and tear, decay, exhaustion or obsolescence of the property? If not, the lessor has no right to depreciate the property for tax purposes because the lessor stands to lose nothing even if the property is lost or destroyed.

The second test ordinarily applies in the context of a lessee's entitlement to a deduction for lease payments. The basic test is whether the substance of the transaction is such that the lessee will receive an equity in, or take title to, the property through the payment of rent. If either of those events occurs, the lease payment deduction generally is denied because the lessee is treated as having purchased the property.

Judicially Established Criteria

Many cases have been decided in the lease versus sale area of tax law, most of which have divergent factual scenarios. The courts have considered innumerable factors in their decision making processes. Many of those factors have precedential value, i.e., they may be used in subsequent cases of a similar nature. Sometimes the factors considered in a particular case, because of special facts peculiar to that case, have no general applicability. In addition, the significance of some of the factors changes over time as business conditions and practices evolve and develop. Typically, however, courts are reluctant to diverge from rules established in prior cases. Consequently, there is often a time lag between the changing practices and conditions of business and the courts' adaptation thereto.

The true lease versus conditional sale criteria outlined in Exhibit 5-1 have been gleaned from cases decided over the past three decades. The list is not comprehensive but it is certainly representative of the types of concerns addressed by the courts. Although there are times that one criterion is conclusive in and of itself, more often than not all criteria taken together influence the courts' decisions. Later in this chapter, these criteria are ranked in order of relative importance to facilitate understanding. Most of the crite-

Exhibit 5-1
Judicial Criteria

1. Intent of the parties at the time of execution of the agreement
2. Whether title to the property automatically passes to the lessee upon its payment of the lease rentals
3. Whether the agreement provides that title will not pass to the lessee
4. Whether the lessor retains title during the lease term
5. Whether the lease is a net lease
6. Frequency that equipment is returned to the lessor at lease termination
7. Extent of the lessor's remarketing capabilities
8. Lease term compared to the useful life of the equipment
9. Industry practices
10. Nature of the lessor's business
11. Nature of the lessee's business
12. The extent to which the lessor keeps track of the leased equipment
13. Amount of minimum lease payments compared with original purchase price plus financing charges
14. Amount of the lease payments compared with the fair rental value of the equipment
15. Whether the lease payments are constant, increasing or decreasing
16. Existence of tax avoidance motives
17. Existence of dealer guarantees or repurchase agreements
18. Existence of a purchase option; analysis of the exercise price
    a. side agreements either written or oral
    b. exercise price compared with the original purchase price of the equipment
    c. exercise price compared with total rents
    d. exercise price compared with the equipment's fair market value at the end of the lease term
    e. whether the lessee is economically compelled to exercise the purchase option
       1) lessee improvements to the property
       2) disruption of the lessee's business
    f. whether the lessee is able to exercise the purchase option
    g. whether some portion or all of the rent payments is credited toward the purchase option price
19. Whether the lease agreement contains an automatic renewal provision
20. Type of property that is the subject of the lease
21. Existence of lessor puts or similar options
22. Extent, if any, of the lessor's equity investment
23. Whether the lease transaction is match funded
24. Whether the lease transaction has economic substance
25. Whether the taxpayer accounted for the transaction as a lease in its books and records.

ria have current and general applicability. Some have greater significance and should be scrutinized closely in the planning stages of every transaction. Several of these criteria are illustrated in the following discussion of landmark decisions.

Landmark Decisions

Although literally hundreds of cases have addressed the lease versus sale issue, five cases, listed chronologically, clearly outline some of the most important principles discussed in the preceding sections.

In *Helvering v. F& R Lazarus & Co.*, 308 U.S. 252 (1939), the Supreme Court held that the lessor's retention of title was not an absolute prerequisite to the lessor's entitlement to depreciation deductions. Lazarus & Co. entered into a loan arrangement with a bank in which the form of the transaction was a sale by and leaseback to Lazarus. The Supreme Court analyzed the transaction from the perspective of a lessor, and determined that Lazarus was the party who stood to gain or lose from the exhaustion and wear and tear of the equipment, and who otherwise maintained the attributes and indicia of ownership. This case is important because it requires a court, when questioning the entitlement to depreciation deductions, to look beyond the form of the transaction. Consequently, from the perspective of entitlement to depreciation, who holds the title to the property is only one factor, and not necessarily a conclusive one, in the determination of who the owner is for federal income tax purposes.

Lockhart Leasing Co. v. Commissioner, 446 F.2d 269 (1971), aff'g 54 T.C. 301 (1970), involved the disallowance by the IRS of investment credits taken by Lockhart that were generated in connection with Lockhart's equipment leasing activities. The IRS contended, among other things, that Lockhart was in the financing business, not the leasing business, and that the agreements between Lockhart and its customers, although cast in the form of leases, were in reality loans secured by the underlying equipment. The tax court held (which was affirmed on appeal) that Lockhart was the owner of the equipment for federal income tax purposes and, therefore, it was entitled to the depreciation deductions and investment credits.

This case is important for two reasons. First, it recognizes that finance leasing is an alternative method of financing the acquisition of equipment, and is not the equivalent of a sale or a loan. Second, it confirms that the mere existence of a purchase option in a lease does not render that lease a sale for income tax purposes, nor does the fact that some transactions in a lessor's portfolio are sales taint the validity of the true leases in the balance of the portfolio.

In *The LTV Corp. v. Commissioner*, 63 T.C. 39 (1974), the IRS contested the validity of a lease transaction from the perspective of the lessee, and asserted that LTV, the lessee, was not entitled to deduct the lease payments made pursuant to a lease of IBM computer equipment entered into between LTV and an independent leasing company. The lease term, a five-year standard net lease, provided step-down payments and contained a 10% purchase option. The court held the lease was a true lease for federal income tax purposes, and LTV thus was entitled to deduct the lease payments. The existence of the 10% purchase option, the reasonable estimate of the fair market value of the equipment at the expiration of the term of the lease, the fact that the lease was a standard net lease and the step-down payment structure did not result in LTV taking title to, or acquiring an equity in, the computer equipment.

Frank Lyon Co. v. United States, 435 U.S. 561 (1978), concerned entitlement to depreciation. In this transaction Lyon entered into a complex sale-leaseback of a new building with Worthen Bank which was prohibited by banking regulations from utilizing conventional financing methods to construct its building. Worthen sold the building to Lyon for approximately 7,500,000 and then leased it back for 25 years. Lyon made a down payment of 500,000 and obtained the balance of the purchase price from a third-party lender. Worthen negotiated for a series of repurchase options that, if exercised, would have provided Lyon with a return of its down payment together with interest at the rate of 6%. The transaction was match funded, i.e., the lease payments exactly matched the loan payments, and the lease was a net lease. The IRS disallowed Lyon's depreciation deductions, contending that Lyon was not really the tax owner of the building.

The Supreme Court ruled in favor of Lyon, holding that the form of the transaction should be respected so long as the lessor retains significant and genuine attributes of a traditional lessor, and provided the transaction was motivated by a business purpose and could be supported by economic substance. This case is especially important because it intimates a presumption in favor of the taxpayer, as long as (1) it can support the form of the transaction with a legitimate business purpose and (2) the transaction would be viable on its own without tax benefits.

Finally, in *Rice's Toyota World, Inc. v. Commissioner,* 752 F.2d 89 (4th Cir. 1985), aff'g 81 T.C. 184 (1983), the IRS disallowed the depreciation deductions taken by Rice's Toyota in connection with a complex computer leasing transaction referred to as a wrap lease. The facts in this case were extremely unfavorable to Rice's Toyota. In upholding the IRS's position, the court states it was clear from even a cursory review of the transaction's economics that Rice's Toyota had entered into the transaction solely for tax benefits. With even very optimistic assumptions regarding the value of the computer equipment at the expiration of the wrap lease, the transaction would not have been viable without tax benefits.

The Rice's Toyota case is important because it applies the business purpose/economic substance tests mandated in the Frank Lyon case to computer leasing. It also emphasizes the need for passive investors in tax shelter transactions to conduct a reasonable amount of due diligence with respect to the economics of the transaction.

There have been a number of other cases since the Rice's Toyota case, many of which have been decided in favor of the taxpayer. In those cases, however, although tax benefits played a material role in the taxpayers' decisions to enter into the leasing transactions, they were not the sole motivation.

IRS Tests and Criteria

The U.S. government operates under a system of three branches. The legislative branch (Congress) enacts the laws; the executive branch (the president and administrative agencies) implements and enforces the laws; and the judicial branch (the courts) interprets the laws. In the context of federal income taxation, the IRS is the administrative agency that enforces the tax law.

As part of its enforcement and implementation process, the IRS issues four different types of guidance to help taxpayers comply with the law: regulations, revenue rulings, revenue procedures and letter rulings. Since Congress is unable to consider every aspect of the tax laws it enacts, the IRS is burdened with the responsibility of completing the myriad details left either untouched or not clearly defined by Congress. In that regard, the IRS issues regulations that explain and expound upon the law. Regulations are binding on both the taxpayer and the IRS unless they are determined by a court to be contrary to the congressional intent at the time the law was enacted.

The IRS issues revenue rulings in response to specific taxpayer requests. A revenue ruling sets forth the position of the IRS with respect to a particular set of actual facts submitted to it by a taxpayer. The revenue ruling is binding on both the taxpayer and the IRS if the transaction occurs the way it was represented by the taxpayer. Revenue rulings generally have precedential value, i.e., all taxpayers can rely on the position taken by the IRS in the ruling.

Private letter rulings, on the other hand, set forth the position of the IRS with respect to a particular set of actual facts submitted to it by the taxpayer but have no precedential value. Private letter rulings may be relied on only by the taxpayers to whom they are issued.

Revenue procedures tell the taxpayer how to interact with the IRS. For example, Revenue Procedure (Rev. Proc.) 75-21, 1975-1 C.B. 715, outlines the requirements necessary for a taxpayer to obtain an advance ruling on whether a transaction constitutes a lease from a federal income tax perspective.

REVENUE PROCEDURE 75-21, 1975-1 C.B. 715

Although leveraged leasing has been a method of financing the acquisition of capital for several decades, its utilization began increasing at a geometric rate in the late sixties and early seventies. This increase was in part the result of the tremendous technological advancements occurring in the computer field, among others. The flourishing use of this financing method also was tied to the availability of significant tax benefits, e.g., ITC and accelerated depreciation to the tax owner of the asset.

The combination of the increasing popularity of leveraged leasing and the significance of the tax benefits attendant to that structure prompted the IRS to issue Rev. Proc. 75-21. In order to obtain an advance ruling from the IRS as to whether the IRS considers a lease in a leveraged lease transaction to be a true lease for federal income tax purposes, the lease must comply with the requirements of that revenue procedure. For purposes of the revenue procedure, a leveraged lease is generally a lease (1) involving three parties: the lessor, the lessee and the lender; (2) in which the responsibilities of maintenance, insurance and taxes (not including the lessor's income taxes) rest with the lessee (a net lease); (3) the term of which covers a substantial part of the property's useful life; and (4) with respect to which the lease payments are sufficient to discharge the lessor's nonrecourse loan payments to the lender.

It is important to recognize that the definition of a leveraged lease in Rev. Proc. 75-21 is not the same as the definition used for financial reporting purposes. (Refer to Chapter Nine for the Financial Accounting Standards Board Statement No. 13 (FASB 13) definition of a leveraged lease.) In addition, what the leasing industry considers to be a leveraged lease may or may not be a leveraged lease for purposes of Rev. Proc. 75-21. From an industry perspective, a leveraged lease is one in which the lease payments fully amortize the nonrecourse loan obtained by the lessor from a third-party lender. It is not necessary that the lease term cover "a substantial part of the property's useful life," as suggested in the revenue procedure, although most leveraged leases in the marketplace do so.

The revenue procedure contains six requirements with which a taxpayer must comply before the IRS will issue an advance ruling as to the transaction's true lease status. Compliance with these requirements does not ensure true lease status but, as a practical matter, does provide virtual protection against an IRS argument on the issue (even without a ruling request). Both the courts and the marketplace in general, however, do not suggest that meeting these requirements is necessary to have a true lease for tax purposes. In fact, the Rev. Proc. 75-21 guidelines are much more restrictive than the standards and criteria established by the courts. In addition, the revenue procedure itself states the guidelines are not intended to be used by revenue agents for audit purposes, implying the advance ruling requirements are more conservative than what the tax law requires.

The Requirements

The six requirements of Exhibit 5-2 must be complied with to obtain the advance ruling.

The 20% Minimum Unconditional At-risk Investment

As indicated, the lessor must have made a "minimum unconditional investment in the property (the Minimum Investment) at the inception of the lease. The lessor also must maintain such Minimum Investment throughout the entire lease term, and such Minimum Investment must remain at the end of the lease term" [Rev. Proc. 75-21, Sec. 4(1)]. The purpose of this requirement appears to be to ensure the lessor has and maintains a significant depreciable interest in the property.

The revenue procedure further provides:

> *The Minimum Investment must be an equity investment (the 'Equity Investment') which, for purposes of this Revenue Procedure, includes only consideration paid and personal liability incurred by the lessor to purchase the property. The net worth of the lessor must be sufficient to satisfy any such personal liability. [Rev. Proc. 75-21, Sec. 4.(1)]*

The greater the level of Equity Investment, the more interest the lessor has in the property. The revenue procedure analyzes the Minimum Investment at three different times: at the inception of the lease (the Initial Minimum Investment), during the term of the lease (the Maintenance of the Minimum Investment) and at the end of the lease term (the Residual Investment).

Exhibit 5-2
Rev. Proc. 75-21 Requirements

1. The lessor must have a 20% minimum at-risk investment in the property at the inception, during and at the end of the lease term

2. The exercise price of any lessee purchase option must not be less than fair market value

3. The lessee may not make an investment in the lease, nor can it lend to the lessor any purchase money or guarantee any lessor loans

4. The value of the property at the end of the lease term must be equal to at least 20% of the property's original cost, and the useful life of the property at the end of the lease term must be at least equal to the greater of (a) one year or (b) 20% of the originally estimated useful life

5. The lessor must have positive cash flow and a profit from the transaction independent of tax benefits

6. A lease with step-up or step-down payments must fall within certain guidelines.

To satisfy the Initial Minimum Investment requirement, the Minimum Investment must be equal to at least 20% of the cost of the property when the property is first placed in service or use by the lessee. Although it is not directly prohibited by that language, it certainly appears that the placed-in-service requirement precludes a sale-leaseback.

In addition, the Minimum Investment must be unconditional. In other words, after the property is placed in service or use by the lessee, the lessor cannot be entitled to a return of any portion of the Minimum Investment through any arrangement with the lessee, any shareholder of the lessee or any party related to the lessee (collectively, the Lessee Group). Compensation to the lessor from other than the Lessee Group, however, is permissible if the property fails to satisfy written specifications for the supply, construction or manufacture of the property.

In order to comply with the Maintenance of the Minimum Investment requirements, the Minimum Investment must remain equal to at least 20% of the cost of the property at all times throughout the entire lease term. Put another way, the net cash flow to the lessor during the lease term cannot result in a return to the lessor that has the effect of reducing the Initial Minimum Investment below 20%. To ensure that the Minimum Investment is maintained, the revenue procedure contains the following textual formula:

> ... *the excess of the cumulative payments required to have been paid by the lessee to or for the lessor over the cumulative disbursements required to have been paid by or for the lessor in connection with the ownership of the property must never exceed the sum of (i) any excess of the lessor's initial Equity Investment over 20 percent of the cost of the property plus (ii) the cumulative pro rata portion of the projected profit from the transaction (exclusive of tax benefits). [Rev. Proc. 75-21, Sec. 4.(1)(B)]*

The projected profit from the transaction is determined in accordance with a similar textual formula:

> ... *the aggregate amount required to be paid by the lessee to or for the lessor over the lease term plus the value of the residual investment . . . exceed an amount equal to the sum of the aggregate disbursements required to be paid by or for the lessor in connection with the ownership of the property and the lessor's Equity Investment in the property, including any direct costs to finance the Equity Investment . . . [Ibid. at Sec. 4.(6)]*

To illustrate, assume that a lessor agreed to lease to a lessee for five years equipment constituting 5-year recovery property. Assume further that the lease was a net lease and that the required lease payments were 23,261 annually in advance for five years. The lessor's cost was 100,000 and the residual value at the end of the lease term was reasonably estimated to be 20,000. The lessor purchased the equipment from the manufacturer using 25,000 of its own funds and obtaining a nonrecourse loan in the principal amount of 75,000, with an interest rate of 12.5%, payable in five equal annual installments, in advance. To determine whether the lessor maintained at least a 20% minimum investment in the equipment, the lessor must apply the above stated formula. The formula, restated in a simplified fashion, is presented in Exhibit 5-3.

Application of the Maintenance of Minimum Investment test, which is applied on a cumulative basis, is set forth in Exhibit 5-4.

To meet the Residual Investment criterion, the lessor must comply with two requirements. First, it must show that an amount equal to 20% of the original cost of the property is a reasonable estimate of what the fair market value of the property will be at the end of the lease term. In that regard, fair market value must be determined (1) without including in such value any increase or decrease for inflation or deflation during the lease term, and (2) after subtracting from such value any cost to the lessor for removal and

---

Exhibit 5-3
Minimum Investment Formula

	Cumulative cash inflow from lessee	(a)
-	Cumulative cash outflow of lessor	(b)

Less than or equal to

	Initial equity over 20%	(c)
+	Cumulative pro rata profit	(d)

The profit formula is as follows:

	Profit = (lease payments + value of residual)
-	(loan payments + equity investment)

Exhibit 5-4
20% Minimum
Unconditional At-risk Investment

			Year		
Cash flow item	**1**	**2**	**3**	**4**	**5**
Equity investment	(25,000)	0	0	0	0
Loan payments	(18,724)	(18,724)	(18,724)	(18,724)	(18,724)
Lease payments	23,361	23,361	23,361	23,361	23,361
Residual	0	0	0	0	20,000
Net cash flow	(20,363)	4,637	4,637	4,637	24,637

Year 1 test: a-b ≤ c+d
23,361-18,724 ≤ 5,000+3,637
4,637 ≤ 8,637 (test satisfied)

Year 2 test: a-b ≤ c+d
46,722-37,448 ≤ 5,000+7,274
9,274 ≤ 12,274 (test satisfied)

Year 3 test: a-b ≤ c+d
70,083-56,172 ≤ 5,000+10,911
13,911 ≤ 15,911 (test satisfied)

Year 4 test: a-b ≤ c+d
93,444 - 74,896 ≤ 5,000 + 14,548
18,548 ≤ 19,548 (test satisfied)

Year 5 test: a - b ≤ c + d
116,805-93,620 ≤ 5,000+18,185
23,185 ≤ 23, 185 (test satisfied).

delivery of possession of the property to the lessor at the end of the lease term. Second, it must show that a remaining useful life of the longer of one year or 20% of the originally estimated useful life of the property is reasonably expected to exist at the end of the lease term.

Lessee Purchase Options

In order to ensure that the lessee is not obtaining an equity interest in the property, and that the lessor is retaining a significant depreciable interest in the property, Section 4.(3) of the revenue procedure establishes a dual requirement. First, no member of the Lessee Group may have a contractual right to purchase the property from the lessor at a price less than fair market value at the time the right is exercised. Although the fair market value standard is clearly established, it is not unequivocally clear when fair market value must be determined, whether it can be reasonably estimated at the inception of the lease or whether it must be determined at the expiration of the lease term. The language seems to support the latter, although the general position outside of Rev. Proc. 75-21 is that reasonable estimates of fair market value at lease inception are permissible.

Second, when the property is first placed in service by the lessee, the lessor must not have a contractual right, or have the intention to acquire such a right, to cause any party to purchase the property. A manufacturer or vendor repurchase agreement triggered in the event of the property's failure to meet written specifications for the supply, construction or manufacture of the property is apparently permitted. A lessor right of abandonment is tantamount to a contractual right to require a party to purchase the property.

No Investment by the Lessee

In general, no part of the cost of the property or of improvements, modifications or additions to the property (improvements) may be furnished by any member of the Lessee Group. This "no lessee investment" requirement is intended to ensure that the lessee is not taking, or has not taken, title to the property, and is not acquiring an equity in the property. For purposes of this rule, ordinary maintenance and repairs provided by the lessee or any other member of the Lessee Group do not constitute an improvement.

A lessee, however, may furnish some portion or all of the cost of a severable improvement, i.e., an improvement that is readily removable without causing material damage to the leased property, and that is not required to render the leased property complete for its intended use by the lessee. In addition, if certain conditions are met, a lessee may furnish the cost of a nonseverable improvement, i.e., an improvement that is not readily removable without causing material damage to the leased property.

No Lessee Loans or Guarantees

To ensure that the lessee does not have even a semblance of an ownership interest in the leased property, no member of the Lessee Group may lend to the lessor any of the funds necessary to acquire the property. This requirement also prevents the Lessee Group from guaranteeing any indebtedness created in connection with the acquisition of the property by the lessor. This requirement would seem to eliminate sale-leaseback transactions (which include wrap leases) from the transactions in which the IRS will issue an advance ruling on the true lease question.

Fortunately, however, a guarantee by any member of the Lessee Group of the lessee's obligations under the lease (including the obligation to pay rent) does not constitute the guarantee of the indebtedness of the lessor. Similarly, the assignment to a lender in return for a nonrecourse loan from the lender to the lessor, secured by the lease and the leased property, apparently does not violate the "no lessee loans or guarantees" requirement.

Although that position is somewhat inconsistent with the concept of the requirement, it validates the manner in which leveraged leases are typically structured.

Profit and Cash Flow Requirement

As stated in the discussion regarding Maintenance of Minimum Investment, the lessor must represent and demonstrate that it expects to receive a profit from the transaction, completely independent of tax benefits. This is a widely accepted standard generally employed by the IRS and the courts to invalidate business transactions entered into solely for tax avoidance motives. In the leasing context, this test generally is referred to as the economic substance test.

Although articulated only in the textual profit formula, the lessor also must show that it expects to receive a positive cash flow from the transaction during the lease term (thereby excluding the positive cash inflow effect of the realization of the residual value of the equipment at the end of the lease term). Although many Rev. Proc. 75-21 requirements are stringent and conservative, the cash flow test is the one most inconsistent with industry practice. As explained above, most leveraged leases are match funded, i.e., the loan is fully amortized by the lease payments, such that the periodic loan payments are exactly equal to the periodic lease payments. The cash flow aspect of the formula is as follows:

> *... the aggregate amounts required to be paid to or for the lessor over the lease term exceed by a reasonable amount the aggregate disbursements required to be paid by or for the lessor (excluding the lessor's initial Equity Investment, but including any direct costs incurred by the lessor to finance the Equity Investment) in connection with the ownership of the leased property. [Rev. Proc. 75-21 Sec. 4.(6)]*

The Uneven Rent Test

If the lease provides for other than equal payments over the lease term, the issue of prepaid or deferred rent arises. In the case of uneven rent, if such payments do not fall within either of two guidelines, the lessor must request a ruling as to whether any portion of the uneven rent constitutes prepaid or deferred rent. The IRS concern is the timing of (1) the lessor's recognition of lease revenue for tax purposes, irrespective of receipt, and (2) the lessee's deductibility of lease payments, irrespective of payment.

At the time Rev. Proc. 75-21 was pronounced, it was a relatively simple and commonplace endeavor to structure lease transactions to reduce the overall payment of income taxes by providing for step-down lease payments (higher payments in the first part of the term and lower payments thereafter). This type of structure was beneficial when the lessee was a high tax bracket cash basis taxpayer and the lessor was a lower bracket accrual basis taxpayer. Under current tax law, as the result of the uneven rent limitations imposed by IRC §467 as well as other tax deferral limitations, the prepaid/deferred rent game is much less common.

The uneven rent guidelines of the revenue procedure are as follows:

1. The annual rent for any year is not more than 10% above or below the amount calculated by dividing the total rent payable over the lease term by the number of years in such term

2. The annual rent for any year during the first two-thirds of the lease term is not more than 10% above or below the amount calculated by dividing the total rent payable over such initial portion of the lease term by the number of years in such initial portion of the lease term, and the annual rent for any year during the remainder of the lease term is no greater than the highest annual rent for any year during the initial portion of the lease term and no less than one-half of the average annual rent during such initial portion of the lease term.

Application of the two guidelines can be illustrated by the following example:

A taxpayer leases equipment according to the following payment schedule:

Months	Payment	Total payment
1-18	1,800	32,400
19-42	2,000	48,000
43-60	2,200	39,600
		120,000

This payment schedule will not result in an uneven rent determination by the IRS because the payments in any one year are not more than 10% above or below the average annual rental, as shown in Exhibit 5-5.

Limited Use Property

The IRS, at the time of issuance of Rev. Proc. 75-21, had not yet decided whether it would issue advance rulings involving limited use property. Limited use property is property expected not to be useful or usable by the lessor at the end of the lease term except for purposes of continued leasing to the lessee or transfer to any member of the Lessee Group. In Rev. Proc. 76-30, 1976-2 C.B. 647, the IRS announced that it would not issue an advance ruling under Rev. Proc. 75-21 when the leased property was limited use property. The later revenue procedure stated that:

> . . . in the case of limited use property, at the end of the lease term[,] there will probably be no potential lessees or buyers other than members of the Lessee Group. As a result, the lessor of limited use property will probably sell or rent the property to a member of the Lessee Group, thus enabling the Lessee Group to enjoy the benefits of the use or ownership of the property for substantially its entire useful life [Rev. Proc. 76-30, Sec. 3].

Exhibit 5-5
Uneven Rent Test

Average annual rental   24,000 (120,000 ÷ 5)

Year	Annual rent	+ 10%	-10%
1	21,600	26,400	21,600
2	22,800	26,400	21,600
3	24,000	26,400	21,600
4	25,200	26,400	21,600
5	26,400	26,400	21,600

Although the leasing of limited use property, in and of itself, does not result in the transaction being recharacterized as a sale under federal income tax law, the IRS position in Rev. Proc. 76-30 is consistent with the balance of the conservatism contained in Rev. Proc. 75-21.

REVENUE RULING 55-540, 1955-C.B.

Although leveraged leasing did not begin to flourish until the mid-sixties, leasing began to take hold in the U.S. after World War II. The increase in leasing led to a need for guidelines for the purpose of defining a lease from a sale. The IRS provided taxpayers with general guidelines to distinguish a lease from a sale in Revenue Ruling 55-540 (Rev. Rul. 55-540). Although far from definitive, the guidance contained in that ruling did provide some insight into the IRS approach to the issue, and contained a fair recap of prior case law on the issue. For 20 years (from 1955 to 1975, when Rev. Proc. 75-21 was issued), Rev. Rul. 55-540 was the most significant and comprehensive statement from the IRS that addressed the lease/sale question.

The revenue ruling approached the analysis from the viewpoint of the lessee, i.e., whether the lessee was entitled to a deduction for rent payments. The ruling initially stated that "it is necessary to determine whether by virtue of the agreement the lessee has acquired or will acquire title to or an equity in the property" (IRC §162).

After repeating the rhetoric contained in many cases about the relevance of the intent of the parties, and stating that no general rule could be laid down, the IRS noted that:

> . . . *in the absence of compelling persuasive factors of contrary implication, an interest warranting treatment of a transaction for tax purposes as a purchase and sale rather than as a lease or rental agreement may in general be said to exist if, for example, one or more of the following conditions are present:*
>
> (a) *Portions of the periodic payments are made specifically applicable to an equity to be acquired by the lessee.*
>
> (b) *The lessee will acquire title upon the payment of a stated amount of rentals which under the contract he is required to make.*
>
> (c) *The total amount which the lessee is required to pay for a relatively short period of use constitutes an inordinately large proportion of the total sum required to be paid to secure the transfer of the title.*

(d) The agreed rental payments materially exceed the current fair rental value. This may be indicative that the payments include an element other than compensation for the use of property.

(e) The property may be acquired under a purchase option at a price which is nominal in relation to the value of the property at the time when the option may be exercised, as determined at the time of entering into the original agreement, or which is a relatively small amount when compared with the total payments which are required to be made.

(f) Some portion of the periodic payments is specifically designated as interest or is otherwise readily recognizable as the equivalent of interest. [Rev. Rul. 55-540 Sec. 4.]

The standards set forth in subsections (a) and (b) are derived directly from IRC §162, which proscribes the lessee's acquisition of title to or an equity in the property. The standards enumerated in subsections (d) and (e) are attempts to preclude the building of equity by the lessee during the lease term. Subsection (f) is an attempt to properly characterize a transaction that truly is, and was in all likelihood intended by the parties to be, a loan. Subsection (c) sets forth a total consideration test: if the lease payments are substantially equal to the payments that would have been required had the lessee purchased the equipment, then the transaction should be characterized as a purchase. Although the ruling provides a reasonably concise summary of the standards established by the case law, it has not added anything new and, in fact, perpetuates some of the erroneous tests and criteria established by the courts.

Application of the Judicial and Administrative Factors

From a quick review of the case law and the IRS pronouncements, it is clear only a few hard and fast rules are applicable in the true lease versus sale controversy. Those rules are derived from IRC §162 (from the lessee's perspective) and IRC §167 (from the lessor's viewpoint). In fact, upon very close scrutiny, it becomes evident that only IRC §162 contains an ostensibly black and white test: did the lessee acquire title to, or is it acquiring title to, or an equity in the property through the payments denominated as rent? Even that test occasionally can have some shades of gray. The depreciable interest test of IRC §167 also provides little in the way of firm definitional guidance.

Of all the factors considered by the courts and the IRS, four appear to be of utmost importance because they either determine the essence of a leasing transaction or they have been elevated to this level by Congress or the Supreme Court:

1. Whether title to the property has passed or will pass to the lessee for no consideration beyond the required lease payments

2. Whether the agreement contains bargain purchase and/or renewal options

3. Whether the lease term is substantially equivalent to the useful life of the asset

4. Whether the transaction has economic substance.

The reason for the first factor is obvious. IRC §162 prohibits passage of title upon the payment of the lease payments. If title does pass, with no additional consideration from the lessee, Congress has concluded that the lessee cannot deduct the lease payments. If the lessee does not have a leasehold interest, it would then seem to have an ownership interest for federal income tax purposes. Therefore, the transaction is not a lease for federal income tax purposes.

The second factor, which also derives its relevance from IRC §162, is critical to the tax and theoretical ownership of the property. IRC §162 provides, among other things, that lease payments are nondeductible if the lessee acquires title to or an equity in the asset upon the payment of the rentals. If the lessee is able to purchase the asset or use it at less than its fair market or fair rental value, then arguably the lessee has acquired an equity in the property during the original lease term.

From a theoretical perspective, the question of whether the lessor has retained a significant residual interest in the leased asset needs to be answered in two different ways. First, at the end of the lease term, does the property have any significant value? Second, if it does, does that value inure, at least primarily, to the benefit of the lessor? If the answer to the first part of the question is no, then the transaction is not a lease, because the lessor has retained nothing – all of the value of the asset has been transferred to and used by the lessee, even though legal title may have been retained by the lessor. If, however, the first part of the question is answered in the affirmative, the second part must be addressed. If the value at the end of the lease term, although significant, does not inure to the benefit of the lessor, then again the lessor has not retained the residual interest in the asset. In many instances, the way to transfer the residual value from the lessor to the lessee is either a fair market value purchase option or a fair rental value renewal option.

The third factor also has its roots in the essence of a lease analysis. If the lease term is substantially equivalent to the asset's useful (economic) life, then the lessor has not retained a significant residual interest in the asset. In circumstances in which, pursuant to the initial lease term, the lessee has used the asset for substantially all of its economic life, the lessee should be treated as having purchased the asset.

Conversely, the fourth factor is entirely tax related. The Supreme Court (and several lower courts) has consistently held that a transaction cannot be entered into solely for tax avoidance motives; there must be a legitimate business purpose. Therefore, if the lessor cannot reasonably expect to realize a profit in the transaction completely independent of tax benefits, the form of the transaction will be collapsed. (The lessor will not be treated as the owner of the asset for federal income tax purposes and, consequently, will not be entitled to the tax benefits that normally attend ownership, e.g., depreciation and credits.)

It does not necessarily follow that the lessee is entitled to the tax benefits simply because the lessor is not. Because the economic substance test is entirely tax related, a business purpose must exist in all transactions. If not, the normal tax benefits (to the party who entered into the lease without a proper purpose) can be denied, without having any effect whatsoever on the other party to the transaction.

Although only four factors are of utmost importance, two other factors are quite important. Although not analytically sound, they are important because they have their roots in the two applicable IRC sections, and are, therefore, used to help determine whether the statutes are being complied with. The fifth factor is the relationship between fair rental value and the lease payment. The more the lease payment exceeds fair rental value, the more it looks as if the lessee is building equity in the property. Otherwise, why would the lessee be paying more than required in the marketplace?

The theoretical and practical problem with that factor is that, in and of itself, the payment of an amount in excess of fair rental value cannot create an equity in the asset for the lessee. Any equity can be realized only by the lessee through below market purchase or renewal options. Therefore, unless excess lease payments are coupled with a transfer of title (which itself violates §162) or bargain purchase and/or renewal options, the only effect is that the lessee, by definition, paid too much for the use of the equipment, and the lessor made a disproportionate amount of profit. Nevertheless, the courts and the IRS continually focus on this factor.

Finally, because of the desire to ensure that the lessor has a depreciable interest in the asset, the IRS and the courts, to a lesser degree, focus on the amount the lessor has at-risk in the transaction. The at-risk analysis in this context has nothing to do with loss deductibility or eligibility for the investment credit. The at-risk requirement in the true lease/conditional sale controversy approaches the "retention of a significant residual interest" test from the opposite direction. Rather than looking at the end of the lease term, the at-risk requirement attempts to ensure that the lessor truly has something to lose if the residual value is not realized by imposing a lease inception equity investment on the lessor.

As the result largely of Rev. Proc. 75-21, many lessors seem to believe that, in order to maintain true lease status for federal income tax purposes, it is essential to comply with the revenue procedure's 20% at-risk test. That simply is not true. The dynamics of the marketplace together with the lessor's residual value expectations dictate the amount of equity insertion that a lessor is willing to put into lease transactions – not a conservative IRS pronouncement issued over 20 years ago. In defense of those practitioners and commentators espousing the 20% requirement, however, there is little question that a lessor can expect to fare more favorably under IRS audit the closer it complies with the conservative requirements of Rev. Proc. 75-21.

JUDICIAL HISTORY

Numerous cases and letter rulings support the importance of the six factors discussed above. The following list represents a sampling of these cases.

In *Charles Smith v. Commissioner,* T.C. Memo. 1976-114, April 12, 1976, tax deductions were taken for rental payments in a lease by the defendant. The defendant had leased several pieces of construction equipment and had in most cases exercised his purchase option within six months of entering into the agreement. In question were four particular equipment leases. Three of the four had been entered into when the defendant was just starting his business. The fourth was entered into several years later.

The first three were held to be true leases as the court ruled that the intent of the parties was in fact a lease. The company was a start-up company and was unsure of future economic events. The fact that the defendant actually bought the equipment six months later did not override the intent of the parties. The fourth lease was held to be a conditional sales contract. Once again the intent of the parties was examined by the court and two critical factors were cited. The company was no longer a start-up company with economic uncertainties. The intent was a sale as was evidenced by the defendant's purchase of the equipment six months later. In addition, the defendant was required to pay minimum payments equaling over 92% of the original purchase price. This meant the defendant could have purchased the equipment at the end of the first year for less than one month's rent.

In *H. Lawerence Kaufman v. Commissioner*, T.C. Memo. 1987-350, July 21, 1987, the court focused on the economic substance factor. Contrary to various IRS challenges, the tax court found that a taxpayer who acquired a 50% interest in computer equipment that was already leased would be the owner of that portion for tax purposes. The tax courts reasoned that the investment was profit motivated and therefore allowed the tax deductions. The court also stated there was a chance for gain apart from the tax consequences.

In *Trans Coastal Equipment Leasing, LTD v. Commissioner*, T.C. Memo. 1990-67, February 13, 1990, the courts held the transaction, a purported 7purchase of a mining dredge by a limited partnership, formed for the purpose of leasing equipment, was not a bona fide arms-length transaction. The same individual controlled both the limited partnership and the company that manufactured the equipment. The sales price was inflated to maximize the tax benefits and the partnership was created to flow through the tax deductions to the individuals in the partnership.

The tax court held that this transaction was, in essence, a sham because it lacked economic substance. The partnership never acquired a depreciable interest in the dredge and there was no profit or positive cash flow motive in the transaction.

In *David Kramer v. Commissioner,* T.C. Memo. 1988-475, September 28, 1988, the focus was again on the economic substance of the transaction. A doctor was denied loss deductions and ITC claimed in connection with a sale-leaseback of tractor-trailer trucks. The court ruled that the agreement lacked a business purpose and had no economic substance. Neither the doctor nor his accountant was familiar with the tractor-trailer leasing business and neither had analyzed the transaction for profit potential. The doctor also had sold his interest at the time when cash flow profit began to occur.

Finally, in an IRS private letter ruling, *LTR 8642009*, July 9, 1986, Rev. Rul. 55-540 was cited. This ruling was issued to a lessor who was trying to establish the right to depreciation deductions. In reaching its decision the IRS noted that two of the six factors included in Rev. Rul. 55-540 were violated. First, the lessee was required to pay the total sum required to secure the transfer of title over the relatively short period of 12 to 18 months.

The second factor violated was the nominal purchase option factor. Lessees were entitled to a cash purchase option that declined each time the contract was renewed. The contract automatically renewed each month when the lease payment was made, which meant that the purchase option declined each month. The purchase option would reach zero sometime between 12 to 18 months when the equipment still had substantial useful life remaining. The IRS also noted that it considered the intent of the parties and how the lessor dealt with other lessees.

The importance of this decision is that the IRS and the courts still consider Rev. Rul. 55-540 useful in deciding the tax status of a lease. The ruling is old and somewhat vague, but the broad guidelines it provides help create the environment in which true leases are structured.

The TRAC Lease

Notwithstanding the preceding discussion about the essential elements of a lease, if a transaction meets the requirements enumerated by Congress in IRC §7701(h), the parties to the transaction are permitted to treat it as a lease – even though it would not meet the criteria for a true lease.

In general, any lease that contains a TRAC shifts the risk of depreciation to the lessee. A TRAC is a provision in a lease agreement that requires a rental adjustment at the end of the lease term. The amount of this adjustment depends on the actual value of the vehicle as compared with the originally estimated value of the vehicle upon which the lease payments were based. If the actual value is less than the estimated value, the lessee is required to pay the deficiency to the lessor as the final rental. If, on the other hand, the actual value is greater than the estimated value, the lessor may pay to the lessee the surplus, which payment reduces the amount of the final lease payment.

The Qualified Motor Vehicle Operating Agreement provisions originally enacted as part of the Tax Equity and Fiscal Responsibility Act of 1982 allow TRAC leases to be treated as leases rather than sales. (See *Swift Dodge v. Commissioner*, 692 F. 2d 651 (9th Cir. 1982).) If the lease falls within the parameters of the TRAC provisions, the existence of a terminal rental adjustment clause will not invalidate the characterization of an agreement as a true lease, provided the lease otherwise would be treated as a lease for federal income tax purposes.

To comply with the TRAC provisions, the lease must be a qualified motor vehicle operating agreement, which is an agreement with respect to a motor vehicle (including a trailer) that meets the following three requirements. First, the sum of (1) the amount the lessor is personally liable to repay and (2) the net fair market value of the lessor's interest in any property pledged as security for property subject to the agreement equals or exceeds all amounts borrowed to finance the acquisition of property subject to the agreement. In other words, all debt used to finance the leased property must be recourse.

Second, the lessee must sign a separate written statement in which the lessee certifies, under penalty of perjury, that it intends that more than 50% of the use of the leased property is to be in a trade or business of the lessee, and that clearly and legibly states that the lessee has been advised it will not be treated as the owner of the lease property for federal income tax purposes. Third, the lessor must not know the lessee's certification described above is false.

In light of the significance of compliance with the TRAC provisions of the IRC, those lessors involved with automobile and tractor and trailer leasing should periodically review both their lease agreements and their practices and procedures to ensure compliance.

CONCLUSION

This chapter is not intended to be an exhaustive analysis of the complex and continually changing standards employed by the tax authorities with respect to the true lease issue. It does, however, provide a basic understanding of the issues and insights into the various factors the IRS and the courts consider in making a true lease determination. Nevertheless, it is always important to obtain the opinion of tax counsel with regard to the true lease versus conditional sale issue when tax benefits constitute a material portion of the yield on a lease transaction.

Chapter Six

Income Tax Benefits

Congress is always contemplating different ways to modify the Internal Revenue Code (IRC) as it addresses the goals of the nation. As evidenced by the past, some of these modifications directly impact the leasing industry. Others, such as those involving tax rates, depreciation rules, acquisition incentives and the alternative minimum tax (AMT), affect all aspects of equipment acquisition, both leasing and purchasing. Once provided with the new rules, however, the leasing industry analyzes the rules and reacts quickly with new products and services.

In its present format, the IRC does not contain many tax benefits associated with the ownership of property available to the leasing industry . Those that do exist, however, are discussed in this chapter. (These discussions focus on the consequences of ownership, not the determination thereof. Issues regarding true leases versus conditional sales contracts are discussed in Chapter Five.) Income tax benefits discussed include:

- Corporate Tax Rates
- Modified Accelerated Cost Recovery System
- Deferred Intercompany Transactions
- Investment Tax Credit.

CORPORATE TAX RATES

The current corporate tax rates are contained in Exhibit 6-1. This rate structure provides tax breaks for smaller corporations, and also incorporates two different make-up adjustments. The first occurs at 100,000 of taxable income, at which point a 5% surcharge is added to the base rate of 34%.

Exhibit 6-1
Corporate Tax Rates

Taxable income	Tax rate
Not more than 50,000	15%
50,000 to 75,000	25%
75,001 to 100,000	34%
100,001 to 335,000	34% + 5% = 39%
335,001 to 10,000,000	34%
10,000,001 to 15,000,000	35%
15,000,001 to 18,333,333	35% + 3% = 38%
18,333,334 and above	35%

This surcharge eliminates the benefit of the lower 15% and 25% rates. The second adjustment occurs for taxable income greater than 15,000,000. For the next 3,333,333 of taxable income above 15,000,000, a 3% surcharge is added to the base rate of 35%. This surcharge adjusts the 34% rate charged on the first 10,000,000 of taxable income to a 35% rate.

For companies with taxable income of less than 10,000,000, the top rate is 34%. Only companies with taxable income in excess of 10,000,000 are impacted by the 35% tax rate surcharge. Furthermore, no distinction is made between ordinary income and capital gains income, so the tax rates are the same for both types of corporate income.

Timing of Taxes Paid

Tax benefits are realized, and tax costs are incurred, on the date the corporation is required to pay its federal income taxes. A corporation with a reasonably estimated taxable income of 40 or more is required to remit 25% of its projected tax liability for the current year on the 15th day of months 4, 6, 9 and 12 of its current fiscal year. The due dates for a calendar year taxpayer are shown in Exhibit 6-2. Current underpayment penalty provisions do not impose a penalty if 100% of the required installment is made on or before the respective due date.

Even if the percentage requirement is not met, no underpayment penalty will be imposed if the total of the corporation's estimated tax payments made on or before the respective due dates would have been sufficient. The sufficiency test is met if the estimated tax for the current taxable year equaled the lesser of:

1. **The preceding year method** – The amount of tax shown on the corporation's original return (or an amended return filed on or before the due date of the original return) for the preceding year, as long as the preceding year covered 12 months and a tax liability was incurred for that year. In other words, the percentage test can be applied to last year's income to determine this year's estimated tax payments. This route, however, is not available for large corporations

2. **The annualized income method** – The amount of the required annual installment under the annualized method is the excess, if any, of:

   a. the applicable percentage of the tax for the year computed by placing on an annualized basis the taxable income for the months in the tax year ending before the due date of the installment, over

   b. the aggregate amount of any earlier required installments for the year

Exhibit 6-2
Due Dates and Amounts

Due dates	Percentage of tax
April 15	25%
June 15	25%
September 15	25%
December 15	25%

The applicable percentages under the annualized income method are:

25% for the first installment

50% for the second installment

75% for the third installment

100% for the fourth installment

Annualized estimators must elect, at the time of their first quarter payments, which months' incomes will be used in the computation. The alternatives are as follows:

Payment for	General rule	Alternative A	Alternative B
1st quarter	3 months	2 months	3 months
2nd quarter	3 months	4 months	5 months
3rd quarter	6 months	7 months	8 months
4th quarter	9 months	10 months	11 months

3. **The seasonal income method** – The amount of the required annual installment under the seasonal income method is the excess, if any, of:

   a. 100% of the adjusted seasonal installment, over

   b. the aggregate amount of all prior required installments for the tax year.

Most companies pay their estimated taxes in accordance with Exhibit 6-2. When a corporation pays its taxes it must consider their impact on a present value (PV) basis in order to determine the actual value of the tax benefits (or, conversely, the actual cost of the tax payments). This concept is known as tax timing. In addition, whether the transaction is budgeted or incremental must be factored into the analysis, as it will affect the tax timing calculation.

A budgeted transaction is one that is part of the company's overall plan for the taxable year. Although the specifics of the particular transaction are not known at the time the plan is formulated (generally, sometime the year before), many companies are able to predict with a fair degree of certainty the timing and amount of transactions that will be consummated during the year. The tax savings and costs from those budgeted transactions are reflected in each estimated tax payment, even though the actual transaction may not occur for several months.

For example, assume a calendar year corporation consummates a lease on December 31, and the lease is part of its budgeted transactions. The value of the Modified Accelerated Cost Recovery System (MACRS) deduction attributable to that transaction would be 104.88% of its face value, as calculated in Exhibit 6-3 (assuming a cost of capital of 12%).

It should be noted that the analysis of Exhibit 6-3 applies to the entire lease transaction. The amount of lease revenue includable for the year, together with any interest expense and other expenses associated with that particular transaction, also must be considered to determine the overall tax effect of the transaction.

An incremental transaction, on the other hand, is one that was not part of the planned transactions for the year. Its tax consequences are reflected only in the remaining future estimated tax payment dates. Using the same example, the value of the MACRS deduction taken in the first year would be only 97.54% of its face value, because the benefit of the deduction would not be realized until April 15 of year two. Incremental transactions generally cause the attendant tax benefits or costs to have a PV less than the face value. Budgeted transactions, on the other hand, depending on the consummation date, cause the tax benefits or costs to be greater or less than the face value of the actual payment or savings.

Exhibit 6-3
PV of Tax Benefits

Estimated tax dates	Estimated tax percentages	Number of months to FV or PV taxes	Future value (FV) or PV
April 15	25	8.5 (FV)	.2720
June 15	25	6.5 (FV)	.2667
September 15	25	3.5 (FV)	.2588
December 15	25	.5 (FV)	.2513
Total			1.0488

MODIFIED ACCELERATED COST RECOVERY SYSTEM

MACRS was enacted in 1986 as part of the Tax Reform Act of 1986 (TRA 86) and modified the Accelerated Cost Recovery System (ACRS). MACRS was a means for Congress to raise more revenue. Certain property was assigned longer recovery periods and the actual methodology was modified to slow down the depreciation deductions taken on tax returns. MACRS is the current depreciation methodology.

Recovery Classes

Property, under MACRS, has been classified into eight categories. Six of these categories deal with personal property and two with real property. Personal property cost recovery for the 3-, 5-, 7- and 10-year classes is based on the 200% declining balance method with a maximizing switch to straight-line. Cost recovery for the 15- and 20-year classes is based on the 150% declining balance method with a maximizing switch to straight-line.

Reference must be made to the Asset Depreciation Range (ADR) mid-point lives and to certain changes enacted by TRA 86 in order to determine the appropriate recovery class for property. The ADR tables were introduced in 1970 by the Internal Revenue Service (IRS) to provide guidance to taxpayers with respect to depreciable lives. Although the MACRS recovery periods generally are shorter than the class lives set forth in the ADR tables, the tables provide the reference point for recovery period classifications.

For example, property having an ADR midpoint life of four years or less, except automobiles and light trucks, is considered 3-year MACRS property. Property with an ADR midpoint life of more than four years and less than 10 years (which is the majority of leased property), together with automobiles, light trucks, qualified technological equipment, research and experimentation property, as well as some other property, falls in the 5-year class. Property with an ADR midpoint of at least 10 years and less than 16 years and property without an ADR midpoint life, and not classified elsewhere, are classified as 7-year property.

Cost Recovery Methodology

The cost of property generally is depreciated over the applicable MACRS recovery period. For 3-year class property, that period is four years (because of application of the half-year convention). Similarly, the recovery period is six years for 5-year property, eight years for 7-year property and so on.

For the first four recovery classes (3-, 5-, 7- and 10-year property), the 200% declining balance method with an optimal switch to straight-line is utilized to calculate the cost recovery deductions. To illustrate the principles involved, the cost recovery percentages for 5-year property are calculated below. First, the straight-line rate is computed:

$$100\% \div 5 \text{ years} = 20\% \text{ per year}$$

Second, the double declining percentage is calculated by doubling the straight-line rate.

$$20\% \times 200\% = 40\%$$

This percentage is applied to the beginning undepreciated balance each year to determine the cost recovery deductions for that year. It is applied for all years except the year of acquisition and the year of disposition.

Third, the half-year convention must be applied. This convention allows only one-half of the normal deduction in the year property is acquired and the year property is disposed. Therefore, the first year's deduction for 5-year property is 20% (40% x 1/2).

Fourth, the declining balance method is applied to each of the succeeding years until switching to the straight-line method results in a greater deduction. Exhibit 6-4 sets forth this process and its results. The MACRS cost recovery percentages for 5-year property are 20%, 32%, 19.2%, 11.52%, 11.52% and 5.76%, for years one through six, respectively. These percentages incorporate the requirements of the methodology including the half-year convention. Exhibit 6-5 contains the cost recovery percentages for each of the six personal property MACRS recovery classes.

Effective Dates

MACRS generally applies to property placed in service on or after January 1, 1987. The ACRS rules generally apply to property placed in service on

Exhibit 6-4
Derivation of MACRS Percentages
(5-year Recovery Property)

Year	Undepreciated basis	200% declining balance	Prospective straight-line depreciation	MACRS depreciation
1	1.0000	**.2000** (40% x 1/2)	.10 (20% x 1/2)	.2000
2	.8000	**.3200** (40% x .8)	.1778 (.8 ÷ 41/2)	.3200
3	.4800	**.1920** (40% x .48)	.1371 (.48 ÷ 31/2)	.1920
4	.2880	**.1152** (40% x .288)	.1152 (.288 ÷ 21/2)	.1152
5	.1728	.0691 (40% x .1728)	**.1152** [1] (.1728 ÷ 11/2)	.1152
6	.0576		**.0576** (.1152 x 1/2)	.0576
				1.0000

[1] Crossover to straight-line

or after January 1, 1981 and before January 1, 1987. In addition, MACRS does not apply to property falling within the antichurning rules, which are discussed in Chapter Seven.

Value of Depreciation

Lessors oftentimes seek the tax benefits of tax ownership, which affect the pricing of the lease transaction. The value of tax depreciation is nothing more than the timing value between MACRS and the principal exclusion in a nontax lease. This section quantifies the value of the depreciation tax benefit in a tax lease and highlights how it affects lessor pricing.

The following assumptions are used to illustrate the value of depreciation:

Equipment cost: 100,000

Depreciable life: 5-year MACRS benefits versus principal repayment

Pretax equivalent loan rate : 10.50%

Cost of capital: 7.15%

Payment: 2,149.39 per month, in arrears

Lease inception date: December 31.

Exhibit 6-5
MACRS Classlife Percentages

Recovery year	3-year class (200%)	5-year class (200%)	7-year class (200%)	10-year class (200%)	15-year class (150%)	20-year class (150%)
1	33.33	20.00	14.29	10.00	5.00	3.75
2	44.45	32.00	24.49	18.00	9.50	7.22
3	14.81	19.20	17.49	14.40	8.55	6.68
4	7.41	11.52[1]	12.49	11.52	7.70	6.18
5		11.52	8.93[1]	9.22	6.93	5.71
6		5.76	8.92	7.37	6.23	5.29
7			8.93	6.55[1]	5.90[1]	4.89
8			4.46	6.55	5.90	4.52
9				6.56	5.91	4.46[1]
10				6.55	5.90	4.46
11				3.28	5.91	4.46
12					5.90	4.46
13					5.91	4.46
14					5.90	4.46
15					5.91	4.46
16					2.95	4.46
17						4.46
18						4.46
19						4.46
20						4.46
21						2.23

[1] Year of switch to straight-line to maximize the depreciation deduction.

This example illustrates, in a quantitative manner, the value to the lessor of classifying the transaction as a tax lease rather than as a conditional sales contract or nontax lease. This analysis is from the lessor's viewpoint, not the lessee's.

Exhibit 6-6 details the taxable income recognized by the lessor if the transaction is a nontax lease. The interest income recognized by the lessor from the loan, on an annual basis, is based on the amortization in Exhibit 6-6.

The income recognized if the transaction is characterized as a tax lease is shown in Exhibit 6-7. Notice that the total income recognized is the same under both alternatives over the 60-month term. Only the nature and the timing of the income vary.

Exhibit 6-8 shows a year-by-year comparison of the income recognized under each alternative. In the first year, which lasts only one day, the tax lease alternative generates a MACRS deduction of 20,000 because of application of the half-year convention. The nontax lease alternative, on the other hand, generates neither income nor expense because payments are in arrears. In year two, the tax lease shows a tax loss of 6,207, whereas the nontax lease shows taxable income of 9,742. The net difference between the two alternatives is 15,949 (9,742 - (6,207)).

The last column of Exhibit 6-8 illustrates the differences in taxable income recognition. The timing of the deductions and taxable income, of course, affects the timing of the cash flows resulting from the tax benefits and tax expenses. A time value of money benefit, therefore, can be realized by the lessor if the end-user of the equipment selects the tax lease alternative. The amount of this benefit is determined by computing the present value of the difference column times the tax rate. The amount of 2,892 represents the value of depreciation in this transaction and is calculated as follows:

HP-12C			HP-17B (#TIMES PROMPTING: OFF)			
	f	REG				FIN
7.15		i				CFLO
20,000	g	CFo		■ CLEAR DATA		YES
15,949	g	CFj	FLOW (0)=?	20,000		INPUT
1,381	g	CFj	FLOW (1)=?	15,949		INPUT
8,263	CHS g	CFj	FLOW (2)=?	1,381		INPUT
10,443	CHS g	CFj	FLOW (3)=?	8,263	+/-	INPUT
18,624	CHS g	CFj	FLOW (4)=?	10,443	+/-	INPUT
	f	NPV 8,262	FLOW (5)=?	18,624	+/-	INPUT
.35	x	2,892				EXIT
						CALC
				7.15		I%
				NPV = 8,262		
				x	.35 = 2,892	

Exhibit 6-6
Nontax Lease Income

HP-12C

	f	REG
	g	END
100,000	CHS	PV
2,149.39		PMT
10.5	g	12÷

Tax year	Keystrokes			Interest income
1				-0-
2	12	f	AMORT	9,742
3	12	f	AMORT	7,973
4	12	f	AMORT	6,010
5	12	f	AMORT	3,829
6	12	f	AMORT	1,409
Total interest income				28,963

HP-17B (12 P/YR END MODE)

		FIN
		TVM
	■	CLEAR DATA
100,000	+/-	PV
2,149.39		PMT
10.5		I%YR
		OTHER
		AMRT
12		P#

Tax year	Keystrokes		Interest income
1			-0-
2		INT	9,742
3	NEXT	INT	7,973
4	NEXT	INT	6,010
5	NEXT	INT	3,829
6	NEXT	INT	1,409
Total interest income			28,963

Exhibit 6-7
True Lease Income

Tax year	Rental income	MACRS	Total income (expense)
1	-0-	(20,000)	(20,000)
2	25,793 [1]	(32,000)	(6,207)
3	25,792	(19,200)	6,592
4	25,793	(11,520)	14,273
5	25,792	(11,520)	14,272
6	25,793	(5,760)	20,033
	128,963	(100,000)	28,963

[1] (2,149.39 x 12)

In this transaction, the tax lease alternative is worth an additional 2,892 to the lessor. This represents the amount, on a present value basis, of the tax savings from the accelerated depreciation deductions compared to the principal reductions in the nontax lease. The additional cash flow, realized purely from timing differences in income recognition, either contributes to the lessor's yield in the lease or allows the lessor to offer a lower payment to the lessee.

Exhibit 6-8
Taxable Income Comparison

Year	Loan income	Lease income	Difference
1	-0-	(20,000)	20,000
2	9,742	(6,207)	15,949
3	7,973	6,592	1,381
4	6,010	14,273	(8,263)
5	3,829	14,272	(10,443)
6	1,409	20,033	(18,624)
	28,963	28,963	-0-

The above example assumes an inception date of December 31, which, because of the half-year convention, maximizes the timing differences of the two alternatives. If the inception date had been January 1 instead, the value of depreciation would be diminished. A comparison of year one illustrates this point.

In the example, because of payments in arrears, the lessor did not record any rental income, yet, under the half-year convention, it recognized a depreciation expense of 20,000. If the start date had been January 1 instead, a full year's rental income of 25,793, along with the depreciation of 20,000, would be recognized. Furthermore, a full year of principal would be excluded from income in the nontax lease. Although still beneficial, the impact of depreciation is greatly diminished for tax transactions completed early in the year. This diminution in benefits is reflected in the lessor's pricing.

This analysis highlights why lease rate factors can be lower at the end of the year. A tax lease that starts in the fourth quarter is more sensitive to the value of depreciation because of the half-year convention. The lessor is able to realize more of the yield in the lease from tax benefits, thereby relying less on the periodic payment. Hence, the lessee's payment in a tax lease typically is lower if structured in the fourth quarter.

Elective Alternatives to MACRS

As mentioned earlier, there are exceptions to the general rule with regards to the utilization of MACRS. U.S. tax law provides four broad methods of depreciation (or cost recovery) that may be elected by taxpayers. First, a taxpayer may elect to recover the cost of its property under the normal MACRS, as discussed above. Second, a taxpayer may recover the cost on a straight-line basis over the MACRS recovery period, with the half-year convention generally applicable.

The third method of depreciation was introduced in the Tax and Miscellaneous Revenue Act of 1988. It allows taxpayers to elect to recover the cost of 3-, 5-, 7- and 10-year property using the 150% declining balance method over the ADR midpoint with the maximizing switch to straight-line. This method mirrors depreciation calculated for AMT purposes and, like the other elections, represents a tax planning option.

Fourth, a taxpayer can recover the cost of its property in accordance with the Alternative Depreciation System (ADS). The ADS generally requires the use of the straight-line method over the ADR classlife, not the MACRS classlife. The ADS is discussed more fully in the next section.

Generally, leasing companies use MACRS because it is the most accelerated depreciation method available. (MACRS reduces taxable income and minimizes the amount of taxes payable to the IRS.) Situations exist, however, in which a company may want to elect another method. For example, if a company is in a taxable loss position or is subject to the AMT, using an alternative depreciation method may be the most advantageous tax planning strategy possible.

ALTERNATIVE DEPRECIATION SYSTEM

Although the ADS is usually an election of the taxpayer, the ADS must be used in certain circumstances. It is required, for example, when property is used predominantly outside the U.S., or when the property is tax-exempt use property. In general, the ADS requires the use of straight-line depreciation over the ADR life. The ADS also requires that the 150% declining balance method with a maximizing switch to straight-line be used for purposes of calculating the AMT.

Predominantly Used Outside the U.S.

If property is physically located (whether by the owner-user or the user-lessee) outside the U.S. for more than 50% of the taxable year, it generally is considered used predominantly outside the U.S. Property used predominantly outside the U.S. generally must be depreciated straight-line over the ADR life of the equipment. However, exceptions to the general rule exist. These exceptions are found in IRC §168(g)(4). Under this section the following equipment is exempt from the "outside the U.S." rules and, therefore, can be depreciated using MACRS:

> *(A) IN GENERAL. – Except as provided in subparagraph (B), the term "section 38 property" does not include property which is used predominantly outside the United States.*
>
> *(B) EXCEPTIONS. – Subparagraph (A) shall not apply to –*
>
> *(i) any aircraft which is registered by the Administrator of the Federal Aviation Agency and which is operated to and from the United States or is operated under contract with the United States;*
>
> *(ii) rolling stock which is used within and without the United States and which is –*

(i) of a domestic railroad corporation providing transportation subject to subchapter I of chapter 105 of title 49, or

(ii) of a United States person (other than a corporation described in subclause (I)) but only if the rolling stock is not leased to one or more foreign persons for periods aggregating more than 12 months in any 24-month period;

(iii) any vessel documented under the laws of the United States which is operated in the foreign or domestic commerce of the United States;

(iv) any motor vehicle of a United States person (as defined in section 7701(a)(30)) which is operated to and from the United States;

(v) any container of a United States person which is used in the transportation of property to and from the Untied States

(vi) any property (other than a vessel or an aircraft) of a United States person which is used for the purpose of exploring for, developing, removing, or transporting resources from the outer Continental Shelf (within the meaning of section 2 of the Outer Continental Shelf Lands Act, as amended and supplemented; (43 U.S.C. 1331));

(vii) any property which is owned by a domestic corporation (other than a corporation which has an election in effect under section 936) or by a United States citizen (other than a citizen entitled to the benefits of section 931 or 933) and which is used predominantly in a possession of the United States by such a corporation or such a citizen, or by a corporation created or organized in, or under the law of, a possession of the United States;

(viii) any communications satellite (as defined in section 103(3) of the Communications Satellite Act of 1962, 47 U. S. C. 702(3)), or any interest therein, of a United States person;

(ix) any cable, or any interest therein, of a domestic corporation engaged in furnishing telephone service to which section 46(c)(3)(B)(iii) applies (or of a wholly owned domestic subsidiary of such a corporation), if such cable is part of a submarine cable system which constitutes part of a communication link exclusively between the United States and one or more foreign countries;

(x) any property (other than a vessel or an aircraft) of a United States person which is used in international or territorial waters within the northern portion of the Western Hemisphere for the purpose of exploring for, developing, removing, or transporting resources from ocean waters or deposits under such waters; and

> *(xi) any property described in subsection (1)(3)(A)(ix) which is owned by a United States person and which is used in international or territorial waters to generate energy for use in the United States.*
>
> *For purposes of clause (x), the term "northern portion of the Western Hemisphere" means the area lying west of the 30th meridian west of Greenwich, east of the international dateline, and north of the Equator, but not including any foreign country which is a country of South America.*

The exceptions of IRC § 168(g)(4) can have a significant impact on the economics of transactions involving a domestic lessee using the equipment predominantly outside the U.S. Because tax benefits represent cash flows the lessor uses to recover its investment, differences in the timing of those tax benefits caused by different depreciation rules affect the pricing of the lease. Care should be taken to fully understand these rules before entering into such transactions.

In certain circumstances the recovery property ceases to be used predominantly outside the U.S., but continues to be used by the taxpayer. In these situations, taxpayers can elect one of two methods for calculating cost recovery deductions. The first method allows the taxpayer to assume the property was placed in service in the year of cessation, using the property's remaining basis as the cost. The normal cost recovery rules of MACRS then are used for the first and all subsequent years. Alternatively, the taxpayer can continue to depreciate the property as though the cessation had not occurred.

For example, for three years a taxpayer has leased 7-year MACRS property with a 12-year classlife to a firm outside the U.S. At the end of the third year the lease expires and the taxpayer takes back the equipment, re-leasing it to a firm located in the U.S. Assuming the equipment originally cost 100,000, and its remaining basis is 75,000, the taxpayer has two options. First, it can continue using 12-year straight-line depreciation for the remaining nine years:

$$\frac{100{,}000}{12} \quad = \quad 8{,}333 \text{ depreciation each year}$$

Second, the taxpayer can apply the 7-year MACRS rate to the remaining basis over the MACRS life (i.e., 14.29% x 75,000), resulting in 10,717.50 of depreciation in the first year.

Tax-exempt Use Property

In general, tax-exempt use property means that portion of any tangible property (other than nonresidential real property) leased to a tax-exempt entity. A tax-exempt entity is any entity that, by statute, is not required to pay U.S. income tax. Tax-exempt entities include (1) the U.S., any state or political subdivision thereof, U.S. possessions or any agency or instrumentality of any of the foregoing; (2) most charitable organizations; and (3) any foreign person or entity.

The general ADS rule mentioned above (i.e., straight-line over the ADR class life) is modified slightly in the case of property leased to a tax-exempt entity. In general, a lessor must compute cost recovery deductions on a straight-line basis over a recovery period equal to the ADR class life or 125% of the lease term, whichever is greater. This methodology, frequently referred to as Pickle depreciation (named for the congressman who sponsored the legislation), impacts the timing of the tax benefits. As a result, the pricing or structuring of the transaction also is affected. For example, a lease of property with a five-year lease term and 6-year ADR midpoint would be depreciated over 6.25 years (5 x 1.25 > 6).

There are two exceptions to the general rule applicable to tax-exempt use property. First, property leased to a tax-exempt entity under a short-term lease is not considered to be tax-exempt use property. A short-term lease is any lease with a term of less than (1) three years and (2) the greater of one year or 30% of the property's present ADR class life. As an example, a taxpayer leases equipment to a governmental entity on an 18-month lease. The equipment has a 6-year ADR class life. The lease qualifies as a short-term lease because the lease term of 18 months is less than (1) three years and (2) the greater of one year or 30% of the property's present class life of six years (22 months).

The second exception to the general tax-exempt use property rule involves qualified technological equipment. The IRS defines qualified technological equipment as tangible personal property that is:

1. Computer or peripheral equipment (which does not include typewriters, calculators, adding machines or copiers)

2. High technology telephone station equipment installed on the customer's premises, e.g., teletypewriters, telephones, private exchanges, but only if such equipment has a high technology content making it reasonably likely that it will become obsolete prior to the expiration of its physical useful life

3. High technology medical equipment, e.g., electronic, electro-mechanical or computer-based high technology equipment used in screening, monitoring, observing, diagnosing or treating patients in a laboratory, medical or hospital environment. Some specifically mentioned items are CAT scanners, nuclear magnetic resource equipment, clinical chemical analyzers, drug monitors, diagnostic ultrasound scanners, nuclear cameras, radiographic and fluoroscopic systems, Holter monitors and bedside monitors. Such property qualifies even if it is used for research. As with the telephone station equipment, it must be reasonably likely that the medical equipment will become obsolete before the expiration of its useful physical life.

If the lease term with respect to qualified technological equipment is less than or equal to five years, the lessor can use standard MACRS. If the lease term is more than five years, however, the cost is recovered using straight-line depreciation, with the half-year convention, over the MACRS recovery period.

Short Taxable Years

In general, for any recovery year in which there are fewer than 12 months, the cost recovery deduction is determined by multiplying the deduction that would have been available in a full year by:

$$\frac{\text{number of months and part months in the short year}}{12}$$

This rule generally prevents a taxpayer not previously in business from starting a business toward year end, placing depreciable property in service and then claiming a full year's deduction. Complications arise, however, when the half-year or midquarter conventions are applied. Revenue Procedure 89-15 sets forth the guidelines necessary to apply these conventions in a short taxable year. The rules usually are applied by the IRS in the case of noncorporate taxpayers entering into year-end tax shelters.

HALF-YEAR CONVENTION

For a short taxable year beginning on either the first day of the month or ending on the last day of the month, the midpoint of the short taxable year is calculated as follows:

$$\frac{\text{number of full months in the short taxable year}}{2}$$

The midpoint calculated is then considered the placed-in-service date of the property. For example, assume Company X has a short taxable year that begins March 15, 19X1 and ends December 31, 19X1. The tax year ends on the last day of the month so this is a 10-month taxable year. Property placed in service during this short taxable year is, therefore, treated as being placed in service on the first day after the fifth month in this taxable year. Allowable depreciation deductions for 5-year MACRS property are calculated as follows:

Year	Deduction
1	16.67%
2	32.00%
3	19.20%
4	11.52%
5	11.52%
6	9.09%
	100.00%

For a short taxable year not beginning on the first day of a month or ending on the last day of a month, the arithmetic midpoint must be calculated as follows:

$$\text{arithmetic midpoint} \quad = \quad \frac{\text{number of days in short taxable year}}{2}$$

If the arithmetic midpoint is a day other than the first or the midpoint of the month, the property is treated as placed in service on the nearest preceding first or midpoint of the month. After the placed-in-service date has been determined, actual cost recovery allowances may be computed using either the allocation method or the simplified method.

Allocation Method

This method requires cost recovery to be calculated by determining which recovery years are included in the taxable year. For each recovery year included, cost recovery attributable to that year is multiplied by a fraction calculated as follows:

$$\frac{\text{number of months in both the taxable and recovery year}}{12}$$

As an example, the allowable deductions given the following assumptions can be computed:

Equipment cost: 10,000

Depreciable life: 5 years

Depreciation method: MACRS

Applied convention: Half-year

Short taxable year beginning: March 1, 19X1

Taxpayer status: Calendar year.

Since this short taxable year ends on the last day of a month, i.e., December 31, the deemed placed-in-service date is August 1. (Number of full months (10) divided by 2 = 5, March + 5 months = August). Deductions are calculated as follows:

Year	Computation	Deduction
1	(40% x 10,000 x 5/12)*	1,666.67
2	(40% x 10,000 x 7/12) + (40% x 6,000 x 5/12)	3,333.33
3	(40% x 6,000 x 7/12) + (40% x 3,600 x 5/12)	2,000.00
4	(40% x 3,600 x 7/12) + (40% x 2,160 x 5/12)	1,200.00
5 **	1,800 x $\dfrac{1}{(1 + 7/12)}$	1,137.00
6		663.00
		10,000.00

  * Ten-month year divided by 2

  ** Year of switch to straight-line

Simplified Method

The simplified method also may be used to calculate subsequent years' cost recovery deductions. This method follows the basic methodology of MACRS. Each year the unrecovered basis of the property is multiplied by the applicable declining balance rate. Using the same assumptions from the previous example, cost recovery deductions are:

Year	Computation	Deduction
1	(40% x 10,000 x 5/12)*	1,666.67
2	(40% x 8,333.33)	3,333.33
3	(40% x 5,000.00)	2,000.00
4	(40% x 3,000.00)	1,200.00
5 **	1,800 x $\dfrac{1}{(1 + 7/12)}$	1,137.00
6		663.00
		10,000.00

  * Ten-month year divided by 2

  ** Year of switch to straight-line

MIDQUARTER CONVENTION

For a short taxable year consisting of four or eight months, quarters are determined on the basis of whole months. For example, in an eight-month taxable year, each quarter would be two months. The computation of depreciation in a short taxable year not consisting of four or eight months requires several steps. First, the quarters are determined by dividing the number of days in the tax year by four. Next, the arithmetic midpoint of each quarter is calculated. Finally, using the nearest first day or midpoint of the month, the deemed placed-in-service dates are determined.

The tax year of the taxpayer placing property in service does not include any month before the month in which the taxpayer begins engaging in a trade or business or holding recovery or depreciable property for the production of income. It generally is not possible to circumvent application of the short year rule by placing a relatively small amount of property in service early in the year (just to attempt to comply in form with the rule) and then later in the year placing a significant amount in service. The IRS takes the position that, in such a case, the taxable year begins in the month in which the significant amount of property was placed in service, not earlier in the year.

DEFERRED INTERCOMPANY TRANSACTIONS

A fundamental facet of U.S. tax law is that a transaction that occurs between two members of the same consolidated group of corporations does not generate a tax consequence. From a federal income tax perspective, nothing has happened. (An oversimplified analogy is taking of money out of the right pocket and putting it into the left. The total amount of money has not changed.) In such a deferred intercompany transaction, profit realized on the sale of property by one member of the controlled group to another member of the group generally is deferred. This deferred profit is restored later in accordance with the deferred intercompany transaction rules. However, once the transaction involves a party outside the consolidated group, a taxable event has occurred, and all the deferred profit must be recognized.

Requirements

A deferred intercompany transaction must occur between members of an affiliated group during a consolidated return year. An affiliated group exists when at least 80% of each corporation (except the common parent) is owned directly by one or more of the other corporations, and the common parent owns directly at least 80% of at least one of the other corporations. A consolidated return year is any taxable year in which all corporations, which at any time during the taxable year have been members of the affiliated group, file a consolidated return.

To determine the amount of gross profit or loss generated in connection with a deferred intercompany transaction, reference must be made to the selling member's cost (manufacturer's cost). In general, manufacturer's cost is the sum of direct and indirect production costs computed under the uniform capitalization rules. Under the uniform capitalization rules, production costs, which must be either deducted currently or capitalized, are allocated to goods produced during the taxable year, whether sold during the taxable year or remaining in inventory at the close of the taxable year.

Application to Leasing

Manufacturing parents that sell their goods to a subsidiary (captive), or through a division, generate gross profit. The captive can enter into a transaction with its customer in one of four forms. The transaction can be a true lease, a conditional sales contract, a money-over-money lease or an outright cash sale. The gross profit of the parent for a true lease (the lessor remains the owner) is recognized differently than for the other three forms (a sale has occurred for tax purposes).

Assume, for example, that the parent produces a computer that costs 550,000 to manufacture. Further assume that the captive purchases the computer from the parent for its fair market value, which is 1,000,000. The gross profit of the parent on this transaction is 450,000. This gross profit is deferred and later restored if the lease is a true lease.

TRUE LEASE

If the captive leases the property to its customer under a true lease, the parent restores the gain (brings it into income) according to the cost recovery methodology used by the captive. The rule states that if the property is depreciable, amortizable or depletable in the hands of the purchaser, the seller (parent) restores the gain as the depreciation, depletion or amortization deductions are taken by the purchaser (captive).

$$\text{Gain recognized} = \text{Total deferred gain} \times \frac{\underline{\text{Current year cost recovery}}}{\text{Purchaser's basis}}$$

A simpler way of looking at this calculation is to multiply the total deferred gain by the cost recovery percentage. For example, assuming that equipment under a tax lease is 5-year MACRS property, the captive lessor's cost recovery deductions would be 20%, 32%, 19.2%, 11.52%, 11.52% and 5.76%, for years one through six, respectively. Applying the rules above, in year one, the parent would recognize income equal to 20% (the MACRS deduction of the captive) times the gross profit on the sale. If the asset is not transferred outside of the consolidated group, the same process would be applied for years two through six.

By deferring income, and, thus, the tax liability, the consolidated group realizes a present value tax savings when compared to a cash sale outside the group. The following illustration quantifies this tax benefit.

Assume once more that the cost of the 5-year MACRS property to the parent is 550,000 and the sales price to the captive (and the fair market value) is 1,000,000. In addition, assume a five-year lease and a discount rate of 10%. Because of the deferral of the taxes on the gross profit, the consolidated group realizes an after-tax, present value benefit of 2.73%, calculated as follows.

The tax due in the year of sale if the asset is sold for 1,000,000 to a party outside of the consolidated group is 157,500.

$$1,000,000 - 550,000 = 450,000 \times .35 = 157,500$$

The taxes due over the recovery period if the asset is sold to the captive, which then leases the equipment to a third party, are shown in Exhibit 6-9. The present value of the tax liability over the recovery period is 130,200, compared to the liability of 157,500 if the taxes were payable in the year of sale. The difference is 27,300, which is approximately 2.73% of the fair market value of the equipment. Of course, changes in the amount of gross profit, the depreciation methodology, the tax rate and the discount rate will affect the magnitude of the benefit.

CONDITIONAL SALE

As discussed in Chapter Five, many transactions called leases are, in substance, treated as sales by the IRS. If the transaction between the captive

| | Exhibit 6-9 | |
| | Tax Deferral Schedule | |

Year	Gross profit restored	Tax liability
1	90,000	31,500
2	144,000	50,400
3	86,400	30,240
4	51,840	18,144
5	51,840	18,144
5	25,920	9,072
	450,000	157,500

and the third party is deemed a sale, the parent must immediately recognize gross profit on the sale to the captive because of changes enacted in the Revenue and Pension Protection Act of 1987.

The 1987 act repealed the installment method of accounting. This means that all payments on transactions entered into subsequent to the applicable date of the act are deemed to be received in the first year of the transaction. The result is the recognition of all gross profit in the first year. Therefore, in a conditional sale, income is recognized, and taxes are paid, as if a sale has been made to a third party outside the consolidated group.

MONEY-OVER-MONEY LEASE

A money-over-money lease also is a transaction characterized by the parties as a lease, but which, in reality, is a sale. All gross profit, therefore, must be recognized by the parent in the year of the transaction. Also of importance in money-over-money transactions are the rules regarding interest income recognition. Rental payments made by the lessee must be split into interest and principal. No interest rate is stated in a money-over-money lease, so the IRC requires an interest rate to be imputed. The total interest paid by the customer must be included by the captive as income on an actuarial basis.

CASH SALE

If the captive sells the property to the customer for cash, all deferred gain is recognized immediately. In this circumstance, the property has been disposed of outside the controlled group.

INVESTMENT TAX CREDIT

The Investment Tax Credit (ITC), as the name implies, is a credit (dollar for dollar reduction) against income taxes. The ITC has had a very tumultuous history. ITC was originally enacted during the Kennedy Administration, at a 7% level, to stimulate investment in new assets to be used in a trade or business or held for the production of income. In 1969 it was repealed. It was restored in 1971 and then increased to 10% in 1975. It was repealed again by TRA 86 for years beginning after 1985. It is often rumored the ITC may be reinstated, although reinstatement has not yet occurred. However, because the credit has a 15-year carryforward period, some leasing companies still are recognizing it in their tax returns.

CONCLUSION

The tax laws related to equipment ownership play an integral role in the leasing industry. Although the tax benefits associated with leasing are few, they must be incorporated into transactions if the lessor is to be competitive. Because of this requirement, and the complexity of many tax provisions, lessors must study and understand the tax aspects of leasing. Unfortunately, obtaining an understanding of the tax issues is not easy and is complicated by the fact that tax laws are in a continuous state of flux. As many lessors have found, benefits here today may be gone, or at least changed, by tomorrow.

Chapter Seven

Income Tax Limitations

Over the years Congress has attempted, through tax legislation, to raise more revenue to offset the budget deficit facing the country. The result of this legislation is that tax benefits have diminished and more tax limitations have emerged.

Tax limitations, for the most part, affect the amount or timing of various tax deductions allowed in the Internal Revenue Code (IRC). These limitations impact lessors in several ways. First of all, tax limitations affect the way lessors price transactions, as they directly impact the cash flows of the lease. The limitations also affect the different types of products offered by the lessor and the marketplace in which those products are offered. This chapter, therefore, discusses the various income tax limitations that exist today and their potential impact on the way lessors conduct business. The following topics are addressed:

- Midquarter Convention
- Antichurning Rules
- Alternative Minimum Tax
- Uneven Rents
- At-risk Provisions
- Passive Losses.

MIDQUARTER CONVENTION

As discussed in Chapter Six, the cost recovery percentages under the Modified Accelerated Cost Recovery System (MACRS) generally are calculated using the half-year convention. This means that, regardless of when the property is placed in service, the property is deemed placed in service in the middle of the tax year. The half-year convention also results in a half-year's deduction in the year of disposition. This method of depreciation represents a benefit that can best be illustrated by the following scenario.

Assume a lessor purchases a computer for 1,000,000 and enters into a lease agreement with a lessee on December 31, 19X1. It also collects an advance rental from the lessee in the amount of 3% of the equipment cost. The lessor is taxed on only one month's rent of 30,000, yet receives a full half-year MACRS deduction of 200,000. Assuming a corporate tax rate of 35%, the lessor receives a tax benefit in the amount of 59,500. It is apparent from this example that taxpayers can maximize the value of their tax deductions under the half-year convention by deferring equipment purchases to later in the tax year.

In order to prevent companies from waiting until the fourth quarter to purchase all their equipment (and reducing revenues to the treasury), Congress created a limitation called the midquarter convention. Under this limitation, if more than 40% of all personal property placed in service during the year is placed in service in the last three months of the taxable year, the midquarter convention replaces the half-year convention. The rule requires that all MACRS property placed in service during the year be subject to the midquarter convention.

The impact of the midquarter convention is that previously calculated MACRS deductions have to be recalculated. This recalculation generally results in cost recovery deductions slower than regular MACRS for the taxpayer, whether a lessor or a lessee. The slower depreciation and, hence, slower cash flow realization directly impact lessor yields on tax leases and could act as a deterrent to purchasing for lessees.

The midquarter convention treats all MACRS recovery property placed in service during a quarter as having been placed in service at the midpoint of such quarter. Compared to the half-year convention, the midquarter convention provides greater first-year cost recovery deductions for property placed in service during the first and second quarters, but lower first-year deductions for property placed in service during the third and fourth quarters.

The original provisions of the midquarter convention were modified slightly in 1988. The Technical and Miscellaneous Revenue Act of 1988 (TAMRA 88) provided that property placed in service and disposed of within the same tax year is disregarded in applying the midquarter convention. Also, transfers between members of the same affiliated group filing a consolidated return are not included for purposes of the 40% test.

Calculation of the deductions under the midquarter convention is as follows (assuming 5-year property). Using the midpoint of the first, second, third and fourth quarters, the midquarter convention treats MACRS recovery property placed in service in the fiscal year as having been placed in service for 10.5, 7.5, 4.5 and 1.5 months, respectively. In order to compute the amount of depreciation, the amount of property placed in service in a given quarter is multiplied by a fraction, the numerator of which is the number of months the property is deemed to have been placed in service (e.g., 10.5, 7.5, 4.5 or 1.5 months), and the denominator of which is 12. That fraction is then multiplied by the declining balance percentage, which, as discussed in Chapter Six, is 40% for 5-year property.

Based on this methodology, the cost recovery in the first year is 35% for property placed in service in the first quarter (10.5/12 x 40%). On the other end of the spectrum, the cost recovery for property placed in service in the last quarter is only 5% (1.5/12 x 40%). If the midquarter convention is not applicable (i.e., the half-year convention applies), the recovery for property placed in service during the fourth quarter is 20%.

Although the 35% allowed for property placed in service in the first quarter is greater than the 20% allowed under the half-year convention, remember what caused the midquarter to apply in the first place – more than 40% of the property was placed in service in the fourth quarter. Therefore, at least 40% of the equipment placed in service during the year is generating a depreciation deduction of only 5%. For the remaining years, the process is identical to that set forth in Exhibit 7-1. The 5-year property midquarter percentages are reproduced in Exhibit 7-2.

Property that is depreciated under the midquarter convention is still depreciated over the same period as under the half-year convention. For example, 5-year MACRS property costing 100,000 is depreciated over six years under either convention, as shown in Exhibit 7-3.

The impact of the midquarter convention is one of timing. It is the timing of the deductions not the amount of the deductions that is changed. There is, therefore, a time value of money penalty associated with property placed in service under the midquarter convention, as highlighted in the following example:

Exhibit 7-1
Derivation of Midquarter Percentages
(Fourth Quarter)

Year	Undepreciated basis	200% declining balance	Prospective straight-line deductions	MACRS depreciation
1	1.0000	**.0500** (40% x .125)	.0250 (20% x .125)	.0500
2	.9500	**.3800** (40% x .95)	.1949 (.95 ÷ 4.875)	.3800
3	.5700	**.2280** (40% x .57)	.1471 (.57 ÷ 3.875)	.2280
4	.3420	**.1368** (40% x .342)	.1190 (.342 ÷ 2.875)	.1368
5	.2052	.0821 (40% x .2052)	**.1094** [1] (.2052 ÷ 1.875)	.1094
6	.0576		**.0958** (.1094 x .875)	.0958
				1.0000

[1] Crossover to straight-line

Assumptions:

Equipment acquired in 19X1: 10,000,000

MACRS life: 5-years.

Scenario one: Half-year convention applies

Quarter 1	500,000
Quarter 2	2,000,000
Quarter 3	3,500,000
Quarter 4	4,000,000
Total	10,000,000
MACRS (half-year)	x 20%
Deduction	2,000,000
Tax rate	x 35%
Tax benefit	700,000

Scenario two: Midquarter convention applies

Quarter 1	500,000	x 35% =	175,000
Quarter 2	2,000,000	x 25% =	500,000
Quarter 3	3,499,999	x 15% =	525,000
Quarter 4	4,000,001	x 5% =	200,000
Total	10,000,000		1,400,000
Deduction			1,400,000
Tax rate			x 35%
Tax benefit			490,000

Exhibit 7-2
Midquarter Recovery Percentages

Quarter	Year					
	1	2	3	4	5	6
1st	.35	.26	.156	.1101	.1101	.0138
2nd	.25	.30	.18	.1137	.1137	.0426
3rd	.15	.34	.204	.1224	.1130	.0706
4th	.05	.38	.228	.1368	.1094	.0958

In scenario one, fourth quarter acquisitions equal exactly 40% of the total acquisitions for the year; therefore the half-year convention applies. In this scenario, the equipment owner (lessor or lessee) receives first-year cash flow of 700,000 from the tax benefits. In scenario two, one more dollar of equipment acquisition in the fourth quarter places this company under the midquarter convention. The result is a recalculation of the first-year MACRS deductions, resulting in tax benefits of only 490,000, a reduction of 210,000 compared to the half-year convention.

Exhibit 7-3
Comparison of Conventions

Yr.	Midquarter convention		Half-year convention		Difference	
	Amount	Cumulative	Amount	Cumulative	Amount	Cumulative
1	5,000	5,000	20,000	20,000	(15,000)	(15,000)
2	38,000	43,000	32,000	52,000	6,000	(9,000)
3	22,800	65,800	19,200	71,200	3,600	(5,400)
4	13,680	79,480	11,520	82,720	2,160	(3,240)
5	10,944	90,424	11,520	94,240	(576)	(3,816)
6	9,576	100,000	5,760	100,000	3,816	- 0 -

It is easy to see from this example why lessors try to avoid the midquarter convention – the timing difference in the cash flows from tax benefits adversely affects their yield. Lessees can avoid the midquarter convention by leasing instead of owning the equipment.

ANTICHURNING RULES

The antichurning rules are designed to prevent a taxpayer from converting property depreciated under one system (e.g., Accelerated Cost Recovery System, or ACRS) to a newer more favorable system such as MACRS. As an example of how the antichurning provisions are applied, ACRS must be used regarding certain pre-1987 property involved in post-1986 churning transactions entered into to obtain the benefits of MACRS (even if the taxpayer acquired the property after January 1, 1987) for which:

1. Such property was owned or used at any time during 1986 by the taxpayer or a person related to the taxpayer

2. Such property is acquired from a person who owned such property at any time during 1986 and, as part of the transaction, the user of the property does not change

3. Such property is leased by the taxpayer to a person (or a person related to such person) who owned or used such property at any time during 1986

4. Such property is acquired in a transaction in which the user of such property does not qualify for MACRS in the hands of the person from whom the property is so acquired due to condition 2 or 3 above.

If, however, application of the antichurning rules would result in a more favorable deduction than if the rules did not apply (assuming utilization of the half-year convention), the antichurning rules do not apply. This may occur when property has been reclassified under MACRS into a longer recovery period.

Examples

The following examples illustrate the application of the antichurning rules.

EXAMPLE ONE

DC Corporation leased equipment from AC Company in 1986 for a nine-year term. In 1995, DC exercised its fair market value purchase option and acquired the equipment formerly leased from AC. DC must use ACRS because it used the equipment during 1986.

EXAMPLE TWO

DC, the owner of a manufacturing system, entered into a sale-leaseback in 1994 with AC, whereby DC sold the equipment to AC and leased it back from AC for a five-year term. (DC owned the equipment in 1986.) AC must use ACRS because it acquired the equipment from DC, and the user of the property (DC) did not change.

EXAMPLE THREE

AC entered into a lease of railcars in 1986 with DC. In 1995, AC sold the equipment subject to the lease and assigned the lease to Equity Source. Equity Source is required to use ACRS because it acquired the equipment from AC, which owned the equipment during 1986, and the user (DC) did not change.

EXAMPLE FOUR

AC entered into a lease of aircraft in 1986 with DC. In 1996, AC sold the equipment subject to the lease and assigned the lease to First Equity Source. First Equity Source then sold the equipment subject to the lease and assigned the lease to Second Equity Source. Second Equity Source must use ACRS because the equipment is leased, by assignment, by Second Equity Source to DC, a user of the property during 1986.

The antichurning rules have had limited application for most lessors since the last change in depreciation methodology (from ACRS to MACRS) occurred in 1986. Typically, only leasing companies involved in lease and sale-leaseback transactions for long-lived assets such as manufacturing facilities, aircraft or railcars need to be concerned with the antichurning rules. However, any changes to the existing depreciation methodology would generate a new series of churning transactions.

ALTERNATIVE MINIMUM TAX

The alternative minimum tax (AMT) has been a part of the system of taxation for over two decades. The AMT originally was enacted under the Tax Reform Act of 1969 to curb congressionally perceived abuses of tax preference items. Until 1986, the provisions of the AMT affected specific industries, such as mining, oil and gas and real estate. Revisions to the tax law enacted in 1986, however, expanded the items of tax preference in such a way that now all corporations must be concerned with the AMT. Several of these tax preferences have a direct impact on leasing companies.

The AMT provisions are among the most complex found in the IRC. The provisions impose a heavy administrative burden on taxpayers. The AMT is conceptually simple, but actual application is often very difficult. As is illustrated in this section, a thorough understanding of a variety of tax rules is required in order to comply with the law. The rules relating to the minimum tax credit, tax preference items and credit limitations, to name but a few, are difficult to understand. Help, in the form of either a full-time staff of tax professionals or outside tax resources, has become a necessity for many companies.

General Provisions

The framework for the revised AMT, which is effective for tax years beginning after December 31, 1986, and modified for years beginning after December 31, 1993, diverges sharply from the pre-1986 law. The AMT is now based on an entirely supplemental tax recording system. A taxpayer must maintain a separate set of AMT records side-by-side with the existing regular tax system. The items of income and deductions that apply for regular tax purposes do not, in many cases, apply in the AMT environment. The effect is a much stronger relationship between a corporation's books used for financial reporting purposes and its tax books. At the very minimum (and ignoring the idiosyncrasies of state and local tax laws), three sets of books are maintained by U.S. companies: financial reporting books, regular tax books and AMT books.

DETERMINING THE TAX LIABILITY

Both the regular tax for the taxable year and the AMT for the taxable year are computed. As shown in Exhibit 7-4, the AMT is equal to 20% of alternative minimum taxable income (AMTI) for the taxable year.

```
┌─────────────────────────────────────────────────────────────┐
│                      Exhibit 7-4                             │
│                    Tax Comparison                           │
│                                                             │
│          Regular tax                    AMT                 │
│     Income before taxes          Income before taxes        │
│     (-) Adjustments              (-) Adjustments            │
│        Taxable income               Taxable income          │
│                                  (+) Preferences            │
│                                     AMTI                     │
│           x  35%                     x  20%                 │
│        Taxes payable              AMT payable               │
└─────────────────────────────────────────────────────────────┘
```

This amount is compared to the regular taxes payable and the higher of the two is due to the IRS. As shown in the example, the AMTI consists of regular taxable income plus or minus preference items. This simplified example does not include the impact of the exemption or any tax credits, which are discussed later.

The indifference point between regular tax and AMT status occurs when 20% of AMTI equals 35% of taxable income. Once 20% of AMTI exceeds 35% of taxable income, a corporation is in AMT and is paying higher overall taxes. If this point is not reached, the corporation pays regular taxes just as it always had before the AMT rules were expanded. The breakeven (indifference) point can be calculated by comparing the relationship of taxable income to the amount of preferences. (Preferences are a component of the AMT that are discussed in the next subsection.)

An analysis of Exhibit 7-5 indicates that until preferences exceed 75% of taxable income, a corporation is not in AMT. However, when the total amount of the preferences exceeds 75% of the taxable income, the corporation is in AMT and will have a higher effective tax rate. The following example illustrates this "75%" rule.

	Regular tax	AMT
Taxable income	500,000	500,000
Tax preference item	N/A	400,000
Total	500,000	900,000
Rate	x 35%	x 20%
Applicable tax	175,000	180,000

Exhibit 7-5
AMT Breakeven Analysis

If TI = taxable income and P = preferences, breakeven occurs when

$$.35TI = .20AMTI, \text{ where AMTI equals (TI + P)}$$

$$.35TI = .20(TI+P)$$

$$.35TI = .20TI + .20P$$

$$.35TI - .20TI = .20P$$

$$.15TI = .20P$$

$$.75TI = P$$

This corporation must pay 180,000 in taxes. The effective tax rate to the corporation is now 36% (180,000/500,000) instead of the regular tax rate of 35%. Notice that the preferences of 400,000 exceed 75% of the taxable income (500,000 x 75% = 375,000) and that AMT is greater than regular tax. If preferences were equal to 375,000, the corporation would be at a breakeven point between regular taxable income and AMT, with total taxes due of 175,000.

Tax Preference Items

In computing AMTI, a corporation is required to redetermine taxable income by including preference items. Preference items supplant certain items of income and deductions used in the calculation of regular taxable income with those required under the AMT. They arise when certain items of income and deductions are utilized in excess of prescribed levels. Generally, the AMT methodology results in greater income and lower deductions than under the regular tax system. Companies must consider many types of preference items when computing their AMT. The following tax preference items, however, are those most commonly encountered in the equipment leasing industry.

ACCELERATED DEPRECIATION ON PERSONAL PROPERTY

The Tax Reform Act of 1986 (TRA 86) changed the law with respect to personal property, which is property other than land and real estate. The pre-TRA 86 law applies for leased equipment placed in service before 1987 and for transitional property. (This pre-TRA 86 preference applies only to leased personal property owned by an individual or a personal holding company. The amount of the preference is the excess of the accelerated depreciation taken by the taxpayer for regular tax purposes over depreciation calculated under the straight-line method, using the same useful lives.)

TRA 86 expanded this preference to include all corporations, although these rules vary from those for individuals and personal holding companies. The TRA 86 rules directly impact the leasing industry and apply for property placed in service after 1986, and for transitional property placed in service after July 31, 1986 and before January 1, 1987, for which MACRS was elected. For this property, the depreciation deduction for AMT purposes is calculated using the 150% declining balance method with a maximizing switch to straight-line over the alternative depreciation system (ADS) life, i.e., the asset depreciation range (ADR) midpoint life.

The mechanics of the AMT calculation require that depreciation used in calculating regular taxable income (usually MACRS) be added back to taxable income, and then AMT depreciation subtracted, to arrive at AMTI. Since AMT depreciation is not as accelerated as regular MACRS, AMTI generally will be higher than taxable income in the early years of ownership. Furthermore, if the 75% threshold is exceeded, the corporation will pay taxes sooner to the IRS.

Several depreciation alternatives to MACRS, for computing regular taxable income, were discussed in Chapter Six. Exhibit 7-6 recaps the interrelationship between the four regular tax depreciation methods and the method required under the AMT provisions. The depreciation amounts applicable to 100,000 of 5-year MACRS property for regular tax and AMT purposes are shown in Exhibit 7-7. Although the total depreciation for AMT purposes is the same as under MACRS, the AMT deductions are less accelerated, resulting in lower tax benefits on a present value basis.

The AMT depreciation preference has widespread impact in both pricing and lease versus buy decisions because the cash flows from the depreciation deductions are altered. Many lessors and lessees are of the opinion that using straight-

Exhibit 7-6
Depreciation Methods

Regular tax method	AMT method	Preference
MACRS	150% declining balance over ADR	Yes
Straight-line over MACRS	Straight-line over ADR	Yes, if ADR life > MACRS life
Straight-line over ADR	Straight-line over ADR	No
150% declining balance over ADR	150% declining balance over ADR	No

line depreciation is more beneficial economically. Although it certainly does not create preferences, use of the straight-line method can result in economic loss, because the amount of the taxes saved on the preference amount may be less than the tax savings associated with the foregone MACRS.

It is easy to see that for lessors who are writing tax leases, AMT presents a potentially severe problem. The more assets the lessor owns, the more depreciation it deducts in the tax return. The more deductions taken, the more likely it is that a lessor will generate preferences in amounts that exceed 75% of taxable income and, therefore, fall into AMT.

TAX-EXEMPT INTEREST

Although tax-exempt interest is not includable in gross income for regular tax purposes, tax-exempt interest on private activity bonds (other than qualified § 501(c)(3) bonds) issued generally on or after August 15, 1986 is fully includable in income for AMT purposes. Federal income tax is imposed on the interest of a state or local bond if it constitutes a private activity bond that is not a qualified bond.

A private activity bond is any bond that meets the private business use test (greater than 10% of the bond issue proceeds are used for a private business) and the private payment test (the payment of principal or interest on more than 10% of the proceeds is secured by an interest in property used for private business). A bond also qualifies as a private activity bond if greater than 5% of the proceeds, or 5,000,000, is used to finance loans to entities other than governmental units.

A qualified § 501(c)(3) bond is any bond in which all property provided by the bond issue proceeds is owned by a 501(c)(3) organization or governmental unit and the face amount of the issue is less than 150 million. A 501(c)(3) organization is defined as any nonprofit corporation, foundation or fund organized and operated exclusively for religious, charitable, scientific, literary or educational purposes, etc., that does not participate in any political activities.

ADJUSTED CURRENT EARNINGS (ACE) ADJUSTMENT

The ACE adjustment is the most complex aspect of the AMT provisions. This preference has a pervasive effect on the business community for two reasons. First, corporations with a significant difference between income calculated for book purposes and income as reported for federal income tax purposes are impacted directly and adversely by the ACE adjustment. The timing of income taxes payable is altered to increase the present value of taxes paid. As has been seen with many of the other tax limitations, pricing strategies have to be altered to protect lessor yields in true lease transactions.

Exhibit 7-7
Depreciation Comparison

Year	MACRS	150% declining balance	Straight-line MACRS	Straight-line ADR
1	20,000	15,000	10,000	10,000
2	32,000	25,500	20,000	20,000
3	19,200	17,850	20,000	20,000
4	11,520	16,660	20,000	20,000
5	11,520	16,660	20,000	20,000
6	5,760	8,330	10,000	10,000
Total	100,000	100,000	100,000	100,000

Second, it is administratively costly for corporations to properly keep track of this preference. This preference partially bridges the gap between a corporation's financial reporting books and its tax books. Congress, through the ACE adjustment, is attempting to impose income taxes on a base that more closely approximates economic income.

ACE was an original provision of TRA 86; however, because of its complexity, Congress provided for a three-year phase-in period. During tax years 1987, 1988 and 1989, a temporary adjustment referred to as the Business Untaxed but Reported Profits (BURP) adjustment was used by taxpayers in lieu of the ACE adjustment. The BURP adjustment was 50% of the difference between pretax book income and the AMTI before this preference, often referred to as other AMTI. Pretax book income was the income reported by a corporation for financial reporting purposes (excluding any impact of foreign or federal income taxes). Other AMTI consisted of the AMTI before taking this preference into consideration.

For tax years beginning after 1989, the BURP adjustment was replaced by the originally enacted ACE adjustment. The amount of the preference is 75% of the difference between the IRS-defined ACE and preadjusted AMTI before this preference. The adjustment may be positive or negative. However, negative ACE adjustments are limited to the positive adjustments of prior years. An example of the computation is as follows:

	19X1	**19X2**
Other AMTI	2,000	1,000
ACE adjustments:		
Depreciation	<u>3,000</u>	<u>(1,300)</u>
Adjusted current earnings	5,000	(300)
Less: Other AMTI	<u>(2,000)</u>	<u>(1,000)</u>
	3,000	(1,300)
ACE inclusion factor	x 75%	x 75%
ACE preference	2,250	(975)
Plus: Other AMTI	<u>2,000</u>	<u>1,000</u>
AMTI	4,250	25

The 975 reduction in AMTI is allowed in 19X2 because AMTI had been increased at least that amount by the ACE preference in 19X1.

The calculation of the ACE adjustment is complex and requires knowledge of a variety of tax issues. In theory, the various components that make up the adjustment attempt to create the true economic income of a corporation.

For example, existing tax law allows for interest income from state or local obligations to be eliminated from book income when arriving at taxable income. The interest, though, has been received by the company and is, therefore, included or added back to arrive at ACE. As shown in Exhibit 7-8 many such adjustments enter into the calculation of ACE, which in its final form is intended to approximate book income.

The most confusing component of the ACE adjustment was the depreciation component computed per IRC § 312(k). IRC § 312(k) refers to IRC § 168(g), which requires that, for property placed in service before December 31, 1993, the difference between depreciation calculated for AMT purposes (150% declining balance over the ADR life), and depreciation calculated per the following schedule, is a component of the ACE adjustment:

1. **Property placed in service after 1989** – straight-line over the ADR mid-point life

2. **Property placed in service between January 1, 1987 and December 31, 1989 (MACRS, including transitional MACRS)** – AMT basis at December 31, 1989 is depreciated straight-line over the remaining ADR mid-point life at December 31, 1989

Exhibit 7-8
Taxable Income

Common additions	**Common subtractions**
1. Dividends received deduction	1. Depreciation computed per § 312(k)
2. Net operating loss (NOL) carryover or carryback	2. Disallowed travel and entertainment expenses
3. Tax-exempt interest income	3. Interest and other expenses related to tax-exempt income
4. Regular tax depreciation	4. Federal tax liability
5. Installment sales	5. Charitable contributions in excess of 10% limit.
6. Capital loss carryover and carryback.	

3. **Property placed in service between January 1, 1981 and December 31, 1986 (ACRS)** – regular tax basis at December 31, 1989 is depreciated straight-line over the remaining ADR midpoint life at December 31, 1989

4. **Property placed in service before 1981** – the same method used for regular tax depreciation.

The addition of another layer of depreciation-related preferences exacerbated the AMT impact of owning equipment. This double impact created a tax trap that impacted lessor yields and resulted in a significant acceleration of the payment of taxes.

Congress in the Tax Reform Act of 1993 (TRA 93) decided that two layers of AMT depreciation preferences were an unfair tax burden to taxpayers and an administrative nightmare. They concluded that the AMT rules as they existed might be a deterrent to new equipment purchases. Therefore, for property placed in service after December 31, 1993, the depreciation component of the ACE adjustment is eliminated. ACE depreciation continues, though, for property placed in service between December 31, 1989 and December 31, 1993, thereby extending the administrative burden for companies. The following example highlights the first-year impact of the elimination:

Assumptions:

> MACRS life: 5-years
>
> ADR life: 5-years
>
> Asset cost: 100

Prior law - preference amount

I	II	III	IV	V	
Regular	AMT	ACE	Depreciation	ACE	Total
MACRS	depreciation	depreciation	preference	preference	preferences
			(I-II)	(II-III x .75)	(IV + V)
20	15	10	5	3.75	8.75

TRA 93 - preference amount

Regular	AMT	Total preference
I	II	(I-II)
20	15	5

The total first year preference for 5-year property is reduced from 8.75% of the equipment cost to 5%. Theoretically, with fewer preference items, fewer companies should be in AMT.

Credits and Losses

The AMT may not be reduced by the credit for targeted jobs, producing fuel from a nonconventional source, qualified clinical testing expenses and (except as noted) the general business credit. These credits generally are referred to as incentive tax credits.

A corporation's ITC, however, may be used to offset the greater of (1) either the regular tax liability for the taxable year or the excess of its regular tax liability over 75% of its AMT, whichever is less, or (2) 25% of its tentative minimum tax. For example, if the corporation's regular tax liability for the year was 600,000 and its tentative minimum tax liability was 1.5 million, the corporation could use available investment credits to offset its AMT liability by 375,000.

If, on the other hand, the corporation's regular tax liability was 1.5 million and its AMT liability was 600,000, the corporation could use up to 1,050,000 of ITC to reduce its regular tax liability to 450,000. Except as set forth in the preceding formula, ITC cannot reduce the regular tax below the AMT.

Foreign tax credits (FTCs) also are allowed against the AMT. They cannot, however, offset more than 90% of the AMT (determined prior to application of FTCs and NOLs). Assuming AMT of 5,000,000 and AMT FTCs of the same amount, AMT of 500,000 would still be paid, as follows:

AMT	5,000,000
Limitation	x 90%
Amount available	4,500,000

$$5,000,000 - 4,500,000 = 500,000$$

NOLs cannot offset more than 90% of AMTI; any unutilized losses, however, may be carried forward. As an example, a company's AMTI (before NOLs) is 7,500,000 and it has minimum tax NOLs of 8,250,000. The maximum amount of minimum tax NOLs that can be offset against AMTI is 6,750,000.

AMTI	7,500,000
Limitation	x 90%
	6,750,000

The taxpayer's AMTI would be reduced to 750,000 (7,500,000 - 6,750,000), resulting in a tentative AMT of 150,000. Minimum tax NOLs of 1,500,000 (8,250,000 - 6,750,000) would be carried forward.

An illustration combining the various limitations previously discussed is presented below to demonstrate the interaction (and overall view) of the limitations. Assume the following:

AMTI (pre-NOL): 10,000,000

AMT NOL: 8,000,000

AMT FTC: 350,000

The floor to which the tax can be reduced is 200,000.

(10,000,000 x .20 x .10)

Utilization of the available credits would occur as follows:

AMTI (pre-NOL)	10,000,000
AMT NOL	(8,000,000)
AMTI	2,000,000
	x .20
AMT	400,000
AMT FTC	(200,000)
Tentative minimum tax	200,000

AMT Small Corporation Exemption

There is an exemption from the taxpaying requirements of the AMT (but not necessarily the bookkeeping requirements) for small corporations. The amount of the exemption, 40,000, is used to reduce AMTI before the tax rate of 20% is applied to determine the AMT. That exemption, however, is phased out by 25 cents for every one dollar of AMTI over 150,000. For example, if AMTI is 225,000, the AMT exemption amount would be calculated as follows:

AMTI	225,000
Base amount	(150,000)
Excess	75,000
	x .25
Reduction	18,750
Total AMT exemption	40,000
Reduction	(18,750)
AMT exemption	21,250

Minimum Tax Credit

The AMT is a timing tax in that it accelerates the taxes paid by a corporation. This acceleration increases the amount of taxes paid on a present value basis. The AMT does not, however, increase the total amount of taxes paid. Any taxes paid in excess of the regular tax (because of AMT) can be used to offset future regular taxes. This amount is referred to as the minimum tax credit.

The minimum tax credit is equal to the excess, if any, of (1) the AMT for all prior taxable years beginning after 1986 over (2) the regular tax liability for such years. The credit is reduced by any minimum tax credits already taken, and limited each year to the amount by which the regular tax for the taxable year exceeds the AMT for that taxable year. The minimum tax credit can be carried forward indefinitely and is measured without regard to other credits. For example, assume the following:

	19X1	19X2	19X3	Total
Regular tax	200,000	210,000	220,000	630,000
AMT	250,000	200,000	180,000	
AMT credit	50,000			
AMT credit used		10,000	40,000	
AMT credit carryforward	50,000	40,000	0	
Taxes paid	250,000	200,000	180,000	630,00

In 19X1, regular tax is higher than AMT. In accordance with the rules, this corporation pays the higher of the two taxes, or 250,000. In paying the higher AMT, the corporation generates an AMT credit that can be used in subsequent years when regular tax is higher than AMT. Such is the case in both 19X2 and 19X3. In 19X2, regular tax is 10,000 higher than AMT (210,000 - 200,000). The corporation actually pays 200,000 instead of 210,000 because 10,000 of the existing AMT credit is applied against the regular tax liability. As noted above, the credit is limited in that it cannot reduce the regular taxes payable below the minimum tax for that taxable year. Therefore, only 10,000 of the 50,000 can be used in 19X2. The balance is carried forward and used in subsequent years. In this example, the balance of 40,000 is used in 19X3, reducing the regular tax liability to 180,000.

As shown in Exhibit 7-9, this corporation has paid no more in taxes over the three-year period than it would have if the AMT did not exist. It did, however, pay the taxes sooner. The AMT credit, which reduces the future regular tax liability by the taxes paid sooner under the AMT, makes the AMT a time value of money penalty. In the example above, the reversal of the credit occurred in two years, but in the real world it may take many years for a corporation to utilize its AMT credits. In fact, many companies in AMT experience several years of increasing minimum tax credits (especially those in a growth mode) before the trend reverses and the credit is utilized.

The AMT negatively impacts the profitability of leasing companies in a very competitive marketplace. Effective tax rates for companies in AMT in excess of 50% can occur. Strategies to pull out of AMT and reduce the tax liability are limited, and generally only help speed up the process, not immediately eliminate the problem. The first strategy adopted by many companies is to stop writing tax leases and begin doing more nontax or money-over-money leases in which tax ownership resides with the lessee. Remember, excess depreciation on personal property is the cause of the preferences that create AMT problems. A second strategy would be to sell the tax leases that are generating the preferences. This strategy will depend on the turnaround point of the existing preferences. Another action the

		Exhibit 7-9 **Tax Comparison**		
	19X1	**19X2**	**19X3**	**Total**
Regular tax	200,000	210,000	220,000	630,000
AMT	250,000	200,000	180,000	630,000

lessor may take is to sell all tax leases as soon as they are originated, which prevents the generation of preferences.

UNEVEN RENTS

Prior to the enactment in 1984 of the uneven rent limitations codified in IRC §467, it was very common for an accrual basis lessor and a cash basis lessee (or vice versa) to enter into a stepped payment lease in which the payments either increased or decreased over the lease term. Such arrangements created substantial timing differences in the payment of taxes. For example, in a step-up lease (in which the payments increase), a cash basis lessor could defer taxation of income by recognizing the lower payments up front, whereas an accrual basis lessee, in the same transaction, could take current deductions based on a straight-line lease payment approach.

The uneven rent limitation, in an effort to restrict the scope for taxpayers to play these types of deferral games, consists of a series of rules placing lessors and lessees on an accrual basis regarding most leases. It also requires the use of present value principles for those lease transactions affected. TRA 86, however, required all corporations to use the accrual method of accounting for tax purposes, somewhat limiting the applicability of the uneven rent rules. (An exception was provided for corporations with average annual gross receipts of less than 5 million.)

Applicable Leases

Even if a lease agreement meets the definition set forth below, it will not be subject to the uneven rent limitation if the value of all consideration (including rental payments) received by the lessor for the use of the property does not exceed 250,000. The §467 limitation applies to what are termed §467 rental agreements, i.e., any rental agreement for the use of tangible property in which:

1. At least one payment allocable to the use of property during a calendar year is to be paid after the close of the calendar year following the calendar year in which such use occurs

2. There are increases or decreases in the amount to be paid as rent under the agreement.

Criterion 1 addresses a blatant attempt to defer inclusion of rent whereas

Criterion 2 addresses stepped payment leases. In order to illustrate Criterion 1, assume that AC Corporation leases a computer to DC Company in September 19X1 for a 36-month term. The lease agreement requires lease payments to be paid for the months of September and October of 19X1, although they are not required to be paid by DC until August of 19X3. Because the September and October payments are not required to be paid until after 19X2, which is the calendar year following the calendar year of use, the lease is a §467 rental agreement.

Application of the Rules

Irrespective of receipt, the lessor must include two items in income each year (for which the lessee obtains a corresponding deduction):

1. Accrued rent

2. Interest on previously accrued rent that remains unpaid (calculated at 110% of the applicable federal rate, compounded semi-annually).

Except as provided below, accrued rent consists of the amount allocated under the lease to the taxable year, plus the present value of any consideration to be paid after the end of the lease period to which it relates. Interest on previously accrued rent that remains unpaid imposes an additional penalty on the lessor and applies present value principles to the accrued rent concept.

For example, assume a lessor and lessee have entered into a five-year lease that is deemed to be a §467 rental agreement. The lease calls for annual payments, in advance, of 40,000, 50,000, 60,000, 70,000 and 80,000 and a 50,000 payment at lease termination. If the present value of the 50,000 payment due at lease termination is 28,000 (using as the discount rate the applicable federal rate under §1274(d)), the lessor will have to include 45,600 as lease revenue for year one [40,000 + (28,000 ÷ 5)]. This inclusion is the amount allocated under the lease to year one (40,000), together with the pro rata portion of the present value of the 50,000 lease termination payment (5,600). If the additional 5,600 is not paid by the end of year two, the lessor must include 698.10 of interest income for year two (assuming the applicable federal rate is 11%). In addition, the lessor will have 55,600 of rent income [50,000 + (28,000 ÷ 5)] due in that year.

RENT LEVELING

Accrued rent has a different and more restrictive meaning in certain cases. Accrued rent is equal to a pro rata share of the present value of the total lease consideration in two circumstances: (1) when tax avoidance is a principal purpose of the structure of the transaction, and (2) when either (a) the lease agreement does not allocate the payments, e.g., the agreement simply provides for a lump sum payment at some point during the term of the lease, or (b) the lease is a disqualified leaseback or a long-term agreement. Accrued rent as defined in this fashion results in what is referred to as rent leveling.

A disqualified leaseback is a lease to any person who had an interest in the property at any time within two years prior to the lease. Therefore, all traditional sale-leaseback transactions constitute disqualified leasebacks. A long-term lease is a lease with a term in excess of 75% of the MACRS recovery period, i.e., for 3-year property the lease term must be greater than 27 months; for 5-year property the lease term must be greater than 45 months, etc. Therefore, a large percentage of leases in the marketplace are long-term, as defined under the uneven rent rules.

Consequently, the key ingredient is the definition of a tax avoidance purpose, a concept that Congress left vague and ambiguous. The Committee Reports do indicate, however, two situations in which a tax avoidance purpose is most likely. The first is when one of the parties to the lease is a high bracket taxpayer and the other is a low bracket taxpayer. The second occurs when a tax-exempt entity is sandwiched between the lessor and the lessee. Both of these situations give rise to the potential for tax deferral abuse and will be scrutinized closely by the IRS.

Congress instructed the IRS to issue regulations defining with more specificity the meaning of tax avoidance purpose in this context. In addition, the IRS was instructed to incorporate certain specified allowances, such as changes in lease payments, that are tied to the Consumer Price Index, lease payments based on the lessee's receipts or similar amounts, reasonable rent holidays (not to exceed 12 months generally, and in no event more than 24 months) and changes in lease payments based on changes in amounts paid to unrelated parties. Those situations constitute exceptions to the meaning of tax avoidance purpose.

RECAPTURE

If the lease is a disqualified leaseback or a long-term lease, but there is no tax avoidance purpose (so that rent leveling is not required), the lessor is subject to recapture upon its disposition of the property. The purpose of this recapture provision is to prevent the recharacterization of what should be ordinary income into capital gain income.

The recapture amount (which constitutes ordinary income) is the difference between the amount that would have been accrued under rent leveling and the amount that was actually accrued. The recapture amount is limited to gain realized on the disposition (which is reduced by the recapture required under §1245 and §1250).

Assume, for example, that a computer is leased for four years, and the annual payments, in advance, are 30,000, 60,000, 90,000 and 120,000. If the present value of the total lease payments is 240,730, under rent leveling the lessor would have to recognize 60,182.50 of rental income in year one, even though it actually received only 30,000. If no tax avoidance purpose existed, however, and if the lessor sold the computer at the end of year three for 15,000 when its adjusted basis was 12,600, the amount of the §467 recapture would be zero, calculated as follows.

First, the difference between the rent leveling inclusion and the actual inclusion must be determined. Under rent leveling, the inclusion in the first three years of the lease would have been 180,547.50. The lessor actually included 180,000. The difference, therefore, is 547.50. Consequently, the maximum recapture under §467 is 547.50.

Second, §467 recapture is limited to the gain realized on the sale, which gain is reduced by any recapture required under §1245 or §1250. The gain realized on the sale is 2,400 (15,000 - 12,600), all of which must be recaptured under §1245. Therefore, no recapture is required under §467.

AT-RISK PROVISIONS

Originally enacted with the Tax Reform Act of 1976, the at-risk rules of §465 are designed to limit the deductibility of losses arising from the activities of certain taxpayers to the amount the taxpayer has at-risk in the activity (i.e., the amount the taxpayer may lose by virtue of participating in the activity). These rules have been expanded over the years to apply to virtually all activities, the availability of ITC and, most recently, real estate. The original abuse sought to be curbed by Congress, however, was the common taxpayer practice of purchasing equipment with little or no down payment and a nonrecourse loan, and then depreciating and deducting other expenses relating to the asset based on its full purchase price.

Affected Taxpayers

A limitation on certain taxpayers with regard to the deductibility of losses arising in connection with trade or business or income producing activities is imposed by §465. The rules apply to individuals, partnerships, S corporations and closely-held C corporations (i.e., a corporation in which more than 50% of the value of the outstanding stock of the corporation is owned, directly or indirectly, at any time during the last half of the taxable year, by or for not more than five individuals). Those taxpayers were the greatest abusers in this area, as perceived by Congress. Therefore, regular C corporations are exempt from the provisions.

Notwithstanding the general applicability of the at-risk rules to closely-held corporations, those actively engaged in equipment leasing are excluded from the purview of §465. Both the terms "actively engaged" and "equipment leasing," however, have very specific meanings. For purposes of the exclusion from the at-risk rules, equipment leasing is defined as the leasing of §1245 property and the purchasing, servicing and selling of such equipment. In general, a corporation is actively engaged in equipment leasing, for purposes of the §465 exclusion, if at least 50% of the corporation's gross receipts for the taxable year is attributable to equipment leasing.

The component members of a controlled group of corporations generally are treated as a single corporation for purposes of the actively engaged in equipment leasing test. It often is impossible, therefore, for a controlled group to meet the 50% test. To address that problem, if members of the controlled group constitute a qualified leasing group, the rules required to meet the exception are applied at that level, although these rules are more restrictive than the general 50% test.

A qualified leasing group is a controlled group of corporations that, for the current taxable year and each of the two immediately preceding taxable years, satisfies the following requirements:

1. During the entire year the group had at least three full-time employees, substantially all of whose services were directly related to the equipment leasing activity of the qualified leasing members

2. During the year, the qualified leasing members (in the aggregate) entered into at least five separate equipment leasing transactions.

A qualified leasing member refers to a component member of the controlled group that, for each of the three taxable years referred to above, derives at least 80% of its gross receipts from equipment leasing activities.

In summary, for a controlled group of closely-held corporations to qualify for the equipment leasing exception to the application of §465, the gross receipts test is increased to 80% and the group must have at least three full-time employees and have entered into at least five separate equipment leasing transactions for the current taxable year as well as the two preceding taxable years.

Limitations

The following are the limitations that apply to affected taxpayers under §465.

LOSS

Losses are deductible for a taxable year only to the extent of the taxpayer's at-risk amount at the close of the taxable year. The definition of a loss is the excess of allowable deductions for the taxable year over the income received or accrued by the taxpayer during the taxable year. In the typical equipment leasing transaction the loss is the excess of MACRS and interest deductions over lease revenue. Nondeductible losses may be carried forward indefinitely and deducted when the amount at-risk increases sufficiently.

AMOUNTS AT-RISK

The amount the taxpayer is at-risk is the amount of money and the adjusted basis of other property (not to exceed its fair market value net of encumbrances) contributed by the taxpayer to the activity. The at-risk amount also includes amounts borrowed for use in the activity for which the taxpayer is personally liable for repayment or has pledged property, other than property used in such activity, as security for repayment. Such pledged property must have a fair market value net of encumbrances at least equal to the loan amount. In general, therefore, equity and recourse debt constitute amounts at-risk.

Any amounts borrowed from a person who has an interest in the activity, or from a person related to a person (other than the taxpayer) having such an interest, are not considered at-risk. Borrowing from a partner in the activity, even on a full recourse basis, will not provide an at-risk basis.

Borrowing from a person who has an interest in the activity solely as a creditor, however, does not jeopardize the at-risk status of the loan. A corporation that borrows from one of its shareholders, for example, does not tarnish the at-risk status. A lender has an interest other than as a creditor only if the lender has either a capital or net profits interest in the activity. A capital interest is an interest in the assets of the activity that is distributable to the owner of the capital interest upon the liquidation of the activity. Partners of a partnership and shareholders of a corporation, for example, have capital interests.

The definition of an interest in net profits is a little more elusive. It is not necessary for a person to have any incidents of ownership in the activity (such as a capital interest) to have an interest in net profits. An employee or independent contractor, any part of whose compensation is determined with reference to the net profits of the activity, is considered to have an interest in the net profits of the activity.

Applicable Activities

When §465 was first enacted as part of the Tax Reform Act of 1976, it was directed primarily at motion films and videotapes, farming, oil, gas and geothermal exploration and equipment leasing. Since that time, it has been expanded to include each activity engaged in by a taxpayer in carrying on a trade or business or for the production of income, including the holding of real property. To make things even more complex, §465 is generally applied separately to each film or videotape, each farm, each oil and gas property, each geothermal property, each equipment lease, etc. Therefore, except as noted below, the at-risk rules are applied separately to each equipment lease transaction.

Fortunately, all activities with respect to §1245 properties leased or held for lease by a partnership or S corporation, and placed in service in any taxable year of the partnership or corporation, are treated as a single activity. In addition, if the applicable activities constitute a trade or business, the taxpayer actively participates in the management of the trade or business or the trade or business is carried on by a partnership or S corporation and at least

65% of the losses for the taxable year is allocable to persons who actively participate in the management of the trade or business, the trade or business shall be treated as one activity and §465 shall be applied to the entire activity.

PASSIVE LOSSES

The focus of this chapter is on the federal income tax limitations of equipment leasing as they apply to corporations. The passive loss limitation rules, however, have a pervasive effect on the industry's equity marketplace, so it is important to become familiar with their application. These rules limit the ability of individual taxpayers to utilize tax benefits arising from certain activities to reduce their salary and portfolio income. Since 1976 and the enactment of the at-risk rules, there has been a systematic curtailment of available tax deferral loopholes. This curtailment is the result of an emerging policy position within the government that tax benefits can add to the attractiveness of an investment; however, they should not be the primary incentive to enter into the transaction. The passive loss rules shift the emphasis (at least for the taxpayers affected) of an investment from the tax benefits to the economic merits.

Affected Taxpayers

The passive loss limitation rules, codified as §469 of the IRC, apply generally to individuals, estates, trusts and personal service corporations. The rules also apply to partners and to shareholders in S corporations. For purposes of these rules, a personal service corporation is one in which the principal activity is the performance of personal services substantially carried out by owner-employees, i.e., any employee who owns any of the outstanding stock of the corporation. In addition, to a more limited extent as discussed below, the passive loss rules apply to closely-held corporations, i.e., corporations with respect to which at least 50% of the outstanding stock is owned at any time during the last half of the taxable year by or for not more than five individuals.

Application of the Rules

For affected taxpayers, the passive loss rules establish three different types of income and losses: active or trade or business income, portfolio income and passive income. The first category consists of salary, wages and income from general business pursuits in which the taxpayer materially participates in the income earning activity. It is the catch-all category, i.e., if it is not portfolio income or passive income, it is active or trade or business income, and as such, is the broadest of the three categories.

Portfolio income, as the name implies, consists of interest, dividends, royalties, annuities and gain or loss from the sale or exchange of portfolio assets. Portfolio income retains its character, even if it is generated in connection with a passive activity.

The third category, passive income, is any activity that involves the conduct of a trade or business and in which the taxpayer does not materially participate. It also includes any rental activity in which payments are primarily for the use of tangible property, which conclusively includes equipment leasing. Material participation is defined as involvement by the taxpayer in the activity on a regular, continuous and substantial basis. Although there is certainly some gray area in this definition, the most commonly encountered investment vehicle for which the law conclusively presumes material participation not to exist is a limited partnership. Therefore, all losses generated in connection with limited partnership interests are passive losses.

LIMITATION

The third category, of course, is the primary focus of this section and provides a challenge for taxpayers and sellers of investments alike. For all affected taxpayers other than closely-held corporations, losses from passive activities cannot be used to offset income generated in either the active or portfolio categories. Instead, passive activity losses can be used to offset income only from passive activities. The rule is not applied on an activity-by-activity basis; passive activities are viewed in the aggregate. Therefore, a passive activity loss is the amount by which the aggregate losses from all passive activities for the taxable year exceed the aggregate income from all passive activities for such year.

For closely-held corporations, passive activity losses can be used to offset passive income as well as trade or business income. The only restriction is that passive losses of a closely-held corporation cannot be used to offset portfolio income. Disallowed passive losses are not lost; they are carried forward indefinitely until usable. Upon disposition by the taxpayer of its entire interest in a passive activity, allowance of all theretofore suspended passive losses attributable to that activity is triggered.

To the extent that any loss recognized on the disposition is from the sale or exchange of a capital asset, the capital loss limitation is applied before the passive loss allowance, i.e., the suspended passive loss is limited to the amount of gains from the sales or exchanges of capital assets plus 3,000.

The intended and general effect of the passive loss rules is to mitigate the ability of taxpayers to defer income taxes through the use of investments generating tax losses in their early years. However, as is always the case when the tax rates are anything above insignificant, taxpayers attempt to find methods to utilize restrictions and limitations to their benefit.

With respect to the passive loss rules, one such method involves the purchase by a taxpayer (who has passive investments generating nondeductible losses) of investments that generate passive gains, so as to maximize the benefit of the otherwise suspended passive losses. Conversely, taxpayers whose passive investments are now in the phantom income stage can purchase passive investments that generate losses. These losses can offset income that would otherwise create current tax liability. There is, therefore, still some scope for tax deferral. However, the limitations to tax deferral created over the past several years by Congress (of which the passive loss rules are the capstone) make deferral too complex or burdensome for many taxpayers to pursue.

RENTAL REAL ESTATE EXCEPTION

To provide some relief for the middle income taxpayer, Congress created a small exception to the blanket application of the passive loss rules: up to 25,000 of losses and credits arising from the ownership and rental of real property can be used to offset the nonpassive income of the taxpayer. The Tax Reform Act of 1993 carved out an exception to the rule that provides that all rental activities are passive activities. Rental real estate activities will still be treated as passive unless the taxpayer materially participates in them. If material participation is shown, the activity will be nonpassive and losses will therefore be able to offset other nonpassive income. Material participation occurs if:

1. More than half of the personal services performed by the taxpayer in trades or businesses during the year are performed in real property trades or businesses in which the taxpayer materially participates

2. The taxpayer performs more than 750 hours of service during the tax year in real property trades or businesses in which the taxpayer materially participates.

Material participation has the same meaning as previously discussed.

CONCLUSION

Many of the issues discussed in this chapter affect the way leasing companies do business and, more specifically, the lease products offered. The tax limitations that exist within the IRC, for the most part, affect the timing of the various tax benefits currently allowed. For lessors, this leads to a direct impact on the pricing of the lease transaction. An understanding, therefore, of these limitations is critical to the overall success of leasing companies. Unfortunately, the rules continue to change and evolve as Congress addresses the many needs of the country. Remaining current with respect to these changes often requires lessors to rely on their own independent tax counsel to resolve the specific and myriad issues that arise in this fascinating and challenging industry.

Chapter Eight

State and Local Taxes

State and local tax issues, in addition to the federal income taxes previously discussed, can affect the equipment leasing transaction. Furthermore, state and local taxes differ from state to state in both structure and rates. Problems of multiple taxation can arise because of state-to-state variations, particularly with apportionment and allocation of business income. Furthermore, some local governmental units impose miscellaneous business license, rental receipt or similar taxes.

The more salient state and local taxes are discussed in this chapter:

- Franchise and Income Taxes

- Sales Tax

- Personal Property Taxes.

FRANCHISE AND INCOME TAXES

Income taxes (and franchise taxes measured by net income) generally may be viewed as the state analog of the federal income tax. These taxes are levied by states upon businesses that do business in, or derive income from, sources within the state. The taxes are imposed on corporations (or other entities) incorporated within the state, on foreign (including other state) corporations qualified to do business within the state and on foreign corporations deriving income from property or operations within the state.

Income taxes are measured by net income, which typically is defined by reference to the federal income tax, with certain modifications. These modifications include special state tax benefits not available under the federal system as well as disadvantages such as less favorable depreciation allowances or denial, in whole or in part, of net operating loss carryovers.

Some states impose a franchise tax not measured by net income in addition to taxes based on net income. A franchise tax often consists of an annual fee imposed on corporations chartered or qualified to do business in the state. It also may refer to a tax on capital, similar to a capital stock tax in which the capital of the corporation employed in the state is subject to tax. This type of franchise tax is in the nature of a fee or ad valorem tax.

Tax Structure

In analyzing the applicability of a state income tax (or franchise tax measured by net income) to a lease transaction, two fundamental questions are relevant: (1) does the state have the power (or jurisdiction) to impose an income tax and (2) what amount of income is subject to tax? Generally these questions are most relevant to taxpayers located outside the state seeking to impose the tax.

AUTHORITY TO TAX

The first question involves a determination of whether the taxpayer has sufficient connection (or nexus) with the taxing state to support the imposition of the tax. The primary restrictions upon each state's power to impose taxes on out-of-state taxpayers are contained in the Commerce Clause and Due Process Clause of the U.S. Constitution.

The issues under the Commerce Clause are whether the state's taxing activity unreasonably interferes with interstate commerce, which is an area reserved for regulation by the federal government. For example, Congress decided in Public Law 86-272 (discussed below) that certain sales promotion activities conducted by an out-of-state taxpayer could not form the basis for the imposition of a state net income tax. A more difficult situation arises when no precise federal legislation is in existence but the effect of a state tax on interstate commerce must be determined under general constitutional principles relating to the Commerce Clause.

The issue under the Due Process Clause is whether the imposition of the state income tax meets minimum constitutional standards of fairness. The resolution of this issue requires a balancing of the constitutional rights of the parties involved, including an evaluation of many factors such as the taxpayer's activities in the state, the amount of tax burden imposed and the benefits derived by the taxpayer.

To support the imposition of a net income tax, the courts have indicated that the taxpayer must have some physical presence in the state, such as property or personnel. The recent case of *Geoffrey, Inc. v. South Carolina Tax Commissioner* (discussed below) has raised the issue of whether intangible property located in a state can provide sufficient nexus for an income tax. (Taxable nexus for an income tax can differ from taxable nexus for another tax, such as sales tax.)

AMOUNT OF TAX

The second question, the amount of income properly taxable, arises only after it is determined that a taxpayer is subject to tax. This second question is most acute for taxpayers subject to tax in more than one state. When a corporation or other taxpayer has income from sources both within and outside the state, the income must be allocated or apportioned to sources within and outside the state.

This division of income can be accomplished in a variety of ways, such as separate accounting, formula apportionment and specific allocation. About half the states follow the Uniform Division of Income for Tax Purposes Act (UDITPA), albeit with some modifications on a state-by-state basis. This model act, the result of the Multistate Tax Compact (the Compact), provides a uniform statutory framework for the multijurisdictional state taxation of income.

Under UDITPA, income is classified into either business income or non-business income. Business income is apportioned to sources within and outside the state by application of a three-factor formula consisting of property, payroll and sales (or gross receipts). A typical three-factor formula is:

$$\text{State apportionment factor} = 1/3 \left(\frac{\text{State property}}{\text{Total property}} + \frac{\text{State payroll}}{\text{Total payroll}} + \frac{\text{State sales}}{\text{Total sales}} \right)$$

The above formula weights each factor equally (i.e., 1/3 each).

Some states weight the factors differently, for example, by double-weighting the sales factor. Business income generally means income arising from the transactions and activities in the regular course of a taxpayer's trade or business. It includes income from tangible and intangible property if the acquisition, management and disposition of the property constitute integral parts of the taxpayer's trade or business operations.

Unitary Method

Some states require or permit the use of the unitary method in the course of determining a taxpayer's business income. Under the unitary method, the taxpayer and its affiliates are viewed collectively in order to determine the business of the taxpayer. The business may be conducted by one or more taxpayers (not necessarily all the same type of entity) and may comprise all or part of each taxpayer's activities. For example, a taxpayer may have more than one trade or business, one or more of which may be combined, for state tax purposes, with an affiliated taxpayer under the unitary concept.

A taxpayer involved in a unitary business files a combined report with the other entities engaged in the same unitary business. The business income is apportioned according to the method of apportionment adopted by the taxing state, such as the three-factor formula. The tax imposed by the state is then divided among the entities engaged in the business.

The determination of whether a taxpayer is engaged alone or with others in a unitary business is dependent upon the facts and circumstances of each case and the rules of the state regarding the definition of a unitary business. For example, one test of a unitary business is whether the activities of various commonly owned or controlled entities are integrated with, depend upon or contribute to each other and their operations as a whole. In a circumstance such as this, the activities of the various entities constitute a single business.

A second test provides that, if there is (1) unity of ownership (e.g., more than 50% common ownership directly or indirectly), (2) unity of operation (e.g., centralized purchasing, accounting or advertising) and (3) unity of management (e.g., common executive officers or systems of management) among various entities, their activities constitute a single business.

A final test seeks to determine whether there is a flow of goods or value between the entities in the conduct of a single business. These tests have been established judicially and are not mutually exclusive (i.e., failing one test and meeting another results in unitary taxation). They have been incorporated into the administrative schemes of states permitting the unitary method.

Unitary taxation has been the subject of several legal challenges over the past 20 years. The U.S. Supreme Court has ruled that the unitary method, whether applied to a group of corporations (including foreign operations) with a domestic (U.S.) parent or with a foreign (other nation) parent, is constitutionally permissible. These rulings as well as extensive discussions from a legal perspective of the unitary method are contained in *Container Corporation of America v. Franchise Tax Board of California,* 463 U.S. 159 (1983); *Barclays Bank PLC v. Franchise Tax Board of California,* U.S. 114 S. Ct. 2268 (1994) and *Colgate-Palmolive Company v. Franchise Tax Board of California,* U.S. 114 S. Ct. 2268 (1994).

During the last 10 years many states that had a worldwide unitary system of income taxation modified their laws to eliminate or make elective for the taxpayer the inclusion of foreign (i.e., offshore) business operations. In California, a taxpayer may elect to eliminate these offshore businesses from a combined report upon payment of a water's edge election fee.

Multistate Tax Compact

The Compact was formed to mitigate the incongruities between the income tax systems of the various states and to address the problems, such as double taxation, associated with them. The Compact consists of a group of 20 member states and 12 associate member states. UDITPA, as developed by the Compact, provides that any multistate taxpayer can, at its option, elect to use the uniform act for making allocations and apportionment of income among the party states. Each state also retains its existing division of income provisions but is required to make UDITPA available to any taxpayer desiring to use it. In this way, a taxpayer achieves multijurisdictional uniformity among the states adopting UDITPA.

Many of the Compact's provisions are self-executing, but some provisions require administration or other further activity, such as research. For these purposes, the Compact established the Multistate Tax Commission (MTC), composed of representatives from the party states that have responsibility for multistate tax matters. The MTC has undertaken a number of projects including recommended interpretive regulations for UDITPA for both regular business corporations and financial institutions. Exhibit 8-1 lists each state and shows whether it has adopted UDITPA and the MTC interpretive regulations and whether it apportions income.

Nexus

The location within a state of an out-of-state taxpayers' tangible property generally affords sufficient nexus for a state to impose a net income tax on that taxpayer. The presence of tangible property gives the taxpayer a physical presence within the state. In the context of equipment leasing, the lessor of equipment (which by definition is tangible property) pursuant to an operating lease will be regarded as the owner of the property.

OPERATING LEASES

Operating leases can be illustrated by the case of *American Refrigerator Transit Company v. State Tax Commissioner of Oregon*. A non-Oregon corporation owned railroad refrigerator cars and leased them to various operating railroads, which used them in their own transportation business. The taxpayer had no lease agreements with railroads operating in Oregon. However, through various interchange arrangements between railroads, some of the taxpayer's equipment was used in Oregon by railroads operating in Oregon. The taxpayer had paid Oregon property tax on the value of its railroad cars, prorated for the amount of usage in the state. The Oregon Tax Commission assessed the non-Oregon owner income tax on the basis that payments received by the taxpayer with respect to the Oregon usage were income from tangible property located in the state (and, therefore, were income derived from sources within the state). The taxpayer claimed that Oregon lacked jurisdiction because of insufficient nexus for an income tax.

The Oregon Supreme Court upheld the tax with the following explanation.

> *To establish nexus it is necessary to show that the taxpayer has, in the conduct of his business, taken advantage of the economy of the taxing state to produce the income which is subjected to tax. This is readily seen, where, as in the instant case, the taxpayer's property itself is employed in the taxing state to produce income.*

Once nexus is established, such as through leased equipment located within the state (even for part of the time), the amount of income taxable by the state is determined by rules concerning division of income (such as UDIT-PA) and not by the nexus rules. It is not unusual to find that the value of tangible property located with the taxing state is one of the factors used in determining the amount of income taxable by the state.

CAPITAL LEASES

In *Geoffrey, Inc. v. South Carolina Tax Commissioner,* 126 L.Ed. 2d 451, U.S. 114 S. Ct. 550 (1993), a Delaware corporation (Geoffrey) with no physical presence in South Carolina licensed a trademark ("Toys R Us") to a company doing business in South Carolina and other states. The company used the trademark in the course of its business operations. Geoffrey had no operations in South Carolina or any other state and its business consisted strictly of holding and licensing intangibles to other (affiliated) companies.

The South Carolina trial court and Supreme Court held that Geoffrey was subject to income tax in South Carolina. The U.S. Supreme Court declined to review the decision. The state courts cited a variety of grounds for their decision, chiefly market exploitation by Geoffrey, which created taxable nexus for state income tax purposes (as distinguished from sales tax purpose, which was the subject of *Quill Corporation v. North Dakota*).

However, an alternative basis for the rulings of the South Carolina courts was that taxable nexus for purpose of the income tax was created by the presence of Geoffrey's intangible property, the "Toys R Us" trademark, within the state and of the accompanying account receivable due from the licensee to Geoffrey for use of the trademark. Although noting that intangible property, such as trademarks and accounts receivable, normally has its situs or location at the domicile of the owner of the property "until that property has been integrated with an activity carried on in another state," the South Carolina trial court determined (at page 15 of the Final Order of the Trial Court) that Geoffrey's intangible property had acquired a situs in South Carolina because :

> . . . *it is clear that the income is earned in South Carolina . . . [and the] license is in South Carolina since it is integrated with the business carried on here. The same is true with the debts receivable by [Geoffrey] from . . . [the licensee]. Those debts are created solely as a result of the license agreement. The debt is just as integral to the activities in South Carolina as is the license agreement. In short, the intangibles are integrated with the royalty producing activity in South Carolina.*

Exhibit 8-1
Adoption of UDITPA

State	UDITPA adopted	MTC business income regulations adopted	Apportionable income
Alabama	Yes (foreign corporations only)	Similar provisions	Business income
Alaska	Yes	Yes	Business income
Arizona	Yes	No	Business income
Arkansas	Yes	Similar provisions	Business income
California	Yes	Yes	Business income
Colorado	Yes (optional)	Yes	Business income
Connecticut	No (similar provisions)	No	All income
Delaware	No (similar provisions)	No	All income (except income specifically allocated)
District of Columbia	No (similar provisions)	No	Business income
Florida	Yes	Similar provisions	Business income
Georgia	No (similar provisions)	No	Business income
Hawaii	Yes (optional)	No	Business income
Idaho	Yes	Yes	Business income
Illinois	Yes	Similar provisions	Business income
Indiana	No (similar provisions)	Similar provisions	Business income
Iowa	No (similar provisions)	Similar provisions	Business income
Kansas	Yes	Yes	Business income
Kentucky	Yes	Similar provisions	Business income
Louisiana	No (some similar provisions)	No	All income
Maine	No	No	All income
Maryland	No	No	All income
Massachusetts	Yes	No	All income
Michigan	Yes	No	All income
Minnesota	No	No	Business income
Mississippi	No	No	Business income
Missouri	Yes (optional)	Yes	Business income
Montana	Yes	Yes	Business income

Exhibit 8-1 (continued)
Adoption of UDITPA

State	UDITPA adopted	MTC business income regulations adopted	Apportionable income
Nebraska	No	No	All income
Nevada	No corporate tax	N/A	N/A
New Hampshire	No (similar provisions)	No	All income
New Jersey	No	No	All income
New Mexico	Yes	Similar provisions	Business income
New York	No	No	All income (except income specifically allocated)
North Carolina	No (similar provisions)	Similar provisions	Business income
North Dakota	Yes	Yes	Business income
Ohio	No (similar provisions)	No	All income (except income specifically allocated)
Oklahoma	No	No	All income (except income specifically allocated)
Oregon	Yes	Yes	Business income
Pennsylvania	Yes	No	Business income
Rhode Island	No	No	All income
South Carolina	No	No	Business income
South Dakota	No corporate tax	N/A	N/A
Tennessee	Yes	Similar provisions (with some differences)	Business income
Texas	No	No	Business income
Utah	Yes	Similar provisions	Business income
Vermont	No	No	Business income
Virginia	No	No	All income (except dividends)
Washington	No corporate tax	N/A	N/A
West Virginia	No	Similar provisions	Business income
Wisconsin	Yes	No	All income (except income specifically allocated)
Wyoming	No corporate tax	N/A	N/A

The South Carolina Supreme Court affirmed the trial court's decision.

The South Carolina decisions rejected a number of conventional rules:

1. An intangible asset is located at the owner's commercial domicile. The South Carolina courts ruled that intangible property is located everywhere it is used

2. An account receivable is located at the commercial domicile of either the creditor or the debtor. The South Carolina courts ruled that accounts receivable are wherever the underlying transactions occurred

3. A taxpayer must have physical presence in a state in order to be subject to that state's net income tax. The South Carolina Courts ruled that the presence of an intangible asset, under their interpretation of "presence," was a sufficient nexus.

The absence of substantive U.S. Supreme Court review has caused considerable uncertainties in this area. The potential applications of *Geoffrey* to finance leases that are the equivalent of a secured loan are of particular concern.

Several states have responded to *Geoffrey*. In California, where an operating entity and a nonoperating entity holding intangibles are part of a unitary group, no change is likely. In Florida, the corporate regulations may be revised (by proposed rule 12C-1.-011) such that the sale or licensing of intangibles will create taxable nexus. In Massachusetts, the state tax authority has indicated informally that it will not follow *Geoffrey*.

Other legislation that would prohibit the deduction of licensing fees for intangibles to Delaware corporations has been proposed. In New York, the "physical presence" rule will be followed but the state can require a combined return of an operating affiliate doing business in New York with a nonoperating affiliate owning intangibles used in the business. The MTC has recommended a review to establish the appropriateness of the establishment of a de minimus rule. The MTC's draft regulations for apportionment of income of financial institutions do not address economic nexus.

PUBLIC LAW 86-272

Public Law 86-272 was enacted by the U.S. Congress and became law in 1959. This law was passed in response to the decisions of the U.S. Supreme Court in *Williams v. Stockham Valves and Fittings, Inc.,* 358 U.S. 450 (1959) and *Northwestern States Portland Cement Co. v. Minnesota,* 358- U.S. 450 (1959). These cases held that states had broad jurisdiction to impose income taxes on foreign (other state) corporations even though their activities within the taxing states occurred exclusively in the course of interstate commerce.

In Public Law 86-272, the federal government prohibits states and their political subdivisions from imposing or collecting a net income tax on income derived within those states by a taxpayer from interstate commerce, provided that the only business activities within those states by, or on behalf of, the taxpayer are either or both of the following:

1. The solicitation of orders, by the taxpayer's employees or other representatives, which are (a) for the sale of tangible personal property, (b) sent out-of-state for approval and (c), if approved, filled by shipment or delivery from out-of-state

2. The solicitation of orders by employees or other representatives of the taxpayer in the state in the name of, or for the benefit of, a customer of the taxpayer, and the orders by the customer to the taxpayer are orders of the nature described in 1.

The prohibition of Public Law 86-272 also applies to the solicitation of orders through a sales office within the state maintained by independent contractors.

Some states have issued their own interpretations of Public Law 86-272 and under some of these interpretations any activity (such as inspecting equipment) in excess of the statutorily described solicitations can result in a state determination of tax liability.

Public Law 86-272 creates situations in which an out-of-state taxpayer having taxable nexus with a state is not taxable in that state. In these situations, many states apply as part of their apportionment mechanism a so-called throwback or throwout rules. These rules are intended to result in redirecting the income that has escaped taxation to a state with nexus that taxes the income. The throwback rule redirects the untaxed income to a particular states, such as the taxpayer's commercial domicile. The throwout rule redirects the untaxed income ratably to all states in which the taxpayer pays tax by eliminating from the numerator and denominator of the three-factor (or other) apportionment formula the factors in the nontaxable state.

In states applying the unitary method, Public Law 86-272 can have important consequences. If a corporation included in a combined report has activity that cannot be taxed in a state because of the prohibitions of Public Law 86-272, but has sales or payroll factors in the state, the three-factor apportionment formula will attribute income from that activity to the corporation that has sales or payroll factors. Some states applying the unitary method, such as California, now take the position that, if another member of the unitary group is taxable in the state, the sales and payroll factors of the nontaxable corporation will be included in the state's factors in apportioning the entire group's income. This position results in taxation, through another member of the group, of income attributed to the nontaxable corporation. In this way, use of throwback or the throwout rules can be obviated.

Miscellaneous Issues

Several miscellaneous issues may apply to the net income taxes of certain states. These other issues are discussed in this section.

TAX STATUS

Many states distinguish, for income tax purposes, between regular business corporations and financial intermediaries, such as banking corporations. This distinction results in a tax scheme different for financial intermediaries than for regular business corporations. The differences can range from special rules regarding allocation and apportionment of income to special tax rates for financial intermediaries. At one time, some states observed nexus standards for out-of-state banks that were different from the nexus standards applied to regular business corporations.

In some states, a financial intermediary may be required to pay tax at a rate higher than a regular business corporation. In exchange for a higher income tax rate, the financial intermediary may be relieved of a variety of other state and local taxes such as tax on personal (but, perhaps, not real) property. Such is the case in California. Corporations whose principal activity is the leasing of property generally do not qualify for the special bank rate in California, unless their activity is part of a unitary business that would so qualify.

The bank rate can be a benefit to a business, including equipment leasing, if taxable income is not generated. In these cases, the business is shielded by the bank rate from the more regressive local taxes, which typically apply whether or not taxable income exists. On the other hand, if taxable income is generated, the taxpayer pays income tax at the higher bank rate, which may be an adequate offset for relief from other taxes or may be a burden. For example, if a taxpayer subject to the bank rate leases property located in another state (or leases property through an affiliate located in another state), it may be subject to lower personal property taxes in the other state and have no need for the relief from local taxes provided by the bank rate.

When regular businesses and financial intermediaries file a combined return in a state following the unitary method, issues can arise concerning dividing the income apportioned to the state between the regular business corporation and the financial intermediary. The financial intermediary will pay tax at a higher rate in those states in which a special higher bank rate applies.

Lastly, the MTC published "Recommended Formula for the Apportionment and Allocation of Net Income of Financial Institutions," on November 17, 1994. Generally, these regulations recognize that financial institutions deal in money and money equivalents and that special apportionment rules are needed to reflect income fairly. These draft regulations do not contain a definition of financial institutions and let each state provide its own definition.

The MTC regulations contain various rules pertinent to equipment leasing. For example, "tangible personal property owned" means property (1) on which the financial institution claims depreciation for federal income tax purposes or (2) to which the financial institution holds legal title and for which no other person may claim depreciation for federal income tax purposes. The receipts factor of the three-factor apportionment formula includes receipts from the rental of tangible personal property owned by the financial institution, if the property is located within the state when it is first placed in service by the lessee. There are special rules for prorating the use of transportation property.

MODIFICATIONS FOR DEPRECIATION

One feature of the federal income tax that typically is modified for states that base their income tax systems on the federal income tax is the amount of the allowance for depreciation for property. This allowance generally is granted for obsolescence and wear and tear from the time an item of depreciable property is first placed in service. The allowance continues over the useful life of the item.

The current federal system for depreciation is the Modified Accelerated Cost Recovery System (MACRS), which replaces a former system known as the Accelerated Cost Recovery System (ACRS) and Asset Depreciation Range (ADR).

Many states have adopted the federal system as it currently exists, although the state effective date of the adoption may be later than the effective date of the federal provisions.

For states that have adopted the federal system the following items of federal tax are typical of items that are modified by the states:

1. The effective date of adoption of MACRS. (States have varying dates of adoption)

2. Availability of Internal Revenue Code §179 asset expense rules. (Some states that have adopted MACRS may not have adopted the §179 expense deduction)

3. The type of property subject to depreciation. (States may enlarge or restrict the types of property eligible for depreciation. In some cases, certain types of equipment such as pollution control equipment may require certification from a state pollution control agency to be eligible for state depreciation allowances)

4. The depreciation schedule. (States vary significantly the available depreciation allowance by modifying the rate of depreciation, the useful life of the property or both. For example, a state may adopt the former federal scheme of ADR.)

It is necessary, therefore, to review the depreciation scheme for each state involved in a transaction to determine the depreciation deduction available with respect to the computation of net income for that state.

In addition to depreciation allowances, several states permit tax credits for qualified equipment. Such credits typically are available for solar (or alternative) energy equipment, pollution control equipment and other equipment serving a state's governmental policies.

The depreciation, asset expense and tax credit benefits available in a particular state might be altered if the equipment is located in (or used by a business in) a special economic zone. Frequently, accelerated depreciation, special investment or other tax credits, and other tax benefits are available for activities within such zones. The tax laws of each state involved in a transaction must be considered to determine the availability of these benefits.

Finally, the interplay between liberal depreciation allowances within a state and the availability of net operating loss carryovers is important in planning transactions. The benefits of liberal depreciation allowances can be lost when a resulting tax loss cannot be allowed to be carried forward or back to another taxable year.

APPORTIONMENT: SALES FACTOR

Of the factors in the three-factor apportionment formula (property, payroll and sales or receipts), the application of the sales factor has created the most difficulties in practice. These difficulties occur not only in the area of conventional sales of goods or services but also in the specialized area of financial transactions, such as equipment leasing pursuant to a nonoperating lease.

The inclusion of the sales factor in the formula reflects the notion that income is generated at the location of a transaction producing gross receipts and that it is appropriately measured by the amount of those gross receipts. Sales or those gross receipts for this purpose usually mean all gross receipts of the taxpayer, except for those receipts subject to specific allocation.

The difficulties in applying this factor, which carry over into equipment leasing, arise because there is no established legal principle for determining the location of a sale and no other generally accepted standard for determining a location for a sale. Several competing guidelines are in use by the various states.

One guideline attributes a sale to the state of destination, which is the delivery site. Another guideline attributes a sale to the state of origin, which is the location of the factory, warehouse or other place of appropriation to the order. A third guideline attributes a sale to the state of solicitation, which is the location of the sales office to which the sales personnel are attached or where the sales negotiations occurred.

Within these guidelines, details of particular transactions must be considered to appropriately determine a location for the sale. These complexities are aggravated because the states employ multiple standards for sourcing gross receipts, particularly for nonoperating (capital) leases of equipment. The complexities associated with capital leases occur because the rules for receipts are oriented toward a sales transaction. These rules, therefore, must be applied by analogy to a financing transaction such as a loan or lease.

UDITPA

UDITPA sources sales to the state of destination. It specifically allocates net rents from the use of tangible personal property to the state in which the property is utilized (or, if the taxpayer is not subject to tax in the state of utilization, entirely to the taxpayer's state of commercial domicile). The act does not distinguish between operating leases and nonoperating leases. Furthermore, it does not indicate whether nonoperating leases are to be treated as leases or as some other type of transaction, such as a conditional sale or a secured loan.

As a result of these various sales sourcing rules, it is necessary to review the state's administrative practice with respect to nonoperating equipment leases in order to determine the proper sourcing of gross receipts from the lease for that state. The taxpayer should conduct this review whether the state is a UDITPA state or not. If the state does not follow UDITPA, it will be necessary to ascertain which sourcing standard the state has adopted and then determine how a nonoperating lease is classified within those rules. If the state follows UDITPA, and does not distinguish between operating and nonoperating leases, the lease receipts are sourced to the situs of the equipment. If the state follows UDITPA, but distinguishes between operating and nonoperating leases, the receipts from a nonoperating lease might be sourced in one of two ways.

First, the receipts might be sourced as a loan (such as to the state of servicing or booking, the state of commercial domicile of the creditor or the state of commercial domicile of the debtor). Second, the receipts could be sourced as a conditional sale, which may be treated as a conventional sale and sourced to the destination state.

California Presumptions

California has adopted UDITPA and apportions business income in accordance with the three-factor formula. The sales factor is double-weighted in California. Intangible property generally is excluded from the property factor. UDITPA was not designed to apply to certain specialized industries, such as finance companies, banks and financial institutions, and it contains no special rules for those industries. However, UDITPA contemplates administrative deviations from its statutory formula in appropriate circumstances. Accordingly, California has fashioned variations on the standard apportionment formula for special situations as contemplated by UDITPA.

In the case of finance companies, the California Franchise Tax Board, which administers UDITPA and the state income tax, has used an apportionment formula consisting of three factors: (1) average loans outstanding, (2) payroll and (3) interest earned. Loans outstanding are viewed as analogous to the property factor of UDITPA. Consequently, they are sourced to the situs of the originator or the servicer, depending on the facts and circumstances. The interest earned factor is viewed as analogous to sales in the standard formula and is sourced to the place the loans were solicited.

In the case of financial corporations, the California Franchise Tax Board has developed a three-factor formula that includes intangible property (such as loans) in the property factor and sources property and sales (including interest) on the basis of where the loan (or other transaction) is properly booked for regulatory purposes. This modified formula, with its inclusion of intangibles, tends to produce a result comparable to the standard double-weighted sales formula with origination (rather then destination) sourcing.

Under these rules, for purposes of the property factor, the cost of leased tangible property, such as equipment, is sourced to the state of the taxpayer's (i.e., lessor's) commercial domicile. This sourcing applies unless the taxpayer or the California Franchise Tax Board can establish a location for the property in another state for the entire year and in which the taxpayer is taxable. Also under these rules, for purposes of the sales factor, receipts are sourced to the state to which the underlying intangible is sourced. Thus rental receipts from the lease of tangible property are attributed to the commercial domicile of the taxpayer, unless the lease is attributable elsewhere under the aforementioned rules.

Financial corporation is not defined in the California Revenue and Taxation Code. However, the California Franchise Tax Board has provided a definition in its specialized apportionment rules. A financial corporation is defined as a corporation that predominantly (i.e., more than 50%) deals in money or moneyed capital in substantial competition with some or all lines of business permitted to national banks.

Although the California Revenue and Taxation Code does not specifically define financial corporation, its §23183(b) excludes from the term financial corporation any corporation, including a subsidiary of a bank or bank holding company, the principal business of which consists of leasing tangible personal property. After promulgation of the financial corporation regulations, the California Franchise Tax Board issued its Notice 91-4 in which it determined that the statutory leasing company exclusion was ambiguous because it failed to define leasing as meaning only nonfinance leasing.

The notice interpreted the statute as applying only to nonfinance leasing, with the result that finance lease companies are included in the definition of financial corporation. Because the California Franchise Tax Board thought Notice 91-4 was invalid, erroneous or unworkable (in its definition of finance lease), it issued Legal Ruling 94-2, which withdrew FTB Notice 91-4. This ruling reached the same conclusions as FTB Notice 91-4 as to the need to interpret the term "leasing" in § 23183(b). This ruling also links the definition of finance lease to transactions that are the economic equivalent of extensions of credit within the meaning of Regulation Y of the Federal Reserve Board and that do not constitute leases for federal income tax purposes (i.e., where the lessor is treated as the owner for federal income tax purposes).

A corporation engaged in finance leasing will be presumed by the California Franchise Tax Board to be in substantial competition with the business of national banks if it meets the 50% predominance test of the financial corporation regulations. Accordingly, such a leasing company will be subject to the special apportionment rules discussed above applicable to financial corporations. The presumption can be overcome by showing that national banks are prohibited from engaging in the type of leases used by the taxpayer.

SAFE HARBOR LEASES

Safe harbor leases were created by §168 (f)(8) of the Internal Revenue Code for the period 1982 through 1983. Safe harbor leases were recognized as true leases for purposes of federal income tax law, although the transactions were not required to constitute a lease for commercial law purposes. As a result, safe harbor leases are a special feature of the federal income tax.

For states that base their income tax schemes on the federal statute, one must determine whether the safe harbor provision of the Internal Revenue Code has been adopted, rejected or modified. For jurisdictions that do not base their tax on the Internal Revenue Code, one must determine whether the state or locality has adopted a provision similar to the safe harbor lease rules. States that recognize safe harbor leases include Hawaii, Illinois (with modifications possible if the transaction lacks economic substance, as determined by state tax authorities), Missouri, Ohio and Pennsylvania. California and New York do not recognize safe harbor leases.

In evaluating the state income tax effect of a safe harbor lease, a taxpayer that conducts operations in more than one state, and is subject to apportionment of business income under a three-factor or similar formula, must consider the effect of a safe harbor lease on the application of the formula. For example, from the lessor's perspective, will the deemed rental receipts and property be included in the receipts and property factors, and will interest deemed to be paid on an acquisition note be a deduction from income?

From the lessee's perspective, will the lessee include the property but not the deemed interest on the acquisition note, and will the lessee adjust the basis of its property subject to the lease by the amount of the cash received from the lessor? These issues must be reviewed for each state involved in a leasing transaction in order to properly assess the state income tax effect of the transaction. The state sales and use tax effect and property tax effect may not follow the state income tax treatment.

SALES TAX

Sales taxes are a major source of revenue for states and their political subdivisions. The tax is an excise tax on transactions imposed upon retailers for the privilege of selling tangible personal property at retail within the state. Although the tax generally may not be imposed on the purchaser, the retailer ordinarily passes the tax on to the purchasers. Many states exempt certain transactions from the sales tax, either by exempting the item of property from the tax or by exempting the purchaser from the tax. Some states do not impose sales taxes.

Although the concept of sales tax often is discussed in broad terms, there are typically two taxes: a sales tax (imposed on sellers) and a use tax (imposed on purchasers). Also, generally the sales tax and use tax are complementary such that only one tax applies in transactions that constitute both a sale and a purchase for use. This relationship often is achieved by exempting from use tax any purchases for use in which the sales price has been included in the measure of sales tax or by crediting against the use tax the amount of sales tax paid on the transaction.

The sales tax imposed on retailers is measured by their gross receipts from the sale of tangible personal property. Some states include certain services in the sales tax base. A retail sale generally consists of any sale of tangible personal property other than a sale for resale. The tax applies to certain rental transactions, which are regarded as continuing sales, and to many sales by persons not ordinarily thought of as retailers.

Continuing Sale

In the context of equipment leasing, the lessor generally is viewed as the retail seller and the lessee as the purchaser. Often the acquisition of equipment to be leased by the lessor is a sale-for-resale and, thereby, excluded from the definition of sale and from the imposition of sales tax. The rental to the lessee is regarded as the retail sale and, therefore, subject to tax, often as the lease payments are made (on a continuing sale theory). Some states allow the lessor an option to pay the entire sales tax upon acquisition of the equipment or to pay the tax on a continuing sale basis as rent payments are made. The exercise of a purchase option contained in a lease usually constitutes a sale and is subject to tax at the time of exercise based on the option exercise price.

It is important in evaluating the availability of continuing sale treatment to determine whether a lease transaction meets the definition of a lease for purposes of the state's sales tax law. The definition of lease for sales tax purposes often differs from the definition for state or federal income tax purposes. Certain full payout leases and finance leases constitute present sales with a security arrangement rather than leases (i.e., continuing sales) for sales tax purposes, particularly when there is a purchase option the lessee is likely to exercise (i.e., because it is nominal or because of some other economic compulsion). If a nominal lease transaction is classified as a present sale, the sales tax will be due in its entirety at inception of the transaction.

Generally, the sales tax (or the use tax, if applicable) is collected by the seller and remitted to the state. Sellers "engaged in business" within a state, as defined by the state's sale tax statute, usually are required to hold a seller's license or permit.

Considerable controversy concerns the power of a state to impose a sales tax on an out-of-state seller for sales occurring within the state or to require an out-of-state seller to collect sales or use tax with respect to such sales. Generally, there is no difficulty in determining whether a sale (or a purchase for use) of tangible personal property has occurred within a state for purpose of the sales tax, because the property will be delivered or otherwise located in the state. Public Law 86-272, which prohibits states from imposing a net income tax on out-of-state vendor companies on the basis of sales of tangible personal property sold within the states, does not apply to the sales tax.

Nexus

In 1967, the United States Supreme Court rendered a decision in *National Bellas Hess, Inc. v. Department of Revenue,* 386 U.S. 753, (1967) regarding nexus. It held that an out-of-state mail order company was not required to collect and remit use tax on sales made to Illinois residents when the company's only activity within the state was solicitation of sales by catalogs and flyers and if the subsequent delivery of goods to Illinois purchasers was by mail or common carrier. The Court held that the state's attempt to require collection of the use tax was barred by the Commerce Clause and the Due Process Clause of the U.S. Constitution in the absence of physical presence of the catalog company in the state.

In 1992, the U.S. Supreme Court rendered a decision in *Quill Corporation v. North Dakota*, by and through its Tax Commissioner, Heidi Heitkamp, 504 U.S. 298, (1992), which upheld the physical presence test of *National Bellas Hess* with respect to the Commerce Clause but which held that physical presence was not required to satisfy the Due Process Clause. The U.S. Supreme Court ruled that the Due Process Clause by itself would permit a state to require an out-of-state seller to collect use tax if the seller had an economic presence in the state (i.e., regular, continuous and substantial solicitation of business in the state).

As a result of the *Quill Corporation* decision, the issue of whether states can impose use tax collection obligations on out-of-state sellers can be legislatively determined by Congress under the Commerce Clause. Congress has not specifically addressed the imposition of such tax obligations to date.

In determining whether an out-of-state seller has a physical presence in a state for purposes of establishing taxable nexus under the Commerce Clause, the activities of the seller's subsidiaries, other affiliates, licensees and independent contractors within the state, particularly in the case of indirect leasing programs, are considered. The activities of these persons might be attributed, under the governing state sales tax statute or under general legal principles, to the out-of-state sellers for purposes of sales and use tax nexus.

Sales for Resale

Generally, a state's sales tax regime will assume that all sales of tangible personal property within the state are subject to sales tax until otherwise established.

If a transfer is a nontaxable sale, the purchaser delivers to the seller, on a timely basis, an appropriate exemption certificate. In the case of a sale for resale, the purchaser delivers (generally at the time of sale) a resale certificate identifying the property acquired. Typically, state sales tax administrative agencies publish a form of a resale certificate acceptable to the agency. Use of these forms is usually not mandatory. The timely delivery of the resale certificate can be important in states that do not allow resale certificates to be effective retroactively. The resale certificate, if properly taken, relieves the seller from liability for the sales tax and the duty of collecting the use tax.

Some states impose special requirements to establish the exclusion from sales tax of certain property, such as manufacturing machinery and equipment, pollution control equipment or certain transportation equipment. These requirements may involve use of a special form of resale certificate (or certifications as to suitability of the property for its intended use).

Exempt Property

Various types of tangible personal property are exempt from state sales tax. This exempt property varies greatly from state to state, as the exemptions reflect state and local political and economic considerations.

Typical exempt property includes:

1. Farm machinery and equipment used primarily in agricultural production

2. Machinery and equipment for use primarily in manufacturing tangible personal property for sale or lease

3. Small aircraft and small aircraft replacement parts

4. Equipment sold to educational institutions

5. Transportation equipment and component parts used to transport passengers or cargo in foreign or interstate commerce

6. Property exempted by the federal government or U.S. Constitution

7. Property used in special enterprise zones.

The effect of exempt property is to exempt only that particular property from imposition of the sales tax. To establish the exemption, either the seller or purchaser, as appropriate under state law, must produce an exemption certificate, forms of which are prescribed by state sales tax agencies.

EXEMPT LESSEE

In addition to exemptions for certain items of tangible personal property, states also establish exemptions from the sales tax for various purchasers (lessees). The effect of status as an exempt purchaser is an exemption of all sales transactions with that purchaser from sales tax. In some states, exemption of the purchaser from sales and use tax can have the effect of shifting the tax onto the seller, depending upon how the sales and use taxes are structured.

For example, in California the use tax imposed on the lessee is the primary tax in an equipment lease and the lessor is relieved of sales tax because the rent payments are included in the use tax base. As a result, if the lessee is exempt from sales and use tax, the rent payments will no longer be included in the use tax base and the lessor (if not exempt) will become liable for the sales tax.

Typical exempt purchasers include:

1. Federal, state and local governments

2. Educational and religious organizations

3. Nonprofit charitable organizations

4. Specified industries (e.g., insurance companies).

Other Issues

Some variation between the states exists with respect to when the sales tax must be paid in connection with a lease of equipment. In states that do not recognize a lease as a continuing sale and purchase, the tax usually must be paid either at the time the lessor acquires the property or at the time a lessee first uses the property. The tax does not apply to the rental stream.

In states that recognize a lease as a continuing sale and purchase, collection of the tax may be permitted or required over the term of the lease as rent payments are made. If the state requires continuing sale treatment, installment payment of the tax based on the amount of rent paid will be the only option for payment of the tax. If the state, as an alternative, permits and the lessor elects payment of the entire tax at inception of the transaction based on the equipment acquisition cost, then tax is not paid with respect to the rental stream. Typically any election to pay the entire sales tax at inception is irrevocable and is made at inception.

For equipment located in several states during the course of the lease, payment of the sales tax with respect to the rental stream may be advantageous as it will automatically prorate the various states' sales taxes to the time the equipment is located within the state. The alternative would be double taxation or the claiming of credits for taxes paid to another state to avoid double taxation. To the extent that the purchase price of the equipment is less than the aggregate rental payments, an opportunity arises to reduce the sales tax burden on the transaction by paying the entire tax up front.

LEASE RECEIVABLES

A lessor can transfer lease receivables in several ways. Depending on the status of the lease for sales tax purposes (whether the transfer is a collateral assignment for security or a change in title to the leased equipment), sales tax may be imposed with respect to the transfer of the lease receivable.

Generally, when a finance lease (i.e., an existing lease that does not constitute a continuing sale) is transferred, the rental payments are not subject to tax before or after the transfer. If title to the leased equipment also is transferred, sales tax will apply, measured by the sales price, unless a sale-for-resale exclusion or an appropriate exemption applies (such as an exempt assignee or exempt property). Because such a lease does not constitute a continuing sale, the entire sales tax most likely will be due upon assignments with no option to pay the tax as rents are paid.

When an existing lease constituting a continuing sale subject to tax (as measured by the rental payments) is transferred to a new lessor, together with all right and title to the leased equipment, it is usually a sale for resale. Generally no sales tax is imposed on the transfer price and the rental payments remain subject to sales tax. Also, there is not an option to measure the sales tax on the remaining lease payments by the transfer price. In these types of transfers, the old lessor generally retains no substantial rights of ownership in the lease or the leased equipment. The new lessor may be required to hold a seller's permit and to collect and remit sales tax on post-transfer rent payments. The transferor should obtain a resale certificate from the new lessor.

If an existing lease is transferred for security purposes only (i.e., lease receivables are pledged and the lessor may or may not grant a security interest in the leased equipment), the transfer usually does not meet the definition of a sale. The lessor would remain subject to the obligation to collect and pay sales tax, if it is measured by the rent payments. To the extent the assignee receives any payments of tax from the lessee or the assignee forecloses on its security interest and takes title to the leased equipment, a sale will occur at that time and the sales tax will apply, subject to any available exclusions or exemptions.

In some transfers of nonfinance leases that constitute assignments for security, title to the equipment also may be transferred to the assignee (title to the equipment will be reconveyed to the assignor after termination of the transaction.) Depending on the state's administrative policies, the assignee may have assumed the position of the lessor for sales tax purposes and, as a result, may be required to hold a seller's permit and to collect and remit sales tax on any continuing rent payments subject to sales tax (i.e., if sales taxes were not paid up front). In these transfers, the assignor should obtain a resale certificate.

SERVICE CONTRACTS

Some transactions involving the transfer of possession or use of equipment also may involve the provision of services. In states that do not tax all services, an issue can arise as to whether a lease transaction involving both equipment and services is taxable in part or in whole as a sale of tangible personal property. The issue of whether an equipment lease transaction constitutes, for sales tax purposes, a sale of property or services usually cannot be resolved by the simple device of determining the existence of a transfer of title, use or possession of property.

If a transaction involves both a transfer of property and the rendition of services, the comparative importance and value of the services and the equipment are one basis for classifying a transaction as a sale of property or services. One resolution to the problem is to state separately in the governing documents the charges for the equipment and the charges for the services. This segregation can be particularly appropriate when equipment is acquired by the lessor from the manufacturer for lease to the lessee and when the manufacturer will provide training or other services directly to the lessee with respect to the equipment. In most states, if the charges for services are stated separately, there will be no sales tax on them.

INCLUSION FOR OTHER TAXES BORNE BY THE LESSEE

When an equipment lease is subject to sales tax measured by the rentals payable, an issue arises as to what the term rent means for purposes of the sales tax base. Many forms of lease documents will include within the contractual definition of rent all amounts owed by the lessee under the lease. Typical amounts owed are basic rent for use of the equipment (which may include an implicit interest component), late charges, property tax reimbursement, insurance and other charges associated with administration of the lease or the equipment.

Generally, rents subject to tax include any payments required by the lease, including amounts paid for personal property taxes on the leased equipment (whether paid by the lessor with reimbursement or directly by the lessee).

The following amounts paid to the lessor often are excluded from the definition of rent for sales tax purposes:

1. Collection costs, including attorney fees, court costs, repossession charges and storage fees (but not delinquent rent collected, including through court action)

2. Costs incurred in defending court actions or paying tort judgments arising out of the lessee's use or operation of the equipment or in purchasing insurance for court actions or tort judgments

3. Costs of insuring, repairing or refurbishing the equipment following lease termination

4. Costs incurred in disposing of the equipment at lease termination

5. Late charges and interest for failing to pay rent in a timely manner

6. Reimbursement of separately stated optional insurance charges, maintenance charges, maintenance or warranty contracts.

SALE-LEASEBACKS

A sale-leaseback occurs when there is a sale of equipment by a person and a leaseback to that same person of the equipment. In the absence of an exemption, the sales tax consequences of a sale-leaseback typically are a tax-free sale (i.e., sale-for-resale exclusion) and a taxable leaseback. Because a sale-leaseback does not involve a change in possession or use of the property (which remains with the seller-lessee), a significant sales tax cost may be associated with the transaction.

Many states provide immunity from sales tax for sale-leaseback transactions as defined in their statutes. For example, transactions structured as sales-leasebacks may be treated as financing transactions rather than as taxable sales and leasebacks. A transaction in which (1) the leaseback constitutes a sale under a security arrangement, (2) the lessor-purchaser does not claim tax benefits of ownership (e.g., depreciation) for federal or state income tax purposes and (3) the implicit interest does not violate applicable usury laws is viewed for sales tax purposes as a secured financing.

Another type of sale-leaseback exempt from sales tax is the acquisition sale-leaseback that occurs when the seller-lessee has paid sales tax with respect to its original purchase of the equipment and the transaction is completed within 90 days of the seller's first functional use of the property. Acquisition sale-leasebacks are viewed as a nontaxable acquisition financings for purposes of the sales tax and, therefore, are excluded from the tax.

The definitions of nontaxable sale-leasebacks vary and are applied with differing degrees of technical compliance. Accordingly, it is advisable to review the statutes and administrative practices of each state involved in a proposed sale-leaseback.

PERSONAL PROPERTY TAXES

Generally, states impose value-based taxes on the owners of personal property located within their borders. These ad valorem personal property taxes usually are imposed at a specific rate of tax on the value of property owned on a specified date and not on the total value of property owned during a specified period. The tax is assessed and collected at predetermined intervals and is payable whether the property has been used or not during that time. Ad valorem property tax schemes tax all personal property unless immune or exempt from taxation.

Personal property definitions range from negative such as "all property that is not real property" to the more specific "all property that may be seen, weighed, measured, felt or touched or which is in any manner perceptible to the senses, except land and improvements." Statutes generally will provide for exceptions to the definition of personal property. For instance, motor vehicles typically are subject to a license fee in lieu of a property tax and some states do not tax possessory interests in tangible personal property. Further, states generally do not tax personal property held for personal use unless it is held or used in a trade or business or for the production of income.

The U.S. Constitution places restrictions on the states' ability to tax property. Thus, unless Congress specifically consents to its taxation, federally owned property is immune from state taxation. National banks are an example of federal property immune from state taxation without the consent of Congress. As recently as 20 years ago Congress consented to tax personal property of national banks, and then only if local banks are taxed in the same manner.

States also generally are precluded via the Commerce Clause of the U.S. Constitution from taxing goods that are in interstate or foreign commerce. The courts held early on that such goods become immune from state taxation when they commence their movement in foreign or interstate commerce. The goods remain immune until the transit has stopped and the owner disposes of the property within the state or determines its shipment elsewhere.

Generally, the property tax is assessed and collected by the counties within the state. The lien date is the date the property taxes are assessed to an owner, persons claiming to own or persons possessing the personal property located within (having a situs in) the county. The applicable rate of tax is applied against the value of the property on the lien date.

Owner of Record

A typical personal property tax statute requires the county assessor to assess all taxable property in the county to persons who own, claim, possess or control it on the valuation date. Generally, the person who holds legal title (i.e., the owner) will be the person who is considered to be primarily liable and thus responsible for payment of the personal property tax. If the owner has sold the property, and has retained title only as a security interest, the purchaser of the property is properly assessable.

Although the owner of personal property is typically the assessed party, some states specifically allow the assessor to assess the possessor on the valuation date.

The property tax on property in the process of being sold typically will be assessed to the owner up to the time of closing. Thus, if the closing date falls after the valuation date, unless otherwise agreed upon in the sales contract, the owner will be responsible for the payment of the property tax.

The assessing body, although it varies by state, will assess the owner of property that is subject to a lease, in lieu of the lessee. However, states generally allow the assessment of either the lessor or the lessee. The owner will be assessable even though the property may be leased to an exempt lessee. Conversely, if the owner is exempt from property tax, the assessor may be empowered to assess the lessee. If the lessor is a business exempt from property tax (e.g., a bank), states may provide that the lessee is to be considered the owner for property tax purposes. It is common practice for a lessee to be assessed when the owner is unknown or cannot be located.

An assessed owner of leased property may seek reimbursement of the payment of such tax from the lessee. Such right of reimbursement may be pursuant to a contractual agreement.

Situs of Personal Property

Tangible personal property with a fixed situs generally is taxed at the location regardless of the owner's domicile. To determine the tax situs, states apply different rules depending on the type of property at issue. Situs issues arise when the property is not permanently located.

In the case in which the property is transient, states have enacted various rules to determine the situs. Such rules may be dependent on the length of time the property remained in one place during the tax period, as well as how long it is anticipated to remain in a fixed location for a specified period of time. The situs may be determined by the location to which the property normally is returned. If there is not a location to which the property is returned, it may be taxed at the situs of the principal place of business of the owner.

Rules obviously will vary by state with respect to leased personal property. In California, if the property is leased for less than six months it is treated as having a situs where the lessor normally keeps the property. If the lease term is for an unspecified period of time, or more than six months, the situs is deemed to be where the lessee uses the property.

Effect of Contractual Obligations Borne by the Lessee

Personal property tax assessors typically are empowered to assess either the lessor or the lessee of personal property. However, the lessor (i.e., the owner) usually will be assessed. Even if the lessor and lessee have allocated the payment of personal property taxes pursuant to the lease agreement, the assessed party remains liable to the state irrespective of such an agreement. Thus, if the personal property tax is paid by the assessed party, even if it is not responsible for such payments under the lease agreement, such party must recover the payment from the liable party pursuant for a contract claim. The provisions of the lease agreement are not a valid defense for nonpayment of the tax.

Valuation Issues

Because the personal property tax is imposed each year on the value of the property, valuation issues are a critical part of the tax. Valuation issues obviously are dependent upon the state in which the property is taxable. There are varying methods of valuing personal property, most of which attempt to determine the property's fair market value or full cash value. Fair market or full cash value is defined as the value of property a willing buyer is prepared to pay a willing seller in the open market when neither is under any compulsion to buy or sell and when both are fully aware of all the relevant facts. Each state typically has a variation on this definition; however, some states provide a presumption for property sold during the year that the fair market value is the price at which the property was sold.

States generally will value the property at its highest and best use. The use of the property and its appreciation or depreciation affect the property and consequently its value. Restrictions upon the use of the property are also a valuation consideration. Methods of valuation include comparable sales, replacement cost or income. Typically, states also provide special valuation methods for specified types of property.

COMPARABLE SALES METHOD

The comparable sales method is the preferred method of valuing property. When sales or property are sufficient to establish a market, property sold in such market that is similar to the property at issue with respect to location, size, model, etc., can be used to determine the value of the property to be assessed. Because properties rarely are identical, adjustments between the price of the property sold in the market and the value of the property nearly always are required.

REPLACEMENT COST METHOD

Valuing property using the replacement cost method assumes that the property is not necessarily replaced with comparable property. This method is particularly appropriate when a market of similar property has not been established and/or when income derived from the property is not easily determined.

INCOME METHOD

The income method typically applies to property that is used for its income producing potential. The future income stream over the predicted life of the property is determined by a variety of factors concerning the property. The anticipated expenses over the same life also are determined and are deducted from the projected future income stream. Once the net income has been determined, the present value of the future net income stream is computed. States employ various factors for this computation. The resultant figure is considered the value of the property.

Exempt Tangible Personal Property

Most states provide for exemptions of property based on its type, and also exempt property owned by specific types of businesses. Reasons for exempting certain property from tax include revenue gain being outweighed by administrative expenses, subsidies to the user and use of property to provide a service that would otherwise be required to be provided by the government. Although property may be exempted, such an exemption must be defensible under federal and state constitution equal protection provisions.

Classes of exempted property include state owned property, local government owned property, educational institutions, libraries and museums, welfare property and churches and other religious property. The reasons for exempting property owned by certain types of business are as varied as the classes of property that can be exempt. For instance, in California, insurance companies, banks and other financial institutions are exempt from personal property taxes. However, personal property leased to banks or insurance companies does not exempt the lessor unless the lease is a financing device.

Exempt Lessee

Exempt lessees are typically federal or state governmental agencies and entities states determine to exempt for various policy reasons (e.g., churches, schools and other nonprofit entities). When a lessee is exempt from personal property tax, the assessor generally is required to look only to the lessor to pay the tax. Issues that vary by state include whether the assumption of property tax liability by the lessee in the lease agreement is enforceable and whether the state is empowered to place a tax lien on the property leased to an exempt lessee.

CONCLUSION

Unlike the federal income tax, which is uniform in its application throughout the U.S., state and local taxes vary from state to state in both structure and rates. Such variation makes it very difficult for lessors to remain in compliance on each of their leases. This chapter discusses the principal state and local taxes likely to affect an equipment lease and explores the application of those taxes to a leasing transaction. State-by-state tax law summaries may be found in the *State Tax Manual (1994 ed.)* published by the Equipment Leasing Association of America.

Section Three

Financial Reporting

Chapter Nine

Introductory Lease Accounting

The importance of accounting in the leasing industry becomes more evident each day from both lessee and lessor viewpoints. Not only accountants, however, need to understand accounting for leases. Managers, financial analysts, corporate planners and many others also must recognize and understand the impact of leases on the financial statements. With this need in mind, this chapter provides, through the following topics, an understanding of the issues and basic concepts of accounting for leases.

- Accounting and Leasing

- An Introduction to FASB 13

- Capital Versus Operating Leases.

ACCOUNTING AND LEASING

Accounting has been defined as the art of recording, classifying and summarizing transactions and events and interpreting their results. The various components of this definition are applied to the lease transactions of a company through the guidelines set forth by the accounting rule-making body, the Financial Accounting Standards Board (FASB).

Accounting Perspective

It is clear from the above definition that accounting amounts to more than the recording of transactions (i.e., bookkeeping). Note particularly the emphasis in the definition placed on the interpretation of the results of the accounting process. The accounting information must be recorded in such a manner that interpretation of the results is possible, i.e., the information is useful in making economic decisions. There are two broad groups of decision-makers who may utilize accounting information: internal users and external users.

Internal decision-makers are the managers responsible for planning the future of the entity, implementing plans and controlling operations on a day-to-day basis. These users require different and often more detailed information than do external users. Because of their internal relationship to the entity, they also can command whatever financial data they may need, at dates of their choice. Further, the information is for their sole use and generally is not intended to be communicated to outsiders. The process of developing and reporting financial information to internal users usually is called management accounting, and the reports are referred to as internal management reports. Clearly, these reports should be structured to conform to the particular decision-making needs of the management team.

In contrast, the external decision-makers (i.e., the external users of financial information) make distinctly different types of decisions regarding the entity, such as to invest or disinvest, to loan funds and so forth. External decision-makers comprise present and potential investors and creditors, investment analysts, governmental units and the public at large.

These diverse external users, because of their detachment from the entity, cannot directly command specific financial information from the company; therefore, they must rely primarily on general-purpose financial statements, developed by the accounting profession. These statements are developed in a phase of accounting known as financial accounting. The accounting profession, in order to serve external users, has developed a network of accounting standards designed to assure that external financial statements are fair representations of the economic circumstances of the company. These standards, which must be followed in financial statement presentation, are referred to as generally accepted accounting principles (GAAP). Outside auditors provide independent assurance to external users that GAAP has been followed in preparing the financial statements.

GAAP is established through the practices of the accounting profession and formalized by the FASB. The FASB issues statements that outline the accounting principles to be followed in different situations. In November, 1976, the FASB issued Statement No. 13 (FASB 13), "Accounting for Leases." The requirements of FASB 13, which establish the accounting for leases by both lessors and lessees, are covered later in this chapter.

HISTORY OF ACCOUNTING

The history of accounting, although not as lengthy as that of leasing, is certainly as colorful. In fact, it was a peer of Leonardo da Vinci, an Italian monk named Fra Luca Pacioli, who first outlined the fundamental principles of accounting (see Figure 9-1).

This 15th century Italian monk is known as the "Father of Accounting." A true Renaissance man, Pacioli collaborated with the masters of his day in mathematics, commerce and the arts. Although the accounting techniques he described were being used in Venice as far back as the 13th century, Pacioli was the first to bring these many diverse elements together into a coordinated system. This system is the foundation of our modern double-entry bookkeeping system. Pacioli documented his work in *Summa de Arithmetica, Geometria, Proportioni et Proportionalita,* published in 1494.

DEVELOPMENT OF ACCOUNTING STANDARDS

There are many lease accounting standards. These standards provide the underpinnings of the entire profession of lease accountancy. It is important, therefore, to understand their origins and how they are developed, debated and finalized, where they originate and the processes that bring them to fruition.

The Formulation of GAAP

What is GAAP? Before 1964, the pronouncements of the Committee on Accounting Procedure and the Accounting Principles Board (APB) were viewed by practitioners as only recommendations of GAAP. However, because there was a lack of enforcement power, accountants did not necessarily comply with the recommendations of GAAP. This approach to accounting led external users of financial statements to question the validity of the accountants' product.

In 1964, therefore, the Council of the American Institute of Certified Public Accountants (AICPA) incorporated Rule 203 into its rules of ethics. This rule stated:

> *A member shall not express an opinion that financial statements are presented in conformity with generally accepted accounting principles if such statements contain any departure from an accounting principle promulgated by the body designated by Council to establish such principles which has a material effect on the statements taken as a whole, unless the member can demonstrate that due to unusual circumstances the financial statements would otherwise have been misleading....*

Exhibit 9-1
Original Page from the Principles of Accounting Manuscript

Diſtinctio quinta .Tractatus primus. 6 7

rum:e partendo ſoldi per.20.neuē 8.ꝑer che la lira vbiqꝫ ſi tene ſoldi.20.Ɫe 8.poia ſarne
oꝛo:ſi partano per la valuta ꝺe quel oꝛo occurrente:ſecondo li luoghi.Ɇ quello cħ auança
ꝺe li ꝺ.partendoli in.12.ſonno ꝺ.Ɇ cio che auança ꝺe li ſ.partiriī.20.ſono ſ.Ɇ cio che auā
ça ꝺe le 8.partire in la valuta ꝺe loꝛo occurrente ſonno.8.Ɇt ſic in ceteris diſcurrendo: ver
bi gratia.Poniamo che tu habi aredure ale magioꝛi valute ouer magioꝛi monete queſta q̃
tita ꝺe picioli:cioe picioli numero.96598.Dico che pꝛima facci commo feſti ꝺi ſopꝛa in li pe
ſi oꝛdinamente reducendo pꝛima ala immediata moneta ſequente:quale e el ſoldo in que
ſto modo.Partendo la ꝺitta ſumma ꝺe picioli per.12.neuen.8049.e ſono ſoldi e auança.10
che ſon.10.picioli.Ɇ poi ſarne 8.partirai queſti ſoldi venuti per.20.neucue.402.Ɇ que
ſte ſono 8.ꝺe valuta:e auança.9.che ſon.9.ſoldi.Ɇ poi per ſarne oꝛo.Partirai le ſ.per la
valuta ꝺel ꝺitto oꝛo a 8.Ɇ virratte loꝛo.Ɇ quello che auançara ſira ſ.Cõmo ſe voleſſe far
ꝺuɇ.li quali in queſto hauemo poſto valere ſ.7.luno.Ɫe ꝺitte 8.venute partirai per .7. ne
uen.57.Ɇ ſon ꝺuɇ.e auança.3.che ſon 8.Si che ꝺe pꝛimo ad vltimun reducendo li ꝺitti pi
cioli ala magioꝛ moneta ſiranno ꝺuɇ.57.8.3.ſ.9.ꝺ.10.Ɇ coſi regerate in tutte valute meno
ri:reducendole ale magioꝛ:vt in iſta.

Tertium notandum.Ɇadem via pꝛocedens.

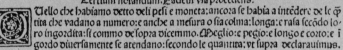

Vello che habiamo ꝺetto ꝺeli peſi e moneta:ancoꝛa ſe habia a intēdere ꝺe le q̃
tita che vadano a numero:e anche a meſura o ſia colma:longa:e raſa ſecõdo lo
ro ingoꝛdita:ſi commo ꝺe ſopꝛa ꝺicemmo.Meglio:e pegio:e longo e coꝛto:e i
goꝛdo ꝺiuerſamente ſe atendano:ſecondo le quantita:vt ſupꝛa ꝺeclarauimus.
Si che hauendo tu octaui ꝺe bꝛaccio ꝺe panno numero.46595.ꝺe panni a volerli redu
re a canne:la qual communiter ſe tien bꝛaccia.4.Pꝛima partirai ꝺitti octaui per.2. e virrat
te quarte:per che ſempꝛe in ogni q̃atita.2.octaui fanno.ƚ.e lo remanēte ſira octauo. Ɇ poi
le quarte partirai per.4.e virratte bꝛaccia per che.4.fanno bꝛaccio.1.Ɇ lauançꝺ ſira quar
te.Ɇ poi li bꝛacci partirai per.4.e virratte cāne:e lauançꝺ ſiran bꝛaccia.Si commo haueſſe
li octaui pꝛeditti partili in.2.neuen.23297.Ɇ ſon quarti.Ɇ auança.1.che e.1.octauo.Ɇ poi
parti.23297.per.4.e virranne.5824.Ɇ ſonno bꝛaccia e auāça.1.che e.1².quarta.Ɇ poi par
ti li bꝛaccia per.4.neuen.1456.e ſonno canne:e auança nulla che ſon:nullo bꝛaccio.Siche
ꝺe pꝛimo adultimum la ꝺitta reducictione fa canne.1456.bꝛaccia o quarte.1.octaui.1.Ɇ tu i
tutte altre ſimili per te farai zɇ.

Quartum notandum ꝺe caratteribus pꝛaticis hoc in opere vſitatis.

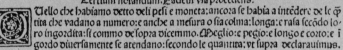

Eſtiero e ancoꝛa ꝺa notare quello impoꝛtino li caratteri per noi in queſt opera
vſitati acio le loꝛo abbꝛeuiature ſien inteſe per chi legera hauenga che molti per
le pꝛopoſte queſtioni per ſe ſteſſi le apꝛendino.Non ꝺimanco piu ſonno quelli
ꝺi poca pꝛatica (per li quali pꝛincipalmente queſto libꝛo ſi fa) che non ſonno
quelli che intendano.Ɇ impero qui ſequente tutti li caratteri:e abꝛeuiature che per noi cõ
munamente in queſto libꝛo ſe vſaranno:ꝺechiararemo:ſi in larte menoꝛe ouer mercatozia:
commo in arte magioꝛe:ouer algebꝛa.Ɫe quali piu per li peſi:e monete:e meſure:che p al
tro ſonno trouari:excepto in algebꝛa che per foꝛça (ꝺifferentie cauſa)ſo biſogno trouare.
Per che non ſi potte a tutte quantita metter nome.Jdeo zɇ.

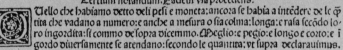

Queſti caratteri e abꝛeuiature commo vedi.Alcuni ſonno che piu ꝺe vna coſa
repꝛeſentano.Peroche ale volte peſo:e ale volte valuta ꝺi monete.Si commo
queſto 8.che ꝺici lira e valuta ꝺe moneta:che ſintende ſoldi.20.Ɇ libꝛa a peſo
che ſintende once.12.e coſi queſta.p.che ꝺici.piu.picioli.pecçe.piedi.Per la q̃l
coſa tu nelli luoghi ꝺoue le trouerai per tuo ingegno chiaro cognoſcerai quale ꝺe luno ꝺe
queſti te repꝛeſentara:ſecondo el ſuon ꝺe la materia che liſe contira.Onde fra le valute.p.
ꝺenota picioli.Fra meſure piedi.Fra quantita ꝺe panni pecça.Jn operatione ꝺe algebꝛa
piu:e coſi ꝺe ciaſcuna ꝺe laltre:ſecondo li techi e le materie te repꝛeſentarāno ſuna ꝺe le co
ſe ꝺitte qui al ſuo incontro ſiche tu per te vſarai lo ingegno tuo:el qual biſogna ſia ſupple
mento a quello chio mancaſſe.Quia ſupplerio ſit loco ꝺefectus.Per che non e poſſibile
mai ponere tutto quello che alarte ſe ricerca:ſi commo e manifeſto a quelli che ꝺi compone
re volumi ſe ꝺelettano.Jurta illud.Dicite pierides non omnia poſſumus omnes:e coſi fa
rai ꝺele ſequenti che ſon per algebꝛa.

Jdem notādum ꝺe caratteribus algebꝛaticis.]

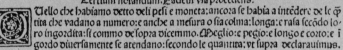

Er loperare ꝺe larte magioꝛe:ꝺitta val vulgo la regola ꝺe la coſa ouer algebꝛa
e amucabala ſeruaremo noi in queſto le qui ꝺa lato abꝛeuiature ouer caratteri:

...guage added the necessary teeth to GAAP. The eagerness of financial statement users to litigate, the economics of litigation defense and the desire to keep their licenses compelled accountants to comply with GAAP. As previously mentioned, GAAP is now promulgated by the FASB.

Establishing the FASB

The latter half of the 1960s was a period of stress for the accounting profession in general, not just lease accountancy. The rapid expansion of accounting firms, the new issue boom, increasingly complex and innovative business practices and the corporate merger movement caused problems that created a wave of criticism of corporate financial reporting. Much of this criticism focused on the APB, the 13-year-old group previously responsible for GAAP. The productivity of the APB was questioned not only by members of the accounting and financial community but, more importantly, by regulatory agencies such as the Securities and Exchange Commission (SEC).

In response, the AICPA established a committee to study how the AICPA's standards-setting role could be made more responsive to the needs of those who rely on financial statements. This committee recommended establishing a new, full-time body, the FASB, which would replace the existing APB. The structure of the FASB was designed to ensure that financial reporting standards would be practical and in the public interest. The desired result of this reorganization was to increase public confidence in financial information, while keeping the development of accounting principles in the private sector.

The FASB is the body designated to establish GAAP. The SEC, through its administrative powers, gives FASB statements the full force of law. In this role, the FASB has to resolve complex and highly controversial issues of diverse groups with often conflicting interests. As a result, its system of extensive and thorough due process also must leave room for the flexibility necessary for developing a broad consensus.

Each of the leasing-related pronouncements has been issued in accordance with the due process procedures of the FASB. They consist of Statements, Interpretations and Technical Bulletins. The Statements are directed towards broad accounting issues, whereas Interpretations and Technical Bulletins clarify specific points of the Statements. A careful reading of a given pronouncement and the FASB's basis for conclusions yields a wealth of information as to the derivation of the ruling and how it is to be applied.

Role of Accounting in the Leasing Industry

Lease accounting has been evolving since 1949 when Accounting Research Bulletin No. 38, "Disclosure of Long-term Leases in Financial Statements of Lessors," appeared. For many years, virtually all leases from a lessee perspective were accounted for as operating, or off balance sheet, leases. However, accounting theorists contended that long-term leases that primarily reflected the characteristics of a financing transaction (and, hence, were called financing leases) should be recorded by the lessor as a sale involving recognition of a long-term receivable. Consistent accounting for the lessee requires capitalization of the leased asset and recognition of a long-term liability.

Although many theorists found this approach to be conceptually sound, relatively few entities accounted for leases in this manner. Because capitalization was not required by GAAP, lessees continued to take advantage of off balance sheet reporting, resulting in an increasing amount of footnote disclosure about lease terms and obligations during this period. All in all, however, there was very little consistency in application.

In 1973, the SEC brought the matter of inconsistent treatment of leases to a head by putting pressure on the newly formed FASB to establish comprehensive lease accounting rules. After issuing several exposure drafts and considering a multitude of letters of comments, position papers and oral presentations from interested parties, the FASB released FASB 13.

FASB 13 substantially changed the accounting treatment of lease commitments and established the standards to be followed by lessors and lessees in accounting for and reporting lease transactions. It requires that certain leases be recorded on the lessee's balance sheet as a liability and the leased property be reported as an asset. This procedure is referred to as "capitalizing the lease" or "capitalization." For leases that fail to meet the tests specified by FASB 13, the lessee is required to disclose certain information regarding its lease commitments in a footnote.

At the time FASB 13 was issued, lessees and lessors were very fearful that its capitalization requirement for lessees, under certain circumstances, would discourage leasing and reduce volume. However, the net effect was just the opposite, as the guidelines were interpreted liberally by the accounting profession. The result was that leasing continued its explosive growth.

Most of the discussion in this and subsequent accounting chapters is derived from issues addressed in FASB 13. This statement describes the difference between capital and operating leases, details how to account for them, and defines many terms pertinent to the accounting classification of leases. FASB 13 sets forth comprehensive guidelines for both lessor and lessee accounting. Although it provided much greater uniformity to the financial reporting of equipment leases, other pronouncements subsequently have been issued by the FASB in an attempt to further clarify FASB 13.

Since its original issuance in 1976, FASB 13 has been amended and clarified by numerous FASB Statements, Interpretations and Technical Bulletins and has become extremely complex. The pronouncements relating to leasing issued as of publication of this text are shown in Exhibit 9-2. When the list from Exhibit 9-2 is combined with the existing body of general accounting literature, the enormity of the task of properly accounting for leases becomes easy to appreciate.

AN INTRODUCTION TO FASB 13

History has shown that as leasing volume increases, so too does its complexity. This complexity is found in all facets of leasing, including payment structure, flexible termination and other options and tax ramifications. To account properly for the increasing complexity of leases, accountants have endeavored to define and compartmentalize the various aspects of the lease product.

Definitions of a Lease

Regulation of various aspects of the leasing industry is a concern to several groups, including the accounting and legal professions, the Internal Revenue Service (IRS), the SEC and a host of state and local taxing authorities. In their attempts to regulate leasing, there has emerged from each group a body of rules and regulations designed to establish what a lease is and how leases should be managed.

Consequently, there are several definitions of a lease, including industry, tax, accounting and legal. A graphic representation of these is shown in Exhibit 9-3. In general, a lease is viewed as any agreement that conveys to the asset user (lessee) the right to use the asset for a stated period of time. In exchange for the use of the asset, the lessee pays the owner (lessor) a fee. In this respect, a lease is viewed as a rental of an asset for a certain portion of its useful life.

Exhibit 9-2
Leasing–related Pronouncements

Number	Title	Date
FASB Statements		
13	Accounting for Leases	1.1.77
17	Accounting for Leases — Initial Direct Costs (Superseded 12/16/87)	1.1.78
22	Changes in Provisions of Lease Agreements Resulting from Refundings of Tax-exempt Debt	7.1.78
23	Inception of the Lease	12.1.78
27	Classifications of Renewals or Extension of Existing Sales-type or Direct Financing Leases	9.1.79
26	Profit Recognition on Sales-type Leases of Real Estate (Superseded 7/1/88)	8.1.79
28	Accounting for Sales with Leasebacks	9.1.79
29	Determining Contingent Rentals	10.1.79
91	Accounting for Nonrefundable Fees and Costs Associated with Originating or Acquiring Loans and Initial Direct Costs of Leases	12.86
98	Accounting for Leases: —Sale-leaseback Transactions Involving Real Estate —Sales-type Leases of Real Estate —Definition of the Lease Term —Initial Direct Costs of Direct Financing Leases	7.1.88
FASB Interpretations		
19	Lessee Guarantee of the Residual Value of Leased Property	1.1.78
21	Accounting for Lease in a Business Combination	5.1.78
23	Leases of Certain Property Owned by a Government Unit or Authority	12.1.78
24	Leases Involving Only Part of a Building	12.1.78
26	Accounting for Purchase of a Leased Asset by the Lessee During the Term of the Lease	12.1.78
27	Accounting for a Loss on a Sublease	3.1.79

Exhibit 9-2 (continued)
Leasing–related Pronouncements

Number	Title	Date
FASB Technical Bulletins		
79-10	Fiscal Funding Clauses in Lease Agreements	12.28.79
79-11	Effect of a Penalty on the Term of a Lease (Superseded 7/1/88)	12.28.79
79-12	Interest Rate Used in Calculating the Present Value of Minimum Lease Payments	12.28.79
79-13	Applicability of FASB 13 to Current Value Financial Statements	12.28.79
79-14	Upward Adjustment of Guaranteed Residual Values	12.28.79
79-15	Accounting for a Loss on the Sublease Not Involving the Disposal of a Segment	12.28.79
79-16(R)	Effect of a Change in Income Tax Rate on the Accounting for Leveraged Leases	2.29.80
79-17	Reporting Cumulative Effect Adjustment from Retroactive Application of FASB 13	12.28.79
79-18	Transition Requirement of Certain FASB Amendments and Interpretations of FASB 13	12.18.79
85-3	Accounting for Operating Leases with Scheduled Rent Increases	11.15.85
86-2	Accounting for an Interest in the Residual Value of a Leased Asset: —Acquired by a Third Party or —Retained by a Lessor That Sells the Related Minimum Rental Payments	6.18.86
88-1	Issues Relating to Accounting for Leases: Time Pattern of the Physical Use of the Property in an Operating Lease —Lease Incentives in an Operating Lease —Applicability of Leveraged Lease Accounting to Existing Assets of the Lessor —Money-over-money Lease Transactions —Wrap Lease Transactions	1.1.89

Exhibit 9-3
Definitions of a Lease

Industry		Accounting	Tax	Legal
Lessor	Lease	Operating lease Capital lease	Tax lease Nontax lease	True lease Secured transaction
Lessee	Lease	Operating lease Capital lease	Tax lease Nontax lease	True lease Secured transaction

There also are leases that more closely resemble long-term commitments to purchase the asset. A distinct difference exists between these two types of leases. The definition the leasing industry uses for a lease, however, does not make a distinction between a lease that is a usage agreement and one that is an ownership agreement. From an industry perspective, as long as the document contains the word "lease" the agreement is referred to as such.

FASB 13

The primary focus of FASB 13 is to differentiate between a usage or rental agreement (an operating lease) and an ownership agreement (a capital lease). The characteristics of a capital lease, such as an automatic transfer of title to the lessee, are indicative that the lessee is acting in the capacity of owner. A capital lease is, in substance, an ownership agreement.

If the lease is classified as a capital lease, the lessee records the liability for the lease payments as debt in the liability section of its balance sheet. The balance sheet also shows the corresponding asset to which the lease obligation pertains. When the leased asset is recorded as an asset on the balance sheet, it is capitalized, hence, the term capital lease. This type of accounting treatment is similar to loan treatment by a borrower that acquires an asset using an installment loan.

In a capital lease, the asset's legal title may not transfer to the lessee until after the final payment is made. There also are instances in which the lessee may be exercising effective instead of actual ownership. In these cases, the lease is still capitalized and treated as though the lessee is buying the equipment, as the lessee is the owner, in substance.

Most lessees would rather not show the debt obligation of a lease on their balance sheet, for a variety of reasons. If they can avoid capitalizing the asset and disclosing the liability, they appear to be in much better financial health to potential lenders and investors. Lessees with this objective in mind prefer to show their leases as operating.

An operating lease is treated as though the lease is a rental agreement in which ownership of the asset resides with the lessor. At the end of the lease an option to renew the lease, purchase the asset or return it may be exercised by the lessee. In the meantime, as each rental payment is made, it is expensed in the lessee's income statement. This type of lease is, in substance, a usage agreement.

Generally, the FASB believes that allowing the debt to remain off the balance sheet is misleading unless the lease contract is truly a usage arrangement. In a usage agreement, the lessee is not contractually obligated to pay for the entire cost of the equipment, and the lessee will not completely use it up or wear it out.

In practice, there is enough ambiguity in lease contracts that it may be unclear what is intended by the lessor and the lessee as to usage versus ownership. On one extreme, a lease may be intended to be simply a rental of an asset by a lessee for a certain short-term need. On the other end of the spectrum, the lease may be intended to be a full financing of the asset in the form of a lease due to some accounting, regulatory or managerial need.

The objective of FASB 13, in part, is to establish the line of demarcation between these two extremes. When is the lease a true rental (operating lease) and when is it, instead, a disguised loan, or sale and purchase (capital lease)? The FASB, much like the IRS, makes this distinction based on the concept of substance over form.

ACCOUNTING PRODUCTS

The FASB distinguishes among various lease types for both lessors and lessees. This distinction is very important, as both the balance sheet and income statement presentation of the lease is a function of how it is classified. The different types of leases that may be written for financial reporting purposes are shown in Exhibit 9-4.

Exhibit 9-4
Types of Leases

Lessee
Capital lease
Operating lease

Lessor
Sales-type lease
Direct financing lease
Leveraged lease
Operating lease

A lessee must show a lease as either operating or capital. From the lessor's perspective, if a lease is not operating, it can be a direct financing, sales-type or leveraged lease. Although not technically defined as such, these last three leases generally are referred to as capital leases. To explain the different characteristics of these capital lease types, reference is made to the definitions in paragraph .102 of FASB 13.

.102 For purposes of applying the accounting and reporting standards [herein], leases are classified as follows:

    a. Classifications from the standpoint of the lessee:

        *(1) **Capital leases.** Leases that meet one or more of the criteria in paragraph .103.*

        *(2) **Operating leases.** All other leases.*

    b. Classifications from the standpoint of the lessor: [FAS13,¶6]

        *(1) **Sales-type leases.** Leases that give rise to manufacturer's or dealer's profit (or loss) to the lessor (that is, the **fair value of the leased property** at the **inception of the lease** is greater or less than its cost or carrying amount, if different) and that meet one or more of the criteria in paragraph .103 and both of the criteria in paragraph .104, except as indicated in the following sentence. A lease involving real estate shall be classified as a sales-type lease only if it meets the criterion in paragraph .103(a), in which case the criteria in paragraph .104 do not apply. [FAS98,¶22c] Normally, sales-*

*type leases will arise when manufacturers or dealers use leasing as a means of marketing their products. Leases involving lessors that are primarily engaged in financing operations normally will not be sales-type leases if they qualify under paragraphs .103 and .104, but will most often be **direct financing leases,** described in paragraph .102(b)(2) below.*

However, a lessor need not be a dealer to realize dealer's profit (or loss) on a transaction, for example, if a lessor, not a dealer, leases an asset that at the inception of the lease has a fair value that is greater or less than its cost or carrying amount, if different, such a transaction is a sales-type lease, assuming the criteria referred to are met. [FAS13,¶6] Leases of a manufacturing company's equipment sold to a leasing subsidiary that are accounted for as direct financing leases on the subsidiary's financial statements normally would be sales-type capital leases in the consolidated financial statements. [FAS94,¶52] . . .

(2) ***Direct financing leases.*** *Leases other than **leveraged leases** that do not give rise to manufacturer's or dealer's profit (or loss) to the lessor but that meet one or more of the criteria in paragraph .103 and both of the criteria in paragraph .104. In such leases, the cost or carrying amount, if different, and fair value of the leased property are the same at the inception of the lease. [FAS13,¶6] An exception arises when an existing sales-type or direct financing lease is renewed or extended[4] during the term of the existing lease. [FAS27,¶7] In such cases, the fact that the carrying amount of the property at the end of the original lease term is different from its fair value at that date shall not preclude the classification of the renewal or extension as a direct financing lease (refer to paragraph .113(f)).*

(3) ***Leveraged leases.*** *Leases that meet the criteria of paragraph .144. [FAS13,¶6]*

(4) ***Operating leases.*** *All other leases, including leases that involve real estate and give rise to manufacturer's or dealer's profit (or loss) to the lessor but do not meet the criterion in paragraph .103(a). [FAS98,¶22d]*

---

[4] *Refer to paragraph .419 [FAS13, ¶6,fn10]*

CAPITAL VERSUS OPERATING LEASES

A lease must be classified, at the inception of the lease, as one of the lease products discussed above. The classification of a lease as either operating or capital impacts its financial statement presentation. Each type of lease classification has its own unique income characteristics. It is important, therefore, that leases be classified properly.

Four Criteria

The FASB has established four criteria in its attempt to draw the line between which leases should be treated as capital and which as operating. These criteria are described in FASB 13 and apply to both lessees and lessors. They generally are referred to as the capital lease criteria because, if the terms of a lease meet any one of them the lease is classified as a capital lease, otherwise the lease is considered an operating lease.

Lessees and lessors refer to the same criteria in determining whether a lease should be reported as a capital or an operating lease. Depending on a particular lease contract's characteristics, a lease may be construed by one party, lessor or lessee, to be a capital lease whereas the other party treats it as an operating lease, or vice versa. Unlike the tax law, there is no mirror requirement in FASB 13. In fact, many leases are treated as capital leases by lessors and as operating leases by lessees. (Certain short-term leases may be considered neither capital nor operating if they are for a term of less than 12 months. Such contracts are rentals and need not be disclosed in the lessee's footnotes.)

The capital lease criteria are listed in paragraph .103 of FASB 13, Section L10. The lessor and lessee both must look at these criteria at the inception of the lease. Once the lease is classified, the accounting treatment remains the same throughout the term of the lease. The four capital lease criteria are outlined in Exhibit 9-5.

CRITERION ONE

The first criterion determines whether the lease automatically transfers ownership of the property to the lessee by, or at, the end of the lease term. Such a transfer is similar to a conditional sales contract in which title to the asset automatically transfers to the borrower after it makes a specified number of payments. If, indeed, the contract provides for an automatic transfer of title, the transaction is considered to be a purchase in the guise of a lease and, hence, is classified as a capital lease. This criterion tests if the lessee has actual ownership.

CRITERION TWO

If the lease contains a bargain purchase option, it is treated as a capital lease. When an option allows the lessee to purchase the asset for an amount far below fair market value, it is almost certain the option will be exercised (i.e., it is too much of a bargain to pass up). Furthermore, the only reason a lessor would offer a bargain purchase option to the lessee is the lessee already has paid for the equipment through the rentals.

This criterion is similar to the first in that title will most likely transfer to the lessee; therefore, the lease is treated as a capital lease. The lessee capitalizes the lease and accounts for the transaction similar to other installment debt obligations. In other words, through the bargain purchase option, the lessee has potential ownership.

CRITERION THREE

The third criterion states that the lease shall be treated as a capital lease if the lease term is greater than or equal to 75% of the estimated economic life of the leased property. In a lease meeting this criterion, the lessee uses the asset for most of its useful life. The lessee is, in substance, the owner and not just a short-term renter of the asset because asset exhaustion occurs in the hands of one user. The lessee uses up the asset just the same as if it were to buy it and wear it out. The lessee has effective ownership.

Exhibit 9-5
Capital Lease Criteria

Criterion one	Automatic transfer of title
Criterion two	Bargain purchase option
Criterion three	Lease term ≥ 75% of the asset's economic useful life
Criterion four	Present value of minimum lease payments ≥ 90% of fair market value (less any investment tax credit).

CRITERION FOUR

The last criterion states that if the present value of the minimum lease payments, at the beginning of the lease term, equals or exceeds 90% of the fair value of the leased property less any investment tax credit (ITC) retained by the lessor, the lease is capital. If the present value of the payments is greater than or equal to 90% of the fair market value of the leased asset, the lessee is effectively paying for it.

The substance of this lease is the same as if the lessee were to buy the asset outright, because the lessee is paying for a substantial portion of the asset on a present value basis. In this situation, the lessee has effective ownership and the lease is accounted for as a capital lease.

It is apparent from the above criteria that a capital lease is recognized when ownership occurs, either in actuality or in substance. The following relationships can be seen by correlating the capital lease criteria to the various forms of ownership being tested:

1. Automatic transfer of ownership – actual ownership is obtained outright during or at the end of the lease term

2. Bargain purchase option – potential ownership is available through the exercise of a bargain purchase option

3. Lease term greater than or equal to 75% of the economic life – effective ownership occurs through the use, or the wearing out, of the asset

4. Present value of the payments greater than or equal to 90% of the fair market value – effective ownership results when a substantial portion of the property's original fair market value is paid for on a present value basis.

These criteria must be applied at the inception of the lease by both lessors and lessees. If at least one of the criteria is met, the lease is classified as a capital lease, otherwise it is classified as an operating lease. The accounting treatment for a capital lease is different from that of an operating lease, so proper classification is critical.

Lessees and lessors both must apply the four capital lease criteria against the terms of the lease in order to classify the lease. Additionally, from the lessor's standpoint only, if a lease meets any one of the capital lease criteria it also must meet both the following criteria in order to be classified as a capital lease. Otherwise it will be classified as an operating lease (FASB 13 paragraph .104 (a) and (b)).

> a. *Collectibility of the minimum lease payments is reasonably predictable. A lessor shall not be precluded from classifying a lease as a sales-type lease, a direct financing lease, or a leveraged lease simply because the receivable is subject to an estimate of uncollectibility based on experience with groups of similar receivables. [FAS98, ¶22f]*
>
> b. *No important uncertainties surround the amount of unreimbursable costs yet to be incurred by the lessor under the lease.[7] Important uncertainties might include commitments by the lessor to guarantee performance of the leased property in a manner more extensive than the typical product warranty or to effectively protect the lessee from obsolescence of the leased property. . .*
>
> [7] *If the property covered by the lease is yet to be constructed or has not been acquired by the lessor at the inception of the lease, the classification criterion of paragraph .104(b) shall be applied at the date that construction of the property is completed or the property is acquired by the lessor. [FAS23, ¶7]*

It should be noted that neither the third nor the fourth capital lease criteria applies when the lease is for used equipment (paragraph .103d). The leased equipment is considered to be used property for this definition if the beginning of the lease term falls within the last 25% of the total estimated economic life of the leased property, including earlier years of use.

Application of the capital lease criteria is an accounting issue only. Although the contract is labeled a lease and, in form, is viewed as such, the FASB wants the accounting to reflect the substance of the transaction. Keep in mind, therefore, that the question of lease classification arises only as the lessor and lessee determine how to report the lease in their financial statements. Lease classification for accounting purposes should not be confused with other tax, economic or managerial issues.

Also, because these accounting issues are governed by the FASB, they are pertinent only when the lessor's or lessee's financial statements are being audited or reviewed. If a lessor's or lessee's statements are not being audited, they may not be following FASB 13 accounting. Often, in this case, all the leases are treated as operating (off balance sheet).

FASB 13 Terminology

In order to better understand and apply the capital lease criteria, it is important to define certain relevant terms. What exactly do lease term and economic life mean, for example? Or, how does one determine present value? What constitutes minimum lease payments? These and other terms are defined in this section.

INCEPTION OF THE LEASE

The inception of the lease is defined by FASB 13 as the date of the lease agreement, or commitment, if earlier. For purposes of this definition, a commitment shall be in writing, should be signed by the parties in interest to the transaction and shall specifically set forth the principal provisions of the transaction. The inception date is viewed as the point at which the economics of the transaction have been determined.

The inception date is extremely important because this is the date the determination is made as to whether a lease is capital or operating. Changes in the accounting treatment of the lease after this time are inappropriate unless the lease is changed through a renegotiation of the terms of the lease. The combination of this rule and the attributes of a valid commitment is intended to match the classification of a lease to its economics. It precludes the parties putting together a skeleton of a lease that qualifies as operating and then altering the economics such that the lessee, in actuality, is acting as owner.

BARGAIN PURCHASE OPTION

A bargain purchase option is a provision allowing the lessee, at its option, to purchase the leased property for a price below fair market value. This option price should be sufficiently lower than the expected fair value of the property at the date the option becomes exercisable, such that the exercise of the option appears, at the inception of the lease, to be reasonably assured. It is apparent from this definition that a bargain purchase option is one that can reasonably be expected to be exercised.

Who determines whether or not a particular purchase option is low enough to be considered a bargain? It is the responsibility of the lessor and lessee to make this determination individually, based on their own best estimates of future events and asset values. The company's auditor, however, through the audit process, passes final judgment as to the appropriateness of the determination.

LEASE TERM

The lease term includes the period covered by each of the following elements contained in Exhibit 9-6. What, specifically, do these events mean? A lease is considered to be noncancellable, for instance, if it is cancellable only upon the occurrence of some remote contingency, only with the lessor's permission or only if the lessee enters into a new lease with the same lessor.

A bargain renewal option is an option to renew the lease in which the renewal payments are so far below fair market value, or normal rentals for the same equipment, that it is reasonably assured the lessee will renew. Because renewal is reasonably assured, the lease term during the renewal period is considered part of the overall lease term.

There also may be an optional renewal period. Failure to renew the lease for a specified length of time, however, imposes a penalty on the lessee. The penalty may be minimal or it may be high enough to ensure that the lessee will renew to avoid the penalty. If the lease contract contains a significant nonrenewal penalty, the definition of the lease term is extended to cover this period.

The lease term also includes periods during which the lessee guarantees or provides all or part of the debt used by the lessor to acquire the asset. In

---

Exhibit 9-6
Lease Term

1. The fixed, noncancellable term of the lease

2. Bargain renewal option periods

3. Periods attributable to significant nonrenewal penalties

4. Periods covered by lessee loans to the lessor, or guarantees of the lessor's debt

5. Ordinary renewal periods preceding a bargain purchase option

6. Renewal periods at the lessor's option (puts).

---

this instance, it is assumed that, as long as the lessee is at risk for any of the lessor's debt, the lessee will continue to use the asset and pay the lease payments for at least that period of time.

Renewal periods preceding a bargain purchase option also must be considered. The lease term is extended to include any time period prior to a bargain purchase option. In this case, the assumption is made that the lessee will remain in the lease at least that long because, by doing so, the asset can be acquired at a bargain price.

Finally, if there is a clause in the contract that allows the lessor to require the lessee to renew the lease, the term is extended to include the additional renewal period. This is known as a put option because the lessor can put the lessee in the position of having to renew. Any put renewal periods are considered part of the lease term definition.

It would be unlikely to have all of these events occur in the same lease contract. Whenever any of them do, however, they serve to lengthen the basic lease term. The lease term used in the third capital lease criterion and the definition of minimum lease payments includes all of these possible events.

ESTIMATED ECONOMIC LIFE

The estimated economic life of leased property is the estimated remaining period during which the property is expected to be economically usable by one or more users. The asset's usable life includes normal repairs and maintenance without limitation by the lease term. The asset should be used for the purpose for which it was intended at the inception of the lease. Again, the lessor and lessee independently determine the economic useful life of the asset.

MINIMUM LEASE PAYMENTS

Minimum lease payments include all the payments the lessee is obligated to make or can be required to make in connection with the leased property. From the standpoint of the lessor, minimum lease payments include all such payments to be received by the lessor. The basic lease payments required by the lease contract are, of course, considered as minimum lease payments. However, if the basic lease term is extended for any of the reasons discussed in the lease term definition above, the additional payments also are considered minimum lease payments. Minimum lease payments include the items in Exhibit 9-7.

Exhibit 9-7
Minimum Lease Payments

FASB 13 paragraph .417 (1), (2), and (3):

(1) The minimum rental payments called for by the lease over the lease term.

(2) Any guarantee by the lessee or any party related to the lessee of the residual value at the expiration of the lease term, whether or not payment of the guarantee constitutes a purchase of the leased property.[407] When the lessor has the right to require the lessee to purchase the property at termination of the lease for a certain or determinable amount, that amount shall be considered a lessee guarantee. When the lessee agrees to make up any deficiency[408] below a stated amount in the lessor's realization of the residual value, the guarantee to be included in the minimum lease payments shall be the stated amount,[409] rather than an estimate of the deficiency to be made up.

(3) Any payment that the lessee must make or can be required to make upon failure to renew or extend the lease at the expiration of the lease term, whether or not the payment would constitute a purchase of the lease property. In this connection, it should be noted that the definition of lease term (refer to paragraph .413) includes "all periods, if any, for which failure to renew the lease imposes a penalty on the lessee in an amount such that renewal appears, at the inception of the lease, to be reasonably assured." If the lease term has been extended because of that provision, the related penalty shall not be included in minimum lease payments.

[407] *A guarantee of the residual value obtained by the lessee...*

[408] *A lease provision requiring the lessee to make up a residual...*

[409] *If a lease limits the amount of the lessee's obligation...*

The minimum lease payments from the standpoint of the lessor include the payments described in Exhibit 9-7 plus any guarantee of the residual value or of rental payments beyond the lease term by a third party unrelated to either the lessee or the lessor. (The third party must be financially capable of discharging the obligations that may arise from the guarantee.)

An adjustment may have to be made to the total lease payment required by the contract in some circumstances to arrive at that portion that is defined as the minimum lease payment. For instance, FASB 13 requires that executory costs and contingent rentals be removed from the total lease payment when calculating the minimum lease payment. These terms are defined next.

EXECUTORY COSTS

Executory costs are those costs such as insurance, taxes and maintenance, whether paid by the lessor or the lessee. They are sometimes built into the lease payment by a lessor as a matter of convenience to the lessee. Although charged to the lessee each month, these amounts are not part of the basic cost of financing the leased asset.

For example, a typical monthly lease payment for a piece of equipment might be structured as follows:

360	(rental)
18	(sales tax)
50	(maintenance)
428	(total payment)

The lessee's total monthly payment is 428. However, for accounting purposes, the minimum lease payment is only 360. Sales taxes and maintenance fees are examples of executory costs and are subtracted from the total lease payment and accounted for separately.

If the portion of the minimum lease payments representing executory costs, including profit thereon, cannot be determined from the provisions of the lease, then an estimate of the amount should be made by the lessee if such executory costs exist.

CONTINGENT RENTALS

Contingent rentals, like executory costs, are deducted from total lease payments when computing minimum lease payments. Contingent rentals are dependent on certain unknown future events and are in addition to the basic lease payment. A common type of contingent rental is an additional charge to a lessee each month for excessive use beyond a certain base level of activity.

For example, a lease for a photocopy machine may require a basic monthly rental of 200 for the first 8,000 copies, plus 0.02 per copy for copies in excess of the 8,000-copy base. If the lessee makes 9,000 copies in a particular month, it is charged a contingent rent of 20.00 (1,000 x .02). The total lease payment for the month, including the contingent rent, is 220. The contingent rent of 20 is subtracted from the total payment to arrive at the minimum lease payment of 200 for purposes of lease classification.

Other types of contingent rentals, such as percentage or indexed rents, are common in other areas of leasing. Contingent rentals should be shown in the income statements of the lessor and lessee as they accrue.

FAIR MARKET VALUE

Fair market value is the price for which the property to be leased could be sold in an arm's-length transaction between unrelated parties. This amount is not necessarily the price the lessor pays for the asset, or a list price quoted by a manufacturer or dealer. It should be viewed as the normal selling price the lessee would pay to purchase the asset.

ESTIMATED RESIDUAL VALUE

The estimated residual value is the lessor's estimate of the fair value of the leased asset at the end of the lease term. Several industries, such as the auto industry and the computer industry, have had enough experience with equipment that they publish anticipated values of used equipment. Such information, when available, may be used by the lessor or the lessee to help in estimating future values of leased assets.

Other lessors and lessees secure estimates from qualified appraisal firms that charge a fee to give appraisals for certain types of assets. Sometimes insurance or other leasing companies will guarantee all or a portion of the future estimated value. In any event, the lessor and the lessee independently assess the anticipated value of the asset in order to negotiate the terms of the lease, as well as account for it.

The value of the estimated residual impacts not only the calculation of the lessor's implicit rate, but also the amount of income to be recognized by the lessor. For either of these two purposes, the estimated residual is that amount estimated at the inception of the lease.

DISCOUNT RATE

The fourth capital lease criterion requires that the present value of the minimum lease payments be compared to the fair market value of the asset. Compliance with this test requires determination of a discount rate. FASB 13 describes the appropriate discount rate to be used. The discount rate may be different, however, depending on whether the lessor or the lessee is making the present value determination.

Implicit Rate

FASB 13 requires a lessor to compute the present value of the minimum lease payments using the interest rate implicit in the lease. A lessee must compute the present value of the minimum lease payments using its incremental borrowing rate. However, if the lessee knows, or can determine, the lessor's implicit rate, and it is less than the lessee's incremental borrowing rate, the implicit rate should be used by the lessee. Normally, the lessee does not know the lessor's implicit rate if a residual position is taken by the lessor; therefore, the lessee uses its incremental borrowing rate.

The implicit rate measures the percentage yield or return to the lessor from the lease from an accounting perspective. It is the discount rate that, when applied to (1) the minimum lease payments (excluding executory costs and contingent rentals) and (2) the unguaranteed residual value accruing to the benefit of the lessor, causes the aggregate present value at the beginning of the lease term to be equal to the fair value of the leased property to the lessor at the inception of the lease, minus any ITC retained by the lessor and expected to be realized by it. An implicit rate calculation is illustrated on page 258.

In simpler terms, the implicit rate in the lease is the internal rate of return (IRR) of the fair market value (less ITC), the minimum lease payments and the unguaranteed residual. This definition does not include all the factors a lessor might recognize in determining its true economic yield from the lease. The implicit rate of FASB 13 is defined solely for purposes of the 90% test, as contained in the fourth capital lease criterion. It should not be confused with other economic returns.

Lessee's Incremental Borrowing Rate

The lessee's incremental borrowing rate is defined by FASB 13 as the rate, at the inception of the lease, the lessee would have incurred to borrow, over a similar term, the funds necessary to purchase the asset rather than lease it. Referencing prime rate or treasury bills (unless as a base to which a spread is added) is not appropriate as these rates do not reflect long-term borrowing rates. Notice that this rate is neither the lessee's imbedded cost of borrowing nor its cost of capital.

This definition refers not just to the length of the lease, but also to other parameters or terms of the lease, such as fixed rate financing, no down payment or a balloon payment comparable to the residual estimate, etc. Such an interpretation does not make sense, however, if the lessee normally would not borrow under such restrictions. Incremental means the borrowing rate should be based on the cost to borrow additional funds for this incremental project.

The incremental borrowing rate is used as the lessee's discount rate for purposes of the 90% test, if the lessor's implicit rate is either unknown or is greater than the lessee's borrowing rate.

INITIAL DIRECT COSTS

Certain costs incurred by the lessor in order to consummate a leasing transaction are allowed by the FASB to be measured separately and amortized over the term of the lease. By doing so, these costs are separated from other overhead costs that are otherwise deducted from income in the month they are accrued. Not all costs of the lessor are treated in this manner, though. A specific definition of initial direct costs is found in paragraph .411 of FASB 13 (as derived from FASB Statement 91, paragraph 24). The impact of initial direct costs on the lessor's accounting is discussed in a subsequent chapter.

> *.411 Initial direct costs.[402a] Only those costs incurred by the lessor that are (a) costs to originate a lease incurred in transactions with independent third parties that (i) result directly from and are essential to acquire that lease and (ii) would not have been incurred had that leasing transaction not occurred and (b) certain costs directly related to specified activities performed by the lessor for that lease. Those activities are: evaluating the prospective lessee's financial condition; evaluating and recording guarantees, collateral, and other security arrangements; negotiating lease terms; preparing and processing lease documents; and closing the transaction. The costs directly related to those activities shall include only that*

portion of the employees' total compensation and payroll-related fringe benefits directly related to time spent performing those activities for that lease and other costs related to those activities, . . . soliciting potential lessees, servicing existing leases, and other ancillary activities related to establishing and monitoring credit policies, supervision, and administration. Initial direct costs shall not include administrative costs, rent, depreciation, any other occupancy and equipment costs and employees' compensation and fringe benefits related to activities described in the previous sentence, unsuccessful origination efforts, and idle time. [FAS91,¶24]

> 402a   *Initial direct costs shall be offset by nonrefundable fees that are yields adjustments as prescribed in Section L20 [FAS91, ¶24 fn) the provisions of paragraphs .104 and .018 of section L20 apply to lessors determining the net amount of initial direct costs (FAS91, ¶23)*

Although the determination of initial direct costs is not needed to classify the lease, they must be measured separately in order to subsequently account for it.

The 90% Test

Of the four capital lease criteria, the 90% test (fourth criterion) is the most difficult to assess. It also is the one most commonly encountered by those trying to achieve off balance sheet financing. This criterion requires several calculations and involves a discount rate and minimum lease payments. In the case of a lessor, it also necessitates calculating an implicit rate.

IMPLICIT RATE CALCULATION

The implicit rate must be calculated by lessors in order to compute the present value of the minimum lease payments for purposes of the 90% test. The following illustration demonstrates the calculation of the implicit rate for a sample lease.

Assumptions

The assumptions for this illustration consist of the following:

    Inception date: January 1
    Term: 60 monthly lease payments, in advance
    Equipment cost: 100,000
    Payment amount: 2,041
    Unguaranteed residual: 15,000.

Calculation

The calculation of the implicit rate is based on the earlier definition from FASB 13, paragraph .412. It is the IRR of the minimum lease payments, the unguaranteed residual value and the fair value of the leased property to the lessor at the inception of the lease. The implicit rate in this example is calculated as follows:

HP-12C				**HP-17B (12 P/YR BEGIN MODE)**	
	f	REG			FIN
	g	BEG			TVM
100,000	CHS	PV		■	CLEAR DATA
2,041		PMT	60		N
60		n	2,041		PMT
15,000		FV	100,000	+/-	PV
		i	1.0319	15,000	FV
	12	x	12.3831		I%YR=12.3831

The present value must be entered into the calculator as a negative amount, because, from the lessor's viewpoint, this is an outflow, or out-of-pocket cash flow. Thereafter, the payments to the lessor and the unguaranteed residual are treated as positive cash flows as they are received from the lessee. Because the payments are due at the beginning of each period, rather than the end, the calculator must be placed in the begin mode.

The lessor uses this implicit rate as a discount rate to solve for the present value of the minimum lease payments in the fourth accounting test. The present value is then compared to 90% of the fair market value of the asset in order to classify the lease as either capital or operating.

PRESENT VALUE CALCULATION

The fourth capital lease criterion requires a computation of the present value of the minimum lease payments by both lessor and lessee. This present value is compared to 90% of the fair market value of the asset. The discount rate to be used to solve for the present value is established by FASB 13. Lessors must use the implicit rate in the lease and lessees typically use their incremental borrowing rate. However, lessees must use the lessor's implicit rate if it is known and if it is lower than the incremental borrowing rate.

The previous example regarding the implicit rate calculation will be expanded to illustrate computing the present value of the minimum lease payments for the 90% test.

Assumptions

The assumptions for this expanded illustration are the same as the previous example, with the addition of several more factors.

> Inception date: January 1
>
> Term: 60 monthly lease payments, in advance
>
> Equipment cost: 100,000
>
> Payment amount: 2,041
>
> Unguaranteed residual: 15,000
>
> Implicit rate (lessor discount rate): 12.3831%
>
> Incremental borrowing rate (lessee discount rate): 10.25%
>
> Executory costs and contingent rentals: None.

FASB 13 Comparison Base

The present value of the minimum lease payments is calculated separately by both the lessee and the lessor. The present value is then compared to 90% of the fair market value of the leased asset (the comparison base).

100,000	Fair market value of the leased asset
x 90%	
90,000	Comparison base

The 90,000 is compared to the present value of the minimum lease payments to classify the lease. In order to be classified as an operating lease, the present value must be less than 90,000. If the present value of the minimum lease payments is equal to or greater than 90,000, the lease is classified as a capital lease.

Lessor Calculation

The keystrokes for calculating the present value of the lessor's minimum lease payments are shown below. This amount exceeds the 90,000 comparison base; therefore, this lease would be classified as capital by the lessor.

		HP-12C			**HP-17B (12 P/YR BEGIN MODE)**
	f	REG			FIN
	g	BEG			TVM
2,041		PMT		■	CLEAR DATA
60		n		60	N
12.3831	g	12 ÷		2,041	PMT
		PV -91,898.27	12.3831	I%YR
					PV=-91,898.27

Lessee Calculation

The keystrokes for calculating the present value of the lessee's minimum lease payments are shown below. This amount exceeds the 90,000 comparison base; therefore, this lease also would be classified as capital by the lessee.

		HP-12C			**HP-17B (12 P/YR BEGIN MODE)**
	f	REG			FIN
	g	BEG			TVM
2,041		PMT		■	CLEAR DATA
60		n		60	N
10.25	g	12÷		2,041	PMT
		PV -96,322.33	10.25	I%YR
					PV=-96,322.33

Remember that some leases contain additional elements besides the basic lease payments that are treated as minimum lease payments. Such other elements might include fees paid by the lessee, residual guarantees by the lessee or by parties related to the lessee, any other residual guarantees (from the lessor's viewpoint), bargain purchase options and nonrenewal penalties. It also is important to exclude from the basic periodic lease payment the amount of any executory costs or contingent rentals present in the lease. Several of these issues are discussed in the next chapter.

Disclosure Requirements

FASB 13 requires that, in addition to the financial statement information regarding a company's leasing activities, there also should be certain other details disclosed in the footnotes to those statements. These disclosure requirements apply to both lessors and lessees for capital and operating leases.

LESSEES

The disclosure requirements for lessees are contained in FASB 13, paragraph .112.

> *.112 The following information with respect to leases shall be disclosed in the lessee's financial statements or the footnotes thereto. (Refer to paragraphs .151 and .152 for illustrations.)*
>
> a. *For capital leases:*
>
> > (1) *The gross amount of assets recorded under capital leases as of the date of each balance sheet presented by major classes according to nature or function. This information may be combined with the comparable information for owned assets.*
> >
> > (2) *Future minimum lease payments as of the date of the latest balance sheet presented, in the aggregate and for each of the five succeeding fiscal years, with separate deductions from the total for the amount representing executory costs, including any profit thereon, included in the minimum lease payments and for the amount of the imputed interest necessary to reduce the net minimum lease payments to present value.*
> >
> > (3) *The total of minimum sublease rentals to be received in the future under noncancelable subleases as of the date of the latest balance sheet presented.*
> >
> > (4) *Total contingent rentals actually incurred for each period for which an income statement is presented. [FAS13,¶16]*
> >
> > (5) *Assets recorded under capital leases and the accumulated amortization thereon shall be separately identified in the lessee's balance sheet or in footnotes thereto. Likewise, the related obligations shall be separately identified in the balance sheet as obligations under capital leases and shall be subject to the same considerations as other obligations in classifying them with current and noncurrent liabilities in classified balance sheets. Unless the charge to income resulting from amortization of assets recorded under capital leases is included with depreciation expense and the fact that it is so included is disclosed, the amortization charge shall be separately disclosed in the financial statements or footnotes thereto. [FAS13,¶13]*
>
> b. *For operating leases having initial or remaining noncancelable lease terms in excess of one year:*
>
> > (1) *Future minimum rental payments required as of the date of*

the latest balance sheet presented, in the aggregate and for each of the five succeeding fiscal years.

(2) The total of minimum rentals to be received in the future under noncancelable subleases as of the date of the latest balance sheet presented.

c. For all operating leases, rental expense for each period for which an income statement is presented, with separate amounts for minimum rentals, contingent rentals, and sublease rentals. Rental payments under leases with terms of a month or less that were not renewed need not be included.

d. A general description of the lessee's leasing arrangements including, but not limited to, the following:

(1) The basis on which contingent rental payments are determined.

(2) The existence and terms of renewal or purchase options and escalation clauses.

(3) Restrictions imposed by lease agreements, such as those concerning dividends, additional debt, and further leasing. [FAS13, ¶6]

LESSORS

The disclosure requirements for lessors are contained in paragraph .119 of FASB 13.

.119 When leasing, exclusive of leveraged leasing, is a significant part of the lessor's business activities in terms of revenue, net income, or assets, the following information with respect to leases shall be disclosed in the financial statements or footnotes thereto (refer to paragraphs .151 and .153 for illustrations):

a. For sales-type and direct financing leases: [FAS13, ¶23]

(1) The components of the net investment in sales-type and direct financing leases as of the date of each balance sheet presented:

(a) Future minimum lease payments to be received, with separate deductions for (i) amounts representing executory costs, including any profit thereon, included in the minimum lease payments and (ii) the accumulated allowance for uncollectible minimum lease payments receivable.

      (b) *The unguaranteed residual values accruing to the benefit of the lessor.*

      (c) *For direct financing leases only, initial direct costs (see paragraph .411).*

      (d) *Unearned income (refer to paragraphs .113(b) and .114(b)). [FAS91,¶25d]*

  (2) *Future minimum lease payments to be received for each of the five succeeding fiscal years of the date of the latest balance sheet presented.*

  (3) *[Deleted 12/86 because of the issuance of FASB Statement No. 91, Accounting for Nonrefundable Fees and Costs Associated with Originating or Acquiring Loans and Initial Direct Costs of Leases.]*

  (4) *Total contingent rentals included in income for each period for which an income statement is presented.*

b. *For operating leases:*

  (1) *The cost and carrying amount, if different, of property on lease or held for leasing by major classes of property according to nature or function, and the amount of accumulated depreciation in total as of the date of the latest balance sheet presented.*

  (2) *Minimum future rentals on noncancelable leases as of the date of the latest balance sheet presented, in the aggregate and for each of the five succeeding fiscal years.*

  (3) *Total contingent rentals included in income for each period for which an income statement is presented.*

c. *A general description of the lessor's leasing arrangements. [FAS13,¶23]*

CONCLUSION

Accounting for leases remains one of the more challenging segments of the leasing industry. It is complex and involves many different factors, due in large part to the creativity and innovation applied to the structuring of lease transactions. That is why today's leasing companies have such a great need for knowledge of FASB 13. Additionally, both accounting and sales professionals are finding this knowledge to be important.

The basic issue of what constitutes a capital versus an operating lease is crucial to understanding the other accounting and managerial reporting topics addressed. Such an understanding requires a knowledge of the accounting guidelines of FASB 13 and subsequent FASB pronouncements. This knowledge includes the rules and definitions necessary to properly account for the various lease accounting products.

Although the rules of accounting for leases are set forth in FASB 13, how they relate to transactions is not always clear. The background provided in this chapter, including an understanding of the lease classification rules and terminology, serves as an essential foundation for their application.

Chapter Ten

Lessor Accounting

Financial Accounting Standards Board Statement No. 13 "Accounting for Leases" (FASB 13) provides the framework for accounting for leases from a lessor perspective. How to apply FASB 13, however, is not clear. Consequently, and in spite of a plethora of pronouncements, numerous practice and implementation problems have developed over the years.

These problems arise for a number of reasons, including a lack of clarity and definitive guidance in the literature and an increase in transactions not originally contemplated in FASB 13. This chapter addresses accounting for leases from a lessor perspective as promulgated by FASB 13. Lessor accounting for the following types of lease transactions is explained:

- Direct Financing Leases

- Sales-type Leases

- Operating Leases.

DIRECT FINANCING LEASES

Direct financing leases constitute a significant portion of lessors' portfolios. This high proportion is the result of the large volume of nontax leases and the accelerated earnings curve of a direct financing lease compared to that of an operating lease.

A direct financing lease is a lease, other than a leveraged lease, that does not give rise to manufacturer/dealer profit (or loss) to the lessor. It also meets one or more of the four classification criteria and both of the additional lessor criteria, as promulgated by FASB 13. (These classification criteria are discussed in detail in Chapter Nine.) In such leases, the cost or carrying amount and the fair value of the leased property are the same at the inception of the lease.

The most prominent characteristic of this type of lease is, as its name implies, direct financing. The lease is just that: a pure financing in which no sale is involved (i.e., gross profit). The lessor finances the acquisition of an asset for the lessee. In the direct financing lease, interest income serves as the source of income to the lessor; therefore, a direct financing lease is accounted for much as though the lessor had provided a loan to the lessee.

Nonetheless, the accounting requirements are more complex than an installment loan because of the numerous variables frequently encountered in leasing. These variables include set-up fees, refundable security deposits, tax depreciation, residual values and initial direct costs. Initial direct costs are those costs necessary to consummate a lease. Initial direct costs incurred in a direct financing lease are amortized to income over the life of the lease, as an adjustment to yield. Because these costs are incurred to create a financial instrument, they are matched against interest income as it is earned over the term of the lease.

Another complexity of direct financing leases is that many are treated as true tax leases for purposes of reporting income to the Internal Revenue Service (IRS). As mentioned, direct financing leases, which do not reflect depreciation in the lessor's financial statements, are treated somewhat akin to loans for accounting purposes. For those leases that are tax leases, however, depreciation is recognized for tax purposes because the lessor retains tax ownership. Such completely opposite accounting and tax treatment gives rise to interperiod tax allocation, or deferred taxes. This concept is illustrated later in this section.

FASB 13 Requirements

FASB 13, as amended by FASB Statement No. 91 (FASB 91) and FASB Statement No. 98 (FASB 98), requires direct financing leases to be accounted for by the lessor as follows (FASB 13 .114 (a), (b) and (d)):

> a. *The sum of (1) the minimum lease payments (net of amounts, if any, included therein with respect to executory costs, such as maintenance, taxes, and insurance, to be paid by the lessor, together with any prof-*

it thereon) and (2) the unguaranteed residual value accruing to the benefit of the lessor shall be recorded as the gross investment in the lease. [20a] *The estimated residual value used to compute the unguaranteed residual value accruing to the benefit of the lessor shall not exceed the amount estimated at the inception of the lease.[21]* [FAS98, ¶22h]

b. *The difference between the gross investment in the lease in (a) above and the cost or carrying amount, if different, of the leased property shall be recorded as unearned income. The net investment in the lease shall consist of the gross investment plus any unamortized initial direct costs less the unearned income. The unearned income and initial direct costs shall be amortized to income over the lease term[21a] so as to produce a constant periodic rate of return on the net investment in the lease.[22] However, other methods of income recognition may be used if the results obtained are not materially different from those which would result from the prescribed method in the preceding sentence. The net investment in the lease shall be subject to the same considerations as other assets in classification as current or noncurrent assets in a classified balance sheet. Contingent rentals shall be included in the determination of income as accruable.* [FAS98, ¶22i]

d. *The estimated residual value shall be reviewed at least annually [24] and, if necessary, adjusted in the manner prescribed in paragraph .113(d).* [FAS13, ¶18]

[20a] Paragraphs .536 and .537 further discuss residual value retained by a lessor that sells rental payments.]

21 If the lease agreement or commitment, if earlier, includes a . . .

[21a] The practice of accelerating the recognition of lease . . .

22 This is the interest method described in Section 169, . . .

[24 Paragraphs .514 through .517 discuss upward adjustment of guaranteed residual values.]

From this definition it can be seen that future benefits (lease payments and residual) are shown as receivables. This treatment reflects the characteristics of the direct financing lease. The lessor has, in substance, sold the asset to the lessee at cost, and is financing that sale.

Any difference between future receipts and the cost of the asset (including initial direct costs) is the total income to be recognized over the term of the lease. The total income to be earned is known on the first day of the lease. Appropriately enough, the net investment (as defined) at the inception of the lease is exactly equal to the net cash outflow of the lessor at that time.

Initial direct costs are treated as an adjustment to the yield of the lease; that is, the earnings of the lease are reduced over time by the amortization of the initial direct costs. Because of this matching of costs to revenues over the term, it is important to include in initial direct costs only those costs that are proper. For instance, prior to the issuance of FASB 91 (which altered the definition of initial direct costs), there was considerable debate about the propriety of including the allowance for doubtful accounts as part of initial direct costs. A careful reading of the definition of initial direct costs in FASB 91, however, clearly indicates that such inclusion has been precluded.

Direct Financing Lease Example

The example illustrating the process of booking a direct financing lease is broken into separate parts for clarity: (1) initial entries to set up the lease, (2) accounting for subsequent interest income, including any related tax effects and (3) the lease in financial statement form.

ASSUMPTIONS

The assumptions for this example are as follows:

Inception date: July 1

Term: 60 months, with one payment in advance

Equipment cost: 100,000

Monthly payment: 2,010

Unguaranteed residual: 18,000

Initial direct costs: 2,500

Refundable security deposit: 5,000

Machine delivery date: June 15

Tax status: Tax lease of 5-year MACRS property

Tax rate: 35%.

INITIAL SET-UP

Certain preliminary steps must be completed before accounting for a lease, the first of which is determining its classification. Is the lease operating? It is assumed that the first three classification criteria were not met; therefore, the remaining criterion to be evaluated is the 90% test. If the present value of the minimum lease payments is greater than or equal to 90% of the fair market value of the asset, less any lessor retained investment tax credit (ITC), the lease is a capital lease.

The discount rate to be used to determine present value is the implicit rate in the lease. This rate must be calculated by the lessor. The implicit rate is the IRR of the fair market value, minimum lease payments and the unguaranteed residual value (as shown in Exhibit 10-1). It is calculated as follows:

HP-12C			HP-17B (#TIMES PROMPTING: ON)		
	f	REG			FIN
97,990	CHS g	CFo			CFLO
2,010	g	CFj	■ CLEAR DATA		YES
59	g	Nj	FLOW (0)=?	97,990 +/-	INPUT
18,000	g	CFj	FLOW (1)=?	2,010	INPUT
	f IRR	1.0396	# TIMES (1)=1	59	INPUT
12	x	12.4747	FLOW (2)=?	18,000	INPUT
			# TIMES (2)=1	1	INPUT
					EXIT
					CALC
			IRR% = 1.0396		
			X 12 = 12.4747		

The calculated annual implicit rate is 12.4747%. This rate is the discount rate used to present value the minimum lease payments in applying the 90% test.

Exhibit 10-1
Implicit Rate Cash Flows

	Inception cash flow	Subsequent cash flow	Residual cash flow
Equipment cost	(100,000)	59 payments of	18,000
Advance payment	2,010	2,010	
	(97,990)		

271

Completion of the 90% test is a three-step process. The first step involves computing 90% of the fair market value. This base is compared to the present value of the minimum lease payments, which is calculated in the second step.

Step One

100,000	Fair market value of the equipment
x 90%	
90,000	Comparison base

Step Two

HP-12C   **HP-17B (12 P/YR BEGIN MODE)**

	f	REG			FIN
	g	BEG			TVM
2,010		PMT		■	CLEAR DATA
60		n		2,010	PMT
12.4747	g	12÷		60	N
	PV	-90,321.93		12.4747	I%YR
					PV= -90,321.93

Step Three

The present value of the minimum lease payments (90,321.93) is greater than 90% of the fair market value; therefore, the lease is not operating.

Furthermore, assume that both of the additional lessor criteria described in Chapter Nine are met. This lease meets one of the four classification criteria and both of the additional criteria. The lease is classified as a direct financing lease because there is no gross profit. It now can be set up on the books of the lessor by making the following entries.

1.	Minimum lease payments receivable	120,600	
	Unguaranteed residual	18,000	
	Initial direct costs	2,500	
	Unearned income		38,600
	Cash		102,500

     To record the minimum lease payments, unguaranteed residual and initial direct costs.

Per FASB 13, the minimum lease payment receivable of 120,600 (60 months x 2,010 per month) and the unguaranteed residual of 18,000 are recorded as the gross investment in the lease. This separation serves two purposes. First, it allows the lessor to track its credit exposure and second, the lessor can monitor its dependence on future residual values. This residual monitoring is important because such values are not as certain of realization as are the minimum lease payments. The unamortized balance of initial direct costs must be shown for disclosure purposes and is, therefore, recorded as a separate account that becomes part of the net investment. If all components were buried in one investment account, these managerial/investor objectives would not be met.

The difference between the gross investment and the cost of the equipment is recorded as the unearned income:

Gross investment	138,600
Equipment cost	(100,000)
Unearned income	38,600

The equipment cost and initial direct costs are credited to either cash or accounts payable, depending on the timing of the payments. As a practical matter, the amount of initial direct costs booked with each lease will represent the lessor's best estimate of such costs, based upon experience and historical data. This estimate generally is made on an annual basis and is reviewed by the auditors.

The difference between the gross investment plus the initial direct costs and the unearned income in the lease is the net investment. The lessor's net investment in the lease at this point is 102,500. In general, this net investment is the only item shown on the face of the balance sheet. The components of the net investment, however, must be disclosed in the footnotes to the financial statements.

Next, the receipt of the advance payment and the refundable security deposit are recorded.

2. Cash	2,010	
Minimum lease payments receivable		2,010

> To record the receipt of the advance payment as a reduction in the gross investment in the lease.

3. Cash   5,000

     Refundable security deposit   5,000

     To record receipt of the refundable security deposit.

With the completion of entries 1, 2 and 3, the entire lease has been booked. A good check to ascertain whether the lease has been booked correctly is to compare the beginning net investment with the net cash outflow at the inception of the lease. They should be equal, as the net investment represents the lessor's cash investment in the lease. The refundable security deposit is not considered part of the net investment for financial reporting purposes. It is a form of credit enhancement and really does not belong to the lessor. The net of the account balances represents the net investment of 100,490.

Minimum lease payments receivable	118,590	
Unguaranteed residual	<u>18,000</u>	
Gross investment		136,590
Initial direct costs		2,500
Unearned income		<u>(38,600)</u>
Net investment		100,490

The lease has been booked correctly because the net investment of 100,490 is equal to the net cash outflow at the inception of the lease.

Equipment cost	(100,000)
Initial direct costs	(2,500)
Advance payment	<u>2,010</u>
Net cash outflow	(100,490)

ACCRETION OF INCOME

Many companies prefer to further improve the informational value of their accounting records by identifying the earnings associated with any unguaranteed residuals booked. This is the first step in the process referred to as accretion accounting, or the walking up of income.

It is easy to see that a leased asset generates earnings, as evidenced by the amount in the unearned income account. These earnings, however, come from two sources: the lease payments and any expected residual value. Examination of the unearned income calculation indicates that earnings flow from both the lease payments and the residual. Because there are two different sources of income, proponents of this method prefer to monitor each source separately.

This monitoring is accomplished by splitting the total unearned income into components – receivable and residual – and then separately recognizing interest earnings on both the minimum lease payments and on the unguaranteed residual. To effectuate this separate income recognition involves presenting the unguaranteed residual at its present value, using the implicit rate of the lease as the discount rate. This present value represents the principal portion of the residual, or the amount of the financing attributable to the future residual payment.

HP-12C			HP-17B (12 P/YR BEGIN MODE)	
	f	REG		FIN
12.4747	g	12 ÷		TVM
18,000		FV	■	CLEAR DATA
60		n	12.4747	I%YR
	PV	-9,678	18,000	FV
			60	N
				PV=-9,678

The present value, or principal portion, of the 18,000 residual value to be received 60 months in the future is 9,678. The difference between this present value and future value of 8,322 represents the earnings component of the residual; in effect, the unearned income to be recognized on the residual. The unearned residual earnings are journalized as follows:

4. Unearned income (minimum lease payments) 8,322
        Unearned income (residual)   8,322

> To record the unguaranteed residual at its present value and recognize the unearned income on the residual.

The total income to be recognized over the life of the lease cannot be changed just by moving accounts around. It is important to note in this example, therefore, that, although the unearned income has been allocated to its various sources, the total unearned income (and the net investment) remains the same.

Minimum lease payments receivable	118,590	
Unguaranteed residual	18,000	
Gross investment		136,590
Initial direct costs		2,500
Unearned receivable income	30,278	
Unearned residual income	8,322	
Unearned income		(38,600)
Net investment		100,490

The value of this methodology is that it allows management to track the company's dependence on residual earnings. If the company has heavy residual dependence in a certain equipment category, and residuals begin to soften in that category, the impact on earnings is evident.

It is interesting to note that, as residual earnings are recognized, the unearned residual amount declines, serving to increase the net investment in residuals; hence, the term accretion. This phenomenon is illustrated in Exhibits 10-2 and 10-3.

The increase in the present value of the residual should make sense conceptually. After all, as the lease approaches maturity, the net investment in the residual approaches its future value. By the end of the term the present value of the residual has been accreted, or walked up, to its future value. Residual earnings occur whether the accretion method is used or not. The accretion method identifies the specific increase.

The T-accounts for the initial booking of the lease are shown in Exhibit 10-4. There has not been any income recognized at this point. Earnings recognition is the next topic.

THE EARNING PROCESS

The earnings in a direct financing lease consist of interest income. This interest income is a function of the beginning-of-period net investment in the lease times the earnings rate (principal times interest). There are several methods of applying this principle to direct financing leases.

Earning Methods

The amount of unearned income booked at inception, less the full amortization of initial direct costs, is the total earnings to be recognized over the

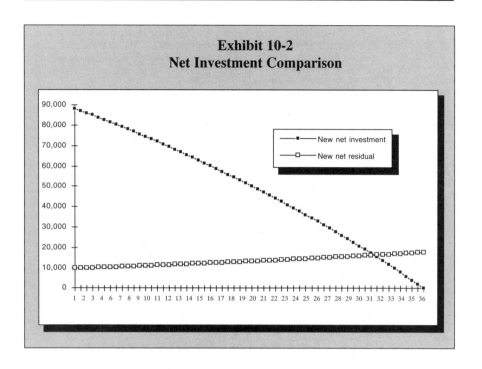

Exhibit 10-2
Net Investment Comparison

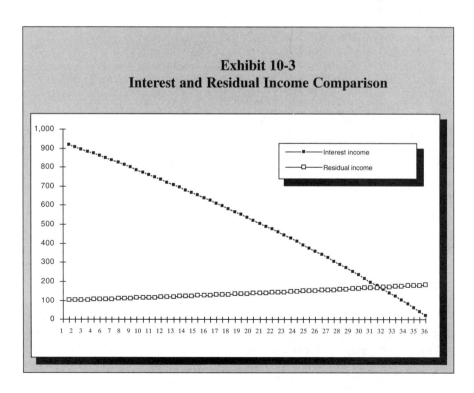

Exhibit 10-3
Interest and Residual Income Comparison

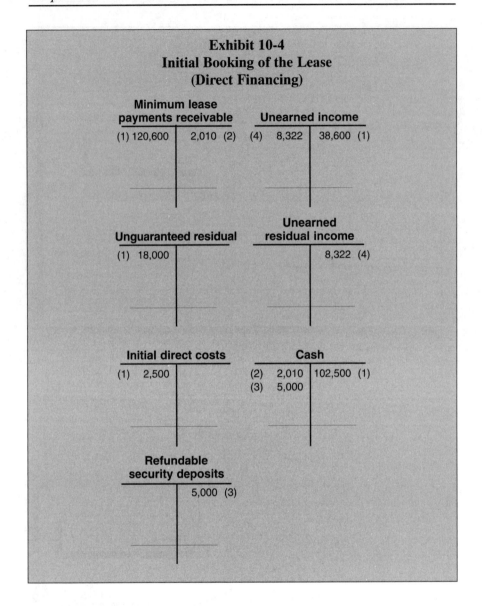

Exhibit 10-4
Initial Booking of the Lease
(Direct Financing)

Minimum lease payments receivable		Unearned income	
(1) 120,600	2,010 (2)	(4) 8,322	38,600 (1)

Unguaranteed residual		Unearned residual income	
(1) 18,000			8,322 (4)

Initial direct costs		Cash	
(1) 2,500		(2) 2,010	102,500 (1)
		(3) 5,000	

Refundable security deposits	
	5,000 (3)

life of the lease. Interest earnings are computed each period on the net investment in the lease, utilizing a constant periodic rate of return, as required by FASB 13.

The use of different constant periodic rates of return, or methods of recognizing income, does not affect the total income to be recognized in a lease over its life. Each method allocates income in a different manner, however. What are these methods of income allocation and which one is most appropriate?

There are three potential methods of income allocation to recognize income: (1) the pretax rate, (2) an after-tax return on assets method and (3) an after-tax return on equity method. (Another method of income allocation referred to as the Rule of 78 that accelerates the recognition of interest income. Although popular in the past, this method is no longer acceptable for GAAP purposes.)[1] The two after-tax methods are highly sophisticated and have very limited acceptance for GAAP purposes. As previously discussed, the Rule of 78s materially misstates income and, therefore, is not permissible for GAAP purposes. Hence, only the pretax method is discussed.

The nature of the revenue to be recognized in a finance lease is finance, or interest, income. As in any other form of financing, this income is a function of the yield (or rate of return) in the lease times the outstanding principal. In a direct financing lease, the outstanding principal is synonymous with the net investment. The periodic finance income to be recognized is equal to the yield times the net investment in the lease at any time.

The pretax rate is the most common method of income recognition for direct financing leases. Under the pretax rate method, the rate or yield that amortizes the cash flows (minimum lease payments, unguaranteed residual and initial direct costs) to the fair market value of the asset is applied against the net investment. The pretax rate in the example is 11.4711%.[2]

---

[1] The Rule of 78 draws its name from the formula for computing one year of interest. This formula uses a reverse sum-of-the years digits methodology. The denominator is expressed as $n(n+1)/2$, where n is equal to the number of periods. For one year (12 periods), the denominator is 78 (hence the name), computed as follows:

$$\frac{12(12+1)}{2} = 78$$

As an example, if the total interest to be earned in the lease for the 12-month period was 1,000, the first month's interest would be 153.85. Total interest is multiplied by the ratio of remaining months divided by the formula. In this example:

$$1,000 \times \frac{(12)}{78} = 153.85$$

[2] The pretax earnings rate is computed by considering the minimum lease payments, residual value and the initial direct costs.

HP-12C					HP-17B (#TIMES PROMPTING: ON)		
	f	REG					FIN
100,490	CHS	g	CFo				CFLO
2,010		g	CFj			■	CLEAR DATA
59		g	Nj	FLOW (0)=?	100,490	+/-	INPUT
18,000		g	CFj	FLOW (1)=?	2,010		INPUT
	f	IRR	0.9559	#TIMES (1) = 1	59		INPUT
	12	x	11.4711	FLOW (2) = ?	18,000		INPUT
				#TIMES (2) = 1	1		INPUT
							EXIT
							CALC

IRR% = 0.9559
X   12 = 11.4711

The monthly rate of .9559% (11.4711% ÷ 12) times the declining net investment in the lease equals the net interest earned for that month. For instance, the net interest earned for the first month for the example lease is 960.58 (100,490 x .9559%). Unfortunately, this earnings process is not quite as simple as it appears, because of the amortization of initial direct costs required by FASB 91.

Initial Direct Costs

FASB 91 requires that initial direct costs be reflected as an adjustment to the yield of the lease. Rather than being offset or capitalized to unearned income, initial direct costs are to be shown and amortized separately as a component of the net investment in the lease. Under this method, interest earned on the investment is offset by the amortization of the initial direct costs, which is, in reality, an expense. The result is net interest earnings, which is the amount presented in the income statement.

To satisfy this requirement requires several layers of computation. One must first compute the yield without including initial direct costs. This yield represents the gross, or pure, interest earnings. Next the yield is computed with the effect of initial direct costs included. This yield represents the net interest earnings.

Mathematically, the difference between the two yields must be attributable to the initial direct costs. This amount represents the amortization of initial direct costs against gross interest earnings. An illustration is needed to clarify this concept.

The net interest earned of 960.58 calculated earlier actually consists of gross interest earned less amortized initial direct costs. How are these two components identified? Following the methodology of FASB 91, the first step is to compute the yield without including the initial direct costs. This yield is equal to the previously computed implicit rate of 1.0396% per month (or 12.4747% annually). The yield of 1.0396% is applied to the "without initial direct costs" net investment of 97,990 to determine the first month's gross interest earnings of 1,018.70.

Next, the yield with initial direct costs is computed. This yield of .9559% per month (11.4711% annually) also has been computed, and is applied against the "with initial direct costs" net investment of 100,490 to arrive at the net interest of 960.58.

The difference in earnings between the two amounts of 58.12 represents the amortization of the initial direct costs. The monthly amortization amount is credited against the initial direct cost component of the net investment and reduces interest income. These differences for the first month and over the term are illustrated in Exhibit 10-5.

Exhibit 10-6 isolates the overall net investment in the lease by its components into the net investment in the lease receivable and the net investment in the residual. Just as the net investment represents the principal in the lease, the components of the net investment represent the principal associated with both the lease receivable and the unguaranteed residual.

Earlier, the unearned income attributable to the residual was calculated and set up as a separate account. This is necessary to calculate the net investment in the residual. As shown in Exhibit 10-6, the net investment in the residual is the amount of the unguaranteed residual booked (18,000) less the unearned income calculated earlier (8,322), or 9,678. The net investment in the lease receivable is the outstanding lease receivable (118,590) minus the remaining unearned income (30,278). Earnings on both the outstanding net investment in the lease receivable and the net investment in the unguaranteed residual are computed by multiplying the outstanding net investment times the pretax earnings rate in the lease, as shown in Exhibit 10-6.

Exhibit 10-5
Amortization of Initial Direct Costs

	1 Earnings without initial direct costs	2 Earnings with initial direct costs	(1-2) Amortization of initial direct costs
Net investment	97,990	100,490	
x rate	x .010396	x .009559	
First month's earnings	1,019	961	58
Earnings over the term	38,600	36,100	2,500

Exhibit 10-6
Net Investment Components

	1 Net investment in lease receivable	2 Net investment in residual	3 Initial direct costs	Overall net investment (1+2+3)
Gross investment	118,590	18,000		
Unearned income	(30,278)	(8,322)		
Net investment	88,312	9,678	2,500	100,490
Pretax earnings rate	x 1.0396%	x 1.0396%		
First month's earnings	918	101	(58)	961

Given the above discussion, and using the data from Exhibits 10-5 and 10-6, receipt of the payment and earnings recognition for the first month can be journalized as follows:

Cash	2,010	
Unearned income	918	
Unearned residual	101	
G & A expense	58	
Minimum lease payments receivable		2,010
Interest earned		918
Residual earned		101
Initial direct costs		58

> To record receipt of the first month's payment and earnings recognition.

The result of this entry is to reduce the net investment by the amount of principal received. The principal received is equal to the difference between the payment and the interest earned. As illustrated in Exhibit 10-7, the net investment in the lease receivable was reduced by 1,092. This amount is equal to the payment of 2,010 less the interest earned of 918. The pretax earnings rate is multiplied by the new net investment each month until the end of the lease term, at which time the net investment in the lease receivable will equal zero and the net investment in the residual will have accreted to the future value of 18,000.

Note that, in the income recognition for the first month, the advance payment was applied 100% to the net investment (principal). None of the advance payment was considered to be income. Finance income was recognized for the first month, however, even though the next payment does not occur until next month.

Recognition of income in the first period of a lease is correct accounting under an accrual concept. This is true for leases in advance or arrears. Income recognition is proper because the lessor has made an investment at the beginning of the lease. Income should accrue, therefore, on that investment from day one.

Earnings for the first year are journalized as follows:

5.	Cash	10,050	
	Unearned income	4,476	
	Unearned residual	514	
	G & A expense	287	
	Initial direct costs		287
	Interest earned		4,476
	Residual earned		514
	Minimum lease payment receivable		10,050

To record receipt of the first year's payments.

Exhibit 10-8 recaps the pure interest, residual earnings and initial direct costs amortization over the life of the lease. A complete recap by month of

---

Exhibit 10-7
First Month's Payment Allocation

	Net investment in lease receivable	Net investment in residual
Beginning balance	88,312[a]	9,678
Payment	(2,010)	–
Interest earned	918	101
Ending balance	87,220	9,779
Net change	1,092	101

[a] From Exhibit 10-6

Exhibit 10-8
Recap of Earnings Amortization

		Pure interest	Residual interest	Initial direct costs
Year 1	July			
	August	918	101	58
	September	907	102	58
	October	895	103	57
	November	884	104	57
	December	872	105	57
	Total	4,476	514	287
Year 2	January	860	106	57
	February	848	107	56
	March	836	108	56
	April	824	109	55
	May	812	110	55
	June	799	112	55
	July	787	113	54
	August	774	114	54
	September	761	115	54
	October	748	116	53
	November	735	117	52
	December	722	119	52
	Total	9,505	1,347	653
Year 3	January	708	120	52
	February	695	121	51
	March	681	122	50
	April	667	124	50
	May	653	125	49
	June	639	126	49
	July	625	128	48
	August	610	129	48
	September	596	130	47
	October	581	132	47
	November	566	133	46
	December	551	134	46
	Total	7,574	1,524	583

Exhibit 10-8 (continued)
Recap of Earnings Amortization

		Pure interest	Residual interest	Initial direct costs
Year 4	January	536	136	45
	February	521	137	44
	March	505	139	43
	April	490	140	43
	May	474	142	41
	June	458	143	41
	July	442	144	40
	August	426	146	40
	September	409	148	39
	October	392	149	37
	November	376	151	37
	December	<u>359</u>	<u>152</u>	<u>36</u>
	Total	5,387	1,726	486
Year 5	January	341	154	35
	February	324	155	34
	March	307	157	33
	April	289	159	32
	May	271	160	31
	June	253	162	31
	July	235	164	29
	August	216	165	28
	September	198	167	28
	October	179	169	26
	November	160	171	25
	December	<u>140</u>	<u>172</u>	<u>23</u>
	Total	2,912	1,954	355
Year 6	January	121	174	23
	February	101	176	21
	March	81	178	21
	April	61	180	19
	May	41	181	21
	June	21	183	16
	July	<u>-2</u>	<u>185</u>	<u>15</u>
	Total	<u>424</u>	<u>1,257</u>	<u>136</u>
		30,278	8,322	2,500

the interest earnings, residual earning and amortization of initial direct costs may be found in Appendix One.

INTERPERIOD TAX ALLOCATION

Once interest earnings have been ascertained, taxes must be provided on those earnings. To determine the interperiod tax allocation entries necessary to reflect the temporary differences between the tax and accounting books, the rules of FASB Statement No. 109 (FASB 109), "Accounting for Income Taxes," must be followed. First, the tax liability per the tax books is calculated as shown in Exhibit 10-9. Second, deferred taxes are calculated. The deferred tax methodology requires that the difference between the book and tax basis in the assets and liabilities be multiplied by the existing tax rate. Remember, this lease is considered to be a true tax lease for tax purposes, in contrast to its direct financing lease status for accounting purposes.

Based on the methodology of FASB 109, deferred taxes are calculated as follows:

Exhibit 10-9
Computation of the Tax Provision

	Tax books
Advance rental	2,010
Normal rentals	10,050
Other income	8,000
Initial direct costs	(2,500)
G & A expense	(1,320)
Depreciation (MACRS)	(20,000)
Interest expense	(3,000)
Taxable income	(6,760)
Tax rate	x .35
Tax expense (benefit)	(2,366)

Net investment	95,143
Tax basis	80,000

Difference	15,143
Tax rate	x 35%
Deferred taxes	5,300

The following tax entry is made at the end of the first year.

6. Tax expense	2,934	
Taxes payable	2,366	
Deferred taxes		5,300

To provide taxes on the first year's income.

END OF FIRST YEAR T-ACCOUNT SUMMARY

The T-account summaries for the balance sheet and income statement at the end of the first year are shown in Exhibits 10-10 and 10-11, respectively. T-account entries are annotated with the corresponding journal entry number for ease of reference.

Financial Statements

Using the T-account balances in Exhibits 10-10 and 10-11, an income statement (Exhibit 10-12), a balance sheet (Exhibit 10-13) and a cash flow statement (Exhibit 10-14) can be prepared. Some data have been added to present a more representative set of financial statements. The examples provided are common standard formats. Differences in presentation may occur when examining a specific company's financial statements.

Disclosure Requirements

FASB 13 paragraph .119 requires the following footnote disclosures be made with respect to direct financing leases. Actual presentation will vary from company to company; materiality will, of course, affect the presentation. The balance sheet need show only the net investment in the lease receivable.

I.   *The components of the net investment in sales-type and direct financing leases as of the date of each balance sheet presented:*

A.   *Future minimum lease payments to be received, with separate deductions for (i) amounts representing executory costs, includ-*

Exhibit 10-10
T-account Summary – Balance Sheet
(Direct Financing)

Minimum lease payments receivable	
120,600	2,010
	10,050 (5)
108,540	

Unearned income	
8,322	38,600
(5) **4,476**	
	25,802

Cash	
2,010	102,500
5,000	
(5) **10,050**	
	85,440

Unguaranteed residual	
18,000	

Unearned residual	
(5) **514**	8,322
	7,808

Deferred taxes	
	5,300 (6)

Initial direct costs	
2,500	**287** (5)
2,213	

Taxes payable	
(6) **2,366**	

Refundable security deposit	
	5,000

Exhibit 10-11
T-account Summary – Income Statement
(Direct Financing)

Interest earnings		Income tax expense	
	4,476 (5)	(6) 2,934	

Initial direct costs		Residual earnings	
(5) 287			514 (5)

G&A expense		Interest expense	
1,320		3,000	

Exhibit 10-12
Income Statement
(Direct Financing)

Revenue

Interest earnings	4,476	
Residual earnings	514	
Initial direct costs	(287)	
Total lease income		4,703

Operating expenses

G & A expense	1,320	
Interest expense	3,000	
Total operating expense		(4,320)
Operating income		383

Other income/expense

Other income	8,000	
Total other income/expense		8,000

Income from operations before taxes 8,383

Current taxes	(2,366)	
Deferred taxes	5,300	
Income tax expense		(2,934)
Net income		5,449

Exhibit 10-13
Balance Sheet
(Direct Financing)

Assets

Cash		31,560
Accounts receivable		11,000

Net investment in direct financing leases

Minimum lease payments receivable	108,540	
Unguaranteed residuals	18,000	
Gross investment		126,540
Initial direct costs		2,213
Unearned rental income	(25,802)	
Unearned residual income	(7,808)	
Total unearned income		(33,610)
Net investment [1]		95,143

Property, plant and equipment (net)		9,000
Total assets		146,703

Liabilities

Current liabilities

Accounts payable		15,000
Taxes payable		(2,366)
Current portion long-term debt		13,000
Long-term liabilities		50,000
Refundable security deposit		5,000
Deferred taxes		5,300
Total liabilities		85,934

Owners' equity

Contributed capital	55,320	
Retained earnings	5,449	
Total owners' equity		60,769
Total liabilities and owners' equity		146,703

---

[1] FASB 13 requires only that the net investment in lease receivables be shown here, with the components disclosed in the footnotes.

Exhibit 10-14
Statement of Cash Flows
(Direct Financing)

Cash flows from operating activities
Net interest earned	4,476	
Other income	8,000	
Operating expenses paid	(320)	
Interest expense paid	0	
Net cash from operating activities		12,156

Cash flows from investing activities
Initial direct costs capitalized	(2,500)	
Principal received from leases	7,584	
Capital expenditures	(9,000)	
Refundable security deposits received	5,000	
Investment in lease	(100,000)	
Net cash used in investing activities		(98,916)

Cash flows from financing activities
Proceeds from contributed capital	55,320	
Proceeds from long-term debt	63,000	
Net cash provided by financing activities		118,320

Net increase in cash
Net increase in cash		31,560
Cash at the beginning of the year		0
Cash at the end of the year		31,560

Reconciliation of net income to operating activities
Net income		5,449
Adjustments to net income		
Increase in deferred taxes	5,300	
Decrease in taxes payable	(2,366)	
Increase in accounts payable [1]	15,000	
Increase in accounts receivable	(11,000)	
Decrease in initial direct costs	287	
Increase in unguaranteed residual	(514)	
Total adjustments		6,707
Net cash from operating activities		12,156

[1] Includes 3,000 of interest payable and 1,000 of various accrued general and administrative items.

      ing any profit thereon, included in the minimum lease payments and (ii) the accumulated allowance for uncollectible minimum lease payments receivable.

   B.   *The unguaranteed residual values accruing to the benefit of the lessor;*

   C.   *For direct financing leases only, initial direct costs; (see paragraph .411).*

   D.   *Unearned income (refer to paragraphs .113 (b)). FAS91, ¶35d]*

  II. *Future minimum lease payments to be received for each of the five succeeding fiscal years as of the date of the latest balance sheet presented.*

  III. *Total contingent rentals included in income for each period for which an income statement is presented.*

SALES-TYPE LEASES

Sales-type leases have several characteristics that set them apart from direct financing leases. The most prominent of these is the immediate recognition of a sales gain or loss in the transaction. Because of this gain or loss aspect, sales-type leases occur most commonly in the portfolios of manufacturers or dealers who use leasing to market their products. However, leases written by nonmanufacturers/dealers also may result in sales-type treatment.

Characteristics

A lease is classified as a sales-type lease by the lessor whenever (1) it meets one of the four capital lease criterion, (2) it meets the two additional lessor criteria and (3) the fair value of the leased property, at the inception of the lease, is different from its cost or carrying amount. This situation occurs in a manufacturer or dealer environment and when leases are renewed. In fact, renewals represent a growing source of sales-type leases.

Keep in mind that leasing is an alternative means for financing the use of equipment. Direct financing leases, which were discussed in the previous section, reflect financing arrangements. The accounting is very similar to a loan in that interest income on the financing is the only source of earnings. Similarly, the term sales-type lease conveys the nature of this type of financing arrangement.

The transaction is accounted for as if a sale of the equipment has taken place. The revenue on the sale is recognized immediately along with the associated cost of goods sold. Gross profit is recognized on the difference between the cost of the equipment and its fair market value. It is important to be aware that, in this definition, the difference between cost and fair market value can represent either a gain or a loss. This gain or loss is recognized immediately when the lease is booked.

Because a sales-type lease is viewed as the sale and financing of a product, two types of income are recognized – sales revenue and interest income. The recognition of two types of income is the critical element to be remembered in a sales-type lease. It also is the major divergence in treatment between the sales-type and direct financing lease. Another difference is that FASB 13 requires a treatment of initial direct costs different from that for a direct financing lease.

In a sales-type lease, initial direct costs are required to be charged against income in the period in which the sales revenue is recorded. These costs are expensed under the premise that they are incurred primarily to produce sales revenue. This treatment is consistent with the practice of accounting for such costs in a normal sale of goods. The initial direct costs in a sales-type lease are expensed as a part of the cost of goods sold.

Once the sales gain (or loss) on the transaction has been recognized, the sales-type lease is treated the same as a direct financing lease. Interest income is recognized over the term of the lease as though the lessor is providing normal loan financing. As in the direct financing lease, though, the accounting requirements are more complex than a simple loan because of the numerous other variables involved.

FASB 13 Requirements

FASB 13 (L10.113) requires sales-type leases to be accounted for by the lessor as follows:

    *a. The minimum lease payments (net of amounts, if any, included therein with respect to executory costs to be paid by the lessor, together with any profit thereon) plus the **unguaranteed residual value** accruing to the benefit of the lessor shall be recorded as the gross investment in the lease. [13b] [FAS13,¶17] The estimated residual value used to compute the unguaranteed residual value accruing to the benefit of*

> the lessor shall not exceed the amount estimated at the inception of the lease. [14] [FAS23,¶9] . . .

b. The difference between the gross investment in the lease in (a) above and the sum of the present values of the two components of the gross investment shall be recorded as unearned income. The discount rate to be used in determining the present values shall be the interest rate implicit in the lease. The net investment in the lease shall consist of the gross investment less the unearned income. The unearned income shall be amortized to income over the lease term so as to produce a constant periodic rate of return on the net investment in the lease. [15] However, other methods of income recognition may be used if the results obtained are not materially different from those which would result from the prescribed method. The net investment in the lease shall be subject to the same considerations as other assets in classification as current or noncurrent assets in a classified balance sheet. [FAS13,¶17] Contingent rentals shall be included in the determination of income as accruable. [FAS29,¶13]

c. The present value of the minimum lease payments (net of executory costs, including any profit thereon), computed at the interest rate implicit in the lease, shall be recorded as the sales price. The cost or carrying amount, if different, of the leased property, plus any **initial direct costs**, less the present value of the unguaranteed residual value accruing to the benefit of the lessor, computed at the interest rate implicit in the lease, shall be charged against income in the same period.

[13b] Paragraphs .536 and .537 further discuss residual value retained by a lessor that sells rental payments.]

[14] If the lease agreement or commitment . . .

[15] This is the interest method described in Section 169, paragraph .108 and footnote 4. [FAS13,¶12,fn11]

It can be seen from this definition that the lessor in a sales-type lease receives income from two sources. The first is the gross profit on the sale of the leased asset. This gross profit is recognized immediately, and represents the difference between the leased asset's fair value (retail) and its carrying amount (cost).

The second component consists of financing income, and represents the difference between total future receipts and the net investment, or fair value of the leased asset at the beginning of the lease term. The future benefits in the lease are shown as receivables, similar to the direct financing lease.

Sales-type Lease Example

An illustration of booking a sales-type lease is broken down into separate parts for clarity: (1) initial entries to set up the lease; (2) the accounting for subsequent interest income, including taxes and their related effects; and (3) the lease in financial statement format.

ASSUMPTIONS

The same basic assumptions used in the direct financing lease example of the previous section are utilized in order to highlight the differences between these two lease types. Some additional information has been added.

> Inception date: July 1
>
> Term: 60 months, with one payment in advance
>
> Equipment cost: 60,000
>
> Fair market value: 100,000
>
> Monthly payment: 2,010
>
> Unguaranteed residual: 18,000
>
> Initial direct costs: 2,500
>
> Refundable security deposit: 5,000
>
> Equipment delivery date: June 15
>
> Tax lease: 5-year MACRS property
>
> Tax rate: 35%.

INITIAL SET-UP

As always, the first step to be completed before accounting for a lease is to determine its classification. Assume that the first three criteria are not applicable. The remaining criterion to be evaluated, therefore, is the 90% test. If the present value of the minimum lease payments is greater than or equal to 90% of the fair market value of the asset, less any lessor retained ITC, the lease is not an operating lease.

The discount rate to be used is the implicit rate in the lease. This rate must be calculated, and is the same rate as was computed on page 271 in the discussion on direct financing leases. In that example, the annual implicit rate was calculated as 12.4747%. This rate is used to present value the minimum lease payments in the 90% test, as illustrated below.

100,000	Fair market value of the equipment
x 90%	
90,000	Comparison base

HP-12C **HP-17B (12 P/YR BEGIN MODE)**

	f	REG		FIN
	g	BEG		TVM
2,010		PMT	■	CLEAR DATA
60		n	2,010	PMT
12.4747	g	12÷	60	N
		PV -90,321.93	12.4747	I%YR
				PV=-90,321.93

The present value of the minimum lease payments (90,321.93) is greater than 90% of the fair market value; therefore, one of the capital lease criteria is met. (Assume the two additional lessor criteria also are met.) The question must now be asked as to whether the cost of the equipment is equal to the fair market value. In this example, the cost is 60,000 and the fair market value is 100,000. Because these amounts are not equal, this lease is classified as a sales-type lease. The lease now can be set up on the books of the lessor.

JOURNAL ENTRIES

The following entries are required to set up this sales-type lease on the lessor's books. The entries to set up a sales-type lease are more complex than those of a direct financing lease; therefore, each component is explained separately.

1. Minimum lease payments receivable	120,600	
Unguaranteed residual	18,000	
Cost of goods sold		9,678
Unearned income		38,600
Sales revenue		90,322

To record the minimum lease payments, unguaranteed residual, sales revenue and unearned income.

This entry establishes the components of the net investment in the lease per the guidelines of FASB 13. As with direct financing leases, the sum of the lease payments (2,010 x 60) is debited to the minimum lease payments receivable account and the unguaranteed residual account is debited for 18,000. The sum of these two components (138,600) is the gross investment in the lease. This separation allows the lessor to monitor its dependence on the minimum lease payments and the future residual values.

The unearned income account is credited for the difference between the gross investment and the sum of the present values of the minimum lease payments and the unguaranteed residual. In this case, unearned income is computed as follows:

Gross investment:	
Minimum lease payment receivable	120,600
Unguaranteed residual	18,000
Total	138,600
Less:	
Present value of minimum lease payments	(90,322)
Present value of unguaranteed residual	(9,678)
Unearned income	38,600

In the sales-type lease, revenue equal to the present value of the minimum lease payments is recorded. Such treatment is distinctly different from that of the direct financing lease. The minimum lease payments are discounted at the implicit rate in the lease. The keystrokes necessary to calculate the revenue to be recognized are as follows:

HP-12C			**HP-17B (12 P/YR BEGIN MODE)**	
	f	REG		FIN
	g	BEG		TVM
2,010		PMT	■	CLEAR DATA
60		n	2,010	PMT
12.4747	g	12÷	60	N
	PV	-90,321.93	12.4747	I%YR
				PV = -90,321.93

The credit of 9,678 to the cost of goods sold account in entry 1 represents the present value of the unguaranteed residual. This aspect of the entry is required by FASB 13. Because the sales revenue recognized does not include the present value of the residual, this amount also is excluded from the cost of sales. The present value of the unguaranteed residual is excluded from both sales and cost of sales because it represents a reversionary interest in the asset. The sale of this portion of the asset has not been realized; therefore, it cannot be recognized. The present value of the unguaranteed residual is computed as follows:

HP-12C			HP-17B (12 P/YR BEGIN MODE)	
	f	REG		FIN
12.4747	g	12÷		TVM
18,000		FV	■	CLEAR DATA
60		n	12.4747	I%YR
		PV -9,678	18,000	FV
			60	N
				PV = -9,678

In general, the net investment represented by entry 1 is the only item shown on the face of the balance sheet. The components of the net investment, although not displayed on the face of the balance sheet, must be shown in the footnotes to the financial statements.

2. Cash   2,010
       Minimum lease payments receivable   2,010

> To record the advance payment paid at the inception of the lease.

With entries 1 and 2 completed, the net investment, or balance sheet portion, of the lease has been booked. A good check to ascertain whether the lease has been booked correctly is to compare the beginning net investment with the net cash outflow at the inception of the lease. These two amounts should be equal. The net investment of 97,990 is the net of the account balances in Exhibit 10-15. The lease has been booked correctly, because 97,990 is equal to the net cash outflow of the lease (exclusive of items included in cost of goods sold).

Equipment cost	(100,000)
Advance payment	2,010
Net cash outflow	(97,990)

Entries 3 and 4 now may be completed.

3. Cost of goods sold   60,000
       Inventory   60,000

> To relieve inventory to cost of goods sold.

Exhibit 10-15
Net Investment

Minimum lease payments receivable	118,590	
Unguaranteed residual	18,000	
Gross investment		136,590
Unearned income		(38,600)
Net investment		97,990

---

4. Cost of goods sold   2,500
   Cash   2,500

> To recognize initial direct costs as a cost of goods sold.

Entry 4 records the initial direct costs as a part of the cost of goods sold. This practice is consistent with the accounting principle of matching. Because sales revenue is recognized, the costs of generating the sales revenue also are recognized. Therefore, initial direct costs are expensed rather than deferred and amortized, as is the case for direct financing leases.

Many companies prefer to further improve the informational value of their accounting records by identifying the earnings associated with any unguaranteed residuals booked. This is the first step in the process referred to as accretion, or the walking up of income. The concept of accretion is explained in detail on page 274.

5. Unearned income   8,322
   Unearned residual   8,322

> To transfer the income associated with the residual out of unearned rental income.

With the above five entries completed, the entire lease has been booked. The net investment at this point in time equals 97,990, as illustrated in Exhibit 10-16. Viewed from an economic perspective, this net investment

---

Exhibit 10-16
Revised Net Investment

Minimum lease payments receivable	118,590	
Unguaranteed residual	18,000	
Gross investment		136,590
Unearned receivable income	30,278	
Unearned residual income	8,322	
Unearned income		(38,600)
Net investment		97,990

---

consists of the elements of Exhibit 10-17. The gross profit on the lease is calculated as shown in Exhibit 10-18.

THE EARNING PROCESS

The sales revenue and attendant gross profit of the sales-type lease can be easily identified from the journal entries. The other aspect of earnings generated by the lease, interest or finance income, is represented by the amount of unearned income booked at inception. This amount is the total interest earnings to be recognized over the life of the lease.

Each period, interest income on the lease is recognized by relieving the unearned income account. This income is computed on the net investment

---

Exhibit 10-17
Economic Components of the Net Investment

Cost	60,000
Gross profit	37,500
Initial direct costs	2,500
Advance payment	(2,010)
Total	97,990

Exhibit 10-18
Gross Profit Components

Sales revenue		90,322
Less: cost of goods sold		
Inventory	(60,000)	
Initial direct costs	(2,500)	
Present value of unguaranteed residual	9,678	
		(52,822)
Gross profit		37,500

---

in the lease, utilizing a constant periodic rate of return as required by FASB 13. The mathematical process of recognizing earnings involves multiplying the net investment in the lease, representing the principal, by the interest rate in the lease.

Although the use of various earnings methods does not affect the total income to be recognized over the life of the lease, each method allocates income in a different manner. Of the possible methods of income allocation that may be utilized, however, the pretax rate is the most common. (Note that for sales-type leases, the implicit rate and pretax rate methods are the same.)

Under the pretax, actuarial yield method, the rate that amortizes the cash flows (minimum lease payments and unguaranteed residual) to the present value of those cash flows is applied against the net investment. This rate is the implicit rate of 12.4747% previously calculated. The monthly rate of 1.0396% (12.4747% ÷ 12) times the net investment in the lease equals the interest earned for that month.

The amount of interest earned during the first month for the sales-type lease in this example is 1,018.70 (97,990 x 1.0396%). The interest earnings in the first month of this lease are higher than the corresponding amount for the direct financing lease illustrated on page 281. This difference is due to the treatment of initial direct costs of 58.12 (1,018.70 - 960.58).

In the direct financing lease, initial direct costs are amortized over the life of the lease, thereby reducing the amount of periodic interest income recognized. The initial direct costs in a sales-type lease are expensed immediately as a cost of goods sold. As a result, the monthly earnings are higher in the sales-type lease. Receipt of the payment and the earnings recognition for the first month are journalized as follows:

Cash	2,010	
Unearned income	918	
Unearned residual	101	
Interest earned		918
Residual earned		101
Minimum lease payments receivable		2,010

To record the first month's payment.

Exhibit 10-19 breaks out the earnings into two components: earnings on the net investment in the lease receivable and the net investment in the residual. Again, the only difference from the direct financing lease example is that initial direct costs have been totally expensed at the beginning of the lease. Exhibit 10-20 shows the allocation of the first month's payment and the new ending balances of the components of the net investment. The earnings on the components of the net investment over the life of the lease are summarized in Appendix One.

Exhibit 10-19
Net Investment Components

	1 Net investment in lease receivable	2 Net investment in residual	(1 + 2) Overall net investment
Gross investment	118,590	18,000	136,590
Unearned income	(30,278)	(8,322)	(38,600)
Net investment	88,312	9,678	97,990
Pretax earnings rate	x 1.0396%	x 1.0396%	
First month's earnings	918	101	1,019

Exhibit 10-20
First Month's Payment Allocation

	Net investment in lease receivable	Net investment in residual
Net investment	88,312	9,678
Earnings rate	x 1.0396%	x 1.0396%
Interest income	918	101
Beginning balance	88,312	9,678
Payment	(2,010)	----
Ending balance	87,220	9,779

END OF FIRST YEAR T-ACCOUNT SUMMARY

The T-accounts of Exhibits 10-21 and 10-22 represent the balances on the books at year end for this sales-type lease. The first year journal entry is as follows:

6.	Cash	10,050	
	Unearned income	4,476	
	Unearned residual	514	
	Interest earned		4,476
	Residual earned		514
	Minimum lease payments receivable		10,050

> To record the first year's payment.

The T-account entries are annotated with the corresponding journal entry number for ease of reference. Journal entries 6, 7 and 8 represent annualized amounts. The T-account summaries for the balance sheet and income statement are shown in Exhibit 10-21 and Exhibit 10-22, respectively.

INTERPERIOD TAX ALLOCATION

Once interest earnings have been ascertained, taxes must be provided on those earnings. Interperiod tax allocation is necessary to reflect the temporary differences between the tax and accounting books. In order to deter-

Exhibit 10-21
Balance Sheet T-accounts
(Sales-type)

Minimum lease payments receivable				Unearned income			Cash	
(1) 120,600	2,010 (2)		(5) 8,322	38,600 (1)		117,000	60,000	
	10,050 (6)		(6) 4,476			(3) 2,010	2,500 (4)	
						(6) 10,050		
108,540				25,802		66,560		

Unguaranteed residual			Unearned residual			Accounts payable	
(1) 18,000			(6) 514	8,322 (5)			10,680
							1,320
							3,000
				7,808			15,000

Long term debt		Taxes payable		Deferred taxes	
	50,000		434 (7)		15,726 (7)

Property, plant & equipment		Contributed capital	
9,000			55,320

Current portion long-term debt		Accounts receivable		Inventory	
	13,000	3,000		60,000	60,000 (2)
		8,000			
		11,000			

Exhibit 10-22
Income Statement T-accounts
(Sales-type)

Interest earnings	Income tax expense	Sales revenue
4,476 (6)	(7) 16,160	90,322 (1)

Cost of goods sold	Residual earnings	G&A expense
(3) 60,000 9,678 (1)	514 (6)	1,320
(4) 2,500		
52,822		

Other income	Interest expense
8,000	3,000

mine these entries, the tax liability per the tax books and deferred taxes must be determined. Remember, this lease is considered to be a true tax lease for tax purposes, in contrast to its sales-type lease status for accounting purposes. The tax liability per the tax books is shown in Exhibit 10-23.

Once the sales revenue is recognized, the earnings process and journal entries for this sales-type lease are very similar to those of the direct financing lease. The only difference is the deferred taxes. The difference in deferred taxes between the two types of leases is caused primarily by the treatment of gross profit and initial direct costs.

In the sales-type lease, initial direct costs do not create a temporary difference because they are expensed for both book and tax. A key temporary difference, however, is depreciation taken for tax purposes. Notice that the tax depreciation is now based on an asset cost of 60,000 rather than the 100,000 cost used in the direct financing lease example. Deferred taxes are calculated as follows:

Net investment	92,930	
Tax basis	(48,000)	(60,000-12,000)
Difference	44,930	
Tax rate	x 35%	
Deferred taxes	15,726	

The following represents the journal entry for the tax provision:

7.	Tax expense	16,160	
	Taxes payable		434
	Deferred taxes		15,726

To record the first-year tax provision.

Exhibit 10-23
Tax Calculation
(Sales-type)

	Tax books
Advance rental	2,010
Normal rentals	10,050
Other income	8,000
Initial direct costs	(2,500)
G & A costs	(1,320)
Depreciation (MACRS)	(12,000)
Interest expense	(3,000)
Taxable income	1,240
Tax rate	x .35
Tax expense (benefit)	434

FINANCIAL STATEMENTS

Using the T-account balances in Figures Exhibit 10-21 and Exhibit 10-22, an income statement (Exhibit 10-24), a balance sheet (Exhibit 10-25) and a cash flow statement (Exhibit 10-26) can be prepared. Some data have been added to present a more representative set of financial statements.

Exhibit 10-24
Income Statement
(Sales-type)

Revenue		
Sales revenue	90,322	
Interest earnings	4,476	
Residual earnings	514	
Total lease income		95,312
Operating expenses		
Cost of goods sold	52,822	
G & A expense	1,320	
Interest expense	3,000	
Total operating expenses		(57,142)
Operating income		38,170
Other income/expense		8,000
Income from operations before taxes		46,170
Income tax expense		
Current taxes	434	
Deferred taxes	15,726	
Income tax expense		(16,160)
Net income		30,010

Exhibit 10-25
Balance Sheet
(Sales-type)

Assets

Cash		66,560
Accounts receivable		11,000
Net investment in sales-type leases		
Lease receivable	108,540	
Unguaranteed residuals	18,000	
Gross investment		126,540
Unearned rental income	(25,802)	
Unearned residual income	(7,808)	
Unearned income		(33,610)
Net investment		92,930
Property, plant and equipment (net)		9,000
Total assets		179,490

Liabilities

Accounts payable [1]	15,000
Taxes payable	434
Current portion long-term debt	13,000
Long-term liabilities	50,000
Deferred taxes	15,726
Total liabilities	94,160

Owners' equity

Contributed capital	55,320
Retained earnings	30,010
Total owners' equity	85,330
Total liabilities and owners' equity	179,490

[1] Includes 3,000 of interest payable and 1,000 of various accrued general and administrative items.

Exhibit 10-26
Statement of Cash Flows
(Sales-type)

Cash flows from operating activities

Net interest earned	4,476	
Other income	8,000	
Initial direct costs incurred	(2,500)	
Operating expenses paid	(320)	
Interest expense paid	0	
Net cash from operating activities		9,656

Cash flows from investing activities

Principal received from sales-type leases	7,584	
Capital expenditures	(9,000)	
Investment in sales-type lease	(60,000)	
Net cash used in investing activities		(61,416)

Cash flows from financing activities

Proceeds from contributed capital	55,320	
Proceeds from long-term debt	63,000	
Net cash provided by financing activities		118,320

Net increase in cash		66,560
Cash at the beginning of the year		0
Cash at the end of the year		66,560

Reconciliation of net income to operating activities

Net income		30,010
Adjustments to net income		
Increase in deferred taxes	15,726	
Increase in taxes payable	434	
Increase in accounts payable [1]	15,000	
Increase in accounts receivable	(11,000)	
Increase in unguaranteed residual	(514)	
Sales-type lease gross profit	(40,000)	
Total adjustments		(20,354)
Net cash from operating activities		9,656

[1] Includes 3,000 of interest payable and 1,000 of various accrued general and administrative items.

OPERATING LEASES

Operating leases are a rapidly growing segment of the leasing industry. This growth is fueled by lessee demand and is attributable to the many advantages of the operating lease product, including off balance sheet financing and hedging against technological obsolescence. As a result of these benefits, lessors are finding more of these leases in their portfolios.

Compared to the accounting for other leases, operating lease accounting is quite straightforward. Unique problems and issues are associated with operating leases, however.

Characteristics

The prime characteristic of an operating lease is the residual dependence of the lessor, which connotes continued asset ownership by the lessor beyond the lease term. The lessee obtains temporary use of the asset through the operating lease. Because the lessor retains ownership of the asset, the accounting treatment is different from that of a direct financing, sales-type or leveraged lease.

The lessor, because of its ownership of the asset, treats operating leases on balance sheet. The lessor records the leased asset as an asset on the balance sheet and depreciates it for accounting purposes along with its other fixed assets. The lease payment is recognized as revenue in the lessor's income statement.

DEFINITIONS

The term operating lease is generally understood to be an accounting definition. In the leasing industry, however, the term operating is sometimes used to describe other types of leases. Several of these other types are described in this section.

ACCOUNTING USAGE

An operating lease, for accounting purposes, is one that does not meet any of the four capital lease criteria below (also refer to Chapter Nine):

1. Automatic transfer of title

2. Bargain purchase option

3. Lease term greater than or equal to 75% of the asset's economic useful life

4. Present value of the minimum lease payments greater than or equal to 90% of fair market value.

In addition to these four criteria, the collectibility of the minimum lease payments must be reasonably predictable and there can be no important uncertainties surrounding the amount of unreimbursable costs yet to be incurred by the lessor under the lease. If either of these criteria is not met, the lessor must treat the lease as an operating lease regardless of the determination based on the first four criteria.

TAX USAGE

The IRS never uses the term operating to describe the tax attributes of leases. Many people in the marketplace, however, do use this term to describe leases that are treated as true tax leases from a tax perspective. The term operating lease should be used only when describing accounting attributes to avoid confusion.

INDUSTRY USAGE

The term operating lease, as used in the industry, describes the lease's economic characteristics rather than either its accounting or tax classification. In this general setting the term operating usually means a short-term lease and residual-based pricing. Shorter term, non-full-payout leases, which more closely resemble a true rental than an asset financing, are called operating leases. Again, this usage can be confusing because the term operating is intended to describe the accounting attributes of the lease.

FINANCIAL REPORTING RAMIFICATIONS

The accounting advantages of operating leases are primarily lessee-oriented. The lessor is subject to several financial statement ramifications, both detrimental and beneficial. For instance, the income recognition pattern is less accelerated in a lease classified as an operating, as opposed to direct financing, sales-type or leveraged lease. The operating lease is recorded as an asset by the lessor and depreciated for accounting purposes, usually on a straight-line basis. The lease income is the difference between the revenue from the lease payment and the depreciation expense for the period.

Lease income in a direct financing lease is the interest income on the declining net investment in the lease (as calculated using the interest method). As is the case with a loan, there is more interest and less principal in the earlier payments; therefore, the lessor has more income in the earlier years of the direct financing lease and less in the latter years when compared to the operating lease. For this reason, some lessors force their operating leases into direct financing classification through the purchase of residual guarantees and puts.

Another financial reporting aspect of operating leases relates to the impact on income of a growing operating lease portfolio. Operating leases generally throw off losses during the first several years. These losses are a function of the lower lease payment, depreciation and funding attributes. The treatment of initial direct costs also contributes to the loss. Some lessors expense the total of these costs immediately under the premise that a bit more loss is not going to hurt. This immediate expensing provides greater income in the later years of the operating lease.

Because of these unique income characteristics, the lessor must carefully manage the operating lease portfolio to alleviate the negative income aspects. One such method would be to do broker business or some other activity to generate fee income until the residuals start to come in and the portfolio begins to turn around.

FASB 13 Requirements

Properly recording the lease requires an understanding of the lessor accounting provisions for operating leases as outlined in FASB 13. These requirements, which are quite simple and concise, are summarized below. (FASB 13, Paragraph .115 (a), (b) and (c))

.115 Operating leases shall be accounted for by the lessor as follows:

a. *The leased property shall be included with or near property, plant, and equipment in the balance sheet. The property shall be depreciated following the lessor's normal depreciation policy, and in the balance sheet the accumulated depreciation shall be deducted from the investment in the leased property.*

b. *Rent shall be reported as income over the lease term as it becomes receivable according to the provisions of the lease. However, if the rentals vary from a straight-line basis[24a], the income shall be recognized on a straight-line basis unless another systematic and rational basis is more representative of the time pattern in which use benefit from the leased property is diminished, in which case that basis shall be used.*

c. *Initial direct costs shall be deferred and allocated over the lease term in proportion to the recognition of rental income. However, initial direct costs may be charged to expense as incurred if the effect is not materially different from that which would have resulted from the use of the method prescribed in the preceding sentence.*

[24a} Refer to paragraphs .525 through .527f for...

Operating Lease Example

An example is the most effective method to illustrate the booking of an operating lease. The example is broken down into three parts: (1) the initial entries to set up the lease, (2) the earnings process and (3) the lease in financial statement format.

ASSUMPTIONS

The following assumptions are used in the operating lease example:

Inception date: September 1

Lease term: 48 months (two payments in advance)

Payment amount: 2,175

Unguaranteed residual: 25,000 (fair market value purchase option)

Initial direct costs: 2,400

Refundable security deposit: 2,000

Equipment fair market value: 100,000 (cost to the lessor)

Lessor tax rate: 35%

Accounting depreciation: Five-year life, with a salvage value of 10,000

Tax status: Tax lease to the lessor, 5-year MACRS property.

INITIAL SET-UP

The classification of the lease must be determined before recording the lease in the accounts of the lessor. The first three capital lease criteria are assumed to be not applicable; therefore, only the 90% test is evaluated.

Lease Classification

As part of verifying whether or not the lease meets the fourth capital lease criterion (90% test), the lessor must present value the minimum lease payments. The lessor uses the implicit rate in the lease as defined by FASB 13 as the discount rate to make the present value determination. The implicit rate is computed for this example as follows:

		HP-12C		HP-17B (# TIMES PROMPTING: ON)		
	f	REG				FIN
98,050[3]	CHS g	CFo				CFLO
2,175	g	CFj		■ CLEAR DATA		YES
46	g	Nj	FLOW (0)=?	98,050[3]	+/-	INPUT
0	g	CFj	FLOW (1)=?	2,175		INPUT
25,000	g	CFj	# TIMES (1)=1	46		INPUT
	f	IRR 0.8937	FLOW (2)=?	0		INPUT
12	x	10.7249	# TIMES (2)=1	1		INPUT
			FLOW (3)=?	25,000		INPUT
			# TIMES (3)=1	1		INPUT
						EXIT
						CALC

IRR% 0.8937
x 12 =10.7249

The present value of the minimum lease payments must be compared to 90% of the asset's fair market value. This amount is referred to as the comparison base. If the present value of the minimum lease payments is less than the comparison base, the lease is classified as an operating lease, computed using the lessor's implicit rate in the lease. The implicit rate is 10.73% (12 x .89%), as previously calculated. The lease is classified as an operating lease because the present value of the minimum lease pay-

---

[3] Net inception cash flow:

(100,000)	Fair market value
(2,400)	Initial direct costs
4,350	Two advance rentals
(98,050)	Net inception cost

ments is less than the basis of comparison (86,082 versus 90,000, respectively).

100,000	Fair market value
x 90%	
90,000	Comparison base

Next, the present value of the minimum lease payments is computed:

HP-12C			**HP-17B (# TIMES PROMPTING: ON)**		
	f	REG			FIN
4,350	g	CFo			CFLO
2,175	g	CFj	■ CLEAR DATA		YES
46	g	Nj	FLOW (0)=?	4,350	INPUT
10.73	g	12÷	FLOW (1)=?	2,175	INPUT
	f	NPV 86,082.23	# TIMES (1)=1	46	INPUT
					EXIT
					CALC
			10.73 ÷ 12		I%
			NPV = 86,082.23		

Once the lease has been properly classified, the initial journal entries recording the lease are made. The asset is recorded on the balance sheet at its cost, or carrying amount. Depreciation expense attributable to the asset is shown in the income statement and accumulated depreciation for the asset is recorded. Rentals in an operating lease are recorded as revenue over the lease term as they become receivable. Lease commitment fees, closing fees, origination fees and other fees collected by the lessor at the beginning of the lease are offset against the initial direct costs of the lessor. This offsetting of the fees generally results in a deferral of the revenue over the noncancellable lease term on a straight-line basis.

The journal entries necessary to account for this lease are shown below. Both the balance sheet and income statement entries are included.

1. Leased equipment	100,000	
Cash		100,000

To record the cost of acquiring the equipment to be leased.

2. Cash   6,350

      Refundable security deposit   2,000

      Deferred rent revenue   2,175

      Rent revenue   2,175

> To record the receipt of the security deposit and deferral of one advance payment. The other advance payment is recognized as revenue.

3. Deferred initial direct costs   2,400

      Cash (or accounts payable)   2,400

> To defer the costs incurred to set up the operating lease at its inception.

4. Cash   100,000

      Contributed capital   100,000

> To record the source of cash used to acquire the equipment.

The operating lease has been properly recorded in the books of the lessor at this point. The initial set-up T-accounts are shown in Exhibit 10-27. Note that the lessor does not record the unguaranteed residual in a separate account as is the case in direct financing, sales-type or leveraged leases. Instead, the residual in an operating lease is referred to as the salvage value. The residual/salvage is represented by the net book value of the asset under operating lease.

EARNINGS PROCESS

Income recognition in an operating lease consists of rent revenue less depreciation expense and the amortization of initial direct costs. Rentals in an operating lease generally are recorded as revenue over the lease term as they become receivable. As a general rule, this method results in the recognition of rent revenue on a straight-line basis.

Rent Revenue

If the actual rentals vary from a straight-line basis, FASB 13 paragraph .115 (b) requires that revenue still be recognized straight-line.

> *.115 (b.) Rent shall be reported as income over the lease term as it*

Exhibit 10-27
Initial Set-up T-accounts
(Operating)

Balance sheet

Leased equipment	Cash	Deferred initial direct costs
(1) 100,000	(2) 6,350 | 100,000 (1) (4) 100,000 | 2,400 (3)	(3) 2,400
	——————————	
	3,950 |	

Refundable security deposit	Deferred rent revenue	Contributed capital
| 2,000 (2)	| 2,175 (2)	| 100,000 (4)

Income statement

Rent revenue
| 2,175 (2)

> *becomes receivable according to the provisions of the lease. However, if the rentals vary from a straight-line basis,[24a] the income shall be recognized on a straight-line basis unless another systematic and rational basis is more representative of the time pattern in which use benefit from the leased property is diminished, in which case that basis shall be used.*

[24a] *Refer to paragraphs .525 through .527f...*

FASB 13 was issued in 1976. Since that time, the leasing market has changed appreciably. Competition has become more intense and more creative operating lease structures have emerged. Many of these structures use varied rent schemes such as step-ups and -downs, rent holidays and skipped payments. Consequently, many lessors in recent years have questioned the straight-line methodology. The FASB readdressed this issue in Technical Bulletin 85-3.

The FASB's response to the question raised in this Technical Bulletin did not change its original position. Variation from straight-line income recognition is appropriate only if the variation matches the physical use of the leased property. Variations are not appropriate if they are designed around other characteristics such as lessee cash flow needs, marketing motivations, inflation and the time value of money.

The FASB, in requiring straight-line recognition, is attempting to properly match revenues (lessor) and expenses (lessees) with the use of the asset. If the rental stream differs from straight-line because of marketing motivations only, the usage of the asset does not change. If the asset is being used on a consistent basis, the rent and expense should be so recognized. If the pattern of physical usage does, indeed, differ from a straight-line basis, the revenue may be recognized on that basis. The lessor, however, must justify that other methods more accurately match the physical use or wearing out of the leased asset.

Depreciation Expense

The depreciation for this operating lease is computed to be 1,500 per month, based on a 10,000 salvage value and a 60-month asset life.

100,000	Fair market value (original cost)
(10,000)	Salvage value estimate
90,000	
÷ 60	Expected life of the leased asset
1,500	Monthly depreciation charge

The lease income in an operating lease is the net of rent revenue and depreciation expense. The pattern of lease income recognition is typically straight-line because the lessor recognizes rent revenue on a straight-line basis and deducts depreciation expense on a straight-line basis. If the lessor utilizes another method of depreciation, the pattern of the lease income changes. Lessor income recognition, therefore, is a function of the method of depreciation employed.

Depreciation Techniques

Some lessors prefer to estimate the total useful life of the asset as used by all potential lessees. The ultimate salvage value at the end of all potential leases is used as the estimated salvage value for determining the depreciation expense. This causes the lessor's depreciation to be even throughout the entire life of the asset rather than changing in amount each time the lessor re-leases the asset. Depreciating an operating leased asset to its ultimate salvage value in this manner distorts the lease income (rent minus depreciation).

This distortion occurs during the life of the asset because of the nature of operating leases. By depreciating the asset to its salvage value at the end of the asset's economic life, the lessor causes depreciation to remain constant over the asset's life. The asset's life, however, includes several lease terms because operating leases generally are renewed or the asset is re-leased. However, because the asset has declined in value, the secondary lease rate is at a lower amount than the rate over the initial or previous term. The lease becomes, in essence, a step-down lease.

The result of these step-down leases is a rental payment that is declining with the fair market value of the asset. The declining rent revenue is matched with depreciation that does not decline with the asset's fair value. This concept is graphically represented in Exhibit 10-28.

To avoid this distortion, many lessors depreciate the leased asset over the term of the lease based on the asset's estimated residual value at the end of each individual lease term. The residual value is considered to be the salvage value of the asset. If the lessor retains the asset at the end of the lease and re-leases it to the same lessee or to a new lessee, the lessor continues to depreciate the asset. The depreciation to be matched with the new lease revenue is calculated based on the expected residual value at the end of the new lease. This process continues until the lessor disposes of the asset. Each time the asset is leased, the depreciation amount changes to reflect the

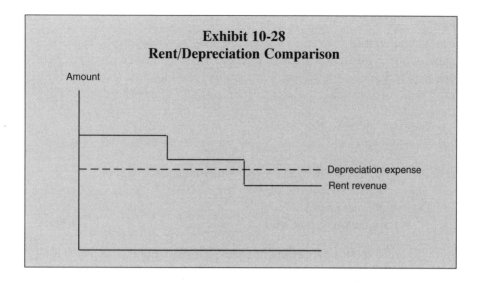

Exhibit 10-28
Rent/Depreciation Comparison

change in fair value and, hence, the lease payment. This method of depreciating operating leases is referred to as the rent curve method of depreciation.

Initial Direct Costs

FASB 13 requires that initial direct costs in an operating lease be deferred and recognized over the life of the lease in the same manner as income. Generally, the amortization will be on a straight-line basis. If the results are not material, however, an alternate method of expensing the initial direct costs may be used. One alternate method is to expense them immediately.

There are several reasons for a lessor to immediately expense its initial direct costs. One is that these costs are not material to the transaction. Another and more complex reason has to do with the income patterns created in an operating lease. Because of the rent recognition, residual position, depreciation expense and funding costs in an operating lease, the lease usually creates a book loss in the early years. These patterns were discussed in more detail earlier in this section.

Because the operating lease is spinning off book losses during the first part of its term, many lessors take the hit on the initial direct costs expense at that time. By taking the additional loss in a loss year, the profitability of the lease is enhanced in the later years of the lease. This enhancement occurs because interest expense is very low and there is no initial direct costs expense.

Journal Entries

The journal entries to account for the monthly lease payments, depreciation expense and amortization of initial direct costs are the same each month. Only one tax entry is recorded at year-end in this example. The journal entries in the months of September through December for the example are shown below:

Cash	2,175	
Rent revenue		2,175

      To record the monthly lease payment and revenue.

Depreciation expense	1,500	
Accumulated depreciation		1,500

      To record depreciation expense for the month.

Initial direct cost expense	50	
Deferred initial direct costs		50

      To recognize 1/48th of the deferred initial direct costs.

INCOME TAX ENTRY (YEAR-END)

The income tax entry at the end of the first calendar year is shown. It is based on the tax computation in Exhibit 10-29 and the following FASB 109 calculation:

Exhibit 10-29
Tax Calculation
(Operating)

	Tax return
Advance rentals	4,350
Regular payments	6,525
Initial direct costs	(2,400)
MACRS depreciation	(20,000)
Taxable income (loss)	(11,525)
Tax rate	x 35%
Tax benefit	(4,034)

Book basis

Asset	94,000	
Deferred revenue	(2,175)	
Initial direct costs	2,200	
		94,025
Tax basis		(80,000)
Difference		14,025
Tax rate		x .35
Deferred taxes		4,909

A deferred tax credit is generated in this example based on the differences between book and tax accounting.

Taxes receivable	4,034	
Income tax expense	875	
Deferred taxes		4,909

To record the year-end provision for taxes.

END OF FIRST-YEAR SUMMARY

The initial set-up of the lease and earnings recognition for the first four months of the lease, including the tax entries, have been completed. The journal entries can now be recorded in T-accounts and the financial statements prepared.

T-accounts

The T-accounts in Exhibits 10-30 and 10-31 summarize the journal entries completed as of the end of the first year. In addition to the initial set-up entries to the balance sheet accounts, the earnings for the sum of the first four months of the lease (September - December) are shown in bold.

Financial Statements

The financial statements in the accompanying exhibits reflect the data from the preceding journal entries and T-accounts as of the end of the calendar year. The lease is four months into its term as of the balance sheet date of December 31. Two advance and three regular payments have been received. The income statement, balance sheet and cash flow statement are shown in Exhibits 10-32, 10-33 and 10-34, respectively.

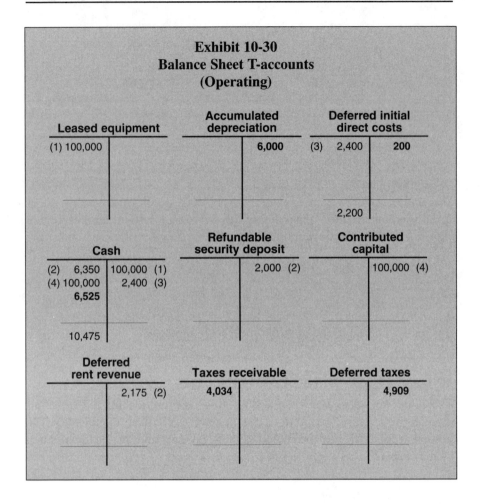

Exhibit 10-30
Balance Sheet T-accounts
(Operating)

Leased equipment		Accumulated depreciation		Deferred initial direct costs	
(1) 100,000			6,000	(3) 2,400	200
				2,200	

Cash		Refundable security deposit		Contributed capital	
(2) 6,350	100,000 (1)		2,000 (2)		100,000 (4)
(4) 100,000	2,400 (3)				
6,525					
10,475					

Deferred rent revenue		Taxes receivable		Deferred taxes	
	2,175 (2)	4,034			4,909

CONCLUSION

The accounting methodologies explained in this section follow the rules and regulations of FASB 13. Actual practice from company to company, however, varies significantly. Most companies, though, stay within the basic framework of FASB 13 and account for their leases similarly to the methods presented here.

The characteristics of the different types of leases presented in this section follow the principle of substance over form. Direct financing leases are accounted for as a loan arrangement. Sales-type lease accounting takes a lease that in substance looks like a sale, and requires an accounting treatment that resembles a sale and subsequent financing. Operating leases are rental arrangements and the accounting treatment reflects ownership by the lessor and use by the lessee.

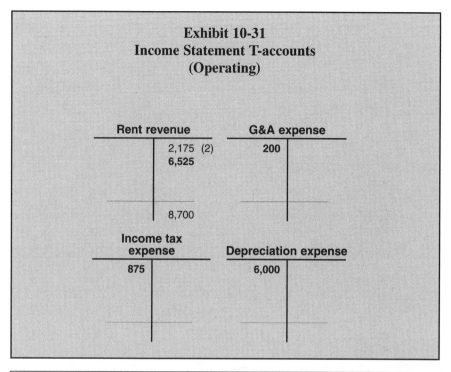

Exhibit 10-31
Income Statement T-accounts
(Operating)

Rent revenue			G&A expense	
	2,175	(2)	200	
	6,525			
	8,700			

Income tax expense		Depreciation expense	
875		6,000	

Exhibit 10-32
Income Statement
(Operating)

Revenue		
Rent		8,700
Operating expenses		
Depreciation	6,000	
Initial direct costs	200	
G & A	0	
Total operating expenses		(6,200)
Operating income		2,500
Other expenses		
Interest expense		0
Income before taxes		2,500
Current taxes	(4,034)	
Deferred taxes	4,909	
Income tax expense		(875)
Net income		1,625

Exhibit 10-33
Balance Sheet
(Operating)

Assets

Cash		10,475
Taxes receivable		4,034
Property, plant and equipment (net)		0
Leased equipment	100,000	
Less: depreciation	(6,000)	
Net leased equipment		94,000
Initial direct costs		2,200
Total assets		110,709

Liabilities

Taxes payable	0
Refundable security deposit	2,000
Deferred lease payment	2,175
Deferred tax credit	4,909
Total liabilities	9,084

Owners' equity

Contributed capital	100,000	
Retained earnings	1,625	
Total owners' equity		101,625
Total liabilities and owners' equity		110,709

Exhibit 10-34
Statement of Cash Flows
(Operating)

Cash flows from operating activities

Operating lease rentals	10,875
Security deposits received	2,000
Initial direct costs paid	(2,400)
Net cash provided by operations	10,475

Cash flows from investing activities

Purchase of equipment to be leased	(100,000)

Cash flows from financing activities

Proceeds from issuance of common stock	100,000

Net increase in cash	10,475
Cash at the beginning of the year	0
Cash at the end of the year	10,475

Reconciliation of net income to operating activities

Net income		1,625
Adjustments:		
Depreciation	6,000	
Increase in taxes receivable	(4,034)	
Net increase in initial direct costs	(2,200)	
Increase in security deposits	2,000	
Increase in deferred tax credits	4,909	
Increase in deferred lease payments	2,175	
Total adjustments		8,850
Net cash provided by operating activities		10,475

Chapter Eleven

Lessee Accounting

Several of the rules and guidelines of Financial Accounting Standards Board Statement No. 13 "Accounting for Leases" (FASB 13) overlap between lessors and lessees. This overlap includes the definitions and classification criteria contained in Chapter Nine. Other areas of overlap include the application of FASB 13 to early terminations, upgrades and similar issues. However, certain aspects, rules and issues are specific to accounting for leases by lessees.

This chapter discusses lessee lease accounting requirements, including sale-leasebacks, and illustrates their application in detail. Accounting procedures, journal entries and other techniques are addressed under the following headings:

- Capital Lease Accounting

- Operating Lease Accounting

- Comparative Differences

- Sale-leasebacks.

CAPITAL LEASE ACCOUNTING

From the point of view of the lessee, a lease considered to be a capital lease for accounting purposes must be capitalized in the financial statements. A lease that is capitalized is recorded as an asset in the balance sheet along with a corresponding liability for the same amount. The income statement attributes of the transaction include expensing the interest on the lease obligation and depreciating the leased asset for book purposes.

If the lease meets one of the first two capital lease criteria, the capital leased asset is depreciated following the lessee's normal depreciation policies. If either of the last two capital lease criteria is met, the leased asset is depreciated over the term of the lease. The debt, on the other hand, is amortized to principal and interest using the lessee's incremental borrowing rate. (This is the same rate that is used to classify and capitalize the leased asset.)

The rules to be followed in accounting for a capital lease according to FASB 13 are presented in the following pages. After a review of the rules from FASB 13, a comprehensive illustration is used to show the appropriate journal entries, T-accounts and financial statement presentation.

FASB 13 Requirements

The rules from FASB 13 regarding capital leases are summarized below, as a preface to the illustration. (FASB 13 .106 - .108)

> *.106 The lessee shall record the capital lease as an asset and an obligation at an amount equal to the present value at the beginning of the lease term of minimum lease payments during the lease term, excluding that portion of the payments representing executory costs to be paid by the lessor, together with any profit thereon. However, if the amount so determined exceeds the fair value of the leased property at inception of the lease, the amount recorded as the asset and the obligation shall be the fair value.[8] If the portion of the minimum lease payments representing executory costs, including profit thereon, is not determinable from the provisions of the lease, an estimate of the amount shall be made. The discount rate to be used in determining present value of the minimum lease payments shall be that prescribed for the lessee in paragraph .103(d) (refer to paragraph .150 and Exhibit 150c for an illustration) [FAS13,¶10]*
>
> [8] *If the lease agreement or commitment, . . .*
>
> *.107 Except as provided in paragraphs .121 and .122 with respect to lease involving land, the asset recorded under a capital lease shall be amortized as follows:*
>
> a *If the lease meets the criterion of either paragraph .103(a) or .103(b), the asset shall be amortized in a manner consistent with the lessee's normal depreciation policy for owned assets.*
>
> b *If the lease does not meet either criterion .103(a) or .103(b), the asset shall be amortized in a manner consistent with the lessee's normal depreciation policy except that the period of amortization shall be the lease term. The asset shall be amortized to its*

> *expected value, if any, to the lessee at the end of the lease term. As an example, if the lessee guarantees a residual value at the end of the lease term and has no interest in any excess which might be realized, the expected value of the leased property to (the lessee) is the amount that can be realized from it up to the amount of the guarantee [FAS13,¶11]*

> *.108 During the lease term, each minimum lease payment shall be allocated between a reduction of the obligation and interest expense so as to produce a constant periodic rate of interest on the remaining balance of the obligation.[9] (Refer to paragraph .150 for illustrations.) In leases containing a residual guarantee by the lessee or a penalty for failure to renew the lease at the end of the lease term,[10] following the above method of amortization will result in a balance of the obligation at the end of the lease term that will equal the amount of the guarantee or penalty at that date . . . .*

> [9] *This is the interest method described in Section I69 . . .*

> [10] *Residual guarantees and termination penalties . . .*

The accounting procedures for a capital lease can be summarized in three steps.

STEP ONE

Capitalization of the leased asset and recognition of the lease liability or obligation. The capitalized asset amount is determined by calculating the present value of the minimum lease payments. The amount booked must not exceed the actual fair market value of the asset.

STEP TWO

Depreciation of the asset in a manner consistent with the applicable classification criteria of the lease. The capital leased asset should be depreciated using the lessee's normal depreciation policy (in terms of both method and period) when the lease is classified as capital because it meets either of the first two capital lease criteria. Otherwise, the depreciable life is limited to the lease term.

STEP THREE

Amortization of the lease obligation. The capital lease obligation is amortized in a manner similar to a simple interest loan (i.e., at a constant rate over the lease term). This amortization separates the lease payments into principal payments and interest expense.

Illustration

The accounting requirements for a capital lease have been reviewed; therefore, an illustration that clarifies and expands on the conceptual accounting requirements can be presented.

ASSUMPTIONS

The following assumptions are used in the illustration:

Inception date: January 1

Lease term: 36 months, in advance

Payment amount: 1,500

Unguaranteed residual: 5,000

Equipment fair market value: 50,000

Lessee tax rate: 35%

Capital lease criteria: The present value of the minimum lease payments exceeds 90% of the fair market value

Discount rate: The lessor's implicit rate of 10.78% is unknown to the lessee. The lessee's incremental, pretax borrowing rate is 10%

Tax status: Tax lease to the lessor, 3-year MACRS property

Other closing costs, fees, etc.: None.

INITIAL SETUP

Before actually accounting for the lease, it is important to review the process of determining its accounting classification. The assumptions suggest that the only reason for treating the lease as capital is the fourth capital lease criterion. In this test the lessee must determine the present value of the minimum lease payments. The lessee uses its incremental borrowing rate of 10% as the discount rate when determining the present value of the minimum lease payments. This rate is used unless the lessee knows the lessor's implicit rate and the implicit rate is lower than the incremental borrowing rate.

As discussed earlier, application of the fourth capital lease criterion, or 90% test, is a three-part process. The first step in this process is to establish the comparison base. The comparison base is equal to 90% of the asset's fair market value.

50,000	Fair market value
x 90%	
45,000	Comparison base

Next, the present value of the minimum lease payments is calculated using the lessee's pretax, incremental borrowing rate of 10%.

HP-12C			**HP-17B (12 P/YR BEGIN MODE)**	
	f	REG		FIN
	g	BEG		TVM
1,500		PMT	■	CLEAR DATA
36		n	1,500	PMT
10	g	12÷	36	N
	PV	-46,874.24	10	I%YR
				PV = -46,874.24

The lease in this example is classified as a capital lease because the present value of the minimum lease payments exceeds the comparison base (46,874 versus 45,000).

CAPITALIZATION OF THE LEASED ASSET (STEP ONE)

The present value of the minimum lease payments calculated above (46,874) is first compared to the fair market value of the asset. Because the present value of the minimum lease payments does not exceed the fair market value of the asset, this present value amount is capitalized as the asset. The present value amount of 46,874 is used as the original amount for both the asset and the lease obligation in the lessee's balance sheet.

DEPRECIATION OF THE LEASED ASSET (STEP TWO)

Depreciation of the leased asset is limited to the lease term because the lease meets the fourth capital lease criterion. The lessee has chosen to use the straight-line method to depreciate its assets.

46,874	
÷ 3	Years
15,625	Annual depreciation

AMORTIZATION OF THE LEASE OBLIGATION (STEP THREE)

The capital lease obligation of 46,874 must be split into its current and long-term portions if the lessee classifies its balance sheet. The current portion at any time is the amount of the lease liability that will be paid off during the following 12 months. The long-term portion is the balance of the total obligation.

The lease payments must be separated into their interest and principal components through an amortization. The lease payments are amortized using the lessee's pretax, incremental borrowing rate, which is the same interest rate used to calculate the present value of the asset (10% in this example). The amortization of the obligation for this example is shown in Exhibit 11-1.

JOURNAL ENTRIES

The preceding calculations are used to make the journal entries necessary to account for the capital lease.

1. Capital leased equipment   46,874
        Lease payable (current)   15,597
        Lease payable (long-term)   31,277

        To record the initial capital leased asset and the capital lease obligation (current and long-term).

The next journal entry appears at the end of the first year of the lease on December 31.

Exhibit 11-1
Lease Amortization Schedule

Year	Interest	Principal	Balance
1	3,903	15,597	31,277
2	2,427	15,573	15,704
3	796	15,704	0
Total	7,126	46,874	

2.	Interest expense	3,903	
	Lease payable (current)	15,597	
	Cash		18,000
	Lease rental payable		1,500

> To record the payment of the first 12 lease
> rentals plus the accrual of the last month's rental.

| 3. | Depreciation expense | 15,625 | |
| | Accumulated depreciation | | 15,625 |

> To record depreciation expense and accumulated
> depreciation for the first 12 months of the lease.

| 4. | Lease payable (long-term) | 15,573 | |
| | Lease payable (current) | | 15,573 |

> To transfer the current amount due from long-term
> liabilities to current liabilities.

5.	Taxes receivable	6,300	
	Deferred tax charge	535	
	Tax benefit		6,835

> To provide for taxes on the lease payment expense.

T-ACCOUNT SUMMARY AT THE END OF THE FIRST YEAR

The deferred tax computation for the first year is shown in Exhibit 11-2. The impact of the above journal entries is summarized in T-account form in Exhibits 11-3 and 11-4. The T-accounts are shown as they appear at the end of the first year of the lease and the entries are identified by the number of the applicable journal entry. The income statement (Exhibit 11-5), balance sheet (Exhibit 11-6) and cash flow statement (Exhibit 11-7) as of the end of the first year also have been presented. The balance sheet in Exhibit 11-5 includes given amounts of 40,000 each for other fixed assets and common stock in order to make a more realistic presentation.

Exhibit 11-2
Deferred Tax Computation
(Capital Lease)

	Books	Tax return
Rent expense	—	18,000
Interest expense	3,903	—
Depreciation expense	15,625	—
Total	19,528	18,000
Tax rate	x 35%	x 35%
Tax benefit	6,835	6,300
Increase in deferred tax charge	—	535
	6,835	6,835

OPERATING LEASE ACCOUNTING

A lease that does not meet any of the four capital lease criteria is considered to be an operating lease. An operating lease, for financial reporting purposes, is treated as off balance sheet financing from the viewpoint of the lessee. Neither the leased asset nor the corresponding obligation appears on the balance sheet. Footnote reference to the future rental obligations is the only disclosure requirement. The lease payments are shown as rental expense in the income statement.

The rules to be followed in accounting for an operating lease according to FASB 13 are presented in the following pages. After a review of these rules, a comprehensive illustration is used to show the appropriate journal entries, T-accounts and financial statement presentation.

FASB 13 Requirements

The rules from FASB 13 are summarized below as a preface to the illustration.

> *.111   Normally, rental on an operating lease shall be charged to expense over the lease term as it becomes payable. If rental payments are not made on a straight-line basis,[13a] rental expense nevertheless shall be recognized on a straight-line basis unless another systematic and rational basis is more representative of the time pattern in which use benefit is derived from the leased property, in which case that basis shall be used. [FAS13¶15]*

[13a]   *Refer to paragraphs .525 through .527f for supplemental...*

Exhibit 11-3
Balance Sheet T-accounts
(Capital Lease)

Lease payable (current)		Lease payable (long-term)		Cash	
(2) 15,597	15,597 (1)	(4) 15,573	31,277 (1)		18,000 (2)
	15,573 (4)				
	15,573		15,704		

Capital leased equipment		Accumulated depreciation		Lease rental payable	
(1) 46,874			15,625 (3)		1,500 (2)

Deferred tax charge		Taxes receivable	
(5) 535		(5) 6,300	

Exhibit 11-4
Income Statement T-accounts
(Capital Lease)

Depreciation expense		Interest expense		Tax benefit	
(3) 15,625		(2) 3,903			6,835 (5)

Exhibit 11-5
Income Statement
(Capital Lease)

Revenue		0
Operating expenses		
Depreciation expense		(15,625)
Operating income		(15,625)
Other expenses		
Interest expense		(3,903)
Income before taxes		(19,528)
Current	(6,300)	
Deferred	(535)	
Tax benefit		6,835
Net income (loss)		(12,693)

Illustration

The requirements for accounting for an operating lease of the lessee have been reviewed; therefore, an illustration is presented to clarify and expand on the conceptual accounting requirements.

ASSUMPTIONS

The following assumptions are used in the illustration:

Inception date: January 1

Lease term: 48 months, in advance

Payment amount: 2,175

Fair market value purchase option

Equipment fair market value: 100,000

Lessee tax rate: 35%

Capital lease criteria: None are met

Discount rate: The lessor's is implicit rate of 11.49% is unknown to the lessee. The lessee's incremental pretax borrowing rate is 11%

Tax status: Tax lease to the lessor, 5-year MACRS property

Other closing costs, fees, executory costs, etc.: None.

Exhibit 11-6
Balance Sheet
(Capital Lease)

Assets
Current assets
    Cash .... (18,000)
    Taxes receivable 6,300
        Total current assets .... (11,700)

Fixed assets
    Capital leased equipment 46,874
    Less accumulated depreciation .... (15,625)
        Net 31,249
    Other property, plant and equipment (net) 40,000
        Total fixed assets 71,249

Deferred tax charge 535
        Total assets 60,084

Liabilities
Current liabilities
    Lease rental payable 1,500
    Lease payable (current) 15,573
        Total current liabilities 17,073

Long-term liabilities
    Lease payable (long-term) 15,704
        Total liabilities 32,777

Owners' equity
Common stock 40,000
Retained earnings .... (12,693)
        Total equity 27,307
        Total liabilities and equity 60,084

Exhibit 11-7
Statement of Cash Flows
(Capital Lease)

Cash flows from operating activities		
Interest paid		(3,903)
Cash flows from investing activities		0
Cash flows from financing activities		
Principal payments (15,597 - 1,500)		(14,097)
Net decrease in cash		(18,000)
Cash at the beginning of the year		0
Cash at the end of the year		(18,000)
Reconciliation of net income to operating activities		
Net income		(12,693)
Adjustments:		
Depreciation	15,625	
Increase in taxes receivable	(6,300)	
Increase in deferred tax charge	(535)	
Total adjustments		8,790
Cash flows from operating activities		(3,903)
Noncash investing activities		
Assets acquired (capital lease)		46,874
Liabilities assumed		
Current	15,597	
Long-term	31,277	
Total liabilities		46,874

INITIAL SET-UP

The assumptions suggest the reason for treating the lease as operating is that none of the capital lease criteria are met. Although the first three criteria must be accepted as given, the fourth capital lease criterion, or 90% test, can be calculated. In this test the lessee determines the present value of the minimum lease payments. The lessee uses its incremental borrowing rate of 11% as the discount rate unless it knows the lessor's implicit rate and the implicit rate is lower than the incremental borrowing rate.

Application of the 90% test is a three-part process. The first step in this process is to establish the comparison base. The comparison base is equal to 90% of the asset's fair market value.

100,000	Fair market value
x 90%	
90,000	Comparison base

Next, the present value of the minimum lease payments is calculated using the lessee's incremental borrowing cost. The lease is classified as an operating lease because the present value of the minimum lease payments is less than the comparison base (84,925 versus 90,000).

HP-12C			**HP-17B (12 P/YR BEGIN MODE)**	
	f	REG		FIN
	g	BEG		TVM
2,175		PMT	■	CLEAR DATA
48		n	2,175	PMT
11	g	12÷	48	N
		PV -84,925.25	11	I%YR
				PV = -84,925.25

The lease has been properly classified as an operating lease, so the income statement entries can be determined. Rentals for an operating lease usually are charged to expense over the lease term on a straight-line basis. Lease commitment fees, closing fees, origination fees, lease bonuses and leasehold improvements paid at the inception of the lease by the lessee to the lessor generally are deferred. These expenses are allocated as expenses to the income statement over the noncancellable lease term on a straight-line basis. Any tax credits that are passed to the lessee are accounted for separately from the operating lease expenses.

JOURNAL ENTRIES

There are no journal entries for the balance sheet in an operating lease. The following journal entries pertain to the income statement.

1.	Lease expense	26,100	
	Cash		26,100

To record the first 12 months of lease payment expense.

2. Taxes receivable	9,135	
Tax benefit		9,135

To record the tax consequences of the first 12
lease payments.

T-ACCOUNT SUMMARY AT THE END OF THE FIRST YEAR

The deferred tax computation for the first year is shown in Exhibit 11-8.
The impact of the above journal entries is summarized in T-account format
in Exhibits 11-9 and 11-10. The T-accounts are shown as they appear at the
end of the first year of the lease. The T-account entries are identified by the
number of the applicable journal entry.

The income statement (Exhibit 11-11), balance sheet (Exhibit 11-12) and
statement of cash flows (Exhibit 11-13) as of the end of the first year also
are presented. The balance sheet in Exhibit 11-12 includes given amounts
of 40,000 each for other fixed assets and common stock in order to make a
more realistic presentation.

COMPARATIVE DIFFERENCES

The comprehensive example that follows contrasts the lessee's accounting
and reporting for the same lease, reflected as an operating and a capital
lease. The same lease is shown side by side as both operating and capital
in this comparison. This method of illustration most effectively demonstrates the impact of the off balance sheet nature of the operating lease and
the capitalization of the leased asset.

Exhibit 11-8
Deferred Tax Computation
(Operating Lease)

	Books	Tax return
Rent expense	26,100	26,100
Tax rate	x 35%	x 35%
Tax benefit	9,135	9,135

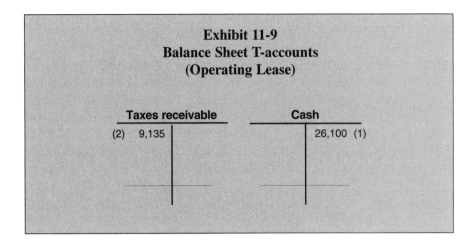

Exhibit 11-9
Balance Sheet T-accounts
(Operating Lease)

Taxes receivable
(2) 9,135

Cash
26,100 (1)

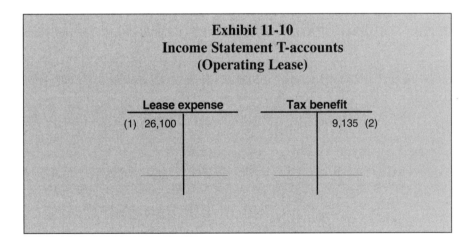

Exhibit 11-10
Income Statement T-accounts
(Operating Lease)

Lease expense
(1) 26,100

Tax benefit
9,135 (2)

The impact of the two lease types on the income statement and cash flow statement is shown as well, in addition to that on the balance sheet. It is important to remember that, regardless of the book accounting treatment of the lease as capital or operating, the tax status and treatment of the lease remain the same. This illustration assumes that the lease, in either case, is a true lease for tax purposes.

Exhibit 11-11
Income Statement
(Operating Lease)

Revenue		0
Operating expenses		
Lease expense		(26,100)
Operating income		(26,100)
Other expenses		
Interest expense		0
Income before taxes		(26,100)
Current	(9,135)	
Deferred	0	
Tax benefit		9,135
Net income (loss)		(16,965)

Exhibit 11-12
Balance Sheet
(Operating Lease)

Assets	
Current assets	
Cash	(26,100)
Taxes receivable	9,135
Total current assets	(16,965)
Fixed assets	
Other property, plant and equipment (net)	40,000
Deferred tax charge	0
Total assets	23,035
Liabilities	
Current liabilities	0
Long-term liabilities	0
Owners' equity	
Common stock	40,000
Retained earnings	(16,965)
Total equity	23,035
Total liabilities and owners' equity	23,035

Exhibit 11-13
Statement of Cash Flows
(Operating Lease)

Cash flows from operating activities
Lease rentals paid .... (26,100)

Cash flows from investing activities 0

Cash flows from financing activities 0

Net decrease in cash .... (26,100)
Cash at the beginning of the year 0
Cash at the end of the year .... (26,100)

Reconciliation of net income to operating activities
Net income .... (16,965)
Increase in taxes receivable .... (9,135)
   Net cash used in operating activities .... (26,100)

Assumptions

The following assumptions are utilized in the illustration for Lightshow, Inc.:

Inception date: January 1

Equipment cost: 100,000

Lease term: 60 months in arrears

Lease payment amount: 2,000

Purchase option: Fair market value

Lessee's incremental borrowing rate: 11%

Accounting depreciation: Straight-line over five years (no salvage value).

CAPITALIZATION OF THE LEASED ASSET

A lease that is deemed to be a capital lease for accounting purposes is capitalized on the lessee's balance sheet. The present value of the lease payments is recorded as an asset and a corresponding amount is recorded as a liability.

In substance, the lease is treated similar to an asset purchase financed with an installment loan. Each lease payment is amortized to its interest and principal components. The interest component is recorded as an expense in the income statement, whereas the principal component reduces the lease obligation in the balance sheet.

When the lease is capitalized, it is shown as an asset in a category separate from other property, plant and equipment. The leased asset is depreciated following the lessee's normal depreciation policy. If the lease meets either of the first two capital lease criteria, the asset is depreciated over the asset's useful economic life. If either of the last two criteria is met, the depreciation life of the capital leased asset is limited to the lease term.

The value at which the asset is capitalized may not necessarily be the fair market value of the asset. The lessee must determine the capitalization amount by computing the present value of the minimum lease payments. However, the capitalized amount can never exceed the fair market value of the asset. The lessee uses its incremental borrowing rate, which is the same discount rate used in the 90% test. The lessee's discount rate for this illustration is 11%.

The present value of the minimum lease payments is calculated as follows:

	HP-12C			**HP-17B (12 P/YR END MODE)**
	f	REG		FIN
	g	END		TVM
2,000		PMT	∎	CLEAR DATA
60		n	2,000	PMT
11	g	12÷	60	N
	PV	-91,986.07	11	I%YR
				PV =-91,986.07

The present value of the minimum lease payments is 91,986. This is the amount at which the leased asset is capitalized in the balance sheet of the lessee, because it does not exceed the fair market value of the asset.

RECORDING THE LEASE LIABILITY

The capital lease obligation is recorded in the balance sheet at the present value of the minimum lease payments (91,986,) the same amount as the asset. In a classified balance sheet, the liability is presented in its current and long-term components. The portion of the total liability that will be paid off during the next 12 months of the lease is recorded as a current liability under the current leases payable. The remaining liability is recorded under long-term leases payable.

The calculator can be used to amortize the lease liability into its interest and principal components. The keystrokes for this amortization are displayed in Exhibit 11-14. The amortization process identifies the periodic interest expense and separates the remaining principal into its current and long-term portions.

Exhibit 11-14
Interest and Principal Amortization

HP-12C

	f	REG
	g	END
91,986	CHS	PV
2,000		PMT
11	g	12÷
0		n

Year	Interest 12 f AMORT	Principal (X ⋛ Y)	Balance (RCL PV)
1	9,397	14,603	77,383
2	7,707	16,293	61,090
3	5,821	18,179	42,911
4	3,718	20,282	22,629
5	1,371	22,629	0
Total	28,014	91,986	

HP-17B (12 P/YR END MODE)

		FIN
		TVM
	■	CLEAR DATA
91,986	+/-	PV
2,000		PMT
11		I%YR
0		N
		OTHER
		AMRT
12		#P

Year	Interest (INT)	Principal (PRIN)	Balance (BAL NEXT)
1	9,397	14,603	77,383
2	7,707	16,293	61,090
3	5,821	18,179	42,911
4	3,718	20,282	22,629
5	1,371	22,629	0
Total	28,014	91,986	

The current and long-term portions of the lease obligation are shown separately in the financial statements. Exhibit 11-14 shows the amount of principal that is paid each year. In the first year, the principal portion (debt payoff) is 14,603. The total debt is reduced by this amount, leaving a balance of 77,383.

The financial statements presented for this illustration reflect the amortization at the end of the first year of the lease. The remaining balance of 77,383 is broken down between its current and long-term portions. The current portion from the second year of the amortization is 16,293 and the long-term portion is 61,090. The interest portion of the first year's payments of 9,397 is recorded as interest expense in the income statement.

DEPRECIATION

The amount of the capital leased asset, 91,986, is used as the original basis for recognizing accounting depreciation. The annual depreciation expense is 18,397, as calculated below:

91,986	Original basis
0	Estimated salvage value
91,986	
÷ 5	Number of years
18,397	Depreciation per year

It is assumed in this illustration that the lessee has the option to acquire the asset for its fair market value purchase at the end of the lease. Ownership after the basic lease term, therefore, is not assured. Because of this assumption, it can be deduced that one of the third and fourth capital lease criteria was met. For this reason the depreciation life is limited to the lease term only.

ACCOUNTING FOR THE CAPITAL LEASE

The interest and principal amounts previously calculated and the depreciation expense each year are necessary to account for the income statement impact of the capital lease. The present value of the minimum lease payments is recorded as the initial amount of both the capital leased asset and the capital lease obligation. The asset is depreciated over the lease term using the straight-line depreciation of 18,397 each year. Additionally, the interest component of the payments is shown as interest expense on the capital lease obligation in the income statement.

ACCOUNTING FOR THE OPERATING LEASE

Accounting for the operating lease is much simpler than for the capital lease. Because the operating lease is considered a rental for financial reporting purposes, the amount of the lease payment is expensed each period. The amount of the annual lease expense is the sum of 12 payments of 2,000, or 24,000. Because this is an operating lease, neither an asset nor an obligation is recorded in the balance sheet (i.e., the lease is off balance sheet). Although the lease obligation is off balance sheet, the future minimum lease payments pertaining to the operating lease must be disclosed in a footnote to the financial statements.

Comparative Financial Statements

Now that the accounting information pertaining to the sample lease has been compiled, the impact of the two lease types on each financial statement of the lessee can be illustrated. The operating and capital lease presentations are shown side by side. The balance sheet, income statement and cash flow statement are shown in Exhibits 11-15, 11-16 and 11-17, respectively. Additionally, a reconciliation of the difference between the tax expense for book and tax purposes is shown in Exhibit 11-18.

BALANCE SHEET

Many of the accounts in the balance sheet are the same for both types of leases. Notice that none of the current asset accounts are affected by the lease accounting. The total amount of current assets in both columns is 33,155. The cash account is the same irrespective of how the lease is treated for book purposes, because the lessee is making the same cash payment no matter how it is allocated for accounting purposes. The tax status and attributes also are the same whether the lease is treated as capital or operating. (This lease is considered a true lease for tax purposes.)

A deferred tax charge appears only for the capital lease accounting. This deferred tax amount of 1,328 represents the difference between the tax expense for the period of 27,547 for book purposes and 28,875 for income tax purposes. (Alternatively, the deferred tax charge can be viewed as representing expenses that have been recognized in the tax return, but not yet in the books.) The operating lease tax expense of 28,875, on the other hand, is the same for both book and tax purposes. The net income amounts for both alternatives appear on the balance sheet as current year's retained earnings.

Exhibit 11-15
Comparative Balance Sheet

Assets

Current assets	Capital	Operating
Cash	17,355	17,355
Accounts receivable	11,200	11,200
Inventory	4,600	4,600
Total current assets	33,155	33,155

Fixed assets		
Deferred tax charge	1,328	—
Property, plant & equipment	220,000	220,000
Capital leased equipment	91,986	—
Less: accumulated depreciation	(98,397)	(80,000)
Total fixed assets	214,917	140,000
Total assets	248,072	173,155

Liabilities

Current liabilities		
Accounts payable	4,300	4,300
Wages payable	2,100	2,100
Lease contract payable	16,293	—
Total current liabilities	22,693	6,400

Long-term liabilities		
Contract payable	42,000	42,000
Notes payable	7,750	7,750
Lease contract payable	61,090	—
Total long-term liabilities	110,840	49,750
Total liabilities	133,533	56,150

Owners' equity

Common stock	32,000	32,000
Retained earnings		
Prior years	31,380	31,380
Current year	51,159	53,625
Total equity	114,539	117,005
Total liabilities and equity	248,072	173,155

Exhibit 11-16
Comparative Income Statement

Revenue	Capital	Operating
Revenue	714,000	714,000
Cost of goods sold	(428,000)	(428,000)
Gross profit	286,000	286,000
Operating expense		
General & administrative expense	(94,000)	(94,000)
Selling expenses	(53,500)	(53,500)
Depreciation expense	(46,397)	(28,000)
Lease expense	—	(24,000)
Operating income	92,103	86,500
Other income & expense		
Interest expense	(13,397)	(4,000)
Income before taxes	78,706	82,500
Income taxes at 35%	(27,547)	(28,875)
Net income	51,159	53,625

The property, plant and equipment category represents fixed assets (in addition to the new capital leased equipment) that the lessee already has acquired. The new equipment subject to the capital lease is listed in a separate category from the other property, plant and equipment. The leased asset is listed at its original capitalized value of 91,986. This is the present value of the minimum lease payments discounted at the lessee's incremental borrowing rate.

The original property, plant and equipment as well as the capital leased asset generate depreciation expense for book purposes. For the current year the total depreciation is determined as follows:

28,000	Other property, plant and equipment
18,397	Capital leased equipment
46,397	Total depreciation

Exhibit 11-17
Comparative Statement of Cash Flows

Sources of cash	Capital	Operating
Net income	51,159	53,625
Add depreciation expense	46,397	28,000
Deduct increase in deferred tax charge	(1,328)	—
Total sources	96,228	81,625
Uses of cash		
Dividends	(28,000)	(28,000)
Purchase of equipment	(41,000)	(41,000)
Reduction of lease liability	(14,603)	0
Total uses	(83,603)	(69,000)
Net increase in cash	12,625	12,625

Exhibit 11-18
Deferred Tax Reconciliation

Operating lease

	Tax return	Books
Rent expense	24,000	24,000
Tax rate	x 35%	x 35%
Tax benefit	8,400	8,400

Capital lease

	Tax return	Books
Rent expense	24,000	—
Interest expense	—	9,397
Depreciation expense	—	18,397
Total	24,000	27,794
Tax rate	x 35%	x 35%
Tax benefit	8,400	9,728
Increase in deferred tax charge	1,328	—
	9,728	9,728

The accumulated depreciation figure of 80,000 shown in the operating lease column includes the current year's depreciation of 28,000 on the original property, plant and equipment. For the capital lease, notice that the accumulated depreciation is 18,397 higher. This difference represents the first full year's depreciation on the capital leased equipment, as previously illustrated.

The first financial statement impact of the off balance sheet lease is now evident, in that no asset is booked under operating lease accounting. The result is the difference between fixed assets and total assets for the two alternatives.

The total amount of current liabilities is the same as far as the other non-lease-related accounts payable and wages payable for the sample company are concerned. For the capital lease, however, the lease obligation is on balance sheet; therefore, its current portion is shown as of the end of the first year. The total lease obligation as of the end of the first year of 77,383 is comprised of the short- and long-term components, which are derived from the second year of the lease amortization.

16,293	Current portion
61,090	Long-term portion
77,383	Total

The long-term portion of 61,090 appears under long-term liabilities for the capital lease only. This remaining obligation will be paid off during the balance of the lease term. All other liabilities are the same for the two types of lease accounting.

Common stock and prior years' retained earnings are unchanged. The only equity account that is different is the current year's retained earnings. These amounts are derived from the income statement (net income). The total liabilities plus equity for the two alternatives again show the impact of reflecting the operating lease off balance sheet. The company appears to have incurred far more debt if capital lease accounting is used, even though the same obligation exists in either case (i.e., from a cash flow perspective, the same 60 payments of 2,000 are due irrespective of how the lease is accounted for).

INCOME STATEMENT

Sales, cost of goods sold, selling and general and administrative expenses are not impacted by the choice of lease accounting method. The first difference between operating and capital lease treatment in the income statement appears under depreciation expense. Here, the 28,000 of depreciation pertaining to other property, plant and equipment appears in both columns. The additional depreciation expense of 18,397 for the leased equipment appears only in the capital lease column.

No lease expense is recognized under the capital lease because it is viewed as an asset of the lessee. The expenses recognized under a capital lease consist of interest and depreciation. Under the operating lease, on the other hand, rental expense of 24,000 (12 payments of 2,000) is recognized.

The interest expense attributable to the capital lease obligation for the first year is shown in the other income and expenses category. This figure is derived from the amortization schedule in Exhibit 11-14. The lease interest expense of 9,397 is combined there with 4,000 of other interest expense the lessee has incurred.

Income before taxes is measurably different for the two alternatives. This difference highlights another benefit to the lessee of off balance sheet leases. The difference in reported income is due primarily to the different pattern of expense recognition between the two types of lease accounting. As is seen in Exhibit 11-16, the lease payments are expensed directly for the operating lease (24,000). For the capital lease, the total expense consists of the interest and depreciation expenses (27,794).

The differences between the two accounting methods are reflected at each of the different levels of profitability in the income statement. The impact of operating leases on the lessee's profitability measures is an additional motivation for lessees to use leasing. Many managers, for example, are compensated in part through bonuses that usually pertain to one of these levels of income measurement. Operating leasing may maximize the appropriate income measurement and, consequently, the manager's bonus.

CASH FLOW STATEMENT

The impact of the lease payments in the cash flow statement is summarized in Exhibit 11-17 in a condensed format. Note that the differences in net income and depreciation expense from the income statement are both shown. From the balance sheet, the deferred tax charge and the reduction of the lease principal (first year principal from Exhibit 11-14) are both listed. Other assumed items (dividends and other equipment purchased) are added to make the statement more complete.

It is important to note in this example that the end-of-year cash balance is exactly the same (17,355) for both lease presentations. No matter how the lease payment is allocated to expense, the method of accounting for the leases does not impact either the tax consequences or the actual cash flow of the lease payments.

FINANCIAL RATIOS

Exhibit 11-19 summarizes some of the key ratios used by financial statement analysts for making credit and investment decisions. Each of these measures of financial health is more favorably impacted by the operating lease accounting. Later in the lease these benefits reverse, as do the income statement differences. In the early years of the lease, however, the demonstrated impact provides sufficient motivation for many companies to take advantage of off balance sheet leases.

Liquidity

These three ratios measure a company's short-term capacity to meet its obligations. Theoretically, if a company has at least as many current assets at its disposal as it has current obligations, it will be able to pay its bills. All three liquidity ratios favor the operating lease, suggesting an improved capacity to pay current obligations. In reality, the same obligations exist in either case and the lessee's cash flow requirements are exactly the same. Because current obligations must be paid with cash, and not current assets or working capital, the operating lease advantage is one of perception only.

Solvency

Solvency is a measure of a firm's long-term ability to meet its debt and other obligations. The times-interest-earned ratio measures the number of times a company could meet its interest obligation for the period using available net income. This ratio also appears to favor the operating lease. Actually, the lessee has the same ability to pay its interest in either case because the interest attributable to the capital lease is an allocated, rather than real, amount.

Financial Leverage

These ratios attempt to measure a company's dependence on debt by comparing the ratio of total debt to total equity. Because the debt liability for the operating lease is hidden, reliance on these ratios favors the operating lease. The actual obligations are the same in either case, however.

Exhibit 11-19
Measurements of Financial Impact

		Capital		Operating	
Liquidity					
Current ratio	Current assets / Current liabilities	33,155 / 22,693	= 1.46	33,155 / 6,400	= 5.18
Net working capital	Current assets – current liabilities	33,155 -22,693 / 10,462		33,155 -6,400 / 26,755	
Solvency					
Times interest earned	Net income + interest + taxes / Interest	92,103 / 13,397	= 6.87	86,500 / 4,000	= 21.63
Debt position					
Debt to equity	Debt / Equity	133,533 / 114,539	= 1.17	56,150 / 117,005	= .48
Debt %	Debt / Assets	133,533 / 248,072	= .54	56,150 / 173,155	= .32
Earnings & profitability					
Net profit margin	Net income / Sales	51,159 / 714,000	= .07	53,625 / 714,000	= .08
x asset turnover	Sales / Assets	714,000 / 248,072	= 2.88	714,000 / 173,155	= 4.12
= ROA	Net income / Assets	51,159 / 248,072	= .21	53,625 / 173,155	= .31
x leverage factor	Assets / Equity	248,072 / 114,539	= 2.17	173,155 / 117,005	= 1.48
= ROE	Net income / Equity	51,159 / 114,539	= .45	53,625 / 117,005	= .46
EPS	Net income / Total shares	51,159 / 12,000	= 4.26	53,625 / 12,000	= 4.47

Profitability

Each of the measurements of profitability in Exhibit 11-19 appears to favor the operating lease. Even the very important measurement of earnings per share is 21 cents greater using operating lease accounting.

The favorable impact of operating lease accounting is evident as one reviews each of the financial statements and measurement ratios. They all tend to make the off balance sheet treatment of the lease appear more favorable. For instance, the lessee appears to have less debt, and to be better able to service it. In spite of the fact the company is in the same cash flow and risk position under each lease type, the operating lease accounting presents a more favorable picture. These advantages motivate many companies to seek operating lease financing for their new asset acquisitions.

SALE-LEASEBACKS

Sale-leasebacks involve the sale of property by the owner-user of the asset to an investor. The seller (which becomes the lessee) then leases the property back from the investor (which becomes the lessor). These transactions allow the original owner to maintain use of the property even though it has been sold to the investor. The leaseback may include all or a portion of the original assets sold.

From a financial reporting perspective, the normal characteristics of a sale and a lease pertain to the sale-leaseback transaction; therefore, the new leaseback is classified as either a capital lease or an operating lease for accounting purposes. The accounting classification of the leaseback drives the timing of how the gain on the sale of the asset is recognized.

Reasons for Entering Into Sale-leasebacks

There are many reasons for equipment owners to enter into sale-leaseback transactions. For instance, various tax, accounting and economic benefits can be obtained through utilization of this form of financing. Several of the primary motivations are addressed below.

SOURCE OF LIQUIDITY

The sale-leaseback transaction generates cash from the sale of existing equipment – cash that can be used for current operations or investment in new production capacity. Through this process, nonliquid assets are converted to cash without losing the use of those assets.

ACCOUNTING GAIN

Accounting profit is realized from the transaction to the extent the fair market value of the asset exceeds its current book value. As is demonstrated later, not all of this gain is necessarily recognized in the period of sale. Depending on the accounting characterization of the leaseback, some or all of the gain may have to be deferred and recognized over the term of the leaseback. Nevertheless, the sale-leaseback may generate an accounting gain.

OFF BALANCE SHEET DEBT

The leaseback of an asset is, in effect, a refinancing of the asset. The refinanced (lease) debt is treated off balance sheet, however, if the leaseback is structured so as to be classified as an operating lease. Only a footnote reference to the asset and the debt is required. All of the benefits of operating lease accounting become available to the seller-lessee.

TAX BENEFITS

In a properly structured transaction the leaseback payments are tax-deductible for the seller-lessee. The deductibility of the lease payment, in effect, allows the deduction of both principal and interest (the entire payment amount). In this manner, the seller-lessee is able to "redepreciate" the asset effectively, because the principal portion of the lease payments (over the life of the lease) has the same effect as depreciation. This new "depreciation" may be based on an inflated, or appreciated, asset value.

TAX DEDUCTION FOR THE VALUE OF THE LAND

Normally, the purchase of land does not provide for a tax depreciation benefit. Only the tax basis of buildings or equipment placed on the land is deductible via depreciation. In a sale-leaseback transaction of land and buildings (and equipment), the entire lease payment is deductible if the leaseback is structured as a true tax lease. Because the leaseback payment also includes the leaseback of the land, the seller-lessee is able to receive tax benefits for the value of the land.

OTHER TAX MOTIVATIONS

Several provisions of the tax law have a negative impact on asset owners. In particular, the alternative minimum tax (AMT) rules, the 40% midquarter convention and foreign tax credit rules all work to the disadvantage of certain owners of depreciable assets. In each case, the effect of these rules is mitigated by selling assets and leasing them back. Because the seller-lessee is no longer the tax owner of the assets, it is no longer impacted by these various tax penalties.

Utilization of NOL or ITC Carryforwards

When a sale-leaseback is structured as a sale for tax purposes, the seller-lessee pays taxes on the gain. The gain is the difference between the sale price of the asset and its remaining tax basis. A company having a carryforward of a net operating loss (NOL), investment tax credits (ITC) or other credits can offset these carryforwards against the taxable gain of the sale-leaseback. Some companies may risk losing all or a portion of such carryforwards if they cannot be used within a certain time frame. The sale-leaseback provides the means of creating taxable income to absorb the carryforward tax benefits.

Accounting Requirements

Reference must be made to original FASB Statements 13, 28 and 98 in order to understand the proper accounting for sale-leasebacks. The primary concern in accounting for sale-leasebacks is the timing of any gain or loss recognition on the sale portion of the transaction. The recognition of gain on the sale-leaseback is a function of continuing involvement in the asset by the seller and is measured by the portion of the original asset that is leased back by the seller-lessee. This proportion is derived by comparing the present value of the minimum lease payments to the fair market value of the asset sold. The methodology and discount rate used to solve for present value in this case are the same as those used for lease classification in the 90% test.

For purposes of gain recognition, FASB 13 separates sale-leasebacks into three basic categories. These categories are illustrated in Exhibit 11-20. The FASB 13 requirements for sale-leasebacks and the subsequent gain recognition are detailed in paragraphs .128 - .130, as follows:

Exhibit 11-20
Categories of Sale-leasebacks

Minor leaseback	Present value of the minimum lease payments is less than or equal to 10% of fair market value of the asset sold
Intermediate leaseback	Present value of the minimum lease payments is greater than 10% and less than 90% of fair market value of the asset sold
Major leaseback	Present value of the minimum lease payments is greater than or equal to 90% of fair market value of the asset sold.

.128 Sale-leaseback transactions involve the sale of property by the owner and a lease of the property back to the seller. A sale of property that is accompanied by a leaseback of all or any part of the property for all or part of its remaining economic life shall be accounted for by the seller-lessee in accordance with the provisions of paragraph .129 [except that a sale-leaseback involving real estate, property improvements, or integral equipment[27a] shall be accounted for in accordance with the provisions of paragraphs .130A through .130M]. A sale of property that is accompanied by a leaseback of all or any part of the property for all or part of its remaining economic life shall be accounted for by the [buyer-lessor] in accordance with the provisions of paragraph .130 [FAS28, ¶2]. . . .

.129 If the lease meets one of the criteria for treatment as a capital lease (refer to paragraph .103), the seller-lessee shall account for the lease as a capital lease; otherwise, as an operating lease. Any profit or loss on the sale[28] shall be deferred and amortized in proportion to the amortization of the leased asset,[29] if a capital lease, or in proportion to the related gross rental charged to expense over the lease term, if an operating lease, unless:

a. The seller-lessee relinquishes the right to substantially all of the remaining use of the property sold (retaining only a minor portion of such use),[30] in which case the sale and the leaseback shall be accounted for as separate transactions based on their respective terms. However, if the amount of rentals called for by the lease is unreasonable under market conditions at the inception of the lease, an appropriate amount shall be deferred or accrued, by adjusting the profit or loss on the sale, and amortized as specified in the introduction of this paragraph to adjust those rentals to a reasonable amount.

b.   *The seller-lessee retains more than a minor part but less than substantially all[31] of the use of the property through the leaseback and realizes a profit on the sale[32] in excess of (1) the present value of the minimum lease payments over the lease term, if the leaseback is classified as an operating lease, or (2) the recorded amount of the leased asset, if the leaseback is classified as a capital lease. In that case, the profit on the sale in excess of either the present value of the minimum lease payments or the recorded amount of the leased asset, whichever is appropriate, shall be recognized at the date of sale. For purposes of applying this provision, the present value of the minimum lease payments for an operating lease shall be computed using the interest rate that would be used to apply the 90 percent recovery criterion of paragraph .103(d).*

c.   *The fair value of the property at the time of the transaction is less than its undepreciated cost, in which case a loss shall be recognized immediately up to the amount of the difference between undepreciated cost and fair value. [FAS28,¶3]*

.130 If the lease meets the criteria in paragraphs .103 and .104 the [buyer-lessor] shall record the transaction as a purchase and a direct financing lease; otherwise, the [buyer-lessor] shall record the transaction as a purchase and an operating lease. [FAS13,¶34]

[27a] *The terms property improvements and integral equipment...*

[28] *Profit or loss on the sale is used...*

[29] *If the leased asset is land only,...*

[30] *Substantially all is used here in the context...*

[32] *Profit or loss on the sale is used in this...*

To determine whether a leaseback is to be treated as minor, intermediate or major, the present value of the minimum lease payments must be calculated and compared to the fair market value of the asset. The lessee's incremental borrowing rate normally is used as the discount rate in solving for present value. The lessor's implicit rate is used if it is known and if it is lower than the lessee's borrowing rate.

MINOR LEASEBACKS

If the leaseback is deemed to be minor (the present value of the minimum lease payments is less than or equal to 10% of the fair market value of the asset sold), the sale and the leaseback are accounted for as separate transactions. Sale treatment requires removal of the asset and its accompanying accumulated depreciation from the balance sheet. Any consequent gain or loss is recognized in the period of the sale. The leaseback is classified as either capital or operating based on the four capital lease criteria and accounted for over the term of the lease.

INTERMEDIATE LEASEBACKS

If the leaseback is an intermediate leaseback (the present value of the minimum lease payments is greater than 10% but less than 90% of the fair market value of the asset sold), a portion of the gain from the sale of the asset may be deferred. If the intermediate leaseback is classified as capital, any accounting gain in excess of the recorded amount of the capitalized asset (usually the present value of the minimum lease payments) is recognized by the seller-lessee in the current period.

If the leaseback is classified as operating, any accounting gain in excess of the present value of the leaseback payments is recognized in the current period. For both types of leases, the portion of the gain that is not recognized currently is deferred and recognized over the term of the lease. For the capital lease, the deferred gain is amortized in proportion to the amortization of the leased asset (accounting depreciation). In an operating lease, the deferred gain is amortized in proportion to the related gross rental charged to expense by the seller-lessee over the lease term. This amortization is usually straight-line.

MAJOR LEASEBACKS

Major leasebacks are always classified as capital leases, because the criterion for treating the sale-leaseback as major is that the present value of the minimum lease payments is greater than or equal to 90% of the fair market value of the asset sold. Meeting this criterion also makes the lease a capital lease. For major leasebacks, all of the accounting gain is deferred and recognized subsequently in proportion to the amortization (accounting depreciation) of the asset.

Sale-leaseback Illustrations

The three categories of sale-leaseback transactions and their impact on the accounting gain or loss are illustrated in the following section. Of course, many other combinations of events may make it more complex to determine the gain and the subsequent accounting. Variations of the same example are used in each illustration.

MINOR SALE-LEASEBACK

The assumptions for this example are as follows:

    Original asset cost: 100,000

    Original asset accumulated depreciation: 60,000

    Sale-leaseback fair market value (sale price): 80,000

    Lessor pays 80,000 cash to the lessee (seller) for the asset

    Seller-lessee leases back a portion of the asset for four years

    Leaseback payment amount: 2,500, in arrears

    Fair market value purchase option

    Lessee incremental borrowing rate: 10%

    The accounting classification of the lease is operating.

The present value of the minimum lease payments must be computed to determine whether the leaseback is to be treated as minor, intermediate or major, and whether it is classified as capital or operating. The appropriate discount rate to be used by the lessee in solving for present value is the lessee's incremental borrowing rate of 10%.

HP-12C			HP-17B (1 P/YR END MODE)	
	f	REG		FIN
	g	END		TVM
2,500		PMT	■	CLEAR DATA
4		n	2,500	PMT
10		i	4	N
		PV -7,924.66	10	I%YR
				PV = -7,924.66

The present value of the minimum lease payments is 7,925. This amount is less than 8,000 (10% of the fair market value of the asset sold); therefore, the sale-leaseback is accounted for as a minor sale-leaseback. The sale and the leaseback are accounted for as separate transactions and any accounting gain is recognized immediately. The total accounting gain generated by the sale of the asset to the lessor-investor is 40,000, all of which is to be recognized in the current period.

100,000	Original book value
(60,000)	Accumulated depreciation
40,000	Remaining book value
80,000	Sales price paid to the lessee
(40,000)	Remaining book value (carrying value)
40,000	Accounting gain

The sale portion of the transaction is accounted for as follows:

Accumulated depreciation	60,000	
Cash	80,000	
Asset		100,000
Gain		40,000

To remove the asset sold and its related accumulated depreciation and to recognize currently the gain from the sale.

The leaseback portion of the transaction, in each of the four years of the leaseback, is recognized with the following journal entry:

Lease payment expense	2,500	
Cash		2,500

To record the operating lease payment expense.

INTERMEDIATE SALE-LEASEBACK (OPERATING)

The assumptions for this example are as follows:

Original asset cost: 100,000

Original asset accumulated depreciation: 60,000

Sale-leaseback fair market value (sale price): 80,000

Lessor pays 80,000 cash to the lessee (seller) for the asset

Seller-lessee leases back a substantial portion of the asset for four years

Leaseback payment amount: 21,000, in arrears

Fair market value purchase option

Lessee incremental borrowing rate: 10%

The accounting classification of the lease is operating.

The present value of the minimum lease payments must be computed to determine whether the leaseback is to be treated as minor, intermediate or major, and whether it is classified as capital or operating. The appropriate discount rate to be used by the lessee in solving for present value is the lessee's incremental borrowing rate of 10%. The amount of the accounting gain is the same as in the earlier illustration (40,000).

HP-12C			**HP-17B (1 P/YR END MODE)**	
f	REG			FIN
g	END			TVM
21,000	PMT		■	CLEAR DATA
4	n	21,000		PMT
10	i	4		N
	PV -66,567.17	10		I%YR
				PV =-66,567.17

The present value of the minimum lease payments is 66,567. This amount is more than 10% of the fair market value of the asset sold (8,000), but less than 90% (72,000); therefore, the sale-leaseback is accounted for as an intermediate sale-leaseback. If the accounting gain exceeds the present value of the lease payments, the excess is recognized currently and the balance is deferred. In this example, the gain (40,000) is less than the present value of the minimum lease payments (66,567) so the entire gain is deferred. Because this leaseback is classified as operating, the deferred gain is amortized in proportion to the lease payment expensed by the seller-lessee.

The sale portion of the transaction is accounted for as follows:

Accumulated depreciation	60,000	
Cash	80,000	
Asset		100,000
Deferred gain		40,000

> To remove the asset sold and its related accumulated depreciation and to defer the gain from the sale.

The journal entry for the leaseback portion of the transaction, in each of the four years of the leaseback period, is as follows:

Lease payment expense	21,000	
Cash		21,000

> To record the operating lease payment expense.

Deferred gain	10,000	
Gain		10,000

> To recognize 1/4th of the gain from the sale of the asset (40,000 ÷ 4 years = 10,000).

INTERMEDIATE SALE-LEASEBACK (CAPITAL)

The assumptions for this example are exactly the same as the previous intermediate sale-leaseback example except it is assumed that the lease meets the third capital lease criterion and is classified as capital. Because the assumptions are the same as the previous example, the present value of the minimum lease payments is the same (66,567). The leaseback is classified as capital, so the deferred gain is amortized in proportion to the depreciation expensed by the seller-lessee. The sale portion of the transaction and the initial set-up of the capital lease are recorded as follows:

Accumulated depreciation	60,000	
Cash	80,000	
Asset		100,000
Deferred gain		40,000

> To remove the asset sold and its related accumulated depreciation from fixed assets and to defer the gain from the sale.

Capital leased asset	66,567	
Current lease liability		14,343
Long-term lease liability		52,224

> To record the capital leased asset and the related lease liability at the present value of the minimum lease payments.

The journal entries for the leaseback portion of the transaction, in each of the four years of the leaseback, are as follows. The first entry represents the format of the entry amortizing the lease debt. (The portions of the payment allocated to principal and interest in each of the periods will be different.)

Lease interest expense	6,657	
Current lease liability	14,343	
Cash		21,000

> To record the capital lease interest expense and the reduction of the lease liability.

Depreciation expense	16,642	
Accumulated depreciation		16,642

> To record straight-line depreciation for the capital leased asset (66,567 ÷ 4 years = 16,642).

Deferred gain	10,000	
Gain		10,000

> To recognize 1/4th of the gain from the sale of the asset (40,000 x [16,642 ÷ 66,567]).

MAJOR SALE-LEASEBACK (CAPITAL)

The assumptions for this example are as follows:

Original asset cost: 100,000

Original asset accumulated depreciation: 60,000

Sale-leaseback fair market value (sale price): 80,000

Lessor pays 80,000 cash to the lessee (seller) for the asset

Seller-lessee leases back a substantial portion of the asset for four years

Leaseback payment amount: 24,000, in arrears

Fair market value purchase option

Lessee incremental borrowing rate: 10%

The accounting classification of the lease is capital.

The present value of the minimum lease payments must be computed to determine whether the leaseback is to be treated as minor, intermediate or major, and whether it is classified as capital or operating. The appropriate discount rate to be used by the lessee in solving for present value is the lessee's incremental borrowing rate of 10%. The amount of the accounting gain on the sale also is the same as in the earlier illustrations.

HP-12C		**HP-17B (1 P/YR END MODE)**	
f	REG		FIN
g	END		TVM
24,000	PMT	■	CLEAR DATA
4	n	24,000	PMT
10	i	4	N
	PV -76,076.77	10	I%YR
			PV =-76,076.77

The present value of the minimum lease payments is 76,077. This amount is more than 90% of the fair market value of the asset sold (72,000); therefore, the sale-leaseback is accounted for as a major leaseback and the total amount of the accounting gain is deferred. Because this leaseback is classified as capital, the deferred gain is amortized in proportion to the depreciation expensed by the seller-lessee. The sale portion of the transaction and the initial set-up of the capital lease are recorded as follows:

Accumulated depreciation	60,000	
Cash	80,000	
Asset		100,000
Deferred gain		40,000

> To remove the asset sold and its related accumulated depreciation from fixed assets and to defer the gain from the sale.

Capital leased asset	76,077	
Current lease liability		16,393
Long-term lease liability		59,684

> To record the capital leased asset and the related lease liability at the present value of the minimum lease payments.

The journal entries for the leaseback portion of the transaction, in each of the four years of the leaseback, are as follows. The first entry represents the format of the entry amortizing the lease debt. (The portions of the payment allocated to principal and interest in each of the periods will be different.)

Lease interest expense	7,608	
Current lease liability	16,392	
Cash		24,000

To record the capital lease interest expense and the reduction of the lease liability.

Depreciation expense	19,019	
Accumulated depreciation		19,019

To record straight-line depreciation for the capital leased asset (76,077 ÷ 4 years = 19,019).

Deferred gain	10,000	
Gain		10,000

To recognize 1/4th of the gain from the sale of the asset (40,000 x [19,019 ÷ 76,077]).

It is apparent from the above illustrations that the main differences in the accounting for the three sale-leaseback categories, minor, intermediate and major, are the method and timing of the recognition of accounting gain from the sale, if any. (Any loss incurred in a sale-leaseback transaction is recognized immediately.) Many sale-leasebacks more closely resemble loans (refinancings). If the transaction is a refinancing, it is not appropriate to recognize a gain because the asset has not been sold. The gain recognition criteria relating to sale-leasebacks are intended to distinguish between those transactions that represent true sales and those that are, in substance, refinancings.

CONCLUSION

Knowledge of accounting for leases is critical for maximizing the financial reporting benefits of this form of financing. The basics of lessee accounting, for both operating and capital leases, have been introduced in this chapter along with accounting for sale-leasebacks. These provisions of FASB 13 must be understood if lessees are to manage the financial statement impact of lease financing. The benefits of the material in this chapter are not limited to lessees, however.

Lessees and lessors alike can derive value from this information. Lessees can use it to record the lease product more effectively. Lessors will benefit through a greater understanding of their clients' product needs. In today's dynamic environment, neither party can afford to not understand the accounting for, and reporting of, the lessee's leases.

Chapter Twelve

Structuring FASB 13 Operating Leases

In many lease transactions, the financial statement impact of a lease is the single most important reason the lessee chooses to lease. It is important, therefore, for lessors to understand how to structure off balance sheet leases. This knowledge also is extremely beneficial for the lessee seeking such leases. This chapter discusses a variety of methods used to structure operating leases from the lessee's viewpoint and relies heavily on the accounting definitions in Chapter Nine. The following topics are addressed:

- FASB 13 and Operating Lease Structuring

- FASB 13 Operating Lease Test

- Operating Lease Structuring Methodology

- Structuring Operating Leases.

FASB 13 AND OPERATING LEASE STRUCTURING

For a lease to be classified as an operating lease, the classification criteria contained in Financial Accounting Standards Board Statement No. 13 (FASB 13) must be met. FASB 13 does not actually define the operating lease, which somewhat clouds the definitional issues in operating lease structuring. Instead, FASB 13 defines a capital lease and states that any lease not meeting the capital lease criteria is, by default, an operating lease.

Many techniques that are used to structure operating leases are described in this chapter. Some of these techniques are more conservative than others; some are less conservative. All of them, however, attempt to create a usage (operating lease) agreement in substance, not just in form. It is important to remember that merely changing the form of the lease rather than the substance may lead to an improper classification. Fortunately, FASB 13 allows sufficient latitude for structuring operating leases without unduly increasing the risk of improper classification.

A key factor for lessors to remember is that any operating leases they structure must be acceptable to the lessee's audit firm. The lessee's auditors have the final say as to whether or not a transaction is an operating lease on the lessee's books.

Chapter Nine describes the capital lease criteria in depth. The first three criteria are relatively straightforward and are easily avoidable in a lease transaction. For example, a lease either provides for an automatic transfer of title or it does not; it contains a bargain purchase option or it does not. Even the loosely defined third criterion or 75% test is easily avoided when structuring operating leases. This leaves the fourth criterion as the only criterion that will, in most situations, create problems in structuring operating leases.

The fourth classification criterion of FASB 13 states that a lease is deemed operating only if the present value of the minimum lease payments is less than 90% of the leased equipment's fair market value (FMV) reduced by any lessor retained tax credits. If meeting this criterion can be avoided through legitimate lease structuring variables, without creating a substance over form problem, operating lease treatment can be achieved.

FASB 13 OPERATING LEASE TEST

In order to structure an operating lease, it is first necessary to understand how to apply the 90% test. (A review of Chapter Nine, particularly in regards to minimum lease payments and lessee discount rates, may be appropriate before proceeding with the steps used in determining capital versus operating lease status.) There are three steps to determine whether a lease is capital or operating.

Step One

Calculate the FASB 13 comparison base. The FASB 13 comparison base represents the right hand side of the calculation or 90% of the fair market value. The present value of the minimum lease payments must be less than this number to be classified as operating. The comparison base is calculated as follows:

Comparison base = 90% x (FMV- tax credits)

Step Two

Determine the present value of the minimum lease payments. This step requires discounting the minimum lease payments with the appropriate discount rate. The minimum lease payments represent the noncancellable lease payments a lessee must pay or can be required to pay. Executory costs, plus any profit thereon, must be deducted from the minimum lease payments. Executory costs include insurance, maintenance and taxes incurred for leased property, whether paid by the lessor or the lessee.

Furthermore, any anticipated contingent rentals are excluded from minimum lease payments because of their uncertain and speculative nature. Cash flows that are defined by FASB 13 as part of the minimum lease payments include, among others, bargain purchase options, lessee guaranteed residuals, nonrefundable origination, closing, processing fees, etc. required to be paid by the lessee at the lease's inception, and any lessor purchase option puts.

The lessee must present value the minimum lease payments – this process requires a discount rate. FASB 13 requires the lessee to use a discount rate that is the lower of the lessor's implicit rate in the lease, if known, or the lessee's incremental borrowing rate. Sometimes the incremental borrowing rate is referred to as the IBR. The lessee seldom knows the rate implicit in the lease (as it is difficult to obtain the lessor's residual assumptions); therefore, it generally uses its incremental borrowing rate.

The incremental borrowing rate is a pretax, coterminous borrowing rate. Coterminous is a borrowing rate that would be available on an installment loan covering the same term as the lease. Incremental is today's borrowing rate rather than some past or embedded borrowing rate (previous bond issuance, etc.).

Step Three

Compare the present value of the minimum lease payments (Step Two) to the FASB 13 comparison base (Step One). If the present value of the minimum lease payments is less than the FASB 13 comparison base, the lease is considered an operating lease from an accounting viewpoint. If the present value of the minimum lease payments is equal to or greater than the FASB 13 comparison base, the lease is classified as a capital lease. If this occurs the lease must be restructured using the techniques described in this chapter to obtain operating lease classification.

Examples of the FASB 13 Test

The preceding three steps will be applied to several examples in order to illustrate how the capital lease criteria of FASB 13 are used to classify a lease as capital or operating from the lessee's viewpoint.

EXAMPLE ONE

Determine, from the lessee's perspective, whether the lease is a capital or an operating lease. Use the following assumptions:

Lessee's incremental borrowing rate: 8% (implicit rate unknown to the lessee)

Lease payments: 48 payments of 1,500, in advance

FMV of equipment: 70,000.

Solution

The three steps for determining capital versus operating lease status must be completed in order.

Step One

Calculate the FASB 13 comparison base.

Asset's FMV	70,000
Less tax credits	0
Subtotal	70,000
	x .90
FASB 13 comparison base	63,000

Step Two

Determine the present value of the minimum lease payments.

	HP-12C		**HP-17B (#TIMES PROMPTING: ON)**		
	f	REG			FIN
8	g	12 ÷			CFLO
1,500	g	CFo	■ CLEAR DATA		YES
1,500	g	CFj	FLOW (0) = ?	1,500	INPUT
47	g	Nj	FLOW (1) = ?	1,500	INPUT
	f	NPV 61,852.49	#TIMES (1) = 1	47	INPUT
					EXIT
					CALC
			8 ÷ 12		I%
			NPV = 61,852.49		

Step Three

Compare the present value of the minimum lease payments to the FASB 13 comparison base.

FASB 13 comparison base	63,000.00
Present value of the minimum lease payments	(61,852.49)
Difference	1,147.51

The lease is operating because the present value of the minimum lease payments is less than the comparison base and, therefore, qualifies for off balance sheet treatment by the lessee.

EXAMPLE TWO

Determine, from the lessee's perspective, whether the lease is a capital or an operating lease. Use the following assumptions:

Implicit rate in the lease: 10% (unknown to the lessee)

Lessee's incremental borrowing rate: 9%

Lessee's embedded borrowing rate: 8%

Lease payments: 60 monthly payments at 1,696 (payments in advance)

Sales tax: 96 of each payment

Refundable security deposit: 1,000

Nonrefundable origination fee: 500

Unguaranteed residual: 20,000

FMV of equipment: 100,000

Energy tax credit retained by the lessor: 10,000.

Solution

The three steps for determining capital versus operating lease status must be completed in order.

Step One

Calculate the FASB 13 comparison base.

Asset's FMV	100,000
Less energy tax credit	(10,000)
Subtotal	90,000
	x .90
FASB 13 comparison base	81,000

Step Two

Determine the present value of the minimum lease payments. The appropriate discount rate is 9%, the lessee's incremental, pretax, coterminous borrowing rate, because the implicit rate was unknown.

	HP-12C		HP-17B(#TIMES PROMPTING: ON)	
	f	REG		FIN
9	g	12 ÷		CFLO
2,100	g	CFo [1]	■ CLEAR DATA	YES
1,600	g	CFj [2]	FLOW (0) = ? 2,100	INPUT [1]
59	g	Nj	FLOW (1) = ? 1,600	INPUT [2]
	f	NPV 78,155.48	#TIMES = 1 59	INPUT
				EXIT
				CALC
			9 ÷ 12	I%
			NPV = 78,155.48	

[1] Advance payment plus fee

[2] Regular payments

Note that the minimum lease payment equals 1,600. This represents the base payment of 1,696 less 96 of executory costs (sales tax). The refundable security deposit of 1,000 is not included.

Step Three

Compare the present value of the lease payments to the FASB 13 comparison base.

FASB 13 comparison base	81,000.00
Present value of the minimum lease payments	(78,155.48)
Difference	2,844.52

Because the present value of the minimum lease payments is 2,844.52 below the comparison base, the lease is operating. Neither the refundable security deposit nor the unguaranteed residual is included in the solution because neither is designated by FASB 13 as being part of the minimum lease payments.

EXAMPLE THREE

Determine, from the lessee's perspective, whether the lease is capital or operating. Use the same assumptions as Example Two, except the lease contains a lessee guaranteed residual in the amount of 5,000.

Solution

The result of Step One is the same as in Example Two. Steps Two and Three, however, are different.

Step One

No change from Example Two.

Step Two

Determine the present value of the minimum lease payments. The lessee guarantee of the residual becomes part of the minimum lease payments at the lease termination.

	HP-12C			HP-17B (#TIMES PROMPTING: ON)		
	f	REG				FIN
9	g	12 ÷				CFLO
2,100	g	CFo[1]		■ CLEAR DATA		YES
1,600	g	CFj[2]		FLOW (0) = ?	2,100	INPUT[1]
59	g	Nj		FLOW (1) = ?	1,600	INPUT[2]
5,000	g	CFj[3]		#TIMES (1) = 1	59	INPUT
	f	NPV	81,348.98	FLOW (2) = ?	5,000	INPUT[3]
				#TIMES (2) = 1	1	INPUT
						EXIT
						CALC
					9 ÷ 12	I%
				NPV = 81,348.98		

Step Three

Compare the present value of the lease payments to the FASB 13 comparison base.

FASB 13 comparison base	81,000.00
Present value of the minimum lease payments	(81,348.98)
Difference	(348.98)

The lease has now changed from an operating lease, as in Example Two, to a capital lease because the present value of the minimum lease payments exceeds the FASB 13 comparison base.

OPERATING LEASE STRUCTURING METHODOLOGY

The criteria that determine whether a lease should be treated as capital or operating are such that many leases are capitalized on the lessee's balance sheet. This is not surprising because, from a pricing perspective, most lessors prefer to minimize risk by placing as little emphasis on residuals as possible. This allows the lessor to recoup most of its investment and profit from the lease rentals themselves. Consequently, the present value of the lease payments is generally higher than 90% of the asset's fair market value (the fourth capital lease criterion).

---

[1] Advance payment plus origination fee
[2] Regular payments
[3] Guaranteed residual

The desire of lessors to minimize residual risk as opposed to the preference of many lessees for operating leases makes it extremely challenging to structure the transaction. Nonetheless, several techniques used in the marketplace alone or in combination result in the lease being classified as operating. This section discusses many of the options and techniques available to structure operating leases. Examining the components of the fourth criterion highlights the opportunities to structure operating leases. The components, which include the discount rate, the comparison base and the minimum lease payments, along with other structuring variables, are discussed below.

Increase the Lessee's Discount Rate

One method for structuring an operating lease is to increase the discount rate used to present value the minimum lease payments. This involves determining the highest discount that is verifiable by, as well as acceptable to, the lessee's auditor.

The lessee discount rate used to present value the minimum lease payments is a pretax borrowing rate. It should be an incremental rate that reflects a borrowing period equal to the lease term. This parity between terms is important because longer term borrowing usually costs more than shorter term. Prime rate, for example, is a short-term rate and would not be deemed appropriate as a lessee discount rate for a five-year lease.

The purpose in selecting the highest discount rate possible is obvious – higher discount rates result in lower present value amounts. A high discount rate makes it more likely that the present value of the minimum lease payments will be less than 90% of the fair market value of the leased asset. If this is the case, the lease is treated as operating.

Another way to increase the incremental borrowing rate is to incorporate the cost of origination fees and compensating balances associated with certain loans. These types of costs increase the effective cost of borrowing and should be reflected in the discount rate to be used for the 90% test. As a practical matter, many companies solve for the break-even discount rate necessary to classify the lease as operating. If it is a reasonable rate, given the lessee's circumstances, no additional work is necessary. If it is too low, the above-discussed techniques may be used to raise it.

The classification of the lease based on the following assumptions is capital:

Fair market value: 10,000

Terms: 60 payments at 1,961 per month, in advance

Lessee incremental borrowing rate: 11%

Unguaranteed residual: 20,000

Lessor implicit rate: 12.02%.

The break-even discount rate of 11.511%, however, is easily computed. Notice in the computation that the number used to represent the present value (89,999) is less than 90% of the fair market value of the asset.

HP-12C			HP-17B (12 P/YR BEGIN MODE)	
	f	REG		FIN
	g	BEG		TVM
60		n	■	CLEAR DATA
1,961		PMT	60	N
89,999	CHS	PV	1,961	PMT
		i 0.9593	89,999	+/- PV
		12 x 11.5110		I%YR = 11.5110

High Fair Market Value

Another approach is to make certain the FASB 13 comparison base (90% of the asset's fair market value) has been correctly determined. In those instances in which the lessee does not actually purchase the asset, the lessee may not know the actual cost of the leased asset. The lessee must, therefore, independently determine the asset's fair value.

The higher the fair value of the asset, the higher the 90% basis of comparison will be. A higher comparison base makes it more likely that the present value of the minimum lease payments will be lower than the base, thus allowing classification as an operating lease. As in all cases, any amount chosen as fair value must be reasonable (and verifiable under audit). The lessee's estimate, however, does not have to be the same as that of the lessor.

Reduce the Minimum Lease Payments

The lessor also may attempt to decrease the amount of the minimum lease payments. One way to accomplish this is for the lessor to take a higher residual value. Another is to accept a lower yield. These methods are, of course, generally unacceptable to the lessor, so other approaches must be used. One of these approaches is to offer a lower lease payment in conjunction with a corresponding increase in other cash payments that are not considered to be minimum lease payments.

For example, the lessor may offer slightly lower lease payments in exchange for a refundable security deposit, which is not deemed to be a minimum lease payment. The lessor can easily solve for the amount of the refundable security deposit necessary to achieve operating lease treatment.

SOLVING FOR SECURITY DEPOSIT

As an illustration of this technique, the same assumptions presented on page 380 are used. The objective of the lessor in this case is to solve for the payment structure utilizing a refundable security deposit that will maintain its yield and provide operating lease treatment for the lessee.

The first step in this process is to solve for the payment that causes the lease to be classified as operating. (Using 89,900 as the present value assures a present value of less than 90%.) This payment is 1,936.89.

	HP-12C			**HP-17B (12 P/YR BEGIN MODE)**		
	f	REG			FIN
	g	BEG			TVM
89,900	CHS	PV		■	CLEAR DATA
11	g	12÷	89,900	+/-	PV
60		n	11		I%YR
	PMT	1,936.89	60		N
				PMT =	1,936.89

The next step is to determine the difference between the lessor's required payment of 1,961 and the lessee's required operating lease payment of 1,936.89.

1,961.00	Payment required for lessor 12.02% yield
1,936.89	Maximum lessee operating lease payment
24.11	Difference

The present value, at the lessor's yield, of the monthly difference between the two payments must be computed. This present value of 1,094.23 is the net amount that must be received by the lessor after collecting the security deposit up front and returning it to the lessee at the end of the lease.

HP-12C			HP-17B (12 P/YR BEGIN MODE)	
	f	REG		FIN
	g	BEG		TVM
24.11		PMT	■	CLEAR DATA
12.02	g	12÷	24.11	PMT
60		n	12.02	I%YR
	PV	1,094.23	60	N
				PV = 1,094,23

Unfortunately, the 1,094.23 is a net amount reflecting the receipt and subsequent return of the security deposit. The lessor must solve for the gross amount of the deposit. The solution involves a two-part process. The first part involves solving for, on a present value basis, the receipt and return of the unknown security deposit, letting one dollar equal the deposit.

HP-12C			HP-17B (#TIMES PROMPTING: ON)			
	f	REG				FIN
12.02	g	12÷				CFLO
1	g	CFo	■ CLEAR DATA			YES
0	g	CFj	FLOW (0) = ?	1		INPUT
59	g	Nj	FLOW (1) = ?	0		INPUT
1 CHS	g	CFj	# TIMES(1) =?	59		INPUT
f	NPV	0.4501	FLOW (2) = ?	1 +/-		INPUT
			#TIMES (2) = 1	1		INPUT
						EXIT
						CALC
			12.02 ÷12			I%
			NPV = 0.4501			

In the second part, the lessor determines the refundable security deposit by dividing the amount to be recovered (1,094.23) by the present value of the unknown security deposit, letting one dollar equal the deposit.

$$\frac{1,094.23}{.4501} = 2,431.08$$

If the lessor charges the lessee 1,936.89 per month, and collects a refundable security deposit of 2,431.08, it will realize a yield of 12.02%. Furthermore, the lease will be off balance sheet to the lessee.

A refundable security deposit should not be excessive, however, because a high deposit may begin to appear like a down payment for tax purposes. Such a lessee investment also might suggest capital lease treatment because it is apparent (substance over form) the lessee is actually buying the asset, not just renting it. Regarding the treatment of other cash payments, up-front fees collected from the lessee are considered to be part of minimum lease payments. Pricing these fees into the structure would not, therefore, lower the overall present value of the minimum lease payments.

Contingent Rentals

An increasingly common structuring technique is to replace part of the total lease payment with a contingent portion. FASB 13 excludes the portion of the lease payments that is contingent upon some uncertain future event from the definition of minimum lease payments.

For example, suppose a lease payment for a particular machine has been quoted as 1,000 per month, with expected usage of the machine at 200 hours per month. In order to be classified as an operating lease, the amount of the payment cannot exceed 900. This requirement could be met by alter-ing the lease agreement to include a requirement stating that if the asset is used more than 170 hours per month, an additional 100 of rent is required from the lessee. Economically, of course, the lessor would have to be fair-ly certain of the actual usage levels to be willing to allow the contingency.

In this example, the lessor still expects to receive the full 1,000 per month and maintain its yield, yet the lease is treated as operating. This is because the present value of the minimum lease payments, excluding the contingent portion, is less than 90% of the asset's fair value. Contingent payments also are based on other indices such as revenue generated by the asset, prime rate or the consumer price index.

Executory Costs

Another similar technique for obtaining operating lease status is to allocate a larger portion of the total lease payment as executory costs. Executory costs, like contingent rents, are excluded from the definition of minimum lease payments. For example, if a full-service lease provides maintenance, the maintenance portion of the lease payment is excluded as an executory cost. Given that the payment to the lessee is fixed, the lessor can reduce the amount of the minimum lease payments by allocating a larger portion of the total payment to maintenance and a smaller portion to the actual financing. The financing portion is the only amount considered as minimum lease payments.

For instance, a lease quote that normally would be 800 per month for the equipment, plus 200 per month for maintenance, could be altered to accommodate the lessee's desire for off balance sheet financing. By changing the quote to require 700 for the equipment and 300 for the maintenance service, the lessor does not alter its yield. Furthermore, the lessee's overall cash outlay and tax expense recognition have not changed. However, the lessee now has a lower minimum lease payment to be used in determining the accounting status of the lease.

Along similar lines, if the lease contains a labor and repair contract, the cost of which is not apparent to the lessee, the value of this service must be estimated by the lessee. This amount is deducted from the regular lease payments as an executory cost in determining minimum lease payments. Correspondingly, any other service provided by the lessor for which a dollar amount has not been stated should be estimated by the lessee and treated as an executory cost, including any lessor profit thereon.

Higher Residual

As mentioned earlier, an easy approach for the lessor in structuring operating leases is to depend more on the future residual value of the asset. This allows the lessor to charge a lower lease payment during the basic lease term. This approach is riskier for the lessor, however, unless the residual value can be guaranteed in whole or in part. Any guarantee must be provided by a party independent from the lessee such as the vendor, manufacturer, an insurance company or some other lessor. If the lessee is the guarantor, the amount of the guarantee is included as a minimum lease payment, thus potentially defeating the objective of making the lease operating.

Shorter Lease Term

In order to qualify a lease term as less than 75% of the economic life of the asset or to have fewer minimum lease payments included in the 90% test, the basic noncancellable lease term can be shortened. If the lease term is shortened, there are fewer payments and the residual reliance generally increases. Many lessors believe this method increases their residual exposure to an unacceptable level. Because this approach may be considered too risky by the lessor, one alternative is to shorten the lease term by offering a series of options. This technique is difficult to use successfully, however, as such options are considered part of the minimum lease payments if their exercise is highly probable.

Step Payments

Utilizing a step lease structure oftentimes can lower the present value of the minimum lease payments without altering the lessor's yield. This technique, although effective, depends on the relationship of the lessor's implicit rate to the lessee's discount rate. Exhibit 12-1 illustrates the relationships between discount rates and the required step structures. By trading against the lessee's time preference for money, the lessor can, through creative structuring, take the lease off balance sheet. Consider the following two illustrations.

STEP-DOWN

The illustration of using a step-down lease to lower the present value of the minimum lease payments utilizes the following assumptions:

Equipment cost: 1,000

Term: 48 monthly payments of 21.84, in advance

Unguaranteed residual: 196

Lessor yield: 10%

Lessee discount rate: 8%.

Exhibit 12-1
Implicit Rate Versus Borrowing Rate

Relationship	Structure required to lower the present value
Implicit rate > borrowing rate	Step-down structure
Implicit rate = borrowing rate	Structure does not effect present value
Implicit rate < borrowing rate.	Step-up structure.

This lease is classified as a capital lease by the lessee.

HP-12C			HP-17B (12 P/YR BEGIN MODE)	
	f	REG		FIN
	g	BEG		TVM
8	g	12÷	■	CLEAR DATA
48		n	8	I%YR
21.84	CHS	PMT	48	N
		PV 900.57	21.84 +/-	PMT
				PV = 900.57

The lessor can create a step-down lease by taking two payments in advance instead of only one. A lease with two payments in advance at 21.66 per month provides the lessor with its necessary 10% yield. It also creates an operating lease for the lessee by lowering the present value of the minimum lease payments to 898.96, which is less than 90% of the fair market value.

STEP-UP

The illustration of using a step-up lease to lower the present value of the minimum lease payments utilizes the following assumptions:

Equipment cost: 1,000

Term: 48 monthly payments of 23.47, in advance

Unguaranteed residual: 99.65

Lessor yield: 10%

Lessee discount rate: 12%.

This lease is classified as a capital lease by the lessee.

HP-12C			HP-17B (12 P/YR BEGIN MODE)	
	f	REG		FIN
	g	BEG		TVM
12	g	12÷	■	CLEAR DATA
48		n	12	I%YR
23.47	CHS	PMT	48	N
		PV 900.16	23.47 +/-	PMT
				PV = 900.16

The lessor can create a step-up lease by taking payments in arrears instead of payments in advance. A lease with payments in arrears of 23.67 per month provides the lessor with its necessary 10% yield. It also creates an operating lease for the lessee by lowering the present value of the minimum lease payments to 898.84, which is less than 90% of the fair market value.

Short-term Loan Followed by a Sale-leaseback

An interesting but rather complex method of structuring an operating lease is to create a short-term loan followed by a sale-leaseback. The leaseback is timed such that the present value of the leaseback payments would be less than 90% of the asset's fair market value at the time of the leaseback. This works when the asset subject to the sale-leaseback retains its value well, allowing the 90% basis of comparison to remain high. The leaseback payments will be smaller relative to the comparison base because the previous loan will have already amortized much of the balance due the lender.

Splitting the Transaction

If there are two or more pieces of equipment being leased, the lease can be split into two separate transactions. The largest of the two leases, or as large a portion of the two leases as possible, can be structured so as to be operating. The balance of the equipment is then attributed much higher rates such that this lease will be considered capital. Through this technique at least some, if not most, of the assets and the debt can be taken off balance sheet. This approach also can be considered for existing capital leases. Upon renegotiation of an existing lease, the capital lease criteria are again reviewed in order to properly classify the new lease or leases.

As each of these operating lease structuring methodologies is considered, there arises an increased need to assess the issue of substance over form. If the intent is to manipulate an otherwise capital lease into the form of an operating lease, the lessee's auditors may challenge the lease classification. This issue becomes more relevant as more exotic structures are created. If the lease is in reality the equivalent of a loan and a purchase, the auditors may ignore the effect of some of these structuring suggestions and still require that the lease be capitalized. This is the position the Securities and Exchange Commission has taken.

Early Out

A lessor also can provide the lessee with an early out to reduce the number of noncancellable lease payments a lessee must pay. This, however, increases the lessor's risk in the lease. For example, a 60-month lease may allow the lessee to get out of the lease after 48 months. Should this occur, the lessor needs to sell or re-lease the returned equipment for enough to cover any unrecouped costs in order to protect its yield in the lease.

Because of the risk of this approach, some lessors consider similar but less risky methods. For instance, the lessor could structure the lease in the first place as a 48-month lease and add a 12-month renewal option that, if not renewed, triggers a nonrenewal penalty. The penalty cost (if not too exorbitant) will be included as part of the minimum lease payment but on a present value basis may be much smaller in amount than the renewal payments would be. Other lessors add restrictive return requirements, such as 'all or none' provisions, that effectively force renewal.

STRUCTURING OPERATING LEASES

A basic understanding of pricing is useful in structuring and performing sensitivity analysis of operating leases. This understanding can be used to determine the maximum rental a lessee can pay on a lease and still keep it operating. Also, given a known lease payment, the maximum amount of a lessee guaranteed residual that is required to maintain operating lease status can be calculated.

Computing the Maximum Payment

Computation of the maximum operating lease payment a lessee can pay and still keep the lease off balance sheet requires four structuring steps. Knowledge of this payment amount is important in applying several of the operating lease techniques previously described. For example, before maintenance expense can be substituted for rental expense in a full-service lease, the final lease payment that achieves operating lease status must be known.

EXAMPLE FOUR

Utilizing the following assumptions, determine the maximum lease payment the lessee may be charged and still have the lease classified as a FASB 13 operating lease.

Safety margin for comparison base: 500

Lease term: 60-month lease with two payments in advance

Fair market value of equipment: 100,000

Nonrefundable commitment fee: 600

Tax credits taken by the lessor: None

Lessee guarantees of the residual: None

Lessee incremental borrowing rate: 9%.

Solution

Computation of the maximum operating lease payment is very similar to regular payment structuring. It is accomplished in four steps.

Step One

Compute the FASB 13 comparison base less (1) any nonrefundable commitment or closing fees, etc., (2) the present value of any lessee guaranteed residuals and (3) a safety margin.

Asset's FMV	100,000
Less tax credits	0
Subtotal	100,000
	x .90
FASB 13 comparison base	90,000
Commitment fee	(600)
Present value of the guaranteed residual	0
Safety margin	(500)
Adjusted FASB 13 comparison base	88,900

Step Two

Find the present value of the unknown operating lease payments, letting one dollar equal each payment. Use the lessee's borrowing rate (or the lessor's implicit rate, if lower and known) as the discount rate.

	HP-12C	**HP-17B (#TIMES PROMPTING: ON)**	
	f REG		FIN
9	g 12÷		CFLO
2	g CFo	■ CLEAR DATA	YES
1	g CFj	FLOW(0)=? 2	INPUT
58	g Nj	FLOW(1)=? 1	INPUT
	f NPV 48.891184	#TIMES (1)=1 58	INPUT
			EXIT
			CALC
		9 ÷ 12	I%
		NPV = 48.891184	

Step Three

Divide Step One by Step Two, the quotient of which is the maximum payment the lessee can make and still maintain operating lease status, incorporating a 500 safety margin.

$$\frac{88,900}{48.891184} = 1,818.32 \text{ per month}$$

Step Four

Prove that the present value of the 1,818.32 monthly lease payments and the commitment fee of 600 equals 89,500 (the FASB 13 comparison base of 90,000 less the 500 safety margin).

	HP-12C	**HP-17B (#TIMES PROMPTING: ON)**	
	f REG		FIN
9	g 12÷		CFLO
4,236.64	g CFo	■ CLEAR DATA	YES
1,818.32	g CFj	FLOW(0)=? 4,236.64	INPUT
58	g Nj	FLOW(1)=? 1,818.32	INPUT
	f NPV 89,499.82	#TIMES(1)=1 58	INPUT
			EXIT
			CALC
		9 ÷ 12	I%
		NPV = 89,499.82	

EXAMPLE FIVE

Utilizing the following assumptions, determine the maximum lease payment the lessee may be charged and still have the lease classified as a FASB 13 operating lease.

Lease term: 60-month lease with payments in advance

Safety margin for comparison base: 500

FMV of equipment: 50,000

Nonrefundable commitment fee: 750

Lessee guarantee of residual: 4,000

Lessee borrowing rate: 8%.

Solution

Computation of the maximum operating lease payment is accomplished in four steps.

Step One

Compute the FASB 13 comparison base less (1) any nonrefundable commitment or closing fees, etc., (2) the present value of any lessee guaranteed residuals and (3) a safety margin.

Present value the lessee guaranteed residual using the lessee's borrowing rate as the discount rate.

HP-12C			HP-17B (12 P/YR BEGIN MODE)		
	f	REG			FIN
8	g	12÷			TVM
4,000	CHS	FV		■	CLEAR DATA
60		n	8		I%YR
		PV 2,684.84	4,000	+/-	FV
			60		N
					PV = 2,684.84

Compute the FASB 13 comparison base.

Asset's FMV	50,000
	x .90
FASB 13 comparison base	45,000
Commitment fee	(750)
Present value of the guaranteed residual	(2,685)
Safety margin	(500)
Adjusted FASB 13 comparison base	41,065

Step Two

Find the present value of the unknown operating lease payments, letting one dollar equal each payment. Use the lessee's borrowing rate as the discount rate.

HP-12C			**HP-17B (#TIMES PROMPTING: ON)**	
f	REG			FIN
8 g	12 ÷			CFLO
1 g	CFo	■ CLEAR DATA		YES
1 g	CFj	FLOW(0)=?	1	INPUT
59 g	Nj	FLOW(1)=?	1	INPUT
f	NPV 49.6472	#TIMES(1)=1	59	INPUT
				EXIT
				CALC
			8 ÷ 12	I%
		NPV = 49.6472		

Step Three

Divide Step One by Step Two, the quotient of which is the maximum payment the lessee can make and still maintain operating lease status, incorporating a safety margin of 500.

$$\frac{41,065}{49.6472} = 827.14$$

Step Four

Prove that the present value of the 827.14 lease payments, the 4,000 lessee guarantee and the 750 commitment fee equals 44,500 (the comparison base less the 500 safety margin).

HP-12C			HP-17B (#TIMES PROMPTING: ON)	
	f	REG		FIN
8	g	12÷		CFLO
1,577.14	g	CFo	■ CLEAR DATA	YES
827.14	g	CFj	FLOW(0)=?1,577.14	INPUT
59	g	Nj	FLOW(1)=? 827.14	INPUT
4,000	g	CFj	#TIMES(1)=1 59	INPUT
	f	NPV 44,500.05	FLOW(2)=? 4,000	INPUT
			#TIMES(2)=1 1	INPUT
				EXIT
				CALC
			8 ÷ 12	I%
			NPV = 44,500.05	

Computing the Maximum Guaranteed Residual

The computation of the maximum guaranteed residual a lessee can pay, given a known lease payment, and still keep the lease off balance sheet requires five structuring steps. This technique is commonly used in Terminal Rental Adjustment Clause (TRAC) leasing. In some circumstances, for instance, a lessee guarantees the residual, but the lessor limits the amount of the guarantee to preserve operating lease status for the lessee.

EXAMPLE SIX

Compute, from the lessee's perspective, the maximum lessee guaranteed residual allowable in order to still maintain an operating lease, given the following assumptions:

Safety margin for comparison base: 500

Lease term: 60-month lease with monthly payments of 1,700 (two in advance)

FMV of equipment: 100,000

Nonrefundable commitment fee: 600

Lessee borrowing rate: 9%, which is lower than the lessor's implicit rate in the lease.

Solution

Computation of the maximum guaranteed residual is accomplished in five steps.

Step One

Compute the FASB 13 comparison base, less a safety margin.

Asset's FMV	100,000
Less tax credits	0
Subtotal	100,000
	x .90
FASB 13 comparison base	90,000
Safety margin	(500)
Adjusted FASB 13 comparison base	89,500

Step Two

Calculate the present value of the minimum lease payments, including any commitment fees, etc., at the lessee's borrowing rate.

HP-12C			HP-17B (#TIMES PROMPTING: ON)	
	f	REG		FIN
9	g	12÷		CFLO
4,000	g	CFo	■ CLEAR DATA	YES
1,700	g	CFj	FLOW(0)=? 4,000	INPUT
58	g	Nj	FLOW(1)=? 1,700	INPUT
	f	NPV 83,715.01	#TIMES(1)=1 58	INPUT
				EXIT
				CALC
			9 ÷ 12	I%
			NPV = 83,715.01	

Step Three

Subtract Step Two from Step One. This amount equals the present value of the maximum guarantee the lessor can require of the lessee and still maintain operating lease status for the lessee.

89,500
(83,715)
5,785

Step Four

Find the future value of the difference from Step Three, using the lessee's borrowing rate (or the lessor's implicit rate, if lower) as the appreciation rate.

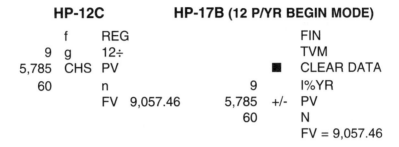

	HP-12C			HP-17B (12 P/YR BEGIN MODE)
	f	REG		FIN
9	g	12÷		TVM
5,785	CHS	PV	■	CLEAR DATA
60		n	9	I%YR
		FV 9,057.46	5,785 +/-	PV
			60	N
				FV = 9,057.46

The 9,057.46 represents the maximum residual value amount the lessee can guarantee and still have an operating lease, given lease rentals of 1,700, a 600 commitment fee and a 500 safety margin.

Step Five

Prove the lease has achieved operating lease status by finding the present value of the minimum lease payments, including the newly computed lessee guaranteed residual. The total should be 89,500 (Step One).

	HP-12C			HP-17B (#TIMES PROMPTING: ON)		
	f	REG				FIN
9	g	12÷				CFLO
4,000	g	CFo	■	CLEAR DATA		YES
1,700	g	CFj	FLOW(0)=?	4,000		INPUT
58	g	Nj	FLOW(1)=?	1,700		INPUT
0	g	CFj	#TIMES(1)=1	58		INPUT
9,057.46	g	CFj	FLOW(2)=?	0		INPUT
	f	NPV 89,500.01	#TIMES(2)=1	1		INPUT
			FLOW(3)=?	9,057.46		INPUT
			#TIMES(3)=1	1		INPUT
						EXIT
						CALC
				9 ÷ 12		I%
			NPV = 89,500.01			

CONCLUSION

Lessees frequently favor operating leases because of the off balance sheet benefits of such leases. Because of this it is important to be familiar with the steps necessary to structure an operating lease. The primary criterion that must be met for purposes of structuring operating leases is the 90% test. Two of the means by which a lease is made operating are minimizing the cash flows included in minimum lease payments and increasing the lessee's discount rate used to present value those payments.

Various cash flow substitution techniques as well as alteration of cash flows through stepping up or down of lease payments, creating skipped payments, etc., also can be used as viable means of creating operating leases. Development of the skills for structuring operating leases definitely adds another important selling tool to the lessor's marketing repertoire.

Section Four

Finance

Chapter Thirteen

Lease Versus Buy

The question of whether to lease or buy equipment, although outwardly simple, is actually quite complex. This complexity begins with a blurring of the distinction between the investing and financing decisions, and increases with tax requirements and the various analytical techniques that can be used. In spite of all this complexity, practical applications are commonly oversimplified.

This chapter addresses the complex aspects of the lease versus buy decision:

- The Investment Decision
- Financing Alternatives
- Decision Methodology
- Examples
- Advanced Issues.

THE INVESTMENT DECISION

The acquisition of an asset must be justified through the capital budgeting process before the method of financing that asset is chosen. The capital budgeting process determines whether the cash flows generated from an asset are sufficient to meet the company's capital investment criteria. The capital budgeting decision is based on either a net present value (NPV) or an internal rate of return (IRR) analysis. In NPV analysis, the cash flows are discounted at a targeted hurdle rate, which is a rate at least equal to the firm's weighted, average cost of capital (WACC).

Once the decision to acquire the asset is made, the methods available to finance the equipment must be considered. Exhibit 13-1 illustrates the various stages of the traditional asset acquisition process, of which lease versus buy is but one.

The focus of this chapter is on the lease versus buy decision. Even so, one must be familiar with the capital investment decision process, given the interrelationship between the investment and financing decisions. For example, traditional lease versus buy methodology views leasing as an alternate form of financing the acquisition, with no impact on the capital budgeting decision. There is a flaw in this view, however, in that lease versus buy analysis ignores some of the capital productivity implications of the two alternatives. In this respect, the more traditional view of lease versus buy may be inadequate to measure fully the impact on capital investment.

An asset provides cash flow benefits whether it is purchased or leased. Because maximizing net cash flow is the primary objective of acquiring an asset, the best financing alternative is the one that requires the lowest capital expenditure. Therefore, the proper methodology for determining the best financing alternative is one that measures both the capital investment implications and the inherent financing characteristics of each alternative.

Changing the Investment Profile

A classic lease versus buy decision compares an operating lease to an asset purchase. Each of these alternatives generates a different set of after-tax cash flows. The present value obligation of an operating lease, by definition, always will be something less than 90% of the asset's cost; therefore, there is a real difference in the initial capital committed to acquire the asset. The implication of this difference is significant. A company can obtain the use of an asset (and its operating cash flows) through an operating lease for an initial capital investment lower than for a purchase.

The question then becomes whether or not it is beneficial to invest the additional capital required in the purchase to obtain the deferred tax and salvage value cash flows available from owning the asset. The following example illustrates this point.

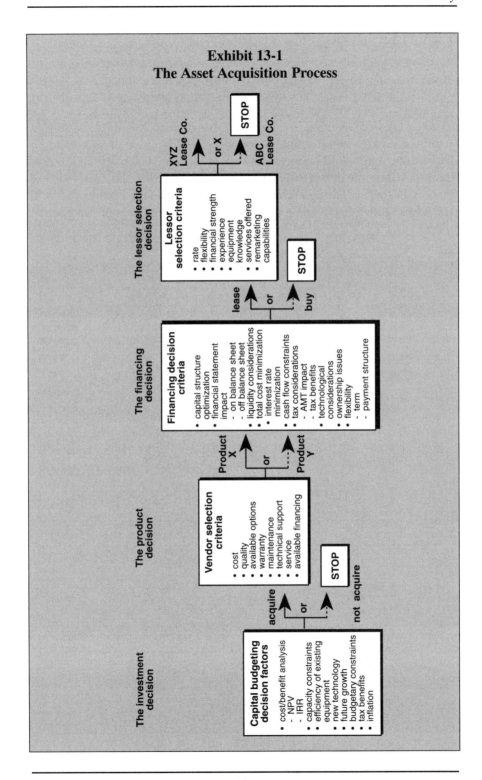

Exhibit 13-1
The Asset Acquisition Process

EXAMPLE

An investment under consideration consists of an asset costing 100,000. The lessee can either pay 100,000 in cash or borrow the same amount in some fashion. Irrespective of the alternative chosen, the present value cost, at the debt rate, will be 100,000. The lessee's capital budgeting hurdle rate is 13%.

Exhibit 13-2 contains a simple model for evaluating this investment. The NPV of the net cash flow of this investment is 9,897 (109,897 - 100,000) at the required hurdle rate of 13%. The IRR on the net cash flow of this investment is 17.05%. (The deferred taxes in this example are attributable to the tax depreciation benefit being generated through ownership of the asset.)

HP-12C			HP-17B (#TIMES PROMPTING: OFF)			
	f	REG				FIN
13		i				CFLO
33.2	g	CFj	■	CLEAR DATA		YES
37.2	g	CFj	FLOW (0)=?		0	INPUT
26.8	g	CFj	FLOW (1)=?		33.2	INPUT
24.2	g	CFj	FLOW (2)=?		37.2	INPUT
21.6	g	CFj	FLOW (3)=?		26.8	INPUT
13.0	g	CFj	FLOW (4)=?		24.2	INPUT
	f	NPV 109.897	FLOW (5)=?		21.6	INPUT
			FLOW (6)=?		13.0	INPUT
						EXIT
						CALC
					13	I%
				NPV	= 109.897	

Exhibit 13-2
Investment Cash Flows
(000s)

	1	2	3	4	5	Salvage
Operating profit	44.0	44.0	44.0	44.0	44.0	20.0
Taxes @ 35%	(15.4)	(15.4)	(15.4)	(15.4)	(15.4)	(7.0)
After-tax profit	28.6	28.6	28.6	28.6	28.6	13.0
Deferred taxes	4.6	8.6	(1.8)	(4.4)	(7.0)	0.0
Net cash flow	33.2	37.2	26.8	24.2	21.6	13.0

Now, assume the asset in this investment can be leased for 60 months with payments of 1,731.64, in advance. Also assume that the company's incremental borrowing rate for debt of this term is 8.5%. If all leases were capitalized at their present value, this lease obligation and the corresponding asset would be capitalized at approximately 85,000. A decision to lease the asset changes the investment's profile. The investment decision is now 85,000 versus 100,000. The revised investment's cash flow characteristics are shown in Exhibit 13-3.

HP-12C			HP-17B (#TIMES PROMPTING: ON)		
	f	REG			FIN
13		i			CFLO
28.6	g	CFj	■ CLEAR DATA		YES
5	g	Nj	FLOW (0)=?	0	INPUT
	f	NPV 100.593	FLOW (1)=?	28.6	INPUT
			#TIMES (1)=1	5	INPUT
					EXIT
					CALC
				13	I%
				NPV	= 100.593

The NPV of the net cash flow of the lease is 15,593 (100,593 - 85,000) at the required hurdle rate of 13%. The IRR on the net cash flow of the lease is 20.3%. There are no deferred taxes in this example because no tax depreciation benefit is generated through ownership of the asset.

Exhibit 13-3
Revised Investment Cash Flows
(000s)

	1	2	3	4	5	Salvage
Operating profit	44.0	44.0	44.0	44.0	44.0	N/A
Taxes @ 35%	15.4	15.4	15.4	15.4	15.4	N/A
After-tax profit	28.6	28.6	28.6	28.6	28.6	N/A
Deferred taxes	0.0	0.0	0.0	0.0	0.0	N/A
Net cash flow	28.6	28.6	28.6	28.6	28.6	N/A

It can be seen from this example that the financing method can affect the investment decision. Conventional lease versus buy analysis ignores the capital budgeting ramifications of the financing method. It does not measure the change in the investment's profile or the impact on the investment's cash flow characteristics.

The Mini-investment Decision

Most lessees fail to recognize that a decision to lease includes an investment decision. (Although a mini-investment decision, it is an investment decision, nonetheless.) In the previous example, the asset costs the lessee 100,000, on a present value basis, to own, but can be leased for a present value cost of 85,000. Furthermore, the asset generates the operating cash flows expected in the original investment decision, no matter how it is financed.

If the asset generates the same operating cash flows no matter how it is financed, what benefits can be gained by investing the additional 15,000 in capital to own it? The answer, of course, is the deferred tax and salvage value cash flows that occur over time. The return on this incremental capital investment should be held to the same standard (hurdle rate) as the original investment decision.

The implications of the financing method for the capital budgeting process generally are ignored. One school of thought, however, suggests these implications should be factored into the capital budgeting decision. Some analysts, on the other hand, are of the opinion that the lease versus buy decision adequately reflects the capital budgeting implications. With regard to these arguments, lessors and lessees must make up their own minds and choose the methodology with which they are most comfortable.

FINANCING ALTERNATIVES

Every company needs financial resources to fund ongoing capital investment needs. Even mature companies, with relatively few new investment opportunities, require capital to replace or modernize the existing asset base as it is consumed by the enterprise. Where a company is in its life cycle will greatly influence the amount of capital required and the form in which funding should be obtained. The major forms of capital financing are discussed in this section.

Debt

Leveraging capital investment with debt enables a company to invest in more projects than otherwise might be possible using only equity capital. Value is created when the return on invested capital is greater than the company's WACC.

Consider a project that yields a return on assets (ROA) of 15%, after taxes. If the WACC for the project is 12%, the difference of 3% represents economic value added (EVA). Therefore, additional value is created when the return exceeds the cost of capital. Value is preserved when the return equals the cost of capital and value is destroyed when the return on capital is less than its cost. Leveraging capital investment can reduce the WACC and increase the EVA derived from the investment.

Debt financing also can put equity at risk. The more debt financing that is employed the greater is the risk to equity. From a financial management standpoint, every company has an optimum leverage threshold or point at which more leverage unduly exposes equity to risk. The optimal leverage is based on the relationship between the ability of the assets to generate cash flow (operating leverage) through a business cycle and the cash flow required to pay debt obligations through a business cycle. Stated another way, a company should not leverage more than can be repaid during a down business cycle.

Deferred Taxes

Deferred taxes are the difference between book and tax income and represent interest-free debt. Inclusion of this interest-free debt in the capital structure alters the company's WACC. In theory, deferred tax obligations must be paid back in the future, as the assets and liabilities generating the deferred taxes turn around. In practice, however, if a company continues to grow, its deferred taxes may never reverse. In this respect, the deferred taxes are a form of quasi-equity.

Retained Earnings and Equity

Equity represents more of a variable obligation in that shareholders expect some business cycle volatility. In fact, they require a higher return because they are subject to the business cycle risks inherent in the business. Equity can, however, have the impact of a fixed obligation, at least in terms of the continued employment of executive management that fails to meet shareholder expectations through a business cycle.

Optimizing Capital Investment Through Leasing

Both the return on capital and the velocity at which capital is employed provide a company an opportunity to create value. Lease financing can accelerate capital investment. Provided a company has other investment opportunities, the use of leasing can increase the pace at which those investments can be funded.

As discussed earlier, leasing changes an investment's profile and cash flow characteristics. The present value of the lease payments, if the lessor assumes a residual value, always will be less than the present value of ownership. Instead of expending 100% of an asset's value initially, and receiving deferred tax benefits and the residual value over time, a company need expend only the present value investment inherent in the lease obligation. The key is whether it makes sense for the lessee to make the incremental investment necessary to obtain those future cash flows or pass them to a lessor in return for a capital credit equal to their present value.

Who should invest capital in order to receive the deferred tax benefit and residual value, the lessor or the lessee? Most nonfinancial companies employ between 25% to 50% debt in their balance sheets. Lessors, on the other hand, carry significantly greater leverage. The typical lessor employs 80% to 90% debt in its capital structure. This high degree of leverage is possible because the operating or business cycle risk associated with the assets being financed rests with the lessee. The lessor is taking only the credit risk associated with the credit quality of the lease and the value of the underlying collateral or assumed residual value.

The lessor's ability to apply more leverage to make the mini-investment discussed earlier drives down its WACC and increases the future value of the deferred tax and residual cash flows. In this respect, it makes more sense for the lessor to own the equipment. The lessee, on the other hand, can increase the velocity of its capital by leasing instead of buying. If leasing requires less capital investment, on a present value basis, the lessee can invest the incremental capital savings in the next available project. Because the lessee is able to invest in additional projects with the same amount of available cash, it has increased the velocity of its capital and enhanced capital productivity.

Financial managers must focus on the importance of capital productivity. Their challenge is to earn the highest possible return on investments so that company management can attract additional investment to fund new opportunities. Leasing, under the right conditions, and after proper analysis, can provide a capital productivity advantage to an equipment user. It increases the velocity of capital investment by allowing a company to trade future cash flows for a lower initial capital outlay.

DECISION METHODOLOGY

The lease versus buy decision, from a quantitative perspective, is one of cost minimization. The time value of money impacts the cost minimization decision, because an expense incurred today is more costly than an expense incurred five years from today. Costs, of course, must be converted to an after-tax basis before they are present valued, because tax benefits play such an important part in the decision. Therefore, the lease versus buy decision is to choose that financing alternative, lease or buy, with the lowest, after-tax, present value cost.

Other time value of money approaches, in addition to present value analysis, may be used, including future value analysis, also known as terminal value analysis (TVA), and IRR analysis. IRR analysis often is used because of practitioner preference to express decisions in terms of yields and money costs. The decision methodology chosen, however, is one of preference.

If the NPV approach is chosen, two different methods may be used to discount the cash flows. The first, and, by far, most common, is the single discount rate method. Under this method, all the cash flows from the lease and purchase alternatives are discounted at the same rate. (The appropriate discount rate to be used is discussed in a subsequent section.)

The second method, multiple discount rate, as the name implies, utilizes more than one rate to discount the cash flows. The application of the different discount rates is a function of the cash flows being considered. Some cash flows, such as residual, for instance, are more risky than those associated with the debt payments. It is because of these differences in the risk and nature of the cash flows that more than one discount rate is utilized. The multiple discount rate method, although theoretically more sound, is not commonly utilized because of practical problems in implementing the method.

Decision Inputs

Care must be taken to ensure the primary data and information upon which the decision is based are accurate and complete. This implies that all input premises, such as residual and salvage assumptions, timeline issues and loan terms, etc., are truly reflective of the anticipated borrowing or leasing scenario.

A problem often arises in the lease versus buy decision if the expected economic life of the equipment exceeds the term of the lease being used to finance the equipment. Some equipment may be expected to last seven years, for instance, yet the lessee is contemplating a five-year lease. To compare seven years of ownership expenses with only five years of lease expenses is an inappropriate matching of holding periods. To be valid, the two financing alternatives must be compared over the same holding period.

Equation of the purchase term to the lease term can be accomplished many ways. The method most indicative of the expected holding pattern should be chosen, however. Exhibit 13-4 depicts numerous holding pattern alternatives used to equate buying with leasing. The anticipated disposition of a purchased asset is described in the first column and the corresponding disposition of the asset (necessary to equate the terms) had it been leased is described in the second column.

Exhibit 13-4 assumes the economic life of the asset is seven years, which exceeds the five-year lease term, as it is very common in the leasing industry for the economic life of a particular piece of equipment to exceed its respective lease term. (Just a note on the 35-year alternative in Exhibit 13-4. Although seemingly absurd to forecast so far in the future, this method is effective because it prevents residual assumptions from influencing the decision, because no salvage is assumed under either the purchase or lease alternatives.)

In a situation in which it is not absolutely certain which disposition alternative will occur, the decision maker can choose several and determine a weighted average outcome. The percentage weights are assigned on the basis of the relative probability of occurrence of each alternative.

Another important issue relates to the assumed length of the loan used to fund the equipment's purchase (a cash acquisition without borrowing also can be assumed). Generally, in the absence of actual quotes from lending institutions to the contrary, the terms of the loan should match those of the

Exhibit 13-4
Equating Holding Patterns

Purchased equipment disposition	Leased equipment disposition
Salvage the equipment at the end of five years	Return the equipment to the lessor at the end of the five-year base term
Retain the equipment and continue its use until the end of its economic life	Purchase the equipment and continue its use until the end of its economic life
Retain the equipment and continue its use until the end of its economic life	Renew the lease after five years and continue to use the equipment until the end of its economic life
Salvage the equipment at the end of five years	Purchase the equipment after five years and immediately sell it to others
Lease the equipment to others at the end of five years	Purchase the equipment after five years and immediately lease it to others
Lease the equipment to others at the end of five years	Renew the lease after five years and immediately sublease the equipment to others
Lease the equipment to others at the end of five years	Return the equipment to the lessor at the end of the five-year lease term
Sell the equipment on an installment basis to others at the end of five years	Return the equipment to the lessor at the end of the five-year lease term
Buy, in succession, five more pieces of equipment totaling 35 years (5 x 7 years). Equation of the total buy holding term to the leasing term obviates any need for residual assumptions	Lease, in succession, seven more similar assets subject to five-year leases, totaling 35 years (7 x 5 years)
Trade in the existing equipment for new equipment at the end of five years.	Purchase the equipment and trade it in for new equipment at the end of five years.

lease. Terms to be matched include the down payment amount, the number of months in the loan term and a balloon payment equal to the lease purchase option that is expected to be exercised.

Skip, step-up and step-down payments should be the same. Loan origination fees, refundable security deposits and compensating bank balances should not be assumed to exist unless they really do. When these fees do exist, they should be evaluated as is, without being made to conform to any corresponding cash flows of the lease.

Actual loan quotes that represent the best borrowing terms available should be used. The assumed borrowing rate also should be indicative of rates charged on borrowings with similar terms. When the lessee's after-tax cost of debt is applied to the debt costs as the discount rate, loan terms are not important; however, use of rates higher than the cost of debt makes loan assumptions material in their impact on the lease versus buy decision.

All pertinent costs should be included in the analysis. Such costs represent differential expenses that occur under each alternative, but that vary in amount (e.g., sales tax), or those costs that impact only one alternative (e.g., interim rent in a lease). Costs that are exactly the same in either the lease or buy alternative can be excluded or included without impacting the final decision. Maintenance costs, for example, frequently cost the same whether the equipment user leases or buys the equipment.

Additional revenues, benefits, costs and expenses that must be included in a complete lease versus buy analysis are:

1. Sales and/or use tax

2. Property tax

3. Closing, documentation, origination fees, etc.

4. Installation costs

5. Shipping costs: freight in and out

6. Deinstallation: removal costs, etc.

7. Maintenance and any other bundled services included in a full-service lease

8. Security deposits and compensating bank balances

9. Tax benefits derived from items such as Modified Accelerated Cost Recovery System (MACRS)

10. Alternative minimum tax (AMT) impact

11. Foreign tax credit (FTC) impact

12. Insurance (product liability and casualty, etc.).

RISK ADJUSTMENTS

The lease versus buy decision is heavily dependent upon residual assumptions. If the lessee returns the equipment at the end of the lease, a salvage value must be assumed on the buy side in order to equate the term (as explained earlier in the chapter). Furthermore, should the lessee decide to exercise a purchase option, or renew the lease, the exercise price or the renewal rate must be predicted. Predictions necessarily involve risk and uncertainty that must be dealt with. As always, the decision is only as good as the estimates used in the lease versus buy decision.

Although there are many ways of addressing risk (such as use of a higher discount rate applied to residual assumptions), one of the best is the expected value approach, which makes use of decision tree and probability analysis. In order to illustrate this concept, an example of a five-step process that might be followed in ascertaining the expected cost of exercising a fair market value purchase option in a lease is presented.

Assume a lessee has compiled the following information concerning the possible prices that might be paid to purchase equipment at the end of the lease term:

Commercial appraisal of the estimated future value	1,000
Lessor's verbal estimate	800
Best possible exercise price	1,200
Worst possible exercise price	600
Lessee's best point estimate	900

Step One

Determine the alternative outcomes (given above), along with their probability of occurrence, using a decision tree analysis. At least three alternative outcomes should be used, along with their probabilities of occurrence; however, if there are no clear probabilities of occurrence, the following probabilities can be used:

Best outcome	.16
Average expected outcome	.68
Worst outcome	.16

In this case there are five possible outcomes. The probability of their occurrence is assessed in Exhibit 13-5.

Step Two

Compute the expected value of the option (EVO) exercise price by multiplying the probability of the event (or joint probabilities when there are additional branches in the decision tree) by the dollar outcome of the event. Then total the resulting products. This step is summarized in Exhibit 13-6.

Step Three

Calculate the standard deviation of the EVO. The standard deviation indicates the degree of risk or variability in the EVO caused by the breadth of the range (1,200 to 600) of options and the relative certainty of events (5 to 45%), both of which are subjective guesses. Although guesswork cannot be eliminated from predictions, at least the variability of the guess can be dealt with scientifically in this and the next two steps.

Exhibit 13-5
Assessment of Outcome

Event	Outcome	Dollar value	Probability
1	Best exercise price feasible	1,200	.10
2	Commercially appraised value	1,000	.25
3	Lessee's best point estimate	900	.45
4	Lessor's verbal estimate	800	.15
5	Worst possible exercise price	600	.05

Exhibit 13-6
EVO Computation

Event	Outcome		Probability		Weighted outcome
1	1,200	x	.10	=	120
2	1,000	x	.25	=	250
3	900	x	.45	=	405
4	800	x	.15	=	120
5	600	x	.05	=	30
EVO					925

The EVO standard deviation is computed using the following formula:

$$\sqrt{\sum_{i=1} (0_i - EVO)^2 P_i}$$

where: P_i = probability of the first through the last outcome

0_i = The first through the last outcome

EVO = expected value of the option cost (Step Three)

The standard deviation of the EVO is 129.90. ($\sqrt{16,875}$ = 129.90). The standard deviation is then used to derive the expected outcome.

$(1,200 - 925)^2$	=	75,625	x	.10	=	7,562.50
$(1,000 - 925)^2$	=	5,625	x	.25	=	1,406.25
$(900 - 925)^2$	=	625	x	.45	=	281.25
$(800 - 925)^2$	=	15,625	x	.15	=	2,343.75
$(600 - 925)^2$	=	105,625	x	.05	=	5,281.25
Total						16,875.00

Step Four

Compute the EVO cost given a required level of confidence that the exercise price will be equal to or less than a certain amount. This requires use of the following equation:

$$EVO_{Expected} = [EVO_{Step\ Two} + (EVO_{Standard\ Deviation} \times C)],$$

where C is a confidence coefficient taken from the following table of probabilities of an event being less than or equal to a certain amount:

98%	=	2.06
95	=	1.65
90	=	1.28
85	=	1.04
80	=	.84
75	=	.67
70	=	.52
65	=	.38
60	=	.26

Using a probability of occurrence of 90% (determined by the degree of the lessee's risk averseness), the expected value of the option cost is calculated as follows:

$$EVO_{Expected} = [EVO_{Step\ Two} + (EVO_{Standard\ Deviation} \times C)],$$
$$EVO_{Expected} = 925 + (129.90 \times 1.28) = 1,091.27$$

Step Five

Based on the foregoing calculations, the unknown purchase option price will be equal to or less than 1,091.27, given a 90% degree of confidence (bear in mind that this number also is predicated on the degree of guesswork, the range and the outcomes resulting in a 129.90 standard deviation). This amount then could be used as one of the lease versus buy assumptions. The expected value would have been smaller had the range or magnitude of the outcomes been smaller or had some of the outcomes been more likely. However, because the guess was so broad, a higher than expected option price is anticipated.

QUALITATIVE ISSUES

Leasing is a viable alternative to conventional forms of equipment financing, and frequently offers substantial cost savings to the lessee. Expense reductions, however, represent only part of the numerous reasons why leasing might be preferable to conventional financing methods. For example, a properly structured lease with a low down payment might alleviate liquidity problems experienced by a growing company whose cash is tied up in working capital. Additionally, a lease might be preferable to the purchase alternative because of certain flexibilities in the lease, such as cancelling early, upgrading or swapping. Although the value of flexible lease terms is difficult to quantify, such flexibilities nevertheless influence the lease versus buy decision.

Proper integration of all quantitative and qualitative factors and variables impacting the decision is essential to a reliable and relevant conclusion. Numerous qualitative factors influence the lease versus buy decision. To the degree possible, some quantitative dollar value should be placed on these qualitative issues; however, in many cases this is impossible. Nevertheless, unquantified or not, these quality attributes of the decision still need to be integrated into the decision process because of their significant impact on the overall conclusion. Following is a list of many of the qualitative factors that typically favor leasing, instead of buying equipment:

1. **Off balance sheet financing:** If the lease qualifies as operating from an accounting viewpoint, neither the leased asset nor the corresponding lease liability appears on the face of the lessee's balance sheet. Operating leases favorably impact profitability ratios such as ROA, as well as financial ratios (current ratio, etc.)

2. **Down payment affordability:** A lease with only one advance payment (1.5 to 3.0% of equipment cost) is quite affordable relative to typical bank financing for equipment, which requires down payments of 10 to 20%

3. **Excessive use of leased asset:** When excessive wear and tear of the asset is anticipated, certain lessees are more apt to lease. If the lease document does not require reimbursement of the lessor for such excess usage, then, to that degree, the lessee has gained economically

4. **Ability to hold vendor lessors accountable:** If the lessor also is the manufacturer of the equipment, the lessee might feel more confident about lessor service regarding warranties and maintenance, because of the lessee's perceived ability to withhold lease payments until the equipment is properly working or adequately serviced

5. **Payment for the lease out of an operating budget:** When an equipment user's capital acquisition budget has been spent, the only remaining option to obtain additional equipment is leasing, because the rentals will be paid out of an operating expense budget as opposed to a capital acquisition budget

6. **Working capital credit lines kept intact:** If credit lines will be unduly consumed through equipment acquisition, the result might be a serious impairment of the company's growth, because of an inability to obtain working capital. Leases represent an additional source of funding not otherwise available

7. **Flexible structuring options:** Swaps, skipped payments and upgrades commonly used in leasing are not found as frequently in commercial lending

8. **On-the-spot financing:** Product financing when it is offered by vendor or manufacturer lessors, saves the lessee time, as it alleviates the need to shop for funding

9. **Avoidance of salvage problems:** The disposal of purchased equipment can be uncertain, risky and time consuming, all of which can be avoided through leasing

10. **Greater credit leniency:** Sales driven vendor lessors often are willing to take greater credit risks in order to make a sale.

Appropriate Discount Rates

Whenever cash flows are discounted, as in a lease versus purchase analysis, the issue of discount rate arises. Which discount rate is most appropriate in a lease versus purchase analysis? The answer depends on the method of the analysis (single versus dual rate) and the characteristics of the lessee. However, certain rules govern the choice of discount rate. Generally, when liquidity preference is not a consideration, the following discount rates should be used:

1. Single rate method   - after-tax cost of debt

2. Dual rate method

    a.   Equivalent loan costs   - after-tax cost of debt

    b.   Obsolescence avoidance   - after-tax cost of capital

    c.   Tax benefits   - after-tax cost of capital

    d.   Indirect costs   - after-tax cost of capital.

When liquidity preference is an issue, the after-tax cost of equity should be used on all costs.

LIQUIDITY PREFERENCE

What is liquidity preference and why is the cost of equity the appropriate discount rate in the lease versus buy decision when the lessee has a liquidity preference? Liquidity preference represents the lessee's time preference for cash; that is, the lessee's degree of preference for the extra cash flow generated by a lease, even though the lease may have a higher interest rate than the loan alternative. The extra cash flow a lease generates usually represents a timing benefit to the lessee.

The argument for liquidity preference states that the extra cash flow generated by the lease in its early years, when reinvested in working capital, more than compensates for any extra interest cost in the lease. A higher priced funding alternative is deemed acceptable as long as it generates cash flow savings that can be reinvested at a sufficiently high enough rate to compensate for any extra interest expense in the lease. The lessee, in essence, prefers cash (liquidity) today, rather than tomorrow.

Leases typically create cash savings in their early years because of low down payments (one or two rentals in advance). Installment and commercial lenders, on the other hand, frequently require down payments of 10 to 20%. This down payment requirement, when coupled with sales taxes and other soft costs, can be substantial. Of course, there are other reasons a lease might have preferable cash flow savings, e.g., the lessee is in an AMT position and tax lease payments do not create tax preferences.

Actually, the liquidity preference argument is more complex than cited above. For example, excess cash flow in a lease is created primarily from the additional financial leverage created by low down payments, long terms and residual emphasis. The generation of cash flow simply from borrowing creates several hurdles relating to capital structure theory. These hurdles must be overcome before the liquidity preference approach can be fully justified.

Several implicit assumptions must be made when the liquidity preference approach is applied. The more financial leverage the better, as long as:

1. The company does not care about maintaining a constant debt-to-equity ratio. Indifference to capital structure may occur if a company has not yet reached its optimal debt-to-equity ratio

and is in need of more debt. Such a company would probably be nonpublic and, most likely, not be financially rated by Moodys or Standard and Poors. The company, therefore, would not be overly concerned about maintaining a constant debt-to-equity ratio

2. The company cannot obtain debt (of equal terms) at a lower cost. Obviously, if one seeks financial leverage to enhance cash flows it should be done at the lowest cost. Frequently, lending institutions will match the terms of any lease, including low down payments and balloon payments, etc. Therefore, leasing should not be preferred based on the assumption that it alone can produce cash flow savings, because other financing alternatives might be able to produce the same effect. However, in the absence of equally structured financing alternatives, leasing still might produce the best cash flows

3. The extra cash flow resulting from the leverage can be reinvested at a rate greater than the IRR of the cash flow differential between the lease and buy alternatives. Lessee reinvestment rates that are lower than the IRR of the differential cash flow favor buying. The IRR of the differential cash flow is the implied borrowing cost of the cash flow savings. If these cash flow savings cannot be invested at a rate high enough to cover the incremental cost of the savings, they are not worth having

4. The borrower can absorb the extra risk caused by increased leverage. Extra debt relative to equity increases the overall economic risk of the firm should a recession occur. Additionally, the more a firm leverages itself, the more its additional borrowings will cost; therefore, the borrower must be willing to assume such increased risk

5. The proposed debt is self-liquidating and as much financial leverage as possible should be maintained. For example, an investment in an apartment house that is subject to a fixed-rate, fixed-term mortgage represents a self-liquidating investment. As rentals are received, and the mortgage paid, the investment's debt-to-equity ratio is constantly lowered. To minimize the lowering of this ratio, the debt term could be stretched out. This particular reason, along with the next two, helps to further justify the liquidity preference approach

6. Future rates are expected to increase. More financial leverage allows one to lock in a fixed interest cost

7. Leasing is viewed as an additional source of capital not otherwise available, thereby leaving working capital lines intact. Working capital lines typically are restricted in amount for small to intermediate size companies. Because expansion of credit lines to accommodate equipment acquisition is restricted, leasing becomes the only viable alternative borrowing source for these smaller companies.

INTEREST MINIMIZATION

When liquidity preference is not an issue, the equipment user is said to be making an interest minimization or equivalent loan decision. No emphasis is placed on the impact of financial leverage in this decision. The following are the basic assumptions justifying the interest minimization approach.

1. Debt is readily available (other than timing) and, therefore, cash flow from financial leverage always is available and should be obtained at the lowest cost

2. The lessee attempts to maintain a constant debt-to-equity ratio. Debt funding comparisons should not include the impact of various degrees of leverage because this would be contradictory to the assumption of maintaining a constant debt-to-equity ratio

3. The company is attempting to lower its financial leverage so it should not place a preference on higher amounts of debt

4. Costs of debt are dropping over the investment horizon; thus, higher leverage should be avoided because higher borrowing rates would be inappropriately locked in

5. The lease is capital and, therefore, on balance sheet. If a constant debt-to-equity relationship is desired, an equally leveraged debt alternative must be compared to the lease, or undue preference will be given to financial leverage.

Cost of Equity

The interest minimization approach requires the after-tax cost of debt as a discount rate, whereas the liquidity preference approach requires the after-tax cost of equity as a discount rate. The cost of equity should be used as the discount rate under liquidity preference because the difference in cash flows between two funding alternatives, over the equipment holding period, represents return on equity cash flows. In other words, the savings derived from using one method of financing over another inure solely to the benefit of the equity holders. Therefore, the larger return on equity (ROE) cash flow is the better financing alternative as long as the time value of money has been considered. The time value of equity returns is the required ROE the company normally expects. This yield is greater than the firm's cost of debt or cost of capital.

The primary problem with the ROE discount rate approach is not so much the use of a high ROE discount rate as it is the use of a constant ROE discount rate over the equipment's economic life. General financial theory requires the use of higher ROE discount rates for higher degrees of financial leverage and, hence, risk.

A second problem with an ROE discounting is interpretation of the final answer. For example, assume, after having discounted the lease and the loan cash flows at a 16% ROE, a present value of 10,000 results in favor of leasing. Compare this to another lease with lower up-front costs (resulting in more leverage) that has a present value total of 15,000. In reality, if the second alternative were chosen it would be implied that more financial leverage is better than less (given the company can assume the risk of more financial leverage). Certainly, a lease versus buy analysis need not be performed to ascertain this basic financial truth. However, when particular lease versus buy alternatives represent two mutually exclusive ways of funding an equipment acquisition, use of the ROE discount rate will give the proper financial answer.

After-tax Cost of Debt

Discounting lease or loan costs with the after-tax cost of debt does not consider the impact of financial leverage; therefore, this rate is used in the interest minimization approach. A cost of debt discount rate values only the interest in the funding alternative.

For example, the after-tax, present value of an installment loan over 48 months is the same as that of a commercial loan in which the total principal plus interest is due in a lump sum in 48 months. Use of a higher discount rate favors the commercial loan, not because it has a lower interest cost, but because of the additional financial leverage it provided (100% principal outstanding for four years versus paying down principal each month in the installment loan).

Cost of Capital

Cost of capital is used in nonliquidity preference situations. It is, however, applied only to cash flows that normally would be discounted at the cost of capital were the analysis solely that of capital budgeting. For example, MACRS depreciation normally is offset against revenues in capital budgeting to determine tax benefits or expenses. The resulting after-tax cash flows are then discounted at the cost of capital. Therefore, MACRS tax benefits in a lease versus buy decision still will be valued at the cost of capital.

APPROPRIATE DISCOUNT PERIODS

The standardization of discount periods is as important as the appropriateness of the discount rate. The general rule is that all cash flows, whether occurring monthly, quarterly or semiannually, should be discounted at the same periodic discount rate. Thus, if 1% per month is the appropriate monthly discount rate, an annual cash flow should be discounted over 12 months at 1%.

This treatment is different from discounting the event at 12% over one year, because a 12% annual, nominal rate does not have the effect of monthly compounded interest built in. Had the annual cash flow been discounted at 12.682503% per year (the annual effective rate of 12% with monthly compounding), the answer would have been the same as discounting it at 1% per month for 12 months. Inconsistent discounting could erroneously favor one alternative over another.

Methods of Analysis

Several techniques can be used for making the lease versus purchase decision, including NPV, IRR and TVA. These techniques, and the differences between them, are illustrated in this section. A simple set of assumptions is used to highlight these techniques.

Equipment assumptions

Equipment cost: 1,000

MACRS classlife: 5-year property

Sales tax: 6%, on both the initial purchase and the purchase option

Acquisition date: January 1 of the current year.

Equipment user information

Income tax bracket: 35%, calendar year taxpayer

After-tax cost of debt: 6.5%

After-tax, weighted average cost of capital: 12%

After-tax cost of equity: 18.72% (the company is capitalized with 55% debt and 45% equity).

Lease information

Lease rentals: three annual payments of 372, in arrears

Purchase option: 100, expected to be exercised at the end of the third year.

Loan information

Loan amount: 1,000

Pretax interest: 10%

Loan payments: 402.11 each, payable in three annual payments in arrears.

NET PRESENT VALUE ANALYSIS

A presentation of the cash flows of the lease versus loan decision appears in Exhibits 13-7 and 13-8. Applying the cost of debt as the discount rate to the after-tax cash flows in Exhibit 13-7 and 13-8 results in a present value of leasing cost of 738.70.

	HP-12C			HP-17B (#TIMES PROMPTING: OFF)			
		f	REG			FIN	
6.5			i			CFLO	
256.31		g	CFj	■	CLEAR DATA	YES	
2		g	Nj	FLOW (0)=?	0		INPUT
354.89		g	CFj	FLOW (1)=?	256.31		INPUT
11.87	CHS g		CFj	FLOW (2)=?	256.31		INPUT
7.12	CHS g		CFj	FLOW (3)=?	354.89		INPUT
10.68	CHS g		CFj	FLOW (4)=?	11.87	+/-	INPUT
	f	NPV	738.70	FLOW (5)=?	7.12	+/-	INPUT
				FLOW (6)=?	10.68	+/-	INPUT
							EXIT
							CALC
					6.5		I%
					NPV	= 738.70	

Exhibit 13-7
Present Value of Lease Costs

	0	1	2	3	4	5	6
Lease rentals	0.00	372.00	372.00	372.00	0.00	0.00	0.00
Purchase option	0.00	0.00	0.00	100.00	0.00	0.00	0.00
Sales tax	0.00	22.32	22.32	28.32	0.00	0.00	0.00
Subtotal	0.00	394.32	394.32	500.32	0.00	0.00	0.00
Tax impact	0.00	(138.01)	(138.01)	(145.43) [1]	(11.87) [2]	(7.12)	(10.68)[3]
Net cash flow	0.00	256.31	256.31	354.89	(11.87)	(7.12)	(10.68)

[1] 394.32 x .35 =   138.01 (year 3 rent expense)

    100.00 x .20 x.35 =   7.00 (MACRS on the purchased asset)

    6.00 x .20 x.35 =   .42 (sales tax)

                  145.43

[2] (100 + 6) x .320 x .35 = 11.87 (purchase option + sales tax) x MACRS % x tax rate.

[3] (100 + 6) x .288 x .35 = 10.68 (purchase option + sales tax) x remaining tax basis %
    x tax rate.

The present value cost of the loan alternative is 747.61, or a value of 8.91 in favor of the lease alternative.

HP-12C			**HP-17B (#TIMES PROMPTING: OFF)**		
	f	REG			FIN
6.5		i			CFLO
60	g	CFo	■ CLEAR DATA		YES
292.91	g	CFj	FLOW (0)=?	60	INPUT
258.96	g	CFj	FLOW (1)=?	292.91	INPUT
318.08	g	CFj	FLOW (2)=?	258.96	INPUT
42.74 CHS	g	CFj	FLOW (3)=?	318.08	INPUT
2	g	Nj	FLOW (4)=?	42.74 +/-	INPUT
21.37 CHS	g	CFj	FLOW (5)=?	42.74 +/-	INPUT
	f	NPV 747.61	FLOW (6)=?	21.37 +/-	INPUT
					EXIT
					CALC
				6.5	I%
				NPV	= 747.61

Exhibit 13-8
Present Value of Loan Costs

	0	1	2	3	4	5	6
Loan payments	0.00	402.11	402.11	402.11	0.00	0.00	0.00
Sales tax	60.00	0.00	0.00	0.00	0.00	0.00	0.00
Interest benefits[1]	0.00	(35.00)	(24.43)	(12.80)	0.00	0.00	0.00
MACRS benefits[2]	0.00	(70.00)	(112.00)	(67.20)	(40.32)	(40.32)	(20.16)
Sales tax benefits[3]	0.00	(4.20)	(6.72)	(4.03)	(2.42)	(2.42)	(1.21)
Net cash flow	60.00	292.91	258.96	318.08	(42.74)	(42.74)	(21.37)

[1]
    Year
      1   100.00 x.35 = 35.00
      2   69.79 x.35 = 24.43
      3   36.56 x.35 = 12.80

[2]
    Year
      1   200.00 x.35 = 70.00
      2   320.00 x.35 = 112.00
      3   192.00 x.35 = 67.20
      4   115.20 x.35 = 40.32
      5   115.20 x.35 = 40.32
      6   57.60 x.35 = 20.16

[3]   The sales tax of 60 is amortized over the MACRS life. Each year's amortization amount times 35% represents the tax benefit.

TERMINAL VALUE ANALYSIS

An equally valid method of evaluating the choice between borrowing and leasing is TVA, which measures the future value of the cash flows. This technique always provides the same conclusion as NPV analysis. It does, perhaps, give a better answer, however, in that the true magnitude of the difference between the alternatives is known. This future value represents the income statement (profit and loss) difference between the two alternatives that appears over the life of the lease or buy alternative. NPV analysis understates the income statement magnitude even though the correct choice is made. In this example the future value difference between the two methods is 13.00.

IRR DIFFERENTIAL

Another technique used in lease versus buy analysis is to compute the IRR of the cash flow differences between the two alternatives, which are shown in Exhibit 13-9. This particular decision method differs from NPV or TVA analysis in that a discount rate is not applied to the cash flows. Instead, the implicit cost of the lease cash flows over the loan cash flows is computed. The IRR of the cash flow differential is calculated as follows:

HP-12C			HP-17B (#TIMES PROMPTING: OFF)			
	f	REG				FIN
60.00	g	CFo				CFLO
36.60	g	CFj	■	CLEAR DATA		YES
2.65	g	CFj	FLOW (0)=?	60.00		INPUT
36.81	CHS g	CFj	FLOW (1)=?	36.60		INPUT
30.87	CHS g	CFj	FLOW (2)=?	2.65		INPUT
35.62	CHS g	CFj	FLOW (3)=?	36.81	+/-	INPUT
10.69	CHS g	CFj	FLOW (4)=?	30.87	+/-	INPUT
	f	IRR 3.7693	FLOW (5)=?	35.62	+/-	INPUT
			FLOW (6)=?	10.69	+/-	INPUT
						EXIT
						CALC
			IRR%	= 3.7693		

		Exhibit 13-9		
		Cash Flow Differences		
Year	After-tax loan cash flow	After-tax lease cash flow	Cash flow difference	
0	60.00	0.00	60.00	
1	292.91	(256.31)	36.60	
2	258.96	(256.31)	2.65	
3	318.08	(354.89)	(36.81)	
4	(42.74)	11.87	(30.87)	
5	(42.74)	7.12	(35.62)	
6	(21.37)	10.68	(10.69)	

In this case, the IRR of the cash flow differentials is 3.7693%, after-tax. If it can borrow at less than 3.7693%, on an after-tax basis, the lessee should choose the loan alternative. However, because the cost of borrowing is greater than this rate, the lease alternative is selected as the better choice. Had the cost of cash savings been equal to or greater than the cost of debt, the loan alternative would have been preferable.

Conversely, if liquidity preference is an issue, any IRR of the cash flow differential that is less than the cost of capital favors leasing. As long as the lessee can earn greater than 3.7693% on the excess cash flows generated by the lease, it should choose the lease alternative. Rates equal to or greater than the cost of capital favor buying, but only when liquidity preference is an issue.

If the previous example was an actual lease versus loan analysis, the following refinements would be made:

1. Generally, lease and loan cash flows would be analyzed on a month-by-month basis, a process that is too cumbersome and lengthy to be shown here

2. Tax benefits or liabilities would be spread over the estimated tax payment dates for each tax year

3. Other termination options, explained earlier, also might be assumed

4. Other pertinent cash flows, such as maintenance, that impact the decision also should be included

5. Were the lessee in a net operating loss (NOL) or Investment Tax Credit (ITC) carryforward position, additional adjustments would be required. The same is true if the lessee expected to enter or exit an AMT position during the lease.

EXAMPLES

Lease versus purchase analysis is illustrated in this section through several examples, utilizing the single discount rate method of NPV analysis. The single rate method does not recognize any differences in the risk attributable to the various cash flows in the analysis; therefore, a standard discount rate is used throughout the analysis. (Refer to the discount rate discussion for what is considered to be the appropriate discount rate to use.)

This section consists of a base case (Case One) that assumes the lessee is an interest minimizer (liquidity preference is not applicable). Sensitivity of the conclusion to changes in payment, discount rate and residual is then performed. Following Case One, the impact of liquidity preference is shown in Case Two. In the next section, in which advanced issues are discussed, the dual rate methodology is shown. The examples are based on the following assumptions:

Equipment assumptions

Equipment cost: 100,000, payable January 1, 19X5

MACRS classlife: 5-year

Expected pretax salvage value: 12,000 at the end of 60 months.

Equipment user information

Federal income tax rate: 35%, for a calendar year taxpayer

AMT position: none

Capital costs (all stated after-tax):

	Annual nominal	Monthly nominal
Cost of debt	5.5770%	.4648%
Cost of capital	11.4630%	.9553%
Cost of equity	16.2789%	1.3566%

Capital structure: 45% debt, 55% equity

Liquidity preference: not an issue.

Lease information

Payments: 60 monthly payments of 1,875, in advance

Refundable security deposit: 1,000

Purchase option: lessee does not expect to exercise the 12,000 purchase option at the end of the 60th month.

Loan information

Down payment: 10,000

Loan: 90,000, with interest at 8.58% per annum, requiring 60 payments in arrears at 1,850 per month

Closing fee: 625 (nonrefundable)

Compensating bank balance: 1,200, which is refundable at the end of the loan term

General issues: considered to be the best financing alternative available; no one else will lend with a lower down payment.

Case One

In this case, liquidity preference is not an issue. However, the same case is shown later (Case Two), with liquidity preference considered. When liquidity preference is not an issue, the after-tax cost of debt is used for all costs and benefits when the single rate method of discounting is employed.

Other factors must be discussed before presenting the quantitative analysis. For instance, the intraperiod present value factor (IPVF) describes the present value of the four quarterly estimated tax payments during the year. The following cases ignore the IPVF calculation for simplicity of presentation. However, current software packages incorporate the quarterly payment of taxes and the impact on cash flow.

As in any lease versus purchase, the term of the purchase alternative must match that of the lease. Exhibit 13-4 indicates the various options available that will equate the terms. In this particular case, the asset is assumed to be purchased by the lessee at the end of the lease term. All pertinent costs also must be considered.

Pertinent costs are those that vary under the loan versus the lease alternative or that occur in only one or the other case. The pertinent costs beyond the basic lease and loan payments in this case are refundable deposits and compensating bank balances, residual and salvage values, cost recoveries and closing fees. Some lease versus buy decisions have even fewer variables than this particular case.

PRESENT VALUE SUMMARY

Exhibit 13-10 and Exhibit 13-11 illustrate the cash flows for the lease and the loan alternatives in Case One, respectively. Calculations are footnoted when necessary. This analysis shows that, when discounted at the cost of debt, purchasing the asset is less costly than leasing by 258.

Lease	Buy	Difference
62,849	62,591	258

	0	**1**	**2**	**3**	**4**	**5**
	Exhibit 13-10					
	Lease Alternative					
Lease payments	1,875	22,500	22,500	22,500	22,500	20,625
Tax savings	(656)	(7,875)	(7,875)	(7,875)	(7,875)	(7,219)
After-tax subtotal	1,219	14,625	14,625	14,625	14,625	13,406
Refundable security deposit	1,000					(1,000)
Net cash cost	2,219	14,625	14,625	14,625	14,625	12,406

Lease alternative

	HP-12C		**HP-17B (#TIMES PROMPTING: ON)**		
	f	REG			FIN
5.577		i			CFLO
2,219	g	CFo	■ CLEAR DATA		YES
14,625	g	CFj	FLOW (0)=?	2,219	INPUT
4	g	Nj	FLOW (1)=?	14,625	INPUT
12,406	g	CFj	#TIMES (1)=1	4	INPUT
	f	NPV 62,849	FLOW (2)=?	12,406	INPUT
			#TIMES (2)=1	1	INPUT
					EXIT
					CALC
				5.577	I%
				NPV	= 62,849

Loan alternative

	HP-12C		**HP-17B (#TIMES PROMPTING: OFF)**		
	f	REG			FIN
5.577		i			CFLO
11,606	g	CFo	■ CLEAR DATA		YES
12,701	g	CFj	FLOW (0)=?	11,606	INPUT
8,972	g	CFj	FLOW (1)=?	12,701	INPUT
13,965	g	CFj	FLOW (2)=?	8,972	INPUT
17,211	g	CFj	FLOW (3)=?	13,965	INPUT
6,803	g	CFj	FLOW (4)=?	17,211	INPUT
	f	NPV 62,591	FLOW (5)=?	6,803	INPUT
					EXIT
					CALC
				5.577	I%
				NPV	= 62,591

Exhibit 13-11
Loan Alternative

	0	1	2	3	4	5
Down payment	10,000					
Closing fee	406					
Compensating balance	1,200					(1,200)
Loan payments	0	22,200	22,200	22,200	22,200	22,200
Interest benefit[1]		(2,499)	(2,028)	(1,515)	(957)	(349)
MACRS benefit[2]		(7,000)	(11,200)	(6,720)	(4,032)	(2,016)
Salvage value[3]						(11,832)
Net cash cost	11,606	12,701	8,972	13,965	17,211	6,803

1 Set-up calculator for amortization:

	HP-12C				**HP-17B (12 P/YR END MODE)**
	f	REG			FIN
	g	END			TVM
8.58	g	12÷		■	CLEAR DATA
90,000		PV		8.58	I%YR
1,850	CHS	PMT		90,000	PV
				1,850 +/-	PMT
					OTHER
					AMRT

Amortize annual loan payments:

Year	**HP-12C Keystrokes**			**HP-17B Keystrokes**			**Amount**
1	12	f	AMORT	12	#P	INT	7,139.00
2	12	f	AMORT	12	#P	INT	5,795.00
3	12	f	AMORT	12	#P	INT	4,330.00
4	12	f	AMORT	12	#P	INT	2,735.00
5	12	f	AMORT	12	#P	INT	998.00

Calculate interest tax benefit:

Year	Interest		Tax rate		Tax benefit
1	7,139	x	.35	=	2,499
2	5,795	x	.35	=	2,028
3	4,330	x	.35	=	1,515
4	2,735	x	.35	=	957
5	998	x	.35	=	349

2 Year	Equipment cost		MACRS %		Annual deduction		Tax rate		Tax benefit
1	100,000	x	.20	=	20,000	x	.35	=	7,000
2	100,000	x	.32	=	32,000	x	.35	=	11,200
3	100,000	x	.192	=	19,200	x	.35	=	6,720
4	100,000	x	.1152	=	11,520	x	.35	=	4,032
5	100,000	x	.1152/2	=	5,760	x	.25	=	2,016
					88,480				

3			
Pretax salvage value			12,000
Less remaining tax basis			
Original basis	100,000		
Less depreciation taken	(88,480)	(11,520)	
Pretax gain		480	
(x) tax rate		x .35	
Tax liability		(168)	
Salvage value		12,000	
Net salvage value		11,832	

SENSITIVITY ANALYSIS

Sensitivity analysis consists of studying the impact of changes in assumptions on the final lease versus buy decision. In the following examples, the discount rate, pretax salvage and payment amount necessary to equate leasing with buying in Case One are calculated.

Discount Rate

Solve for the indifference or breakeven rate that equates the present value cost of leasing to the present value cost of buying. This rate is equal to the IRR of the differential cash flows between the two financing alternatives. Based on the differential cash flows, as shown below, the breakeven IRR (discount rate) is 6.6213%.

	0	1	2	3	4	5
Cash flow differential	(9,387)	1,924	5,653	660	(2,586)	5,603

HP-12C			**HP-17B (#TIMES PROMPTING: OFF)**		
f	REG				FIN
9,387 CHS g	CFo				CFLO
1,924 g	CFj	■	CLEAR DATA		YES
5,653 g	CFj	FLOW (0)=?	9,387 +/-	INPUT
660 g	CFj	FLOW (1)=?	1,924	INPUT
2,586 CHS g	CFj	FLOW (2)=?	5,653	INPUT
5,603 g	CFj	FLOW (3)=?	660	INPUT
f	IRR 6.6213	FLOW (4)=?	2,586 +/-	INPUT
		FLOW (5)=?	5,603	INPUT
				EXIT
				CALC
			IRR% = 6.6213	

At a discount rate of 6.6213%, the lessee would be indifferent between leasing and buying, given the above assumptions. At a discount rate higher than this amount, leasing is favored.

Pretax Salvage Value

Solve for the pretax salvage value that would equate leasing to buying. This solution requires future valuing the present value difference between the two alternatives at the cost of debt. The present value difference is 258, as previously computed.

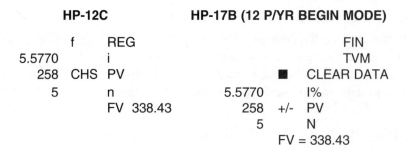

	HP-12C			**HP-17B (12 P/YR BEGIN MODE)**	
	f	REG			FIN
5.5770		i			TVM
258	CHS	PV		■	CLEAR DATA
5		n		5.5770	I%
		FV 338.43		258 +/-	PV
				5	N
					FV = 338.43

The future value difference, on an after-tax basis, is 338.43. This future value must be converted to its pretax equivalent of 520.66, because the salvage value will be received in pretax dollars.

$$338.43 \div (1 - \text{tax rate}) =$$

$$338.43 \div (.65) = 520.66$$

These calculations indicate that, if the salvage value in the purchase alternative was 11,479 (12,000 - 520.66), leasing would cost the same as buying.

Breakeven Payment Amount

Calculate the reduction in the lease payment that would equate the present value cost of the lease and buy alternatives. The buy alternative is less costly by 258. This is the amount, on a present value, after-tax basis, by which the lease payment must be reduced. The first step is to calculate the present value structuring factor:

	HP-12C			**HP-17B (12 P/YR BEGIN MODE)**	
	f	REG			FIN
	g	BEG			TVM
1	CHS	PMT		■	CLEAR DATA
5.577	g	12÷		1 +/-	PMT
60		n		5.577	I%YR
		PV 52.4984		60	N
					PV = 52.4984

Next, convert this factor to its after-tax equivalent.

$$52.4984 \times (1 - \text{tax rate}) =$$

$$52.4984 \times (.65) = 34.124$$

This factor of 34.124 is applied to the present value difference between the two alternatives of 258. The quotient, 7.56, represents the amount the lease payment must be reduced in order for the lessee to be quantitatively indifferent between the two alternatives.

$$\frac{258}{34.124} = 7.56$$

Case Two

Case Two reflects the lease versus purchase analysis of a lessee with a liquidity preference. All cash flows, therefore, are present valued at the 16.2789% cost of equity. The computations are completed in the same manner as the base case just presented, with the sole difference being the discount rate applied to all the cash flows. The summary of cash flows for this case is shown in Exhibit 13-12.

Lease alternative

	HP-12C			HP-17B (#TIMES PROMPTING: ON)		
	f	REG				FIN
16.2789		i				CFLO
2,219	g	CFo	■	CLEAR DATA		YES
14,625	g	CFj	FLOW (0)=?	2,219		INPUT
4	g	Nj	FLOW (1)=?	14,625		INPUT
12,406	g	CFj	#TIMES (1)=1	4		INPUT
	f	NPV 48,752	FLOW (2)=?	12,406		INPUT
			#TIMES (2)=1	1		INPUT
						EXIT
						CALC
				16.2789		I%
				NPV	=	48,752

Exhibit 13-12
Present Value Analysis

	Lease	Buy	Difference
After-tax cost of equity	48,752	50,662	(1,910)
After-tax cost of debt	62,849	62,591	258

Loan alternative

	HP-12C		HP-17B (#TIMES PROMPTING: OFF)		
	f	REG			FIN
16.2789	i				CFLO
11,606	g	CFo	■ CLEAR DATA		YES
12,701	g	CFj	FLOW (0)=?	11,606	INPUT
8,972	g	CFj	FLOW (1)=?	12,701	INPUT
13,965	g	CFj	FLOW (2)=?	8,972	INPUT
17,211	g	CFj	FLOW (3)=?	13,965	INPUT
6,803	g	CFj	FLOW (4)=?	17,211	INPUT
	f	NPV 50,662	FLOW (5)=?	6,803	INPUT
					EXIT
					CALC
				16.2789	I%
				NPV	= 50,662

The difference of 1,910 in favor of leasing indicates that leasing generally is favored when liquidity preference is an issue. When liquidity preference was not an issue, buying was favored by 258.

ADVANCED ISSUES

Some lessees choose to use more advanced analytical techniques, such as the dual rate method. In addition to advanced analytical techniques such as the dual rate method, certain unique tax issues affect the lease versus purchase decision: the AMT and the FTC, both of which tend to favor the lease alternative. Each of these tax aspects must be incorporated into the lease versus purchase decision whenever they are applicable.

Dual Rate Method

The lease versus buy decision embodies typical capital budgeting costs and benefits such as obsolescence avoidance, salvage values, indirect costs and tax benefits. Yet, at the same time, the decision includes financial costs such as loan interest expense. The real problem is not so much that four basic cost categories complicate the decision, but that two (at least) different discount rates should be used in the discounting process because of the nature of those categories.

Lease versus purchase cash flows that normally are part of the capital budgeting process should be discounted at the equipment user's cost of capital. However, equivalent loan costs normally are discounted at an after-tax cost of debt. Use of two different discount rates is called the dual rate discounting method.

The dual rate method can be used in lieu of the single rate method. The basic difference between the two methods is that cash flows are categorized according to their nature, i.e., equivalent loan costs, obsolescence avoidance, tax benefits and indirect costs. Under the dual discount rate method, equivalent loan costs are discounted at the after-tax cost of debt; all other costs are discounted at the cost of capital. Additionally, the lease payments are separated into their principal and interest components so that the equivalent loan costs, as well as cost recovery, can be discounted at the appropriate rates.

DUAL RATE COMPONENTS

Determination of the overall cost of leasing is a complex process because leasing costs include four separate financial elements, each of which must be separately valued. The first three of the following costs generally are considered capital budgeting elements. The fourth is a true lease versus buy financing cost.

1. Obsolescence avoidance

2. Tax benefits (MACRS, etc.)

3. Indirect costs

4. Equivalent loan costs.

It is essential to an understanding of the dual discount rate method of lease versus buy to see how these costs interrelate; therefore, each is discussed, followed by an illustration using numbers.

Obsolescence Avoidance

A portion of the payments represents the principal portion of the loan or lease paid to the creditor or lessor. If the lessor prices a 10% residual into the lease, the lease rentals amortize only 90% of the equipment cost. If a lessee anticipates the equipment's future value to be below 10% of the cost, it has hedged against obsolescence through leasing. However, if the equipment is worth more than 10% of cost, the lessee would have been in a better economic position through borrowing.

If the equipment user anticipates buying the equipment, then each of the total acquisition costs would be compared as in Exhibit 13-13. To the degree the purchase option exercise price is below 10%, the lessee again would have had a lower total net cost through leasing. However, purchase option costs in excess of 10% would favor buying.

Tax Benefits

The owner of equipment can take depreciation deductions on 100% of the equipment cost over six tax years, in the manner indicated in Exhibit 13-14,

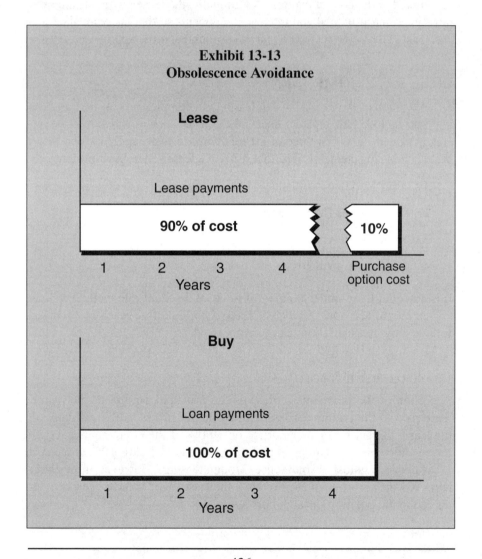

Exhibit 13-13
Obsolescence Avoidance

Lease

Lease payments

90% of cost   **10%**

1   2   3   4   Purchase option cost
Years

Buy

Loan payments

100% of cost

1   2   3   4
Years

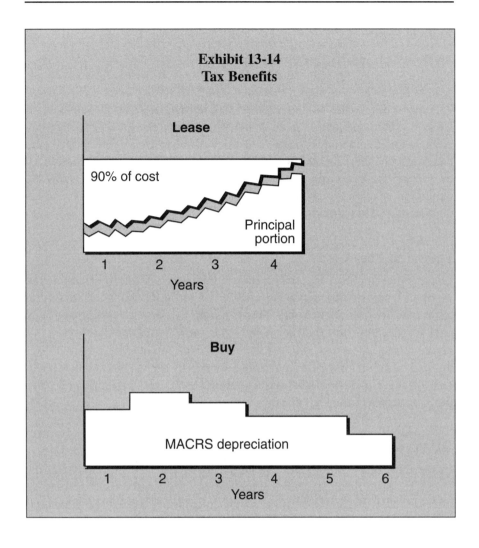

Exhibit 13-14
Tax Benefits

for 5-year MACRS classlife equipment. The lessee of the equipment could take as a deduction the cost recovery in the lease (the principal portion of the lease rentals) over the lease term of 90% of equipment cost, which would also include any additional time required for the depreciation of purchase options (at 10%) if exercised. To the degree the MACRS tax deductions are received faster than the principal portion of the tax lease payments, buying is favored. However, when tax leases are written over terms shorter than the MACRS classlife, leasing is favored.

Indirect Costs

Indirect costs such as sales tax influence the lease versus buy decision based upon their present value costs. Sales tax on leases, for instance, is paid over the lease term as a percentage of each lease payment. The disadvantage of more sales tax being paid when leasing (sales tax is paid on both lease principal and interest) can be overcome when the future costs are discounted and compared to the present value of the sales tax paid at time zero (when purchasing). In addition, tax law requires sales tax to be capitalized as part of the tax basis when purchasing equipment; thus the sales tax deduction is spread over the MACRS classlife in proportion to the annual depreciation deductions.

Equivalent Loan Costs

Lease payments, like loan payments, can be separated into principal and interest. Usually, interest is imputed in the lease payments at the equipment user's pretax debt cost. This process, in essence, assigns the loan cost to the lease alternative; hence, the term equivalent loan cost. To arrive at the amount of interest in the lease payments, the payments are amortized (split into principal and interest) using the pretax debt cost. Use of the equivalent loan costs method provides uniformity of comparison between the two alternatives.

DUAL RATE THEORY

In the dual rate method, the equivalent loan costs are discounted at the lessee's cost of debt. The residual and salvage values are discounted at the after-tax cost of capital because of the uncertainty associated with their realization. The MACRS cost recovery benefits and the indirect costs also are discounted at the lessee's cost of capital because such tax deductible expenses are considered to be typical capital budgeting costs. (In capital budgeting, revenue from an investment is adjusted for indirect expenses as well as tax deductible expenses, which include tax depreciation. The adjusted, after-tax cash flow is then compared to the net investment on an NPV or IRR basis to establish whether the investment is sufficiently profitable.)

The key point is that MACRS and indirect costs are included in the process of establishing the investment's after-tax net cash flow. The cash flow then is discounted at the cost of capital to determine an NPV, or the IRR is compared to the cost of capital because the cost of capital is the appropriate rate to use with capital budgeting elements. Debt-related elements, such as loan payments and interest tax benefits, typically are discounted at the cost of debt.

This dual rate method of evaluating purchase and lease costs is theoretically more correct, although it is not commonly used in the industry. Most analysts still use one discount rate (the cost of debt or of capital) for all cash flows. When the single rate method is used, the process is simplified because the costs do not need to be separated into component parts.

The dual rate method discounts each element of the lease versus loan decision at an appropriate rate: cost of debt for loan equivalent costs and cost of capital for capital budgeting components. Some financial analysts argue that the tax benefits associated with either the lease or loan decision are an integral part of the cost of borrowing and should, therefore, be discounted at a single rate – the after-tax cost of debt. However, the tax benefits associated with the choice of financing actually are a separate issue, even though they occur simultaneously with the borrowing.

It could be argued that the real choice in lease versus loan is one of maximizing tax benefits. The financing is ancillary, thus requiring all cash flows to be discounted at the cost of capital. Neither of these single rate arguments is cogent, however, because the decision is much more complex. In reality, two decisions are being made simultaneously – one requiring the cost of debt as a discount rate and the other the cost of capital.

Another argument in favor of the dual rate method is illustrated in the case in which a company that has no debt is attempting to determine whether to purchase with cash or to lease. Clearly, the MACRS depreciation is the only tax benefit available on the buy side of the decision because there are no debt components. MACRS tax benefits must be discounted at the cost of capital since the cost of debt is irrelevant (because there is no debt). On the lease side, the cost recovery portion of the lease payment must be discounted at the cost of capital in order to be consistent.

The single rate method of discounting is an oversimplification of the complex nature of lease versus buy. This oversimplification appears to favor buying to the exclusion of leasing. The complexity of the lease versus purchase decision is more than a simple comparison of one financing alternative versus another. Rather, the decision embodies a purchase financing decision plus an obsolescence avoidance decision, in addition to tax benefits and indirect costs. These facets of the buy decision are compared to similar costs on the leasing side.

The comparison would be more obvious if the decision were between a loan and a money-over-money lease (the previous examples have pitted a loan against a tax lease). The money-over-money lease is a nontax lease accounted for on the tax books of the lessee as a loan, resulting in lease payments separated into principal and interest and MACRS deductions accruing to the benefit of the lessee. The point is that leases do have two components: debt and cost recovery. Each component has to be evaluated on its own merits without assuming one is a function of the other. In fact, they are coexistent, not cause and effect related.

DUAL RATE ILLUSTRATION

Exhibits 13-15 and 13-16 illustrate the lease versus purchase analysis under the dual rate method, using the same example as the single rate method illustration on page 427. Note that two discount rates are used to present value the cash flows.

The present value cost of leasing is 66,856 under the dual rate method (see Exhibit 13-15). The cost of leasing is 1,118 less than the present value cost of the loan alternative of 67,974, which is shown in Exhibit 13-16.

Alternative Minimum Tax Impact

When an equipment user is in an AMT position, there is a direct impact on the lease versus buy decision. The MACRS depreciation creates a tax preference on the purchase side. The tax lease payment on the lease side, however, does not create a tax preference. A penalty is attached to equipment ownership because any tax preferences attributable to accelerated depreciation are taxed at 20%. Thus, tax leasing should be considered as a viable funding alternative to avoid or mitigate an AMT problem.

The existence of an AMT problem requires certain adjustments to the lease versus buy decision. Assuming a lessee is in an AMT position, the basic lease versus buy methodology is the same as described earlier, except a 20% tax rate is used. However, the difference between the 35% regular tax rate and the 20% AMT rate becomes a tax benefit or liability in the year the AMT position reverses.

Exhibit 13-15
Present Value of Lease Costs
(Dual Rate Method)

	Present value	0	1	2	3	4	5
Equivalent loan costs							
Lease payments		1,875	22,500	22,500	22,500	22,500	20,625
Refundable security deposit [1]		1,000					(1,000)
Interest tax benefits [1]		0	(2,807)	(2,354)	(1,862)	(1,325)	(740)
After-tax costs	88,579 [2]	2,875	19,693	20,146	20,638	21,175	18,885
Obsolescence avoidance							
None							
Tax benefits							
Cost recovery in the lease rentals	(21,723) [3]		(5,068)	(5,521)	(6,013)	(6,550)	(7,135)
Indirect costs							
None	0						
Net cost of leasing	66,856						

1 See Exhibit 13-17

2 Discounted at 5.577%

3 Discounted at 11.463%

Exhibit 13-16
Present Value of Loan Costs
(Dual Rate Method)

	Present value	0	1	2	3	4	5
Equivalent loan costs							
Down payment		10,000					
Loan payments			22,200	22,200	22,200	22,200	22,200
Compensating balance		1,200					(1,200)
Interest tax benefits [1]			(2,400)	(2,028)	(1,515)	(957)	(349)
After-tax cost	98,376 [2]	11,200	19,701	20,172	20,685	21,243	20,651
Obsolescence avoidance							
Salvage value	(6,877) [3]	0	0	0	0	0	(11,832)
Tax benefits							
MACRS benefit [1]	(23,931) [3]	0	7,000	11,200	6,720	4,032	2,016
Indirect costs							
Loan closing fee	406	406					
Net cost of buying	67,974						

1 See Exhibit 13-11
2 Discounted at 5.577%
3 Discounted at 11.463%

Exhibit 13-17
Tax Benefit Calculations

Interest

Year	Interest [1]	Tax rate	Tax benefit
1	8,019	.35	2,807
2	6,727	.35	2,354
3	5,319	.35	1,862
4	3,786	.35	1,325
5	2,115	.35	740
Total	25,966		9,088

Cost recovery

Year	Cost recovery [1]	Tax rate	Tax benefit
1	14,481	.35	5,068
2	15,773	.35	5,521
3	17,181	.35	6,013
4	18,714	.35	6,550
5	20,385	.35	7,135
Total	86,534		30,287

[1] See Exhibit 13-18

In performing a lease versus buy analysis under AMT, it is important to recognize that any tax preference items create additional tax liabilities equal to 20% of their total each tax year. These tax liabilities, in most situations, reverse automatically over time. The following are tax preference issues that occur in the lease versus buy decision when the lessee is in an AMT situation.

1. Purchasing equipment creates a depreciation tax preference equal to the difference between the MACRS deductions and 150% declining balance depreciation over the asset's Asset Depreciation Range (ADR) midpoint life

2. Leasing might create the same tax preferences as above if the equipment is purchased during the lease term

3. Tax lease rentals do not generate depreciation tax preferences.

Exhibit 13-18
Lease Amortization Schedule

HP-12C

	g	BEG
	f	REG
1,875		PMT
100,000	CHS	PV
0		n
8.58	g	12÷

Months			Interest		Principal		Balance
12	f	AMORT	8,019	X ≷ Y	14,481	RCL PV	85,519
12	f	AMORT	6,727	X ≷ Y	15,773	RCL PV	69,746
12	f	AMORT	5,319	X ≷ Y	17,181	RCL PV	52,565
12	f	AMORT	3,786	X ≷ Y	18,714	RCL PV	33,851
12	f	AMORT	2,115	X ≷ Y	20,385	RCL PV	13,466
		Total	25,966		86,534		

HP-17B (12 P/YR END MODE)

		FIN
		TVM
■		CLEAR DATA
100,000	CHS	PV
1,875		PMT
0		N
8.58	g	I%YR
		OTHER
		AMORT

Months			Interest		Principal		Balance
12	#P	INT	8,019	PRIN	14,481	BAL	85,519
12	#P	INT	6,727	PRIN	15,773	BAL	69,746
12	#P	INT	5,319	PRIN	17,181	BAL	52,565
12	#P	INT	3,786	PRIN	18,714	BAL	33,851
12	#P	INT	2,115	PRIN	20,385	BAL	13,466
		Total	25,966		86,534		

AMT EXAMPLE

Exhibits 13-19 and 13-20 depict a lease and a purchase analysis, respectively, the tax benefits of which have been adjusted for AMT considerations. (This is the same example from Exhibits 13-10 and 13-11.) The lessee is assumed to be in an AMT position for five full tax years. At the end of the fifth tax year, the lessee exits its AMT position, which means that any AMT credits will be utilized fully in this reversal year.

Note that the lease alternative cash flows do not change, other than to reflect the AMT rate of 20%. The difference between the AMT rate of 20% and the regular tax rate of 35% is recognized (turns around) in year five, when the lessee comes out of its AMT position. This timing difference reduces the value of the deductions for the lease payments.

The value of the deductions also decreases under the loan alternative because of the 20% rate. In addition to the effect of the 20% tax rate, the tax depreciation benefit is reduced because the lessee must use AMT depreciation, which is a 150% declining balance methodology. It is this slower depreciation (the depreciation preference) that penalizes ownership in the lease versus purchase analysis. Although both the slower depreciation and lower tax rate turn around when the lessee comes out of AMT, the time value of the deductions is lost.

Exhibit 13-19
Lease Alternative (AMT)

	0	1	2	3	4	5
Lease payments	1,875	22,500	22,500	22,500	22,500	20,625
Tax rate savings	(375)	(4,500)	(4,500)	(4,500)	(4,500)	(4,125)
After-tax subtotal	1,500	18,000	18,000	18,000	18,000	16,500
AMT impact	0	0	0	0	0	(16,875)
Refundable security deposit	1,000					(1,000)
Net cash cost	2,500	18,000	18,000	18,000	18,000	(1,375)

Exhibit 13-20
Loan Alternative (AMT)

	0	1	2	3	4	5
Down payment	10,000					
Closing fee	500					
Compensating balance	1,200					(1,200)
Loan payments	0	22,200	22,200	22,200	22,200	22,200
Interest benefit[1]		(1,428)	(1,159)	(866)	(547)	(200)
Depreciation benefit[2]		(3,000)	(5,100)	(3,570)	(3,332)	(1,666)
AMT turnaround		0	0	0	0	(16,442)
Salvage value[3]						(12,932)
Net cash cost	11,700	17,772	15,941	17,764	18,321	(10,240)

1   After-tax interest benefit calculated as follows:

Year	Interest		Tax rate		Tax benefit
1	7,139	x	.20	=	1,428
2	5,795	x	.20	=	1,159
3	4,330	x	.20	=	866
4	2,735	x	.20	=	547
5	998	x	.20	=	200

2   After-tax AMT depreciation computed as follows:

Year	Equipment cost		AMT %		Annual deduction		Tax rate		Tax benefit
1	100,000	x	.15	=	15,000	x	.20	=	3,000
2	100,000	x	.255	=	25,500	x	.20	=	5,100
3	100,000	x	.1785	=	17,850	x	.20	=	3,570
4	100,000	x	.1666	=	16,660	x	.20	=	3,332
5	100,000	x	.1666 / 2	=	8,330	x	.20	=	1,666
					83,340				

3   After-tax salvage value computed as follows:

Pretax salvage value:		12,000
Less remaining tax basis		
Original basis	100,000	
Less depreciation taken	(83,340)	(16,660)
Pretax gain (loss)		(4,660)
x tax rate		.20
Tax benefit		932
Pretax proceeds		12,000
Net salvage value		12,932

This lost time value must be reflected in the lease versus purchase analysis. The calculation of the AMT turnaround for the loan alternative is as follows:

Interest	3,148 [1]
Depreciation	12,501 [2]
Basis	699 [3]
Fee	94 [4]
Total	16,442

[1] Turnaround of tax rate on interest benefit calculated as follows:

Year	Interest		Tax rate		Tax benefit
1	7,139	X	.15	=	1,070
2	5,795	X	.15	=	869
3	4,330	X	.15	=	650
4	2,735	X	.15	=	409
5	998	X	.15	=	150
Total					3,148

[2] Turnaround of tax rate on AMT depreciation computed as follows:

Year	Equipment cost		AMT %		Annual deduction		Tax rate		Tax benefit
1	100,000	X	.15	=	15,000	X	.15	=	2,250
2	100,000	X	.255	=	25,500	X	.15	=	3,825
3	100,000	X	.1785	=	17,850	X	.15	=	2,678
4	100,000	X	.1666	=	16,660	X	.15	=	2,499
5	100,000	X	.1666	=	8,330	X	.15	=	1,249
			2		83,340				12,501

[3] Turnaround of tax rate on salvage value computed as follows:

Pretax salvage value	12,000
Less remaining tax basis	(16,660)
Pretax loss	(4,460)
(x) tax rate	.15
Tax rate turnaround	699

[4] Turnaround of tax rate on fee computed as follows:

Pretax fee	625
(x) tax rate	.15
Tax rate turnaround	94

What is the impact on the equipment user's decision to lease or purchase if it is in an AMT position? The answer is found by comparing the present values of the net changes in tax benefits between the two alternatives. Note that an AMT taxpayer's cost of capital and after-tax cost of debt increase when it is in an AMT position. These increases occur because the tax benefits attributable to the interest expense deduction at a 35% rate are reduced to 20%.

Although the 15% tax benefit foregone (the difference between a 35% and a 20% tax rate) becomes a tax benefit in the year of AMT reversal, the lessee loses the time value of the benefit. This loss affects not only the deductions, but also the discount rate that is used. In the example, the taxpayer's after-tax cost of debt increased from 5.5770% to 6.8640% (8.58% x (1-.2)).

Using the AMT-adjusted discount rate of 6.8640%, and the net changes in tax benefits between leasing and buying, results in the present value totals shown in Exhibit 13-21. (The present value of each alternative is calculated at both the cost of debt and the cost of capital.)

In this example, the leasing alternative benefitted from the taxpayer's AMT position. Research has shown this to be the general conclusion regarding the impact of AMT. Other variables, however, impact this conclusion: (1) the AMT entry and exit date, (2) whether MACRS or another depreciation method is used by the taxpayer and (3) the length of the lease relative to the MACRS classlife of the asset. Additionally, use of a higher AMT-adjusted discount rate generally favors leasing.

Exhibit 13-21
Present Values (AMT)

	Cost of debt (6.8640%)	Cost of capital (12.0422%)
Leasing present value	62,671	56,345
Loan present value	(63,546)	(58,716)
Difference (favoring leasing)	(875)	(2,371)

The marketing implications of these facts for lessors should be apparent. For example, lessees in an AMT position might favor leasing even if they have never tried it. Also, leasing can not only help prevent a lessee from ever going into an AMT position, but it also can aid the lessee in coming out of the AMT position more quickly.

Foreign Tax Credit Impact

The FTC was instituted by Congress as a means of eliminating double taxation on the foreign earned income of domestic corporations. As a credit, it provides U.S. taxpayers with a dollar-for-dollar reduction in their U.S. tax liability on worldwide income for income taxes paid to foreign countries, subject to certain limitations. (Refer to Chapter Four for a detailed discussion of the FTC provisions, as this section primarily addresses the lease versus buy implications.)

The general formula for calculating the maximum credit allowed is as follows:

$$\text{FTC limitations [5]} = \frac{\text{Foreign source taxable income}}{\text{Worldwide taxable income}} \times \frac{\text{Total U.S. tax liability}}{\text{on worldwide income}}$$

As this equation illustrates, by increasing foreign source taxable income relative to worldwide taxable income, a corporation can increase the amount of the FTC limitation. This, in turn, increases the amount of foreign taxes paid that can be utilized as credits against the U.S. tax liability. As a result of this relationship, taxpayers, over the years, have devised several methods for converting U.S. source income to foreign source income in an attempt to increase the FTC limitation.

Recognizing the potential for manipulation, Congress, in the 1986 tax act, tightened the sourcing rules in an attempt to eliminate this practice. Perhaps the most critical of these sourcing rules, with respect to its impact on leasing, is the mandatory method of allocating interest expense to foreign source income. The changes in this specific methodology have caused many corporations to consider leasing equipment rather than purchasing it with borrowed funds.

---

[5] Corporations are required to classify types of income from both foreign and domestic sources into various categories or baskets as defined in the law. Therefore, corporations must calculate separate FTC limitations for each basket of income using the above formula. The sum of these amounts is equal to the total allowable FTC. Currently there are 10 separate baskets or income categories.

Under prior law, interest expense could be allocated on a separate company basis. This allowed corporations to manage the amount of interest expense allocated to foreign income by arranging borrowings within an affiliated group of corporations, such that the interest expense was incurred by a company within the group that had only U.S. income and assets. In doing so, interest expense would be allocated entirely to U.S. source income, thus maximizing the FTC limitation by leaving foreign source income intact.

The current law requires interest expense to be allocated as if all members of an affiliated group are branches of a single corporation. This treatment of interest expense is based upon the principle that money is fungible, such that interest is considered properly attributable to all a corporation's business activities and properties, regardless of the specific purpose for which the debt was incurred.

The current law also requires the allocation to be made on the basis of assets. Congress reasoned that interest expense should be allocated between U.S. and foreign income based on the proportion of U.S. to foreign asset values, as interest expense is related more closely to the amount of capital utilized in an activity than to the subsequent gross income generated.

This change in methodology has resulted in more interest expense being allocated to foreign source income than under prior law, effectively lowering foreign source income. Lower foreign source income, relative to worldwide income, decreases the FTC limitation.

This decrease in the FTC limitation reduces the amount of foreign taxes paid that can be credited against the U.S. tax liability, thus increasing U.S. taxes payable.

For corporations with foreign income, therefore, a tax penalty is associated with incurring additional recourse debt. Given that this penalty is the direct result of interest expense, U.S. corporations with foreign operations will need to modify their lease versus purchase (loan) analysis to reflect this penalty on interest. The lease rentals in a tax lease are not subject to foreign allocation although the rentals contain, in theory, an element of interest.

The following lease versus purchase (loan) analysis illustrates how the lease versus purchase decision is affected by the FTC. Assumptions include:

General assumptions
Equipment: computer system
Cost: 100,000
Inception date: January 1
Discount rate (after-tax cost of debt): 5.3625%
Tax rate: 35%
Foreign tax rate: assumed to be equal to or greater than the U.S. rate.

Lease information
Payments: five annual payments of 23,361, in arrears
Sales tax: 4% of each lease payment (24,295 total payment)
Purchase option: fair market value, not exercised.

Buy information
Loan structure: five annual payments of 25,211, in arrears, at 8.25%
Sales tax: 4% of cost (4,000)
MACRS: 5-year classlife
Estimated salvage value: 15,000.

Given these assumptions, the following present value comparison illustrates the base case lease versus purchase decision without taking the loss of FTC (due to interest allocation) into account. The present value of the cash flows (net cash cost) is:

Buy	64,663
Lease	(67,691)
Disadvantage to leasing	(3,028)

Lease

	HP-12C			HP-17B (#TIMES PROMPTING: ON)	
f	REG				FIN
5.3625	i				CFLO
15,792	g	CFj	■ CLEAR DATA		YES
5	g	Nj	FLOW (0)=?	0	INPUT
f	NPV 67,691		FLOW (1)=?	15,792	INPUT
			#TIMES (1)=1	5	INPUT
					EXIT
					CALC
				5.3625	I%
				NPV =	67,691

Loan

	HP-12C		HP-17B (#TIMES PROMPTING: OFF)	
	f REG			FIN
5.3625	i			CFLO
20,198	g CFj	■	CLEAR DATA	YES
12,124	g CFj	FLOW (0)=?	0	INPUT
17,101	g CFj	FLOW (1)=?	20,198	INPUT
20,241	g CFj	FLOW (2)=?	12,124	INPUT
8,768	g CFj	FLOW (3)=?	17,101	INPUT
	f NPV 67,889	FLOW (4)=?	20,241	INPUT
		FLOW (5)=?	8,768	INPUT
				EXIT
				CALC
			5.3625	I%
			NPV	= 67,889

Purchasing, in this example, has approximately a 5% (3,028 ÷ 64,663) advantage over leasing on a present value basis. However, if the loss of FTC due to interest allocation is taken into account, leasing is favored, as illustrated in the present value comparison of Exhibit 13-22. (This example assumes the ratio of U.S. to foreign assets is 60:40.)

	Without FTC	**With FTC**
Buy	64,663	67,889
Lease	(67,691)	(67,691)
Advantage to leasing	(3,028)	198
Decision	Buy	Lease

The penalty associated with incurring additional interest expense reverses the lease versus purchase decision in this example. It is important to note that this penalty increases as the percentage of a corporation's foreign assets relative to total assets increases. Because of the adverse impact of interest expense allocation on the FTC limitation, it becomes critical for corporations with foreign operations to analyze carefully the impact of any additional leverage incurred. The impact of existing debt and the associated interest expense also should be reconsidered.

Exhibit 13-22
FTC Comparison

Lease alternative

	1	2	3	4	5
Lease payments	24,295	24,295	24,295	24,295	24,295
x tax rate (.35)	(8,503)	(8,503)	(8,503)	(8,503)	(8,503)
Net cash cost	15,792	15,792	15,792	15,792	15,792

Buy alternative

	1	2	3	4	5
Down payment	0	0	0	0	0
Sales tax	4,000	0	0	0	0
Sales tax benefit	(280)	(448)	(269)	(161)	(81)
Loan payments	25,211	25,211	25,211	25,211	25,211
Interest tax benefit	(2,888)	(2,398)	(1,868)	(1,294)	(672)
MACRS tax benefit	(7,000)	(11,200)	(6,720)	(4,032)	(2,016)
Loss of FTC due to interest allocation [1]	1,155	959	747	517	269
Salvage value	0	0	0	0	(13,943)
Net cash cost	20,198	12,124	17,101	20,241	8,768

[1] The after-tax loss of FTC is computed as follows:

Year	Interest		Tax rate		Percentage of foreign assets		Loss of FTC
1	8,250	x	.35	x	.40	=	1,155
2	6,851	x	.35	x	.40	=	959
3	5,336	x	.35	x	.40	=	747
4	3,696	x	.35	x	.40	=	517
5	1,921	x	.35	x	.40	=	269

Several techniques may be used to manage the lessee's FTC problem: leasing, in lieu of purchasing, using nonrecourse debt to fund assets (as the interest is not subject to allocation[6]) and the use of sale-leaseback transactions. Sale-leasebacks on assets currently encumbered with recourse debt can be used to convert previously incurred interest expense to lease expense. All of the above items are methods of managing (i.e., minimizing) interest expense, and, thereby, maximizing the FTC limitation.

CONCLUSION

Lease versus buy is a decision that encompasses far more than a comparison of debt alternatives. Obsolescence avoidance, tax benefits and numerous other quantitative as well as qualitative costs impact the decision. The logic of the lease versus buy decision also requires an understanding of the appropriate discount rate, as well as whether the single rate or dual rate method should be used. Pulling together all the many factors presented in this chapter requires skill and knowledge, as the lease versus purchase decision is not only very complex, but also strategically important.

---

[6] Regulation §1.861-8(e)(2)(iv).

Chapter Fourteen

Lease Analysis

Many lessors go through elaborate pricing exercises to compute a payment that will meet their targeted yield or required return on investment. Pricing the lease, however, is only the starting point. The lease also must be monitored and analyzed over its term to determine if it is performing as anticipated. This process of measuring performance is called yield analysis.

Several methods are used for analyzing lease profitability. The method chosen by the lessor is a matter of its size, sophistication, management needs and available resources. Furthermore, most analytical techniques can be applied to single lease transactions as well as to entire portfolios of leases. The analytical issues presented in this chapter include:

- Approaches to Yield

- Types of Yields

- Yield Analysis

- Comparing Proposals.

APPROACHES TO YIELD

The method chosen to analyze lease profitability will depend on the decision-maker's goals and objectives. Lessor management must, therefore, carefully examine the characteristics of each yield method and choose that yield most appropriate for their needs. Most of the various analytical methods used in the leasing industry today fall under one of the five broad categories discussed in this section.

Yield-oriented Methods

Yield-oriented methods consist of internal rate of return (IRR) and external rate of return (ERR) analysis. These approaches are used to determine the yield, or interest rate, inherent in the cash flows in the lease. This rate of return is synonymous with the annual percentage rate (APR) that a bank would quote a borrower on a loan. The calculation of the IRR or ERR may include all cash flows from the lease, or may consider only selected cash flows. In addition, the rate can be calculated on either a pretax or after-tax basis as described later in this chapter.

In most cases, the yields used to measure profitability are based on an IRR. The IRR is defined as the discount rate that causes the present value of the cash inflows to be equal to the present value of the cash outflows. The IRR represents a constant earnings rate on the declining principal balance over the lease term. Another way of looking at the IRR is as a measure of the financial quality of the investment. For example, a lessor will identify a targeted IRR to be achieved in the lease. Transactions that meet this benchmark are approved, whereas those that do not are reworked or rejected.

When the lessor uses an IRR approach to yield analysis, it makes two assumptions: (1) all positive cash flows received by the lessor during the lease are reinvested at the IRR of the lease and (2) all negative cash flow needs are met from sinking funds that earn at the IRR of the lease. These assumptions may not hold true in the case of a leveraged lease or a lease with an IRR significantly different from other investment opportunities. The solution to this problem is to use an ERR that assumes a reinvestment rate that is different from the IRR.

Present and Future Value Methods

Calculating the net present value (NPV) of a series of future cash flows removes interest, or the time value of money, from the cash flows. This process, known as discounting, is used in lease analysis. The present value, using the targeted yield as the discount rate, is compared to the original investment. If the present value is greater than or equal to the investment in equipment, the lease is profitable. If the present value is less than the investment, the profitability has been impaired.

Future value methods, sometimes referred to as terminal value analysis (TVA), add reinvestment earnings to the lease cash flows (compounding). The future, or terminal value, is compared to the future value of the original investment. These methods may utilize single or multiple growth rates.

Calculating the NPV or TVA of the lease requires an interest appreciation or discount rate. The actual rate used by lessors varies depending on the particular financial philosophy of the company. A common rate selected is the rate that represents the earnings required by the lessor to justify a particular investment. This rate can be developed by adding operating costs and profit, expressed as a percentage, to the lessor's cost of funds. It commonly is referred to as the hurdle rate, target rate or opportunity rate.

Managerial-oriented Indices

Management is concerned with a variety of issues as it evaluates the performance of the leasing company. As a result, many methods are used to evaluate leases and to address the goals of management. Common managerial-oriented indices include accounting rates of return, cash flow rules of thumb, risk-adjusted return on assets, interest spread analysis and interest accretion. Some techniques, such as payback, measure the time to receive actual cash flow (undiscounted) equal to the investment. These techniques emphasize time at-risk rather than profitability.

Managerial-oriented techniques are not necessarily an accurate reflection of the economic return of the lease, but they are valuable measurement tools for management. For example, two leases with identical IRRs and NPVs can have very different undiscounted net cash flows, which is important to the company when evaluating future cash flow needs. Accounting reported earnings also are important to stockholders and management in terms of earnings per share impact. Although earnings per share does not reflect the actual economic return of the lease, it frequently is evaluated because of the impact on the company's share value.

Marketing-related Techniques

Marketing-related analytical techniques are greatly influenced by industry norms and often reflect the marketing department's attempt to tell the potential lessee what it wants to hear. Because the lessee typically wants to pay the lowest interest rate possible, lessors quote such rates as the street rate, running or stream rates and the lessee's effective or apparent rates.

From a purely economic standpoint, these market rates are incomplete. They frequently ignore such important rate ingredients as tax benefits, residual value, number of advance payments, interim rent, contingent rentals, etc. Although marketing-based yields are incomplete, they are, nevertheless, useful as a tool to compare the relative cost of one lease to another. For example, two lessors may both offer the lessee 48-month leases with equal fees, payments in advance and fair market value purchase options.

If all other variables are the same, the lessee could make a decision regarding the lowest cost lease simply by comparing the street rates. However, leases frequently have variables that differ, making a comparison of quoted rates not valid. In addition, some forms of rate quotes, such as add-on or discount interest, so understate the actual interest cost to the lessee that they are misleading.

What this means to the lessee is that it must do more than simply learn the terminology and the definition of different rates. Because all lessors do not define the same rate in the same way, care must be taken by the lessee to understand the variables used by the lessor when it quotes a rate.

Integrated Approaches

Integrated approaches have been developed because of the variety of conflicting goals within the leasing organization. These methods attempt to optimize overall profitability by prioritizing goals. Economic yield should be maximized simultaneously with the accounting return, cash flow and risk. Integrated approaches deal with balancing the trade-offs that usually occur between these variables. For example, a lessor may decide to give up some economic earnings in order to improve cash flow essential to continued operations. Additionally, this improved cash flow may reduce the credit risk associated with the lease.

It is important for a lessor to evaluate and prioritize profitability goals and objectives in order to develop an appropriate integrated method. All goals cannot be maximized at the same time, and no perfect method exists for evaluating the profitability of the lease. However, integrated approaches can give the analyst a better overall answer than any particular method used in isolation.

Integrated analytical methods of whatever type must deal with two distinct aspects of profitability analysis: quality and quantity. Quality of earnings (NPV, etc.) implies that:

1. Cash flows subject to uncertainty have been risk adjusted. For example, lease cash flows that are not contractually agreed to, such as tax benefits, residual values and contingent rentals, are subject to different risks than the lease payments

2. Other risks, such as general lessee credit risk (allowance for doubtful accounts) and the tax consequences of lessee default under a leveraged lease, have been identified and quantified

3. The appropriate decision method has been used in light of the reinvestment opportunities available to the lessor

4. The required return has been reached or exceeded.

Quantity of earnings implies that sufficient amounts of cash flow and accounting reported earnings have been generated. Examples of integrated methods are debt optimized IRR and cash flow, ERR with optimized cash flow and accounting earnings, and NPV with optimized cash flow and accounting earnings.

TYPES OF YIELDS

Many different types of yields can be calculated for any given lease. These yields are calculated on several different levels and include various characteristics. The type of yield calculated is a function of what the analyst is trying to accomplish. Types of yields include gross, net, pretax, after-tax, return on assets (ROA), return on investment (ROI), return on equity (ROE) and IRR or ERR analysis. Furthermore, the characteristics of several of these yields may be combined (e.g., a net, after-tax ROE calculated on an IRR basis).

Gross Versus Net Yields

Leases may be analyzed on a gross or a net basis. Gross yield analysis takes into consideration pretax lease payments and, possibly, the anticipated residual value. Typically, gross yield analysis ignores the following elements of the lease, although there is no firm definition of what must or must not be included:

1. Initial direct costs (such as commissions, credit checks, etc.)

2. General and administrative (G&A) expenses and other overhead costs

3. Interest expense on the debt used to fund the lease

4. Tax benefits

5. Origination fees

6. Interim rent

7. Allowance for doubtful accounts.

Gross analysis most commonly is used in competitive analysis with other leasing companies in which the omitted items are seldom known by the lessee anyway.

Net analysis includes most or all of the above expenses that impact cash flow. G&A or interest expense sometimes is not included in net analysis. A net analysis, incorporating all cash flows, is utilized by lessors to perform the cost accounting analysis necessary for determining the true, overall profitability of a lease.

Pretax Versus After-tax Yields

Leases also can be analyzed either before or after tax consequences are considered. After-tax analysis takes into account all relevant tax benefits and expenses, such as the tax on the rents, tax depreciation, gross profit tax deferral, taxes on residual disposition and any alternative minimum tax (AMT) problems, etc.

Pretax analysis, on the other hand, deals with tax considerations by either ignoring them or converting the tax benefits and expenses to their pretax equivalents. Conversion to a pretax equivalent can be accomplished by either (1) dividing the after-tax cash flows by one minus the tax rate or (2) utilizing a more complex method that includes the impact of the timing of when taxes are actually remitted.

ROA, ROE and ROI Yields

The yield in a lease represents the relationship between the return being generated by an investment and the investment itself. The return can be measured in several ways and at different levels of completeness. By the same token, the investment can be defined in different ways.

When a lessor buys an asset, it does so with both debt and equity funds. Any income earned by that asset, therefore, belongs to the debt and equity holders. The ROA measures the return on the total assets invested in the lease. This return represents the earnings, after-tax, but before any interest has been paid to the debt holders (sometimes referred to as EBI).

ROE measures the return on the equity investment after the debt portion of the investment has received its return (the interest expense on the debt). The definition of the return in the ROE is the EBI less interest expense. The investment is the actual equity invested in the asset. An ROE considers the amount of the debt used to fund the asset, the cost of that debt and how the debt is repaid. The ROA and ROE, using the income statement and balance sheet of Exhibit 14-1, are calculated as follows:

$$ROA = \frac{EBI}{Assets} = \frac{4{,}125}{55{,}000} = 7.50\%$$

$$ROE = \frac{Net\ income}{Equity} = \frac{1{,}100}{6{,}600} = 16.67\%$$

ROI is a commonly used measure in the leasing industry and is a hybrid of the ROA and the ROE. Its popularity stems from its wide usage in the banking industry, an industry from which many leasing personnel have come. The return in the ROI calculation is defined as the EBI less interest expense, just as in the ROE. The investment, on the other hand, is the total assets invested in the lease, as in the ROA. Based on the information in Exhibit 14-1, the ROI is 2.00%

$$\frac{1{,}100}{55{,}000} = 2.00\%$$

Exhibit 14-1
Financial Information

Income statement

After-tax income before interest	4,125
After-tax interest expense	(3,025)
Net income	1,100

Balance sheet

Assets	55,000
Debt (costing 6.25%, after-tax)	48,400
Equity	6,600
Debt and equity	55,000

Although the ROA, ROE and ROI in this example are presented as static measures, they should incorporate the time value of the cash flows, such as through an IRR calculation. Subsequent examples in this chapter illustrate this concept.

IRR Versus ERR Yields

The IRR, which is the unique discount rate that equates the present value of the cash inflows to the present value of the cash outflows, is the most common method used to compute yields. Although the IRR is commonly used, in certain circumstances the IRR approach to yield analysis is inadequate and ERR analysis is required.

The IRR is calculated based on the assumption that all cash flows (inflows and outflows) have the same reinvestment opportunity or cost. This is not always the case. In some circumstances, such as in leveraged leases, an assumed reinvestment rate different from the IRR of the lease is required. A more complete discussion of ERR analysis is included later in this chapter.

YIELD ANALYSIS

The following example is used to illustrate the various yield calculations presented in this chapter. The assumptions used in this example include:

Lease inception date: January 1

Equipment cost: 100,000 (paid at lease inception)

Tax depreciation: over six tax years (20%, 32%, 19.2%, 11.52%, 11.52% and 5.76% in years one through six, respectively

Payments: 48 monthly payments, in advance, of 2,396.09

Refundable security deposit: 4,000

Income tax rate: 35%

Tax remittance dates: 25% of the total liability is due in March, June, September and December of the current year

Residual value: 20,000, at the end of month 48

Initial direct costs: 2,500, tax deductible in the first tax year

G & A costs: 6,000, spread monthly over the lease term

Bad debt costs: 3,750, spread monthly over the lease term.

Gross, Pretax Yields

Gross, pretax yields measure the basic, pretax cash flows of a lease. The industry often refers to these rates as street rates, running rates, stream rates, lessee effective rates, etc. The distinction between these rates and more complex yields is the components included (or excluded, as the case may be) in the calculation. The types of cash flows in the various pretax yields include lease payments, advance payments, initial direct costs and residual expectations. All pretax yields, of course, ignore the impact of taxation.

The three most common gross, pretax yields are the street rate, the modified street rate and the all-inclusive rate. Variations of these yields may be calculated by including additional or fewer pretax cash flows in the analysis. Occasionally, other pretax yields, such as the Rule of 78 and add-on rates, are used.

STREET RATE

The street rate is the most basic of the lease yields that can be calculated. It represents the lease yield equivalent of the lowest common denominator. As such, the street rate is the yield most often quoted by lessors to lessees. It also may be used by lessors when doing simplified analysis. Because the street rate ignores any residual assumptions built into the payment structure, the yield may even be negative.

When calculating a street rate, the periodic payments and the initial investment are the only cash flows considered. All others are ignored.

Includes: Initial investment and periodic payments

Excludes: Refundable security deposits, purchase options, closing fees, initial direct costs, operating expenses, income tax payments, tax depreciation and tax timing.

When a lessee compares lessors' street rates for a piece of equipment, it is, in essence, comparing only the benefit of the equipment being received to the payments it (the lessee) is required to make. Even the timing impact, such as that attributable to advance payments, is ignored. As mentioned, the street rate puts the analysis of competitive rates on the lowest possible level.

Inception cash flows	Subsequent cash flows	Termination cash flows
(100,000) equipment cost	48 payments at 2,396.09	0

Based on these cash flows, with payments in advance, the monthly yield is 0.5860% and the annual street rate is 7.0316%.

HP-12C			HP-17B (12 P/YR END MODE)	
g	END		FIN	
f	REG		TVM	
100,000 CHS	PV		■ CLEAR DATA	
2,396.09	PMT		100,000 +/-	PV
48	n		2,396.09	PMT
	i	.5860	48	N
12	x	7.0316	I%YR = 7.0316	

MODIFIED STREET RATE

Sometimes the calculation of the street rate is modified to include the impact of advance payments. The modified street rate is not identified as such; instead, even with the advance payments included, it is still referred to as a street rate. As a result, lessees may receive street rate quotes based on different cash flows. Lessors should be careful, therefore, to identify whether the competition is quoting lease costs using a street rate or a modified street rate.

Cash flows		Cash flows	Cash flows
(100,000.00)	equipment cost	47 payments	0
2,396.09	advance payment	at 2,396.09	
(97,603.91)	net outflow		

Based on these cash flows, with payments in advance, the monthly yield is 0.6123% and the annual modified street rate is 7.3471%. By including the advance payment in the analysis, the yield increased by 31.55 basis points. The modified street rate is considered by some lessors to be the most accurate street rate.

HP-12C			HP-17B (12 P/YR END MODE)	
g	END		FIN	
f	REG		TVM	
97,603.91 CHS	PV		■ CLEAR DATA	
2,396.09	PMT		97,603.91 +/-	PV
47	n		2,396.09	PMT
	i	.6123	47	n
12	x	7.3471	I% YR = 7.3471	

ALL-INCLUSIVE RATE

Most lessors rarely quote an all-inclusive gross, pretax yield to their lessees because this yield is (1) much higher than the street rate and (2) the lessee can use it to determine the lessor's residual assumption. Of the three types of gross, pretax yields discussed here, however, the all-inclusive rate most accurately portrays the true yield of the lessor.

Includes: Initial investment, periodic payments, advance payments, refundable security deposits, purchase options, closing fees and initial direct costs

Excludes: Operating expenses, income taxes on revenues, tax depreciation and tax timing.

The cash flows and their timing for the all-inclusive yield are shown below.

Inception cash flows		Subsequent cash flows		Termination cash flows	
(100,000.00)	equipment cost	47 payments		(4,000)	deposit refund
2,396.09	advance payment	at 2,396.09		20,000	purchase option
4,000.00	refundable security deposit			16,000	net inflow
(2,500.00)	initial direct costs				
(96,103.91)	net outflow				

Based on these cash flows, the monthly yield is 1.1397% and the annual all-inclusive gross, pretax yield is 13.6760%.

HP-12C			**HP-17B (#TIMES PROMPTING: ON)**		
	f	REG			FIN
96,103.91	CHS g	CFo			CFLO
2,396.09	g	CFj	■ CLEAR DATA		YES
47	g	Nj	FLOW (0)=? 96,103.91	+/-	INPUT
16,000	g	CFj	FLOW (1)=? 2,396.09		INPUT
	f	IRR 1.1397	#TIMES (1)=1	47	INPUT
12	x	13.6760	FLOW (2)=?	16,000	INPUT
			#TIMES (2)=1	1	INPUT
					EXIT
					CALC
			IRR% =1.1397		
			x 12	=	13.6760

As was mentioned, many different yields can be calculated for any given lease. Three of these yields, on a pretax basis, have been discussed. Note the differences in results between the three methods of computing the yields.

Street rate	7.0316%
Modified street rate	7.3471%
All-inclusive gross, pretax yield	13.6760%

Before going on to after-tax yields, two more pretax yields, the Rule of 78 and add-on interest yields, are presented.

RULE OF 78

The Rule of 78 yield is a pretax yield. It allocates total interest based on a formula that determines each month's interest earned. The total pretax earnings of 32,512.32 in the sample lease on page 462 are used in this illustration. The formula is:

$$\frac{\text{Number of months in reverse order}}{\frac{n\,(n+1)}{2}} \qquad \text{x} \qquad \text{Total interest,}$$

where n = total number of months in the lease.

The first month's interest, therefore, is:

$$\left(\frac{48}{\frac{48\,(48+1)}{2}} \right) \qquad \text{x} \qquad 32{,}512.32$$

$$\frac{48}{1{,}176} \qquad \text{x} \qquad 32{,}512.32 \qquad = \qquad 1{,}327.03$$

The second month's interest is:

$$\frac{47}{1{,}176} \qquad \text{x} \qquad 32{,}512.32 \qquad = \qquad 1{,}299.39$$

To complete a full amortization, which is beyond the scope of this discussion, the numerator is decreased by one each month. The Rule of 78 method of income allocation overstates income early in the lease and understates it later in the lease.

ADD-ON INTEREST

Add-on, or discount, interest rates seldom are quoted to lessees anymore, except abroad and sometimes for certain agricultural equipment. They are used almost exclusively with finance leases. Occasionally, however, lessees will request such quotes for comparative purposes. The following is a description of the computation of add-on interest in a hypothetical 60-month lease.

First, the implied interest is computed

Advance payment	2,000
Remaining payments	118,000
Total costs to the lessee	120,000
Less equipment cost	(100,000)
Implied interest	20,000

Next, the implied interest is divided by the months in the lease

$$\frac{20,000}{60} = 333.33 \text{ interest per month}$$

Finally, the monthly interest (times 12) is divided by the cost of the equipment

$$\frac{333.33}{100,000} \quad \text{x} \quad 12 \quad = \quad 4.000\% \text{ (add-on interest cost)}$$

An approximation of the pretax, actuarial yield can be derived by doubling the quoted add-on interest and subtracting one. This rule-of-thumb provides an approximate conversion to the true, pretax interest rate in the lease of 7.69%.

$$4.000 \times 2 = 8.000 - 1 = 7.000$$

Net, After-tax Yields

Some yields are calculated on a pretax basis. These pretax yields do not accurately reflect the true economics of the transaction, however, because they do not consider the tax attributes of the cash flows. Net, after-tax yields consider the tax attributes of the cash flows. In this respect, they are more accurate than the pretax yields. Several after-tax yields can be calculated, the most common of which are the ROA and the ROE.

NET, AFTER-TAX ROA

A net, after-tax ROA measures the yield the leased asset generates before allocating any of the return to the debt or equity holders. It is based on the net, after-tax cash flows from the asset. Exhibit 14-2 shows the net, after-tax cash flows generated by the sample lease. The cash flows shown are considered net because they include expenses such as G & A and initial direct costs. The cash flows are on an after-tax basis because they include tax expense and tax benefits. Furthermore, tax timing has been included because all the tax expenses and benefits have been allocated to the quarterly estimated tax payment dates.

The after-tax ROA generated by this lease is .55532 per month or 6.6638% per year. This yield can be compared to the pretax, all-inclusive yield of 13.6760%. Exhibit 14-3 includes the HP-17B keystrokes necessary to solve for this yield.

NET, AFTER-TAX ROE

Lessors pay for their assets through a combination of debt and equity funds. Because a substantial portion of the asset's cost is borrowed from a third party, the lessor pays for only a portion of the asset's cost. This portion is the equity. The after-tax ROE yield measures the lessor's return on its equity investment. An after-tax ROE is the most detailed yield that can be computed.

The computation of an ROE requires additional information such as the amount and cost of the debt used to finance the lease. The ROE also is impacted by how the debt is repaid. Is the debt paid back in a manner that maintains a constant debt-to-equity ratio, or with level loan payments over the same term as the lease payments?

Constant Debt-to-equity

Assume the lessor's cost of debt is 9% over the lease term. Furthermore, 88.89% of the asset's net cash cost is funded with debt and a constant debt-to-equity ratio is maintained throughout the lease term. A simple formula for constant debt-to-equity funding can be used to convert an ROA to an approximate ROE. A more accurate method is described later. For example,

$$RODw + ROEw = ROA, \text{ where}$$

RODw = weighted, average after-tax return on debt
ROEw = weighted, average after-tax return on equity
ROA = total after-tax return on assets.

Exhibit 14-2
ROA Cash Flow

Period	Rent/ residual	G&A	Bad debt expenses	Deposit/ IDC	Taxes	Total cash flow
0	2,396	-	-	(98,500)		(96,104)
1	2,396	(167)	(104)	-		2,125
2	2,396	(167)	(104)	-		2,125
3	2,396	(167)	(104)	-		2,125
4	2,396	(167)	(104)	-	(263)	1,862
5	2,396	(167)	(104)	-		2,125
6	2,396	(167)	(104)	-	(263)	1,862
7	2,396	(167)	(104)	-		2,125
8	2,396	(167)	(104)	-		2,125
9	2,396	(167)	(104)	-	(263)	1,862
10	2,396	(167)	(104)	-		2,125
11	2,396	(167)	(104)	-		2,125
12	2,396	(167)	(104)	-	(263)	1,862
13	2,396	(146)	(88)	-		2,163
14	2,396	(146)	(88)	-		2,163
15	2,396	(146)	(88)	-		2,163
16	2,396	(146)	(88)	-	529	2,692
17	2,396	(146)	(88)	-		2,163
18	2,396	(146)	(88)	-	529	2,692
19	2,396	(146)	(88)	-		2,163
20	2,396	(146)	(88)	-		2,163
21	2,396	(146)	(88)	-	529	2,692
22	2,396	(146)	(88)	-		2,163
23	2,396	(146)	(88)	-		2,163
24	2,396	(146)	(88)	-	529	2,692
25	2,396	(104)	(67)	-		2,225
26	2,396	(104)	(67)	-		2,225
27	2,396	(104)	(67)	-		2,225
28	2,396	(104)	(67)	-	(657)	1,569
29	2,396	(104)	(67)	-		2,225
30	2,396	(104)	(67)	-	(657)	1,569
31	2,396	(104)	(67)	-		2,225
32	2,396	(104)	(67)	-		2,225
33	2,396	(104)	(67)	-	(657)	1,569
34	2,396	(104)	(67)	-		2,225
35	2,396	(104)	(67)	-		2,225
36	2,396	(104)	(67)	-	(657)	1,569
37	2,396	(83)	(54)	-		2,259
38	2,396	(83)	(54)	-		2,259
39	2,396	(83)	(54)	-		2,259
40	2,396	(83)	(54)	-	(1,602)	657
41	2,396	(83)	(54)	-		2,259
42	2,396	(83)	(54)	-	(1,602)	657
43	2,396	(83)	(54)	-		2,259
44	2,396	(83)	(54)	-		2,259
45	2,396	(83)	(54)	-	(1,602)	657
46	2,396	(83)	(54)	-		2,259
47	2,396	(83)	(54)	-		2,259
48	20,000	(83)	(54)	(4,000)	(1,602)	14,261
Total	135,008	(6,000)	(3,756)	(102,500)	(7,972)	14,796

Exhibit 14-3
Net, After-tax ROA Solution (HP-17B)

```
FIN
CFLO (#TIMES PROMPTING: ON)
FLOW (0)=?              96,104     +/-    INPUT
FLOW (1)=?              2,125             INPUT
#TIMES (1)=1               3              INPUT
FLOW (2)=?              1,862             INPUT
#TIMES (2)=1               1              INPUT
FLOW (3)=?              2,125             INPUT
#TIMES (3)=1               1              INPUT
FLOW (4)=?              1,862             INPUT
#TIMES (4)=1               1              INPUT
FLOW (5)=?              2,125             INPUT
#TIMES (5)=1               2              INPUT
FLOW (6)=?              1,862             INPUT
#TIMES (6)=1               1              INPUT
FLOW (7)=?              2,125             INPUT
#TIMES (7)=1               2              INPUT
FLOW (8)=?              1,862             INPUT
#TIMES (8)=1               1              INPUT
FLOW (9)=?              2,163             INPUT
#TIMES (9)=1               3              INPUT
FLOW (10)=?            2,692             INPUT
#TIMES (10)=1             1              INPUT
FLOW (11)=?            2,163             INPUT
#TIMES (11)=1             1              INPUT
FLOW (12)=?            2,692             INPUT
#TIMES (12)=1             1              INPUT
FLOW (13)=?            2,163             INPUT
#TIMES (13)=1             2              INPUT
FLOW (14)=?            2,692             INPUT
#TIMES (14)=1             1              INPUT
FLOW (15)=?            2,163             INPUT
#TIMES (15)=1             2              INPUT
FLOW (16)=?            2,692             INPUT
#TIMES (16)=1             1              INPUT
FLOW (17)=?            2,225             INPUT
#TIMES (17)=1             3              INPUT
FLOW (18)=?            1,569             INPUT
#TIMES (18)=1             1              INPUT
FLOW (19)=?            2,225             INPUT
#TIMES (19)=1             1              INPUT
FLOW (20)=?            1,569             INPUT
#TIMES (20)=1             1              INPUT
FLOW (21)=?            2,225             INPUT
#TIMES (21)=1             2              INPUT
FLOW (22)=?            1,569             INPUT
#TIMES (22)=1             1              INPUT
FLOW (23)=?            2,225             INPUT
#TIMES (23)=1             2              INPUT
FLOW (24)=?            1,569             INPUT
#TIMES (24)=1             1              INPUT
FLOW (25)=?            2,259             INPUT
#TIMES (25)=1             3              INPUT
FLOW (26)=?              657             INPUT
#TIMES (26)=1             1              INPUT
FLOW (27)=?            2,259             INPUT
#TIMES (27)=1             1              INPUT
FLOW (28)=?              657             INPUT
#TIMES (28)=1             1              INPUT
FLOW (29)=?            2,259             INPUT
#TIMES (29)=1             2              INPUT
FLOW (30)=?              657             INPUT
#TIMES (30)=1             1              INPUT
FLOW (31)=?            2,259             INPUT
#TIMES (31)=1             2              INPUT
FLOW (32)=?           14,261             INPUT
#TIMES (32)=1             1              INPUT
EXIT                   CALC      TOTAL  14,796
IRR% = .55532
x    12   =    6.66378
```

More specifically, the equation can be shown in the following model.

	Leverage		**Cost/return**		**Tax effect**		**Total**
Debt	debt portion	x	pretax ROD	x	(1-tax rate)	=	RODw
Equity	equity portion	x	after-tax ROE	x	n/a	=	ROEw
							ROA

Since the after-tax ROA of 6.6638% already has been calculated, the ROEw can be computed by replacing the variables in the model with the components that are known.

	Leverage		**Cost/return**		**Tax effect**		**Total**
Debt	.8889	x	9%	x	.65	=	5.2001%
Equity	.1111	x	**ROE**	x	n/a	=	ROEw
							6.6638%

The ROEw of 1.4637% is calculated by subtracting 5.2001% from 6.6638%. Replacing ROEw with 1.4637% and dividing it by .1111 (the equity portion) results in an ROE of 13.1749%. The completed model is as follows, and shows the lease earning a 13.1749% ROE per year, after-tax:

	Leverage		**Cost/return**		**Tax effect**		**Total**
Debt	.8889	x	9%	x	.65	=	5.2001%
Equity	.1111	x	**13.1749%**	x	n/a	=	1.4637
							6.6638%

The inaccuracies of this approximation approach relate to the implicit assumptions that (1) the company constantly maintains debt at 88.89% of its total assets (most companies would do so only at the end of each quarter) and (2) the tax benefits on the interest expense are received concurrently with the payment of interest. In reality, the interest tax benefits are spread over the lessor's estimated tax payment dates.

A more precise ROE can be computed based on the after-tax, equity cash flows. These cash flows incorporate a debt schedule that maintains a constant debt-to-equity ratio each month and also the timing of when interest tax benefits are actually received. The first step in this process requires amortizing the net investment in the lease using the after-tax ROA and cash flows. The amortization schedule of the net investment in the lease at the end of each month is shown in Exhibit 14-4.

The loan balance (Exhibit 14-5) can be derived from this amortization schedule because the loan balance always is assumed to be 88.89% of the net investment. Given the loan balances, the loan amortization is calculat-

Exhibit 14-4
Net Investment Amortization

Period	ROA cash flows	Interest	Principal	Balance
0	(96,104)	-		96,104.00
1	2,125	533.68	1,591.32	94,512.68
2	2,125	524.84	1,600.16	92,912.52
3	2,125	515.96	1,609.04	91,303.48
4	1,862	507.02	1,354.98	89,948.50
5	2,125	499.50	1,625.50	88,323.00
6	1,862	490.47	1,371.53	86,951.47
7	2,125	482.85	1,642.15	85,309.33
8	2,125	473.74	1,651.26	83,658.06
9	1,862	464.57	1,397.43	82,260.63
10	2,125	456.81	1,668.19	80,592.44
11	2,125	447.54	1,677.46	78,914.98
12	1,862	438.23	1,423.77	77,491.20
13	2,163	430.32	1,732.68	75,758.53
14	2,163	420.70	1,742.30	74,016.22
15	2,163	411.02	1,751.98	72,264.25
16	2,692	401.29	2,290.71	69,973.54
17	2,163	388.57	1,774.43	68,199.12
18	2,692	378.72	2,313.28	65,885.84
19	2,163	365.87	1,797.13	64,088.71
20	2,163	355.89	1,807.11	62,281.60
21	2,692	345.86	2,346.14	59,935.46
22	2,163	332.83	1,830.17	58,105.29
23	2,163	322.67	1,840.33	56,264.96
24	2,692	312.45	2,379.55	53,885.41
25	2,225	299.23	1,925.77	51,959.64
26	2,225	288.54	1,936.46	50,023.18
27	2,225	277.79	1,947.21	48,075.97
28	1,569	266.97	1,302.03	46,773.94
29	2,225	259.74	1,965.26	44,808.69
30	1,569	248.83	1,320.17	43,488.52
31	2,225	241.50	1,983.50	41,505.01
32	2,225	230.48	1,994.52	39,510.50
33	1,569	219.41	1,349.59	38,160.91
34	2,225	211.91	2,013.09	36,147.82
35	2,225	200.73	2,024.27	34,123.55
36	1,569	189.49	1,379.51	32,744.05
37	2,259	181.83	2,077.17	30,666.88
38	2,259	170.30	2,088.70	28,578.18
39	2,259	158.70	2,100.30	26,477.88
40	657	147.04	509.96	25,967.91
41	2,259	144.20	2,114.80	23,853.12
42	657	132.46	524.54	23,328.58
43	2,259	129.55	2,129.45	21,199.12
44	2,259	117.72	2,141.28	19,057.85
45	657	105.83	551.17	18,506.68
46	2,259	102.77	2,156.23	16,350.45
47	2,259	90.80	2,168.20	14,182.24
48	14,261	78.76	14,182.24	0.00
Total	14,796			

Exhibit 14-5
Loan Balances

Period	Net investment balance[1]	Constant debt %	Loan balance
0	96,104.00	x .8889	85,426.85
1	94,512.68	x .8889	84,012.32
2	92,912.52	x .8889	82,589.94
3	91,303.48	x .8889	81,159.66
4	89,948.50	x .8889	79,955.22
5	88,323.00	x .8889	78,510.32
6	86,951.47	x .8889	77,291.16
7	85,309.33	x .8889	75,831.46
8	83,658.06	x .8889	74,363.65
9	82,260.63	x .8889	73,121.47
10	80,592.44	x .8889	71,638.62
11	78,914.98	x .8889	70,147.52
12	77,491.20	x .8889	68,881.93
13	75,758.53	x .8889	67,341.75
14	74,016.22	x .8889	65,793.02
15	72,264.25	x .8889	64,235.69
16	69,973.54	x .8889	62,199.48
17	68,199.12	x .8889	60,622.19
18	65,885.84	x .8889	58,565.92
19	64,088.71	x .8889	56,968.45
20	62,281.60	x .8889	55,362.12
21	59,935.46	x .8889	53,276.63
22	58,105.29	x .8889	51,649.80
23	56,264.96	x .8889	50,013.92
24	53,885.41	x .8889	47,898.74
25	51,959.64	x .8889	46,186.93
26	50,023.18	x .8889	44,465.61
27	48,075.97	x .8889	42,734.73
28	46,773.94	x .8889	41,577.36
29	44,808.69	x .8889	39,830.44
30	43,488.52	x .8889	38,656.94
31	41,505.01	x .8889	36,893.81
32	39,510.50	x .8889	35,120.88
33	38,160.91	x .8889	33,921.23
34	36,147.82	x .8889	32,131.80
35	34,123.55	x .8889	30,332.43
36	32,744.05	x .8889	29,106.18
37	30,666.88	x .8889	27,259.79
38	28,578.18	x .8889	25,403.14
39	26,477.88	x .8889	23,536.18
40	25,967.91	x .8889	23,082.88
41	23,853.12	x .8889	21,203.04
42	23,328.58	x .8889	20,736.77
43	21,199.12	x .8889	18,843.90
44	19,057.85	x .8889	16,940.52
45	18,506.68	x .8889	16,450.59
46	16,350.45	x .8889	14,533.91
47	14,182.24	x .8889	12,606.60
48	0.00	-	0.00

[1] From Exhibit 14-4

ed in Exhibit 14-6. The loan principal paid is the difference between the monthly loan balances in Exhibit 14-5. The total loan payment is calculated by adding the loan principal to the interest as shown in Exhibit 14-6.

This exhibit provides sufficient information to solve for the after-tax, equity cash flows in the lease, which are included in Exhibit 14-7. Once these after-tax, after-debt service cash flows are known, the net after-tax ROE for the lease, maintaining a constant debt-to-equity ratio, is determined using the HP-17B (Exhibit 14-8).

The more accurate ROE is 42.54 basis points lower than the approximate ROE previously calculated (13.1749% - 12.7495%). Obviously, a computer makes this calculation much easier and an analyst would never be running lease yields on the portfolio by hand. The purpose of the preceding discussion, therefore, is to describe the logic underlying what the software is doing in the lease analysis.

Level Debt Service

The previous ROE assumed the debt balance always remained at a constant percentage of the monthly net investment in the lease. Not all lessors can fund themselves in this manner, however. Some lessors must use debt that is repaid according to an amortization schedule required by the creditor, which usually is fixed equal payments over the lease term. Such a debt amortization seldom maintains a constant debt-to-equity relationship.

In order to understand how level payment funding alters the ROE, another example is used. Using the sample lease, the level payment debt service (Exhibit 14-9) is deducted from the lease cash flow and the interest tax benefits are added back in the same manner as was done for the constant debt-to-equity ROE. This process is illustrated in Exhibit 14-10. The following assumptions are used to illustrate this point:

Cost of debt: 9% (or .75% monthly)

Payments: 48 payments, in arrears, of 2,125.85.

Given the after-tax, ROE cash flows of Exhibit 14-10, the net, after-tax ROE of the lease can be computed, as shown in Exhibit 14-11. The level payment ROE of 10.67281% is lower than the constant debt-to-equity ROE of 12.7495%. Why does this difference exist? Both funding methods have the same beginning principal balance of 85,426.85, and both loans have 9% interest rates. Why did one method of funding generate an increase in yield?

Exhibit 14-6
Debt Service (Pooled)

Period	Balance[1]	Interest	Principal
0	85,426.85	-	85,426.85
1	84,012.32	640.70	1,414.52
2	82,589.94	630.09	1,422.38
3	81,159.66	619.42	1,430.28
4	79,955.22	608.70	1,204.44
5	78,510.32	599.66	1,444.91
6	77,291.16	588.83	1,219.15
7	75,831.46	579.68	1,459.70
8	74,363.65	568.74	1,467.81
9	73,121.47	557.73	1,242.18
10	71,638.62	548.41	1,482.86
11	70,147.52	537.29	1,491.09
12	68,881.93	526.11	1,265.59
13	67,341.75	516.61	1,540.18
14	65,793.02	505.06	1,548.73
15	64,235.69	493.45	1,557.33
16	62,199.48	481.77	2,036.21
17	60,622.19	466.50	1,577.29
18	58,565.92	454.67	2,056.27
19	56,968.45	439.24	1,597.47
20	55,362.12	427.26	1,606.34
21	53,276.63	415.22	2,085.48
22	51,649.80	399.57	1,626.84
23	50,013.92	387.37	1,635.87
24	47,898.74	375.10	2,115.18
25	46,186.93	359.24	1,711.81
26	44,465.61	346.40	1,721.32
27	42,734.73	333.49	1,730.88
28	41,577.36	320.51	1,157.37
29	39,830.44	311.83	1,746.92
30	38,656.94	298.73	1,173.50
31	36,893.81	289.93	1,763.13
32	35,120.88	276.70	1,772.93
33	33,921.23	263.41	1,199.65
34	32,131.80	254.41	1,789.43
35	30,332.43	240.99	1,799.37
36	29,106.18	227.49	1,226.24
37	27,259.79	218.30	1,846.39
38	25,403.14	204.45	1,856.65
39	23,536.18	190.52	1,866.96
40	23,082.88	176.52	453.31
41	21,203.04	173.12	1,879.84
42	20,736.77	159.02	466.26
43	18,843.90	155.53	1,892.87
44	16,940.52	141.33	1,903.38
45	16,450.59	127.05	489.93
46	14,533.91	123.38	1,916.67
47	12,606.60	109.00	1,927.32
48	0.00	94.55	12,606.60

[1] From Exhibit 14-5

Exhibit 14-7
ROE Cash Flow (Pooled)

Period	ROA cash flows	Interest	Principal	Taxes	ROE cash flows
0	(96,104)	-	85,426.85		(10,677.15)
1	2,125	(640.70)	(1,414.52)		69.77
2	2,125	(630.09)	(1,422.38)		72.53
3	2,125	(619.42)	(1,430.28)		75.30
4	1,862	(608.70)	(1,204.44)	612.97	661.83
5	2,125	(599.66)	(1,444.91)		80.43
6	1,862	(588.83)	(1,219.15)	612.97	666.99
7	2,125	(579.68)	(1,459.70)		85.61
8	2,125	(568.74)	(1,467.81)		88.46
9	1,862	(557.73)	(1,242.18)	612.97	675.06
10	2,125	(548.41)	(1,482.86)		93.73
11	2,125	(537.29)	(1,491.09)		96.62
12	1,862	(526.11)	(1,265.59)	612.97	683.27
13	2,163	(516.61)	(1,540.18)		106.21
14	2,163	(505.06)	(1,548.73)		109.21
15	2,163	(493.45)	(1,557.33)		112.22
16	2,692	(481.77)	(2,036.21)	469.16	643.18
17	2,163	(466.50)	(1,577.29)		119.22
18	2,692	(454.67)	(2,056.27)	469.16	650.22
19	2,163	(439.24)	(1,597.47)		126.29
20	2,163	(427.26)	(1,606.34)		129.40
21	2,692	(415.22)	(2,085.48)	469.16	660.46
22	2,163	(399.57)	(1,626.84)		136.59
23	2,163	(387.37)	(1,635.87)		139.76
24	2,692	(375.10)	(2,115.18)	469.16	670.87
25	2,225	(359.24)	(1,711.81)		153.95
26	2,225	(346.40)	(1,721.32)		157.28
27	2,225	(333.49)	(1,730.88)		160.63
28	1,569	(320.51)	(1,157.37)	308.27	399.39
29	2,225	(311.83)	(1,746.92)		166.25
30	1,569	(298.73)	(1,173.50)	308.27	405.05
31	2,225	(289.93)	(1,763.13)		171.94
32	2,225	(276.70)	(1,772.93)		175.37
33	1,569	(263.41)	(1,199.65)	308.27	414.21
34	2,225	(254.41)	(1,789.43)		181.16
35	2,225	(240.99)	(1,799.37)		184.64
36	1,569	(227.49)	(1,226.24)	308.27	423.54
37	2,259	(218.30)	(1,846.39)		194.31
38	2,259	(204.45)	(1,856.65)		197.90
39	2,259	(190.52)	(1,866.96)		201.52
40	657	(176.52)	(453.31)	163.87	191.04
41	2,259	(173.12)	(1,879.84)		206.04
42	657	(159.02)	(466.26)	163.87	195.58
43	2,259	(155.53)	(1,892.87)		210.60
44	2,259	(141.33)	(1,903.38)		214.29
45	657	(127.05)	(489.93)	163.87	203.88
46	2,259	(123.38)	(1,916.67)		218.95
47	2,259	(109.00)	(1,927.32)		222.68
48	14,261	(94.55)	(12,606.60)	163.87	1,723.72
Total	14,796	(17,763.10)	0.00	6,217.09	3,249.99

Exhibit 14-8
ROE Calculation (Pooled) – HP-17B

```
FIN
CFLO (#TIMES PROMPTING: OFF)
FLOW (0)=?            10,677.15     +/-    INPUT
FLOW (1)=?                69.77             INPUT
FLOW (2)=?                72.53             INPUT
FLOW (3)=?                75.30             INPUT
FLOW (4)=?               661.83             INPUT
FLOW (5)=?                80.43             INPUT
FLOW (6)=?               666.99             INPUT
FLOW (7)=?                85.61             INPUT
FLOW (8)=?                88.46             INPUT
FLOW (9)=?               675.06             INPUT
FLOW (10)=?               93.73             INPUT
FLOW (11)=?               96.62             INPUT
FLOW (12)=?              683.27             INPUT
FLOW (13)=?              106.21             INPUT
FLOW (14)=?              109.21             INPUT
FLOW (15)=?              112.22             INPUT
FLOW (16)=?              643.18             INPUT
FLOW (17)=?              119.22             INPUT
FLOW (18)=?              650.22             INPUT
FLOW (19)=?              126.29             INPUT
FLOW (20)=?              129.40             INPUT
FLOW (21)=?              660.46             INPUT
FLOW (22)=?              136.59             INPUT
FLOW (23)=?              139.76             INPUT
FLOW (24)=?              670.87             INPUT
FLOW (25)=?              153.59             INPUT
FLOW (26)=?              157.28             INPUT
FLOW (27)=?              160.63             INPUT
FLOW (28)=?              399.39             INPUT
FLOW (29)=?              166.25             INPUT
FLOW (30)=?              405.05             INPUT
FLOW (31)=?              171.94             INPUT
FLOW (32)=?              175.37             INPUT
FLOW (33)=?              414.21             INPUT
FLOW (34)=?              181.16             INPUT
FLOW (35)=?              184.64             INPUT
FLOW (36)=?              423.54             INPUT
FLOW (37)=?              194.31             INPUT
FLOW (38)=?              197.9              INPUT
FLOW (39)=?              201.52             INPUT
FLOW (40)=?              191.04             INPUT
FLOW (41)=?              206.04             INPUT
FLOW (42)=?              195.58             INPUT
FLOW (43)=?              210.60             INPUT
FLOW (44)=?              214.29             INPUT
FLOW (45)=?              203.88             INPUT
FLOW (46)=?              218.95             INPUT
FLOW (47)=?              222.68             INPUT
FLOW (48)=?            1,723.72             INPUT
EXIT
CALC
IRR% = 1.062459
x    12    =    12.749506
```

Exhibit 14-9
Debt Service (Level Payment)

Period	Balance	Interest	Principal
0	85,426.85	-	85,426.85
1	83,941.70	640.70	1,485.15
2	82,445.41	629.56	1,496.29
3	80,937.90	618.34	1,507.51
4	79,419.08	607.03	1,518.82
5	77,888.87	595.64	1,530.21
6	76,347.19	584.17	1,541.68
7	74,793.94	572.60	1,553.25
8	73,229.05	560.95	1,564.90
9	71,652.41	549.22	1,576.63
10	70,063.96	537.39	1,588.46
11	68,463.59	525.48	1,600.37
12	66,851.21	513.48	1,612.37
13	65,226.75	501.38	1,624.47
14	63,590.10	489.20	1,636.65
15	61,941.17	476.93	1,648.92
16	60,279.88	464.56	1,661.29
17	58,606.13	452.10	1,673.75
18	56,919.82	439.55	1,686.30
19	55,220.87	426.90	1,698.95
20	53,509.18	414.16	1,711.69
21	51,784.64	401.32	1,724.53
22	50,047.18	388.38	1,737.47
23	48,296.68	375.35	1,750.50
24	46,533.06	362.23	1,763.63
25	44,756.20	349.00	1,776.85
26	42,966.02	335.67	1,790.18
27	41,162.42	322.25	1,803.61
28	39,345.29	308.72	1,817.13
29	37,514.53	295.09	1,830.76
30	35,670.03	281.36	1,844.49
31	33,811.71	267.53	1,858.33
32	31,939.45	253.59	1,872.26
33	30,053.14	239.55	1,886.30
34	28,152.69	225.40	1,900.45
35	26,237.98	211.15	1,914.71
36	24,308.92	196.78	1,929.07
37	22,365.38	182.32	1,943.53
38	20,407.27	167.74	1,958.11
39	18,434.48	153.05	1,972.80
40	16,446.88	138.26	1,987.59
41	14,444.39	123.35	2,002.50
42	12,426.87	108.33	2,017.52
43	10,394.22	93.20	2,032.65
44	8,346.32	77.96	2,047.89
45	6,283.07	62.60	2,063.25
46	4,204.34	47.12	2,078.73
47	2,110.03	31.53	2,094.32
48	0.00	15.83	2,110.03

Exhibit 14-10
ROE Cash Flow (Level Payment)

Period	ROA cash flows	Interest	Principal	Taxes	ROE cash flows
0	(96,104)	-	85,426.85		(10,677.15)
1	2,125	(640.70)	(1,485.15)		(0.85)
2	2,125	(629.56)	(1,496.29)		(0.85)
3	2,125	(618.34)	(1,507.51)		(0.85)
4	1,862	(607.03)	(1,518.82)	606.78	342.92
5	2,125	(595.64)	(1,530.21)		(0.85)
6	1,862	(584.17)	(1,541.68)	606.78	342.92
7	2,125	(572.60)	(1,553.25)		(0.85)
8	2,125	(560.95)	(1,564.90)		(0.85)
9	1,862	(549.22)	(1,576.63)	606.78	342.92
10	2,125	(537.39)	(1,588.46)		(0.85)
11	2,125	(525.48)	(1,600.37)		(0.85)
12	1,862	(513.48)	(1,612.37)	606.78	342.92
13	2,163	(501.38)	(1,624.47)		37.15
14	2,163	(489.20)	(1,636.65)		37.15
15	2,163	(476.93)	(1,648.92)		37.15
16	2,692	(464.56)	(1,661.29)	454.30	1,020.45
17	2,163	(452.10)	(1,673.75)		37.15
18	2,692	(439.55)	(1,686.30)	454.30	1,020.45
19	2,163	(426.90)	(1,698.95)		37.15
20	2,163	(414.16)	(1,711.69)		37.15
21	2,692	(401.32)	(1,724.53)	454.30	1,020.45
22	2,163	(388.38)	(1,737.47)		37.15
23	2,163	(375.35)	(1,750.50)		37.15
24	2,692	(362.23)	(1,763.63)	454.30	1,020.45
25	2,225	(349)	(1,776.85)		99.15
26	2,225	(335.67)	(1,790.18)		99.15
27	2,225	(322.25)	(1,803.61)		99.15
28	1,569	(308.72)	(1,817.13)	287.53	(269.32)
29	2,225	(295.09)	(1,830.76)		99.15
30	1,569	(281.36)	(1,844.49)	287.53	(269.32)
31	2,225	(267.53)	(1,858.33)		99.15
32	2,225	(253.59)	(1,872.26)		99.15
33	1,569	(239.55)	(1,886.30)	287.53	(269.32)
34	2,225	(225.40)	(1,900.45)		99.15
35	2,225	(211.15)	(1,914.71)		99.15
36	1,569	(196.78)	(1,929.07)	287.53	(269.32)
37	2,259	(182.32)	(1,943.53)		133.15
38	2,259	(167.74)	(1,958.11)		133.15
39	2,259	(153.05)	(1,972.80)		133.15
40	657	(138.26)	(1,987.59)	105.11	(1,363.74)
41	2,259	(123.35)	(2,002.50)		133.15
42	657	(108.33)	(2,017.52)	105.11	(1,363.74)
43	2,259	(93.20)	(2,032.65)		133.15
44	2,259	(77.96)	(2,047.89)		133.15
45	657	(62.60)	(2,063.25)	105.11	(1,363.74)
46	2,259	(47.12)	(2,078.73)		133.15
47	2,259	(31.53)	(2,094.32)		133.15
48	14,261	(15.83)	(2,110.03)	105.11	12,240.26
Total	14,796	(16,613.99)	0.00	5,814.90	3,996.91

Exhibit 14-11
ROE (Level Payment) – HP-17B

```
FIN
CFLO (#TIMES PROMPTING: ON)
FLOW (0)=?           10,677.15    +/-    INPUT
FLOW (1)=?                 .85    +/-    INPUT
#TIMES (1)=1                3            INPUT
FLOW (2)=?              342.92           INPUT
#TIMES (2)=1               1             INPUT
FLOW (3)=?                 .85    +/-    INPUT
#TIMES (3)=1               1             INPUT
FLOW (4)=?              342.92           INPUT
#TIMES (4)=1               1             INPUT
FLOW (5)=?                 .85    +/-    INPUT
#TIMES (5)=1               2             INPUT
FLOW (6)=?              342.92           INPUT
#TIMES (6)=1               1             INPUT
FLOW (7)=?                 .85    +/-    INPUT
#TIMES (7)=1               2             INPUT
FLOW (8)=?              342.92           INPUT
#TIMES (8)=1               1             INPUT
FLOW (9)=?               37.15           INPUT
#TIMES (9)=1               3             INPUT
FLOW (10)=?           1,020.45           INPUT
#TIMES (10)=1              1             INPUT
FLOW (11)=?             37.15            INPUT
#TIMES (11)=1              1             INPUT
FLOW (12)=?           1,020.45           INPUT
#TIMES (12)=1              1             INPUT
FLOW (13)=?             37.15            INPUT
#TIMES (13)=1              2             INPUT
FLOW (14)=?           1,020.45           INPUT
#TIMES (14)=1              1             INPUT
FLOW (15)=?             37.15            INPUT
#TIMES (15)=1              2             INPUT
FLOW (16)=?           1,020.45           INPUT
#TIMES (16)=1              1             INPUT
FLOW (17)=?             99.15            INPUT
#TIMES (17)=1              3             INPUT
FLOW (18)=?            269.32     +/-    INPUT
#TIMES (18)=1              1             INPUT
FLOW (19)=?             99.15            INPUT
#TIMES (19)=1              1             INPUT
FLOW (20)=?            269.32     +/-    INPUT
#TIMES (20)=1              1             INPUT
FLOW (21)=?             99.15            INPUT
#TIMES (21)=1              2             INPUT
FLOW (22)=?            269.32     +/-    INPUT
#TIMES (22)=1              1             INPUT
FLOW (23)=?             99.15            INPUT
#TIMES (23)=1              2             INPUT
FLOW (24)=?            269.15     +/-    INPUT
#TIMES (24)=1              1             INPUT
FLOW (25)=?            133.15            INPUT
#TIMES (25)=1              3             INPUT
FLOW (26)=?           1,363.74    +/-    INPUT
#TIMES (26)=1              1             INPUT
FLOW (27)=?            133.15            INPUT
#TIMES (27)=1              1             INPUT
FLOW (28)=?           1,363.74    +/-    INPUT
#TIMES (28)=1              1             INPUT
FLOW (29)=?            133.15            INPUT
#TIMES (29)=1              2             INPUT
FLOW (30)=?           1,363.74    +/-    INPUT
#TIMES (30)=1              1             INPUT
FLOW (31)=?            133.15            INPUT
#TIMES (31)=1              2             INPUT
FLOW (32)=?          12,240.26           INPUT
#TIMES (32)=1              1             INPUT
EXIT                    CALC     TOTAL  3,996.86
IRR% = .8894
x   12   =    10.6726
```

The answer is that, in this example, constant debt-to-equity (pooled) funding provides more financial leverage (debt outstanding over time) during the life of the lease than does level payment funding. The increased leverage in this example is attributable to the residual position being taken by the lessor. This is true even though the debt balance in the lease begins and ends the same under both methods. This greater financial leverage produces a greater yield. Exhibits 14-12 and 14-13 illustrate the differing leverage amounts at the end of each month during the lease for the pooled debt and the level payment debt, respectively.

What creates the difference in financial leverage between the two methods? The primary cause is the residual position taken by the lessor. Because the lessor is anticipating receiving residual proceeds, a larger proportion of the net investment is outstanding over a longer period. Consequently, the debt balance, because it remains at 88.89% of the net investment, also remains outstanding over a longer period.

A second cause has to do with the receipt of tax benefits under constant debt-to-equity funding. Tax benefits, when received, are assumed to pay off debt just like the regular rentals in the lease. This constant paydown of debt

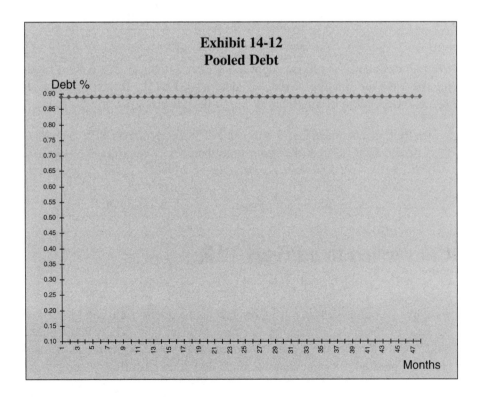

Exhibit 14-12
Pooled Debt

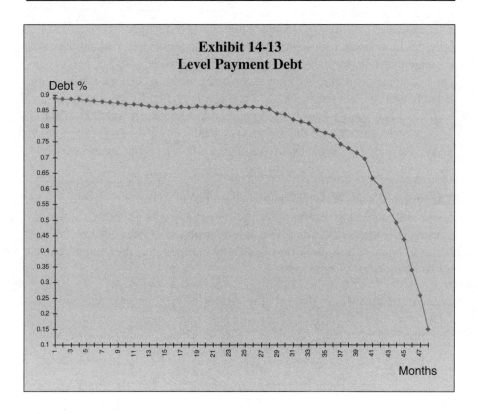

Exhibit 14-13
Level Payment Debt

from all cash sources reduces debt more rapidly than level payment funding, because the funding payback is determined by the funding source. It also is independent of any relationship to the net investment in the lease.

Which ROE is more meaningful is the subject of the section on NPV analysis in this chapter. Note that, at the same time the ROE went from 12.7495% to 10.67281%, total net cash flow increased from 3,249.99 to 3,996.91, respectively. Cash flow was sacrificed for yield in the constant debt-to-equity ROE, which creates an interesting dilemma for the analyst when assessing profitability.

Conversion to a Pretax IRR

So far in this chapter, both pretax and after-tax yields have been discussed. Theoretically, the after-tax yield can be derived by multiplying the pretax yield by one minus the tax rate. Conversely, the pretax yield can be derived by dividing the after-tax yield by one minus the tax rate. These conversions hold true as long as the lease is a nontax lease (no tax depreciation) and taxes are paid on the same date the rents and other cash flows occur.

Of course, this situation rarely happens because most tax authorities require tax remittances on a nonmonthly basis. For example, the pretax, all-inclusive ROA for the sample lease is 13.6760%. Multiplying this rate by one minus the tax rate (1- .35 = .65) gives an after-tax equivalent of 8.8894%.

$$
\begin{array}{r}
13.6760\% \\
\underline{\times \quad .65} \\
8.8894\%
\end{array}
$$

The costs of doing business (e.g., G & A and bad debts) must be deducted from the after-tax equivalent because the all-inclusive yield is a gross yield. These costs decrease the after-tax yield by 2.7822%, leaving a net, after-tax equivalent of the all-inclusive yield of 6.1072%. The actual after-tax ROA, however, is 6.6638%, as was computed in Exhibit 14-3.

The difference between these two yields of .5566% is attributable to the tax depreciation in the lease and how taxes are remitted to the government. The actual after-tax yield is greater than the computed, after-tax equivalent of the pretax yield because of the tax depreciation benefit, slightly offset by the impact of how taxes are paid.

After-tax equivalent	6.1072%
Depreciation benefit	0.5958
Tax timing	(0.0392)
Actual, after-tax yield	6.6638%

External Rate of Return Analysis (ERR)

Occasionally the IRR approach to yield analysis is inadequate. In these circumstances, ERR analysis is required. In order to illustrate the problems with IRR, and how ERR analysis solves them, assume that a 4,500 lease investment (Alternative One) generates the following six annual, after-tax cash flows:

Year	Cash flows
0	(4,500)
1	4,000
2	2,000
3	1,000
4	1,000
5	(3,500)
6	1,000

To begin with, compute the annual after-tax IRR on the Alternative One cash flows.

HP-12C			HP-17B (#TIMES PROMPTING: OFF)			
	f	REG			FIN	
4,500	CHS g	CFo			CFLO	
4,000	g	CFj	■ CLEAR DATA	YES		
2,000	g	CFj	FLOW (0)=?	4,500	+/-	INPUT
1,000	g	CFj	FLOW (1)=?	4,000		INPUT
2	g	Nj	FLOW (2)=?	2,000		INPUT
3,500	CHS g	CFj	FLOW (3)=?	1,000		INPUT
1,000	g	CFj	FLOW (4)=?	1,000		INPUT
	f	IRR	FLOW (5)=?	3,500	+/-	INPUT
		ERROR 3	FLOW (6)=?	1,000		INPUT
			EXIT			
			CALC			
			IRR% =			
			MANY/NO SOLUTIONS . . .			

ERROR 3 most likely will appear in the display of the HP-12C and an error message indicating multiple solutions will appear in the display of the HP-17B. This is because there is more than one answer to the problem and the calculator does not know which one is wanted. For illustrative purposes, negative answers are sought first by choosing a negative guess to the solution. The first guess is negative 75.

HP-12C				HP-17B (#TIMES PROMPTING: OFF)			
75	CHS	RCL	g PSE	75	+/-	STO	IRR%

The calculator should give -65.857931 as a solution. Another solution is sought next by guessing positive 75.

HP-12C				HP-17B (#TIMES PROMPTING: OFF)			
75		RCL	g PSE	75		STO	IRR%

The calculator should display 25.442492 as another solution. This solution, however, is positive.

A sixth degree polynomial (six cash flows) has six answers, some of which are real, some of which are not. Descartes' rule of signs states that a real solution exists for each sign change. Thus, there are three real solutions to this problem, two of which have been calculated. The other solution, which may be negative or positive, may approach infinity, which is beyond the HP's ability to locate. Some analysts view the existence of three solutions as a definite shortcoming of using IRRs.

Another problem with using IRR is that positive cash flows are assumed to be immediately reinvested at the IRR. This assumption has two shortcomings: (1) the actual reinvestment rate available might be materially greater or less than the investment's IRR and (2) the actual reinvestment rate may vary from year to year.

For example, compare Alternative One with the following lease investment (Alternative Two) of the same amount and term.

Year	Cash flows
0	(4,500.00)
1	1,368.07
2	1,368.07
3	1,368.07
4	1,368.07
5	1,368.07
6	1,368.07

The IRR on this lease (Alternative Two) is 20.4425%, which is lower than the 25.4425% IRR of Alternative One. To most lessors, Alternative One would be considered a better investment than Alternative Two. This choice is correct, however, only if the cash flows of Alternative One can be reinvested at 25.4425%.

For instance, which investment alternative should the lessor choose if cash flows can be reinvested only at 12%? Exhibit 14-14 displays the future value of the cash flows for each alternative, reinvested at 12%. Notice that Alternative Two has a higher future value of reinvested cash flows. If 12% is the real reinvestment opportunity, then Alternative Two is superior, even though it has a lower IRR. If, however, the cash flows actually are reinvested at 25.4425%, the future value of the Alternative One cash flows exceeds that of Alternative Two, which earns only at 20.4425%. The reinvestment assumption, therefore, plays a key role in IRR analysis.

Another little-understood problem with IRR concerns the earnings rate assumption on sinking fund balances in the lease. Sinking funds represent money set aside from current lease earnings that will be used to meet neg-

Exhibit 14-14
Future Value of Cash Flows

	Alternative One (IRR: 25.44%)			Alternative Two (IRR: 20.44%)		
	Cash flow	Years	Future value at 12%	Cash flow	Years	Future value at 12%
1	4,000	5	7,049.37	1,368.07	5	2,411.01
2	2,000	4	3,147.04	1,368.07	4	2,152.68
3	1,000	3	1,404.93	1,368.07	3	1,922.04
4	1,000	2	1,254.40	1,368.07	2	1,716.11
5	(3,500)	1	(3,920.00)	1,368.07	1	1,532.24
6	1,000	0	1,000.00	1,368.07	0	1,368.07
Total	5,500		9,935.74	8,208.42		11,102.15

ative cash flows in the future. They occur because the lessor has recovered more principal from the lease than it originally invested in the lease.

The condition in which the lessor recovers more principal from the lease than it puts into the lease also is referred to as a disinvestment balance. (Disinvestment balances are common in leveraged leases.) Leases with only positive cash inflows beyond inception never have disinvestment balances, only normal investment balances. An amortization of the cash flows of Alternative One demonstrates how a disinvestment balance occurs (see Exhibit 14-15).

Notice during the third and fourth year that the investment balances in Exhibit 14-15 are positive (instead of negative, or normal). When this happens a disinvestment balance is created. The lessor, in this example, has recovered a total of 5,420.44 in principal at the end of year three, which is 920.44 in excess of what it invested. Hence, the disinvestment balance is 920.44.

ERR analysis solves the problems associated with IRRs in several ways. First, it assigns an earnings rate to the sinking funds that is different (more economically realistic) from the IRR. Second, it allows the lessor to impose a reinvestment rate on the analysis, if it so desires. Lastly, ERR analysis eliminates the multiple solutions that may occur with IRR analysis. A more detailed discussion of ERRs, particularly as they relate to leveraged leases, is contained in Chapter Twenty-six.

COMPARING PROPOSALS

An adjunct to lease analysis is the comparison by the lessor (or lessee, for that matter) of competing proposals. This comparison may be done to identify competitors' strengths and weaknesses, to specifically sell against a strong competitor or to identify the most economical transaction. The comparison of leases can be made using qualitative factors, such as accounting classification, indemnifications and termination rights, or using quantitative factors. This section discusses quantitative comparisons.

When comparing leases, the lessor should focus on certain characteristics. For instance, any time the periodicity of the leases being compared is different, factors other than the payment should be considered. As an example, assume a 48-month lease on a 50,000 piece of equipment. The pretax yield on the lease is 11%. In addition to the foregoing, Lessor A has based its payment of 1,205.58 on the following data:

Payments: in advance

Fee paid to a broker: 300

Residual: 5,000.

Lessor B, however, computes its payment of 1,212.22 in arrears. Lessor B does not pay a broker fee, and has taken a 4,800 residual position. If the lessee is making its decision based solely on payment, it would choose

---

Exhibit 14-15
Amortization of Alternative One

Cash flow number	Cash flow	Interest	Principal	Balance
0	0.00	0.00	0.00	(4,500.00)
1	4,000.00	1,144.91	2,855.09	(1,644.91)
2	2,000.00	418.51	1,581.49	(63.42)
3	1,000.00	16.14	983.86	920.44
4	1,000.00	(234.18)	1,234.18	2,154.62
5	(3,500.00)	(548.20)	(2,951.80)	(797.18)
6	1,000.00	202.82	797.18	0.00
Total	5,500.00	1,000.00	4,500.00	

Lessor A.

Lessor B	1,212.22
Lessor A	(1,205.58)
	6.64

Implicit Cost

Because the terms are not the same for the two leases, Lessor B should focus the lessee's attention on measures that reflect the time value of money, such as implicit cost and NPV. The implicit cost to the lessee is computed in Exhibit 14-16. If the time value of money is considered,

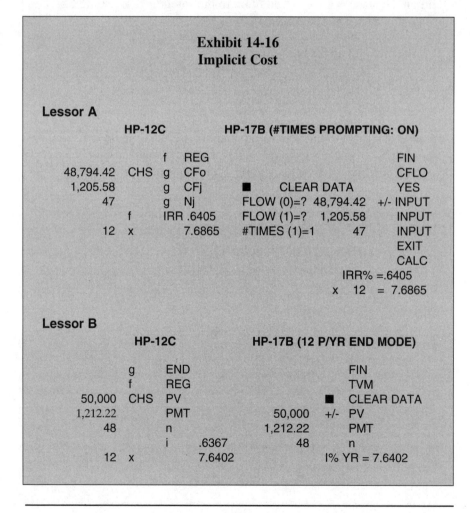

Exhibit 14-16
Implicit Cost

Lessor A

HP-12C				HP-17B (#TIMES PROMPTING: ON)	
	f	REG			FIN
48,794.42	CHS	g CFo			CFLO
1,205.58		g CFj	■ CLEAR DATA		YES
47		g Nj	FLOW (0)=? 48,794.42	+/-	INPUT
	f	IRR .6405	FLOW (1)=? 1,205.58		INPUT
12	x	7.6865	#TIMES (1)=1 47		INPUT
					EXIT
					CALC
			IRR% =.6405		
			x 12 = 7.6865		

Lessor B

HP-12C				HP-17B (12 P/YR END MODE)	
	g	END			FIN
	f	REG			TVM
50,000	CHS	PV		■	CLEAR DATA
1,212.22		PMT	50,000	+/-	PV
48		n	1,212.22		PMT
		i .6367	48		n
12	x	7.6402	I% YR = 7.6402		

Lessor B's lease is less expensive.

Lessor A	7.6865
Lessor B	(7.6402)
	.0463

NPV

Another approach that may be used to overcome the raw payment differential between the leases is to have the lessee evaluate the lease costs on an NPV basis. Assuming a 9.75% borrowing rate, Lessor B's lease is, again, more favorable. The calculations of the NPVs are shown in Exhibit 14-17.

Exhibit 14-17
NPV Comparison

Lessor A

	HP-12C		HP-17B (12 P/YR BEGIN MODE)	
	g	BEG		FIN
	f	REG		TVM
9.75	g	12÷	■	CLEAR DATA
1,205.58	CHS	PMT	9.75	I%YR
48		n	1,205.58 +/-	PMT
		PV 48,148	48	N
				PV = 48,148

Lessor B

	HP-12C		HP-17B (12 P/YR END MODE)	
	g	END		FIN
	f	REG		TVM
9.75	g	12÷	■	CLEAR DATA
1,212.22	CHS	PMT	9.75	I%YR
48		n	1,212.22 +/-	PMT
		PV 48,023	48	N
				PV = 48,023

Lessor A	48,148
Lessor B	48,023
	125

Because leasing is predicated on the time value of money, it is important that lessors incorporate these concepts into their sales strategies. Alternative methods of analysis, such as implicit cost and NPV, accomplish this.

CONCLUSION

Yield analysis is a critical aspect of every leasing company. If the lessor does not analyze the profitability of its leases, it will not know if it is pricing correctly, controlling costs and meeting management's targeted return. As has been illustrated, numerous yields (and combinations, thereof) may be calculated. The yield ultimately used, therefore, is dependent on the needs and sophistication of the user. Irrespective of the yield utilized, the successful lessor must constantly monitor the performance of its leases and overall portfolio.

Chapter Fifteen

Structuring Principles

Structuring (or pricing) a lease transaction integrates so many diverse variables, including lessee acceptance of the transaction, that putting together a well-structured lease requires a great deal of skill and knowledge. (Throughout the next two chapters the terms pricing and structuring will be used interchangeably.) These skills and knowledge range from understanding lessee needs to recognizing the impact of when taxes are paid on the yield. The fundamental principles necessary to successfully structure leases are explored in this chapter:

- Purpose of Structuring

- Structuring Factors To Be Considered

- Pretax Targeted Yield Structuring

- Structuring Unusual Payment Streams.

PURPOSE OF STRUCTURING

Pricing has always played a critical role in the leasing company. If the company's lease transactions are not priced properly, either of two events occurs: (1) the transaction will be unacceptable to the marketplace or (2) it will not meet the lessor's profit requirements. Both events can precipitate the failure of the leasing company. Given the importance of proper pricing, what are its critical elements and how is proper pricing accomplished?

Structuring incorporates many variables, such as lessor requirements, lessee needs, marketplace constraints, funding impact and lessee risk, so each lease will be different. Certain characteristics, however, are fundamental to all lease structures. Two of these characteristics form the basis of lease structuring. Whenever the lessor enters into a lease agreement, it must obtain:

1. A return **of** the principal invested

2. A return **on** the principal invested. (What is an acceptable return is the subject of Chapter Twenty-nine.)

In this respect, leasing should be viewed as any other investment. For example, an investment of 1,000 in the bank today, earning 10% interest, returns to the investor 1,100 at the end of one year (1,000 return **of** principal and 100 return **on** principal.) This pervasive concept must be kept in mind at all times during the pricing process. The pricing specialist must structure the lease so as to recover the leasing company's investment plus management's targeted rate of return. This principle is evident throughout the chapter and underlies all the discussions of the various pricing methods and techniques.

Structuring Theory

If a return of principal invested and a reasonable return on that principal invested are the basic goals of structuring, then it is imperative to understand the concepts of return of and return on principal. The first step is to determine what constitutes the principal in the lease. The largest component is, of course, the cost of the equipment. Principal, however, goes well beyond just the equipment cost.

In lease structuring, principal consists of the total costs, or investment, in the lease, including other costs, such as commissions, legal fees and selling, general and administrative (S,G&A) expenses. Benefits also are generated that reduce the cost of the investment made, such as fees and tax benefits. All these must be considered when determining investment principal for purposes of pricing. This principal is then recovered through a combination of the lease payment and residual. (Some analysts consider the residual to be a reduction, in the future, of principal to be recovered.)

For example, a lessor may lease equipment costing 10,000 for 48 months. Additionally, it will receive 1,800 in net tax benefits, a 250 closing fee, a 300 advance payment and will pay out 400 in initial direct costs. In this simple example, the lessor needs to recover 8,050 of principal (i.e., investment, or cost) through the remaining lease payments (see Exhibit 15-1).

Exhibit 15-1
Summary of Cash Flows

Description	Cash flow	Nature of cash flow
Equipment cost	(10,000)	Outflow
Tax benefits	1,800	Inflow
Closing fee	250	Inflow
Advance payment	300	Inflow
Initial direct costs	(400)	Outflow
Principal to be recovered	(8,050)	Net outflow

The investment does not need to be limited to actual cost. In the case of a dealer who recognizes gross profit on the leases being written, the equipment component of principal to be recovered would be its fair market value. The dealer in this way also would recover, through the lease payment, the gross profit inherent in the transaction.

Keep in mind, though, that a return of principal through the lease payments is only one of the two basic goals of structuring. The other goal is a reasonable return on the principal invested. This return generally is referred to as the earnings, the interest, the rate of return, the yield or simply the rate in the lease.

The rate of return (the interest rate) is applied to the principal to be recovered to generate the lease payment. As a result, payments and lease rate factors are both a function of the rate of return in the lease.

Many rates of return can be used in pricing, several of which are covered in more depth in other chapters. The most common rates are pretax return on assets (ROA), after-tax ROA and after-tax return on equity (ROE). The structuring in this chapter is done on an ROA basis. ROE structuring is discussed in Chapter Sixteen.

The rates used in structuring leases fall into two broad categories: cost accounting rates and market rates. Cost accounting rates of return can be capital budgeting returns, such as cost of capital or ROE, or they can be derived from cost accounting inputs. These inputs include the costs of working capital, uninvested capital, S,G&A, debt, the debt payback method and deferred taxes, inter alia. Based upon these factors the lessor develops a required rate of return, or hurdle rate. This hurdle rate then becomes the minimum acceptable rate at which the leasing company must structure if it is to remain in business.

Market rates, on the other hand, are determined solely by what the market will support. Market rates may exceed or be less than the lessor's hurdle rate. Because market rates are so important, the lessor attempts to establish a target rate when developing a yield to use in pricing. This target rate must be equal to or greater than the hurdle rate, yet still be acceptable in the marketplace. This concept is best shown through an illustration (see Exhibit 15-2). The market rates should exceed the company's hurdle rate, as in Exhibit 15-2.

In addition to the many rates of return that may be targeted in structuring, a variety of structuring methods may be utilized. These methods range from the expediently simple to ultra complex. Some companies, for instance, structure their leases with financial calculators. Others utilize sophisticated software and mainframe computers. The method to be employed is a function of the lessor's needs, its resources and the marketplace it is in.

Other earnings issues in addition to choosing the rate of return used to price leases relate to the quality and the quantity of the earnings generated by a lease. These advanced issues are explained in Chapter Sixteen.

STRUCTURING FACTORS TO BE CONSIDERED

Many inputs must be considered by a lessor when structuring a lease. Some of these inputs impact the investment to be recovered by the lessor, including the cash inflows and outflows, their timing and their importance one to another. Other inputs relate to the return on the investment, including the cost of the lessor's capital.

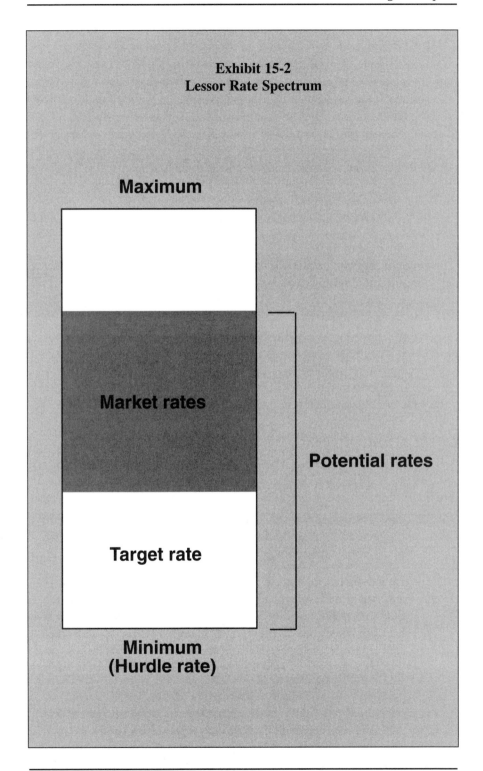

Exhibit 15-2
Lessor Rate Spectrum

Maximum

Market rates

Potential rates

Target rate

Minimum
(Hurdle rate)

Inputs

The most simple form of structuring occurs when a lessor enters the cost of the equipment, its targeted yield and the term into a calculator and solves for the periodic lease payment. For example, assume equipment costing 100,000 is to be leased over a 60-month period. The lessor, targeting a yield of 18%, believes the equipment will not have any residual value when the lease term expires. If the lessor calculates the payment in arrears, the payment is 2,539.34 per month. If calculated in advance, the payment is 2,501.82.

In a more complex approach to structuring, the lessor may include additional inputs in the process, and arrive at its pricing structure in the following manner:

Current cost of funds	9.0%
Amount required to recover expected bad debt expense	2.0%
Amount required to cover overhead costs	3.5%
Required spread	3.5%
The lessor hurdle rate	18.0%

Although this process seems simplistic, it is used by lessors every day to calculate payments quoted to lessees. If the lessee is sophisticated, however, and is able to negotiate with a lessor on a knowledgeable basis, many other factors must be taken into account when pricing a transaction.

Transactions can be priced on either a pretax basis or an after-tax basis. The simplest form of pricing is on a pretax, ROA basis. The most complex is pricing to an after-tax ROE. The input and output elements that must be taken into consideration when pricing a lease are as follows:

1. **The equipment cost:** The equipment cost should include transportation, installation and any other costs associated with placing the equipment in service

2. **Initial direct costs:** This element includes all cash outlays associated with negotiating and consummating a lease transaction. Examples of this type of outlay are sales commissions, brokerage fees, credit investigation fees, legal fees and other costs to place the transaction on the books of the lessor

3. **S,G&A and bad debt costs:** These costs normally are allocated based on the historical experience of the lessor. However, they may vary with the creditworthiness of the lessee, ticket size and any unusual characteristics of a transaction

4. **Debt repayment, including servicing of principal and interest:** The method by which transactions are funded impacts the timing of payment outflows, the cost of debt and the ROE

5. **Debt proceeds:** The amount of debt utilized to fund transactions and the method of funding the lessor's transactions both impact the pricing equation. Any delayed funding techniques used may enhance lessor yield and, therefore, enable it to reduce payment amounts and gain a pricing edge

6. **Interest tax benefits:** The single largest expense item for a lessor is debt service. The ability to fully utilize the deduction of interest expense enhances the pricing capability of a lessor

7. **Closing or nonrefundable fees:** Any nonrefundable fees received by the lessor can be used to enhance its yield or lower the lessee's payment. This type of fee may be referred to as a documentation fee or commitment fee or some similar name

8. **When payment of the equipment cost is made by the lessor:** The longer a lessor waits to pay for equipment, the more it is able to enhance its yield and gain a pricing advantage over competitors. Volume purchase agreements and past payment history enable a lessor to take advantage of this technique

9. **Deposits required by the lessor:** Typical deposits include security deposits or excess usage deposits. A refundable security deposit generally is required by a lessor for credit enhancement purposes. However, because the lessor has the use of this money, it is, in effect, an interest free loan from the lessee. The lessor pays the deposit amount to the lessee at lease termination but it has the full use of the funds during the lease term at no cost. Thus the lessee may be subsidizing the cost of the equipment to the lessor

   This value may be passed to the lessee in the form of a lower payment, or it may be used by the lessor to increase its yield. Anticipated excess usage charges function the same as a refundable security deposit and may be required on equipment that is expected to have a high level of wear and tear during the term of the lease. If the excess usage does not materialize, the deposit is repaid to the lessee

10. **Rental payments:** The timing of payments, whether in advance or arrears, skips, step-up or step-down, etc., may be used by the lessor to enhance its yield. On a pretax basis, the lessor recovers its investment and makes a profit from the rental payments and the residual

11. **Tax depreciation benefits:** In a tax lease, the lessor recovers its cost for tax purposes in the form of depreciation instead of principal. The front loading of this cost recovery delays the payment of tax. This delay enhances the lessor's yield because it has the use of the funds before taxes must be paid

12. **Residual:** This element may represent a large or small portion of the return of investment and, hence, the profitability in a transaction. The ability of a lessor to remarket equipment, net of the costs of remarketing, significantly impacts this important source of investment recovery

13. **Miscellaneous income:** This category includes amounts received by the lessor to perform such tasks as maintenance, insurance, payment of property taxes and remittance of sales taxes to the proper authorities. The lessor also may charge a host of fees to cover events such as late payments, early terminations, relocation of equipment and renegotiating the original terms of a lease agreement

14. **Contingent rentals:** Typically, contingent rentals are usage based. Contingent rentals may be charged for excess mileage, excess engine hours, excess revolutions on hub meters and computer processing time in excess of agreed upon amounts. However, they also may be associated with the passing of specific events, such as a change in tax rates (tax indemnification) or changes in economic indicators

15. **Gross profit deferral:** This element of pricing is a tax benefit created in deferred intercompany transactions, typically between a parent and its subsidiary in a captive relationship. The two entities file a consolidated tax return, creating a delay in the payment of taxes on the gross profit on the intercompany sale. The delayed tax payment creates a pricing advantage

16. **Alternative minimum tax:** The alternative minimum tax is designed to assure that profitable companies pay income taxes. The alternative minimum tax rate, although less than the regular tax rate, is applied to a higher base. As a result, the value of a tax deduction is reduced and costs are increased on an after-tax basis

17. **Tax rates:** Corporate tax rates vary depending on the level of reported taxable income. Thus, on an after-tax basis, the value of deductions and revenues will vary. These changing values can be priced into a transaction. Tax loss carryforwards and other tax complexities will have varying impacts on lessor pricing

18. **Tax timing:** Corporate taxes generally are paid in periods other than when they are incurred. In the U.S., for instance, income taxes are paid on a quarterly basis with the amount of each remittance based on the taxpayer's expected income. If a lessor is able to take advantage of a tax deduction before a transaction is executed, a pricing advantage may be gained. Conversely, transactions that occur before tax remittance dates may create a lessor disadvantage

19. **Leverage:** The ratio of debt and equity on the balance sheet of a lessor has a direct impact on the hurdle rate the lessor must charge (see Chapter Twenty-nine). The leverage affects not only the weighting of the cost of funds, but also the cost itself

20. **Targeted ROE:** The ROE is another key component of the lessor's hurdle rate. The higher the lessor's targeted ROE, the more it must charge the lessee. The effect of the ROE can be altered through the amount of leverage the lessor maintains

21. **Working capital:** A lessor requires funds to meet its daily operating obligations. Thus the levels of working capital will impact the cost requirements of a lessor when determining lease pricing. The greater the size and the competitiveness of a transaction, the greater the need to manage the working capital of a lessor

22. **Uninvested capital:** A lessor generates revenue by leasing the equipment it acquires. Not all the lessor's capital is invested in earning assets, however. Some must be expended for facilities and operating assets such as computers. This uninvested capital has a cost that must be recovered from the lessee.

As can be seen, the inputs considered by a lessor when pricing transactions are many and diverse. The interaction of these inputs must be understood. For instance, at times they function in opposition to one another and at other times they function in synchronization. When performing simple pricing (pretax ROA) a lessor is impacted by few of these items. When pricing to achieve an after-tax ROE, however, it is often a difficult balancing act.

Structuring Variables

Although the terms pricing and structuring often are used interchangeably, they are quite different concepts. Pricing is the mechanical process of achieving the profit objectives of management and shareholders. Structuring is the timing of cash flows to achieve the objectives of the lessor and the payment requirements of the lessee.

Unique structuring variables available to lessors set their product apart from other types of financing such as bank loans. Many of these have been noted in the discussion of pricing inputs. Others require further explanation and an understanding of how they enable lessees and lessors to achieve their objectives.

1. **Advance payments:** The lessor's yield is based on when cash is received or disbursed. Thus the timing and amount of cash at lease inception directly impact the lessor's profitability. The greater the number of advance payments received by a lessor, the less equity contribution it must make and the sooner it recovers its investment

    Sometimes a lessor calculates the payment as if no advance payments are to be received. However, advance payments are then collected from the lessee, thereby increasing the lessor's yield

2. **Security deposits:** Security deposits may be interest bearing or noninterest bearing. They may be refundable or nonrefundable. The use of deposits allows the lessor to gain pricing advantages and manage cash

3. **Origination or service fees:** These amounts represent cash received by a lessor. They may be used to lower either the lease payments or the residual, or to increase the lessor's yield

4. **Interim rents:** If a lessee uses equipment prior to the commencement of the lease payments (the initial billing date) the lessor's yield is reduced because the useful life of the equipment is being consumed. Typically a lessor will charge interim rents or some compensation for this usage

5. **Lease payment variability:** In a lease transaction, the lessee's use of the equipment provides the income to make the payments. The lessee's cash flow is enhanced if payment sched-

ules are designed to fit the income producing capability of equipment. Lessors are willing to structure the payment stream in any way the lessee wishes

6. **Penalties:** If a lessee does not make its payments on time, or if it terminates the lease early, the lessor's expected cash flows are altered, as is its return. The lessor may charge penalties to compensate for the effects of these events

7. **Residuals:** Residual reliance allows the lessor to offer lower lease payments. This factor sets leasing apart from other types of financing because lenders rarely offer payments based on residuals

8. **Renewal options:** A lessor may establish renewal options at the inception of a lease agreement. Doing so allows the lessee the option to continue to use the equipment or to walk away from the equipment at the end of the lease

9. **Capital or operating lease (accounting viewpoint):** The accounting designation of a lease may impact structuring for many reasons. From the lessor perspective, a capital lease front-end loads the recognition of income and an operating lease end-loads the recognition of income. The expense recognition of the lessee, on the other hand, also is altered. Because the lessee has two products to choose from, leasing's value is enhanced

10. **True lease (tax viewpoint):** If a lessor has the ability to utilize tax benefits in a lease transaction, and is willing to pass the timing value of these benefits to the lessee, a lower payment may be achieved. Tax benefits are not available to a lender

11. **Full service leasing:** In a loan, the borrower is required to pay its own insurance, maintenance and property taxes. Leasing is much more convenient if the lessor includes these additional services in the lease payment amount

12. **Contingent rentals:** Contingent rentals generally are usage based. From the lessee's perspective, it is paying only when the equipment is generating revenue, which allows the lessee to match its costs with the revenue the equipment is generating

13. **Flexible lease options:** Flexible options cover a broad range of elements. Upgrades, swaps, skips, and step leases may be included. Profit sharing arrangements and the bundling of other services also represent flexible options. This flexibility sets the lease product apart from other forms of financing

14. **Full payout or not:** In a full payout lease, the lessor does not rely on the receipt of a residual amount to recover its investment and make a profit. If a lessor does assume residual risk, the payment amount to the lessee will decline. The choice between these two products allows the lessor to offer more options than a bank

15. **Fixed payment lease:** In a volatile interest rate environment, most providers of funds will not agree to a fixed payment amount. However, lessees often seek a fixed payment for budget and other costing purposes. Lessors typically are willing to provide the lessee with a fixed payment lease

16. **Economies of scale:** If a lessor has the ability to acquire large quantities of equipment, maintenance or insurance, it may pass the savings on to the lessee in the form of reduced cost.

The many variables available to a lessor when structuring its leases allow it a high degree of flexibility. The advantage of this flexibility is that a lessor is able to meet the needs of a lessee better than the providers of other, less flexible, forms of financing. The ability of a lessor to determine the needs of a lessee and then structure the lease to address those needs sets it apart from the competition.

PRETAX TARGETED YIELD STRUCTURING

Many methods are utilized to structure leases. Typical pricing methods range from lease payment tables to sophisticated pricing software. This section focuses on manual structuring using a targeted pretax ROA. An understanding of manual pricing is important because effectively structuring a lease requires a knowledge of how each variable affects the pricing process. For lessors using pricing software, the manual pricing approach provides valuable insight into the computation and alteration of payments.

In order to price a lease to a targeted ROA, it is critical to correctly identify the timing and amount of all cash flows. Timelines are used throughout this chapter to illustrate these cash flows. The value of the timelines becomes apparent as lease structures become more complex.

The following factors typically are associated with a pretax transaction.

1. Equipment cost

2. Pretax yield required by the lessor

3. Number of lease rental payments

4. Number of advance payments

5. Residual value assumption

6. Initial direct costs (IDC) to package the transaction

7. Fees paid by the lessee

8. Refundable security deposits.

A building block approach is used to illustrate the structuring process. First, a simple lease with no advance payments, no residual and level payments throughout the lease is priced. This example provides the basis for a discussion of residuals, security deposits and closing fees. These additional cash flows can be used by the lessor to either increase the effective yield on the lease or reduce the payment to the lessee while still maintaining the required ROA.

The structuring of more complex leases with irregular payment schedules such as multiple advance payments and step-down leases is covered in the following section. The concepts for level payment leases provide a basis for understanding these more complex lease structures.

The structuring of all leases, whether manually, with a calculator or with software, incorporates a basic algorithm, or process. This process can be distilled into three steps. By following these three steps, any lease may be structured. This three-step structuring method is presented on page 507.

Before proceeding to the three steps, however, several simple calculator examples are presented to increase familiarity with the pricing process. All examples include the HP-12C and HP-17B calculator keystrokes because it is important to be able to utilize standard tools used within the leasing industry. The examples within this section are as follows:

Example One compares payments in arrears to payments in advance

Example Two adds a residual to Example One

Example Three and Four add a refundable security deposit to Example Two

Examples Five through Seven discuss pricing with closing fees and initial direct costs.

Example One

Example One and Example Two utilize the financial keyboard and menu capabilities of HP hand-held calculators to structure the leases. As was previously mentioned, the more flexible Three-step Method is presented later on page 507 so that unusual payment stream leases may be structured.

Using the assumptions below, structure a level payment lease.

Equipment cost: 90,000

Annual pretax yield (required ROA): 12%

Term: 60 months, payments in arrears.

The use of a timeline allows for correct placement of the cash flows at the point at which they actually occur. The known cash flows have been identified on the timeline. The timeline shows both the timing and the amount of these known cash flows.

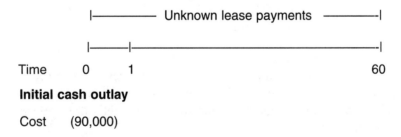

Initial cash outlay

Cost   (90,000)

In this example, the white keyboard on the HP-12C or the TVM menu on the HP-17B can be used because all variables are known except for the amount of the payments. As can be seen, the monthly payment, in arrears, for this lease is 2,002.00.

HP-12C		HP-17B (12 P/YR END MODE)
f	REG	FIN
g	END	TVM
90,000 CHS	PV	■ CLEAR DATA
60	n	END
12 g	12÷	90,000 +/- PV
	PMT 2,002.00	60 N
		12 I%YR
		PMT=2,002.00

What is the payment if this lease is structured with payments in advance instead of arrears? The keystrokes are exactly the same as above, except the calculator is put into "BEGIN" mode. The payment can be computed by replacing the "Payment in arrears" line with the keystrokes below. The new payment can be computed without clearing registers.

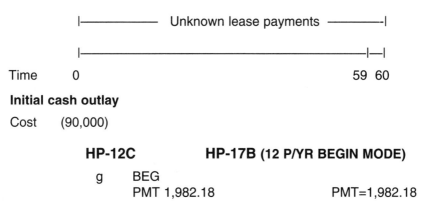

Time   0   59 60

Initial cash outlay

Cost   (90,000)

HP-12C		HP-17B (12 P/YR BEGIN MODE)
g	BEG	
	PMT 1,982.18	PMT=1,982.18

It makes sense that payments in advance of 1,982.18 are lower than those in arrears because the lessor's principal recovery begins one month earlier with advance payments.

This example is a full-payout lease (a lease priced with no reliance on a residual value). Pricing a lease on a pretax basis without a residual value is equivalent to pricing an installment loan with the same terms.

Example Two

Use the same assumptions as Example One, except assume a residual of 10% of equipment cost. Because the lessor expects one additional cash inflow of 9,000 at the end of the lease, the lessee will pay for using less than

100% of the equipment value, as opposed to 100%, as in Example One. Using the following assumptions, structure a level payment lease with payments in advance.

> Equipment cost: 90,000
>
> Annual pretax yield (required ROA): 12%
>
> Term: 60 months, payments in advance
>
> Residual value: 9,000 (10% of equipment cost).

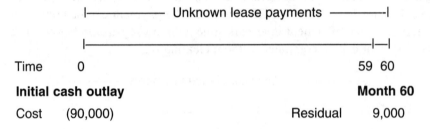

Time	0	59 60
Initial cash outlay		**Month 60**
Cost	(90,000)	Residual 9,000

The white keyboard on the HP-12C and the TVM menu on the HP-17B can still be used because the lease includes level payments with one payment in advance.

HP-12C			**HP-17B (12 P/YR BEGIN MODE)**	
			FIN	
	f	REG	TVM	
	g	BEG	■ CLEAR DATA	
90,000	CHS	PV	90,000	+/- PV
9,000		FV	9,000	FV
60		n	60	N
12	g	12÷	12	I%YR
		PMT 1,873.07		PMT=1,873.07

This payment is 109.11 less than the monthly payments in advance calculated in Example One (without the 9,000 residual). Looked at another way, if 109.11 is deposited in a bank account at the beginning of each month for 60 months, at an annual interest rate of 12% (compounded monthly), the depositor will have a balance of 9,000 at the end of 60 months. In this example, the lessor is able to reduce the lessee's payment because of this anticipated cash flow (the equipment can be either sold or re-leased) at the end of the lease.

The 109.11 reduction in the payment from Example One represents the pretax cash flow advantage of a lease with a residual value over a level payment, fully amortized loan. By relying on a residual value, the lessor calculates payments based only on the amortization of the anticipated decline in equipment value over the lease term. A loan, on the other hand, is fully amortized over its life without considering a future equipment value. The concept of the lessee paying only for the decline in the equipment's value while in its possession is one of the major cash flow benefits of leasing.

The Three-step Method

Now that the concepts of cash flow, timing and the use of timelines have been discussed, the structuring process for more complex leases can be introduced. Any lease can be structured manually on a pretax basis by following three basic steps. These steps provide a solution to simple leases with even payment streams or complex leases with uneven payment streams. The remainder of this section introduces these three steps and applies them to level payment pricing. These three steps will be referred to collectively as the Three-step Method. The next section applies the method to pricing leases with uneven payment streams. At this time the value of the method will become even more obvious.

STEP ONE

Identify and present value all known cash flows in the transaction, using the targeted pretax yield as the discount rate.

This step requires an identification of all known cash flows just as in the previous examples. With this process, however, all future cash flows, such as the residual, are present valued at the pretax targeted yield or internal rate of return (IRR). The sum of all cash flows on a present value basis represents the lessor's net investment, or principal, in the lease. This amount must be recovered through the lease payments.

To illustrate this step, the assumptions for Example Two are used. The residual of 9,000 in this example represents a cash flow in month 60 that must be present valued at the lessor's yield of 12%.

HP-12C		**HP-17B (12 P/YR BEGIN MODE)**	
f	REG		FIN
g	BEG		TVM
9,000	FV	■	CLEAR DATA
60	n	9,000	FV
12 g	12÷	60	N
	PV 4,954.05	12	I%YR
			PV=4,954.05

With all known cash flows identified and present valued at the pretax targeted yield, the first step is complete. The result, 85,045.95, represents the amount of principal to be recovered through the lease payments at the given pretax return of 12%.

Initial cash outlay	(90,000.00)
Residual present value	4,954.05
Net investment at time 0	(85,045.95)

STEP TWO

Determine the present value of the unknown payment stream, using the targeted pretax yield as the discount rate and letting each payment equal one dollar.

This step determines the amount of principal a one dollar payment over the term of the lease will recover. If the payment was known, the amount of principal recovered through the payment stream could be computed. (The present value of any cash flow stream represents the amount of principal inherent in that cash flow stream.) Since the payment is unknown in the pricing process, one dollar is substituted in order to determine the amount of principal to be recovered, given a one dollar payment.

The amount of principal recovered through a one dollar payment can be thought of as an investment recovery unit (IRU). The number of one dollar payments over the lease term required to recover that net investment can be calculated because the net investment to be recovered was determined in Step One.

For example, if the IRU is 50 and the net investment is 500, dividing the net investment by the IRU results in periodic payments of 10. The payment of 10 is the amount necessary to recover the net investment at the required target yield.

$$\frac{\text{Net investment}}{\text{IRU}} = \text{Required pretax payment}$$

This concept can be applied to all net investments and payment structures, no matter how complex. Using the assumptions in Example Two of a 60-month lease with payments in advance, at 12%, the IRU is calculated as follows:

HP-12C		**HP-17B (12 P/YR BEGIN MODE)**	
			FIN
f	REG		TVM
g	BEG	■	CLEAR DATA
1	PMT	1	PMT
60	n	60	N
12 g	12÷	12	I%YR
	PV 45.4046		PV=45.4046

The present value of 45.4046 represents the amount of principal the lessor will recover for each dollar of payment it charges over the lease term of 60 months.

STEP THREE

Divide the net investment from Step One by the IRU from Step Two.

Step Three identifies the number of one dollar payment streams required to recover the net investment. This calculation produces the pretax payment due from the lessee. Given that the IRU for the lease in Example Two is 45.4046, how many IRUs will it take to recover the net investment of 85,045.95?

Step One	÷	**Step Two**	=	**IRUs per month**
85,045.95	÷	45.4046	=	1,873.07

Since each IRU represents a stream of one dollar payments over the lease term at the targeted yield, the monthly payment is equal to:

$$1{,}873.07 \quad \times \quad 1 \quad = \quad 1{,}873.07 \text{ monthly payment}$$

This payment is exactly equal to the payment calculated in Example Two using the white keyboard of the HP-12C and the TVM function of the HP-17B.

The Three-step Method is more complicated for calculating the solution to Example Two than the calculator method. For level payment leases, with no more than one payment in advance, the calculator method used in Example One and Example Two is adequate. However, to calculate payments for a lease with multiple advance payments or uneven cash flows, the Three-step Method is necessary.

The method shown in Examples One and Two will be referred to as the "Calculator Method" because the calculator automatically computes the payment. The Three-step Method, although not required for the remainder of this section, is necessary in the following section to compute solutions for uneven payment streams. The remaining examples in this section are all level payments with one payment in advance; however, the solutions will be shown using both methods to increase reader understanding of the Three-step Method.

Effect of Deposits, Fees and IDC

Refundable security deposits, closing fees and IDCs impact a lessor's true yield in a lease. Each of these three items represents cash flows to the lessor but may or may not be included in the pricing calculations. A refundable security deposit is paid by the lessee at the inception of the lease (time zero), and the exact amount is returned to the lessee at the end of the lease assuming the lessee has met all its contractual obligations. This deposit effectively is an interest free loan from the lessee to the lessor, unless the lessor lowers the monthly payment as a result of the deposit. If the payment is not affected by the deposit, the lessor has enhanced the yield on the lease.

Closing fees are paid by the lessee and lower the lessor's net cash investment. If considered in pricing the lease, the closing fee reduces the lessee's payment. However, closing fees often are used to enhance the lessor's yield and reduce credit risk, not to impact the lessee's payment.

Unlike refundable security deposits and closing fees, IDCs are cash outlays for lessors. Including IDCs in lease pricing will increase the periodic lease payment because the lessor's net investment at the inception of the lease (time zero) is increased by the amount of the IDCs. The remaining examples in this section deal with the impact of these additional cash flows on lease payments and the lessor's effective (true) yield.

EXAMPLE THREE

Refundable security deposits can provide at least two advantages to a lessor. First, the lessor reduces its credit risk by holding the deposit. If the lessee fails to meet its obligations, the security deposit can help offset any losses. Second, assuming the lessee is not paid interest on the security deposit and the lessor is allowed to commingle these funds, a lessor is provided with an interest free source of capital. If this interest free use of funds is not priced into the lease, the effective yield on the lease is enhanced. If the interest free use of funds is priced into the lease, the refundable security deposit reduces the lease payment, which helps in marketing the lease.

In this example, assume the lease in Example Two also includes a refundable security deposit of 10%. It was not priced into the lease because the lessor intends to utilize the security deposit to enhance the yield on the lease.

What is the lessor's effective yield on this lease? The monthly payment of 1,873.07 was calculated in Example Two and in the Three-step Method explanation based on a required ROA of 12%. Now, the use of the 9,000 security deposit is included to determine the lessor's true yield. Including the receipt of the security deposit at inception, and its return to the lessee at the end of the lease, changes the cash flows at time 0 and month 60.

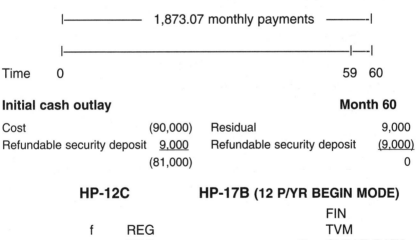

|—————— 1,873.07 monthly payments ———-|

|————————————————————|—-|

Time   0   59 60

Initial cash outlay		**Month 60**	
Cost	(90,000)	Residual	9,000
Refundable security deposit	9,000	Refundable security deposit	(9,000)
	(81,000)		0

	HP-12C			**HP-17B (12 P/YR BEGIN MODE)**		
					FIN	
	f	REG			TVM	
	g	BEG			■ CLEAR DATA	
81,000	CHS	PV		81,000	+/- PV	
0		FV		0	FV	
60		n		60	N	
1,873.07		PMT		1,873.07	PMT	
		i	1.19		I%YR	14.25
		12	x 14.25			

In this case, the interest-free use of 9,000 for 60 months increased the lessor's yield from 12% to 14.25%.

Although the lessor must return the 9,000 security deposit to the lessee at the end of the lease, the lessor is able to invest the money in other leases and earn income. Another way to look at this effect is to view the lessor as paying only 90% of the cost of the equipment at lease inception. The lessor pays the remaining 10% at the end of the lease by refunding the security deposit in dollars that are worth less. Alternatively, the lessor could have decreased the payment to reflect the security deposit.

EXAMPLE FOUR

In the previous example, a refundable security deposit was used to enhance the lessor's yield. However, in order to be competitive with other financing alternatives, the lessor may choose to include the security deposit in the pricing calculation. The security deposit lowers the lessee's monthly payment, thereby increasing the probability of closing the transaction.

Using the following assumptions, structure a level payment lease with the refundable security deposit included in calculating the lease payment.

> Equipment cost: 90,000
>
> Annual pretax yield (required ROA): 12%
>
> Term: 60 months, payments in advance
>
> Residual value: 9,000
>
> Refundable security deposit: 9,000.

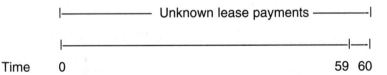

| | Time | 0 | 59 60 |

Initial cash outlay   **Month 60**

Cost	(90,000)	Residual	9,000
Refundable security deposit	9,000	Refundable security deposit	(9,000)
	(81,000)		0

HP-12C			HP-17B (12 P/YR BEGIN MODE)		
				FIN	
	f	REG			TVM
	g	BEG		■	CLEAR DATA
81,000	CHS	PV	81,000	+/-	PV
0		FV	0		FV
60		n	60		N
12	g	12÷	12		I%YR
		PMT 1,783.96			PMT=1,783.96

Using the Three-step Method, the payment is calculated as follows:

Step One

Cost	(90,000.00)
Refundable security deposit	9,000.00
Present value of security deposit refund	(4,954.05)
Present value of residual	4,954.05
Net investment	(81,000.00)

Step Two

HP-12C			HP-17B (12 P/YR BEGIN MODE)		
				FIN	
	f	REG			TVM
	g	BEG		■	CLEAR DATA
1		PMT	1		PMT
60		n	60		N
12	g	12÷	12		I%YR
		PV 45.4046			PV=45.4046

For every dollar of payment over the lease term, 45.4046 of net investment will be recovered.

Step Three

$$\text{Net investment} \div \text{IRU} = \text{Monthly payment}$$
$$81,000 \div 45.4046 = 1,783.96$$

This payment is 89.11 less than the payment of 1,873.07 calculated in Example Two, which did not include the 9,000 refundable security deposit. The difference represents the effect on the payment of monthly interest of 1% (12% annually) on the lessee's investment (security deposit) of 9,000. In effect, the lessee is receiving interest on the security deposit, at the lessor's earnings rate, through the reduction in the required lease payment.

A lessor reduces credit risk and either enhances the yield on the lease or reduces the monthly payment for the lessee through the use of a refundable security deposit. The lessee also may benefit from this arrangement. If the security deposit is priced into the lease, the lessee is, in effect, paid interest on the security deposit at the lessor's required rate of return (12% in this example). It is possible this rate is higher than the lessee's alternative investment opportunities.

EXAMPLE FIVE

A lessor may include its IDCs in the pricing of a lease. IDCs are those costs directly associated with negotiating and consummating a lease, including commissions, legal fees, credit investigation expenses and other costs that can be attributed to a specific lease. If included in the pricing, IDCs increase a lessor's net investment in the lease that must be recovered through an increase in the periodic payments.

Using the following assumptions, structure a level payment lease with all cash flows, including IDCs, considered in calculating the lease payment.

> Equipment cost: 90,000
>
> Annual pretax yield (required ROA): 12%
>
> Term: 60 months, payments in advance
>
> Residual value: 9,000
>
> Refundable security deposit: 9,000
>
> Initial direct costs: 1,800.

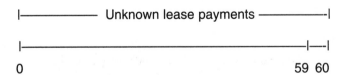

| Time | 0 | | 59 60 |

Initial cash outlay   **Month 60**

Cost	(90,000)	Residual	9,000
Refundable security deposit	9,000	Refundable security deposit	(9,000)
Initial direct costs	(1,800)		0
	(82,800)		

HP-12C			**HP-17B (12 P/YR BEGIN MODE)**		
				FIN	
f	REG			TVM	
g	BEG		■	CLEAR DATA	
82,800	CHS	PV	82,800	+/-	PV
0		FV	0		FV
60		n	60		N
12	g	12÷	12		I%YR
		PMT 1,823.60			PMT=1,823.60

Using the Three-step Method, the payment is calculated as follows:

Step One

Cost	(90,000.00)
Refundable security deposit	9,000.00
Present value of security deposit refund	(4,954.05)
Present value of residual	4,954.05
Initial direct costs	(1,800.00)
Net investment	(82,800.00)

Step Two

HP-12C			**HP-17B (12 P/YR BEGIN MODE)**		
				FIN	
f	REG			TVM	
g	BEG		■	CLEAR DATA	
1		PMT	1		PMT
60		n	60		N
12	g	12÷	12		I%YR
		PV 45.4046			PV = 45.4046

For every dollar of payment over the lease term, 45.4046 of net investment will be recovered. Note that the amount of principal to be recovered per dollar of payment remains constant between the examples being discussed, because the pattern of the lease payments does not change.

Step Three

Net investment ÷ IRU = Monthly payment

82,800 ÷ 45.4046 = 1,823.60

This payment is 39.64 more than the payment of 1,783.96 calculated in Example Four, which did not include the 1,800 of IDCs. The difference represents monthly payments on a present value of 1,800, at 12%, for 60 months.

In this example the net investment in the lease was increased by the amount of the IDCs. However, a lessor also could price to a higher yield on all leases, with the increase in the required target yield attributable to an average effect of IDCs. However, for pricing purposes, if IDCs are not considered in the target yield or the net investment, the lessor will fail to achieve its targeted yield.

EXAMPLE SIX

Closing, documentation and origination fees can provide an additional source of income to lessors. Through charging fees up front, the lessor can offset all or a portion of its IDCs, thereby reducing the net investment in the lease. By reducing the net investment, the lessor reduces credit risk. If a lessor prices a lease based on the net investment without considering the closing fees, the true yield on the lease will be greater than the targeted yield used for pricing. A lessor also may reduce the lessee's payments for competitive reasons.

Building upon Example Five, assume the lessor charges a fee of 1% of equipment cost to originate the lease. What is the lessee's payment if a 1% closing fee is paid?

> Equipment cost: 90,000
>
> Annual pretax yield (required ROA): 12%
>
> Term: 60 months, payments in advance
>
> Residual value: 9,000
>
> Refundable security deposit: 9,000
>
> Closing fee: 900.

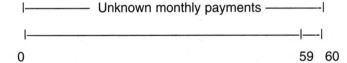

| Time | 0 | | 59 | 60 |

Initial cash outlay   **Month 60**

Cost	(90,000)	Residual	9,000
Refundable security deposit	9,000	Refundable security deposit	(9,000)
Initial direct costs	(1,800)		0
Closing fee	900		
	(81,900)		

HP-12C			HP-17B (12 P/YR BEGIN MODE)		
				FIN	
	f	REG			TVM
	g	BEG	■		CLEAR DATA
81,900	CHS	PV	81,900	+/-	PV
0		FV	0		FV
60		n	60		N
12	g	12÷	12		I%YR
	PMT	1,803.78		PMT = 1,803.78	

Using the Three-step Method, the payment is calculated as follows:

Step One

Cost	(90,000.00)
Refundable security deposit	9,000.00
Present value of security deposit refund	(4,954.05)
Present value of residual	4,954.05
Initial direct costs	(1,800.00)
Origination fee	900.00
Net investment	(81,900.00)

Step Two

HP-12C			HP-17B (12 P/YR BEGIN MODE)		
				FIN	
	f	REG			TVM
	g	BEG	■		CLEAR DATA
1		PMT	1		PMT
60		n	60		N
12	g	12÷	12		I%YR
	PV	45.4046		PV=45.4046	

For every dollar of payment over the lease term, 45.4046 of net investment will be recovered.

Step Three

$$\text{Net investment} \div \text{IRU} = \text{Monthly payment}$$
$$81,900 \div 45.4046 = 1,803.78$$

This payment is 19.82 less than the payment of 1,823.60 calculated in Example Five, which did not include the 900 closing fee. The difference is equivalent to monthly payments on a present value of 900 (the amount of the closing fee), at 12%, for 60 months.

By collecting the fee, the lessor is able to reduce the monthly payment by 19.82. Alternatively, the lessor could keep the payment constant at 1,823.60 and increase its yield. If the lessor collects the 1% closing fee, but does not reduce the lessee's payment, the lessor can increase the yield on the lease from 12.0% to 12.5%.

Equipment cost: 90,000

Annual pretax yield (required ROA): 12%

Term: 60 months, payments in advance

Residual value: 9,000

Refundable security deposit: 9,000

Monthly payment: 1,823.60

Closing fee: 900.

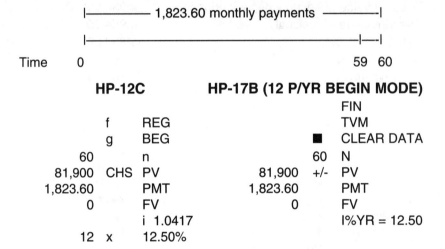

By charging the lessee a 1% closing fee, the lessor is able to reduce its net investment to 81,900. However, the payment was still calculated based on an investment of 90,000. As has been discussed before, the lessor increased the true yield on the lease and the credit risk was reduced because the lessor's net investment has been reduced.

STRUCTURING UNUSUAL PAYMENT STREAMS

A lessee may have unique cash flow requirements. To meet them, a lessor can offer skip, step-up or step-down payment streams. If a lessor is unable or unwilling to meet the lessee's needs, the lessee will seek other funding alternatives. The Three-step Method of structuring leases presented in the previous section allows the lessor to tailor unique payment streams and address the specific needs of the lessee.

For example, a lessee has cash flow limitations early in the lease, but anticipates greater cash flow in later periods. To accommodate the lessee's cash flow restrictions, the lessor may create a step-up lease, structuring payments that increase (step-up) at some point during the lease term. A lease, for instance, may be structured that requires payments of 1,000 for the first 12 months, followed by 36 monthly payments of 1,200.

A step-down lease may be used by a lessor to compensate for additional credit risk. This is a lease with larger monthly payments early in the lease, and payments decreasing at some point during the term of the lease. For example, a lease may be structured with monthly payments of 2,000 for the first 12 months, and payments reduced to 1,200 for the remaining 24 months of the lease term. The greater cash inflow to the lessor provides a hedge against credit risk.

A step-down lease also may be used for a lessee that is currently generating a level of revenue that may or may not continue (such as a company with a few large contracts). This type of lease reduces payments when the lessee is less certain of its cash flow situation.

Another unusual payment stream is a skipped-payment lease. The purpose of this type of lease is to match the timing of lease payments with the lessee's generation of revenue. For example, ski resorts generate a majority of their income during five or six months of winter. Structuring a lease with level payments throughout the lease term would require lease payments during a period when the lessee is not generating revenue. This obviously increases the risk of default by the lessee. A skipped-payment lease could be structured requiring payments only during those six months when revenue is expected. This structure accommodates lessees with seasonal or cyclical business such as ski resorts, construction and agriculture. Other payment patterns may be offered, of course, depending on the various needs of the lessee.

Structuring Step-up or Step-down Leases

Structuring step-up or step-down leases requires a modification of how Step Two is computed in the Three-step Method. In a stepped lease, the stepped-up or -down payment is expressed as a percentage of the base one dollar rental. This concept is illustrated in the following examples.

EXAMPLE SEVEN

Structure a step-up lease consisting of 24 monthly base rentals, in arrears, followed by 24 rentals that are 12% higher than the base rentals. Use the following assumptions.

Equipment cost: 100,000

Purchase option: 15,000, expected to be exercised after a 48-month non-cancellable lease term

Refundable security deposit: 1,500

Initial direct costs: 2,500

Annual pretax yield: 12.00%.

Step One

Identify and present value all known cash flows in the transaction, using the targeted pretax yield as the discount rate.

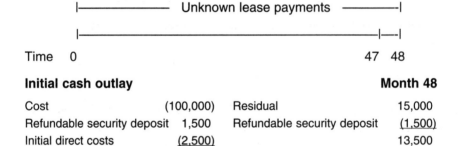

Initial cash outlay		Month 48	
Cost	(100,000)	Residual	15,000
Refundable security deposit	1,500	Refundable security deposit	(1,500)
Initial direct costs	(2,500)		13,500
	(101,000)		

Present value the end-of-term (month 48) cash flows:

HP-12C			**HP-17B (12 P/YR BEGIN MODE)**	
				FIN
	f	REG		TVM
	g	BEG	■	CLEAR DATA
13,500		FV	13,500	FV
48		n	48	N
12.00	g	12÷	12.00	I%YR
		PV 8,373.52		PV =8,373.52

The lessor's net investment at time zero is 92,626.48.

Initial cash outlay	(101,000.00)
Residual present value	8,373.52
Net investment	(92,626.48)

Step Two

Step Two is calculated by determining the present value of the unknown payment stream, using the targeted pretax IRR as the discount rate, and letting each base payment equal one dollar. The stepped-up payments are set equal to 1.12, which is 12% higher than the base rental of one dollar. The present value of this payment stream is 39.9816.

	HP-12C			**HP-17B (#TIMES PROMPTING: ON)**		
					FIN	
					CFLO	
	f	REG	■	CLEAR DATA	YES	
12.00	g	12÷	FLOW (0) = ?	0	INPUT	
1	g	CFj	FLOW (1) = ?	1	INPUT	
24	g	Nj	#TIMES (1) = 1	24	INPUT	
1.12	g	CFj	FLOW (2) = ? 1.12		INPUT	
24	g	Nj	#TIMES (2) = 1	24	INPUT	
	f	NPV 39.9816	EXIT			
			CALC			
			12.00 ÷ 12	I%		
			NPV = 39.9816			

Step Three

Divide the 39.9816 IRU from Step Two into the present value total from Step One of 92,626.48. The quotient is the required base payment. The stepped-up payment will be 112% of the base payment.

Base payment:

$$\frac{92,626.48}{39.9816} = 2,316.73$$

Stepped-up payment:

$$\begin{array}{r} 2,316.73 \\ \times\ \ \ \ 1.12 \\ \hline 2,594.74 \end{array}$$

If the lessor charges the lessee 24 payments of 2,316.73, followed by 24 payments of 2,594.74, in arrears, it will achieve its targeted yield of 12%.

EXAMPLE EIGHT

In a situation in which a lessee requests a step-down lease, a similar procedure to the step-up lease is required. In this example, assume the lessee wishes to pay 36 base payments, with one in advance, followed by 12 reduced payments that are 87% of the base payment.

Step One

Step One, which is to identify and present value all the known cash flows, is exactly the same as Example Seven (92,626.48).

Step Two

Determine the present value of the unknown payment stream, using the targeted pretax IRR as the discount rate, and letting each base payment equal one dollar and each stepped-down payment equal 87% of the one dollar base rental. The present value of this payment stream is 37.3208.

	HP-12C		HP-17B (#TIMES PROMPTING: ON)		
12.00	g	12÷	FLOW (0)=?	1	INPUT
1	g	CFo	FLOW (1)=?	1	INPUT
1	g	CFj	#TIMES (1)=	35	INPUT
35	g	Nj	FLOW (2)=?	.87	INPUT
.87	g	CFj	#TIMES (2)=	12	INPUT
12	g	Nj	EXIT		
	f	NPV 37.3208	CALC		

$$12.00 \div 12 \quad I\%$$
$$NPV = 37.3208$$

Step Three

Divide the 37.3208 from Step Two into the present value total from Step One of 92,626.48. The quotient is the required base payment. The stepped-down payment will be 87% of the base payment.

Base payment:

$$\frac{92{,}626.48}{37.3208} = 2{,}481.90$$

Stepped-down payment:

$$
\begin{array}{r}
2,481.90 \\
\times \quad .87 \\
\hline
2,159.25
\end{array}
$$

If the lessor charges the lessee 36 payments of 2,481.90, followed by 12 payments of 2,159.25, in advance, it will achieve its targeted yield of 12%.

Structuring Leases With Known Initial Payments

Each lessee has a different set of needs, depending on its circumstances. In those situations in which the lessee can pay only a limited amount of rent during the early months of a lease, there will be several changes in structuring methodology. A lessee with a limited budget in the current year may fall in this category.

EXAMPLE NINE

Using the base assumptions of Example Seven, and assuming the lessee can pay only 1,800 per month, in arrears, for the first 12 months of the lease, structure the 36 remaining level payments to provide the lessor its required pretax, 1% monthly yield. (The primary adjustment required is the inclusion of the known cash flows of 1,800 per month as part of Step One, in which all known cash flows are identified and present valued.) The following process reflects the necessary adjustments to the structuring steps.

Step One

Identify and present value all known cash flows in the transaction using the required pretax IRR as the discount rate. The present value of the 12 payments of 1,800 must be added to the (92,626.48) present value of the known cash flows from the preceding examples.

First, present value the known lease payments.

HP-12C			HP-17B (12 P/YR END MODE)	
				FIN
	f	REG		TVM
	g	END	■	CLEAR DATA
12	g	12÷	12	I%YR
1,800		PMT	1,800	PMT
12		n	12	N
		PV 20,259.14		PV 20,259.14

Next, compute the net inception outflow.

Previous present value net cash flows	(92,626.48)
Present value of the 12 rentals at 1,800 each	20,259.14
Net inception outflow	(72,367.34)

Step Two

Determine the present value of the payment stream, using the targeted pre-tax IRR as the discount rate, and letting each regular payment equal one dollar. This step is modified by using a zero in place of the twelve 1,800 payments already considered in Step One. The present value of the remaining unknown payment stream is 26.7189.

HP-12C			HP-17B (#TIMES PROMPTING: ON)		
					FIN
					CFLO
	f	REG	■ CLEAR DATA	YES	
12.00	g	12÷	FLOW (0)=?	0	INPUT
0	g	CFj	FLOW (1)=?	0	INPUT
12	g	Nj	#TIMES (1)=1	12	INPUT
1	g	CFj	FLOW (2)=?	1	INPUT
36	g	Nj	#TIMES (2)=1	36	INPUT
	f	NPV 26.7189	EXIT		
			CALC		
			12.00 ÷ 12	I%	
			NPV = 26.7189		

Step Three

Divide the net investment (from Step One) by the pretax IRU (from Step Two). This step results in the remaining 36 lease payments necessary to achieve the targeted pretax return on investment.

$$\frac{72,367.34}{26.7189} = 2,708.47 \text{ per month}$$

Structuring a Skipped Payment Lease

The following example illustrates how to structure a skipped payment lease. A skipped-payment lease also requires a modification of Step Two.

EXAMPLE TEN

Structure a skipped payment lease using the assumptions of Example Seven, with the following modifications:

Lease term: 48 months, payments in arrears, beginning May 1, with the second, third and fourth payments (June, July, August) skipped each year.

Step One

Cost	(100,000.00)
Refundable security deposit	1,500.00
Present value of deposit refund	(930.39)
Present value of residual	9,303.91
Initial direct costs	(2,500.00)
Net investment	(92,626.48)

Step Two

Determine the present value of the unknown payment stream, using the targeted pretax yield as the discount rate and letting each payment equal one dollar.

		HP-12C		HP-17B (#TIMES PROMPTING: ON)		
						FIN
						CFLO
	f	REG	■	CLEAR DATA	YES	
12.00	g	12÷	FLOW (0)=?		0	INPUT
1	g	CFj	FLOW (1)=?		1	INPUT
0	g	CFj	#TIMES (1)=1		1	INPUT
3	g	Nj	FLOW (2)=?		0	INPUT
1	g	CFj	#TIMES (1)=1		3	INPUT
9	g	Nj	FLOW (3)=?		1	INPUT
0	g	CFj	#TIMES (1)=1		9	INPUT
3	g	Nj	FLOW (4)=?		0	INPUT
1	g	CFj	#TIMES (1)=1		3	INPUT
9	g	Nj	FLOW (5)=?		1	INPUT
0	g	CFj	#TIMES (1)=1		9	INPUT
3	g	Nj	FLOW (6)=?		0	INPUT
1	g	CFj	#TIMES (1)=1		3	INPUT
9	g	Nj	FLOW (7)=?		1	INPUT
0	g	CFj	#TIMES (1)=1		9	INPUT
3	g	Nj	FLOW (8)=?		0	INPUT
1	g	CFj	#TIMES (1)=		3	INPUT
8	g	Nj	FLOW (9)=?		1	INPUT
	f	NPV 28.1495	#TIMES (1)=		8	INPUT
						EXIT
						CALC
			12.00 ÷ 12			I%
				NPV = 28.1495		

The IRU of this skipped payment lease stream is 28.1495.

Step Three

Divide the net investment from Step One by the IRU from Step Two.

$$\text{Net investment} \div \text{IRU} = \text{Unknown payment}$$
$$92{,}626.48 \div 28.1495 = 3{,}290.52$$

This is the base rental amount for each month of the 48-month lease, excluding June, July and August of each year. The payment amount for the three summer months was defined in Step Two as zero. The base rental amount always will be the payment for the period in which the payment in Step Two is assumed to be one dollar.

Base rental (September to May)	=	3,290.52
June, July and August rental	=	0.00

By offering a skipped payment lease, the lessor is able to meet the lessee's seasonal cash flow. The Three-step Method allows for the calculation of the payment amount by identifying the relationship of payment levels in Step Two. Any lease structure can be calculated by matching the pattern of the payments in Step Two.

Uneven or Step Payments (IRS Tests)

The lessor must take care not to violate the Internal Revenue Service (IRS) uneven rent tests when structuring uneven rent leases. The purpose of these tests is to eliminate any potential tax avoidance through either acceleration of expense or deferral of revenue. In general, the IRS ordinarily will not raise any questions about prepaid or deferred rent if the uneven rents meet either of two tests:

1. The annual rent does not vary more than 10% above or below the average annual rent during the initial period

2. The annual rent during the first two-thirds of the lease is not more than 10% above or below the average annual rent during the initial period and the annual rent during the remaining period is no greater than the highest annual rent during the initial phase and no less than one-half of the average annual rent during the initial period.

These tests are referred to collectively as the 90-110 rule. If the uneven rent tests are not met, the IRS may designate portions of the rent as either prepaid or accrued to eliminate any tax avoidance. By doing so, the IRS, in essence, levels the rent stream. Rent levelling could occur, for example, in a step-down lease in which the IRS denies the lessee an immediate deduction for some or all of the higher rentals paid in excess of the average rentals during the earlier part of the lease term (see Exhibit 15-3). Such excess rent would be considered prepaid (deferred) and not yet incurred as an expense for tax purposes and, therefore, would not be deductible.

Accrued rent occurs in a step-up lease in which the IRS requires the lessor to recognize revenue not yet received, but which has been deferred to the latter part of the lease term in the form of higher payments. The pattern of this payment stream is shown in Exhibit 15-4. Average annual rentals include rental holidays, other skipped payments, partial and stepped-up or

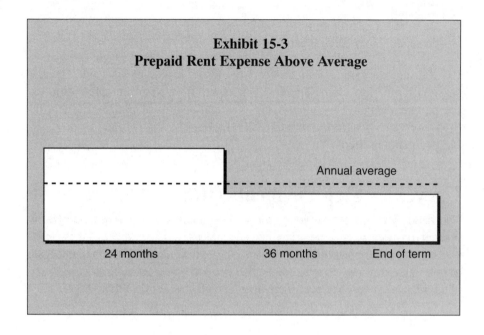

Exhibit 15-3
Prepaid Rent Expense Above Average

Annual average

24 months   36 months   End of term

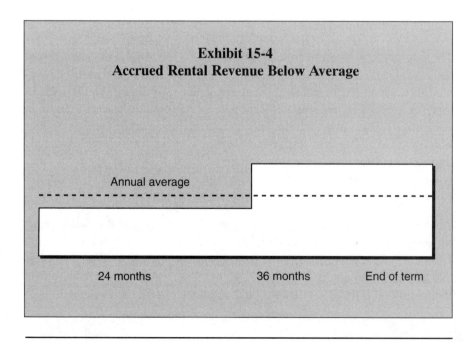

Exhibit 15-4
Accrued Rental Revenue Below Average

Annual average

24 months   36 months   End of term

stepped-down payments occurring within a given year. If the IRS test did not consider annual averages, a lease with only one skipped monthly payment per year would be in violation of the rule.

FORMULAE FOR DETERMINING STEP LEASE MAXIMUMS

When the number of low annual rents is equal to the number of high annual rents, the following formula is used to determine the maximum difference between the high and low rents the IRS test will allow:

L =.8182H, where L equals the low payment and H equals the high payment

Thus, the low payments can be no lower than 81.82% of the high payments. This formula is proven by an example that assumes three years of high rentals at 20,000, followed by three years of low rentals at 16,364 (.8182 x 20,000).

$$\frac{(3 \times 20,000) + (3 \times 16,364)}{6} = 18,182 \text{ average}$$

18,182 x .10 = 1,818
High limit   18,182 + 1,818 = 20,000
Low limit   18,182 - 1,818 = 16,364

Note the high and low payments are at the absolute limits of IRS acceptability. Another way to view this test is following the 90-110 formula.

High limit   18,182 x 110% = 20,000

Low limit   18,182 x 90% = 16,364

When the number of low annual rents is greater than the number of high annual rents (L > H), the following formula is used (if a lease contains a partial year, as in a 42-month lease, the partial year should be annualized).

$$H = \frac{(1.1 \, L) \, (X)}{X - .1 \, (Y)},$$

where, L = Low payment
H = High payment
X = Number of annual low payments
Y = Number of annual high payments

Assuming three years of low rentals followed by two years of high rentals (step-up lease), the high rental can be calculated in relationship to the low.

$$\frac{(1.1 \, L) \, (3)}{3 - .1 \, (2)} = \frac{3.3 \, L}{2.8} = 1.1786 \, L$$

Thus, H = 1.1786 L, or the high payments can be no higher than 117.86% of the low payments. If the annual low payments were 20,000, the high payments would be 23,572 (20,000 x 1.1786).

$$\frac{3\ (20{,}000) + 2\ (23{,}572)}{5} \quad = \quad 21{,}429 \text{ average}$$

$$21{,}429 \times .10 \quad = \quad 2,\ 143$$

High limit   21,429 + 2,143 = 23,572
Low limit   21,429 - 2,143 = 19,286

Note the high and low payments fall within the limits; however, the high payment is at the extreme limit, whereas the low payment is above the lower limit. The low payment can never meet the lower limit as long as the low payment years are in excess of the high payment years. When the number of low annual rents equals the number of high annual rents, both the upper and lower limits can be met.

When the number of low annual rents is less than the number of high annual rents (L < H), the following formula is used:

$$L = \frac{(.9\ H)\ (Y)}{.1\ (X) + Y,} \quad \text{where} \quad \begin{array}{l} L = \text{Low payment} \\ H = \text{High payment} \\ X = \text{Number of annual low payments} \\ Y = \text{Number of annual high payments} \end{array}$$

Assuming three years of high rentals followed by two years of low rentals (step-down lease), the relationship between the low rental and the high can be calculated.

$$L = \frac{.9\ H\ (3)}{.1\ (2) + 3}$$

$$L = \frac{2.7\ H}{3.2}$$

$$L = .8438\ H$$

If the annual payments were 20,000, then the annual high rentals would be 23,702 (20,000 ÷ .8438).

$$\frac{3\ (23,702) + 2\ (20,000)}{5} \qquad = \qquad 22,222 \text{ average}$$

$$22,222 \times .10 \qquad\qquad = \qquad 2,222$$

High limit	22,222 + 2,222 = 24,444	
Low limit	22,222 - 2,222 = 20,000	

Note the high and low payments fall within the limits; however, the low payment is at the extreme limit, whereas the high payment is below the limit. The high payment can never meet the higher limit as long as the number of high payment years is in excess of the low payment years.

When structuring unusual payment streams the lessor should be cognizant of the IRS uneven rent tests, and also of any alternative minimum tax ramifications of the proposed structure.

CONCLUSION

Pricing, at a fundamental level, is a simple, relatively straightforward process. Even complex leases, however, can be structured when the basic principles are understood and correctly implemented. The objectives of pricing always must be to achieve acceptable lessor profitability and to meet customer (lessee) needs. If this is accomplished, all sides will be satisfied with the transaction. The procedures explained in this chapter allow a lessor to add value to a transaction, thereby enhancing customer satisfaction and lessor profitability.

Chapter Sixteen

Advanced Structuring

The fundamental principles necessary to successfully structure leases were explained in the previous chapter. These principles are just that, however – fundamental. The material in this chapter builds on those core structuring principles, but takes them well beyond the basics by addressing how to ensure maximum profitability and competitiveness. Because of the interrelationship between the topics discussed in this chapter and Chapter Fifteen, it is suggested that Chapter Fifteen be reviewed before reading this chapter.

The specialized problems and techniques of advanced structuring are presented in the following sections:

- Pricing Theory

- Quantification of Tax Variables

- After-tax Structuring Techniques.

PRICING THEORY

Although the lessor's rate of return in the lease is a major component of lease pricing, factors beyond rate must be considered when structuring leases. One of these factors is the earnings in the lease, from both a qualitative and quantitative perspective.

Quality of Earnings

Quality of earnings implies several conditions, which are discussed in this section. Once these conditions have been assessed, the appropriate structuring technique for those conditions must be chosen. First, the risk in the structure must be addressed.

RISK

Risk in a lease can take many forms – tax risk, default exposure, residual risk, contingent rental risk and lessee credit risk, to name but a few. If a lessor loses or cannot utilize its tax benefits, for instance, the profitability of the structure has been affected adversely. Likewise, in case of default, the profitability is impacted. In those tax leases with nonrecourse debt, creditor repossession may create unsheltered tax liability. Such a disposition also can trigger recapture of tax benefits.

Another risk, residual or market risk, takes several forms. Technological obsolescence, poor maintenance by the lessee or an oversupply of the equipment type at the end of the lease term can lead to loss of residual value. If such a loss is incurred, either through loss on sale or lack of re-lease opportunities, the lease profitability again has been impaired.

All of the above risks should be dealt with through adjustment of inputs rather than increasing the targeted rate, because increasing the rate assumes risk increases over time. For instance, if residual remarketing results are uncertain, the residual position must be reduced. Lessee risk may be dealt with by increasing yield, which is an approach consistent with traditional lending theory.

TIME VALUE ASSUMPTIONS

Earnings must meet either the company's hurdle rate or the targeted rate of return. The targeted rate should be equal to or greater than the hurdle rate, as the hurdle rate represents the absolute minimum rate of return the lease company must earn.

The earnings in a lease are generated through a mathematical application of the time value of money. This application imposes conditions on how the earnings are calculated, e.g., reinvestment opportunities. As a result, reinvestment of cash flows and sinking fund assumptions must be addressed properly. The lessor's actual reinvestment opportunities must be reflected accurately in the structuring process and the appropriate sinking fund assumptions established. To do so necessitates the selection of a structuring technique appropriate for the reinvestment scenario.

Reinvestment assumptions are critical in any pricing exercise. When a lessor invests in equipment, the leased equipment generates cash flows. These cash flows are reinvested in other lease investments at a rate of return that may or may not be the same as the rate of return on the initial investment. To the extent the reinvestment rate is different from the priced interest rate, the return on the initial investment will be altered. This potential alteration of the rate of return must be considered in pricing. To understand this concept more fully it is necessary to examine how the reinvestment of cash flows occurs in internal rate of return (IRR) structuring, the most common structuring methodology.

Two basic assumptions of an IRR are that (1) all positive cash flows are immediately reinvested at the IRR of the investment and (2) any negative cash flow needs are met from sinking funds earning at the IRR of the investment. These concepts are best illustrated by an example. Given the following cash flows, the IRR of 6.82% can be computed and the validity of the reinvestment assumptions proven (Exhibit 16-1).

Year	Cash flow
0	(1,000)
1	500
2	350
3	(100)
4	400

It can be seen from this example that if the reinvestment rate (6.82% in this case) is equal to the IRR, the actual return will be the IRR. If the lessor's actual reinvestment opportunities differ from the IRR it is using, the lessor's actual rate of return will be altered. Differences in reinvestment opportunities require changes in pricing strategies. For example, if a lessor writes an atypical lease with an after-tax return of 15%, yet normally earns only 7% on its portfolio, a modification to the method of structuring should be made.

Highly inflationary or deflationary environments require structuring methods other than IRR because the reinvestment conditions of the IRR calculation have been altered. These modified methods are used to evaluate various structures of the same transaction so the optimal structure can be chosen. IRR, as a structuring methodology, is appropriate only when the cash flow from the lease can be reinvested at the IRR of that lease.

ALTERNATIVE METHODS

The alternative methods of structuring are presented next and discussed further. Each methodology is dependent on the lessor's reinvestment opportunities (Exhibit 16-2).

NPV Methodology

One modified structuring method is the net present value (NPV) methodology. An example is helpful in understanding this method. Assume a lessor can make the following two investments, one with an IRR of 20% and one with an IRR of 16%. The lessor's reinvestment rate is 10%.

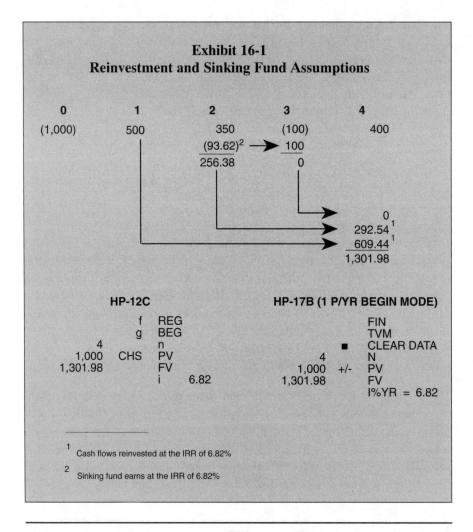

Exhibit 16-1
Reinvestment and Sinking Fund Assumptions

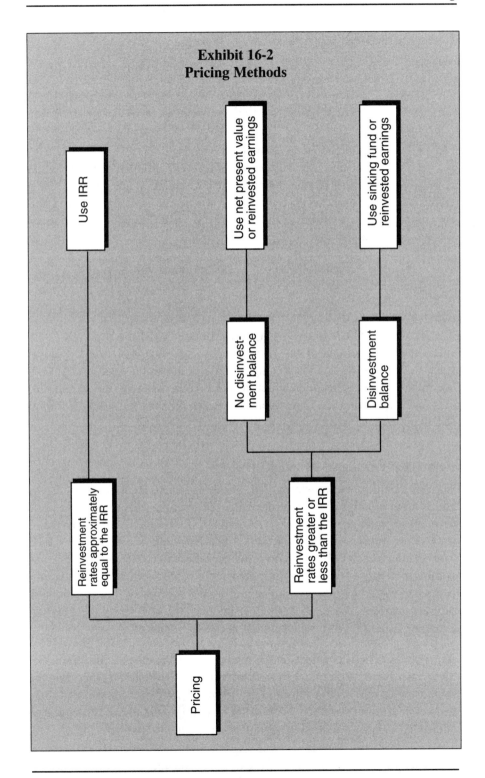

**Exhibit 16-2
Pricing Methods**

Which investment should the lessor make?

Year	0	1	2	3	4	IRR
A	(3,000)	3,585	3	3	18	20%
B	(3,000)	1,072	1,072	1,072	1,072	16%

Most lessors would choose investment A because it has a higher IRR. This is a poor choice because the lessor cannot reinvest at the 20% rate, but only at the 10% rate. The conditions of the IRR calculation are not met. NPV analysis must be used because the reinvestment rate is substantially different from the IRR. Looking at the NPV of the cash flow at 10%, the lessor would choose investment B.

Investment	Net present value
A	276
B	398

The NPV should be selected when NPV contradicts IRR because NPV considers the reinvestment of cash flows at the true reinvestment opportunity. Cash flows must be analyzed using the rate at which they can be reinvested. When choosing between structures, if the reinvestment opportunity differs materially from the investment's IRR, an NPV or reinvested earnings (RE) approach should be used, as shown in Exhibit 16-2.

Reinvested Earnings Methodology

The RE technique is an external rate of return (ERR) method of structuring and is an alternative to NPV structuring. The result is expressed as a yield percentage, making it very easy to compare to targeted returns on assets (ROAs) or returns on equity (ROEs.) The RE yield is calculated by reinvesting all the cash flows in an investment at the actual reinvestment rate and coming up with a terminal value. This appreciated terminal value is then compared to the original investment and a yield computed. The RE methodology has been applied to both investments A and B from the previous example, using the 10% reinvestment rate (see Exhibits 16-3 and 16-4).

After considering the effect of the actual reinvestment rate on the investment cash flows, B is the preferred investment. To reiterate, any time the reinvestment rate differs substantially from the IRR in the lease, and there is no disinvestment balance, NPV or RE structuring should be utilized as an additional means of assessing various structuring alternatives.

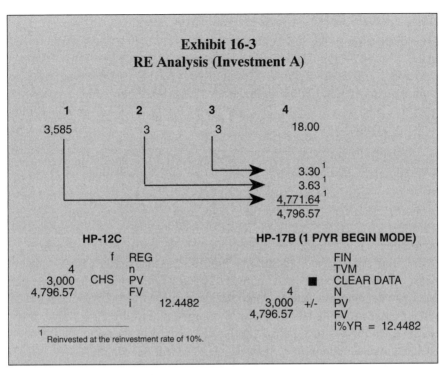

Exhibit 16-3
RE Analysis (Investment A)

1	2	3	4
3,585	3	3	18.00

$3.30\ ^1$
$3.63\ ^1$
$\underline{4,771.64}\ ^1$
$4,796.57$

HP-12C

	f	REG
4		n
3,000	CHS	PV
4,796.57		FV
	i	12.4482

HP-17B (1 P/YR BEGIN MODE)

	FIN
	TVM
■	CLEAR DATA
4	N
3,000 +/-	PV
4,796.57	FV
	I%YR = 12.4482

^{1} Reinvested at the reinvestment rate of 10%.

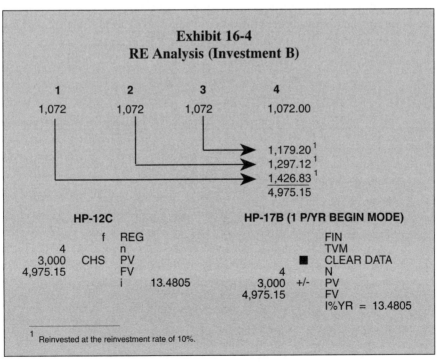

Exhibit 16-4
RE Analysis (Investment B)

1	2	3	4
1,072	1,072	1,072	1,072.00

$1,179.20\ ^1$
$1,297.12\ ^1$
$\underline{1,426.83}\ ^1$
$4,975.15$

HP-12C

	f	REG
4		n
3,000	CHS	PV
4,975.15		FV
	i	13.4805

HP-17B (1 P/YR BEGIN MODE)

	FIN
	TVM
■	CLEAR DATA
4	N
3,000 +/-	PV
4,975.15	FV
	I%YR = 13.4805

^{1} Reinvested at the reinvestment rate of 10%.

Disinvestment Balances

The discussion so far has centered on leases without a disinvestment balance. An analysis of Exhibit 16-2 illustrates that a disinvestment balance requires a different structuring methodology. Disinvestment balances are found most often in highly tax-leveraged leases, although they can occur in monthly analyses of single investor leases because of the timing of when taxes are paid.

A disinvestment balance occurs when the initial investment in the lease is completely recovered before the end of the lease, as in Exhibit 16-5. As can be seen, there is a point (year two) at which the lessor has recovered more principal than has been invested. This overrecovered amount of 372.80 (2,000 - 1,093.20 - 1,279.60) is referred to as the disinvestment balance or, sometimes, as the secondary investment. It is almost as if the lessor owes the initial investment 372.80. At this time in the lease, earnings to the lessor become negative (an expense). The key issue from a structuring perspective becomes the rate at which the earnings on the disinvestment or secondary investment balance should be computed. Exhibit 16-6 shows that if earnings were not recognized on the disinvestment balance, the principal balance would remain unamortized.

This example highlights the importance of utilizing the proper earnings assumptions on disinvestment (also known as sinking fund) balances. If the economic earnings assumption is incorrect, then principal will not be recovered and the lease company's quality of earnings goal will not be met.

Exhibit 16-5
Disinvestment Balance

Year	Cash flows	Interest	Principal	Balance
0	(2,000)			(2,000.00)
1	1,800	706.80	1,093.20	(906.80)
2	1,600	320.40	1,279.60	372.80
3	(800)	(131.80)	(668.20)	(295.40)
4	400	104.60	295.40	0

<table>
<tr><td colspan="5">**Exhibit 16-6**
Impact of a Zero Earnings Rate</td></tr>
<tr><td>**Year**</td><td>**Cash flows**</td><td>**Interest**</td><td>**Principal**</td><td>**Balance**</td></tr>
<tr><td>2</td><td>1,600</td><td>320.40</td><td>1,279.60</td><td>372.80</td></tr>
<tr><td>3</td><td>(800)</td><td>0.00</td><td>(800.00)</td><td>(427.20)</td></tr>
<tr><td>4</td><td>400</td><td>151.00</td><td>249.00</td><td>(178.20)</td></tr>
</table>

Sinking Fund With Reinvestment

A structuring technique that can be used to solve the disinvestment balance problem is called sinking fund with reinvestment (SFR). Under this method, a reasonable reinvestment (as discussed earlier) and disinvestment earnings rate are imposed on the analysis.

Utilizing the previous example, the SFR yield can be calculated. The anticipated reinvestment rate on positive cash flows is 18% and the earnings rate on disinvestment balances is 12%. The SFR is computed in Exhibit 16-7.

SFR structuring simultaneously deals with disinvestment balances and reinvestment problems. SFR does not contradict NPV because, under both methods, the reinvestment rates have been considered. NPV, RE and SFR analytical methods can be used to evaluate various structures given reinvestment and disinvestment balance parameters. They are used to ensure that the quality of the lessor's earnings is maintained. A further discussion of lease yields is contained in Chapter Fourteen.

Quantity of Earnings

There are two aspects to the earnings of a lease – quality of earnings and quantity of earnings. Quantity of earnings implies (1) sufficient cash flow has been generated and (2) the reported accounting profit is adequate. A lessor, in structuring the lease, can choose to maximize cash flow, NPV, yield, accounting income or some other variable. Maximizing one variable, however, generally requires a trade-off in the other variables not being maximized. This is particularly true with the relationship between yield and cash flow, as can be seen in Exhibit 16-8.

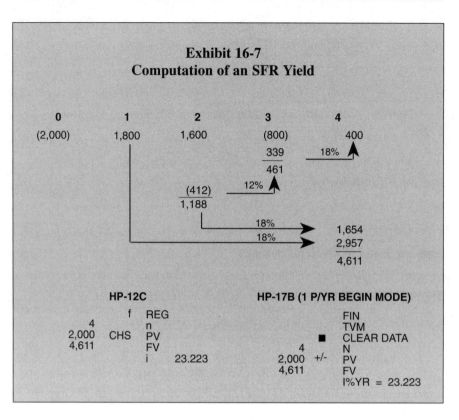

Exhibit 16-7
Computation of an SFR Yield

0	1	2	3	4
(2,000)	1,800	1,600	(800)	400

HP-12C				HP-17B (1 P/YR BEGIN MODE)
	f	REG		FIN
4	n			TVM
2,000	CHS	PV		■ CLEAR DATA
4,611		FV		N
	i	23.223	4	PV
			2,000 +/-	FV
			4,611	I%YR = 23.223

Exhibit 16-8
Cash Flows Versus Yield Comparison

Cash flows

	0	1	2	3	4	5
A	(2,000)	2,100	30	30	30	230
B	(2,000)	0	0	0	0	4,022

Analysis

	IRR	Net cash flow
A	15%	420
B	15%	2,022

If a comparable yield of 15% is maintained for both investments, investment A's net cash flow is significantly less than that of investment B. This difference is a function of how long the average investment is outstanding. Which investment should the lessor choose, given the above information? The decision will depend on the lessor's motivation in the transaction, i.e., is the lessor trying to maximize cash flow or maximize NPV?

MAXIMIZING NPV

For instance, if the lessor wants to maximize NPV, its choice will be based on the lessor's perception of reinvestment opportunities. If reinvestment opportunities are expected to remain at 15%, the lessor would be totally indifferent with regard to investments A and B because the net present value is the same (zero) for both.

If, on the other hand, reinvestment opportunities were expected to rise, investment A would be preferable because the rapid recovery of investment during the first year makes cash available to be reinvested at the expected higher rates. If reinvestment opportunity rates were expected to decline, however, investment B would be selected because the investment has been locked in at 15% and will continue to earn at that rate even if rates decline. (Investment B is very similar to a zero coupon bond.)

When a lessor is faced with rising reinvestment opportunities, it should attempt to structure leases that are front-end loaded. In this way it is able to take advantage of new opportunities more quickly. The converse is true in the case of declining rates. However, the risks associated with end-loading need to be noted. In addition to the additional risk created by end-loading due to residual dependence, other factors, such as credit risk, must be considered.

In the above example, a lessor normally would be indifferent between investments A and B if reinvestment opportunities were constant. Investment B may still be preferable, however, because choosing investment A would cause the lessor to incur the additional costs and risks of locating four new investments to generate the same cash flow as investment B. Another factor to be considered is the cash flow requirements of the lessor over the term of the investment, such as working capital needs. Investment B does not provide interim cash flow.

CASH FLOW

In a discussion of cash flow adequacy it is logical to seek a definition of what is considered to be adequate cash flow. The adequacy or sufficiency of cash flow must be answered by each lessor on a situation-specific basis, but a standard cash flow measurement may be developed. This measurement, termed here the Standardized Investment Liquidity (SIL) index, is defined as the cash flow an investment would generate (at a given IRR or ERR) in equal installments over the full term of that investment. Utilizing the previous 2,000 investment and a 15% yield, a level payment of 597 over the term would be required.

0	1	2	3	4	5
(2,000)	597	597	597	597	597

Based on a level payment of 597, the SIL index can be computed. In this example, 985 is the standardized cash flow.

$$5 \times 597 = \quad \begin{array}{r} 2,985 \\ \underline{(2,000)} \\ 985 \end{array}$$

The SILs on investments A and B from the previous examples are then computed:

$$A \qquad \frac{420}{985} \quad = \quad .43$$

$$B \qquad \frac{2,022}{985} \quad = \quad 2.05$$

In relation to this standard cash flow measure, investment B should be selected as being above the standard. Investment A is below the standard.

If the IRR or ERR remains constant, end-loading will accomplish the objective of improving cash flow. Emphasizing residuals or renewals, employing step-up leases and reducing front-end costs such as advance payments or closing fees are examples of methods to be used. Investment B in the previous example is an excellent example of cash flow enhancement. If the IRR or ERR increases, cash flow should be added pro rata over the lease term to correspond with those increases.

ACCOUNTING EARNINGS

So far, the discussion regarding the quantity of earnings has centered on cash flow. The sufficiency of accounting earnings is the other element implied in quantity of earnings. Accounting earnings and the sufficiency thereof must be considered separately because accounting earnings frequently do not accurately reflect an investment's true economics. Some of the many reasons for these differences include flow-through accounting for ITCs, deferred taxes, the use of implicit rates and residual understatement.

QUANTIFICATION OF TAX VARIABLES

All the structuring examples to this point have been based on a pretax targeted yield. Pretax structuring is widely used, relatively uncomplicated and easy to calculate. Furthermore, for those companies that do not pay taxes, it is entirely accurate. For those lessors that do pay taxes, however, pretax structuring is a less accurate, although acceptable, method of pricing. Since the effect of taxes plays such a significant role in business, after-tax structuring is a more accurate and, therefore, preferable level at which to structure.

Even after-tax structuring can be further stratified into ROA or ROE techniques. ROE is the most sophisticated method of structuring. However, because of its sophistication and accuracy, it is the most complex and difficult to use. For this reason, ROE is not used on a widespread basis for pricing purposes. Before understanding any form of after-tax structuring, however, it is necessary to identify the conceptual differences between pretax and after-tax structuring methodologies.

Because the components included in pretax structuring have been illustrated in the previous chapter, only those items impacting after-tax structuring are identified here. After-tax structuring includes the impact of:

1. **Tax depreciation:** The benefits of the tax depreciation allowed by the government must be included. Tax depreciation is not included in pretax structuring

2. **Tax timing:** The impact of how an entity pays taxes is included in after-tax structuring. The date the transaction is structured, the dates the taxes are remitted, the method of estimation, if applicable, and whether the lessor is a cash versus accrual taxpayer, are considered

3. **Tax effect:** All pretax cash flows are shown net of taxes, or the related taxes are shown separately. A cash outflow, such as interest expense, for example, enters into the calculation at the net amount after any related tax benefits have been recognized. Conversely, cash inflows are shown after any taxes paid on the inflow have been deducted

4. **Targeted rate:** The targeted yield used when structuring the payment must be on an after-tax basis to be consistent with the after-tax nature of the cash flows. The development of targeted yields and hurdle rates is discussed in Chapter Twenty-nine

5. **Tax credits:** Although pretax structuring also may include tax credits, the effect of any form of tax credit, when and if available, always must be included when calculating an after-tax payment. The inclusion of tax credits also would include any recapture of tax credits.

All of the above, plus any other tax benefits/constraints such as gross profit tax deferral (GPTD) or the alternative minimum tax (AMT), are included when structuring on an after-tax basis.

An ancillary aspect of after-tax structuring is the gross-up of an after-tax rate for pricing purposes. A company often will compute a targeted after-tax yield and then convert it to a pretax yield (sometimes referred to as "grossing up"). This pretax yield then is used by the marketing personnel when pricing transactions. Many gross-up approximations are sometimes materially at variance with the true pretax yield. The most common method of grossing up the after-tax yield is to simply divide the after-tax rate by one minus the tax rate. Thus, a 7% after-tax return would be converted to a pretax return as follows, assuming a 35% tax rate:

$$\frac{.07}{(1 - .35)} \quad = \quad 10.77 \text{ pretax equivalent}$$

This method of conversion fails to recognize that the taxes on cash flows received or disbursed are paid on a basis different from the actual receipt or disbursement of those cash flows. The above method does not recognize the timing of tax payments. To achieve an accurate conversion of an after-tax to a pretax yield, the timing of the tax payments must be incorporated into the tax rate, developing, in essence, a timing-effected tax rate. Once this is accomplished, the conversion is:

$$\frac{\text{after-tax rate}}{(1 - t_e)} = \begin{array}{l} \text{pretax equivalent, where } t_e \text{ equals the} \\ \text{timing-effected tax rate} \end{array}$$

A more complete discussion of after-tax yield conversions can be found in Chapter Fourteen.

Structuring Variables

The complexity involved in the pricing of a transaction on an after-tax basis necessitates understanding the impact of numerous variables beyond those discussed in the pretax section. For their effects to be recognized in the pricing of the lease payment, these variables must be quantified, shown after-tax, put on a present value basis and included in the computation of the net investment at lease inception. The following variables are discussed in detail in this section:

1. Nominal versus effective rates

2. Budgeted versus incremental taxpayer

3. Timing of tax payments

4. Gross profit tax deferral

5. Miscellaneous variables.

NOMINAL VERSUS EFFECTIVE RATES

Most of the leases being written today incorporate monthly compounding of the yield. This is not to say they all have monthly payments. Certainly quarterly, semiannual and annual payments are being offered. The point is that, although the payments may not be made on a monthly basis, the yield still is compounded monthly. If the cash flows or benefits occur on other than a monthly basis, therefore, an effective rate must be computed when manually structuring a lease. First of all, what is an effective yield?

A nominal yield is the rate stated in the instrument. If the bank advertises a 5% earning on savings, 5% is the stated or nominal rate. An effective rate, on the other hand, includes the effects of any compounding. Since the interest earnings also are earning, in addition to the principal, the effective rate always will be higher. Using the same bank example, if the nominal 5% rate were to be compounded monthly, the effective rate would be 5.12%. The effective rate is higher because of the monthly compounding.

An annual effective rate is used most commonly in manual structuring to recognize the present value of tax depreciation. Because the allowable percentages are stated at an annual amount, the annual discount rate used must reflect monthly compounding. A monthly compounded annual effective rate accomplishes this. An annual effective rate can be computed a number of ways.

1. With a formula:

$$\left(1 + \frac{\left(\frac{i}{n}\right)}{100}\right)^n$$ where i is the annual nominal rate and n is the number of compounding periods

Using the 5% bank example, with a 12-month period:

$$\left(1 + \frac{\left(\frac{5}{12}\right)}{100}\right)^{12} =$$

$(1.004167)^{12} = 1.0512$

$(1.0512 - 1) = .0512$ or 5.12%

The keystrokes to accomplish the above formula are as follows:

HP-12C	HP-17B
1 ENTER	5 ÷ 12 ÷ 100 + 1
5 ENTER	■ y^x 12
12 ENTER	- 1 = .0512
100 X ÷ +	
12 Y^x	
1 - .0512, or 5.12%	

2. The formula method is a mathematical approach. An approach that makes more conceptual sense to most people is to use the time value function of the calculator. Using this method, the future value of one dollar, invested at the nominal rate for 12 months, is computed. This is appropriate, for the effective growth rate (or earnings) is nothing more than the appreciated value (future value) of an investment less the original investment:

	HP-12C			**HP-17B**
f	REG			FIN
1	CHS PV			ICNV
12	n		■	CLEAR DATA
5	g 12÷			PER
	FV 1.0512	12		P
1	-	5		NOM%
	.0512, or 5.12%			EFF% = 5.12

Both of these methods result in exactly the same answer: which is used depends on the individual lessor's discretion.

Effective rates have efficacy beyond finding the present value of tax benefits. They also can be used to compute nonmonthly payments, such as quarterly payments, and still maintain a monthly compounded yield. In the case of quarterly payments, a quarterly effective rate (with monthly compounding) must be computed. Using the methods previously discussed, and the 5% bank example, the quarterly effective rate can be computed.

1. Formula:

$$\sqrt[4]{(1.004167)^{12}} = \quad \text{(to reflect quarterly compounding)}$$
$$(1.004167)^3 = \quad 1.0126$$
$$1.0216 - 1 = \quad .0126, \text{ or } 1.26\%$$

This formula compounds monthly the nominal annual rate and then removes the subsequent quarterly compounding so there is no double compounding.

	HP-12C			**HP-17B**		
1.004167	ENTER	1.004167	■	y^x	3	
3	Y^x	-	1	=	.0126	
1	- .0126, or 1.26%					

2. Alternative method:

	HP-12C			**HP-17B (12 P/YR BEGIN MODE)**
f	REG			FIN
1	CHS PV			TVM
3	n		■	CLEAR DATA
5	g 12÷	1	+/-	PV
	FV 1.01263	3		N
1	- .0126, or 1.26%	5		I%YR
				FV = 1.0126
		-	1	= .0126

Effective rates are used throughout the remainder of this chapter.

BUDGETED VERSUS INCREMENTAL TAXPAYER

Whether or not a lease represents budgeted or incremental business affects the timing and, hence, the value of tax benefits. This timing impacts the structuring process.

Corporations pay taxes differently than most individuals. A corporation is allowed to estimate all its revenues and expenses for the coming year in arriving at what is termed its budgeted taxable income. Taxes must be computed on this estimated taxable income. In the U.S., these estimated taxes are then remitted over four estimated tax remittance dates. For a calendar year taxpayer, estimated taxes are paid on the following dates in the stated percentages:

April 15	.25
June 15	.25
September 15	.25
December 15	.25

The tax benefits associated with a budgeted lease are received over the four estimated payment dates, irrespective of when during the year it is funded. Conversely, any tax liabilities are likewise recognized.

If a lease is not included in the budgeted taxable income, it is termed an incremental lease. The tax benefits or liabilities are recognized in an incremental lease differently than in a budgeted lease. An incremental lease generates tax benefits in a manner such that the tax benefits are recognized over the remaining tax remittance dates. (This is very similar in concept to a budgeted lease.) Thus, an incremental lease structured June 1 will create tax benefits as follows:

June 15	.333
September 15	.333
December 15	.334

A fiscal year corporation remits taxes in the same sequence, except the first remittance date is 3.5 months into its fiscal year. Because of the timing of when tax benefits are recognized, a budgeted lease should be structured differently than an incremental lease.

TIMING OF TAX PAYMENTS

When a lease is structured impacts the value of the tax benefits. The tax benefits for a budgeted lease funded in December, for instance, are worth more than the tax benefits for a lease funded in March. This is because the tax benefits, and associated cash savings, are realized much earlier, and, hence, earn longer, for the lease written in December. These tax savings then can be reinvested for a period of time before any funds need to be expended for the lease. This phenomenon is seen each year at year-end when lease rates drop. Although not the sole reason, it is certainly a contributing factor.

The impact of the structuring date on tax benefits can be quantified. Once quantified, it then can be incorporated into the structuring computation. The process by which this timing effect is quantified is to present or future value the tax benefits received on each remittance date to the date on which the lease is structured.

Example

Assuming a company's monthly nominal cost of capital is 1% per month, calculate the value of the tax benefits for a lease that has a December 31 inception date, is part of the annual estimated tax budget and has 1,000 of after-tax benefits associated with it.

Solution

In order to determine how much the after-tax benefits are actually worth (due to the December 31 structure date), the tax benefit on each of the remittance dates must be future valued to December 31, the inception date, as in Exhibit 16-9.

The future values of the estimated quarterly tax remittance dates, as shown in Exhibit 16-10, are then calculated. The 1,000 of tax benefits is actually worth 1,048.89 (on a present value basis), because the lease is structured on December 31.

Thus, tax benefits or liabilities in a lease structured on December 31 would be worth 104.9% of face value (1,048.89 ÷ 1,000). This factor is referred to as the intraperiod present value factor (IPVF), and is utilized heavily throughout after-tax structuring. Intuitively, tax benefits from a lease structured in December, such as depreciation, should be worth more than face

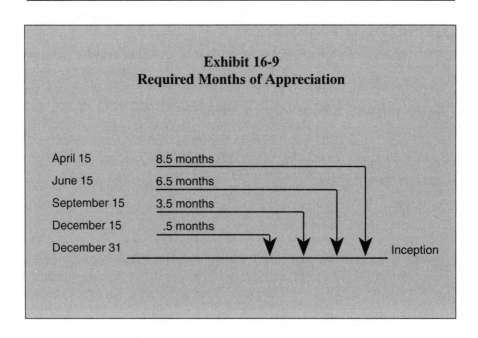

Exhibit 16-9
Required Months of Appreciation

April 15	8.5 months
June 15	6.5 months
September 15	3.5 months
December 15	.5 months
December 31	Inception

Exhibit 16-10
Inception Value of Tax Benefits

Date	Benefit received	Future value of benefit at inception
April 15	1,000 x .25 = 250	272.07
June 15	1,000 x .25 = 250	266.71
September 15	1,000 x .25 = 250	258.86
December 15	1,000 x .25 = 250	251.25
Total		1,048.89

value because 100% of the tax benefits for the year have been received and invested beginning in April of the current year. The concept of IPVF is applied to both tax benefits and liabilities.

TAX DEPRECIATION BENEFITS

Lessor oftentimes seek the tax benefits of tax ownership, which affect the pricing of the lease transaction. These benefits are a result of the timing of when MACRS deductions are received in a tax lease, as opposed to the principal exclusion in a nontax lease. The timing of the deductions and taxable income, of course, affects the timing of the cash flows resulting from the tax benefits and tax expenses. Therefore, a time value of money benefit can be realized by the lessor if the end-user of the equipment selects the tax lease alternative.

The lessor can consider in its pricing process the amount, on a present value basis, of the tax savings from the accelerated depreciation deductions compared to the principal reductions in the nontax lease. The additional cash flow, realized purely from timing differences in income recognition, either contributes to the lessor's yield in the lease or allows the lessor to offer a lower payment to the lessee.

GROSS PROFIT TAX DEFERRAL

If a manufacturing parent sells its products to its captive subsidiary or division, a tax benefit, GPTD, is created. This benefit should be incorporated into the captive pricing. To amplify this concept, any gain realized by the parent on the sale of property to its captive lessor, in a deferred intercompany transaction, is not remitted by the parent at the time of sale. Instead, it is taken into income in proportion to the cost recovery on the financial instrument being recognized by the captive. The benefit of this tax deferral method is in receiving cash proceeds when the transaction is funded, yet paying taxes on those proceeds over the deferral period. (GPTD is further discussed and illustrated in Chapters Six and Twenty-four.)

The benefit from GPTD, which represents a reduction in taxes paid, is included in the calculation of the net investment at time zero for purposes of computing the lease payment. Structuring to incorporate GPTD is illustrated later in this chapter.

MISCELLANEOUS VARIABLES

Before finishing up this section on quantifying tax structuring variables, two other points need to be made. One is the impact of refundable security deposits, which are nontaxable. Refundable security deposits are included, therefore, at face value. The other issue is the Internal Revenue Service (IRS) uneven rent tests for guideline leases, and the Internal Revenue Code §467 uneven rent tests.

Creative structuring often results in an uneven rental stream, such as in a step-up or step-down pattern. The IRS has developed rules to preclude tax avoidance in structuring these kinds of leases. The IRS ordinarily will not raise any question about prepaid or deferred rent if the uneven rents in the payment stream meet either of two tests. These tests are sometimes referred to as the 90-110 tests and are discussed in Chapter Seven, as are the §467 tests. When structuring tax leases, these criteria must be kept in mind. Uneven rent structuring is discussed more fully in Chapter Fifteen.

AFTER-TAX STRUCTURING TECHNIQUES

After-tax structuring is a more accurate and sophisticated method of structuring than pretax structuring. As a result, it is more complex. Although it is not an appropriate, or even necessary, method for all lessors, after-tax structuring allows a lessor to be very price competitive and still know it is earning its required return.

Structuring Steps

After-tax structuring is predicated on the basic principles of pretax structuring. Although there are more variables and a few special steps, the core concept is exactly the same. Five steps must be followed to structure a lease to an after-tax targeted yield using a hand-held calculator.

STEP ONE

Identify and present value all the known cash flows in the transaction, including tax benefits. The required after-tax IRR is used as the discount rate. This step is the same as Step One in pretax structuring. The only differences are the discount rate and the additional variables, such as after-tax residuals, tax depreciation, the effect of GPTD and G & A expenses, etc.

STEP TWO

Determine the present value of the payment stream, using the targeted after-tax IRR as the discount rate, and letting each payment equal one dollar. This step is exactly equal to Step Two in pretax structuring.

STEP THREE

Determine the present value of the annual tax liabilities associated with the one dollar lease payments determined in Step Two. After computing the present value of the lease stream, it is necessary to compute the taxes on the payments being received. This step is done in the same manner as Step Two, by letting one dollar equal the payment.

The appropriate IPVF is applied to the present value of the taxes to reflect the tax payment dates. Taxes typically are not paid at the time rent is received, or when other taxable events occur. In the U.S., for example, taxes are paid on an annual basis over four estimated payment dates; therefore, the present value of the payment stream will be calculated on an annual basis. This present value is then multiplied by the tax rate to arrive at the annual taxes due.

By using the IPVF of allocating the taxes on the payments to the tax year in which they are paid, the proper timing of the tax remittances is recognized. An annual effective rate must be utilized as a discount rate when computing the present value of the taxes. An example will help clarify this step.

The assumptions are for a lease structured on June 1, with two payments in advance, a 48-month term, an annual effective, after-tax discount rate of 9%, a 99.03% IPVF and a 35% tax rate. To calculate the taxes due on this payment stream, the payments first must be placed into the tax years in which they are taxed. Notice this 48-month lease spans five tax years:

Year	Number of payments	
1	8	(six regular and two advance payments)
2	12	
3	12	
4	12	
5	4	
Total	48	

The present value of the annual taxable income (payments) is computed and then multiplied by the tax rate to arrive at the taxes due. The IPVF is multiplied by the present value of the taxes to reflect the four estimated payment dates. The first year payments are placed at time 0 because the IPVF brings all payments to time 0.

HP-12C			HP-17B (#TIMES PROMPTING: ON)		
	f	REG		FIN	
9		i		CFLO	
8	g	CFo	■ CLEAR DATA	YES	
12	g	CFj	FLOW(0)=?	8	INPUT
3	g	Nj	FLOW(1)=?	12	INPUT
4	g	CFj	#TIMES(2)=?	3	INPUT
	f	NPV 41.2092	FLOW(2)=?	4	INPUT
.35	x	14.4232	#TIMES(2)=1	1	INPUT
.9903	x	14.2833		EXIT	
				CALC	
			9	I%	
			NPV =	41.2092	
			x .35 =	14.4232	
			x .9903 =	14.2833	

The total of 14.2833 represents the present value of the taxes payable on the payment stream of 48 months, after reflecting when the taxes are actually paid.

STEP FOUR

Deduct the results of Step Three from Step Two. This step puts the investment recovery unit (IRU) on an after-tax basis, so it can be applied to the after-tax net investment in arriving at the payment.

STEP FIVE

Divide the after-tax net investment (from Step One) by the after-tax IRU (from Step Four). This step results in the pretax payment computed on an after-tax basis. The logic behind this step is exactly the same as Step Three in the pretax structuring chapter. By reducing the IRU by the amount of the taxes, the amount of the payment will be larger. This increase in payment allows the taxes to be paid, yet still returns the lessor's targeted, after-tax yield.

After-tax Structuring Example

The steps to be followed in structuring on an after-tax basis now have been explained. An example of how they are actually applied in structuring a lease will reinforce these concepts. The example is based on the following assumptions:

Equipment cost: 100,000 (purchased June 1)

Refundable security deposit: 1,500

Tax depreciation: 5-year MACRS equipment placed in service June 1, of a calendar year taxpayer

Purchase option: 15,000, expected to be exercised after 48 months

Initial direct costs: 2,500

Federal tax rate: 35%

Annual nominal, after-tax yield required by the lessor: 8.04%

Monthly G & A expenses: 50

The lease is considered part of the annual tax budget and not incremental. The lessor currently can use all tax benefits

Lease term: 48 months, payments in advance.

SOLUTION

Before the five, after-tax structuring steps can be completed, it is necessary to make certain preliminary computations. The results of these computations then are used in the structuring steps.

Preliminary Computations

1. Convert the annual nominal IRR to its monthly nominal rate, as well as its annual effective equivalent

   Monthly nominal rate: $8.04 \div 12 = .67\%$ per month

   Annual effective rate:

$$\left(1 + \left(\tfrac{.67}{100}\right)\right)^{12}$$

HP-12C		HP-17B		
1.0067	ENTER	1.0067	■ y^x	12
12 y^x	1.08343	- 1	= .08343	
1.08343 - 1	.08343			

The annual effective yield is 8.343%

2. Compute the IPVF for a budgeted lease structured June 1, as in Exhibit 16-11. In this example, tax benefits or liabilities are worth 98.529% of face value for a lease structured on June 1.

Exhibit 16-11
IPVF Computation

Remittance date	Required remittance %	Months from inception	Present or future value %
April 15	25	-1.5	25.252
June 1	0	0.0	0.000
June 15	25	.5	24.917 [1]
September 15	25	3.5	24.422
December 15	25	6.5	23.938
Total			98.529

1		HP-12C		HP-17B (1 P/YR BEGIN MODE)		
		f	REG			FIN
	.67		i			TVM
	.25	CHS	FV		■	CLEAR DATA
	.50		n		.67	I%YR
			PV	.24917	.25	+/- FV
					.50	N
						PV = .24917

Step One

Present value, at the required after-tax IRR, all the known cash flows.

1. All the known cash flows must be identified and listed

    Equipment cost
    Initial direct costs (after-tax)
    Refundable security deposit
    Residual value (net of taxes and deposit refund)
    MACRS tax benefits
    G & A costs

2. The present value of the equipment cost must be determined

    a. given at 100,000

    b. had the equipment been paid for at a later date, a present value computation would have been required

3. Any initial direct costs should be identified and expressed at their after-tax equivalent

    a. after-tax conversion formula: Expense x [1 - (tax rate x IPVF)] = after-tax cost

    b. 2,500 x [1 - (.35 x .98529)] = 1,637.87

4. The impact of the refundable security deposit must be identified

    a. given at 1,500, it is not adjusted for tax benefits because it is not tax deductible

    b. the refund of the security deposit is considered as part of the net residual yet to be calculated. The residual value (net of taxes and the deposit refund) must be calculated and then present valued, as in Exhibit 16-12. The present value of the net residual is then computed

	HP-12C				HP-17B (1 P/YR BEGIN MODE)	
	f	REG				FIN
.67		i				TVM
48		n			■	CLEAR DATA
12,299.92	CHS	FV		.67		I%YR
		PV	8,926.87	48		N
				12,299.92	+/-	FV
						PV = 8,926.87

Exhibit 16-12
Calculation of Net Residual Proceeds

Step	Amount
Salvage proceeds	15,000.00
Remaining tax basis	(11,520.00)
(.1152 x 100,000)	
Salvage expenses	0.00
Taxable gain (loss)	3,480.00
Tax rate	x .35
Tax benefit (liability)	(1,218.00)
IPVF	x .98529
Net tax benefit (liability)	(1,200.08)
Proceeds	15,000.00
Security deposit refund	(1,500.00)
Net residual proceeds	12,299.92

5. The value of the MACRS tax benefit is calculated

		HP-12C	**HP-17B (# TIMES PROMPTING: OFF)**		
	f	REG			FIN
8.343		i			CFLO
.20	g	CFo	■ CLEAR DATA		YES
.32	g	CFj	FLOW (0)=?	.20	INPUT
.192	g	CFj	FLOW (1)=?	.32	INPUT
.1152	g	CFj	FLOW (2)=?	.192	INPUT
.0576	g	CFj	FLOW (3)=?	.1152	INPUT
	f	NPV .7913	FLOW (4)=?	.0576	INPUT
					EXIT
100,000	x	79,131.45			CALC
.35	x	27,696.01		8.343	I%
.98529	x	27,288.60		NPV =	.7913
			x	100,000 =	79,131.45
			x	.35 =	27,696.01
			x	.98529 =	27,288.60

The present value of the MACRS benefits is 27,288.60

6. G & A expenses must be converted to an after-tax basis and then present valued. Convert the monthly G & A expense of 50 to its after-tax equivalent

$$50 \times [1 - (.35 \times .98529)] = 32.76$$

The present value of the monthly, after-tax, G&A expense then is computed.

HP-12C			HP-17B (1 P/YR END MODE)	
f	REG			FIN
g	END			TVM
48	n		■	CLEAR DATA
32.76	CHS	PMT	48	N
.67	i		32.76 +/-	PMT
	PV	1,340.88	.67	I%YR
				PV = 1,340.88

The present value of all the known cash flows is 65,263.39. This amount represents the after-tax investment, the lessor must recover through the lease payments.

Equipment cost	(100,000.00)
Initial direct costs (after-tax)	(1,637.87)
Refundable security deposit	1,500.00
Residual value (net)	8,926.87
MACRS tax benefits	27,288.60
G & A costs	(1,340.88)
	(65,263.28)

Step Two

Find the present value of the unknown lease payments, letting one dollar equal each payment.

HP-12C			HP-17B (1 P/YR BEGIN MODE)	
f	REG			FIN
g	BEG			TVM
48	n		■	CLEAR DATA
.67	i		48	N
1	PMT		.67	I%YR
	PV	41.2047	1	PMT
				PV = 41.2047

Step Three

Find the present value of the annual tax liabilities associated with the one dollar lease payments previously determined. Since the payment is being structured on an after-tax basis, the tax impact of the unknown payments that will be received must be considered. The lease payments occur each year in the following manner:

Tax year	Lease payments
1	7
2	12
3	12
4	12
5	5

The present value of 14.2643 represents the taxes associated with the payment stream. The present value of the taxes has been adjusted to reflect the timing of when, during the year, the taxes are paid.

HP-12C			HP-17B (#TIMES PROMPTING: ON)		
	f	REG			FIN
8.343	i				CFLO
7	g	CFo	■ CLEAR DATA		YES
12	g	CFj	FLOW (0)=?	7	INPUT
3	g	Nj	FLOW (1)=?	12	INPUT
5	g	CFj	#TIMES (1)=1	3	INPUT
			FLOW(2)=?	5	INPUT
	f	NPV 41.3636	#TIMES (2)=1	1	INPUT
.35	x	14.4773			EXIT
.98529	x	14.2643			CALC
				8.343	I%
			NPV =	41.3636	
			x .35	= 14.4773	
			x .98529	= 14.2643	

Step Four

Deduct the present value of the tax liability from the present value of the payments. This step will place the structuring factor on an after-tax basis.

41.2047	(pretax structuring factor)
(14.2643)	(tax liability present value)
26.9404	(after-tax structuring factor)

Step Five

Divide the 26.9404 after-tax structuring factor from above into the present value of all the known cash flows. The quotient is the required pretax payment that will result in an 8.04% annual, after-tax return to the lessor.

$$\frac{65,263.28}{26.9404} \quad = \quad 2,422.51$$

The structuring factor is shown as:

$$\frac{2,422.51}{100,000.00} \quad = \quad .024225$$

Structuring Unusual Payment Streams

Lessors frequently accommodate their lessees' unique cash flow requirements by structuring leases with varied or unusual payment patterns. These leases may reflect a skipped, step-up, step-down or other type of payment stream that meets the lessees' needs.

The same steps described in Chapter Fifteen are followed in structuring unusual payment leases, except Steps Two and Three are modified slightly to include the impact of the taxes on revenue. Step Two must be changed by altering the assumed one dollar lease payments for the periods affected and Step Three must be modified to reflect the annual tax liability on the altered one dollar lease payment stream.

SKIPPED-PAYMENT EXAMPLE

Structure a skipped payment lease using the same base assumptions as on page 557. The only difference between those assumptions and this example is the inclusion of skipped payments during the lease.

Equipment cost: 100,000 (purchased June 1)

Refundable security deposit: 1,500

Tax depreciation: 5-year MACRS equipment placed in service June 1, of a calendar year taxpayer

Purchase option: 15,000, expected to be exercised after 48 months

Initial direct costs: 2,500

Federal tax rate: 35%

Annual nominal, after-tax yield required by the lessor: 8.04%

Monthly G & A expenses: 50

The lease is considered part of the annual tax budget and not incremental. The lessor currently can use all tax benefits

Lease term: 48 months, with payments in arrears, beginning May 1,
19X1, with the second, third and fourth payments of each year
(June, July, August) being skipped.

Step One

Step One is exactly the same as the base example, except for when the payments
are received. Therefore, only the calculation of Steps Two through Five is shown.
The summary of the present value of all known cash flows is presented below.

Equipment cost	(100,000.00)
Initial direct costs	(1,637.87)
Refundable security deposit	1,500.00
Residual value (net)	8,926.87
MACRS tax benefits	27,288.60
G & A expenses	(1,340.88)
Net inception outflow	(65,263.28)

Step Two

Step Two is to determine the unknown present value of the payment stream,
using the targeted after-tax IRR as the discount rate. Each regular payment
is equal to one dollar and the skipped payments are equal to zero.

HP-12C			HP-17B (#TIMES PROMPTING: ON)		
	f	REG			FIN
.67		i			CFLO
1	g	CFj	■ CLEAR DATA		YES
0	g	CFj	FLOW (0)=?	0	INPUT
3	g	Nj	FLOW (1)=?	1	INPUT
1	g	CFj	#TIMES (1)=1	1	INPUT
9	g	Nj	FLOW (2)=?	0	INPUT
0	g	CFj	#TIMES (2)=1	3	INPUT
3	g	Nj	FLOW (3)=?	1	INPUT
1	g	CFj	#TIMES (3)=1	9	INPUT
9	g	Nj	FLOW (4)=?	0	INPUT
0	g	CFj	#TIMES (4)=1	3	INPUT
3	g	Nj	FLOW (5)=?	1	INPUT
1	g	CFj	#TIMES (5)=1	9	INPUT

9	g	Nj		FLOW (6)=?	0	INPUT
0	g	CFj		#TIMES (6)=1	3	INPUT
3	g	Nj		FLOW (7)=?	1	INPUT
1	g	CFj		#TIMES (7)=1	9	INPUT
8	g	Nj		FLOW (8)=?	0	INPUT
	f	NPV	30.458475	#TIMES (8)=1	3	INPUT
				FLOW (9)=?	1	INPUT
				#TIMES (9)=1	8	INPUT
				EXIT		
				CALC		
				I%	.67	
				NPV=30.458475		

The present value of this skipped payment lease stream is 30.458475.

Step Three

Find the present value of the annual tax liabilities associated with the one dollar lease payments determined in Step Two.

	Lease payments
Tax year	per tax year
1	5
2	9
3	9
4	9
5	4

HP-12C				**HP-17B (#TIMES PROMPTING: ON)**		
	f	REG			FIN	
8.343		i			CFLO	
5	g	CFo		■ CLEAR DATA	YES	
9	g	CFj		FLOW (0)=?	5	INPUT
3	g	Nj		FLOW (1)=?	9	INPUT
4	g	CFj		#TIMES (1)=1	3	INPUT
	f	NPV	30.954135	FLOW (2)=?	4	INPUT
				#TIMES (2)=1	1	INPUT
.35	x	10.833947			EXIT	
.98529	x	10.674580			CALC	
				I%	8.343	
				NPV =	30.954135	
				x .35	= 10.833947	
				x .98529	= 10.674580	

The present value of the tax liability associated with this skipped payment lease stream is 10.674580.

Step Four

Deduct the results of Step Three from Step Two.

$$
\begin{array}{ll}
30.458475 & \text{(pretax structuring factor)} \\
\underline{(10.674580)} & \text{(tax liability present value)} \\
19.783895 & \text{(after-tax structuring factor)}
\end{array}
$$

Step Five

Divide the 19.783895 remainder from Step Four into the present value total from Step One. The quotient is the required pretax payment that will result in an 8.04% annual, after-tax return to the lessor.

Payment:

$$
\frac{65{,}263.28}{19.783895} = 3{,}298.81
$$

Structuring factor:

$$
\frac{3{,}298.81}{100{,}000.00} = .032988
$$

The key to structuring leases with unusual payment streams is to replicate the pattern of the payments, using one dollar as the payment amount. For example, in the skipped payment leases, the skipped payments are set equal to zero when computing the present value of the one dollar payments and the tax liability on those payments.

ROE Structuring (Match Funded)

Leases can be structured on either an ROA or an ROE basis. ROE level structuring takes into consideration the amount of the debt, the cost of the debt and the way it is repaid. If the lessor chooses to target an ROE, the structuring method will be a function of how the leasing company is funded. Certain lessors, for instance, attempt to maintain constant debt-to-equity ratios in their leasing portfolios, which is a pooled approach. Others match fund each lease with debt that matches the terms of the lease.

When structuring a lease to obtain a targeted ROE, assuming match funded debt, the same structuring procedures are followed as in ROA structuring. The only differences are that all cash flows are discounted at the required ROE (rather than the ROA), the IPVF is computed using the ROE as a discount rate and the known cash flows now include the loan proceeds, loan payments and the tax benefit of the interest deductions on the debt.

Match funding means to fund the underlying debt in a lease investment with a loan, the terms of which are the same as the lease. Therefore, a 48-month lease would have a loan requiring 48 monthly loan payments. Since, at the inception of a lease, the terms of the debt repayment are known (interest rate, payment amounts, etc.), the structuring process revolves around recouping the difference between the investment cost and the debt proceeds. This difference is the equity investment.

ROE STRUCTURING EXAMPLE

The following structuring techniques are used to structure a lease to a targeted ROE, using match funded debt. They incorporate certain procedural modifications to the previously illustrated structuring steps. This example is based on the following assumptions:

Equipment cost: 100,000 (purchased June l)

Refundable security deposit: 1,500

Tax depreciation: 5-year MACRS equipment placed in service June 1, of a calendar year taxpayer

Purchase option: 15,000, expected to be exercised after 48 months

Initial direct costs: 2,500

Incremental federal tax rate: 35%

Annual nominal, after-tax yield required by the lessor: 8.04%

Monthly G & A expenses: 50

The lease is considered part of the annual tax budget and not incremental. The lessor currently can use all tax benefits

Lease term: 48 months, payments in advance

Match funded loan: 85,000, with interest at 7.9707% and 48 loan payments, in arrears, at 2,073.93 per month. Loan proceeds are received at lease inception

Required ROE (annual effective): 17% (1.317% per month nominal)

IPVF: .96975.

The following steps must be followed in ROE, match funding structuring. Except for the aforementioned modifications, these steps are exactly the same as the after-tax structuring steps previously discussed. Because of this repetition, each step is presented in an abbreviated format.

Step One

Present value, at the required after-tax IRR, all the known cash flows.

1. Review of all the known cash flows

    Equipment cost

    Initial direct costs

    Refundable security deposit

    Residual value (net of taxes and deposit refund)

    Loan proceeds

    Loan payments

    Interest tax benefits

    MACRS tax benefits

    G & A expenses

2. Initial direct costs: 2,500 x [1 - (.35 x .96975)] = 1,651.47

3. The residual value (net of taxes and deposit refund) is computed in Exhibit 16-13 as 12,318.84. The present value of the net residual is determined as follows:

	HP-12C			HP-17B (1 P/YR BEGIN MODE)	
	f	REG			FIN
1.3170		i			TVM
12,318.84	CHS	FV		■	CLEAR DATA
48		n		1.3170	I%YR
	PV	6,573.83		12,318.84 +/-	FV
				48	N
					PV = 6,573.83

Exhibit 16-13
Residual Proceeds Schedule

Salvage proceeds	15,000.00
Less remaining tax basis	(11,520.00)
Salvage expenses	0.00
Taxable gain (loss)	3,480.00
Tax rate	x .35
Tax benefit (liability)	(1,218.00)
IPVF	x .96975
Net tax benefit (liability)	(1,181.16)
Proceeds	15,000.00
Security deposit refund	(1,500.00)
Net residual proceeds	12,318.84

4. MACRS tax benefits

HP-12C   **HP-17B (# TIMES PROMPTING: OFF)**

	f	REG			FIN
17		i			CFLO
.20	g	CFo	■ CLEAR DATA		YES
.32	g	CFj	FLOW (0)=?	.20	INPUT
.192	g	CFj	FLOW (1)=?	.32	INPUT
.1152	g	CFj	FLOW (2)=?	.192	INPUT
.0576	g	CFj	FLOW (3)=?	.1152	INPUT
	f	NPV .716429	FLOW (4)=?	.0576	INPUT
					EXIT
100,000	x	71,642.86			CALC
.35	x	25,075.00		17	I%
.96975	x	24,316.48		NPV =	.716429
			x 100,000 =		71,642.86
			x .35 =		25,075.00
			x .96975 =		24,316.48

569

5. G & A expenses

    a. convert the monthly G & A expense of 50 to its after-tax equivalent

$$50 \times [1 - (.35 \times .96975)] = 33.03$$

    b. compute the present value of the after-tax G & A

HP-12C			**HP-17B (1 P/YR END MODE)**	
f	REG			FIN
g	END			TVM
48	n		■	CLEAR DATA
1.317	i		48	N
33.03	CHS	PMT	1.317	I%YR
	PV	1,169.62	33.03 +/-	PMT
				PV = 1,169.62

6. The loan proceeds were given at 85,000

7. Present value the pretax loan payments

HP-12C			**HP-17B (1 P/YR END MODE)**	
f	REG			FIN
g	END			TVM
1.3170	i		■	CLEAR DATA
2,073.93	PMT		1.3170	I%YR
48	n		2,073.93	PMT
	PV	73,439.45	48	N
				PV = 73,439.45

8. Present value the interest tax benefits associated with the loan payments

    a. loan amortization. (The loan could have been present valued on a monthly basis, also.)

Tax year	Payments	Interest expense
1	7	3,739.26
2	12	5,207.35
3	12	3,580.14
4	12	1,818.39
5	5	203.47

b. present value the loan interest per year

	HP-12C			**HP-17B (#TIMES PROMPTING: OFF)**	
	f	REG			FIN
17		i			CFLO
3,739.26	g	CFo	■	CLEAR DATA	YES
5,207.35	g	CFj	FLOW (0)=?	3,739.26	INPUT
3,580.14	g	CFj	FLOW (1)=?	5,207.35	INPUT
1,818.39	g	CFj	FLOW (2)=?	3,580.14	INPUT
203.47	g	CFj	FLOW (3)=?	1,818.39	INPUT
			FLOW (4)=?	203.47	INPUT
	f	NPV 12,049.26			EXIT
.35	x	4,217.24			CALC
.96975	x	4,089.67		17	I%
				NPV	= 12,049.26
			x	.35	= 4,217.24
			x	.96975	= 4,089.67

9. Summary of the present value of the cash flows

Equipment cost	(100,000.00)
Initial direct costs	(1,651.47)
Refundable security deposit	1,500.00
Residual value (net)	6,573.83
Loan proceeds	85,000.00
Loan payments	(73,439.45)
Interest tax benefits	4,089.67
MACRS tax benefits	24,316.48
G & A expenses	(1,169.62)
Net inception outflow	(54,780.56)

Step Two

Find the present value of the unknown lease payments, letting one dollar equal each payment.

	HP-12C			**HP-17B (1 P/YR BEGIN MODE)**	
	f	REG			FIN
	g	BEG			TVM
1.3170		i		■	CLEAR DATA
1		PMT		1.3170	I%YR
48		n		1	PMT
		PV 35.87713		48	N
					PV = 35.87713

Step Three

Find the present value of the annual tax liabilities associated with the one dollar lease payments determined in Step Two above by first computing the taxable income.

Tax year	Total rentals
1	7
2	12
3	12
4	12
5	5

Next, calculate the present value of the liability.

	HP-12C			**HP-17B (#TIMES PROMPTING: ON)**		
	f	REG				FIN
17		i				CFLO
7	g	CFo	■	CLEAR DATA		YES
12	g	CFj		FLOW (0)=?	7	INPUT
3	g	Nj		FLOW (1)=?	12	INPUT
5	g	CFj		#TIMES (1)=1	3	INPUT
				FLOW (2)=?	5	INPUT
	f	NPV 36.18327		#TIMES (2)=1	1	INPUT
.35	x	12.66414				EXIT
.96975	x	12.28105				CALC

$$\begin{aligned} & 17 && \text{I\%} \\ & \text{NPV} && = 36.18327 \\ & \text{x} \quad .35 && = 12.66414 \\ & \text{x} \quad .96975 && = 12.28105 \end{aligned}$$

Step Four

Deduct the results of Step Three from Step Two.

$$\begin{aligned} & 35.87713 \\ & \underline{(12.28105)} \\ & 23.59608 \end{aligned}$$

Step Five

Divide the remainder from Step Four into the present value total from Step One. The quotient is the required pretax payment that will result in a 17%

annual effective, after-tax ROE to the lessor.

Payment:

$$\frac{54{,}780.56}{23.59608} = 2{,}321.60$$

Lease rate factor:

$$\frac{2{,}321.60}{100{,}000} = .023216$$

COMPARISONS TO ROA STRUCTURING

Exhibit 16-14 shows that the ROE, match funding method of structuring results in a lower payment than the ROA method, which incorporates a pooled approach. (It should be noted that the cost of the debt has been held constant between the two examples. In reality, this would not be the case.) The ROE, match funded payment is lower than the ROA payment because match funding in this example provides greater leverage over the lease term than the pooled approach, which maintains a constant debt-to-equity ratio.

Other debt structures can be used in structuring leases at the ROE level. For example, a balloon payment equal to 85% of the purchase option in the preceding example could be assumed. The resulting lease payment will be even lower because of the increase in leverage over the previous example.

Exhibit 16-14
ROA/ROE Comparison

Method	Targeted return	Payment
Pooled (constant debt-to-equity)	8.04% (ROA)	2,422.51
Match funded	17.00% (ROE)	2,321.60

Although the preceding examples are producing the same ROE, their net undiscounted cash flows differ. Refer to Chapter Thirty for an in-depth discussion of yield versus cash flow trade-offs.

GPTD Structuring

In a typical vendor-lessor situation, the parent corporation creates gross profit on the sale of the equipment to its captive subsidiary or division. If the leasing function writes a tax lease, the taxes due on the gross profit are deferred. The parent then remits to its captive subsidiary or division an amount equal to the savings associated with this deferral, which is known as GPTD. (The concept of GPTD is discussed in Chapters Six and Twenty-four.)

In turn, the subsidiary pays this interest-free loan back to the parent in proportion to the rate at which the subsidiary depreciates the asset for tax purposes (MACRS, straight-line over the MACRS life, etc.). What impact does the interest-free loan have on pricing for the captive lessor?

The value of GPTD in structuring a lease is equal to the value of the loan proceeds from the parent less the present value of the loan repayments to the parent, discounted at the lessor's targeted after-tax yield. This value should be incorporated into the structuring process. The loan proceeds and subsequent repayments are not tax-adjusted because they do not enter taxable income. The loan proceeds and repayments, however, are adjusted by the IPVF because they typically are received and paid on the estimated tax payment dates of the parent corporation.

GPTD PRICING EXAMPLE

Assume the gross margin on the lease transaction from page 557 is 10,000, or 10% of the asset's cost to the captive. The parent, therefore, has deferred 35% of 10,000 in taxes, or 3,500. The 3,500 benefit in this incremental transaction will be received pro rata by the parent on June 15, September 15 and December 15 of the current year.

For 5-year MACRS property, the 3,500 tax saving is reduced by the taxes due in the current period, which is the 3,500 multiplied by the 20% MACRS depreciation taken by the captive. Thus, 80% of 3,500, or 2,800, is the actual net amount of the parent's benefit, which is remitted to the captive. The net 2,800 loan from the parent is repaid over the MACRS life of the asset on the quarterly tax remittance dates.

Solution

The actual value of the GPTD is the timing benefit between the parent paying 3,500 in taxes today versus spreading the payment of the taxes over the asset's MACRS life. This timing benefit, which is incorporated into the structuring process, is calculated as follows, using an 8.343% annual effective discount rate.

HP-12C			HP-17B (#TIMES PROMPTING: OFF)		
	f	REG			FIN
8.343		i			CFLO
2,800	g	CFo	■	CLEAR DATA	YES
1,120	CHS g	CFj	FLOW (0)=?	2,800	INPUT
672	CHS g	CFj	FLOW (1)=?	1,120 +/-	INPUT
403.20	CHS g	CFj	FLOW (2)=?	672 +/-	INPUT
403.20	CHS g	CFj	FLOW (3)=?	403.20 +/-	INPUT
201.60	CHS g	CFj	FLOW (4)=?	403.20 +/-	INPUT
	f	NPV 449.040	FLOW (5)=?	201.60 +/-	INPUT
.98529	x	442.43			EXIT
					CALC
				8.343	I%
				NPV	= 449.04
				x .98529	442.43

The GPTD benefit is 442.43. To illustrate the pricing impact of the GPTD on this example, the lease structuring factor of 26.9404 calculated on page 562 is used. (Note the value of GPTD impacts only the cash flows, not the structuring factor.) By dividing the 442.43 present value of the GPTD by this base lease structuring factor, the 16.42 (442.43 ÷ 26.9404) reduction in lease payment due to GPTD can be determined.

Since the 16.42 reduction correlates to a 10% gross profit margin, a company with a 70% margin would receive seven times the 16.42 amount, or a total reduction in lease payment of 114.96. Keep in mind the lessor does not have to lower the lease rate; it can charge whatever the market will bear and keep the GPTD benefit as extra profit.

Alternative Minimum Tax Considerations

If the lessor is in an alternative minimum tax (AMT) position, pricing and analysis become particularly onerous. It is recommended that the AMT section of Chapter Seven be reviewed, as AMT is not discussed here, only its impact on structuring. A simple example, utilizing the following assumptions, will demonstrate the analytical and structuring difficulty of AMT.

Term: four-year lease, in arrears

Annual payments: 2,500

Taxes are paid (or benefits received): December 31 of this calendar year taxpayer

Residual proceeds: 3,000

Equipment cost: 10,000

Initial direct costs: none

Tax depreciation: 5-year MACRS property

Asset class life: 5-year

Required after-tax ROA: 6.7671%

Inception date: January 1, 19X1.

The cash flows (non-AMT) generated by this lease are shown in Exhibit 16-15. As can be seen, the after-tax ROA is the targeted 6.7671%.

Exhibit 16-15
Non-AMT Cash Flow Analysis

	0	1	2	3	4	Total
Cost	(10,000)	0	0	0	0	(10,000)
Rentals	0	2,500	2,500	2,500	2,500	10,000
Residual	0	0	0	0	3,000	3,000
MACRS	0	(2,000)	(3,200)	(1,920)	(1,152)	(8,272)
Tax basis	0	0	0	0	(1,728)	(1,728)
Taxable income	0	500	(700)	580	2,620	3,000
Taxes at 35%	0	(175)	245	(203)	(917)	(1,050)
Net income	0	325	(455)	377	1,703	1,950
MACRS/cost	(10,000)	2,000	3,200	1,920	2,880	10,000
Cash flow	(10,000)	2,325	2,745	2,297	4,583	1,950

HP-12C				HP-17B (#TIMES PROMPTING: OFF)	
	f	REG			FIN
10,000	CHS g	CFo			CFLO
2,325	g	CFj	■ CLEAR DATA		YES
2,745	g	CFj	FLOW (0)=?	10,000 +/-	INPUT
2,297	g	CFj	FLOW (1)=?	2,325	INPUT
4,583	g	CFj	FLOW (2)=?	2,745	INPUT
	f	IRR 6.7671	FLOW (3)=?	2,297	INPUT
			FLOW (4)=?	4,583	INPUT
					EXIT
					CALC
				IRR% =	6.7671

Now, assume the lessor determines it currently is in an overall AMT position (with or without the above lease), and that it will remain so until the third year of the lease. Once the company is in an AMT position, the lessor pays the AMT on all incremental leases for the period the company is in AMT. The only time this would not be the case is when the next transaction is so large relative to the existing portfolio that its non-AMT attributes cause the whole portfolio to leave an AMT position.

The AMT impact on the example cash flows is shown in Exhibit 16-16. The after-tax ROA has decreased to 6.704% as a result of the acceleration of taxes under the AMT.

HP-12C				HP-17B (#TIMES PROMPTING: OFF)	
	f	REG			FIN
10,000	CHS g	CFo			CFLO
2,300	g	CFj	■ CLEAR DATA		YES
2,510	g	CFj	FLOW (0)=?	10,000 +/-	INPUT
2,557	g	CFj	FLOW (1)=?	2,300	INPUT
4,583	g	CFj	FLOW (2)=?	2,510	INPUT
	f	IRR 6.704	FLOW (3)=?	2,557	INPUT
			FLOW (4)=?	4,583	INPUT
					EXIT
					CALC
				IRR% =	6.704

As is apparent from analyzing Exhibit 16-16, the computations associated with the AMT are extremely complex and require several levels of supporting calculations. Exhibit 16-17 details the AMT liability, but, in order to come up with that liability, a preference schedule (Exhibit 16-18) and the AMT reversal schedule (Exhibit 16-19) also must be completed.

Exhibit 16-16
AMT Cash Flow Analysis

	0	1	2	3	4	Total
Cost	(10,000)	0	0	0	0	(10,000)
Rentals	0	2,500	2,500	2,500	2,500	10,000
Residual	0	0	0	0	3,000	3,000
Taxes						
AMT[1]	0	(200)	10	N/A	N/A	(190)
Regular[2]	0	N/A	N/A	(143)	(917)	(1,060)
AMT reversal[3]	0	0	0	200	0	200
Net cash flow	(10,000)	2,300	2,510	2,557	4,583	1,950

[1] From Exhibit 16-17
[2] Regular taxes - AMT credit (e.g., 203 - 60 = 143)
[3] From Exhibit 16-19

Exhibit 16-17
AMT Liability

	1	2	3	4	Total
Taxable income[1]	500	(700)	580	2,620	3,000
Depreciation preference[2]	500	650	135	(257)	1,028
Residual preference[2]	0	0	0	(1,028)	(1,028)
AMT income (AMTI)	1,000	(50)	715	1,335	3,000
AMT at 20%	(200)	10	(143)	(267)	(600)

[1] From Exhibit 16-15
[2] From Exhibit 16-18

Exhibit 16-18
Preference Calculations

	1	2	3	4	Total
Depreciation preference					
MACRS	2,000	3,200	1,920	576	7,696
150% declining balance	(1,500)	(2,550)	(1,785)	(833)	(6,668)
	500	650	135	(257)	1,028
Residual preference					
MACRS basis	8,000	4,800	2,880	2,304	2,304
AMT basis	8,500	5,950	4,165	3,332	3,332
	(500)	(1,150)	(1,285)	(1,028)	(1,028)

Exhibit 16-19
AMT Reversal Computation

	1	2	3	4	Total
Normal liability[1]	(175)	245	(203)	N/A	(133)
AMT liability[2]	(200)	10	(143)	N/A	(333)
AMT credit	(25)	(235)	60	N/A	200
AMT reversal	0	0	(200)	N/A	(200)
Cumulative AMT credit	(25)	(260)	0	N/A	0

[1] From Exhibit 16-15
[2] From Exhibit 16-17

Notice the AMT adjustments have caused the lease's yield to drop seven basis points (6.7671% down to 6.704%). Had the AMT position been prolonged (five or six years, etc.), a greater impact on yield would have occurred.

STRUCTURING CONSIDERATIONS

Assume the lessor wants to restructure the above lease to earn the required 6.7671% after-tax ROA. From a cash flow perspective, it is obvious the payment must go up to reimburse the lessor for the additional taxes paid under AMT. The change in payment does not impact the depreciation preference, which remains constant because changes in payment do not affect the depreciation of the asset. Repricing the transaction becomes a fairly straightforward exercise because the amount of the additional taxes is known.

Unfortunately for those lessors in AMT, not all lessors are in the same position. These non-AMT lessors, therefore, do not have to increase their payment to compensate for the additional taxes paid under AMT. What this means, in terms of the market, is that a lessor in AMT cannot price to the AMT cash flows. It must, instead, price to the non-AMT cash flows and take the difference as a reduction in yield.

Another perplexing yet interesting issue concerning AMT arises when the date the lessor will eliminate its AMT position is beyond the termination of the lease term. In this prolonged case, the lessor will have paid taxes during the lease term at only 20%, instead of the normal 35% rate. This situation generates a deferred AMT liability that will not be paid until the lessor's overall portfolio reverses out of the AMT position.

It is very possible, therefore, that an individual lease written by a lessor with a prolonged AMT problem will generate more present value cash flow than if the AMT position was shorter. The increase in present value cash flow generates a corresponding increase in after-tax yield because of the deferral of the 15% tax rate differential (35% less 20%). This phenomenon provides a false sense of security on a portfolio basis, however, for common sense dictates that the longer a company is in AMT (a penalty situation), the worse off it will be.

If a lessor cannot price its leases to compensate for the AMT, what are some of the remedies to an AMT problem? There is no single solution; however, some of the following might help mitigate an AMT problem.

1. Use straight-line depreciation over the MACRS classlife for regular tax purposes. In this situation, no new tax preferences are created, because there is no accelerated depreciation. It should be noted that, while solving or mitigating AMT, the lessor also is giving up substantial depreciation tax benefits by using straight-line depreciation

2. Use 150% declining balance depreciation for regular tax purposes. In this situation, no new tax preferences are created, because there is not any accelerated depreciation. Furthermore, the lessor gives up less depreciation tax benefits than by using straight-line depreciation

3. Become owned by a parent corporation that can absorb a sufficient amount of the subsidiary's AMT income such that the AMT position is nullified

4. Generate fee income through selling leases to lessors who do not have an AMT problem

5. Diversify the product base into nontax leases or less AMT prone assets

6. Attempt to pass on to lessees at least a portion of the increase in lease payments necessary to earn the required return on investment. If a majority of lessors have an AMT problem this will be a common solution, although it is highly unlikely. The most likely scenario for those lessors with AMT problems is that they will either accept lower yields on the leases being written, or not write any tax leases.

CONCLUSION

Leases can be structured using different components and with varying degrees of complexity. Some of these components include integrating GPTD into the pricing process and the effects of AMT. Furthermore, the more accurate the lessor wishes to be, the more advanced will be its structuring techniques. The pricing analyst, for example, who is familiar with the impact of the various components on the lease rate and how to incorporate them into the pricing process will create additional, profitable business for the lessor.

It should be noted that the purpose of this chapter is not to supplant the use of existing lease structuring software. A computer certainly can be used to structure any lease. It is as important, however, to know why a pricing variable affects a payment as it does as it is to know how to run the software. In this respect, the goal of this chapter is to provide greater insight into the cash flow components that make up a lease.

Appendix One

1. EARNINGS RECAP – PURE INTEREST

	Prior net investment	- Payment	+ Interest earned	= New net investment	x Rate	= Interest
July						
August				88,312	0.010396	918
September	88,312	2,010	918	87,220	0.010396	907
October	87,220	2,010	907	86,117	0.010396	895
November	86,117	2,010	895	85,002	0.010396	884
December	85,002	2,010	884	83,876	0.010396	872
Total		8,040	3,604			4,476
January	83,876	2,010	872	82,738	0.010396	860
February	82,738	2,010	860	81,588	0.010396	848
March	81,588	2,010	848	80,426	0.010396	836
April	80,426	2,010	836	79,252	0.010396	824
May	79,252	2,010	824	78,066	0.010396	812
June	78,066	2,010	812	76,868	0.010396	799
July	76,868	2,010	799	75,657	0.010396	787
August	75,657	2,010	787	74,433	0.010396	774
September	74,433	2,010	774	73,197	0.010396	761
October	73,197	2,010	761	71,948	0.010396	748
November	71,948	2,010	748	70,686	0.010396	735
December	70,686	2,010	735	69,411	0.010396	722
Total		24,120	9,656			9,505
January	69,411	2,010	722	68,123	0.010396	708
February	68,123	2,010	708	66,821	0.010396	695
March	66,821	2,010	695	65,505	0.010396	681
April	65,505	2,010	681	64,176	0.010396	667
May	64,176	2,010	667	62,834	0.010396	653
June	62,834	2,010	653	61,477	0.010396	639
July	61,477	2,010	639	60,106	0.010396	625
August	60,106	2,010	625	58,721	0.010396	610
September	58,721	2,010	610	57,321	0.010396	596
October	57,321	2,010	596	55,907	0.010396	581
November	55,907	2,010	581	54,478	0.010396	566
December	54,478	2,010	566	53,035	0.010396	551
Total		24,120	7,743			7,574

	Prior net investment	- Payment	+ Interest earned	= New net investment	x Rate	= Interest
January	53,035	2,010	551	51,576	0.010396	536
February	51,576	2,010	536	50,102	0.010396	521
March	50,102	2,010	521	48,613	0.010396	505
April	48,613	2,010	505	47,108	0.010396	490
May	47,108	2,010	490	45,588	0.010396	474
June	45,588	2,010	474	44,052	0.010396	458
July	44,052	2,010	458	42,500	0.010396	442
August	42,500	2,010	442	40,932	0.010396	426
September	40,932	2,010	426	39,347	0.010396	409
October	39,347	2,010	409	37,747	0.010396	392
November	37,747	2,010	392	36,129	0.010396	376
December	36,129	2,010	376	34,495	0.010396	359
Total		24,120	5,580			5,387
January	34,495	2,010	359	32,843	0.010396	341
February	32,843	2,010	341	31,175	0.010396	324
March	31,175	2,010	324	29,489	0.010396	307
April	29,489	2,010	307	27,785	0.010396	289
May	27,785	2,010	289	26,064	0.010396	271
June	26,064	2,010	271	24,325	0.010396	253
July	24,325	2,010	253	22,568	0.010396	235
August	22,568	2,010	235	20,793	0.010396	216
September	20,793	2,010	216	18,999	0.010396	198
October	18,999	2,010	198	17,186	0.010396	179
November	17,186	2,010	179	15,355	0.010396	160
December	15,355	2,010	160	13,505	0.010396	140
Total		24,120	3,130			2,912
January	13,505	2,010	140	11,635	0.010396	121
February	11,635	2,010	121	9,746	0.010396	101
March	9,746	2,010	101	7,837	0.010396	81
April	7,837	2,010	81	5,909	0.010396	61
May	5,909	2,010	61	3,960	0.010396	41
June	3,960	2,010	41	1,991	0.010396	19
July	1,991	2,010	19	0	0.010396	0
Total		14,070	565			424
Totals		118,590	30,278			30,278

2. EARNINGS RECAP – RESIDUAL INTEREST

	Prior residual	+	Interest earned	=	New net residual	x	Rate	=	Interest
August					9,678		0.010396		101
September	9,678		101		9,779		0.010396		102
October	9,779		102		9,880		0.010396		103
November	9,880		103		9,983		0.010396		104
December	9,983		<u>104</u>		10,087		0.010396		<u>105</u>
Total			409						514
January	10,087		105		10,192		0.010396		106
February	10,192		106		10,298		0.010396		107
March	10,298		107		10,405		0.010396		108
April	10,405		108		10,513		0.010396		109
May	10,513		109		10,622		0.010396		110
June	10,622		110		10,733		0.010396		112
July	10,733		112		10,844		0.010396		113
August	10,844		113		10,957		0.010396		114
September	10,957		114		11,071		0.010396		115
October	11,071		115		11,186		0.010396		116
November	11,186		116		11,302		0.010396		117
December	11,302		<u>117</u>		11,420		0.010396		<u>119</u>
Total			1,333						1,347
January	11,420		119		11,538		0.010396		120
February	11,538		120		11,658		0.010396		121
March	11,658		121		11,779		0.010396		122
April	11,779		122		11,902		0.010396		124
May	11,902		124		12,026		0.010396		125
June	12,026		125		12,151		0.010396		126
July	12,151		126		12,277		0.010396		128
August	12,277		128		12,405		0.010396		129
September	12,405		129		12,534		0.010396		130
October	12,534		130		12,664		0.010396		132
November	12,664		132		12,796		0.010396		133
December	12,796		<u>133</u>		12,929		0.010396		<u>134</u>
Total			1,509						1,524
January	12,929		134		13,063		0.010396		136
February	13,063		136		13,199		0.010396		137
March	13,199		137		13,336		0.010396		139
April	13,336		139		13,475		0.010396		140
May	13,475		140		13,615		0.010396		142
June	13,615		142		13,756		0.010396		143
July	13,756		143		13,899		0.010396		144
August	13,899		144		14,044		0.010396		146
September	14,044		146		14,190		0.010396		148
October	14,190		148		14,337		0.010396		149
November	14,337		149		14,486		0.010396		151
December	14,486		<u>151</u>		14,637		0.010396		<u>152</u>
Total			1,708						1,726

	Prior residual	+	Interest earned	=	New net residual	x	Rate	=	Interest
January	14,637		152		14,789		0.010396		154
February	14,789		154		14,943		0.010396		155
March	14,943		155		15,098		0.010396		157
April	15,098		157		15,255		0.010396		159
May	15,255		159		15,414		0.010396		160
June	15,414		160		15,574		0.010396		162
July	15,574		162		15,736		0.010396		164
August	15,736		164		15,899		0.010396		165
September	15,899		165		16,065		0.010396		167
October	16,065		167		16,232		0.010396		169
November	16,232		169		16,401		0.010396		171
December	16,401		<u>171</u>		16,571		0.010396		<u>172</u>
Total			1,934						1,954
January	16,571		172		16,743		0.010396		174
February	16,743		174		16,917		0.010396		176
March	16,917		176		17,093		0.010396		178
April	17,093		178		17,271		0.010396		180
May	17,271		180		17,450		0.010396		181
June	17,450		181		17,632		0.010396		183
July	17,632		<u>183</u>		17,815		0.010396		<u>185</u>
Total			1,244						1,257
Totals			8,137						8,322

3. AMORTIZATION RECAP – INITIAL DIRECT COSTS

	Interest (without) -	Interest (with) =	IDC amortization	Unamortized IDC
July				2,500
August	1,019	961	58	2,442
September	1,009	951	58	2,384
October	998	941	57	2,327
November	988	930	57	2,270
December	977	920	57	2,213
Total	4,990	4,703	287	
January	966	909	57	2,156
February	955	899	56	2,100
March	944	888	56	2,044
April	933	878	55	1,989
May	922	867	55	1,934
June	911	856	55	1,879
July	900	846	54	1,825
August	888	834	54	1,771
September	876	822	54	1,717
October	864	811	53	1,664
November	852	800	52	1,612
December	841	789	52	1,560
Total	10,852	10,199	653	
Year 3	9,098	8,515	583	977
Year 4	7,113	6,627	486	491
Year 5	4,866	4,511	355	136
Year 6	1,681	1,545	136	0
Total	38,600	36,100	2,500	

Glossary

Accelerate Payments

A remedy the lessor can execute in the event of lessee default. All future lease payments are due and payable. No additional interest is due.

Accelerated Depreciation

Any depreciation method that allows for greater deductions or charges in the earlier years of an asset's depreciable life, with charges becoming progressively smaller in each successive period. Examples include the double declining balance and sum-of-the-years digits methods.

Acceptance Letter

A letter signed by the lessee signifying the equipment has been delivered. The letter allows the lessor to pay the vendor. Also called D & A.

Accumulated Depreciation

A financial reporting term for a contra-asset account that shows the total depreciation charges for an asset since acquisition.

Actuarial Interest

A constant interest charge (or return) based upon a declining principal balance.

Add-ons

Features and enhancements that may be installed on lease equipment.

Adjusted (or Remaining) Basis

The undepreciated amount of an asset's original basis. Used for tax purposes to calculate the gain or loss on disposition of an asset.

ADR System

A tax depreciation system that establishes the minimum, midpoint and maximum number of years, by asset category, over which an asset can be depreciated. The midpoint life has become synonymous with the term "ADR class life."

Advance Payments

One or more lease payments required to be paid to the lessor at the beginning of the lease term. Lease structures commonly require one payment to be made in advance. This term also refers to leasing arrangements in which the lease payment is due at the beginning of each period.

Advance Rental

Any payment in the form of rent made before the start of the lease term. The term also is used to describe a rental payment arrangement in which the lessee pays each rental, on a per period basis, at the start of each rental payment period. For example, a quarterly, in advance, rental program requires the lessee to pay one fourth of the annual rental at the start of each consecutive three-month period during the lease term.

Alterations

Modifications to leased equipment, generally subject to restoration at the conclusion of the lease.

Alternative Minimum Tax (AMT)

A separate tax calculation in which a taxpayer must pay the higher of its regular tax or AMT liability. The corporate AMT rate, although lower than the regular tax rate, is applied to a different, typically higher, taxable income than for regular taxes. The Tax Reform Act of 1986 substantially modified the AMT, which all taxpayers must calculate.

Amortization

The process of separating payments into their principal and interest components. An amortized loan is one in which the principal amount of the loan is repaid in installments over the life of the loan with each payment comprised partially of interest and partially of principal.

Annuity

A stream of even (equal) cash flows occurring at regular intervals, such as even monthly lease payments. An annuity in advance is one in which the annuity payment is due at the beginning of each period. An annuity in arrears is one in which the annuity payment is due at the end of each period.

Application

A document requesting a leasing company to lease, completed by a prospective lessee, containing information about lessee and equipment.

Arbitrage

Simultaneous purchase in one market and sale in another of a security in order to make a profit on relative price differences.

Arms-length Transaction

A condition whereby two parties in a leasing transaction are independent. Looked at by accountants to determine reasonableness of price.

Arrears Rental

A rental that is due at the end of each period. Compare to advance rental.

Asian Development Bank (ADB)

ADB advises governments of developing member countries in Asia. It aids in establishing industry regulations. ADB concentrates on providing financing to companies for which it would otherwise be unobtainable.

Assessed Value

The value of equipment as determined by a taxing authority for the purposes of assessing personal property tax.

Asset Class Life

The updated ADR midpoint life as modified by the 1986 Tax Reform Act. An asset class life represents the IRS designated economic life of an asset, and is used as the recovery period for alternative tax depreciation computations.

Assign

To transfer or exchange future rights. In leasing, the right to receive future lease payments in a lease is often transferred to a funding source, in return for up-front cash. The up-front cash represents the loan proceeds from the funding source, and is equal to the present value of the future lease payments discounted at the leasing company's cost of borrowing. A lease assigned by the lessor to a funding source is called an assigned lease. The assignment of leases is a very common funding technique used by leasing companies.

Assignment

A provision within a lease agreement that allows either, neither or both parties of a lease transaction to delivery their obligation to a third party in return for immediate compensation. For example, a lessor may assign all current and future lessee's lease payments to a third party in return for cash today.

At-risk Rules

Federal tax laws that prohibit individuals (and some corporations) from deducting tax losses from equipment leases in excess of the amount they have at risk.

Bad Debt

A lease receivable that is written off because of the lessee's unwillingness or inability to pay.

Bad Debt Reserve

An account offsetting gross receivables on the balance sheet, representing estimated writeoffs.

Bai-Muajjal

Under Islamic law, a transaction whereby the seller allows the buyer to pay the price of a commodity at a future date in a lump sum or installments.

Balloon Payment

A large payment at the end of the loan allowing smaller payments to be made during the term.

Bankruptcy

An action taken by a party to legally protect its remaining assets by declaring that it cannot pay its bills. Typically, liabilities exceed assets.

Bankruptcy Court

A court that legally judges the merits of creditors' demands upon a company that can no longer run without outside financial assistance.

Bargain Purchase Option

A lease provision allowing the lessee, at its option, to purchase the leased property at the end of the lease term for a price sufficiently lower than the expected fair market value of the property, such that exercise of the option appears, at the inception of the lease, to be reasonably assured.

Bargain Renewal Option

A lease provision allowing the lessee, at its option, to extend the lease for an additional term in exchange for periodic rental payments sufficiently less than fair value rentals for the property, such that exercise of the option appears, at the inception of the lease, to be reasonably assured.

Base Term

The initial, noncancellable term of the lease used by the lessor in computing the payment. The base term is the minimum time period during which the lessee has the use and custody of the equipment.

Basis

The original cost of an asset plus other capitalized acquisition costs such as installation charges and sales tax. Basis reflects the amount upon which depreciation charges are computed.

Basis Point

One one-hundredth of a percent (.01%).

Broker

A company or person that arranges lease transactions between lessees and lessors for a fee. See "Lease Broker."

Bundled Lease

A lease that includes additional services such as maintenance, insurance and property taxes that are paid for by the lessor. The cost of these additional services is built into the lease payments.

Buyout

The amount a lessee must pay the lessor to terminate a lease early. Usually calculated to include tax recaptures, unpaid property taxes and lost revenues.

Call Option

An option in a lease, such as a purchase or a renewal option, that is exercised at the discretion of the lessee, not the lessor.

Capital Lease

From a financial reporting perspective, a lease that has the characteristics of a purchase agreement, and also meets certain criteria established by Financial Accounting Standards Board Statement No. 13 (FASB 13). Such a lease is required to be shown as an asset and a related obligation on the balance sheet of the lessee.

Capitalize

To record an expenditure that may benefit future periods as an asset rather than as an expense to be charged off in the period of its occurrence.

Capitalized Cost

The amount of an asset to be shown on the balance sheet, from a financial reporting perspective. The total capitalized cost (or basis) also is the amount upon which tax benefits, such as depreciation deductions, are based and may include asset cost plus other amounts such as sales tax.

Captive Lessor

A leasing company that has been set up by a manufacturer or equipment dealer to finance the sale or lease of its own products to end-users or lessees.

Carryover

A term describing the postponing of tax losses until they can be used. Examples include net operating loss and investment tax credit carryovers.

Cash Flow

A measure of an organization's liquidity that compares cash inflows and outflows. Often shown by adding noncash expenses to net income.

Casualty Value (see also Stipulated Loss Value Table)

A schedule included in a lease that establishes the liability of the lessee to the lessor in the event the leased equipment is lost or rendered unusable during the lease term because of casualty loss. The casualty value is the amount that maintains the lessor's yield in the event of casualty.

Certificate of Delivery and Acceptance (D&A)

A document signed by the lessee to acknowledge the equipment to be leased has been delivered and is acceptable. Many lease agreements state that the actual lease term commences once this document has been signed.

Certificate of Participation

A municipal lease fractionalized into shares and assigned or marketed to investors.

Closed-end Lease

A lease that does not contain a purchase or renewal option, thereby requiring the lessee to return the equipment to the lessor at the end of the initial lease term. Also refers to a vehicle lease in which the lessor absorbs the entire risk of the residual.

Collateral

Equipment or other tangible assets such as a house, car or securities pledged by the lessee to the lessor to minimize the risk of default.

Commitment Fee

A fee required by the lessor at the time a proposal or commitment is accepted by the lessee to lock in a specific lease rate and/or other lease terms.

Commitment Letter

A document prepared by the lessor that sets forth its commitment, including rate and term, to provide lease financing to the lessee. This document, if utilized, precedes final documentation, and may or may not be subject to lessor credit approval.

Compensating Balances

The amount of funds that a bank requires a borrower to keep on deposit during the term of a loan. The amount of this noninterest earning deposit typically is based upon some percentage of the loan and effectively increases the borrower's interest cost.

Compound Interest

An interest method that calculates interest on interest earned in prior periods.

Conditional Sales Contract

An agreement for the purchase of an asset in which the lessee is treated as the owner of the asset for federal income tax purposes (and is entitled to the tax benefits of ownership, such as depreciation). The lessee does not become the legal owner of the asset until all terms and conditions of the agreement have been satisfied.

Consumer Price Index (CPI)

A government-produced table indicating how prices increase or decrease during a given period.

Contingent Rentals

Rentals in which the amount of the rents is dependent upon some future event such as a price index or borrowing rate, other than the passage of time.

Corporate Resolution

A document signed by a registered corporate officer, designating company representatives who may sign leases.

Cost of Capital

The weighted-average cost of funds that a firm secures from both debt and equity sources in order to fund its assets. The use of a firm's cost of capital is essential in making accurate capital budgeting and project investment decisions.

Cost of Debt

The costs incurred by a firm to fund the acquisition of assets through the use of borrowings. A firm's component cost of debt is used in calculating the firm's overall weighted-average cost of capital.

Cost of Equity

The return on investment required by the equity holders of a firm. Cost of equity can be calculated using any number of different theoretical approaches and must take into consideration the current and long-term yield requirements of a firm's investors. A firm's component cost of equity is used in calculating its overall weighted-average cost of capital.

Cost-plus Contracts

Government contracts, popular during World War II, to control manufacturer profits on federal work. Often used in conjunction with leasing.

Coupon Book

A book sent to a new lessee containing coupons for all payments of the lease. Some companies use the book instead of invoices.

Covenant and Condition

A formal and binding agreement or promise between two or more parties for the performance of some action. Usually contained in a lease agreement.

Credit Enhancement

A technique to reduce historical loss risk and concentration risk of a lease portfolio in order to achieve a better credit rating and lower borrowing costs.

Credit References

Banks and suppliers used in the lessee's business and listed on the lease application. Lessor will contact them to check lessee payment habits.

Credit Scoring

An objective method of quantifying credit worthiness by assigning numerical values based on meeting established credit criteria.

Cross-border Leases

A lease structured to take advantage of the tax laws in two different countries. Typically, the lessor is located in one country and the lessee is located in a different country

Debt Optimization

A method of borrowing funds in a leveraged lease in which the equity participants borrow and repay the debt in such a manner as to maximize their return on equity, maintain a constant return and offer a lower lease payment, maximize cash flow or maximize a combination of factors.

Debt Participant

A long-term lender in a leveraged lease transaction. Frequently, these transactions have more than one debt participant.

Debt Service

Payment of principal and interest due lenders under a leveraged lease agreement.

Debt-to-equity Ratio

Financial term comparing total liabilities to equity consisting of retained earnings and contributed capital.

Declining Balance Depreciation

A type of accelerated depreciation in which a constant percentage of an asset's remaining basis is depreciated each year. The constant percentage amount is often calculated at 125%, 150% or 200% (double declining balance) of the straight-line percentage over the same recovery period.

Default

A condition whereby the lessee does not make the payments as required by the lease contract.

Deferred Taxes

Income tax calculated on book income but not currently due for payment. Balance is carried on the balance sheet until it is reversed in later years.

Depreciation

A means for a firm to recover the cost of a purchased asset, over time, through periodic deductions or offsets to income. Depreciation is used in both a financial reporting and tax context, and is considered a tax benefit because the depreciation deductions cause a reduction in taxable income, thereby lowering a firm's tax liability.

Direct Financing Lease

A lessor capital lease (per FASB 13) that does not give rise to manufacturer's or dealer's profit (or loss) to the lessor.

Discount Rate

An interest rate used to bring a series of future cash flows to their present value in order to state them in current, or today's, dollars. Use of a discount rate removes the time value of money from future cash flows.

Discounted Lease

A lease in which the lease payments are assigned to a funding source in exchange for up-front cash to the lessor.

Double-dip Lease

A series of lease transactions between parties in two countries. The tax rules for leases are different to the extent that both parties, the lessee and the lessor, receive favorable tax treatment.

Dry Lease

A net lease. This term traditionally is used in aircraft and marine leasing to describe a lease agreement that provides financing only and, therefore, requires the lessee to separately procure personnel, fuel and provisions necessary to operate the craft.

Dun and Bradstreet (D & B)

A financial company that provides credit information on businesses in the U.S.

Early Termination

Occurs when the lessee returns the leased equipment to the lessor prior to the end of the lease term, as permitted by the original lease contract or subsequent agreement. At times, this may result in a penalty to the lessee.

Economic Life of Leased Property

The estimated period during which the property is expected to be economically usable by one or more users, with normal repairs and maintenance, for the purpose for which it was intended at the inception of the lease.

Effective Interest Rate

The interest rate in a lease stated on an annual basis. The rate includes the compounding effect of interest during the year.

End-of-term Options

Options stated in the lease agreement that give the lessee flexibility in its treatment of the leased equipment at the end of the lease term. Common end-of-term options include purchasing the equipment, renewing the lease or returning the equipment to the lessor.

Equipment Schedule

A document incorporated by reference into the lease agreement that describes in detail the equipment being leased. The schedule may state the lease term, commencement date, repayment schedule and location of the equipment.

Equipment Specifications

A specific description of a piece of equipment that is to be acquired, including, but not limited to, equipment make, model, configuration and capacity requirements.

Equipment Trust Certificate

An early form of conditional sale agreements used mostly by railroads, beginning in the 1800s.

Equity Investor or Participant

An entity that provides equity funding in a leveraged lease transaction and thereby becomes the owner and ultimate lessor of the leased equipment.

Escalation Clause

A lease provision that allows the lessor to increase the rents based on an increase in the CPI, bank prime rate or other index rate.

Essential Use

Use of leased property in a well- and-long established program or function.

European Investment Bank (EIB)

Facilitates the balanced development of the European Community. EIB finances fixed assets and contributes to the total cost of projects within the EC. The European Bank for Reconstruction and Development is a major shareholder of EIB.

Evergreen Lease

A lease that self-renews each year unless the lessee gives notice of its termination within a specified period of time.

Executory Costs

Recurring costs in a lease, such as insurance, maintenance and taxes for the leased property, whether paid by the lessor or the lessee. Executory costs also include amounts paid by the lessee in consideration for a third-party residual guarantee, as well as any profits realized by the lessor on any executory costs paid by the lessor and passed on to the lessee.

Extensions

The process of forgiving a specific monthly rent in return for an extension fee and the lessee's promise to pay at a later date.

External Rate of Return (ERR)

A method of yield calculation. ERR is a modified internal rate of return (IRR) that allows for the incorporation of specific reinvestment, borrowing and sinking fund assumptions.

Facts and Circumstances

A tax depreciation method based upon the historical accuracy of a company's experience.

Fair Market Value (FMV)

The value of a piece of equipment if the equipment were to be sold in a transaction determined at arm's length, between a willing buyer and a willing seller, for equivalent property and under similar terms and conditions.

Fair Market Value Cap

A high end limit on a FMV lease that protects the lessee upside risk for executing the residual at the end of the lease.

Fair Market Value Purchase Option

A lessee option to purchase leased property at the end of the lease for fair market value at that time.

Fair Rental Value

The theoretical amount of periodic rental that should be paid for an asset. Used by the IRS as a guideline in Revenue Ruling 55-540.

FASB 13

Financial Accounting Standards Board Statement No. 13, "Accounting for Leases." FASB 13, along with its various amendments and interpretations, specifies the proper classification, accounting and reporting of leases by lessors and lessees.

Finance Lease

An expression oftentimes used in the industry to refer to a capital lease or a nontax lease. It is also a type of tax-oriented lease that was introduced by the Tax Equity and Fiscal Responsibility Act of 1982, to be effective in 1984, but later repealed by the Tax Reform Act of 1986.

Financial Accounting Standards Board (FASB)

The rule-making body that establishes financial reporting guidelines for commercial enterprises.

Financial Institution Lessor

A type of independent leasing company that is owned by, or is a part of, a financial institution, such as a commercial bank, thrift institution, insurance company, industrial loan company or credit union.

Financing Statement

A notice of a security interest filed under the Uniform Commercial Code (UCC).

Fixed Purchase Option

An option contained in the lease agreement allowing the lessee to purchase the equipment at a predetermined price at lease term.

Floating Rental Rate

Rental that is subject to upward or downward adjustments during the lease term. Floating rents sometimes are adjusted in proportion to prime interest rate, commercial paper rate or other changes in the cost of money during the term of the lease.

Foreign Sales Corporation (FSC)

A legal entity created to export U.S. manufactured goods to a foreign country. If a FSC meets the qualifications for FSC status, a portion of its income is exempt from current U.S. taxation. There are two types of FSC structures: Commission FSCs and Ownership FSCs.

Foreign Source Income

Net income earned overseas that is reported to the IRS for federal income tax purposes.

Foreign Tax Credit

Also called FTC. Under § 901 of the U.S. tax code, a foreign tax credit is allowed for taxes paid or accrued to a foreign country or U.S. possession during the taxable year.

Full-payout Lease

A lease in which the lessor recovers, through the lease payments, all costs incurred in the lease plus an acceptable rate of return, without any reliance upon the leased equipment's future residual value.

Full-service Lease

A lease that includes additional services such as maintenance, insurance and property taxes that are paid for by the lessor, the cost of which is built into the lease payments.

Funding

The process of paying the manufacturer of the equipment for the equipment being placed on lease.

Funding Source

An entity that provides any part of the funds used to pay for the cost of the leased equipment. Funds can come from either an equity funding source, such as the ultimate lessor in a lease transaction, or a debt funding source, such as a bank or other lending institution.

Generally Accepted Accounting Principles (GAAP)

Accounting standards established by the Financial Accounting Standards Board to assure that external financial statements are fair representations of the economic circumstances of the company. FASB 13, "Accounting for Leases," details the practices for accounting for leases by both lessors and lessees.

Grantor Trust

A trust used as the owner trust in a leveraged lease transaction or as a special purpose vehicle on a securitized transaction. Usually funded by the equity participant(s) or investors.

Gross Pretax Yield

The yield calculated in a lease before considering tax benefits and costs of doing business such as bad debt and general and administrative expenses.

Gross Receivables

Accounting term representing the total payments remaining to be collected on the lease contract.

Guaranteed Residual Value

A situation in which the lessee or an unrelated third party (e.g., equipment manufacturer, insurance company) guarantees to the lessor that the leased equipment will be worth a certain fixed amount at the end of the lease term. The guarantor agrees to reimburse the lessor for any deficiency realized if the leased equipment is salvaged subsequently at an amount below the guaranteed residual value.

Guarantor

The party that promises to pay the lease payments to the lessor in the event the lessee defaults.

Half-year Convention

A tax depreciation convention that assumes all equipment is purchased or sold at the midpoint of a taxpayer's tax year. The half-year convention allows an equipment owner to claim a half-year of depreciation deductions in the year of acquisition, as well as in the year of disposition, regardless of the actual date within the year that the equipment was placed in service or disposed of.

Hell-or-high-water Clause

A clause in a lease that states the unconditional obligation of the lessee to pay rent for the entire term of the lease, regardless of any event affecting the equipment or any change in the circumstances of the lessee.

Hurdle Rate

The minimum return or reward a company will accept in order to fund a project. In leasing, the hurdle rate is the lowest return a lease company would accept on a given lease.

Ijara

An Islamic expression for a true lease.

Ijara-wa-Iqtina

An Islamic expression for a financial lease or hire-purchase agreement.

Implicit Rate

The discount rate that, when applied to the minimum lease payments (excluding executory costs) together with any unguaranteed residual, causes the aggregate present value at the inception of the lease to be equal to the fair market value (reduced by any lessor retained investment tax credits) of the leased property.

Inception of a Lease

The date of the lease agreement or commitment if earlier. (For technical application, consult FASB 13 and subsequent amendments.)

Income Fund

An investment vehicle sold to investors. The income fund generates its income by investing in leasing transactions. Dividends, which are derived from leasing activities, are declared and paid to investors.

Incremental Borrowing Rate

The interest rate that would be paid by a company to incur the next dollar of debt for similar terms as the lease.

Indemnification

A clause in a master lease agreement that requires lessees to indemnify lessors against any and all claims, suits, actions, damages, liabilities, expenses, cost, including attorney fees, whether or not suit is instituted, arising out of or incurred in connection with the equipment.

Indemnity Clauses

The indemnity provisions in a lease: general indemnity, general tax indemnity and special tax indemnity. In leveraged leases, the tax indemnity clauses can be quite lengthy and sometimes are contained in a special supplement to the lease agreement or in a separate agreement.

Independent Lessor

A type of leasing company that is independent of any one manufacturer, and, as such, purchases equipment from various unrelated manufacturers. The equipment then is leased to the end-user or lessee. This type of lessor also is referred to as a third-party lessor.

Indenture Trust

An agreement between the owner trustee and the indenture trustee. Similar to a mortgage.

Indenture Trustee

The party who holds the security interest in the leased equipment for the benefit of the lenders.

Initial Direct Costs

Costs incurred by the lessor that are directly associated with negotiating and consummating a lease. These costs include, but are not necessary limited to, commissions, legal fees, costs of credit investigations, the cost of preparing and processing documents for new leases acquired and so forth.

Inspection

The act whereby the lessor goes to the lessee site to see if the leased equipment is in good working order.

Installment Sale

A sale in which the lessee pays the lessor several payments over a period of time. Sometimes used to finance the sale of a residual.

Insured Value

An agreed-upon value that the insurance company will pay the beneficiary if the equipment is destroyed while on lease.

Interest

The difference between the total loan payments and original loan amount (principal). Interest is to a loan as earned income is to a lease.

Interest Expense

An amount paid to a lender in return for a loan. Typically the interest is paid out over time, accompanied by a reduction in loan principal.

Interim Rent

A charge for the use of a piece of equipment from its in-service date, or delivery date, until the date on which the base term of the lease commences. The daily interim rent charge typically is equal to the daily equivalent of the base rental payment. The use of interim rent allows the lessor to have one common base term commencement date for a lease agreement having multiple deliveries of equipment.

Internal Rate of Return (IRR)

The unique discount rate that equates the present value of a series of cash inflows (i.e., lease payments, purchase option) to the present value of the cash outflows (equipment or investment cost). IRR is the most common method used to compute yields.

International Accounting Standard 17

A lease accounting standard followed by several major countries. Similar to FASB 13 in the U.S.

International Finance Corporation (IFC)

An affiliate of the the World Bank. The IFC promotes private sector investments in developing countries and assists in the development of the private sector whereas the World Bank primarily focuses on the public sector.

Investment Tax Credit (ITC)

A credit that a taxpayer is permitted to claim on the federal tax return (a direct offset to tax liability) as a result of ownership of qualified equipment. ITC was repealed by the Tax Reform Act of 1986, for all equipment placed in service after 1985.

Joint Ventures

A legal entity formed by two or more parties to conduct a specific business transaction.

Landlord Waiver

A document required by a lessor when a lessee is placing the leased equipment on a property leased from another party, to secure lessor's rights.

Lease

A contract through which an owner of equipment conveys the right to use the equipment to another party.

Lease Acquisition

The process whereby a leasing company purchases or acquires a lease from a lease originator, such as a lease broker or leasing company.

Lease Agreement

The contractual agreement between the lessor and the lessee that sets forth all the terms and conditions of the lease.

Lease Broker

An entity that provides one or more services in the lease transaction, but that does not retain the lease transaction for its own portfolio. Such services include finding the lessee, working with the equipment manufacturer, securing debt financing for the lessor to use in purchasing the equipment and locating the ultimate lessor or equity participant in the lease transaction. The lease broker also is referred to as a packager.

Lease Expiration

The time at which the original term of the lease contract has ended.

Lease Line

A lease line of credit. A lessee can add equipment without having to renegotiate a new lease each time.

Lease Origination

The process of uncovering (through a sales force), developing and consummating lease transactions. Steps in the process include, but are not limited to, prospecting for new lease business, pricing potential transactions, performing credit reviews and completing the necessary documentation.

Lease Payments

Also called rentals. The amount the lessee pays the lessor in return for using the leased equipment.

Lease Rate

A rate widely used in the leasing industry. Computed by dividing the monthly payment by the cost basis of the lease. Also called the lease rate factor (LRF).

Lease Schedule

An addendum to a master lease, stating specific equipment and lease terms.

Lease Term

The fixed, noncancellable term of the lease. Includes, for accounting purposes, all periods covered by fixed-rate renewal options, which for economic reasons appear likely to be exercised at the inception of the lease. Includes, for tax purposes, all periods covered by fixed-rate renewal options.

Lessee

The user of the equipment being leased.

Lessee's Incremental Borrowing Rate

The interest rate that the lessee at the inception of the lease would have incurred to borrow over a similar term the funds necessary to purchase the leased assets. In a leveraged lease, the rate on the leveraged debt normally is used.

Lessor

The owner of equipment leased to a lessee or user. (Legal title under the Uniform Commercial Code may be with the lessee in finance leases and nontax leases.)

Leverage

An amount borrowed. A lease is sometimes referred to as 100% leveraged for the lessee. In a leveraged lease, the debt portion of the funds used to purchase the asset represents leverage of the equity holder.

Leveraged Lease

A specific form of lease involving at least three parties: a lessor, lessee and funding source. The lessor borrows a significant portion of the equipment cost on a nonrecourse basis by assigning the future lease payment stream to the lender in return for up-front funds (the borrowing). The lessor puts up a minimal amount of its own equity funds (the difference between the equipment cost and the present value of the assigned lease payments) and generally is entitled to the full tax benefits of equipment ownership.

Lien

A security interest on property to protect the lender in the event of lessee default.

Limited Partnership

Tax entity formed by individual investors to shelter personal income. Often used to finance leasing operations.

Loan Participant

The party providing the debt on a leveraged lease.

MACRS Class Life

The specific tax cost recovery (depreciation) period for a class of assets as defined by (Modified Accelerated Cost Recovery System (MACRS.) Asset class lives (ADR midpoint lives) are used to determine an asset's MACRS classlife and, hence, its recovery period.

Maintenance Contract

An agreement whereby the lessee contracts with another party to maintain and repair the leased property during the lease term, in exchange for a payment or stream of payments.

Master Lease

A lease agreement containing boiler plate provisions that allows a lessee to obtain additional leased equipment under the same basic lease terms and conditions as originally agreed to, without having to renegotiate and execute a new lease contract with the lessor. The actual lease rate for a specific piece of equipment generally will be set upon equipment delivery to the lessee.

Match Funded Debt

Debt incurred by the lessor to fund a specific piece of leased equipment, the terms and repayment of which are structured to correspond to the repayment of the lease obligation by the lessee.

Midquarter Convention

A depreciation convention (replacing half-year convention for certain taxpayers in certain years) that assumes all equipment is placed in service halfway through the quarter in which it was actually placed in service. Allowable acquisition and disposition year depreciation deductions are prorated based upon the midquarter date of the quarter in which the asset was placed in service.

Minimum Lease Payments

From the lessee perspective, all payments that are required to be made, may be required to be made or, in all probability, will be made to the lessor per the lease agreement. Minimum lease payments for the lessee include, but are not limited to, the lease payments (excluding executory costs) during the noncancellable lease term, bargain purchase options, any put purchase options, the amount of any lessee residual guarantees and nonrenewal penalties that are insufficiently severe to cause renewal. Minimum lease payments for the lessor include all payments to be received from the lessee, as described above, as well as the amount of any residual guarantees by unrelated third-party guarantors.

Modified Accelerated Cost Recovery System (MACRS)

The current tax depreciation system as introduced by the Tax Reform Act of 1986, effective for equipment placed in service after December 31, 1986.

Money-over-money Lease

A nontax lease. This type of lease is a conditional sales contract in the guise of a lease, in which the lessee is, or will become, the owner of the leased equipment by the end of the lease term, and, therefore, is entitled to the tax benefits of ownership.

Mudaraha

A contractual agreement whereby the entire capital of a business enterprise is provided by an Islamic bank or financial institution. Management, however, remains in the hands of the party operating the business. Profit is shared in predetermined proportions, whereas any loss is borne solely by the provider of the capital

Multiple Investment Sinking Fund (MISF)

Method of income allocation used to report earnings on a leveraged lease. This method is similar to the external rate of return (ERR) method of yield calculation except that it assumes a zero earnings rate during periods of disinvestment (a sinking fund rate equal to 0).

Municipal Lease

A conditional sales contract disguised in the form of a lease available only to state and local governments, in which the interest earnings are tax-exempt to the lessor.

Municipal Obligation

Generally, a bond, debt or obligation issued or incurred by a state or local government.

Murabaha

A contract whereby an Islamic bank of financial institution purchases goods or equipment required by a customer and resells them to the customer at a predetermined profit.

Musharaka

An agreement in which an Islamic bank of financial institution provides funds that are intermingled with the funds of others participating in the business enterprise. All such participants are entitled to participate in management. Profit is distributed among the partners in preagreed upon ratios. Losses are borne by each partner in proportion to his or her respective capital contribution.

Net Lease

A lease in which all costs in connection with the use of the equipment, such as maintenance, insurance and property taxes, are paid for separately by the lessee and are not included in the lease rental paid to the lessor.

Net Present Value

The total discounted value of all cash inflows and outflows from a project or investment.

Nominal Interest Rate

Interest rate stated as an annual percentage without including the effect of interest during the year.

Nonappropriation Clause

Contractual provision found in municipal leases that provides that if the governmental lessee fails to appropriate or make available funds to make the lease payments called for under the agreement for the next appropriation period, the agreement terminates at the end of the current appropriation period. Such a clause is used to prevent lease payment obligations in future years from being classified as debt. Exercise of the nonappropriation clause is not an event of default.

Non-fullpayout Lease

A lease in which cash flows from the payments are insufficient to cover the lessor's cost. The lessor assumes that a re-lease or renewal will take place. Often classified as operating leases by lessors.

Nonrecourse

A type of borrowing in which the lessor-borrower is not at-risk for the borrowed funds. The lender expects repayment from the lessee and/or the value of the leased equipment; hence, the lender's credit decision is based upon the creditworthiness of the lessee, as well as the expected value of the leased equipment.

Nonsubstitution Clause

A clause providing that if the lessee in a lease that has a nonappropriation clause exercises the clause to terminate the agreement, the lessee, within a specified time period after such termination, cannot purchase or use property similar in function to the property being leased.

Nontax Lease

A type of lease in which the lessee is, or will become, the owner of the leased equipment, and, therefore, is entitled to all the risks and benefits (including tax benefits) of equipment ownership.

Off Balance Sheet Financing

Any form of financing, such as an operating lease, that, for financial reporting purposes, is not required to be reported on a firm's balance sheet.

On-behalf-of Agency

Autonomous agency created by one or more state or local governments to issue tax-exempt bonds or obligations on its or their behalf.

Open-end Lease

A lease in which the lessee guarantees the amount of the future residual value to be realized by the lessor at the end of the lease. If the equipment is sold for less than the guaranteed value, the lessee must pay the amount of any deficiency to the lessor. This lease is referred to as open-end because the lessee does not know its actual cost until the equipment is sold at the end of the lease term.

Operating Budget

A budget that lists the amount of noncapital goods and services a firm is authorized by management to expend during the operating period.

Operating Lease

From a financial reporting perspective, a lease that has the characteristics of a usage agreement and also meets certain criteria established by the FASB. Such a lease is not required to be shown on the balance sheet of the lessee. The term also is used to refer to leases in which the lessor has taken a significant residual position in the lease pricing and, therefore, must salvage the equipment for a certain value at the end of the lease term in order to earn its rate of return.

Optimized Debt

A method of setting up the debt structure to minimize the lease rental rate to the lessee and to maximize returns to the equity participant.

Original Equipment Cost (OEC)

The amount the lessor pays the vendor for the equipment at the beginning of the lease. Usually includes up-front sales tax.

Overseas Private Investment Corporation (OPIC)

A quasi-public agency that helps exporters by providing insurance on foreign risks.

Overcollateralization

A technique to protect the investor on a securitized transaction. Basically, the lessor can set aside additional funds in a reserve or transfer more than sufficient assets to the investor vehicle. By doing so, the lessor has effectively provided a cushion that can generate cash flow in the event the lessee receivables are not sufficient to provide enough cash to satisfy investors' requirements.

Owner Participant

The beneficial owner under an owner trust. Used in leveraged leasing to represent the owner(s) of the equipment.

Owner Trustee

The party that holds the title to the equipment under a leveraged lease.

Packager

A leasing company, investment banker or broker that arranges a leveraged lease.

Participation Agreement

Same as financing agreement. An agreement that states the obligations of all parties under a leveraged lease transaction.

Pass-through Securitization

A structure that represents the sale of lease receivables to a special purpose vehicle (SPV). Generally, the receivables are sold to a grantor trust which issues securities backed by the assets of the SPV. Distributions of funds from the SPV are made to the investors who provided the original capital.

Payment Stream

The rentals due in a lease.

Payments in Advance

A payment stream in which each lease payment is due at the beginning of each period during the lease.

Payments in Arrears

A payment stream in which each lease payment is due at the end of each period during the lease.

Payoff

Occurs when the lessee purchases the leased asset from the lessor prior to the end of the lease term.

Pay-through Securitization

A structure that allows the lessor to transfer lease receivables to a special purpose vehicle (SPV) in the form of a loan. The SPV then issues bonds to the investors and the receivables are pledged as collateral.

Penetration Rate

A ratio that reflects the amount of leasing activity in a particular country. The ratio divides leasing volume by total financing volume or leases and loans.

Pickle Lease

A lease by a U.S. lessor to a foreign lessee authorized under the 1984 Tax Reform Act. Accelerated depreciation is slowed down to a straight-line basis over a longer recovery period. Named after Congressman Pickle of Texas.

Placed in Service

Delivered and available for use, although the equipment may still be subject to final installation and/or assembly.

Point

One percent, or one percentage point (1.00%). A point also represents 100 basis points.

Pooled Funds

A funding technique used by lessors in which several forms of borrowing are pooled, or grouped, for use in funding leases and are not tied specifically to the purchase of any one piece of leased equipment.

Present Value

The discounted value of a payment or stream of payments to be received in the future, taking into consideration a specific interest or discount rate. Present value represents a series of future cash flows expressed in today's dollars.

Preference Items

Certain tax benefits that may create additional tax liability under the alternative minimum tax.

Pricing

Arriving at the periodic rental amount to charge a lessee. A lessor must factor many variables into its pricing, which may include lease term, lessor targeted yield, security deposits, residual value and tax benefits.

Private Letter Ruling

A ruling by the IRS requested by parties to a lease transaction that is applicable only to the assumed facts stated in the opinion.

Purchase Agreement Assignment

An agreement in which some or all of the lessee's rights under a purchase agreement (including the right to take title to the equipment) are assigned by the lessee to the owner trustee prior to the delivery of the property by the manufacturer. A consent of the manufacturer or supplier that confirms the availability to the owner trustee of the rights of purchaser under the contract. This assignment usually is annexed to the assignment.

Purchase Option

An option in the lease agreement that allows the lessee to purchase the leased equipment at the end of the lease term for either a fixed amount or at the future fair market value of the leased equipment.

Put Option

An option in a lease (e.g., for equipment purchase or lease renewal) in which the exercise of the option is at the lessor's, not the lessee's, discretion.

Qard

Under Islamic law, a regular loan in which the client undertakes to repay the principal at a future date. Generally, no interest is charged. However, a service fee is permissible in some jurisdictions as long as such fee is based on the actual cost of administering the loan.

Quiet Enjoyment Clause

A contractual provision that permits the lessee to use the leased property free from unreasonable interference from the lessor.

Rate Factor

A percentage amount that, when multiplied by the original equipment cost, produces the monthly rental.

Recourse

A type of borrowing in which the borrower (a lessor funding a lease) is fully at-risk to the lender for repayment of the obligation. The recourse borrower (lessor) is required to make payments to the lender whether or not the lessee fulfills its obligation under the lease agreement.

Refundable Security Deposit

An amount paid by the lessee to the lessor as security for fulfillment of all obligations outlined in the lease agreement that is subsequently refunded to the lessee once all obligations have been satisfied. Security deposits typically are returned at the end of the lease term but, according to mutual agreement, can be refunded at any point during the lease.

Regulation Y

A Federal Reserve Board rule that regulates leasing by banks.

Remarketing

The process of selling or leasing the leased equipment to another party upon termination of the original lease term. The lessor can remarket the equipment or contract with another party, such as the manufacturer, to remarket the equipment in exchange for a remarketing fee.

Renewal Option

An option in the lease agreement that allows the lessee to extend the lease term for an additional period beyond the expiration of the initial lease term, in exchange for lease renewal payments.

Rent Holiday

A period of usage, usually up front, in which the lessee is not required to pay rents. Typically, the rents are capitalized into the remaining lease payments.

Repossession

A situation in which a lessor reclaims and physically removes the leased equipment from the control of the lessee; usually caused by payment default.

Residual Value

The value, either actual or expected, of leased equipment at the end, or termination, of the lease.

Residual Value Insurance

An insurance policy stating the guaranteed residual value on leased equipment. The insurance company pays if the residual is not realized.

Retained Transaction

A lease transaction or investment kept for one's own portfolio; a retained transaction is not sold to another lessor or investor.

Return on Assets (ROA)

A common measure of profitability based upon the amount of assets invested; ROA is equal to the ratio of either 1) net income to total assets or 2) net income available to common stockholders to total assets.

Return on Equity (ROE)

A measure of profitability related to the amount of invested equity; ROE is equal to the ratio of either 1) net income to owners' equity or 2) net income available to common stockholders to common equity.

Revenue Procedures

Commonly used in leasing to refer to IRS Revenue Procedures 75-21, 75-28 and 76-30. These guidelines set forth requirements for obtaining a favorable federal income tax ruling that a particular leveraged lease transaction is a true lease.

Revenue Ruling 55-540

A published ruling by the IRS to determine lease eligibility. Issued in 1955 to distinguish a true lease from a conditional sale.

Riba

The Islamic expression for interest. Typically prohibited under Islamic law.

Rollover

A change in lease term and/or payment resulting from a change in equipment, such as in a takeout or upgrade. The rollover finances those costs associated with the change in equipment and may result in the lessor financing an amount greater than the equipment value.

Rule of 78

An accelerated method of allocating periodic earnings in a lease (or a loan) based upon the sum-of-the-years method.

Running Rate

The rate of return to the lessor, or cost to the lessee, in a lease based solely upon the initial equipment cost and the periodic lease payments, without any reliance on residual value, tax benefit, deposits or fees. This rate also is referred to as the street or stream rate.

Sale-leaseback

A transaction that involves the sale of equipment to a leasing company and a subsequent lease of the same equipment back to the original owner, who continues to use the equipment.

Sales-type Lease

A capital lease from the lessor's perspective (per FASB 13) that gives rise to manufacturer's or dealer's profit to the lessor.

Salvage Value

The expected or realized value from selling a piece of equipment.

Sawtooth Rents

Rents that vary throughout the term of the lease, usually to match debt payments and tax payments in a leveraged lease so as to lessen the need for a sinking fund.

Schedule

Listing of equipment to become subject to a lease that describes the equipment in detail. The schedule may reflect the lease term, the commencement date and the location of the equipment and may be incorporated into the basic lease agreement by reference.

Securities Act of 1933

A federal law governing the issuance of securities to the public.

Securities Act of 1934

A federal law governing the operations of stock and securities exchanges. Also governs over-the-counter trading.

Securitization

The process of selling lease receivables to a separate legal entity that issues stocks and bonds to investors. The investors' proceeds flow through to the company that sold the receivables and the investors receive their returns from collecting lessee receivables.

Security Deposit

A dollar amount held by the lessor to protect against default by the lessee. Refundable at the end of the lease.

Security Interest

An interest in property acquired by contract for the purpose of securing payment or performance of an obligation.

Service Lease

A lease for equipment that assigns the lessor the responsibility for maintaining the leased property.

Servicer

The party that performs collections activities, makes appropriate disbursements, handles terminations/buyouts and provides required reports to investors on a securitized transaction.

Severability

A provision in a lease agreement that states that if any part or provision of a lease shall be found unenforceable, it alone shall be discarded and the remaining provisions shall be given their full force and effect.

Simple Interest

Interest on the original principal only. Ignores impact of compounding interest. Accumulated interest in not included in subsequent calculations.

Single Investor Lease

A lease in which the lessor is fully at-risk for all funds (both equity and pooled funds) used to purchase the leased equipment.

Sinking Fund

A reserve set aside for the future payment of taxes (generally applicable only in leveraged leases), or for the purpose of payment of any liability anticipated to become due at a future date.

Sinking Fund Rate

The earnings rate allocated to a sinking fund.

Skipped-payment Lease

A lease that contains a payment stream requiring the lessee to make payments only during certain periods of the year.

Special Purpose Property

Property that is uniquely valuable to the lessee and not valuable to anyone else except as scrap. Also referred to as limited use property.

Special Purpose Vehicle (SPV)

A separate legal entity that purchases lease receivables in order to securitize them through either a pay-through or pass-through structure.

Spread

The difference between two values. In lease transactions, the term generally is used to describe the difference between the interest rate of the lease and the interest on the debt used to fund the lease.

Step-payment Lease

A lease that contains a payment stream requiring the lessee to make payments that either increase (step-up) or decrease (step-down) in amount over the term of the lease.

Stipulated Loss Schedule

A document that sets forth the lessee's remaining liability to the lessor upon the occurrence of a default or casualty. Typically, the lessee has the duty to repair or replace any lost or damaged equipment, as it is typically required to bear the risk of loss during the lease term.

Stipulated Loss Value

An addendum to a master lease that incorporates required lessee payments in the event of a default or casualty. These amounts, often expressed as a percentage of some amount, decline with each passing month, until the residual value remains at the end of the lease term.

Stipulated Loss Value Table

A schedule included in the lease agreement, generally used for purposes of minimum insurance coverage, that sets forth the agreed-upon value of the leased equipment at various points throughout the lease term. This value establishes the liability of the lessee to the lessor in the event the leased equipment is lost or becomes unusable because of casualty loss during the lease term.

Straight-line Depreciation

A method of depreciation (for financial reporting and tax purposes) in which the owner of the equipment claims an equal amount of depreciation in each year of the equipment's recovery period.

Structuring

Pulling together the many components of a lease to arrive at a single lease transaction. Structuring includes, but is not limited to, lease pricing, end-of-term options, documentation issues, indemnification clauses, funding and residual valuations.

Sublease

A transaction in which leased property is re-leased by the original lessee to a third party, and the lease agreement between the two original parties remains in effect.

Substance Versus Form

A concept that implies that the form of a document is subordinate to the intent of the parties involved in the document.

Takeout

A flexible lease option in which the lessor replaces existing leased equipment with either different equipment or newer equipment of the same make.

Tax-exempt Obligation

Bond, debt or another obligation for which the interest paid is exempt from federal income taxes under Section 103 of the U.S. Internal Revenue Code.

Tax-exempt Organization

An organization that may issue or incur tax-exempt obligations. State and local governments are tax-exempt organizations.

Tax-exempt User Lease

A type of tax lease available to tax-exempt or nonprofit entities, in which the lessor receives only limited tax benefits.

Tax Lease

A generic term for a lease in which the lessor takes on the risks of ownership (as determined by various IRS pronouncements) and, as the owner, is entitled to the benefits of ownership, including tax benefits.

Tax Reform Act of 1986 (TRA 86)

Recent tax law that effected a major overhaul of the U.S. tax system by lowering tax rates, modifying the Accelerated Cost Recovery System (now MACRS), repealing the Investment Tax Credit (ITC) and repealing the transitional finance lease.

Terminal Rental Adjustment Clause (TRAC)

A lessee guaranteed residual value for vehicle leases (automobiles, trucks or trailers), the inclusion of which will not, in and of itself, disqualify the tax lease status of a tax-oriented vehicle lease.

Termination Value

The liability of the lessee in the event of termination is set forth in a termination schedule that values the equipment at various times during the lease term. This value is designed to protect the lessor from loss of investment. If the equipment is sold at a price lower than the amount set forth in the schedule, the lessee pays the difference. In the event the resale is at a price higher than in the termination schedule, such excess amounts belong to the lessor. The termination schedule is not the same as the casualty value schedule, insured value schedule or stipulated loss value schedule.

Third-party Lessor

An independent leasing company, or lessor, that writes leases involving three parties: 1) the unrelated manufacturer, 2) the independent lessor and 3) the lessee.

Ticket Size

Refers to the cost of equipment being leased. The leasing marketplace is roughly segmented into the small, middle and large ticket markets.

True Lease

Another term for a tax lease in which, for IRS purposes, the lessor qualifies for the tax benefits of ownership and the lessee is allowed to claim the entire amount of the lease rental as a tax deduction.

Turnaround Time

The time it takes to make a credit decision and inform the lessee after receiving the lease application.

Two-party Lessor

A captive leasing company, or lessor, that writes leases involving two parties: 1) the consolidated parent and/or captive leasing subsidiary and 2) the lessee or end-user of the equipment.

Uniform Commercial Code (UCC)

A set of standard rules, adopted by 49 states, that governs commercial transactions.

UCC-1

A UCC document filed by a lessor informing the public that the filing party legally owns the equipment on lease.

UCC Financing Statement

A document, under the UCC, filed with the county (and sometimes the secretary of state) to provide public notice of a security interest in personal property.

Unearned Income

The portion of income from a lease that must be earned over the life of the lease in accordance with GAAP.

Unguaranteed Residual Value

The portion of residual value for which the lessor is at-risk. The lessor takes on the risk that the equipment may or may not be worth this expected value at the end of the lease term.

Upgrade

An option that allows the lessee to add equipment to an existing piece of leased equipment in order to increase its capacity or improve its efficiency.

Use Tax

A state or local tax for using equipment on lease. The tax usually is billed each month, collected and remitted to the taxing authority.

Useful Life

A period of time during which an asset has economic value and is usable. The useful life of an asset sometimes is called the economic life of the asset.

Usury Laws

Laws regulating the charging of interest rates. Most usury laws protect consumers from unauthorized interest rates.

Variable Interest Rate

Interest rate charged under a lease that is subject to upward and downward adjustment during the lease term.

Variable Term Lease

A lease that ends when all payments are made. The term is flexible to accommodate skips and increased rents.

Vendor Lease

A lease offered by a manufacturer or dealer to its customers for financing its products.

Vendor Leasing

Lease financing offered to an equipment end-user in conjunction with the sale of equipment. Vendor leases can be provided by the equipment vendor (manufacturer or dealer) or a third-party leasing company with a close working relationship with the equipment vendor.

Warehousing

The short-term funding of leases before permanent funding is finalized.

Wet Lease

A lease in which the lessor provides bundled services, such as the payment of property taxes, insurance, maintenance costs, fuel or provisions, and may even provide persons to operate the leased equipment. This type of lease typically is referred to in aircraft leasing and marine charters.

Wintergreen Lease

A lease that requires the lessee to give notice to the lessor in order to renew for another term. Otherwise, the lease terminates on the already established termination date.

Wrap Lease

A lease in which the lessor sells the equipment to an investor for equity and a note payable over the lease term. This method effectively transfers tax benefits to an investor.

Yield

The rate of return to the lessor in a lease investment.

Zakata

Under Islamic law, a wealth tax levied on businesses and individuals as a percentage of total net worth, which includes industrial assets and real estate.

Index

A

Accelerated Cost Recovery System (ACRS): 10, 170

Accelerated depreciation: 44, 797

Accounting Principles Board (APB): 235

Accounting systems: 860-861

Accretion: 274, 300

Ad valorem property tax: 224

Add-on interest: 467

Additional insured: 706

Adequacy of Appropriations Act: 883

Adjusted current earnings (ACE): 177
 depreciation: 180

Administrative rent: 783

Advance payments: 692

After-tax:
 analysis: 460
 cost of debt: 1123
 ROA: 1127
 structuring: 545

Alternative depreciation system (ADS): 96, 892, 894
 150% declining balance: 151

Alternative minimum tax (AMT): 35, 151, 172, 546, 978, 1104
 150% declining balance: 175
 ACE depreciation: 180
 adjusted current earnings (ACE): 177
 alternative minimum taxable income: 172

exemption: 182
minimum tax credit: 183
preferences: 173-174, 440, 787, 788, 976
structuring: 575
turnaround: 447

Alternative minimum taxable income: 172

American Appraisal Association: 843

American Society of Appraisers (ASA): 843

Anti-deficiency Act: 883

Antichurning rules: 170

Apportionment: 199

Appraisals: 957

Appraisers: 853

Arbitrage bond: 902-903

Article 2A – Leases: 704, 737, 1093

Article 9 – Secured Transactions: 750, 770, 1093

Asian Development Bank (ADB): 78

Asset depreciation range (ADR): 144, 175

Asset management: 819
    preevaluation audit: 823

Asset quality: 1063

Asset risk: 1042

Asset turnover: 667, 1054-1055

Assignment of Claims Act: 884

Assignments: 761, 1084, 1176-1177

AT&T: 1106

AT&T Capital: 1107

At-risk: 23, 993
    amount: 190
    qualified leasing group: 189
    qualified leasing member: 190
    rules: 189

Attachment: 771

Audit report: 652

Australia: 87

Automatic renewal: 841

Automatic stay: 784

Automobile leasing history: 8

Average life: 1161

B

Back-to-back lease agreement: 887

Backleverage: 992

Bad debts: 1132

Bailment for hire: 737

Bailments and rentals: 736

Bank Holding Act: 1105

Bank Holding Company Act: 9

Bankruptcy: 635
    amendments of 1994: 783
    automatic stay: 784
    code: 778, 1091
    debtor in possession: 778
    estate: 1091
    plan of reorganization: 782
    prepetition debts: 778
    remote vehicle: 1085
    trustee: 778

Bargain purchase option: 23, 72, 247, 250, 372

Bargain renewal options: 251

Base rate: 1094-1095, 1127

Bell Atlantic: 1106

Bell South: 1106

Beta: 1125

Blanket filings: 774

Blanket lease: 917

Blind pool: 983

Bluebooks: 852

Bona fide offer: 1087

Bond volatility: 1056

Book basis: 796

Book value: 1115-1116

Brazil: 86

Breaches of warranty: 769

Break-even analysis: 648, 667

Break-even discount rate: 380

Bridge loan: 964

Broker: 854

Budget variance: 650

Budgeted lease: 550

Bulgaria: 85

Bundled services: 18, 20-21

Buy rate: 1084

C

Call option: 844

Canada: 84

Capital appropriations: 32

Capital asset pricing model: 1125

Capital budget: 32

Capital budgeting: 404

Capital lease: 24, 113, 242, 329, 332, 378

Capital lease accounting: 349
   capital leased asset: 331, 348
   capital lease obligation: 331, 346

Capital lease criteria: 246, 248, 371
   automatic transfer of ownership: 24
   bargain purchase option: 247, 250
   estimated economic life: 247, 252
   90% test: 372

Capital stock tax: 198

Capital structure: 1149

CAPM-Beta: 653

Captive lessor: 13, 68, 914, 926

Cash flow
  adequacy: 544
  analysis: 681-682
  consistency: 1069
  deficiencies: 1097
  ratios: 686-687

Cash:
  management: 30
  replacement: 1076
  reserves: 1076

Casualty: 794

Certificate of delivery and acceptance (D&A): 720, 756

Certificate of deposit: 694

Chattel paper: 726, 1093

Checks and balances: 1191-1192

Chile: 86

Circular No. A-104: 906-907

Closed-end leases: 20

Closing fees: 510

Collateral: 651, 679

Collateralized borrowing: 1084

Collection period: 670

Colombia: 86-87

Commencement date: 703

Commerce clause: 198, 225

Commission FSC (CFSC): 99

Commitment letter: 699-700

Comptroller of the Currency: 1105

Concentration risks: 1071

Condition of equipment: 841

Conditional sales contract (CSC): 12, 110

Conduit programs: 1067, 1085

Confidence coefficient: 414

Consolidation: 932-933

Constant debt-to-equity: 468
    ratio: 1165-1166

Consumer leasing: 61

Contingent rentals: 19, 254-255

Continuing sale: 216, 221

Conversion risk: 655

Cost:
    of capital: 399, 416, 493, 1122
    of debt: 416
    of equity: 417
    of funds: 1145
    of goods sold: 300
    reimbursement contract: 887
    standard: 1207-1208

Countenances repossession: 713

Covenants not to compete: 1117

Credit:
    application: 698
    decision process: 644
    enhancements: 694, 1043
    investigation: 644
    life insurance: 693
    policy: 659
    risk: 635, 638, 640, 642, 1188
    standard: 659

Credit analysis:
    balance sheet analysis: 661
    income statement analysis: 648, 661
    primary ratios: 664
    pro forma projections: 646
    secondary ratios: 664
    sensitivity models: 689
    trend analysis: 649

Credit scoring: 57, 646, 647, 656
    matrix: 647, 658
    systems: 862-863

Cross-border leases: 88, 655
    double-dip: 88-89
    financing: 86
    triple-dip: 98

Cross-default provisions: 710

Current ratio: 672

D

De minimus rule: 897, 1072

Debt optimization: 992, 1017-1022

Default: 635

Deferred taxes: 286-287, 306, 349, 1026, 1033
    temporary differences: 1033

Degree of involvement: 754

Depreciation: 18, 320, 322, 348
    Accelerated Cost Recovery System (ACRS): 10, 170
    cost recovery percentages: 145
    half-year convention: 145, 165
    limited use property: 130-131
    midquarter convention: 35, 159, 166, 167
    Modified Accelerated Cost Recovery System: 144, 997
    150% declining balance: 151
    Pickle depreciation: 155
    recovery class: 144
    rent curve: 321
    straight-line basis: 151
    tax-exempt use property: 155
    200% declining balance: 145
    used predominantly outside the U.S.: 152
    year of acquisition: 145
    year of disposition: 145

Development process: 870-871

Differential expenses: 410

Diffusion of risk: 1058

Direct financing: 1193
    leases: 245, 267-268

Direct funding: 952-954

Discount rate:
    lease classification: 256, 373
    lease versus buy: 416

Discounted cash flow method: 1116

Disinvestment balance: 486, 540, 1002-1004

Disposition of equipment: 845-846

Documents:
    certificate of delivery and acceptance (D&A): 720, 756
    commitment letter: 699-700
    credit application: 698
    lease application: 697
    lease proposal: 697
    letter of credit activation: 1076
    opinion of counsel: 728
    purchase order: 730

Document storage systems: 864

Double-dip lease: 88-89

Drop dead date: 700

Due diligence: 1053-1054

Due process clause: 198

Dunn & Bradstreet: 652

DuPont formula: 664, 668, 689, 1212

E

Early out: 388, 794

Early termination: 793

Earn-out provisions: 1115, 1117

Earnings and profits distributions: 104

Earnings before interest and taxes (EBIT): 664

Earnings methods:
    pretax rate: 279, 302
    Rule of 78: 279

Economic compulsion: 745

Economic value added (EVA): 405

Economies of scale: 973

Edward J. Altman: 680

Effective yield: 547

Energy tax credit: 375

Environmental liability: 706

Equipment evaluation information form: 832-833, 836-839

Equipment evaluation request form: 832-833, 834

Equipment Leasing Association: 1107

Equipment trust certificates: 1042

Equity exposure: 1059

Equity insertion: 992

Estimated economic life: 247, 252

European Bank of Reconstruction and Development: 79

European currency unit: 79

European Economic Community: 60

European Investment Bank (EIB) 79

Event of default: 708, 794

Evergreen renewal: 719

Excess servicing income: 1069

Excess-use penalties: 651

Exchange risk: 655

Executory costs: 254, 376, 383-384

Exempt property: 219

Eximbank: 75, 76

Expected value: 411

Express warranty: 759

F

Fair market value: 255, 743

FASB: (see Financial Accounting Standards Board)

FASB pronouncements:
    Statement 109: 286

Statement 13: 10, 234, 238, 268, 294-295, 313, 371, 969, 993
Statement 77: 1086
Statement 91: 257, 268, 280
Statement 95: 662, 683
Statement 98: 268
Technical Bulletin 79-10: 910
Technical Bulletin 85-3: 319
Technical Bulletin 86-2: 1089
Technical Bulletin 88-1: 1089
Technical Bulletin 88-2: 1089

Federal Acquisition Regulation (FAR): 904-905

Federal Consumer Leasing Act: 751

Federal Equal Credit Opportunity Act: 698

Federal Information Resources Management Regulation (FIRMR): 876, 904-905

Feedback systems: 650

Finance lease: 751

Financial Accounting Standards Board (FASB): 10, 233, 662

Financial:
    accounting: 234
    intermediary: 208
    leverage: 48, 664, 678
    ratio checklist: 665
    statements analysis: 653, 646

Financing: 244

Financing statements: 723
    four-month rule: 725

Fixture filing: 726, 760, 773

Forecasting methods:
    exponential curves: 689
    geometric curves: 689
    linear curves: 689
    logarithmic curves: 689

Foreign exchange risk: 74

Foreign persons: 96

Foreign Sales Corporations (FSC): 99
    commission (CFSC): 99

controlled foreign corporation (CFC): 93
    foreign trading income (FTI): 104
    ownership (OFSC): 99

Foreign source taxable income: 449

Foreign tax credit (FTC): 92, 181, 976-977
    foreign source taxable income: 449
    limitations: 450
    worldwide taxable income: 449

Foreign tax withholding: 92

Fra Luca Pacioli: 235

France: 85

Franchise tax: 198

Fraudulent conveyance: 722

Freedom of contract: 750

Full-service leasing: 41, 56

Fund accounting: 908

Fund manager: 989

Funding:
    risk: 1153, 1188-1189
    strategy: 1064

Funding methods:
    match funding: 74, 573, 1173, 1175
    matching maturities: 1161, 1163
    pooled debt: 481, 1165, 1170-1173

G

Gap analysis: 1157

GASB: (see Governmental Accounting Standards Board)

GE Capital: 1107

General Accounting Office (GAO): 882

General Agreement on Tariffs and Trade: 99

General and administrative expenses: 18

General obligation debt: 887

Generally accepted accounting principles (GAAP): 234, 652, 654, 661, 686

Generation costs: 1208

Germany: 85

Goodwill: 1118

Governmental Accounting Standards Board (GASB): 237, 909

Grantor trust: 1063

Great Britain: 85

Gross analysis: 459-460

Gross investment:
  direct financing leases: 273
  sales-type leases: 295, 298

Gross margin: 670

Gross profit: 294

Gross profit tax deferral (GPTD): 47, 546, 553, 797, 935

Growth in earnings: 1124

Guaranteed residual: 20

H

Half-year convention: 145, 165

Hardware and software platforms: 865

Hedging techniques: 655

Hell-or-high-water clause: 80, 704, 758, 1074

Holdbacks: 1054, 1097

Hong Kong: 86

Horizontal integration: 50-51

Hungary: 85

Hurdle rate: 494, 534, 1121, 1151, 1205-1206

I

Implicit rate: 256, 258-259, 271, 296, 373

Implied warranties: 759

Income funds: 70, 979
  blind pool: 983
  specific pool: 983

Income tax systems: 863

Incremental borrowing rate: 257, 332, 340

Indenture trusts: 999

Independent leasing companies: 8, 12

Indirect funding: 952-953

Initial direct costs: 18, 257-258, 510
    direct financing leases: 270, 280
    operating leases: 314, 321
    sales-type leases: 294

Initial public offering: 1109

Inspection rights: 833

Interest expense: 18

Interest minimization: 419

Interest rate risk: 1154, 1188-1189
    gap analysis: 1157
    interest rate hedges: 74
    interest rate swap: 1155
    mismatching: 1156

Interest rate swap: 1155

Internal controls: 835

Internal funding: 992

Internal rate of return (IRR): 256, 456, 535, 1001

International Accounting Standard No. 17: 85

International Finance Corporation (IFC): 77-78

International Society of Appraisers (ISA): 843

Interperiod tax allocation: 286, 304

Interstate banking: 1105

Intraperiod present value factor: 551, 555

Inventory analysis: 1220-1221

Investment Company Act of 1940: 1060

Investment recovery unit: 508

Investment tax credit (ITC): 8, 1104, 1107

Islamic leasing:
    Bai-Muajjal: 80

Ijara-wa-Iqtina: 81
Ijara: 81
Islamic law: 79
Mudaraha: 80
Murabaha: 80
Musharaka: 80
Qard: 80
Riba: 79
Zakat: 82
Italy: 85

J

Japan: 86
Joint ventures: 75, 925

L

Lack of privity: 758
Landlord's waiver: 731-732
Large ticket market: 12
Layered hurdle rate: 1136
Lease:
application: 697
broker: 14
definition: 16
disclosure requirements: 261
proposal: 697
receivables: 221
term: 251
Lease-to-ownership-plan (LTOP): 879
Lease versus buy:
dual rate method: 416
liquidity preference: 416
single rate method: 416
Lease-with-option-to-purchase (LWOP): 879
Leaseurope: 85
Leasing systems: 859-860

Lessee:
    bankruptcy: 699
    guaranteed residual value: 23
    incremental borrowing rate: 373
    projections: 690
    remedies: 767-768
    representations and warranties: 705

Lessor-lessee documents: 697

Letter of credit: 694, 1097

Level payment loan: 1166

Leverage: 1017, 1149

Leveraged buyout (LBO): 964

Leveraged leases: 12, 22, 34, 68, 245, 991
    debt optimization: 992, 1017-1022
    disinvestment balance: 486, 540, 1002-1004
    multiple investment sinking fund (MISF): 1001, 1195
    nonrecourse debt: 992

Lien: 637

Limited partnerships: 957

Limited use property: 130-131

Liquidated damage: 711, 765

Liquidity: 648

Liquidity preference: 416

Loss payee: 706

M

Maintenance provisions: 840

Maintenance reserve: 840

Malawi: 87

Management information systems: 859
    evaluation of: 868-869
    implementation issues: 871

Master lease: 41, 696

Match funding: 74, 573, 1173, 1175

Medieval leasing: 5

Mergers and acquisition: 1101-1102

Mexico: 84

Middle market: 12

Midquarter convention: 35, 159, 166, 167

Minimum lease payments: 252, 271, 332

Minimum tax credit: 183

Mobile goods: 725

Modified Accelerated Cost Recovery System: 144, 997

Money-over-money leases: 12, 23

Moody's: 652

Morocco: 87

Multiple investment sinking fund (MISF): 1001, 1195

Multistate Tax Commission: 201

Multistate Tax Compact: 199, 201

Municipal leases: 33-34, 894
   de minimus rule: 897, 1072
   nonappropriation clause: 876
   on-behalf-of entities: 896
   tax-exempt interest: 47, 894, 896

N

Negotiation process: 850

Net:
   analysis: 460
   lease: 749
   loss indemnity agreements: 920
   loss pool: 1098
   operating loss (NOL): 359, 426
   present value: 456
   realizable asset value: 1115

Net investment:
   direct financing lease: 273
   sales-type lease: 295, 297

New Zealand: 87

Nexus: 202, 217

90-110 rule: 527

90% test: 372

Nominal yield: 547

Nonappropriation clause: 876

Nonassignment clauses: 1060

Noncancellable: 703

Noncorporate taxpayers: 156

Nonprofit: 33

Nonrecourse debt: 22, 454, 1024, 1084, 1178

Nonrenewal penalty: 388

Nontax lease: 23

North American Free Trade Agreement: 60, 84

Notice of default: 764

Notification period: 841

O

Off balance sheet financing: 28, 243, 336, 415, 993, 1046, 1055

OMB Circular No. A-94: 907

On-behalf-of entities: 896

On-the-spot financing: 914

One-stop shopping: 38

Operating budget: 32

Operating cycle: 676

Operating leases: 24, 28, 56, 113, 242, 374
   definition: 244
   lessee: 336
   lessor: 311

Origination fees: 516

Orphan subsidiary: 1085

Overcollateralization: 1097

Owner in substance: 115

Owner trusts: 999

Ownership FSC (OFSC): 99

P

Packager: 14

Partial liquidated damages: 704

Parties to a lease: 16

Pass-through: 1048-1049

Passive loss rules: 192, 193

Passive activity losses: 193

Passive income: 193

Pay-through: 1046-1047

Payments:
    advance: 18
    arrears: 18

Payoffs: 794

Penetration rate: 67

People's Republic of China: 86

Perfected secured creditor: 770

Perfected security interest: 1093

Performance standard: 1205

Personal guarantee: 693

Personal property taxes: 224

Pertinent costs: 410

Phantom income: 1018, 1031

Philadelphia plan: 6

Pickle depreciation: 155

Pickle lease: 95

Pledge: 1176-1177

Pledge of receivables: 1079, 1084

Pool of leases: 1062

Pooled debt: 481, 1165, 1170-1173

Pooling of interests: 1117-1118

Portfolio quality: 1214, 1218-1220

Potential growth rate: 668-670

Preferences: 173, 174, 440, 787, 788, 976
    ACE depreciation: 180
    adjusted current earnings (ACE): 177
    business untaxed but reported profits (BURP): 178
    depreciation: 175, 445

Pretax rate:
    direct financing lease: 279
    sales-type lease: 302

Price/earnings multiple: 1115

Pricing methods:
    additive: 1137-1138
    cost of funds: 1142
    layered: 1133
    manual: 502
    pricing model: 1130
    three-step: 507

Pricing model: 1130

Pricing systems: 861-862

Prime contractors: 32-33, 875, 886

Prime rate: 379

Priority remarketing agreements: 920

Private activity bond: 176, 898

Private letter rulings: 121

Probability analysis: 411

Product liability: 1071

Product warranty: 856

Production standards: 1206-1207

Project financing: 70

Prompt Payment Act: 882

Property tax: 224

Public Law 86-272: 207

Public stock offering: 1109

Purchase money security interest: 774

Purchase options: 843

Put: 844, 1097

Q

Qualified bonds: 898
    501(c) (3): 901
    payment test: 899
    private business use test: 898-899
    private loan financing test: 899
    private security: 899
    small issue: 901

Qualified small issuer: 897

Qualified tax-exempt obligations (QTOs): 897

Qualified technological equipment: 155, 894

R

Railroad leasing:
    U.K.: 5
    U.S.: 6

Rate of return: 493, 534

Rating agency: 644

Ratio analysis: 662
    break-even: 648

Real estate leases: 736

Reciprocity: 33

Recourse debt: 21
    pledge: 1180
    provisions: 1081

Recourse sale: 1179, 1084

Refundable security deposits: 377, 510, 694

Regional development agencies: 74

Reinvested earnings: 538, 1081

Reinvestment:
    assumptions: 535
    opportunities: 798
    rate: 535

Remarketing costs: 855

Remedies provision: 711

Remedy of abandonment: 787

Renewal option: 844-845

Rent leveling: 187

Rental credits: 879

Repossession costs: 640

Repurchase agreements: 920

Resale certificate: 218

Reserve fund: 1097

Residual participation:
   strike price: 956

Residual value: 19, 1090
   analysis: 820, 822
   covenants: 44, 679
   documentation: 833
   estimated: 255-256
   evaluation variables: 825
   exposure: 819
   guaranteed: 20
   loss reserves: 831
   participations: 956
   risk: 640, 642, 1186-1187
   risk rating: 830
   scoring: 830
   valuation systems: 864
   write-downs: 831

Restrictive covenants: 44, 679

Restructures: 794

Retail program: 927-928

Retention ratio: 670

Return of principal: 492

Return on assets (ROA): 29, 279, 460, 468, 493, 664

Return on equity (ROE): 279, 460-461, 468, 493, 668, 678, 1001, 1124

Return on investment (ROI): 461

Return on sales: 667

Return options: 845

Revenue bonds: 887

Revenue Procedure (Rev. Proc.) 75-21: 10, 121, 993

Revenue Ruling 55-540: 8, 121, 131

Reversionary interest: 1087

Right of setoff: 1089

Rights and remedies: 763

Risk of loss: 1090

ROA: (see Return on assets)

ROE: (see Return on equity)

ROI: (see Return on investment)

Rollovers: 27, 919-920

Rule of 78: 279, 466, 799, 802

S

Safe harbor leases: 10, 214-215

Sale for resale: 218

Sale versus loan: 1078-1080

Sale-leaseback: 223, 387, 454, 966
   disqualified: 188
   intermediate leasebacks: 362, 971
   major leasebacks: 362, 970
   minor leasebacks: 362, 972

Sale: 1176-1177

Sales tax: 215, 220

Sales-type leases: 293, 1193

Sales/property tax systems: 863-864

Salvage value: 320

Secondary investment: 540, 1031

Secured sale: 110

Secured transaction: 737

Securities Act of 1933: 1060

Securities and Exchange Commission (SEC): 10, 237, 1059

Securities Exchange Act of 1934: 1060

Securitizations: 70, 1042
    default risk: 1061-1062
    orphan subsidiary: 1085
    overcollateralization: 1097
    pass-through: 1048-1049
    pay-through: 1046-1047
    reserves: 1054
    servicer: 1051
    servicer report: 1077
    servicing rights: 1081
    substitution rights: 1069

Security interest: 995

Sellers of leasing companies: 1101

Service contract: 111

Servicing costs: 1208

Short-term lease: 155

Short-term leases: 96

Side agreements: 716

Singapore: 86

Single-investor lease: 21

Sinking funds: 485-486, 540, 1010

Situs: 226

Skipped payment lease: 18, 39, 519, 525

Small ticket market: 12

Socket control: 914

Soft income: 1031

South Africa: 87

South Korea: 86

Special purpose corporation: 1085

Special purpose vehicle (SPV): 1043

Spread: 634, 1154

Staff Accounting Bulletin 70: 1089

Standard and Poor's: 644

Standard cost accounting: 650

Standard deviation: 412

Standardized investment liquidity index (SIL): 544

State tax:
   benefits: 198
   income: 198
   manual: 229
   three-factor apportionment formula: 199, 211

Step leases: 18
   step-down: 18, 39, 385, 519, 522, 692
   step-up: 18, 39, 386, 519, 520

Stipulated loss schedule: 706-707

Stranded asset: 37

Strategic planning: 1108, 1110

Street rate: 463

Structured finance: 1041

Structuring:
   process: 503
   variables: 500

Substance over form: 71, 372, 1078

Supplier credit: 677

Supply contract: 729-730

Surety bond: 1097

Swap lease: 41

Syndications: 75, 957

T

Taiwan: 86

Takeouts: 27, 919

Targeted yield: 1121

Tax acts:
   Economic Recovery Tax Act of 1981 (ERTA 91): 10
   Tax Equity and Fiscal Responsibility Act of 1982 (TEFRA 92): 10
   Tax Reform Act of 1986 (TRA 86): 10, 144, 175, 820, 1107

Tax basis: 796

Tax benefit transfer leases: 10

Tax cases:
    Frank Lyon Co. v. United States: 119
    Helvering v. F&R Lazarus & Co.: 118
    Lockhart Leasing Co. v. Commissioner: 118
    Rice's Toyota World, Inc. v. Commissioner: 120
    Swift Dodge v. Commissioner: 138
    The LTV Corp. v. Commissioner: 119

Tax:
    credits: 797
    indemnities: 705
    leases: 23, 110, 115
    sharing agreement: 939

Tax-exempt:
    interest: 47, 894, 896
    organizations: 96
    use property: 155
    user: 892
    user leases: 55, 892

Technological obsolescence: 26, 59, 853

Terminal rental adjustment clause (TRAC) leases: 110, 137, 393

Terminal value analysis (TVA): 407, 421, 456

Terminations: 19-20
    after-tax method: 804-805
    for convenience: 883
    implicit rate method: 800
    Rule of 78 method: 799, 802

The Competitive Equality Banking Act of 1987: 9

Third-party lessors: 13, 914, 926-927, 948-949

Times interest earned: 675

TRAC: (see Terminal rental adjustment clause)

Trading ratio: 677

Transfer of rights: 1088

Transfers: 761

Trends: 53

Triple-dip lease: 98

True lease: 110, 737

Trust Indentures Act of 1939: 1060

Trustee in bankruptcy: 778

Turnaround time: 644

Two-party lessor: 14-15

U

UCC: (see Uniform Commercial Code)

U.S. West: 1106

Unearned income:
   direct financing: 273
   sales-type: 295, 298

Uneven rent test: 129, 527
   limitations: 185
   90-110 rule: 527
   rent leveling: 187

Uniform Commercial Code (UCC): 114, 736, 1090
   Article 2A – Leases: 704, 737, 1093
   Article 9 – Secured Transactions: 750, 770, 1093

Uniform Division of Income for Tax Purposes Act (UDITPA): 199

Unitary business: 200

Unitary method: 200, 208

Upgrade: 41

Used equipment dealers: 853

V

Valuation issues: 227

Valuation: 1112

Value of used equipment: 852

Value-added taxes (VAT): 92

Vehicle leasing: 61

Velocity: 406, 1054-1055

Vendor:
    guarantees: 920
    leasing: 7, 59, 913-914
    programs: 13, 925

Vendor-in-possession: 751

Venture leasing: 70, 961-962

Vertical:
    analysis: 661
    integration: 50

W

Warranties and disclaimers: 697

Warranties and representations: 1116-1117

Warrants: 962

Warranty of merchantability: 704

Weighted average cost of capital (WACC): 399

Wholesale disposition: 854

Wholesale programs: 927

Window lease: 56

Wintergreen renewal: 719

Working capital: 31, 674, 678
    sources: 683

World Bank: 77

Wrap leases: 70

Y

Yield methods:
    multiple investment sinking fund (MISF): 1001, 1195
    opportunity reinvestment with limited borrowing (ORLB) ERR: 1014
    Rule of 78: 466
    sinking fund with reinvestment (SFR): 541

Yields:
    add-on interest: 467
    after-tax ROA: 1127
    all-inclusive rate: 465
    effective yield: 547
    external rate of return (ERR): 456, 483, 1001

internal rate of return (IRR): 256, 456, 535, 1001
modified street rate: 464
multiple investment sinking fund (MISF): 1001, 1195
nominal yield: 547
street rate: 463

Z

Z score analysis: 680

Advertisements